LOWRY, RAWLINGS AND MERKIN'S INSURANCE LAW

The fourth edition of this leading introductory text – now under the sole authorship of Rob Merkin QC – provides a detailed examination of the developing law of insurance, combining exposition of the law with critical analysis. The book is designed primarily for undergraduate and postgraduate students, but is also a useful resource for those in the insurance industry studying for professional examinations and legal practitioners who need a concise guide to the legal principles. The text is enhanced by extensive citations to case law and academic commentaries; and a new companion website delivers annual case law updates.

This new edition has been substantially rewritten in light of the transformation of insurance law in recent years. The text has been revised to include new legislation and the effects of Brexit. However, the approach and – where possible – the analysis of John Lowry and Philip Rawlings have been retained.

The first part of the book considers the regulation of insurance business and the general principles underlying the law of insurance contracts. The second part examines the way in which those general principles are shaped by the particular insurance context in which they operate. A new chapter with case studies on COVID-19, earthquakes, and mesothelioma applies the principles to the problems and uncertainties for insurance law revealed by catastrophic losses. This authoritative text offers a sound grasp of the current realities of insurance practice.

Online resources to accompany this book are available at bloomsbury.pub/lowry-rawlings-merkin-4e. If you experience any problems, please contact Bloomsbury at: onlineresources@bloomsbury.com

Lowry, Rawlings and Merkin's Insurance Law

Doctrines and Principles

4th Edition

Rob Merkin QC

•HART•
OXFORD • LONDON • NEW YORK • NEW DELHI • SYDNEY

HART PUBLISHING

Bloomsbury Publishing Plc

Kemp House, Chawley Park, Cumnor Hill, Oxford, OX2 9PH, UK

1385 Broadway, New York, NY 10018, USA

29 Earlsfort Terrace, Dublin 2, Ireland

HART PUBLISHING, the Hart/Stag logo, BLOOMSBURY and the Diana logo are trademarks of Bloomsbury Publishing Plc

First published in Great Britain 2022

A catalogue record for this book is available from the British Library.

A catalogue record for this book is available from the Library of Congress.

ISBN: PB: 978-1-50996-204-4
ePDF: 978-1-50996-206-8
ePub: 978-1-50996-205-1

Typeset by Compuscript Ltd, Shannon
Printed and bound in Great Britain by CPI Group (UK) Ltd, Croydon CR0 4YY

MIX
Paper from responsible sources
FSC® C013604

To find out more about our authors and books visit www.hartpublishing.co.uk. Here you will find extracts, author information, details of forthcoming events and the option to sign up for our newsletters.

Contents

Table of Cases

Table of Legislation

United Kingdom

Other Jurisdictions

Australia

Canada

European Union

New Zealand

United States

1

The Insurance Contract

1. The Development of Insurance

Insurance has a history that appears to go back to the Babylonians and was certainly well established among the town guilds of Europe by the mid-fourteenth century. However, it was the rapid growth in international trade by sea from the fifteenth century, which was centred in particular around the great Italian city states, that led to the development by those states of recognisably modern methods of insurance. This trade involved enormous financial risks for the merchant and insurance enabled these risks to be shared, either through an agreement with other merchants to provide cover if one member of the group suffered a loss or through an insurer, who, in exchange for the payment of a premium, agreed to cover specified losses and who would then seek to spread that risk among other insureds.[1] By the seventeenth century, London had established itself as a leading centre for marine insurance, writing hull and cargo policies for both English and continental merchants. Apart from life insurance in the form of death and accident benefits offered by members' societies, and the development of companies offering fire insurance for wooden buildings following the Great Fire of London in 1666, the marine trade represented the core of early insurance business.

The early marine insurers were individual merchants who carried on a variety of financial businesses as well as that of insurance. They included shipowners, who contributed to the insurance of each other's property. Some formed themselves into companies, but the activities of those companies were brought to an abrupt end by the Bubble Act 1720.[2] The background to this legislation was the formation of the South Sea Company by Royal Charter in 1711, a scheme devised to pay for the expenses of a lengthy period of war with France and Spain. The Company agreed to assume part of the national war debt in exchange for exclusive trading and land rights in British colonies in the Americas and the Caribbean. In 1713 it obtained the lucrative licence from Spain to transport slaves from Africa to Spanish colonial plantations. By 1717 the Company's commitment had risen to some £30 million of the total national debt of £51 million, but its shares were trading at an

[1] See W Holdsworth, 'The Early History of the Contract of Insurance' (1917) 17 *Columbia Law Review* 85; Merkin, *Insurance Law: A Legal History* (Cheltenham, Edward Elgar, 2021) ch 2.

[2] 6 Geo I, c 18.

implausible 98 per cent dividend on investments. The success of the South Sea Company prompted the formation and flotation of numerous joint stock companies, but many of these were run incompetently or motivated by fraud. Facing a tsunami of lost fortunes, the Bubble Act 1720 was passed on the recommendation of a House of Commons Committee. The Act prohibited the formation of associations other than by Royal Charter.

Special provision was made for marine insurance, which underpinned British trading ventures but which had, in the words of the preamble to the Act, been characterised by

> particular persons, after they have received large premiums or consideration monies for or towards insuring ships, goods, and merchandise at sea, having become bankrupts, failed in answering or complying with their policies of assurance, whereby they are particularly engaged to make good, or contribute towards the losses which merchants or traders have sustained, to the ruin and impoverishment of many merchants and traders, and to the diminution of the trade, wealth, strength and public revenues of this kingdom.

The solution was to ban the formation of marine insurance companies and to place the business in the hands of a small number of chartered companies. Two companies were granted Royal Charters for this purpose: the Royal Exchange and London Assurance. The promoters of these companies agreed to pay £300,000, and to lend a further £156,000, to the Exchequer[3] for the exclusive right of 'insuring ships or merchandises at sea', with a ban on 'all other corporations and bodies politick … sole or aggregate … and all … societies and partnerships'. The new model was an immediate failure. Weeks after the passing of the Bubble Act, the South Sea Company collapsed in spectacular fashion, making it impossible for the chartered insurers to raise sufficient funds to meet their financial obligations to the Exchequer.[4]

The marine insurance market was ready for new entrants. The ban on associations being formed to offer marine insurance did not extend to individuals. Since 1688 merchants had been meeting at Edward Lloyd's Coffee House to transact ship and landed estate sales, and to receive information on ship movements in newsletters published by the Coffee House. Lloyd himself died in 1713 and the Coffee House was taken over by his daughter. It is not known when the first marine policy was issued from the Lloyd's premises, although the first recorded policy is 1720. What is known is that the chartered companies were unable to meet demand for marine insurance and that the lacuna was filled by 'underwriters'[5] at Lloyd's. Other coffee houses provided temporary competition but were unable to contend with Lloyd's favourable location close to the Thames. Lloyd's thrived for the next century. It standardised policy wording in 1779 with the Lloyd's SG Policy[6] and a report of the House of Commons in 1819 found that Lloyd's underwriters had secured in excess of 90 per cent of the marine market.

The repeal of the Bubble Act in 1825 opened the door to the formation of both marine and non-marine insurance companies. At the same time, the industrial revolution created a series of new risks for which insurance was required. The history of insurance in the

[3] Less generously classified as a bribe to George I.

[4] F Martin, *History of Lloyd's and of Marine Insurance in Great Britain* (London, Macmillan, 1876); CWright and CE Fayle, *A History of Lloyd's* (London, Macmillan, 1928); C Brooks, *Something in the City* (London, Country Life, 1931) 208–24; DEW Gibb, *Lloyd's of London: A Study in Individualism* (New York, St Martin's Press, 1972); R Flower and MWynn Jones, *Lloyd's of London: An Illustrated History* (Newton Abbot, David & Charles, 1974).

[5] So called because individual subscribers each signed the bottom of the policy stating his agreed proportion of the risk.

[6] This remained in use, as amended, until 1983.

nineteenth century is that of response to emerging risks, mainly through specialist insurance companies formed for the purpose. A few examples suffice. The abolition of window tax in 1847 led to the use of glass in houses and shop windows, and the demand for insurance was met by the formation of plate glass insurance companies. The growth of railway transport produced specialist insurers who offered policies that provided a fixed amount in the event of the insured suffering injury or death as the result of an accident,[7] or combined elements of indemnity and contingency insurance: under the accident policy in *Theobald v Railway Passengers Assurance Co*,[8] the insurer promised to pay a fixed sum on death and to compensate for pain and loss suffered up to £1000. The partial reversal by the Employers Liability Act 1880 of the common law doctrine of common employment that an employee injured at work by the negligence of a co-worker had no cause of action against the employer[9] produced a rash of incorporation of employers' liability insurers. The introduction of the internal combustion engine, allowing cars to take to the roads in 1896, saw the development of motor insurance policies covering both damage to the car itself and also liability cover for injuries inflicted on other road users.

The process continued in the twentieth century and beyond. Lloyd's extended its activities into all forms of non-life insurance, offering insurance worldwide, and niche insurance companies were formed to meet new domestic demands. The vast majority of the small specialist companies no longer exist, having been absorbed into major conglomerate insurance undertakings that offer the full range of cover. In more recent times, new forms of insurance are evolving continually to meet legal and economic changes. A few examples suffice: directors' and officers' liability insurance began to appear in the 1980s once the companies legislation removed the prohibition on companies offering to, or funding indemnification for, defaulting directors; cyber insurance has grown to meet the dangers from hacking and other electronic threats; kidnapping and ransom insurance has become widely available for executives and high-profile figures; and the civil law system has become all but reliant on after the event insurance, which, coupled with litigation funding, removes the risk of an unsuccessful claimant being faced with unaffordable costs bills. In parallel, the life insurance industry has developed a range of complex products combining investment and tax planning with pure death cover.

There are profound modern implications for insurance law from the growth of the insurance industry described above. The key principles of insurance law were developed in the context of marine insurance, and were at least in their origins designed for an era where there was relatively little underwriting expertise and the information required to make underwriting judgements was often unobtainable, given the problems of communication with overseas jurisdictions where vessels and their cargos were located. That led to the adoption of draconian legal principles, including the obligation on policyholders to confirm the truth of statements about the insured subject matter and the risks faced by it where the actual position was unknown and unknowable. A feature of some of the early cases was that the losses had, unknown to the parties, actually occurred by the time the risk had been placed.[10] Added to that, the insurance industry was dominated by Lloyd's, and its peculiar practices became enshrined in the law by judges anxious to give effect to, rather

[7] *Dalby v India and London Life-Assurance Co* (1854) 15 CB (NS) 365, 387 (Parke B).
[8] (1854) 10 Ex 45.
[9] *Priestley v Fowler* (1837) 3 M & W 1.
[10] That was the situation in what is widely regarded as the most important of the early decisions, *Carter v Boehm* (1766) Burr 1905, discussed in ch 4 below.

than hamper, the operation of the market. The law and practice from marine insurance placed at Lloyd's, codified in the Marine Insurance Act 1906, were simply carried over to other forms of insurance as and when they developed. As long as insurance was primarily an arrangement between commercial concerns, that was relatively unproblematic. However, the development of a substantial consumer market in the second half of the twentieth century demonstrated the unsuitability of this form of legal transplant. This means that principles shaped in a commercial context have been forced into the very different environment of consumer insurance. As was said by the English and Scottish Law Commissions in July 2014:

> [A] market which was initially based on face-to-face contact and social bonds has developed into one based on systems, procedures and sophisticated data analysis. Furthermore, the types of risks insured have widened and the volume of information available to market participants has grown exponentially. The law has failed to keep pace with the changes. The law does not reflect the diversity of the modern insurance market or the changes in the way people communicate, store and analyse information. Nor does it reflect developments in other areas of commercial contract and consumer law.[11]

Although there had been investigations and reports by the Law Reform Commission in 1957 and the Law Commission in 1980, each recommending reform, the government was content to allow insurers to regulate themselves with series of voluntary measures governing claims handling and dispute resolution. The landscape was transformed by the passing of the Financial Services and Markets Act 2000, under which the self-regulatory controls on the conduct of insurers were converted into statutory duties. This was followed by the decision of the English and Scottish Law Commissions in 2005, prompted by the market itself, which was concerned with its own national and international reputation, to undertake a comprehensive review of insurance law. The original project was to produce an exhaustive reform in the form of a code, but that ambitious approach was abandoned, and the focus shifted to particular areas of concern. The resulting reforms, in the Consumer Insurance (Disclosure and Representations) Act 2012 and the Insurance Act 2015, feature throughout this book.[12]

---

2. What Is Insurance?

2.1. The General Definition of Insurance

The need to define 'insurance' arises from two sources. The first is regulatory. Insurance business is a regulated activity under the Financial Services and Markets Act 2000, and it is a criminal offence for a person to effect and carry out contracts of insurance in the UK without authorisation by the financial service regulators: the Financial Conduct Authority and the Prudential Regulatory Authority.[13] The second is contractual. As will be seen at various points in this book, certain legal doctrines apply only to insurance contracts, notably: the requirement for insurable interest on formation; the obligation to make a pre-contractual fair presentation, including – in non-consumer cases – a duty of disclosure

[11] *Insurance Contract Law* LC No 353, SLC No 238, para 1.17.

[12] R Merkin and O Gürses, 'The Insurance Act 2015: Rebalancing the Interests of Insurer and Assured' (2015) 78 *MLR* 1004.

[13] See ch 2 below.

all but unique in the common law; and the indemnity principle. Insurance contracts are excluded from the Unfair Contract Terms Act 1977; special rules apply to determining the law applicable to an insurance contract; and insurance is compulsory for employment and motor risks.

Despite the significance of the meaning of insurance, the courts and even Parliament have been somewhat reluctant when it comes to producing an all-embracing definition.[14] Megarry V-C in *Medical Defence Union Ltd v Department of Trade* thought this 'a matter of considerable difficulty'[15] and, while prepared to discuss the issue insofar as it assisted in the determination of the case before him, declined the opportunity, remarking instead that 'it is a concept which it is better to describe than to attempt to define'.[16] Similarly, Templeman J believed that 'a general definition was undesirable ... because definitions tend sometimes to obscure and occasionally to exclude that which ought to be included'.[17]

The judgment of Channell J in *Prudential Insurance Co v Commissioners of Inland Revenue*,[18] which concerned the application of stamp duty to insurance policies, is generally regarded as the starting point for the general definition. He said that a contract of insurance is an agreement in which:

> for some consideration, usually but not necessarily in periodical payments called premiums, you secure to yourself some benefit, usually but not necessarily the payment of a sum of money, upon the happening of some event. Then the next thing that is necessary is that the event should be one which involves some amount of uncertainty. There must be either uncertainty whether the event will ever happen or not, or if the event is one which must happen at some time there must be uncertainty as to the time at which it will happen. The remaining essential is that which was referred to by the Attorney-General when he said the insurance must be against something. A contract which would otherwise be a mere wager may become an insurance by reason of the assured having an interest in the subject-matter, that is to say, the uncertain event which is necessary to make the contract amount to an insurance must be an event which is prima facie adverse to the interest of the assured. The insurance is to provide for the payment of a sum of money to meet the loss or detriment which will or may be suffered upon the happening of the event. By statute it is necessary that at the time of the making of the contract there should be an insurable interest in the assured. It is true that in the case of life insurance it is not necessary that the interest should continue, and the interest is not the measure of the amount recoverable as in the case of a fire or marine policy. Still, the necessity of there being an insurable interest at the time of the making of the contract shows that it is essential to the idea of a contract of insurance that the event upon which the money is to be paid shall prima facie be an adverse event.[19]

This definition was very much one of its time. Matters have moved on from the simple model whereby an insurer accepts a premium and provides payment on the occurrence of an event causing loss. Each of these elements may be varied in practice. As will be seen in chapter five below, the premium does not have to take the form of money, although there must be some benefit provided in exchange for the offer of insurance: for example, the Marine Insurance Act 1906, in section 85(2), recognises mutual marine insurance agreements under which members agree to contribute to losses suffered by fellow members,

[14] MA Clarke, *The Law of Insurance Contracts* (London, LLP, 2009) ch 1; R Hodgin, 'Problems in Defining Insurance Contracts' [1980] *Lloyd's Maritime and Commercial Law Quarterly* 14; RL Purves, 'The Expanding (or Shrinking) Scope of Insurance in FSA Regulation' [2001] *Journal of Business Law* 623.
[15] [1980] Ch 82, 95.
[16] ibid.
[17] *Department of Trade and Industry v St Christopher Motorists Association Ltd* [1974] 1 WLR 99, 101.
[18] [1906] 2 KB 658.
[19] ibid 663. See also *Group Life & Health Ins Co v Royal Drug Co*, 440 US 205 (1979).

if and when they arise. Some policies do not require an up-front premium at all, notably After the Event insurance taken out to pay litigation expenses, which requires payment only once the proceedings are complete and the premium is paid out of the damages or costs received from the defendant. The circumstances in which sums are payable do not always depend upon the happening of an unexpected event, as is the case in some forms of life insurance, and the indemnity may take the form of the provision of services rather than the payment of money (notably, motor breakdown or extended warranty cover). Finally, although the insurer must provide an indemnity, it need not be in the form of money, but may comprise a service or other benefit. In *Department of Trade and Industry v St Christopher Motorists' Association*,[20] motorists made an annual payment in exchange for which the association promised to provide a driver if the motorist became unable to drive as a result of injury or disqualification. This was held to amount to an insurance contract since there was an obligation to provide a benefit and that benefit, although not a cash payment, had value.[21] In *Digital Satellite Warranty Cover Ltd v Financial Services Authority*,[22] the Supreme Court firmly rejected the proposition that a contract of insurance had to provide for the payment of a sum of money by the insurer and held that there could be an insurance where the obligation took another form, such as to repair or replace goods, or to provide services.

There must, however, be some form of obligation. Where the relevant party has no obligation to provide a benefit, but only discretion over whether to do so, there will not be a contract of insurance. In *Medical Defence Union v Department of Trade and Industry*,[23] the union provided a scheme for indemnifying members where damages were awarded against them in connection with their medical practices, but while members had a right to advice and to have their claim considered, they had no right to demand indemnification, although in practice proper claims were met. Megarry V-C held that this did not amount to insurance. He regarded the right to a benefit as one of the distinguishing features of an insurance contract: 'When a person insures, I think that he is contracting for the certainty of payment in specified events.'[24] Furthermore, while the benefit under an insurance policy could be in 'money or money's worth ... or the provision of services to be paid for by the insurer', he believed it was important not to adopt too broad a view of what these phrases meant, otherwise 'money's worth' could stretch to cover a whole host of benefits: 'from matters such as peace and quiet to the pleasure of listening to the arguments of counsel in this case, and much else besides'. In his view, the benefit to which the member had a right needed to be more than merely the right to have a claim considered for the agreement to amount to insurance. He therefore decided that this scheme did not amount to insurance because members had no legal right to a benefit of value. In reaching this conclusion, he seems to have been influenced by a concern that to find otherwise would create difficulties by making a wide range of professional bodies subject to the system of statutory regulation applicable to insurance business. In the circumstances of this case, he believed, 'one is in a different world from the world of insurance'.[25] This will, however, depend on the nature of the discretion: where the obligation to meet the hire costs of a replacement motor car only arose if the

[20] [1974] 1 WLR 99.

[21] See *Card Protection Plan Ltd v Customs and Excise Commissioners* [1994] STC 199, 207 (Balcombe LJ).

[22] [2013] UKSC 7.

[23] [1980] Ch 82.

[24] ibid 95. See also *Hampton v Toxteth Co-operative Provident Society Ltd* [1915] 1 Ch 721, 742–43; *CVG Siderurgica del Orinoco SA v London Steamship Owners' Mutual Insurance Association Ltd, The Vainqueur José* [1979] 1 Lloyd's Rep 557; *Re Equity & Provident Ltd* [2006] EWHC 186 (Ch).

[25] *Medical Defence Union Ltd v Department of Trade* [1980] Ch 82, 95 and 97.

company determined that the existing car was unroadworthy and the motorist had not been at fault, this amounted to insurance because the discretion was not absolute and could have been exercised by another party.[26]

Channell J suggested that the agreement must relate to a risk which involves uncertainty in that the loss might or might not occur, or it will occur at a time that cannot be predicted: there is uncertainty in fire insurance because the house might not catch fire and, although in life assurance it is certain that the insured life will die, the time of death is uncertain. In other words, a contract of insurance is a contract upon speculation.[27] Yet, uncertainty is not unique to insurance: the insurers' liability to pay damages in the uncertain event that the insured suffers loss mirrors the liability of any contracting party to pay damages in the uncertain event that it commits a breach.[28]

Channell J's view that this uncertain event had to be one which is prima facie adverse to the interest of the insured might accurately describe most insurance contracts, but it is difficult to understand why it is required and,[29] He may have linked this factor to the requirement that the insured have an interest in the subject matter. The insurable interest distinguishes an insurance contract from a wager. Furthermore, as is discussed in chapter six below, an insurance contract is void under the Marine Insurance Act 1906, section 4(1) and (2) if the insurer agrees to provide cover irrespective of whether the insured has an insurable interest (known as a 'policy proof of interest' or 'ppi' clause), even if the insured does in fact have an interest. Of course, in both wagering and insurance contracts the parties make judgments about the occurrence of uncertain events, whether it is a house that might burn down or a horse that might or might not win a race. The difference lies in the fact that the risk of loss to the house owner exists independently of the contract, whereas the risk on the horse race is created by the contract. Moreover, someone with no interest in the house will lose nothing if it burns down and the only risk that person runs is the loss of the consideration paid in exchange for the promise of payment if the house does burn down. In other words, in a wagering contract the risk is created by the agreement, for without it the contracting party would have suffered no loss, whereas in an insurance contract the risk exists whether or not there is such a contract.[30] Blackburn J put the matter succinctly:

> I apprehend that the distinction between a policy and a wager is this: a policy is, properly speaking, a contract to indemnify the insured in respect of some interest which he has against the perils which he contemplates it will be liable to.[31]

Interestingly, the courts have tended to set themselves against contracts designed to insure against losses from gaming, even though they would seem to fit the definition of an insurance contract in that the risk arises not from the insurance contract but from the gaming contract.[32]

[26] *Everson v Flurry* [1999] CLY 3411 (Slough County Court).

[27] *Re Barrett; ex parte Young v NM Superannuation Pty Ltd* 106 ALR 549 (Fed Court of Australia) (von Dousa J).

[28] As will be seen, the courts characterise the insurers' liability following a covered loss as a claim in damages: see ch 12 below.

[29] See the comments on life assurance in *Gould v Curtis* [1913] 3 KB 84, 92 (Cozens-Hardy MR), 95 (Buckley LJ), 98–99 (Kennedy LJ). Buckley LJ commented that 'some people regard [death] as adverse, and some do not'.

[30] *Carlill v Carbolic Smoke Ball Co* [1892] 2 QB 484, 490 (Hawkins J).

[31] *Wilson v Jones* (1867) 2 LR Exch 139, 150.

[32] This is the implication of *Hill v William Hill (Park Lane) Ltd* [1949] AC 530.

The difficulties involved in defining the constituent features of an insurance contract or in distinguishing it from other contracts have led most judges to resist generalisations and to turn instead to the particular issue before them. As Professor Clarke has put it:

> Insurance contracts are best seen (and defined, if at all) according to the angle or line of approach, that is, the context or issue before the court. With regulatory statutes, courts are concerned with the purpose of the statute, whether, for example, this is the kind of thing that Parliament intended to regulate, or to encourage … and they examine the terms of the contract in that light.[33]

In the New Zealand Court of Appeal, Richardson J suggested:

> The true nature of a transaction can only be ascertained by careful consideration of the legal arrangements actually entered into and carried out: not on an assessment of the broad substance of the transaction measured by the results intended and achieved or of the overall economic consequences. The nomenclature used by the parties is not decisive and what is crucial is the ascertainment of the legal rights and duties which are actually created by the transaction into which the parties entered. The surrounding circumstances may be taken into account in characterising the transaction. Not to deny or contradict the written agreement but in order to understand the setting in which it was made and to construe it against that factual background having regard to the genesis and objectively the aim of the transaction.[34]

The refusal of Megarry V-C in the *Medical Defence Union* case to provide a general definition of an insurance contract might have been wise, but it also allowed him to decide the case according to whether the Medical Defence Union seemed to him to be insurers:

> I also consider that the general nature of the business carried on by the union is too far removed from the general nature of the businesses carried on by those who are generally accepted as being insurers for the unions business to be fairly regarded as the effecting and carrying out of contracts of insurance.[35]

Yet, did he give proper consideration to the objectives of regulation, and in particular to the protection of the members of the scheme? This was a scheme that, for all practical purposes, must have been regarded by the members as insurance: they would have been shocked to discover that there was no right to benefits and the Union would, presumably, have been at pains to emphasise that, normally, they do pay and to underplay the element of discretion. It is, therefore, reasonable to suggest that he should have erred on the side of finding that the scheme amounted to insurance so that it might be appropriately regulated and the members properly protected, rather than, as he seems to have done, approaching the issue from the point of view of the Union and, therefore, seeing regulation as a burden.[36]

2.2. Regulated Insurance Business

Whatever the difficulties may be in providing a comprehensive definition of insurance for contractual purposes, the fact that carrying on insurance business in the UK without

[33] MA Clarke, *The Law of Insurance Contracts* (London, LLP, 1997) 2. See J Hellner, 'The Scope of Insurance Regulation: What Is Insurance for Purposes of Regulation?' (1963) 12 *American Journal of Comparative Law* 494.

[34] *Marac Life Assurance Ltd v Commissioner of Inland Revenue* [1986] 1 NZLR 694 (Court of Appeal, New Zealand). See also *In re Law Guarantee Trust and Accident Society Ltd, Liverpool Mortgage Insurance Co Case* [1914] 2 Ch 614, 631.

[35] *Medical Defence Union Ltd v Department of Trade* [1980] Ch 82.

[36] See also the discussion in *R (on the application of Moreton) v Medical Defence Union Ltd* [2006] ACD 102, where the court held that the Medical Defence Union is not amenable to judicial review.

authorisation attracts criminal sanctions means that there has to be a clear understanding of what is and what is not permitted. The Financial Services and Markets Act 2000 (Regulated Activities) Order 2001 (as amended) does not seek to define contracts of insurance as such, but instead sets out a list of activities that require authorisation by the Financial Conduct Authority (FCA) and the Prudential Regulatory Authority. This is supplemented by the detailed guidance provided by the FCA in the Perimeter Guidance Manual (PERG 6) of its Regulatory Handbook.[37] The guidance is broadly based on the judgment of Channell J in *Prudential Insurance Co v Commissioners of Inland Revenue*, and addresses a number of borderline cases that have given rise to difficulties at common law. The general principle in PERG 6.5.2 is that there is a contract of insurance where

> a provider undertakes in consideration of one or more payments to pay money or provide a corresponding benefit (including in some cases services to be paid for by the provider) to a 'recipient' in response to a defined event the occurrence of which is uncertain (either as to when it will occur or as to whether it will occur at all) and adverse to the interests of the recipient.

The underlying consideration for the FCA is risk transfer. However, not all risk transfers are insurance. It is commonplace for firms to seek ways of guarding against a risk of loss through, for instance, unfavourable changes in commodity prices or currency exchange rates, or adverse weather conditions. Such risks may, of course, be covered by insurance, but there are various other methods which, while transferring the burden of risk away from the firm, are not treated as insurance contracts. An airline concerned at the prospect of oil prices rising might take out insurance, or it might hedge by buying oil futures, which would amount to an investment contract. As is the case at common law,[38] PERG 6.5.4 is concerned with substance rather than form, so the description of the arrangement used by the parties is not decisive.

One of the features of the 2001 Order is that the list of the classes of contract that are regulated as insurance, thereby requiring authorisation, is in some instances wider than pure insurance. This at least saves the need to draw fine distinctions for regulatory purposes, even though those distinctions may be relevant for contractual purposes. The classes of business that attract regulation as 'insurance business' are divided by the Order into two broad groups, general business and long-term, broadly corresponding to non-life and life. An insurer wishing to carry on business in any one of these classes has to be authorised in respect of that class. There are nine classes of long-term business, most importantly contracts of insurance that cover: human life, including benefits linked to an investment fund; marriage or the birth of a child; and long-term injury or disease. Pension fund management is included in this list.

The 18 classes of general business can be divided into groups. Classes 1 and 2 cover personal injury and sickness. Classes 3–9 are concerned with property damage, including vehicles, railway rolling stock, ships, aircraft and goods in transit, as well as buildings and possessions. Classes 1–9 are all 'first party' risks, ie insurance of a person's own property. Classes 10–13 cover motor vehicle, aircraft, ship and general liability: these classes are concerned not with the insured's own property, but with the insured's liability to third parties for injury to them or their property, including their financial interests, hence the general description 'third party insurance'. Classes 14–18 consist of various first party financial insurances, including: credit insurance against bad debts; the issue of bonds and guarantees

[37] For discussion of other elements of the Handbook, see ch 2 below.

[38] *In re Sentinel Securities* [1996] 1 WLR 316; *Fuji Finance Inc v Aetna Life Insurance Co Ltd* [1997] Ch 173.

by way of security; miscellaneous financial loss, including loss of revenue following interruption to business activities; legal and litigation insurance; and assistance for persons who get into difficulties either at home or while travelling. A number of specific issues have arisen with respect to the statutory classification.

First, the contract may consist of both insurance and non-insurance elements. The test applied by the courts and adopted by PERG 6 is not that of predominant purpose, but rather whether any substantial part of the contract contains an element of insurance.[39] It is common for a publishing contract to contain a term under which the writer agrees to indemnify the publisher against liability for libel, but this does not make it an insurance contract.[40] Similarly, a conditional fee agreement which also contains an indemnity against the client having to pay the other side's costs in the event of the claim failing is a contract for legal services and not a contract of insurance because the indemnity is merely a subsidiary part of the contract.[41] On the other hand, investment schemes, which include minor elements of life insurance, would seem to be contracts of insurance because the right to the benefits is, to an extent, related to life or death.[42] A contract may also contain elements from different classes of insurance, which may cause a problem if the insurer is authorised for one class but not another, and once again the test is whether any substantial part of the contract falls within a particular class so as to require authorisation under that class.[43]

Secondly, there is a difficult distinction to be drawn between insurance and contracts of warranty.[44] A warranty is commonly given in connection with the sale of goods and might, for instance, involve a promise to repair goods that are defective on delivery.[45] This would seem not to amount to insurance, since it is merely a promise to do that which the party had promised to do in the sale contract, which was to deliver goods that were not defective.[46] Yet, it could be insurance if the promise goes further, as where the seller promises to replace goods if a fault arises that was not present at the time of sale, if they are lost or damaged by the buyer, or if the promise to repair is made by someone who otherwise has no responsibility for the fault.[47] In the English courts there has been relatively little consideration of this distinction, although the judges have declined the invitation to stipulate that, for insurance, the insurer should have no control over, or responsibility for, the fault that causes the loss.[48] In *Re OT Computers Ltd (In Administration)*,[49] the Court of Appeal left open the

[39] ibid.

[40] *Medical Defence Union Ltd v Department of Trade* [1980] Ch 82.

[41] *Sibthorpe v Southwark LBC* [2011] EWCA Civ 25.

[42] *Fuji Finance Inc v Aetna Life Insurance Co Ltd* [1997] Ch 173.

[43] *Re Digital Satellite Warranty Cover Ltd* [2011] EWHC 122 (Ch) (Warren J) – the point did not arise on appeal, *Digital Satellite Warranty Cover Ltd v Financial Services Authority* [2013] 1 WLR 605.

[44] *First National Tricity Finance Ltd v OT Computers Ltd* [2004] EWCA Civ 653; Competition Commission, *Extended Warranties on Domestic Electrical Goods* (2003); C Twigg-Flesner, 'Consumer Product Guarantees and Insurance Law' [1999] *Journal of Business Law* 279. See generally GL Priest, 'A Theory of the Consumer Product Warranty' (1981) 90 *Yale Law Journal* 1297; T Baker, 'On the Genealogy of Moral Hazard' (1996) 75 *Texas Law Review* 237.

[45] Or are deemed to have been defective on delivery by virtue of the Sale of Goods Act 1979, s 48A.

[46] That was held to be the position by the New Zealand Court of Appeal in *Commissioner of Inland Revenue v Motorcorp Holdings Ltd* (2005) 22 NZTC 19,126. The point has been confirmed by the Insurance (Prudential Supervision) Act 2010, s 7(3)(d), which expressly excludes from the definition of insurance contract 'a product or service guarantee or warranty in relation to any goods or services that is given or made by the manufacturer or supplier'.

[47] *Re Sentinel Securities plc* [1996] 1 WLR 316.

[48] *Medical Defence Union Ltd v Department of Trade* [1980] Ch 82; *Department of Trade and Industry v St Christopher Motorists Association Ltd* [1974] 1 WLR 99.

[49] [2004] EWCA Civ 653.

question of whether an extended warranty provided by a manufacturer amounted to insurance, but perhaps indicated a disinclination to taking this view and did note the additional regulatory burden that would be imposed if it were. At first instance,[50] Morritt V-C had rejected the idea, but had noted his view might be different where the 'warranty' extended to accidental damage and theft. The position may be clearer where the 'warranty' is provided by a third party. In *Re Sentinel Securities*,[51] companies subscribed to a scheme operated by S under which the companies issued a certificate to customers which appeared to promise that S would honour promises made by the companies to make good defects in the products supplied. It was held that the 'warranty' amounted to insurance.

In the USA, where there has been a good deal of case law on this issue, no clear principle has emerged. In *Ollendorf Watch Co Ltd v Pink*,[52] a promise by the seller of a watch to provide a replacement if the watch were lost or stolen was held to amount to a contract of insurance because it covered risks that did not relate to defects in the watch itself. Similarly, in *Griffin Systems, Inc v Washburn*,[53] a court in Illinois decided that a contract of insurance existed where Griffin, who had not supplied the car, promised to repair any damage caused to it by weather, collision, vandalism, negligence or failure to have it serviced. On the other hand, a majority in the Ohio Supreme Court in *Griffin Systems, Inc v Ohio Department of Insurance*[54] said that it was not the status of the party offering the warranty that was important, but the promise made: 'warranties that cover only defects within the product itself are properly characterised as warranties … whereas warranties promising to cover damages or losses unrelated to defects within the product itself are, by definition, contracts substantially amounting to insurance'. The fact that Griffin was not the manufacturer or retailer of the car was irrelevant and a promise to compensate the motorist for repairs caused by defective parts was not insurance. In that case, however, there was a vigorous dissenting judgment by Wright J, who argued that the status of the person providing the promise was crucial: 'This case does not involve a warranty because a warranty is a statement of representation made by the seller or manufacturer of goods contemporaneously with and as part of the contract of sale.'[55]

The FCA has given detailed guidance on this matter in PERG 6.7.8–17. In outline: a warranty of quality is not insurance; a warranty which requires the manufacturer or retailer to provide repairs or replacement products in response to a defined but uncertain event (eg the emergence of a latent defect in the product) might amount to insurance; an extended warranty under which obligations are assumed by a person other than the manufacturer or retailer and is more extensive than the seller's contractual or statutory obligations is likely to be classified as insurance; and a warranty by a manufacturer or seller in a separate contract may amount to a contract of insurance, although the independence of the contract is not of itself an indication of insurance.

Thirdly, the provision of breakdown cover for electrical or mechanical equipment is potentially insurance. The fact that the obligation undertaken by the provider is not the payment of money but rather replacement or repair does not negate the essential insurance

[50] [2003] EWHC 2490 (Ch).
[51] 1996] 1 WLR 316.
[52] 17 NE2d 676 (NY 1938).
[53] 505 NE2d 1121 (IL 1987).
[54] 575 NE2d 803 (Ohio 1991). Other cases where vehicle service agreements were held to be insurance: *Jim Click Ford, Inc v City of Tuscon*, 154 Ariz 48 (1987); *Pugh v North American Warranty Services*, 2000 UT App 121 (2000); *McMullan v Enterprise Financial Group, Inc* 247 P3d 1173 (Okla 2011).
[55] 575 NE2d 803 (Ohio 1991) 810.

element of the transaction. The Supreme Court in *Digital Satellite Warranty Cover Ltd v Financial Services Authority*[56] refused to recognise a distinction between payment for repairs and the provision of repairs, holding them both to constitute insurance business. This reasoning encompasses breakdown contracts of the kind offered by motoring organisations, but the UK has chosen to exclude such organisations from the regulatory regime by regulation 10 of the Regulated Activities Order 2001. The exclusion does not extend to insurance companies offering breakdown services, only to non-insurers.

Fourthly, the common law draws a distinction between a contract of insurance and a contract of guarantee. That point is not significant for regulatory purposes, in that general insurance class 15 encompasses the business of issuing securities in the form of performance bonds and guarantees. However, it remains a live issue for contractual purposes. Harman LJ suggested that the attempt to distinguish between them is fraught with difficulty and 'has raised many hair-splitting distinctions of exactly the kind "which brings the law into hatred, ridicule and contempt by the public"'.[57] In a contract of guarantee, Alex (the guarantor) promises Toytown Bank (the creditor) that, if it will enter into a contract to lend money to Yasmin (the debtor), Alex will be responsible for Yasmin's debt should she default. Under a contract of guarantee, there is a less rigorous duty of disclosure or even no duty at all, and while in insurance the primary liability is on the insurers, in a contract of guarantee that primary liability is on the debtor and the guarantor's liability arises only if the debtor defaults. Furthermore, under section 4 of the Statute of Frauds Act 1677, a guarantee must be in writing, but there is no such requirement in respect of a contract of indemnity. In *Re Denton's Estate*, Vaughan Williams LJ suggested that the key to distinguishing between these contracts lay in whether it was appropriate to apply the duty of disclosure to the agreement:

> The distinction in substance, in cases in which the loss insured against is simply the event of the non-payment of a debt, seems to be, as I read the judgment of Romer LJ [in *Seaton v Heath*[58]], between contracts in which the person desiring to be insured has means of knowledge as to the risk and the insurer has not the same means, and those cases in which the insurer has the same means.[59]

The traditional justification for this approach is that insurance is a commercial relationship in which the insured has knowledge of facts material to the risk, whereas in a guarantee, it has been assumed, the guarantor acts out of motives of friendship and is assumed to be aware of the risk, so that there is no need for disclosure. The problem is that guarantees are generally commercial transactions and guarantors do not necessarily know the facts. To determine whether an agreement is one of guarantee or insurance, the courts will look at the contract as a whole in order to discover its effect, and neither the use by the parties of the words 'insurance' or 'guarantee' nor the fact that one of the parties is an insurance company will be conclusive.[60] Yet, such words will provide indicators, and there are others. Insurance will generally involve the payment by the insured of a premium, whereas usually a contract of guarantee is entered into without any payment, although, having said that,

[56] [2013] 1 WLR 605. See also *Re Cavalier Insurance Co Ltd* [1989] 2 Lloyd's Rep 430.

[57] *Yeoman Credit Ltd v Latter* [1961] 1 WLR 828, 892 (Harman LJ). To add to this confusion, a guarantee entered into by an insurer may be insurance business: *Travelers Casualty & Surety Co of Europe Ltd v Commissioners of Customs and Excise* [2006] Lloyd's Rep IR 63 (VAT Tribunal).

[58] [1899] 1 QB 782.

[59] [1904] 2 Ch 178. See also *United States v Tilleraas* 709 F2d 1088 (US Court of Appeals, 6th Cir, 1983).

[60] *The Zhula K and The Selin* [1987] 1 Lloyd's Rep 151.

fees are charged by a guarantor in a commercial contract. Moreover, in insurance there are normally two parties (insured and insurer), while in a contract of guarantee there are normally three parties (creditor, debtor and guarantor). In *The Zuhal K and The Selin*,[61] an insurer provided a bond to cargo owners at the request of a protection and indemnity (P & I) club to facilitate the release of a ship owned by D, which had been arrested over a claim for damages. The bond provided that in the event of the insurer paying the cargo owners, the P & I club would indemnify the insurer. The insurer made payment, but the club was in financial difficulties and so the insurer sought payment from D. The court did not accept the argument that the agreement was between the insurer and the club. It was held that the bond amounted to a guarantee of D's liability to the cargo owners and that it stated on its face that it was provided at D's request: D was the principal debtor and the insurer was the surety.

As already noted, the activity that has to be authorised is not simply the making of an insurance contract: authorisation is demanded only of a person who carries on by way of business the effecting and carrying out of insurance contracts in the UK. There is no statutory definition of these terms; it has been held that the concepts are concerned primarily with the issue of policies and the payment of claims,[62] although they will also catch an agent who fraudulently purports to issue policies without the authority of the insurer or, indeed, on behalf of a non-existent insurer.[63] The activity is carried on in the UK if the activities in the UK are a 'significant part of the business activity'.[64]

3. International Aspects

Many insurance agreements, particularly commercial policies and reinsurance contracts, have an international element in that the insured or reinsured is domiciled in a jurisdiction different from that of the underwriters' place of business. Further, many risks are subscribed to by a number of insurance companies, often situated in different parts of the world. Whenever a contract does have an international dimension, and proceedings are brought in the English courts, two separate issues will inevitably arise: do the English courts have jurisdiction to resolve the dispute; and, if so, which law governs the rights of the parties? This section will consider both jurisdiction and choice of law, and highlight the provision made for insurance contracts. Readers should note that very many commercial insurance and reinsurance disputes are resolved by arbitration, although this matter is outside the scope of the present text.[65] Jurisdiction and applicable law are quite separate issues in principle: jurisdiction is about where the case is to be heard, whereas applicable law is about the rules of law to be applied to the dispute. However, the two matters do overlap. For example, one of the grounds upon which the English courts have jurisdiction over a dispute is because the contract is governed by English law. A choice of English law does not mean that English jurisdiction has been chosen, and vice versa. Thus, the standard terms

[61] ibid.

[62] *Ackman and Scher v Policyholders Protection Board* [1993] 3 All ER 384.

[63] *R v Wilson* [1997] 1 WLR 1247; *Re Whiteley Insurance Consultants* [2008] Ch 1782.

[64] *Financial Services Authority v Fradley and Woodward* [2005] EWCA Civ 1183 (Arden LJ).

[65] See generally *Mustill & Boyd: Commercial Arbitration*, 2nd edn (London, LexisNexis, 2009); RM Merkin, *Arbitration Law* (London, Informa, 1993).

of London marine policies, that they are subject to 'English law and practice', means that the policy is governed by English law but not that the parties have chosen that their disputes should be litigated in England.[66]

3.1. Jurisdiction

English jurisdictional rules determine whether an action may be brought in the English courts. England has long been a forum for the hearing of international disputes, as England is a convenient neutral forum and English commercial judges are regarded as experts in their field. It may also be important for a person who wishes to sue or be sued under judicial procedures which are familiar to him and which he or she trusts. For the period of UK membership of the EU from 1972 to 2020, it was necessary to draw a distinction between cases in which the defendant was domiciled in the EU and all other cases. Jurisdictional rules for the former were governed by successive versions of what ultimately became the Brussels Regulation Recast[67] – a measure which contained special rules for insurance contracts. In the event of a dispute, their broad effect as between EU countries was: to require the insurer to sue the insured only in the courts of the country of the insured's domicile; to allow the insured to sue the insurers in the country of the domicile of either party, or in the country where the risk was situated; and in the case of an individual domiciled in the UK but injured in the EU – typically in a road or hotel accident – there was a right to bring a direct action against the defendant's insurers in the UK. Brexit put an end to rules which were, from the point of view of a claimant against insurers, highly advantageous.

The jurisdiction of the English courts over a dispute depends upon the procedural question of whether the claim form may be served upon him. Service is possible on a defendant who: is an individual and is within England, temporarily or otherwise;[68] is a company incorporated or with a place of business in England;[69] is not within England but has agreed that an action can be brought only in England[70] or that an action may be brought in England;[71] or is not present in England and has not agreed to be sued in England, but has nevertheless submitted to the jurisdiction of the English court by nominating solicitors to accept service or by participating in the proceedings by submitting a substantive defence.[72] Most importantly, however, the English courts have jurisdiction – generally referred to as 'exorbitant jurisdiction' – over a defendant who is not present in England and has not submitted to jurisdiction by agreement or otherwise, but where the case has a substantial connection with England. The claimant may apply to the English court under Civil Procedure Rules (CPR) Part 6 for permission to serve the claim form on the defendant outside the jurisdiction. Permission will be granted by the court if: it is satisfied that the claim raises a serious question to be tried; that there is a good arguable case that there is a substantial connection with England in that one or more of the numerous grounds of jurisdiction listed in CPR Practice

[66] *Mujur Bakat SDN BHD v Uni Asia General Insurance Berhad* [2011] EWHC 643 (Comm).

[67] European Parliament and Council Directive 1215/2012/EU.

[68] *Maharanee of Baroda v Wildenstein* [1972] 2 QB 283.

[69] Companies Act 2006, s 1139.

[70] Under an exclusive jurisdiction clause.

[71] Under a permissive clause whereby the defendant agrees not to contest the jurisdiction of the English court if an action is brought against him in England.

[72] Appearing to contest jurisdiction is not enough: *Finnish Marine Insurance Co Ltd v Protective National Insurance Co* [1989] 2 All ER 929.

Direction 6B has been made out; and that England is the obvious appropriate forum for the trial of the action.[73] For insurance and reinsurance purposes, the most important of the heads of potential jurisdiction are that the claim is made in respect of: a contract where the contract was made in England, made by or through an agent of the defendant who was trading in England[74] governed by English law or containing a jurisdiction clause nominating England;[75] a breach of contract committed in England;[76] or a declaration that no contract exists.[77]

Assuming that jurisdiction is made out on any of the above grounds, the court has an overriding discretion[78] to refuse to hear the action.[79] That discretion may be exercised on one of two grounds: that England is not the most appropriate forum for the action to be heard (*forum non conveniens*); or that there are proceedings in existence in some other place (*lis alibis pendens*).

The most important of these principles is *forum non conveniens*, an issue which arises in virtually every case where the jurisdiction of the English courts is contested. The basic principle is that the English court will hear the action unless the defendant can show that there is a more convenient forum which has under its domestic law jurisdiction over the dispute and that the claimant in England would not be deprived of a legitimate juridical advantage by proceeding in some other jurisdiction. In considering these questions, the courts will balance all the circumstances in the case, although a number of principles may be derived from the numerous authorities. First, the courts will, other than in exceptional circumstances, give effect to an exclusive jurisdiction clause which nominates the courts of a particular place: if England is nominated, then the action will be heard here;[80] if some other jurisdiction is nominated, then a stay of English proceedings is all but inevitable.[81] Even if the clause simply confers an option on the claimant to sue in a given jurisdiction, once the claimant has chosen to exercise that option the defendant will not be able to argue that the jurisdiction is not a convenient forum, given that the defendant had, under the clause, agreed to be sued there.[82] Secondly, in the absence of agreed jurisdiction provisions, the law applicable

[73] See generally *Seaconsar Far East Ltd v Bank Marzaki Jamhouri Islami Iran* [1994] 4 All ER 456; *Four Seasons Holdings Inc v Brownlie* [2017] UKSC 80.

[74] CPR, r 6.20(5)(b). For this purpose it should be borne in mind that the broker is the agent of the assured and not the agent of insurers: *Lincoln National Life Insurance Co v Employers Reinsurance Corporation* [2002] Lloyd's Rep IR 853; *Tryg Baltica International (UK) Ltd v Boston Compania De Seguros SA* [2004] EWHC 1186 (Comm).

[75] CPR, PD 6B, para 3.1(6).

[76] CPR, PD 6B, para 3.1(7).v. If a sum of money is outstanding, the English rule is that, in the absence of anything in the contract as to the place of payment, the debtor must seek out the creditor, so that if the creditor is situated in England, then non-payment constitutes a breach of contract in England: *Citadel Insurance v Atlantic Union Insurance* [1982] 2 Lloyd's Rep 543; *Overseas Union Insurance v Incorporated General Insurance* [1992] 1 Lloyd's Rep 439.

[77] CPR, PD 6B, para 3.1(8).

[78] The court is in any event obliged to stay its own proceedings where the parties have entered into a binding agreement to refer the dispute to arbitration: Arbitration Act 1996, s 9.

[79] That discretion is, however, removed where the jurisdiction of the English court is conferred by virtue of the defendant's English domicile. This is the effect of the European rules on jurisdiction: see below.

[80] *Youell v Kara Mara Shipping Co* [2000] EWHC 220 (Comm); *Equitas Ltd v Allstate Insurance Company* [2008] EWHC 1671 (Comm). There is a presumption that a jurisdiction clause is exclusive rather than merely permissive: *AIG Europe SA v John Wood Group plc* [2022] EWCA Civ 781.

[81] *Excess Insurance Ace Insurance SA-NV v Zurich Insurance Co* [2001] 1 Lloyd's Rep 504; *Burrows v Jamaica Private Power Co Ltd* [2001] EWHC 488 Comm); *Groupama Insurance Co v Channel Islands Securities Ltd* [2002] Lloyd's Rep IR 843. But see the exceptional circumstances in *Konkola Copper Mines v Coromin* [2006] EWCA Civ 5.

[82] *Excess Insurance v Allendale Mutual Insurance Co* [2001] Lloyd's Rep IR 524; *Munchener Ruckver-sicherungs Gesellschaft v Commonwealth Insurance Co* [2004] EWHC 914 (Comm). A non-exclusive jurisdiction clause should be distinguished from a clause whereby insurers or reinsurers agree that it may be served at a particular address,

to the contract will be an important, although not determinative,[83] factor: if the policy is governed by English law, there is a strong presumption that the dispute should be resolved in the English courts.[84] Thirdly, weight will be given to other matters, including the location of the witnesses and the documents, the fact that it may be necessary to join other parties to the proceedings and the possibility of delay in other jurisdictions. By way of example, where the dispute relates to the right of the underwriters to avoid a contract placed in the London market for breach of the duty of fair presentation, it will normally be appropriate to hear the action in England, given that the relevant evidence will be in England and the contract is almost certainly governed by English law in such circumstances.[85] By contrast, if the issue is whether the insured or reinsured was aware of facts misstated or withheld, then the relevant evidence may be in some other jurisdiction and that will be the most appropriate forum,[86] and if the dispute relates to breach of contract terms in another jurisdiction or the circumstances of a loss, then the place where the breach[87] or loss[88] allegedly occurred is the most appropriate forum. That is all subject to the overriding consideration that the foreign court will apply English law as the law chosen by the parties.[89]

The existence of other proceedings – *lis alibis pendens* – is a matter which will figure large in the court's ultimate conclusion as to whether the English action should be stayed. The English court will refuse to become involved if the parties have agreed that the action should be brought in that other jurisdiction or if that jurisdiction is the most convenient. The existence of other proceedings will necessarily be disregarded where the foreign action is brought in contravention of an exclusive jurisdiction clause nominating England,[90] and indeed in appropriate circumstances the court may grant an anti-suit injunction against the claimant in the foreign proceedings,[91] preventing the claimant from continuing with the action.[92] An anti-suit injunction will be granted as a matter of course where the action is in breach of arbitration, exclusive jurisdiction or other clause, or where the court otherwise regards the foreign action as oppressive. There are numerous illustrations of anti-suit

as this type of clause does not indicate any intention that the proceedings should be heard in that jurisdiction: *Travelers Casualty and Surety Co of Europe Ltd v Sun Life Assurance Co of Canada* [2004] EWHC 1704 (Comm) 6.

[83] So decided by the House of Lords in *Amin Rasheed Shipping Corporation v Kuwait Insurance Co* [1983] 2 All ER 884.

[84] *Islamic Arab Insurance Co v Saudi Egyptian American Reinsurance Co* [1987] 1 Lloyd's Rep 315; *Sea-shell Shipping Corporation of Panama v Mutualidad de Seguros del Instituto Nacional de Insdustria* [198] 1 Lloyd's Rep 47; *Overseas Union Insurance v Incorporated General Insurance* [1992] 1 Lloyd's Rep 439; *Assicurazioni Generali v Ege Sigorta AS* [2002] Lloyd's Rep IR 480; *Brotherton v Aseguardora Colseguros SA* [2002] Lloyd's Rep IR 848; *Stonebridge Underwriting Ltd v Ontario Municipal Insurance Exchange* [2010] EWHC 2279 (Comm).

[85] *Gan Insurance Co v Tai Ping Insurance Co* [1999] Lloyd's Rep IR 472; *Travelers Casualty and Surety Co of Europe Ltd v Sun Life Assurance Co of Canada (UK) Ltd* [2004] Lloyd's Rep IR 846; *Markel International Insurance Company Ltd v La Republica Compania Argentina de Seguros Generales SA* [2005] Lloyd's Rep IR 90; *Royal & Sun Alliance Insurance Plc v Rolls-Royce Plc* [2010] EWHC 1869 (Comm).

[86] *Chase v Ram Technical Services* [2000] 2 Lloyd's Rep 418.

[87] *Stonebridge Underwriting Ltd v Ontario Municipal Insurance Exchange* [2010] EWHC 2279 (Comm); *Mujur Bakat SDN BHD v Uni Asia General Insurance Berhad* [2011] EWHC 643 (Comm).

[88] *Navigators Insurance Co Ltd v Atlantic Methanol Production Co LLC* [2004] Lloyd's Rep IR 418.

[89] *Mujur Bakat SDN BHD v Uni Asia General Insurance Berhad* [2011] EWHC 643 (Comm).

[90] See *Akai v People's Insurance Co* [1998] 1 Lloyd's Rep 90, where the action was brought in Australia in breach of an English exclusive jurisdiction clause and the Australian courts purported to assert jurisdiction under Australian domestic law.

[91] It is to be emphasised that the injunction is against the claimant in the proceedings, not against the foreign court itself, even though the effect of the injunction is to remove the action from the foreign court (unless the claimant is willing to face contempt proceedings in England).

[92] The requirements for the grant of an anti-suit injunction were laid down by the House of Lords in *Société Nationale Industrielle v Le Kul Jak* [1987] 3 All ER 510 and *Donohue v Armco Inc* [2002] Lloyd's Rep IR 425.

injunctions being granted in insurance and reinsurance cases in these circumstances.[93] An anti-suit injunction is a last resort, so if there are other means of achieving the same result, eg granting a declaration which prevents the defendant from reopening the issue in other proceedings, then that approach will be taken.[94]

Many insurance and reinsurance disputes come before the English courts by way of an application for 'negative declaratory relief', ie an application by the underwriters to the English court that they have a right to avoid the policy or are otherwise not liable to meet any claim which may be made against them in future by the policyholder, almost certainly in a foreign court. At one time it was thought that this type of action was 'forum-shopping' and was frowned upon by the courts, but in the landmark decision in *New Hampshire Insurance Co v Philips Electronics North America Corporation*[95] the Court of Appeal confirmed that this type of action was perfectly valid and that the English court should entertain the action as long as it: (a) serves some useful purpose, eg answers a point of English law raised by the policy;[96] (b) does not undermine existing foreign proceedings;[97] and (c) does not require the court to answer a purely hypothetical question or a question in which the claimant has only an indirect interest.[98]

3.2. Applicable Law

At common law, the courts would determine the law applicable to a contract of insurance, and indeed any contract, using a three-step test: had the parties expressly agreed on the applicable law; if not, could the applicable law be determined impliedly from the other terms of the contract; if not, to what system of law was the contract most closely connected? The default close connection test in insurance cases came to rest upon the contract's 'centre of gravity', in which priority would be given to the place in which the contract was negotiated and subsequently administered. That almost inevitably meant that a contract entered into in the London market would be governed by English law.[99]

The common law was superseded in the 1990s by two separate EU initiatives. The first related exclusively to insurance contracts. At one time, running alongside the insurance directives aimed at establishing a single market for insurance[100] was the notion that substantive insurance law would be harmonised within the EU. That project foundered, and in its

[93] See most recently *Catlin Syndicate Ltd v AMEC Foster Wheeler USA Corp* [2020] EWHC 2530 (Comm); *Axis Corporate Capital UK Ltd v ABSA Group Ltd* [2021] EWHC 225 (Comm); *Markel Bermuda Ltd v Caesars Entertainment Inc* [2021] EWHC 1931 (Comm); *AIG Europe SA v John Wood Group PLC* [2022] EWCA Civ 781.

[94] *Noble Assurance Co v Gerling-Konzern General Insurance Co (UK)* [2007] EWHC 253 (Comm).

[95] [1999] Lloyd's Rep IR 58.

[96] As in *Philips* itself (meaning of the policy). See also *Lincoln National Life Insurance Co v Employers Reinsurance Corporation* [2002] Lloyd's Rep IR 881; *CGU International Insurance v Szabo* [2002] Lloyd's Rep IR 196; *Tiernan v Magen Life* 1998, unreported; *Tryg Baltica International (UK) Ltd v Boston Compania De Seguros SA* [2005] Lloyd's Rep IR 40.

[97] See *American Motorists Insurance v Cellstar Corporation* [2003] Lloyd's Rep IR 295; *Chase v Ram Technical Services* [2000] 2 Lloyd's Rep 418.

[98] As where a reinsurer seeks a declaration that the reinsured is not liable to the assured under a policy governed by some other law: *Meadows Insurance Co v Insurance Co of Ireland* [1989] 2 Lloyd's Rep 298; *Limit (No 3) Ltd v PDV Insurance Co Ltd* [2005] EWCA Civ 383; *Royal & Sun Alliance Insurance plc v Retail Brand Alliance Inc* [2005] Lloyd's Rep IR 110.

[99] *Citadel Insurance Co v Atlantic Union Insurance Co SA* [1982] 2 Lloyd's Rep 543; *Cantieri Navali Riunita SpA v NV Omne Justitia* [1985] 2 Lloyd's Rep 428.

[100] See ch 2.

place the European Union adopted measures whereby a policyholder would, irrespective of the domicile of the insurers, be entitled to have the policy governed by his own domestic law. Accordingly, the Second Life Insurance Directive and the Second Non-Life Insurance Directive contained choice of law rules to that effect. The second initiative applied to contracts generally and was designed to achieve a harmonised set of rules for determining the law applicable to a contract. These rules were enshrined in the Rome Convention 1980, implemented in the UK by the Contracts (Applicable Law) Act 1990. These two initiatives resulted in a complex structure under which insurance contracts whose risk was situated in the EU were governed by the insurance directives, whereas insurance contracts whose risk was situated outside the EU, and also reinsurance contracts, were governed by the Rome Convention. This structure was defective in a number of respects and it was ultimately revised by the Rome I Regulation,[101] which applies to contracts entered into on or after 17 December 2009. The Rome I Regulation is a single measure which applies to the vast majority of commercial contracts, it encompasses insurance and reinsurance contracts, and it has direct application in English law so that implementation was not required.[102] The most significant exclusion, in Article 1(2)(e), consists of arbitration agreements and agreements on the choice of court. English law recognises that these provisions, while forming a part of the contract in which they are contained, are potentially separate undertakings in their own right. As far as arbitration is concerned, the severability principle is given statutory effect by section 7 of the Arbitration Act 1996, although if there is an express choice of law for the main agreement, then there is a presumption that the arbitration provision has the same governing law.[103]

The Rome I Regulation applies irrespective of the domicile of the parties. The UK's departure from the EU has not affected the general principles underlying the operation of the Rome I Regulation, although there have been some consequential amendments to the Regulation by the Law Applicable to Contractual Obligations and Non-Contractual Obligations (Amendment etc) (EU Exit) Regulations 2019.[104]

The applicable law rules in the Rome I Regulation relate only to substantive issues arising under the policy. Procedural matters are to be determined by the law of the country in which the dispute is heard. The matters which are governed by the applicable law are listed in Article 12. These are:

(a) interpretation;
(b) performance;
(c) within the limits of the powers conferred on the court by its procedural law, the consequences of a total or partial breach of obligations, including the assessment of damages insofar as it is governed by rules of law;
(d) the various ways of extinguishing obligations, and prescription and limitation of actions; and
(e) the consequences of nullity of the contract.

[101] European Parliament and Council Regulation 593/2008/EC 'On the Law Applicable to Contractual Obligations'.

[102] Minor modifications to English law were, however, required: see Law Applicable to Contractual Obligations (England and Wales and Northern Ireland) Regulations 2009, SI 2009/3064; Insurance Directives (Financial Services and Markets Act 2000 (Law Applicable to Contracts of Insurance) Regulations 2009, SI 2009/3075).

[103] *Enka Insaat Ve Sanayi AS v OOO 'Insurance Company Chubb'* [2020] UKSC 38. The majority held in *Enka* that in the absence of a choice of law for the main agreement, the law applicable to the arbitration clause would normally be that of the juridical seat of the arbitration.

[104] SI 2019/834.

Article 12.2 also states that, 'in relation to the manner of performance and the steps to be taken in the event of defective performance, regard shall be had to the law of the country in which performance takes place'.

If there is a dispute as to the validity of the policy or any of its terms, Article 10.1 states that validity is to be 'determined by the law which would govern it under this Regulation if the contract or term were valid'. In other words, the court must assume validity and then apply the applicable law to test validity.[105] There is an exception in Article 10.2 where a party asserts that he did not give his consent to the contract, in which case he

> may rely upon the law of the country in which he has his habitual residence if it appears from the circumstances that it would not be reasonable to determine the effect of his conduct in accordance with the law specified in [Article 10.1].

If there are legal requirements for the validity of a policy, Article 11 provides as follows: if the parties are in the same country, the law of that country applies; and if the parties are in different countries, the requirements of any one of the applicable law or the law of either of those countries must be satisfied.

As regards assignment of a policy, the relationship between the assignor and the assignee is governed by the assignment agreement (Article 14.1), although the law governing the claim assigned is governed by the law applicable to the policy (Article 14.2). As regards subrogation, the relationship between the insured and the insurers is governed by the law applicable to the insurance policy, whereas the relationship between the insurers and the third party is governed by the law applicable to the claim (Articles 14 and 15). Contribution claims between insurers are, under Article 16, governed by the law applicable to the payment obligation of the insurer seeking contribution.

Although insurance contracts are now part of the wider regime for choice of law rules, important distinctions still have to be drawn, because the rules vary as between different classes of insurance contract. The rules which apply to contracts generally are set out in Articles 3 and 4, but there are special rules for specific contracts, namely contracts of carriage (Article 5), consumer contracts (Article 6), some insurance contracts (Article 7) and employment contracts (Article 8). The rules applicable to insurance contracts are thus to be determined in some cases under Articles 3 and 4, and in others under Article 7. The rules operate as follows:

1. The law applicable to a reinsurance contract, wherever the risk is situated, is determined in accordance with the general rules in Articles 3 and 4.
2. The law applicable to a 'large' risk is determined in accordance with Article 7.2 (which replicates Articles 3 and 4).
3. The law applicable to an insurance contract where the risk is situated outside the UK and is not a 'large' risk is determined in accordance with the general rules in Articles 3 and 4.
4. The law applicable to an insurance contract whose risk is situated within the UK and which is not a 'large' risk is determined in accordance with Article 7.
5. The law applicable to an insurance contract where the risk is a consumer risk situated outside the UK is determined in accordance with Article 6.

[105] *Egon Oldendorff v Libera Corporation (No 1)* [1995] 2 Lloyd's Rep 64.

This classification rests upon a number of important definitions.

The first is that of the situation of the risk, as the rules vary (other than in the case of large risks) depending upon whether the risk is situated inside or outside the UK. The definition as regards life policies is the place of the policy holder's habitual residence or, if the policy holder is a legal person, the situation of the establishment to which the contract relates is situated. There are four possibilities for non-life policies: if the policy relates to buildings and contents, the risk is situated where the property is situated; in the case of a vehicle, the risk is situated in the place of the vehicle's registration; if the policy relates to travel risks and is for a duration of less than four months, the risk is situated where the policy was taken out; and in any other case the risk is situated where the insured has his habitual residence.

The second is that of 'habitual residence', which is relevant both to the question of where a risk is situated and, as we will see later, to the determination of the applicable law itself if there has been no choice. Under Article 19 of the Rome I Regulation, the habitual residence of a company is 'the place of its central administration' and the habitual residence of an individual is 'his principal place of business'. If the contract is concluded through a branch, agency or establishment, the insured's habitual residence is the 'the place where the branch, agency or any other establishment is located'.

The third is that of the 'large risk', which has its own applicable law rules in Article 7.2 of the Rome I Regulation wherever the risk is situated. A large risk is defined as one which relates to: (i) railway rolling stock, aircraft, ships, liability for aircraft and liability for ships; (ii) credit and suretyship, as long as the policyholder is engaged in an industrial or commercial activity or in one of the liberal professions; and (iii) land vehicles, fire and natural forces, motor vehicle liability, general liability and miscellaneous financial loss, as long as the policy holder has any two of a balance sheet total of €6.2 million, a net turnover of €12.8 million or an average of 250 employees during the financial year.

As can been seen from the above paragraphs, the rules in Articles 3 and 4 apply to reinsurance contracts and risks situated outside the UK that are neither large risks nor consumer risks. The common law approach is more or less replicated by these provisions. The starting point is where the parties have chosen the applicable law. Article 3.1 states: 'A contract shall be governed by the law chosen by the parties. The choice shall be made expressly ... By their choice the parties can select the law applicable to the whole or to part only of the contract.'

The law chosen need not be that of a country; the parties can instead incorporate international conventions to govern their agreement.[106] A choice of law need not be in writing, although the courts have held that if the parties have incorporated into their contract another contract which contains a choice of law clause – and it is common for facultative reinsurance contracts to incorporate the terms of the underlying policy[107] – then the choice of law clause itself will not be treated as having been incorporated unless there is express reference to it.[108] There is more or less unlimited freedom for the parties to choose the applicable law, although the Rome I Regulation does provide some public policy grounds for overturning an express choice. These are unlikely to be relevant to insurance or reinsurance contracts,

[106] This will be of particular importance if the EU chooses to adopt as a voluntary code the Principles of European Insurance Contract Law as developed by a group of leading European insurance academics.

[107] See ch 18 below.

[108] *AIG Group (UK) Ltd v The Ethniki* [1998] 4 All ER 301; *Gan Insurance Co Ltd v Tai Ping Insurance Co Ltd* [1999] Lloyd's Rep IR 229.

and in outline relate to mandatory rules of a law which would, but for the choice of the parties, have been the applicable law (Article 3.3), and any rule of the chosen applicable law which is manifestly incompatible with the public policy of the country in which proceedings are brought (Articles 9 and 21). Under Article 3.2, the parties are free to vary the applicable law at a later date. However, what they cannot do is rely upon a clause which provides that the applicable law is to be determined at some future date, eg the law of the place where an action is brought on the policy: a 'floating choice of law' clause is of no effect and the parties will be treated as not having made any choice of law at all.[109]

If there is no express choice of law, Article 3.1 of the Rome I Regulation recognises the possibility of an implied choice of law. Article 3.1 here states that:

> A contract shall be governed by the law chosen by the parties. The choice shall be … clearly demonstrated by the terms of the contract or the circumstances of the case. By their choice the parties can select the law applicable to the whole or to part only of the contract.

The phrase 'clearly demonstrated' was introduced by the Rome I Regulation, replacing the Rome Convention phrase 'expressed with reasonable certainty', and although the Rome I Regulation test for implied agreement may be harder to satisfy, in practice it is likely that the two provisions mean much the same and cases decided under the Rome Convention generally remain good law. Implied choice can arise in one of two ways. The first way is by 'the terms of the contract'. Such terms may include an exclusive jurisdiction clause or an arbitration clause, as it will be assumed that the law follows the forum or the seat of the arbitration.[110] The second way is by 'the circumstances of the case'. The cases show that the parties are taken to have made an implied choice of the law of the country in which the contract is negotiated and underwritten. That means that a London market placement will generally be regarded as governed by English law,[111] and an overseas market placement will generally be regarded as governed by the law of that country.[112]

In most insurance and reinsurance cases either there is an express choice of law or, at the very least, it is possible to ascertain a choice which is 'clearly demonstrated'. If, however, Article 3 is found not to be applicable, default rules are provided. Article 4.1 contains a series of presumptions based upon different classes of contract, and a general presumption in Article 4.2 for all other cases. There is no mention of insurance and reinsurance in Article 4.1;[113] accordingly, the default general presumption set out in Article 4.2 applies. This states that 'the contract shall be governed by the law of the country where the party required to effect the characteristic performance of the contract has his habitual residence'.

[109] *EI Du Pont de Nemours & Co v Agnew* [1987] 2 Lloyd's Rep 585; *CGU International Insurance plc v Szabo* [2002] Lloyd's Rep IR 196; *Heath Lambert Ltd v Sociedad de Corretaje de Seguros* [2004] 1 Lloyd's Rep 495; *CGU International Insurance plc v AstraZeneca Insurance Co Ltd* [2005] EWHC 2755 (Comm); *Wasa International Insurance Co Ltd v Lexington Insurance Co* [2009] UKHL 40.

[110] *Mitsubishi Corporation v Castletown Navigation Ltd, The Castle Alpha* [1989] 2 Lloyd's Rep 383.

[111] *Assicurazioni Generali SpA v Ege Sigorta* [2002] Lloyd's Rep IR 480; *Gan Insurance Co Ltd v Tai Ping Insurance Co Ltd* [1999] Lloyd's Rep IR 229.

[112] *AIG Europe SA v QBE International Insurance* [2002] Lloyd's Rep IR 22. But note the exceptional facts of *Glacier Reinsurance AG v Gard Marine & Energy Ltd* [2010] EWCA Civ 1052, where a reinsurance policy placed in Switzerland with a Swiss reinsurer was held to be governed by English law, but that was because the Swiss reinsurer had been approached to take an unallocated proportion of a risk being placed on a London market slip, and a separate Swiss slip was issued purely for the sake of convenience.

[113] There is a reference to contracts 'for the provision of services', such a contract being presumed to be governed by the law of the country where the service provider has his 'habitual residence'. There is no authority on the point, but the widely held view is that this phrase does not cover insurance or reinsurance arrangements.

However, this is subject to Article 4.3,[114] which provides: 'Where it is clear from all the circumstances of the case that the contract is manifestly more closely connected with a country other than that indicated in paragraphs 1 or 2, the law of that other country shall apply.'

The initial presumption in the absence of an express or implied choice of law is in favour of the law of the country of the party whose performance characterises the contract; that party can only be the underwriter. So, the presumptive test is in favour of the underwriter's place of business,[115] and it is to be ousted only where the contract is manifestly more closely connected with some other country. In the vast majority of cases decided under the Rome Convention, that presumption has held good, and the addition of the word 'manifestly' by the Rome I Regulation makes it clear that Article 4.3 will operate in exceptional circumstances only. Accordingly, if it is ever necessary to consider Article 4 in an insurance or reinsurance case, the applicable law will be that of the underwriter's place of business.[116] The exception in Article 4.3 has been applied only in the case where the policy is subscribed to by a number of underwriters with their head offices in different jurisdictions: although each subscription is a separate contract, it plainly is not sensible to say that each is governed by a different applicable law, and so it is necessary to identify just one country.[117]

The definition of 'large risks' covers policies which are likely to be multinational in their scope. A typical policy would be one taken out by a parent company for the benefit of itself and its worldwide subsidiaries. Such contracts proved problematic under the Rome Convention, and the English courts refused to accept that there were different applicable laws for each jurisdiction and instead focused on the parent company's place of business.[118] Article 7.2 of the Rome I Regulation addresses this problem. If there is no express or implied choice of law, the matter is resolved by Article 7.2:

> To the extent that the applicable law has not been chosen by the parties, the insurance contract shall be governed by the law of the country where the insurer has his habitual residence. Where it is clear from all the circumstances of the case that the contract is manifestly more closely connected with another country, the law of that other country shall apply.

Thus, the habitual residence of the insurer will provide the applicable law unless there is a single other country with which the risk is more closely connected.

If the risk is not a large one, but it is situated in the UK, the applicable law is to be ascertained in accordance with Article 7.3–6 of the Rome I Regulation. These rules impose restrictions on the ability of the parties to choose the applicable law, the principle being that the insured is entitled to the benefit of domestic law unless the insured has freely agreed to the application of some other law. Article 7.3 lays down the basic proposition that the

[114] It is also subject to Art 4.4, which applies where the applicable law cannot be determined under the other provisions of Art 4. However, that is not in practice relevant to insurance and reinsurance.

[115] *AXA Corporate Solutions Assurance SA v Weir Services Australia Pty Ltd* [2016] Lloyd's Rep IR 578.

[116] *AIG Group (UK) Ltd v The Ethniki; Gan Insurance Co v Tai Ping Insurance Co Ltd* [1999] Lloyd's Rep IR 229; *Commercial Union Assurance Co plc v Simat Helliesen & Eichner Inc* [2001] Lloyd's Rep IR 172; *Assicurazioni Generali SpA v Ege Sigorta AS* [2002] Lloyd's Rep IR 480; *Dornoch Ltd v Mauritius Union Assurance Co Ltd* [2006] EWCA Civ 389; *Stonebridge Underwriting Ltd v Ontario Municipal Insurance Exchange* [2010] EWHC 2279 (Comm).

[117] *Lincoln National Life Insurance Co v Employers Reinsurance Corporation* [2002] Lloyd's Rep IR 881; *Travelers Casualty and Surety Co of Canada v Sun Life Assurance Co of Canada (UK) Ltd (No 2)* [2006] EWHC 2716 (Comm); *Glacier Reinsurance AG v Gard Marine & Energy Ltd* [2010] EWCA Civ 1052.

[118] *American Motorists Insurance Co v Cellstar Corporation* [2003] Lloyd's Rep IR 359.

default applicable law is UK law if the insured has UK habitual residence, although the parties can choose any other law if they so wish. Article 7.4 deals with compulsory policies, and states that a Member State may impose restrictions on choice of applicable law, including that the policy must comply with the requirements laid down in respect of compulsory policies. English law does not require a compulsory policy to be governed by English law as long as the policy adheres to the minimum statutory requirements for coverage. The validity of a choice of law clause is to be tested by the law of the place in which the risk is situated.[119]

The law applicable to a consumer policy where the risk is situated outside the UK is determined by Article 6 of the Rome I Regulation. A consumer for this purpose is 'a natural person who has concluded a contract for a purpose which can be regarded as being outside his trade or profession with another person acting in the exercise of his trade or profession' (Article 6.1). The starting point is that the applicable law is that of the consumer's habitual residence, as defined by Article 19, but only if: (a) the insurer performs his commercial or professional activities in the country where the consumer has his habitual residence; or (b) the insurer directs, by any means, such activities to that country, or to several countries including that country, and the contract falls within the scope of such activities. The effect of these conditions is that a consumer who deals with an insurer from the UK has the benefit of his domestic law or, under Article 6.2, the parties may choose another law, but such a choice is without prejudice to the application of the protections given to the consumer under his domestic law. By contrast, if the consumer is sufficiently sophisticated to seek out an insurer trading overseas, the consumer loses the protection of Article 6 and the applicable law is determined in accordance with the rules in Articles 3 and 4.

[119] *Evialis SA v SIAT* [2003] 2 Lloyd's Rep 377.

2

Regulation of Insurance Business

1. Origins of Domestic Regulation[1]

The insurance and reinsurance industry in the UK is vast – by all measures, the fourth largest in the world. The most recent statistics show that in 2019 there were: 388 insurance and reinsurance companies;[2] 200 friendly societies (small mutual[3] bodies specialising in life and accident cover); 13 major protection and indemnity (P&I) clubs, providing insurance and other benefits to shipowners on a mutual basis; and 76 syndicates within Lloyd's of London, each operating as a self-contained insurer and offering various classes of non-life cover. There are also around 40,000 firms that act for and advise customers and insurers. The total estimated premium income for 2024 is €195.8 billion for life insurance and €87.5 billion for general (non-life) insurance.

Insurance companies (but not, until comparatively recently, insurance intermediaries) have long been subject to a greater degree of regulation than most other types of business. The need for insurance regulation is readily explained. The insurance contract is unusual in that, while the insured is required to perform by paying the premium upfront (or at least in fixed instalments), the insurer is only called on to perform (if ever) at some unidentifiable point in the future. This means that, unlike other trading businesses, the solvency of insurers is not immediately obvious on looking at the accounts, and is capable of being affected dramatically by catastrophic events or trends in mortality. Policyholders rely upon private insurance to protect them against unforeseen events. The need to guarantee the solvency of life insurers is of particular significance in that life insurance is both an investment and a means of providing for family members, so that there has to be confidence the insurers will be in a position to pay out when the risk eventually matures. Some forms of third party liability insurance – notably motor vehicle and employers liability – are compulsory. The sudden insolvency of an insurance company is thus potentially a disaster for policyholders, who may be left uninsured or with outstanding claims, as well as for third parties with claims against policyholders holding liability insurance.

[1] P Rawlings, '"A Sacred Trust for the Future": Regulating Insurance, 1800–70' (2018) 77 *CLJ* 570; P Rawlings, 'Bubbles, Taxes, and Interests: Another History of Insurance Law 1720–1825' (2016) 36 *OJLS* 799.

[2] In 2004 there were 673, but most of the decline is accounted for by mergers and acquisitions.

[3] There are no shareholders and the assets are owned by the members.

Regulation of insurers falls under two headings: solvency (ie the ability to pay claims); and conduct (ie assuming solvency, whether claims are actually paid). Until the passing of the Financial Services and Markets Act 2000, the focus of UK statutory regulation was firmly on the former. Until that Act, the history of solvency regulation had been one of response to the failure of insurance companies and to the need to protect particular types of insurance thought to be socially the most important. The solvency of life insurers in particular had become a serious issue by the middle of the nineteenth century, and matters were brought to a head by the collapse in 1869 of the Albert Life Assurance Company along with 24 other companies that it had acquired. The response was the Life Assurance Companies Act 1870, which introduced a requirement for life insurers to lodge a deposit of money in the Court of Chancery as a sign that they were 'substantial people'.[4] The deposit system was extended to workmen's compensation insurance by the Employers' Liability Insurance Companies Act 1907, to afford protection to employees injured in the workplace in circumstances where their employers faced liability,[5] and then to fire, personal accident and bond investment insurance by the Assurance Companies Act 1909. Other classes of business were left unregulated, but the 1909 Act introduced a key principle, which holds good today, namely, the strict separation of life and non-life business for solvency and accounting purposes. Motor insurance was added to the list by the Road Traffic Act 1930.

This piecemeal approach was unsatisfactory. Many classes of business remained free of solvency controls, and the deposit system itself was no guarantee of solvency: a large premium income did not indicate a secure company if that income had been obtained by offering policies on terms that proved too advantageous to the insured when it came to the payment of claims.[6] The system was revised by the Assurance Companies Act 1946, which extended to all classes of business, adopted a licensing obligation and required a minimum share capital of £50,000, as well as a requirement for assets to exceed liabilities by a margin of 10 per cent of premium income. Even this proved inadequate, as demonstrated by the collapse of the Fire, Auto and Marine Insurance Company, and the Companies Act 1967 in consequence introduced a much stricter regime which required assessments of the financial state of the company, the adequacy of its reinsurance cover on the risks carried, and the fitness of its principal officers and main shareholders. The Act gave the Board of Trade the power to intervene in the operation of the company after its initial authorisation. This more comprehensive approach to authorisation and supervision was extended by subsequent legislation. The Insurance Companies Amendment Act 1973 was passed in the wake of the failure of Vehicle and General, and the law was codified in the Insurance Companies Act 1982.

The central concern of the Insurance Companies Act 1982 remained the financial viability of insurers rather than direct protection for the insured, although the Policyholders Protection Act 1975 did establish a fund to compensate certain categories of insureds in the event of the failure of an insurer.[7] Moreover, insureds were given additional rights: for instance, insurers were obliged to provide certain types of information, particularly, as with some life assurance, where an element of investment was involved; cooling-off periods were

[4] *Nelson v Board of Trade* (1904) 84 LT 565, 567 (Lord Alvestone CJ).

[5] Imposed by the Workmen's Compensation Acts 1906.

[6] *Re North & South Insurance Corp Ltd* (1933) 47 Ll L Rep 346. A reasonable prediction of the liabilities that an insurer will face can be made and it is the ability to make such a calculation with a high degree of accuracy that is one of the skills of the industry, but this is not a scientific process and complete accuracy is impossible.

[7] This was replaced by the Policyholders Protection Act 1997.

instituted, allowing some insurance contracts to be cancelled by the insured; and simpler, cheaper and quicker complaints procedures were introduced. Significantly, although some of these changes were the result of law reform, it was the industry itself that introduced the most important measures of consumer protection. The Unfair Contract Terms Act 1977, which imposes constraints on the enforcement of exclusion clauses, was regarded by insurers as both inappropriate for insurance and a challenge to contract certainty, and the insurance industry's representative body, the Association of British Insurers, agreed with the government to adopt a measure of self-regulation as the price for exemption from the Act. The resulting ABI Statements of Practice for General Insurance and for Life Insurance removed the ability of insurers to refuse claims unreasonably. The Statements were not legally enforceable, but were supplemented in 1981 by the formation by a small number of insurers of the Insurance Ombudsman Bureau, a body authorised to hear consumer complaints and to give rulings on them. The Statements of Insurance Practice were strengthened over time and by the 1990s the membership of the Insurance Ombudsman Bureau had expanded to include almost all mainstream insurers, including Lloyd's. The voluntary structure remained in place until it was overtaken by the Financial Services and Markets Act 2000.

In the two decades following the passing of the Insurance Companies Act 1982, there were important structural changes to the financial services industry. Increased competition at home and internationally forced firms operating in the financial sector to cut costs, develop new products and find new markets. As insurers found it more difficult to make profits in their traditional areas of business, some moved into non-insurance business, such as banking. At the same time, other companies, such as banks and supermarkets, developed insurance products for their customers. There was also a new political environment following the election in 1979 of a Conservative government under Margaret Thatcher. The new government took a good deal of interest in private investment and, as a consequence, in the financial services industry. The government wished to promote private investment by, for instance, encouraging people to buy their own homes and to acquire shares. In addition, the government made no secret of its wish to reduce the welfare state. This was presented as a policy aimed at reducing taxation so that people would be able to make their own choices as to how to spend their money, but it was also a response to the alarming prospect that expenditure on the welfare state seemed set to rise beyond the ability of the country to pay for it: for instance, as birth rates fell and people lived longer, the number entitled to state pensions was expected to increase, while the size of the working population, whose taxes funded those pensions, shrank, and at the same time progress in medical science resulted in increased costs of funding the National Health Service. Of course, the danger in giving people a choice to invest for periods of unemployment or ill health or for their retirement was that some might choose not to do so. The government, therefore, encouraged personal investment and insurance to cover events of life, such as unemployment, ill health and retirement, which had previously been seen largely as tasks for the welfare state. Competition in the financial sector was seen as a way of improving efficiency, prices and performance, and of providing investors and consumers with better protection and rights. It also fitted in with the belief that the market – not the government – was the most efficient means of allocating resources. From the point of view of those investors, much of the enthusiasm for investment in the 1980s was fuelled not by ideology or improved consumer protection, but by the expectation of profit through buying shares or houses, which then seemed almost inevitably to rise in value.

The method of regulation used was to divide financial services into different sectors – insurance, deposit-taking, building societies, pensions and so forth – and to give each sector its own supervisory regime and its own supervisor: for instance, insurance business was regulated under the 1982 Act by the Department of Trade and Industry, banking under the Banking Act 1987 by the Bank of England and building societies under the Building Societies Act 1986 by the Building Societies Commission. The investment industry was treated somewhat differently by the Financial Services Act 1986, which introduced self-regulation but was overseen by three different regulators. As a result of the piecemeal development of regulation, by the late 1980s, there were 10 financial regulators (or more, depending on which bodies were included in the count). This fragmented system of regulation did not work because the financial industry did not operate in neat, self-contained segments and multifunctional financial conglomerates had emerged. A single financial institution or group was subject to several regulators, and the inquiry into problems at Equitable Life indicated some of the difficulties this caused when it noted that two regulators had quite different interpretations of the facts leading to the company's problems.[8] The new focus on private investment and the diversification of the activities of financial service providers was coupled with the view that self-regulation was the best form of investor protection.

---

2. International and European Regulation

In addition to purely domestic issues, by the 1970s there were calls for international agreement on the regulation of financial services firms, which led to reforms that have had an important impact on regulation in the UK. Concerns had emerged as a result of the growth of multinationalism (firms operating in more than one country through branches, subsidiaries or direct cross-border selling) and of globalisation (the interconnectedness of financial markets in different countries). In a global market, firms are not constrained by the same national boundaries that limit the authority of regulators. The failure of two large international banks in the 1970s brought a realisation of the interdependence of national financial markets and led to efforts to improve (or, in many countries, to establish) regulation and to develop co-operation between regulators. Central bankers and bank regulators from the richest nations set up the Basel Committee on Banking Supervision in 1974, although its membership has subsequently expanded. This committee has no formal legal authority, but the economic and political power wielded by its member countries means that its proposals on bank regulation have acquired a powerful influence over national laws. The committee developed the idea that the supervisor from the state in which the bank is authorised (the home state) should take the lead in supervising that bank's global operations. Left without qualification, this would have placed a little too much confidence in the home supervisor for the liking of many countries, so the Basel Committee recognised that the host nation (the place where a bank operates) should have a role; in particular, it should be able to restrict the bank's operations if not satisfied about the quality of the supervision. The committee also emphasised the importance of encouraging the exchange of information between supervisors. By the 1980s the committee had become more ambitious, setting out minimum standards for various aspects of bank regulation, in particular in relation to capital adequacy.

[8] Parliamentary Commissioner for Administration, *The Prudential Regulation of Equitable Life*, 4th report (HC 2002–03, 809); The Rt Hon Lord Penrose, *Report of the Equitable Life Inquiry* (HC 2004, 290).

The Basel Committee's work encouraged the establishment of the International Association of Insurance Supervisors (IAIS) in 1994. The IAIS has a broader base than the Basel Committee, with members from over 200 jurisdictions supplemented by a large number of observers from the industry and professional associations. Like the Basel Committee, the IAIS has issued Insurance Core Principles (ICPs) as benchmarks for an effective supervisory system, the latest version being in November 2018[9] These cover: the powers, independence and responsibilities of supervisors, and the interaction of supervisors across jurisdictions;[10] key supervisory issues, including licensing and supervisory techniques such as inspection, monitoring and intervention; qualitative obligations on insurers in the form of governance and risk management; quantitative matters, including capital requirements and valuation issues; and the conduct of business, including the activities of intermediaries. Each of the ICPs consists of statements of principle, requirements for minimum standards and general guidance. The expectation is that national supervisors will use these standards, and certainly the International Monetary Fund employs them when undertaking its financial system stability assessments.[11] The IAIS has also co-operated with the Basel Committee and the International Organisation of Securities Commissions through the Joint Forum, which deals with issues of mutual interest, such as the regulation of financial conglomerates.

In response to the financial crisis, a new set of pan-European supervisory authorities was proposed and became operational in January 2011.[12] The European Systemic Risk Board[13] has representatives from the central banks of all Member States and the European Commission. It collates and analyses issues relating to systemic risk and financial stability. While national regulators will continue to supervise individual firms, their work will be co-ordinated through the European System of Financial Supervision (ESFS), comprising new European supervisory authorities for insurance (European Insurance and Occupational Pensions Authority),[14] banking (European Banking Authority) and markets (European Securities and Markets Authority). The aim is to improve co-operation and, more controversially, to centralise certain matters to develop consistency of practice among national supervisors. There will be a joint committee to oversee collaboration between the new authorities and to provide a mechanism for settling disputes between national authorities.

These international structures, while important, remain voluntary and advisory. Of far greater significance to the UK insurance industry has been the influence of the European Union. There have been EU directives on life assurance and general insurance, and the distribution of insurance, including the role of intermediaries,[15] and on narrower issues, such as motor vehicle liability insurance,[16] legal expenses insurance,[17] aviation insurance,[18]

[9] For full details, see www.iaisweb.org.

[10] A means of regulating insurers operating across borders, the Common Framework for the Supervision of Internationally Active Insurance Groups, was established in November 2019.

[11] International Monetary Fund, *United Kingdom: Financial System Stability Assessment*, Country Report 03/46 (Washington DC, IMF, 2003) Pt VII.

[12] J de Larosière, *The High Level Group on Financial Supervision in the EU* (Brussels, February 2009).

[13] European Systemic Risk Board (europa.eu).

[14] Reg 1094/2010/EU.

[15] Directive 2016/97/EU.

[16] Directive 2009/103/EC.

[17] Directive 87/344/EC.

[18] Regulation No 785/2004, 1008/2008.

credit and suretyship insurance,[19] accounting[20] and the insolvency of insurers.[21] Much of this legislation has been enacted with the objective of establishing a single market in the European Union.[22] The single market seeks to give EU citizens access to a wide range of insurance products and to enable insurers authorised in one Member State to operate freely in other Member States, although it has been suggested that this project often appears more concerned with facilitating access to markets for insurers than with providing consumer protection.[23] The single market requires the breaking down of regulatory and tax barriers, which earlier inhibited free access to markets, but, at the same time, each state is required to have in place certain minimum standards.[24] This has been prompted, in part, by fear that there might be a 'race to the bottom' in which countries would encourage firms to set up by offering weak regulation and that this might have disastrous consequences if poorly regulated firms were able to operate throughout the EU. In practice, the tendency has been towards greater harmonisation through the intervention of the EU.

In establishing the single market European law has used separate measures for non-life and life insurance because of the fundamental differences between them, and, in particular, the role of life insurance in long-term investment. The first wave of directives on non-life insurance in 1973 and on life insurance in 1979 gave insurers established in one Member State the right to undertake business in other Member States.[25] The directives also prohibited new insurers from offering both life and non-life business,[26] although existing insurers that undertook life and non-life business were permitted to continue, subject to certain requirements, with regard to their life business.[27] These directives still obliged insurers to obtain authorisation to operate outside their home state, but prevented a Member State from discriminating against insurers from another Member State. The second wave of directives were influenced by a series of decisions of the European Court of Justice in 1986 that had aimed to combine liberalisation of the market with consumer protection.[28] These directives developed the passport idea in which an insurer authorised in one Member State would be permitted to supply insurance services in all states. Supervision of the insurer was to be conducted mainly by the home state, although the host state retained a role. The directives also sought to focus on consumer protection by distinguishing consumer from commercial insurance. This was achieved in respect of non-life insurance by separating large risks, which are, broadly, large-scale commercial risks, from mass risks, which are consumer products.[29] In life insurance a distinction was drawn between those policies that originated from an approach made to the insured through, for instance, advertising and those policies that were initiated by the insured, with consumer protection measures being targeted mainly at the first type.[30]

[19] Directive 87/343.

[20] eg Directive 91/674/EC.

[21] Directive 2001/17, 2001/24/EC.

[22] Generally, R Merkin and A Rodger, *EC Insurance Law* (London, Longman, 1997); A McGee, *The Single Market in Insurance: Breaking Down the Barriers* (Aldershot, Ashgate & Dartmouth, 1998).

[23] EC Commission, *Communication from the Commission to the Council, the European Parliament, the European Economic and Social Committee and the Committee of the Regions*, COM(2003) 238.

[24] Directive 92/49, rec 18.

[25] Directives 73/239, 73/240, 79/267 (repealed by 2002/83).

[26] It was commonplace for a UK insurer (but not an insurer elsewhere in Europe) to offer both types of business.

[27] Directive 79/267, Art 13.

[28] *Commission v France* [1986] ECR 3663; *Commission v Denmark* [1986] ECR 3713; *Commission v Germany* [1986] ECR 3755; *Commission v Ireland* [1986] ECR 3817. See D Edward, 'Establishment and Services: An Analysis of the Insurance Cases' (1987) 12 *EL Rev* 231; RW Hodgin (1987) *CML Rev* 273.

[29] Directive 88/357.

[30] Directive 90/619 (repealed by 2002/83).

The third wave of directives extended the notion of the single passport based on minimum harmonisation of rules and mutual recognition of supervision regimes.[31] An insurer, which was authorised and had its head office in one Member State, was permitted to sell its products in another Member State, either directly or by setting up a presence in that state, without requiring fresh authorisation. For instance, if an insurer from another Member State undertook business in the UK through a branch, the establishment conditions had to be satisfied, which in essence meant that consent to the branch being established in the UK had to be obtained from the home state; if the intention was to provide services in the UK from offices outside the country, the service conditions had to be met, which merely required the home state to be notified by the insurer of its intention to provide such services.[32] After the third wave of directives, the Financial Services Action Plan was established to speed up the completion of the single market.[33] Some of the changes introduced as a result of the plan were specific to a particular sector,[34] while others were broader in their impact.[35] In 2001 the Commission sought to improve customer confidence in the single market by establishing a network (FIN-NET) to help consumers who were dissatisfied with a financial service to obtain an out-of-court settlement where the supplier was established in another Member State.[36] As a member of the EU, the legislation of the UK was modified from time to time to incorporate the evolving requirements of the directives.

The earlier directives were replaced by the extensive Solvency II Directive,[37] which, although adopted in 2009, by reason of political disagreements did not come into force in the Member States until January 2016. The key features of Solvency II are: the use of a risk-based capital regime mirroring the capital adequacy rules applicable to banking under what is known as Basel II; solvency requirements in the form of a target Solvency Capital Requirement and a mandatory Minimum Capital Requirement of not less than 25 per cent of the Solvency Capital Requirement; control over the investment of assets; strict processes for risk management and audit; and regulatory supervision. The UK, as a member of the EU, adopted Solvency II by amendments to the Financial Services and Markets Act 2000. As a result of its decision to leave the European Union, the UK ceased to be a part of the Single European Market for Insurance on 31 December 2020. That means that UK insurers can no longer exercise 'passporting' rights by selling insurance directly from the UK into EU countries, and UK insurers who wish to establish themselves in EU countries through branches or agencies must go through the full authorisation process. Equally, EU

[31] Directives 92/49 and 92/96.

[32] The host state may impose conditions on an insurer seeking to exercise its passport rights when it is 'in the interests of the general good' of that state: see eg Third Non-Life Directive 92/49, recitals 19, 20, 24 and 29, Arts 28 and 32(4). However, the European Court of Justice has construed this exception narrowly. For a measure to be justified as in the general good, it must not have been harmonised at EC level, must not be discriminatory, must be clearly justified as being in the general interest, objectively necessary and proportionate to the aim sought, and must not reproduce the rules applied in the insurer's home state. Practices that may be justified as in the general good include enforcing professional codes of conduct in a particular Member State and prohibiting the marketing practice of cold calling.

[33] EC Commission, *Financial Services: Implementing the Framework for Financial Markets: Action Plan*, COM(1999) 232.

[34] For instance, the introduction of new solvency requirements for insurers (Solvency II): European Commission, *Note to the Solvency Subcommittee*, MARKT/2539/03 (2003); the regulation of electronic commerce in relation to insurance: European Commission, *Electronic Commerce and Insurance*, MARKT/2541/03 (2003).

[35] See, eg the adoption of the Fair Value Accounting Directive (Directive 2001/65/EC), which implemented the International Accounting Standard as from 1 January 2005.

[36] See http://ec.europa.eu/internal_market/fin-net/index_en.htm.

[37] Directive 2009/138/EC.

insurers cannot sell insurance in the UK or operate branches or offices in the UK without authorisation from the UK's regulators. The Trade and Co-operation Agreement between the EU and the UK, signed on 24 December 2020, makes no provision for financial services in general and insurance in particular, so that until further agreement is reached – possibly by some form of mutual recognition – this will continue to be the position. In practice, UK insurers wishing to sell insurance in the EU have created branches or agencies in other EU countries and have sought local authorisation to allow them to continue trading. Lloyd's of London adopted its own mechanism to overcome the loss of single market membership through Brexit. Lloyd's has established an insurance subsidiary in Belgium, and all of Lloyd's non-UK European business is written by the subsidiary. However, this is done by way of 'fronting', so that the business is written back into the UK market by way of reinsurance.

The principles applicable to insurance regulation under Solvency II remain operative in the UK even though the UK is no longer in the EU. In addition, UK measures implementing the other insurance directives, including those on distribution, motor insurance and legal expenses, have been retained. It is unclear whether, and to what extent, the UK regime will be altered to take advantage of the claimed new-found freedoms. For the time being, therefore, the UK's system is that laid down by Solvency II and the other directives, but not carrying with it EU single market access. The current regulatory structure is examined in the following paragraphs.

3. Regulation of Insurance in the UK

3.1. The Regulators and their Regulatory Principles

Shortly after its election in 1997, the Labour government began to reshape the regulatory environment of the financial sector. This led to the Financial Services and Markets Act 2000 (FSMA), which established the Financial Services Authority (FSA) as the regulator for most of the financial services industry and handed to it prudential supervision (by which is meant, broadly, supervision aimed at reducing the likelihood of a firm becoming insolvent) and conduct of business supervision (that is, supervision of the relationship between firms and customers). The financial crisis has, however, led to major changes in the regulatory structure. The FSA came in for much criticism as a result of perceived failings in its regulation of the financial services industry – in particular, the banks – and, while the Labour government proposed merely to reform some aspects of its work, on power transferring to the Coalition government in 2010, the abolition of the FSA was announced.[38] The central criticism concerned less the FSA's approach, which had become more intensive following the crisis,[39] and more the structure of the regulatory system, in particular the decision to detach regulation from the Bank of England.

The changes in the regulatory structure were brought about by the Financial Services Act 2012, which made substantial amendments to the 2000 Act. Two bodies were established

[38] HM Treasury, *A New Approach to Financial Regulation: Building a Stronger System* (Cm 8012, 2011).

[39] H Sants, speech at BBA Conference, 2 March 2011: http://tinyurl.com/5vlygbv; H Sants, 'Reforming Supervisory Practice', speech at Reuters Newsmakers Event, 13 December 2010: http://tinyurl.com/25zybly.

to replace the FSA: the Financial Conduct Authority (FCA) and the Prudential Regulatory Authority (PRA). The FCA's strategic objective is to ensure that markets function well. Its operational objectives are: securing an appropriate degree of protection for consumers; protecting and enhancing the integrity of the financial system; and promoting effective competition in the markets for regulated financial services in the interests of consumers.[40] The FCA is independent from the Treasury, but must take note of any recommendations made by the Treasury, and it must also maintain a number of advisory panels consisting of industry professionals and consumers to proffer advice.[41] The PRA, which is the Bank of England, is concerned with financial stability rather than conduct. Its general objective is to promote the safety and soundness of financial service providers by: ensuring that business is carried on in a way which avoids adverse effects on the stability of the UK financial system; minimising the adverse effects of the failure of a business and securing an appropriate degree of protection for policyholders; and ensuring that core services are maintained. Specifically for insurance, the PRA's objective is to contribute to the securing of an appropriate degree of protection for those who are or may become policyholders.[42] Decisions taken by the regulators may be appealed to the Tax and Chancery Chamber of the Upper Tribunal, replacing the Financial Services and Markets Tribunal (established by the FSMA) in 2010.

The regulatory principles to be applied by both the FCA and the PRA are:[43]

(a) the need to use the resources of each regulator in the most efficient and economic way;
(b) the principle that a burden or restriction which is imposed on a person, or on the carrying on of an activity, should be proportionate to the benefits, considered in general terms, which are expected to result from the imposition of that burden or restriction;
(c) the desirability of sustainable growth in the economy of the United Kingdom in the medium or long term;
(d) the general principle that consumers should take responsibility for their decisions;
(e) the responsibilities of the senior management of persons subject to requirements imposed by or under this Act, including those affecting consumers, in relation to compliance with those requirements;
(f) the desirability where appropriate of each regulator exercising its functions in a way that recognises differences in the nature of, and objectives of, businesses carried on by different persons (including different kinds of person such as mutual societies and other kinds of business organisation) subject to requirements imposed by or under this Act;
(g) the desirability in appropriate cases of each regulator publishing information relating to persons on whom requirements are imposed by or under this Act, or requiring such persons to publish information, as a means of contributing to the advancement by each regulator of its objectives;
(h) the principle that the regulators should exercise their functions as transparently as possible.

In carrying out their functions, the FCA and PRA are under a duty to co-operate by co-ordinating their activities and providing advice. To that end, they have prepared a memorandum of understanding setting out their respective rights and duties.[44]

[40] ss 1A–1E.
[41] ss 1JA and 1K–1R.
[42] ss 2A–2C.
[43] s 3B.
[44] ss 3D–3L.

The PRA and FCA's rules, statements of principle, directions and general guidance are to be found in their respective publications the *PRA Sourcebook* and *FCA Handbook*. Both are available online. The *PRA Sourcebook* sets out prudential standards, including the operation of the Solvency II Directive into UK law, while the *FCA Handbook* is concerned with conduct. The *FCA Handbook* is divided into blocks and each block is subdivided into sourcebooks, which detail the FCA's requirements and guidance, and manuals, which contain processes to be followed. The first block in the *Handbook* is High Level Standards, which are the standards that apply to all firms and approved persons. They consist of Principles for Businesses (PRIN), Senior Management Arrangements, Systems and Controls (SYSC), Code of Conduct (COCON), Threshold Conditions (COND), Statements of Principle and Code of Practice for Approved Persons (APER), The Fit and Proper Test for Approved Persons (FIT), Financial Stability and Market Confidence sourcebook (FINMAR), Training and Competence (TC), General Provisions (GEN) and Fees Manual (FEES). The second block is titled Prudential Standards, which set out the prudential requirements that apply to firms, and include General Prudential sourcebook (GENPRU) and, in respect of insurance, Prudential sourcebook for Insurers (INSPRU), Prudential sourcebook for Mortgage and Home Finance Firms, and Insurance Intermediaries (MIPRU), and Interim Prudential sourcebook for Insurers (IPRU-INS). The third block is Business Standards, which are the requirements relating to firms' day-to-day business. They include, so far as is relevant to insurance, Conduct of Business sourcebook (COBS), Insurance: Conduct of Business sourcebook (ICOBS) and Client Assets (CASS). The fourth block is called Regulatory Processes, which describe the operation of the FCA's authorisation, supervisory and disciplinary functions and include Supervision (SUP) and Decision Procedure and Penalties Manual (DEPP). The fifth block is Redress, which sets out complaints and compensation procedures. It includes Dispute Resolution: Complaints (DISP), Consumer Redress Schemes sourcebook (CONRED) and Compensation (COMP). There are also the specialist sourcebooks, which include Professional Firms (PROF). Finally, there are the Regulatory Guides. These are not mandatory, but indicate how the FCA will interpret and enforce its rules. They include The Enforcement Guide (EG), which covers the FCA's enforcement process, the Responsibilities of Providers and Distributors for the Fair Treatment of Customers (RPPD), which discusses the fair treatment of customers, the Perimeter Guidance Manual (PERG), which gives guidance on whether authorisation is required and on the activities regulated under the FSMA, and the Unfair Contract Terms Regulatory Guide (UNFCOG), which indicates how the FCA will use its powers under the Consumer Rights Act 2015. References to the sourcebooks and manuals in this chapter will be noted using these abbreviations.

Each sourcebook and manual opens with an explanation of the types of firms and persons to whom it applies and its purpose, and similar information is provided throughout the text. The sourcebook or manual is divided into chapters, the chapters are divided into sections and the sections into numbered paragraphs. Each paragraph has its regulatory status indicated by a letter in the margin. The most common are 'R' and 'G'. 'R' stands for rules made by the FCA under the FSMA, sections 138A to 138I, and breach of a rule may render the firm liable to an enforcement action as well as a private action for damages (section 138D). 'G' usually indicates guidance issued under section 139A, and is used, among other things, to explain the implications of provisions and to recommend particular courses of action. However, guidance is not binding on those to whom the FSMA applies or the courts, nor does it have any evidential effect, so that a breach of the guidance does not mean there has been a breach of a rule, although each regulator will presume that a firm which follows guidance is in compliance with the relevant rule.[45] The GEN manual in the *Handbook* states that 'Every provision in the Handbook must be interpreted in the light of its purpose' (GEN 2.2.1). That purpose is to be gathered from the provision itself and its context. This manual also notes that all communications required by the *Handbook* to be 'in writing' may, unless a contrary intention appears, be given through electronic media (GEN 2.2.14).

Looking at this description (and it should be noted that there are other parts relating to non-insurance aspects of the financial services industry), it may be hard to believe that the *Handbook* has gone through a simplification process under which large parts have been deleted, either because they are adequately covered elsewhere in the *Handbook* or because the rules and guidance have been relegated to Regulatory Guides and advice pamphlets: so, for example, the Authorisation manual has been deleted and much of the material is now in advice given to those seeking authorisation and in PERG.[46]

3.2. General Prohibition and Authorisation

Section 19 of the Financial Services and Markets Act 2000 contains the general prohibition: no one who is not an authorised[47] or exempt person[48] may carry on (or purport to carry on) a regulated activity in the UK (see section 418).[49] An authorised person is someone who has obtained Part IV permission[50] or someone who is otherwise authorised by a provision of the FSMA. A regulated activity is an activity that is within the list in schedule 2 of the FSMA, that is specified by the Treasury and that is carried on as a business (section 22).[51] The list in schedule 2 includes a contract of insurance (paragraph 20) and, under the Financial Services and Markets Act 2000 (Regulated Activities) Order 2001, effecting or carrying out a contract of insurance is a specified activity.[52] Applications for authorisation are made to the PRA, but must be approved by both the PRA and the FCA.

A person who is acting in the course of business and who is not either authorised or acting with the approval of an authorised person may not invite or induce another to engage in an investment activity (FSMA, section 21),[53] and breach of the general prohibition contained in section 19 is a criminal offence (sections 23–25). An agreement made by someone in breach of the general prohibition is unenforceable against the other party unless

[45] See also s 395.

[46] See also eg Approved Persons Regime (Simplification and MiFID) Instrument 2007 (FSA 2007.6).

[47] The Society of Lloyd's is an authorised person: s 315(1); see below. Someone authorised under the Insurance Companies Act 1982 (s 3 or 4) retains their authorisation: Financial Services and Markets Act 2000 (Transitional Provisions) (Authorised Persons, etc) Order 2001 (2001/2636), Art 14.

[48] The term 'person' refers to a legal person and so includes a company. On the definition of an exempt person, see FSMA, ss 38, 39(1); Financial Services and Markets Act 2000 (Exemption) Order 2001 (2001/1201), sch, para 43 (trade unions and employers organisations that provide certain benefits to members) and 14 (someone who ceased to be an underwriter at Lloyd's before 24 December 1996); SUP 12.2.2. Those who provide motor breakdown services do not require authorisation: Financial Services and Markets Act 2000 (Regulated Activities) Order 2001 (2001/544), Art 12.

[49] On the meaning of regulated activity, see below.

[50] See below.

[51] See s 419.

[52] SI 2001/544, para 75; also sch 1.

[53] The term 'engaging in investment activity' is defined as, among other things, 'entering or offering to enter into an agreement the making or performance of which by either party constitutes a controlled activity': s 21(8). See further s 20(9), (10), sch 2; on 'controlled activity', see below.

the court is of the view that enforcement is just and equitable, and discretion will not be exercised in favour of a company that had failed to act with reasonable care by failing to seek authorisation.[54] The other party is entitled to recover any money or property paid or transferred under the agreement and to be compensated for any loss caused by parting with it (sections 26–28; see also section 30(2)–(4)). Where someone who is authorised under the FSMA undertakes a regulated activity that lies outside the limits of their authorisation, this amounts to a contravention of the Act, but, while they may be liable to a disciplinary sanction, it does not render them guilty of an offence or make any transaction void, although it may give rise to an action for breach of statutory duty (section 20(1), (2)).[55] Both the framework within which the regulators must work when granting, suspending, varying and withdrawing authorisation and the rights of applicants or authorised persons affected by decisions on these matters are set out in Part IV of the FSMA. The regulators are empowered to give permission (known as 'Part IV permission') to carry on a regulated activity (section 55A), but are required to ensure that the authorised person 'will satisfy and continue to satisfy, the threshold conditions in relation to all of the regulated activities for which he has or will have permission' (section 55B(3)). These threshold conditions are contained in schedule 6, part 1D (see section 55B(1)) and are the subject to the *FCA Handbook*'s COND and the *PRA Sourcebook*'s Conditions Governing Business. The focus of the PRA is on the resources of the applicant and the suitability of its senior staff, whereas that of the FCA is the business model and the FCA's ability to maintain supervision.

The first threshold condition is that, if the regulated activity involves effecting contracts of insurance, the authorised person must be a body corporate, registered friendly society or member of Lloyd's (FSMA, schedule 6, paragraph 4B(1)). Secondly, where the authorised person is a body corporate constituted under UK law, its head office and registered office, if any, must be in the UK (schedule 6, paragraph 4C; COND 1, Annexes 1 and 2). This aims to prevent problems of supervision caused by a company having its head office in the UK while being authorised elsewhere. There is no definition of 'head office' in any of the relevant legislation; however, the FCA has taken the view that it need not refer to the place of incorporation or where the firm conducts most of its business, or to the place where its central management and administration are located (COND 2.2.3).

The third threshold condition is that, if the authorised person has close links with another person, the regulators must be satisfied that this will not inhibit effective supervision and that those laws will not prevent effective supervision. By 'close links' is meant that the other firm is the parent or subsidiary of the authorised firm, is the parent of a subsidiary of the authorised firm or is a subsidiary of the parent of the authorised firm; the other firm controls 20 per cent of the voting rights or capital of the authorised firm; or the authorised firm controls 20 per cent of the voting rights or capital of the other firm (FSMA, schedule 6, paragraph 4F). It is worth noting that the regulators may have regard to anyone who has, or is likely to have, a relationship that is considered relevant with an applicant or with an authorised person when determining whether to grant permission or to vary or cancel an existing permission (section 49(1)). A key concern here is that the regulators receive adequate information from all these parties to enable it to assess whether the regulatory requirements are being met (COND 2.3 and COND 2, Annex 1).

[54] *Re Whiteley Insurance Consultants* [2009] Lloyd's Rep IR 212.

[55] A limited right of action for breach of statutory duty does exist under s 20(3): see Financial Services and Markets Act 2000 (Rights of Action) Regulations 2000, SI 2001/2256, para 4.

The fourth threshold condition requires the regulators to be satisfied that the authorised person has adequate resources to conduct the regulated activity (FSMA, schedule 6, paragraph 4D). By 'adequate' is meant 'sufficient in terms of quantity, quality and availability', while 'resources' refers not only to financial resources, but also to, for instance, the systems, staff and anyone related to the firm, such as directors, controllers or those with close links (PRIN 3 and 4, see below). As part of this condition, the FCA will expect an applicant for authorisation to present an appropriate business plan (COND 2.4).

Fifthly, the FCA must be convinced that the authorised person 'is a fit and proper person'. Consideration is given to any relevant circumstances, including connections with any other person, the nature of the regulated activity and 'the need to ensure that his affairs are conducted in an appropriate manner having regard to the interests of consumers and the integrity of the UK financial system' (FSMA, schedule 6, paragraph 3D). Obviously, the ability of a firm to satisfy these conditions will be affected by the fitness of those who work in the firm and those who are closely connected with it so that, for instance, an unfit director may render the firm itself unfit. A firm will be expected to conduct its business with integrity and in compliance with the relevant standards of the FCA and of any other regulatory bodies. It must have competent and prudent management, and must conduct its affairs with due skill, care and diligence (COND 2.5). The sixth threshold condition is that an insurer from outside the UK must appoint an authorised UK representative. The insurer must be a body corporate formed under the law of the place where its head office is located and the person carrying on insurance business in the UK must comply with the requirements on assets held in the UK.

To elicit the information required to make a decision about authorisation, the regulators have designed an application pack. After receipt of the application, the regulators may visit premises and arrange discussions with the management. The regulators may grant or refuse permission, or may grant a narrower permission than is sought, and they must describe the regulated activities for which permission is being given, although they may also specify limitations to that permission and requirements that must be fulfilled. The FCA maintains a public register of those to whom have been granted Part IV permission (FSMA, section 347).

3.3. Approved Person

An approved person is an individual within a firm who carries out a controlled function and is approved by the FCA as being fit and proper to carry out that function (FSMA, section 59). The holders of certain posts in an overseas company which has UK branches do not require approval by the regulators, although there must be notification to the FCA ('notified posts'). These posts are: the worldwide chief executive of a firm where that person is situated outside the UK; the person within the overseas firm who has purely strategic responsibility for the UK; and the authorised UK representative of an insurer. A controlled function is one that the regulators regard as key to the obligations under Part V of the FSMA, which deals with the performance of regulated activities. The controlled functions are listed in SUP 10A.4.4 (see FSMA, sections 59(3), 59ZA, 59ZB and 59A), and these are divided into categories.

The application to become an approved person must be submitted by or on behalf of the firm (FSMA, section 60). Under section 61(1), the PRA can only grant approved person status if satisfied that the individual is fit and proper, which falls under FIT. The FCA emphasises the need for honesty, integrity, reputation, competence, capability and financial soundness (FIT 1.3). These matters will be assessed within a context that takes account of the firm's activities and the markets in which it operates. In determining competence and capability, the FCA will, among other things, consider whether the person satisfies the FCA training and competence requirements in relation to the controlled function being performed, has demonstrated suitability by experience and training, and has adequate time to perform the controlled function (the detailed requirements are set out in APER). An authorised person must take reasonable care to ensure that no one who is not approved performs a controlled function in relation to the carrying out of a regulated activity by the authorised person, even if the firm has outsourced the performance of the controlled function (section 59(1), (2)). Finally, there are time limits within which the PRA must make a decision on an application, even though it has been held that breach of these limits does not lead to approval by default, and although the applicant could apply for judicial review, the breach will not result in the regulators' authority to determine the application lapsing.[56]

APER contains seven Statements of Principle. They only apply insofar as the approved person is carrying out a controlled function (APER 1.1A), that is, the standards do not apply to other aspects of the firm's business, although conduct in non-controlled functions could influence the FCA's opinion of whether someone is a fit and proper person (FIT). They must (APER 2.1A.3): (1) 'act with integrity' and (2) 'due skill, care and diligence'; (3) 'observe proper standards of market conduct'; and (4) deal with the FCA, the PRA and other regulators in 'an open and cooperative way' and disclose such information as the FCA would reasonably expect to receive. These first four Statements of Principle apply to all approved persons (APER 3.1.7A). In addition, an approved person performing significant influence functions, which means, broadly, managing and overseeing the business (SUP 10.4.5): (5) 'must take reasonable steps to ensure that the business of the firm for which he is responsible … is organised so that it can be controlled effectively'; (6) 'must exercise due skill, care and diligence in managing the business … for which he is responsible'; and (7) 'must take reasonable steps to ensure that the business of the firm for which he is responsible … complies with the relevant requirements and standards of the regulatory system' (see APER 2.1A.3). The Code of Practice for Approved Persons is also part of this manual (APER 3 and 4; FSMA, section 64(A)–(B)). It sets out the types of conduct that will, in the FCA's opinion, constitute either compliance with or a breach of the Statements of Principle. The approved person will only be in breach of a Statement of Principle where this person is 'personally culpable', that is, their conduct was deliberate or below a reasonable standard of behaviour (APER 3.1.4).

3.4. Appointed Representative

An appointed representative (AR), who may be an individual or firm, carries on a regulated activity on behalf of an authorised firm and is exempt from seeking permission under

[56] *David Thomas v Financial Services Authority*, 22–23 July 2004, www.financeandtaxtribunals. gov.uk, a decision of the now superseded Financial Services and Markets Tribunal. The Tribunal took the view that, while, in *R (Davies and Others) v Financial Services Authority* [2004] 1 WLR 185, the High Court had said judicial review should be permitted sparingly, this was one situation where it would be appropriate because without a decision by (then) the FSA the Tribunal could not intervene. See Gray [2005] *Journal of Financial Regulation and Compliance* 95.

FSMA, section 19 (FSMA, section 39; PERG 5.13; SUP 12.2.7), although the FCA must be notified (SUP 12.7). Anyone who performs a governing function in a firm that is acting as an AR and is carrying on general insurance business[57] must be an approved person. Where the general insurance business is incidental to the main business of the AR, such as a dentist who recommends a particular dental insurance policy offered by a specific firm, only one person in the firm need be approved, although that person must be a director or partner.

To become an AR, the person must not be an authorised person, must have entered into a contract with an authorised person to carry on business described in the Appointed Representatives Regulations and must comply with any requirement in those regulations (SUP 12.2.2). In the contract, the authorised person must expressly agree to the AR acting on its behalf and accept responsibility for the AR's acts or omissions. Indeed, the AR's acts or omissions are deemed to be those of the authorised person (SUP 12.3; FSMA, section 39(3), (4), (6)). The authorised person can permit the AR to undertake regulated activities for which the authorised person is authorised insofar as these extend to the pre-contractual advising and arrangement of deals. The AR can also act in the conclusion, administration and performance of general insurance and pure protection contracts,[58] but cannot undertake these functions in relation to investment business.

Before appointing an AR, the authorised person must establish on reasonable grounds that the appointment will not prevent it from satisfying the threshold conditions and that the proposed AR is solvent, suitable and has no close links which would be likely to prevent the effective supervision of the AR by the authorised person. The authorised person must have adequate controls over the regulated activities performed by the AR and sufficient resources to monitor compliance. The authorised person must be ready to comply with the other requirements in SUP 12 (SUP 12.4.2) and make regular assessments as to the suitability of the AR to undertake the particular tasks assigned to it (SUP 12.4.1A–12.4.5). The regulatory burden with respect to ARs, therefore, lies with those firms on whose behalf they act. As has been seen, the actions of the AR are deemed to be those of the authorised person but, in addition, such an action may also suggest that the authorised person is in breach of the requirement to maintain adequate systems and controls (see SYSC 3). The authorised person must ensure that the AR understands the regulatory provisions relevant to the authorised person's business, that the AR will provide sufficient access to its staff, premises and records to enable supervision by the authorised person, that it complies with requirements of knowledge, ability and good repute, and that it is able to deliver the same level of protection to clients as if the clients had been dealt with by the authorised person themself (SUP 12.4.8A–B). Finally, an AR may work for several principals, but a multiple principal agreement must be in place with all the principals and one must act as lead principal for dealing with complaints (SUP 12.4.5A–C).

An 'introducer appointed representative' (IAR) is an AR whose appointment is limited to effecting introductions to the firm and distributing non-real-time financial promotions relating to the products available from the firm (SUP 12.2.8).[59] A dentist who provides

[57] Broadly, general insurance means any contract of insurance other than long-term insurance: for the definition, see Financial Service and Markets Act 2000 (Regulated Activities) Order 2001 (ST 2001/544), sch 1.

[58] A pure protection product is a long-term insurance contract that is not an investment product. More particularly, it is a contract under which the benefit is paid on death (occurring within 10 years of the contract or before the insured life attains 70), or on illness, injury or infirmity and for which there is no surrender value (unless it is a single premium policy and the surrender value does not exceed the value of that premium), eg critical illness insurance.

[59] The terms of the contract of employment must limit the scope of the appointment to these matters: SUP 12.5.7. A financial promotion involves the communication of an invitation to engage in an investment activity made in the

information on dental insurance and then passes details of interested clients to an authorised firm so that firm can arrange insurance would need to be appointed as an IAR. The full AR regime does not apply, but an IAR must fulfil the qualifications of an AR, and the obligations as between the authorised person and an IAR are the same as apply between an authorised person and an AR (SUP 12.2.8–11, 12.4.6).

For the sake of completeness, and in order to distinguish them from IARs, mention should be made of 'introducers' and 'representatives'. An introducer is an individual appointed by an authorised person or by the AR of an authorised person to effect introductions in the course of designated investment business and to distribute non-real-time financial promotions. An introducer (unless also an IAR) is not an exempt person under FSMA, section 39, and so cannot carry on regulated activities on their own behalf, but must work in the name of the authorised person. Such a person does not come within the Approved Persons regime because they do not perform a controlled function (SUP 12.2.13). A representative is someone appointed by a firm or an AR to advise on investments, arrange deals in investments or deal in investments as an agent.

---

4. High Level Standards

4.1. Principles for Businesses

The first block in the *FCA Handbook* is entitled High Level Standards and applies to all those regulated by the FSMA. The first manual in this block is Principles for Businesses (PRIN).[60] Much of the rest of the *Handbook* rests on these Principles. They 'are a general statement of the fundamental obligations of firms under the regulatory system' (PRIN 1.1.2) and, in particular, they expand on the fit and proper requirement in COND 5, although the implications of that requirement are not exhausted by the Principles. A firm applying for authorisation must be able and willing to abide by the Principles, and a breach of the Principles renders the firm liable to disciplinary sanctions, which include fines and the variation, suspension or termination of authorisation, and may lay open the issue of whether the firm is fit and proper (PRIN 1.1.4).

There are 11 Principles (PRIN 2.1.1). An authorised firm or person must (1) 'conduct its business with integrity' and (2) 'with due skill, care and diligence', (3) 'take reasonable care to organise and control its affairs responsibly and effectively, with adequate risk management systems', (4) 'maintain adequate financial resources' and (5) 'observe proper standards of market conduct'; it must 'pay due regard' both (6) 'to the interests of its customers and treat them fairly'[61] and (7) 'to the information needs of its clients, and communicate information to them in a way which is clear, fair and not misleading'; a firm (8) 'must manage conflicts of

course of business. It may be a real-time or non-real-time communication. A real-time communication is an oral communication (at a meeting or by telephone) initiated by the recipient (solicited) or the maker of the communication (unsolicited). A non-real-time communication is made in a letter, email or brochure, or through a website.

[60] Another manual in this block is Threshold Conditions (COND), discussed above.

[61] See FSA, 'Treating Customers Fairly', www.fsa.gov.uk/pages/doing/regulated/tcf, which seeks to ensure that: products sold are appropriate to the customers; the systems in the firm do not encourage mis-selling (eg through incentives to salespersons); the customer understands the terms, pricing and risks of the product, and is aware of suitable alternatives and of complaint and redress procedures; and subsequent changes in performance of the product are communicated to the customer.

interest fairly' and (9) 'take reasonable care to ensure the suitability of its advice and discretionary decisions for any customer who is entitled to rely upon its judgment'; (10) 'it must adequately protect those client assets for which it is responsible' and it (11) 'must deal with its regulators in an open and cooperative way, and must disclose to the FCA appropriately anything relating to the firm of which the FCA would reasonably expect notice'. The application of the Principles will vary according to the circumstances: for instance, what will be required to fulfil the obligations imposed under PRIN 6–10 will depend on the characteristics of each customer (see PRIN 1.2.1). One of the Regulatory Guides the FCA has issued, RPPD, provides its view on what the combination of the Principles and the rules require of providers and distributors of products and services to treat customers fairly. The guidance is issued under FSMA, section 157. It is, therefore, not binding, and non-compliance does not indicate a breach of the rules; however, the FCA will not take action against someone who adheres to the guidance. The guidance is concerned mainly with PRIN 2, 3, 6 and 7. It addresses what treating a customer fairly should mean to a provider at various stages, such as design, marketing, sales and advice, aftersales information and service, and complaints handling. So, for instance, firms should consider issues such as the customer's needs, risk appetite and understanding.

4.2. Systems and Controls

The second manual in the High Level Standards block is SYSC. This manual expands on PRIN 3 in the Principles for Businesses (SYSC 1.2) in that it aims 'to encourage firms' directors and senior managers to take appropriate practical responsibility for their firms' arrangements on matters likely to be of interest to the FCA because they impinge on the FCA's functions under the Act' (SYSC 1.2.1). The firm must take reasonable care to have systems and controls that are sufficient to ensure compliance and counter the risk of financial crime (SYSC 3.2.6), and 'are appropriate to its business' (SYSC 3.1.1; see also SYSC 13). What this means in practice will depend on the nature, size and complexity of the business, the diversity (including geographical diversity) of its operations, the volume and size of its transactions, and the degree of risk associated with its business (SYSC 3.1.2). The larger, more complex firms will have an audit committee and internal audit process charged with monitoring systems and controls (SYSC 3.2.15, 3.2.16). There are also provisions in this sourcebook that relate to whistleblowing under the Public Interest Disclosure Act 1998 (SYSC 18). The systems and controls mechanisms must ensure that all employees are suitable, which includes assessing their honesty and competence in the context of their role within the firm (SYSC 3.2.13, 3.2.14).[62] Delegation of management responsibilities is, of course, inevitable, but the firm must assess the suitability of the person designated to carry out a task (SYSC 3.2.3), and the manual also covers the means by which a firm can apportion responsibilities among directors and senior managers in a way that is clear, enables the flow of information and facilitates adequate control and monitoring by the management (SYSC 2.1, 3.2.11A). Out-sourcing – that is, contracting someone outside the firm to undertake services – of regulated functions is permitted, but the firm cannot contract out its regulatory obligations, so must take reasonable care to ensure regulated functions are being properly performed by the other party and must have sufficient information to assess the

[62] See also the Training and Competence sourcebook (TC) below.

impact of the outsourcing on its systems and controls (SYSC 3.2.4). Firms are required to consider whether the various requirements under SYSC mean they need to include in their risk-control arrangements the appointment of a chief risk officer, who would be accountable to the firm's governing body for oversight of firm-wide risk management, and (without detracting from the responsibility of the firm's governing body) a governing body risk committee (SYSC 21.1).

4.3. Training and Competence

TC covers the firm's obligations with respect to its employees in recruitment, training, attaining and maintaining competence and monitoring these issues.[63] These provisions originate in the stipulation in PRIN 3 and the requirement in the threshold conditions that firms demonstrate they are organising and controlling their business and they are fit and proper. They must, therefore, ensure both that their staff in general are competent and that those individuals charged with performing controlled functions are, in addition, fit and proper.

4.4. General Provisions

The final manual in the High Level Standards block is GEN, which, as its name suggests, contains a variety of provisions that do not fit in appropriately anywhere else: for instance, what happens when an emergency makes compliance with a rule impossible (GEN 1.3) and general guidance on interpreting the *Handbook* (GEN 2). The manual also includes a provision that seeks to prevent the public from being misled by the fact of authorisation:

> [A] firm must ensure that neither it nor anyone acting on its behalf claims, in a public statement or to a client, expressly or by implication, that its affairs, or any aspect of them, have the approval of the FCA. (GEN 1.2.1 and 1.2.2A(1))

This does not prevent a firm from making a statement explaining that it is authorised or has permission to carry on a specific activity or that the firm's approved persons have been approved by the FCA (GEN 1.2.2A(2)). Indeed, firms are under certain obligations to reveal their authorisation in communications with customers (GEN 4.3, 4.4 and 4, Annex 1):[64] for instance, a firm must take reasonable care to ensure that every letter or electronic communication sent with a view to conducting a regulated activity discloses that the firm is 'authorised and regulated by the Financial Services Authority', and an appointed representative must in addition specify the firm of which they are an appointed representative.[65]

---

5. Prudential Sourcebook for Insurers

The second block in the *Handbook* consists of prudential sourcebooks. GENPRU sets out the general proposition: 'Adequate financial resources and adequate systems and controls

[63] See also SYSC 3.1.1 and 3.2.13.
[64] Based on Principle 7 in PRIN 3.
[65] For the meaning of appointed representative, see above.

are necessary for the effective management of prudential risks.' This is repeated and elaborated in INSPRU, which requires that all insurers maintain adequate provisions to meet their liabilities to policyholders and other liabilities (INSPRU 1.1). They must also meet the minimum capital requirements, although the calculation will differ between general insurance and long-term insurance (INSPRU 1.1; GENPRU 2.1). There must be provision to cover various risks (INSPRU 3): credit risk (the risk of default by a counterparty), market risk (the risk involved in changes in asset values), liquidity risk (the risk that the firm is unable to meet obligations as they fall due), operational risk (the risk associated with management of the firm's operations: see SYSC 14) and group risk (the risks arising from associated companies).

---

6. Business Standards

The third block in the *Handbook* is Business Standards, which deals with the day-to-day business of firms and their relationships with customers. Broadly, long-term insurance business falls within COBS and other insurance is covered by ICOBS. In broad terms, the content of both sourcebooks elaborates PRIN 6, which requires firms, including intermediaries, to treat customers fairly: a firm must act 'honestly, fairly and professionally in accordance with the best of interests of its client' (COBS 2.1.1). In addition, the sourcebooks have been shaped by various pieces of EU law, including parts of the Distance Marketing Directive and the Insurance Distribution Directive. COBS has provisions concerning, among other things: the content and presentation of information about products;[66] the firm and its remuneration; communication with clients, particularly retail clients; financial promotions; advice on product suitability; distance contracts, including e-commerce; record keeping; cancellation; and claims handling. It also covers the provision of advice. In respect of some of these activities, different obligations are owed to retail clients from those owed to other clients (COBS 1, Annex (Application) and COBS 3). The FCA regards financial promotions as a risk area because of the important part they play in the consumer's decision-making process. Of particular concern are products that are not properly described or are described in a way that creates a misleading impression to retail customers. Distinctions are made between the information that must be supplied to retail customers and that to commercial customers, and also between information required in non-distance sales, where there is a degree of face-to-face contact (even if part of the negotiations were by telephone, email, etc), and in distance sales (eg telephone).The provisions in ICOBS are similar but less exacting. Information must be supplied in order to enable the customer to make a choice as to the appropriate product, although the focus is more on the situation where a customer is being advised, for instance, about buying a particular household contents policy offered by Acme Insurance Company, than where the customer is merely being advised as to the general merits of buying a household contents policy. A firm must take reasonable steps to ensure that its communications with customers are clear, fair and not misleading (ICOBS 2.2.2, 2.2.2A and 2.2.3; see also PRIN 7). It may not exclude or restrict the duties or liabilities

[66] Statutory product disclosure obligations were imposed on insurers by European Commission Regulation 2017/1469/EC, a measure made under the Insurance Distribution Directive. This requires basic product information to be given prior to the making of a non-life policy, including the sum insured and the main risks insured.

it owes to a customer under the regulatory system, and may only exclude or restrict other duties or liabilities insofar as it is reasonable for it to do so (ICOB 2.5.1). Before the far-reaching changes to the common law introduced by the Consumer Insurance (Disclosure and Representations) Act 2012 and the Insurance Act 2015, ICOBS imposed important restrictions on the rights of insurers to deny liability for the insured's breaches of fair presentation rules or of policy terms. Those restrictions were rendered all but redundant by the legislation, and ICOBS 8.1.2 now more or less repeats what is set out in these measures.

7. Regulatory Processes

The fourth block in the *Handbook* is titled Regulatory Processes and it includes SUP, which sets out the relationship between the FCA and authorised persons, and DEPP, which deals with the FCA's procedures for making decisions that involve the issue of statutory notices and penalties and the conduct of interviews.

7.1. Supervision

The FCA is charged by section 1L of the FSMA to maintain arrangements for supervising authorised persons, and by section 1K to provide general guidance as to how it exercises its functions. The detail of this is set out in SUP. SUP furthers the FCA's strategic objective of ensuring that markets function well and the FCA's functional objectives of consumer protection, integrity of the financial system and the promotion of competition (SUP 1A.1.3). The FCA's supervisory principles are: looking forward, to pre-empt or address poor conduct; a focus on the firm's strategy and business models; a focus on culture and governance within a firm; a focus on individual accountability within a firm, as well as the overall accountability of the firm itself; a proportional and risk-based approach; communication with consumers and the industry, securing transparency of the FCA's activities; co-ordination with other regulatory bodies; and intervention to put right systemic harm (SUP 1A.3.2A). The FCA uses a number of tools in performing its supervisory function: diagnostic tools to identify and assess risks; monitoring tools to track identified risks; preventative tools, which limit identified risks and prevent them from crystallising or increasing; and remedial tools to respond when risks have crystallised (SUP 1A.4).

In order to monitor a firm's compliance with regulatory requirements, the FCA depends on gathering information. In practice, it seeks to work 'in an open and cooperative relationship with firms', and to obtain information through that relationship rather than by using statutory powers. The FCA also requires firms to disclose, without being asked, anything of which it would reasonably expect notice (SUP 2.1.6; SUP 15.3.8; see PRIN 11). A firm must take reasonable steps to ensure that anyone supplying it with services or outsourcing facilities deals with the FCA in the same spirit of co-operation (SUP 2.3.7). The authorised firm must inform the FCA immediately if it fails to satisfy one of the threshold conditions. It also must inform it of any matter that might have a significant adverse effect on its reputation or its ability to provide adequate services to customers, or of anything that could lead to serious financial consequences to other firms or the financial system. The firm is also required to notify the FCA of any breach of rule or requirement imposed under the FSMA (SUP 15.3.11), any civil, criminal or disciplinary proceedings against the firm (SUP 15.3.15), any fraud, errors or other irregularities (SUP 15.3.17), any insolvency or winding-up proceedings (SUP 15.3.21), changes in the accounting reference date (SUP 16.3.17) and changes of controller (SUP 11.3), auditor (SUP 3.3) or among the approved persons (SUP 10.11–13). Advanced warning of other matters must be given to the FCA (SUP 15.5.1, 15.5.4, 15.5.5, 15.5.7): a change of the firm's name, its principal place of business or its legal status, or a shift to supervision by an overseas regulator.

Information will come, therefore, primarily from the firms themselves (SUP 15–17A), including through the work of the firm's auditors (SUP 3).[67] It may also come from requests made by the FCA (SUP 2.1.6), from visits to the firm and meetings with its representatives (SUP 2.3.1), from the Financial Ombudsman Service, and ultimately from the FCA's use of its powers under Part XI of the FSMA, which requires the provision of information on demand and also enables a report to be commissioned, an inspector to be appointed or a warrant to be granted for entry into premises.[68] The FCA can gather information on how a firm sells its products by mystery shopping techniques (SUP 2.4). The SUP manual contains various other provisions. It explains the procedure by which a firm may vary or cancel its Part IV permission,[69] or may seek either a waiver of rules (SUP 8; FSMA, section 148)[70] or guidance on the application of rules (SUP 9).[71] It covers the powers of the FCA and the PRA to impose additional requirements on a firm or to amend the activities it is permitted to undertake (SUP 7; FSMA, sections 55J–O).

7.2. Enforcement

The FCA possesses a range of enforcement powers (FSMA, Part XIV). Guidance on the use that will be made of them is contained in DEPP. The FCA may: vary or cancel permission and withdraw authorisation (sections 33, 55J–KA, 206A); issue a prohibition order against an individual who is considered not fit and proper to perform functions in relation to a regulated activity (sections 56–58); withdraw approval from an approved person (section 63); or issue a public censure or impose a fine on an approved person (sections 66–66B[72]) or a firm (sections 205–06). It can apply to a court for an injunction where, for instance, there is a reasonable likelihood of a regulatory breach occurring (section 380); it can challenge unfair terms in standard form consumer contracts under powers in the Consumer Rights Act 2015 (section 12); and it can seek a restitution order (sections 382, 384). Moreover, the FCA can prosecute for an offence under the Act and under the rules on money laundering (sections 401–02).

[67] In addition, the auditing regime is covered in general legislation on companies (Companies Act 2006).

[68] See FSMA, ss 165–177A and SUP 5.

[69] SUP 6; FSMA, ss 55H (FCA) and 55I (PRC).

[70] SUP 8 and 9. A waiver may be granted on application by a firm, or the FSA may consider it appropriate to waive the rule with respect to a number of firms, in which case it will notify the firms and each firm may then consent to the waiver. A waiver will only be granted if the FSA is satisfied that compliance by a firm would be unduly burdensome or would not achieve the objective of the rule, and it would not jeopardise persons whose interests the rule was designed to protect: FSMA, s 148(4). Sch 6 of each sourcebook or manual indicates the rules that can and cannot be waived.

[71] Normally, guidance will be given only to a particular person rather than to a class of regulated persons. The FSA may of its own initiative give guidance.

[72] The latter section conferring similar powers on the PRA.

The FCA can issue various types of statutory notice: a warning notice (FSMA, section 387; DEPP 2.2), which gives details of the action proposed; a decision notice (section 388; DEPP 2.3), which gives details of the action the FCA is going to take; a notice of discontinuance (section 389; DEPP 1.2.4, 3.2.26), which identifies the proceedings in a warning or decision notice that are being discontinued; a final notice (section 390; DEPP 1.2.4), which sets out the terms of action being taken; and a supervisory notice (section 395(13); DEPP 2.2, 2.3), which gives details of action the FCA has taken or proposes to take, such as varying a Part IV permission. The procedure for issuing notices seeks to ensure that, among other things, the decision giving rise to the obligation to issue a notice is taken by someone not directly involved in establishing the evidence on which the decision is based (DEPP 1.2.1). DEPP sets out: the decisions requiring the giving of notices and who takes those decisions (DEPP 2); the procedures of the Regulatory Decisions Committee (DEPP 3), which is a committee of the FCA Board, but is separate from the executive structure and, apart from its chair, none of the members is an FCA employee; and the procedures for decision-making by FCA staff under executive procedures and the settlement decision procedure (DEPP 4, 5). Someone affected by such a notice has the right to have it referred to the Upper Tribunal.

The FCA's EG has been extensively amended over time. The guide was issued under FSMA, section 139A. It sets out various principles underlying its approach to enforcement: the importance of 'an open and cooperative relationship' with those the FCA regulate; the need to exercise powers in a way that is 'transparent, proportionate, responsive to the issue, and consistent with [the FCA's] publicly stated policies'; the FCA will seek to ensure fair treatment; the FCA will aim to change the behaviour of the subject of the action, to deter non-compliance by others, to eliminate gain from non-compliance and to remedy harm caused (EG 2.1.2). The guide also notes that enforcement should be directed by the FCA's goal of achieving its regulatory objectives, that enforcement is only one tool at the FCA's disposal and that it may be appropriate to deal with non-compliance through other methods (EG 2.1.3). The guide then discusses investigation methods, settlement, publicity and the use of specific enforcement powers, such as penalties, censures, variation or cancellation of authorisation, injunctions and prosecutions.

8. Transfers of Insurance Business

Under the Insurance Companies Act 1982 a distinction was drawn between transfers of non-life business, which required only regulatory approval, and transfers of life business, which required court approval. Part VII of the FSMA abolished this distinction and requires court sanction in all cases. The regime was extended to reinsurance in 2007. The controls are explained in SUP 18.[73]

An insurance business transfer scheme is one that would result in insurance business carried on in the UK being transferred from a UK-authorised insurer or Lloyd's underwriter to a transferee within the UK. There are four excluded cases: the transfer of the

[73] See also the FCA document, 'The FCA's Approach to the Review of Part VII Insurance Business Transfers', FG18/4 (May 2018).

insurance business of a friendly society;[74] the transfer of the insurance business by a UK insurer to an insurer outside the UK, as long as there are no UK risks included and the transferee has been approved by its own relevant authorities; the business to be transferred is the whole of the business of the authorised person, the policyholders are all controllers of the transferee and they have all consented; and the business to be transferred is confined to reinsurance and all of the policyholders have consented. All of this is set out in FSMA, section 105.

The formalities for application to the court are set out in secondary legislation.[75] The procedures are designed to give maximum publicity to the scheme, so that objections can be lodged by policyholders who believe that their interests may be adversely affected. To that end, the scheme must be sent to policyholders and advertised in two UK national newspapers. The court may waive strict compliance where, for example, the policyholders cannot be traced or where national newspapers are inappropriate.[76] The application must include an expert financial report prepared by a person approved by the regulators (FSMA, section 109) and the report is in practice the key document in the court's consideration, although the court will not merely rubber-stamp the report's recommendations. There have been challenges to reports by policyholders on the grounds that the expert was not independent[77] or had erred,[78] but these have to date been unsuccessful. The court will also take account of the views of the FCA and PRA, as well as policyholders (section 110).

The criteria guiding the court's decision to approve or reject a scheme are not set out in the FSMA itself but have evolved from a series of decisions, summarised most recently by the Court of Appeal in *Re Prudential Assurance Company Ltd*.[79] The overall issue is whether the interests of policyholders overall will be prejudiced, although a scheme will be approved if, on balance, it is fair as between the different classes of policyholders affected. More specifically: (1) the legislation confers an absolute discretion on the court whether or not to sanction a scheme, but the discretion is to be exercised by giving due recognition to the commercial judgement entrusted by the company's constitution to its directors; (2) the court is concerned whether a policyholder, employee or other interested person, or any group of them, would be adversely affected by the scheme; (3) that question is primarily a matter of actuarial judgement involving a comparison between the security and reasonable expectations of policyholders without the scheme and what would be the result if the scheme were implemented – for the purpose of this comparison, the report of the independent expert is to be given close attention; (4) the regulators by reason of their powers could also be expected to have the necessary material and expertise to express an informed opinion on whether policyholders were likely to be adversely affected, and the court is to pay close attention to any views expressed by them; (5) the fact that individual policyholders or groups of policyholders might be adversely affected does not mean that the scheme has to be rejected by the court – the fundamental question is whether the scheme as a whole is fair as between the interests of the different classes of persons affected; (5) it is not the function

[74] Governed instead by the Friendly Societies Act 1992.

[75] Financial Services and Markets (Control of Business Transfers) (Requirements on Applicants) Regulations 2001, SI 2001/3625.

[76] *Re Equitas Ltd* [2009] Lloyd's Rep IR 642.

[77] *Re Norwich Union* [2004] EWHC 2802 (Ch), [2005] BCC 586; *Re Allied Dunbar Assurance Plc* [2005] EWHC 28 (Ch).

[78] *Re Axa Equity & Law* [2001] 2 BCLC 447; *Re Eagle Star Insurance Co Ltd* [2005] EWHC 1850 (Ch).

[79] [2020] EWCA Civ 1626, reviewing the key authorities, including *Re Allied Dunbar Assurance Plc* [2005] EWHC 28 (Ch).

of the court to produce what, in its view, is the best possible scheme – as between different schemes, all of which the court might deem fair, it is the company's directors' choice which to pursue; and (7) the details of the scheme are not a matter for the court provided that the scheme as a whole is found to be fair, so the court would not amend the scheme because it thought that individual provisions could be improved upon.

In practice, no schemes have been rejected. The court's generous approach is demonstrated by *Re Prudential Assurance Company Ltd* itself. The insurer, with a long-established reputation as a market leader, proposed to transfer its annuity business to a relatively new insurer, Rothesay. The expert report found no adverse effects on policyholders and the regulators raised no objections, but the trial judge, Snowden J, nevertheless refused to sanction the scheme because it would have defeated the expectation of many policyholders that they had secured – in the terms of the Prudential's publicity material – 'a lifetime annuity with the Prudential'. The Court of Appeal, reversing the judge and upholding the scheme, held that historic reputation was not a relevant consideration and the question was whether the transfer had actual adverse effects on the security of policyholder benefits. There was nothing to suggest that the transferee was any less risky for them.

Where a scheme is approved, the court may under section 112 impose ancillary conditions. These relate to: the transfer of the undertaking, and any property or liabilities; the allotment or appropriation of shares, debentures or policies; the continuation by or against the transferee of legal proceedings involving the transferor; and such incidental matters as are necessary to secure that the scheme is fully and effectively carried out. The order may also require any reinsurance held by the transferor to be transferred to the transferee.[80] Although most of the transfers for which approval has been sought have been motivated by commercial decisions by insurers to cease a particular class of business or to relocate its operations, the regime is applicable also to companies in difficulties, and in such a case the court has the power to reduce the benefits payable under the transferred policies in order to make a transfer more attractive to the transferee.

---

9. Redress

This block of the *Handbook* is concerned with complaints and compensation.[81] DISP is based on the principle that firms should deal reasonably and fairly with complaints. DISP 1.2 requires firms to publish information regarding their internal procedures for complaints handling, and under DISP 1.3 the procedures must be effective and transparent, and free of charge. Any complaint must be investigated competently, diligently and impartially (DISP 1.4), with a final decision within eight weeks (DISP 1, 6.2). In addition, under FSMA, section 146D, a private person (and, in certain circumstances, other persons) may bring an action to recover loss suffered as a result of the contravention by an authorised person of a regulatory rule, subject to any defences applying to actions for breach of

[80] *WASA International (UK) Insurance Co Ltd v WASA International Insurance Co Ltd* [2003] 1 All ER (Comm) 696, confirmed by the Financial Services and Markets Act 2000 (Control of Business Transfers) (Requirements on Applicants) (Amendment) Regulations 2008, SI 2008/1467, and the Financial Services and Markets Act 2000 (Amendments to Part VII) Regulations 2008, SI 2008/1468.

[81] On the Financial Compensation Scheme, which is part of this block (COMP), see below.

statutory duty, unless this right of action is excluded.[82] A private person is any individual, but an individual who suffers loss in the course of carrying on any regulated activity may not bring an action unless that loss occurs in the course of effecting or carrying out insurance contracts written at Lloyd's. Under section 404, which was amended by the Financial Services Act 2010, if it appears to the FCA that there may have been 'a widespread or regular failure' by a firm to comply with applicable 'requirements' (which presumably means regulations under the FSMA) and that consumers appear to have suffered loss in respect of which relief would be available in legal proceedings (which would, presumably, including a complaint to the Financial Ombudsman Service), and the FCA considers it desirable to make rules to secure redress for consumers, the FCA will make such rules requiring firms to establish a consumer redress scheme. The rules can specify, among other things, what firms must do to carry out an investigation and the kinds of redress that must be put in place, and they can provide for the appointment of someone by the FCA to undertake actions in relation to the redress scheme.

The FCA has assisted policyholders in other respects. It established a mechanism for supervising the handling of complaints by banks concerning their mis-selling of payment protection insurance, in the form of requiring borrowers (sometimes without their knowledge) to insure against default on loans. Many of the policies proved to be unsuitable for their purpose, eg policies against loss of employment being sold to the retired or self-employed. The sums paid by way of compensation since January 2011 have exceeded £38.3 billion. Further, following the outbreak of the COVID-19 pandemic, the FCA initiated a test case on behalf of some 380,000 holders of business interruption policies, and obtained a ruling from the Supreme Court[83] establishing the coverage and causation principles applicable to such policies. This matter is explored in detail below.[84]

10. Lloyd's of London

The Society of Lloyd's of London does not provide insurance; it is a market within which insurance is written: it provides the buildings where trading takes place and the rules under which that trading occurs. Its history goes back to the late seventeenth century and the practice of merchants meeting at Lloyd's Coffee House, although it seemingly did not transact insurance business until 1720, when the Bubble Act ban on insurance companies was introduced. As the market developed, it outgrew the coffee house, but the original name lived on. Lloyd's retained a virtual monopoly on marine insurance business until the repeal of the Bubble Act in 1825. Lloyd's was granted incorporated and self-regulating status by the Lloyd's Act 1870. In the second half of the nineteenth century, Lloyd's expanded its business to cover most forms of non-life insurance, as well as reinsurance, and much of its business came from overseas. Lloyd's international reputation was cemented when, immediately following the San Francisco earthquake on 18 April 1906, underwriter

[82] Financial Services and Markets Act 2000 (Rights of Action) Regulations 2000, SI 2001/2256, para 6. No action lies where the rule breached is one that requires the authorised person to have financial resources: FSMA, s 150(4)(b). Each sourcebook or manual contains rules on the availability of the right to sue (eg see SYSC 1.1.12) and summarises these in the appendix.

[83] *Financial Conduct Authority v Arch Insurance* [2021] UKSC 1.

[84] See ch 18.

Cuthbert Heath issued an instruction to 'pay all of our policyholders in full, irrespective of the terms of their policies'. The cost of some US$50 million was a sound investment.

Lloyd's reorganised its internal regulation by the Lloyd's Act 1982. This measure provides the framework for the management structure and the rules of the market. The main objective of the Act is to provide reasonable safeguards for Lloyd's policyholders and for members of Lloyd's to give people confidence in the market as a place to do business. This is primarily achieved by ensuring that people trading in the market are solvent, competent and honest, that those who use the market are fairly treated, that the market operates with an appropriate degree of transparency and that there is no abuse. Lloyd's and its agents – syndicate managing agents, who are responsible for writing the business, and members' agents, who protect the investment interests of subscribers and brokers accredited by Lloyd's to place business – are regulated by the FCA (FSMA, Part XIX), but since these functions are also carried out by the Council of Lloyd's, the two bodies have an agreement of co-operation in respect of supervision and enforcement. The FCA did issue a separate sourcebook covering Lloyd's, but this has been withdrawn and the rules are now contained in the general parts of the *Handbook*,[85] although the peculiar nature of the market is provided for in special provisions (eg INSPRU 8; COBS 18.6; DISP 1.11).

During the 1970s and 1980s, Lloyd's suffered severe losses, the result of imprudent underwriting in particular in the US liability insurance market. A further problem was the London Market Excess of Loss (LMX) Spiral, under which risks were underwritten and then reinsured over and over again, with the result that much of the premium income was taken up by broker commissions and very little was left to pay actual losses. At the time, all investors at Lloyd's were individuals and they had unlimited liability, with the result that many were forced into bankruptcy. However, the Lloyd's Act 1982 conferred immunity from suit on Lloyd's as a body. A market solution was found in the Reconstruction and Renewal plan of 1996, under which investors received compensation of £3.2 billion and their liabilities under existing contracts were reinsured by Equitas,[86] a reinsurance company established for the purpose. The premiums charged by Equitas were necessarily large, and gave rise to much litigation as to the liability of members to pay the premiums. The vast majority of claims were dismissed. One important consequence of Reconstruction and Renewal was to replace individual investment by corporate investment. New entrants to the Lloyd's market must now be companies, and the only individual members remaining are those who had invested before 1996.

---

11. Insurance Intermediaries

It might seem obvious that the regulation of the insurers who write insurance contracts should be accompanied by the regulation of those who give advice to prospective insureds and who are responsible for passing on premiums and, in some cases, payments under the policy, but until relatively recently there was no statutory supervision of these insurance intermediaries. This meant that anyone could set up as an intermediary and offer advice to the public on insurance. The situation was made worse by the conflict of interest that arose

[85] See The CRD (Consequential Amendments) Instrument 2006 (FSA 2006/53), Appendix R.
[86] The scheme is described in *Re Equitas Ltd* [2010] Lloyd's Rep IR 69.

as a result of intermediaries, from whom consumers expected impartial advice, receiving secret commissions from insurers. A report by the British Insurance Brokers' Association in 1976 and a government White Paper the following year led to a slow process of reform.[87] The Insurance Brokers (Registration) Act 1977 was limited in its scope, and in particular only applied to those who chose to call themselves insurance brokers, so might be avoided by the simple expedient of using some other title to describe the function of their activities. Later, most of those involved in life assurance business came within the terms of the Financial Services Act 1986. Key players in the industry established the General Insurance Standards Council (GISC), with encouragement from the Treasury in the wake of the repeal of the Insurance Brokers Registration Act 1977. Its aim was to maintain and indeed improve standards in the general insurance market through a set of rules and codes of practice. Yet, in spite of initial enthusiasm and a good deal of excellent work, various factors conspired against the GISC. Membership was voluntary, but members were required only to undertake business with other members. A campaign was launched against the legality of this rule that diverted the council from the task of establishing effective regulation and undermined its public credibility. In spite of the GISC's many achievements, it was clear that statutory regulation of intermediaries was required to ensure that consumers would not be exposed to unregulated intermediaries.[88] Since January 2005 the FCA has taken over regulation of those intermediaries involved in general insurance business.[89] However, the FCA has stretched its net wider than the GISC and the new regime now applies to many who advise their clients on insurance, but who doubtless have never thought of themselves (or been seen as) part of the insurance industry, such as doctors, dentists, vets, motor car dealers and removal firms. If they engage in a certain level of insurance business, authorisation is required, and continuing to act without obtaining such authorisation is a criminal offence. We have already seen how one way around this is to become an appointed representative, but the difficulty with this route is that the responsibility placed on an authorised firm means they will be cautious about selecting appointed representatives and are likely to focus on those with whom they have a long-established relationship, which may affect the ability of new firms to progress their businesses.

The current form of regulation was inspired by the EU, in a series of measures designed to provide minimum, albeit high-level, forms of protection, thereby allowing intermediaries to trade throughout the EU. The first initiative was a recommendation by the European Commission in 1991, followed by the Mediation Directive in 2002[90] and, most recently, the Insurance Distribution Directive in 2016.[91] Although the UK is no longer in the EU, the Insurance Distribution Directive was implemented in 2018 by amendments to the Regulated Activities Order[92] and to the *FCA Handbook*, and its principles remain the governing framework.

The effect of the 2018 amendments is to bring within the regulatory regime all channels of insurance distribution, although there is a more restricted form of regulation applicable

[87] Cmnd 6715.

[88] GISC Scrutiny & Consumer Affairs Committee, *Report on GISC Performance against Objectives* (2004) www.gisc.co.uk.

[89] This was also a consequence of the Directive on Insurance Mediation (2002/92), which was implemented by the Financial Services and Markets Act 2000 (Regulated Activities) (Amendment) (No 2) Order 2003 (2003/1476) and the Insurance Mediation Directive (Miscellaneous Amendments) Regs 2002 (2004/1473).

[90] Directive 2002/92/EC.

[91] Directive 2016/97.

[92] By the Insurance Distribution (Regulated Activities and Miscellaneous Amendments) Order 2018, SI 2018/546.

to 'ancillary insurance intermediaries', consisting of persons whose principal activity is something other than insurance but who offer insurance products related to goods and services supplied by them.

It is necessary to have PRA and FSC authorisation to carry on the activity of 'assisting in the administration and performance of a contract of insurance', which includes arranging insurance contracts, providing specific advice on insurance contracts, concluding insurance contracts, assisting in the performance and administration of insurance contracts, and claims-handling. The authorisation requirement does not apply to authorised representatives and employees of authorised insurers, as the insurers themselves must take responsibility for the acts of their own agents. Guidance on who needs authorisation or what activities can only be carried out by an authorised person is provided in PERG, which is issued under FSMA, section 157. All firms must be authorised if they carry out insurance mediation activities in connection with contracts of insurance (PERG 5.3) and those activities are carried on by way of business (PERG 5.4). The overriding requirements of the *FCA Handbook* are that: the business of an intermediary has to be carried out with integrity, skill, care and diligence; the intermediary has adequate financial resources; and conflicts of interest are avoided.

On the first of these matters, the COND 4 and PRIN 3 and 4 require the authorised firm's senior management to ensure that it maintains adequate resources and this includes appropriate management and control systems (SYSC), as well as adequate and competent staff. An insurance intermediary with Part IV permission must allocate responsibility for the firm's insurance mediation activity to a director or senior manager, whose identity must be notified to the FCA for registration in the Financial Services Register (MIPRU 2.2). Various aspects of the *FCA Handbook* focus on the competence and training of intermediaries (TC) and on the reporting by intermediaries of their activities (SUP 15).

As to the second matter, financial stability, the firm must ensure that it is able to meet its liabilities as they fall due and must maintain capital resources equal to or above its capital resources requirement, which is calculated in accordance with the provisions set out in MIPRU (MIPRU 4); the firm must obtain professional indemnity insurance with minimum limits of indemnity for any one claim; and the firm must have systems and controls that enable it to be satisfied of the suitability of such persons (SYSC 3.2.13). CASS deals with the rules concerning the handling of client funds and other assets, and it develops PRIN 10, which requires a firm to provide adequate protection for client assets. In construing the sourcebook, the FCA and the courts will take into account the importance placed by the FSMA on the protection of the consumer.[93] The sourcebook contains rules on holding client funds, on the segregation of such funds from money held as an agent for the insurer and on accounting procedures. It also obliges an intermediary to ensure that its appointed representatives and other agents observe rules on segregating client money (CASS 5.5.19–25). Client money is that which is received and held for a client by an intermediary acting in the course of carrying on insurance business. Client money received by the firm must be paid out or placed in a client bank account as soon as is practicable, which will normally be the next business day after receipt (CASS 5.5.5–6). By segregating funds in this way, the insured is treated as a secured creditor so that if the intermediary becomes insolvent, other creditors have no right to share in the funds in the client account. An insurance intermediary

[93] *Re Lehman Brothers International (Europe) (In Administration)* [2010] EWCA Civ 917.

that holds client money must regularly undertake a calculation to ensure there are sufficient funds to meet obligations to clients (CASS 5.5.62). Where the client money resource is less than the client money requirement, the firm must top it up; where the resource exceeds the requirement, the firm must withdraw the excess.

In practice, client funds consist of two elements: premiums received from the insured for transmission to the insurer; and claims paid by the insurer for transmission to the insured. The effect of CASS is to transfer the risk of default from the insured to the insurer in the event of the intermediary's insolvency. Under CASS 5.2.1, premiums received by the intermediary are deemed to have been received by the insurer, so there is no question of an insurer denying liability for a claim by relying on non-payment of premium if it has been received by the intermediary. However, an insurer to whom the premiums are due has a secured claim against the trust fund for those premiums.[94] Conversely, where an insurer has paid to the intermediary sums due to the insured (claims or, where the risk has been terminated, return of premium) and they have not been transmitted to the insured, they are treated as not having been received and the assured is entitled to claim from the insurer the sum due. Thus, an insured will not have to pay twice, but an insurer may be required to do so.

The third matter is the avoidance of conflict of interest, regulated by ICOBS. An intermediary is required, in good time before the conclusion of the contract of insurance, to provide the customer with information as to its status, in particular whether it has any connections with one or more insurers, and whether it is giving a personal recommendation (ICOBS 4.1). Any advice that is given must be given with reasonable care and must take account of the needs of the customer (ICOBS 5.1). By that means the customer can ascertain whether the advice is based on a fair analysis of the market or on only a limited range of products, and can assume that the product is appropriate. Perhaps the most contentious aspect of conflict of interest is remuneration. Intermediaries have long resisted the imposition of a duty to disclose payment of any sums by an insurer, and ICOBS has settled for a compromise. In all cases the intermediary must disclose the nature of the remuneration (ICOBS 4.1). As regards a commercial customer, the intermediary must on the customer's request disclose any commission received by it in connection with the policy (ICOBS 4.4). By contrast, in the case of a consumer customer, there is no right to demand such information. If, at a later stage, the intermediary becomes involved in claims handling, the intermediary is required to take all reasonable steps to identify any conflict of interest (ICOBS 8.3).

---

12. The Insolvency of Insurers

As has already been seen in this chapter, the focus on prudential regulation of insurers is to protect against the risk of insolvency. There has not been a life insurer insolvency since 1993 (Oaklife), and between 2000 and 2022 only 15 non-life insurers became insolvent, but these were all small organisations offering niche products. If the worst occurs and an insurance company is unable to pay its debts, English law tries to deal with the problem in two ways: by intervention in the usual statutory insolvency procedures, and through the operation of

[94] *Allanfield Property Insurance Services Ltd v Aviva Insurance Ltd* [2015] EWHC 3721 (Ch), [2016] Lloyd's Rep IR 217.

a compensation scheme for policyholders and others with actual or potential claims against insurers.

The most extreme procedure for an insolvent company is liquidation, a process carried out under the Companies Act 2006 and the Insolvency Act 1986 which results in the winding up of the company and its business and subsequently its removal from the register of companies. The purpose of liquidation is to allow the liquidator to distribute the company's assets between its various creditors in a manner that reflects their respective rights and interests. Winding up may be voluntary, by a resolution passed in a general meeting. Where there is such a resolution, if the company is solvent, the winding up is a members' voluntary winding up, and if the company is insolvent, then the procedure becomes known as a creditors' voluntary winding up. Special rules apply to insurers: a life insurer is not permitted to pass a resolution for voluntary winding up (FSMA, section 366); and where there is a voluntary winding up, the regulators may intervene in any court proceedings on the winding up under FSMA, section 365 to protect the interests of policyholders. A compulsory winding up, by contrast, is by application to the court by any creditor or shareholder whose debt has not been satisfied. In the case of an insurer, the regulators themselves may present a winding up petition if the company is insolvent or if it is otherwise just and equitable for the company to be wound up. Once the liquidation has commenced, the liquidator must report to the regulators and they retain the right to participate in any court proceedings (FSMA, sections 367–71). The usual consequence of a winding up petition in the case of an insurer is not liquidation but, rather, a scheme of arrangement under sections 895–901 of the Companies Act 2006 whereby a scheme for settling debts as agreed with creditors may be approved by the court. As an alternative to a scheme of arrangement, the court has, under FSMA, section 377, the power to reduce the value of the insurer's policies, and this may facilitate a transfer of the insurers' business to another insurer. Special rules apply to a life insurer, which, under FSMA, section 376 and the Insurers (Winding Up Rules) 2001,[95] requires the liquidator to continue the insurers' business until arrangements have been made for a reduction in its value or transfer. If a company cannot be rescued and is wound up, the common law rule that policyholders are unsecured creditors and thus are at the end of the queue along with other unsecured creditors where liabilities exceed assets is modified by the Insurers (Reorganisation and Winding Up) Regulations 2004:[96] insurance creditors are given priority over all other unsecured creditors. That process requires insurance debts to be valued at the date of the winding up order (which is backdated to the date when the petition for winding up was presented). In that process, funds representing life and non-life insurance are to be separated into two distinct funds, and the valuation rules in the 2001 Regulations then turn upon whether there is an outstanding claim against the insurer or whether the correct valuation is simply unexpired premium.

The second form of insolvency procedure is administration, a process created by Part II of the Insolvency Act 1986 and designed to effect a corporate rescue. Administration involves the appointment of an administrator charged with the task of finding a means of allowing the company to continue as a going concern. Administration was extended to insurance companies by the Financial Services and Markets Act 2000 (Administration Orders Relating to Insurers) Order 2002.[97] The regulators may themselves initiate the administration procedure.

[95] SI 2001/3635.
[96] SI 2004/353.
[97] SI 2002/1242.

The third process, the company voluntary arrangement (CVA),[98] authorises the creditors to reach agreement on the best means of distributing the company's assets. The CVA is available to insurance companies, subject to the right of the regulators to intervene under FSMA sections 356–62A.

Assuming that an insurer cannot be prevented from insolvency, a further question is the fate of its customers. The Policyholders Protection Acts of 1975 and 1997 were designed to provide consumer insureds with compensation in the event of an insurer being unable to meet claims. That arrangement has been replaced by a scheme established by the FCA under the provisions of FSMA, Part XV. The scheme for compensating consumers is administered by the Financial Services Compensation Scheme Ltd (FSCS) under rules laid down by the FCA in COMP. The FSCS is obliged to carry out its functions efficiently and economically, and it must publish an annual report, must have a procedure to deal with complaints against the FSCS and must keep consumers informed about the process of making a claim (COMP 2). Funding for the scheme comes from levies on authorised firms (COMP 13). The sourcebook lays down the conditions that must be satisfied for a claim to succeed, which are, in broad terms, that the claimant must be eligible (COMP 4), the activity that caused the loss and the firm involved must be covered by the scheme (COMP 5 and 6) and the claimant must assign to the FSCS their rights to bring a claim against the firm, although if the FSCS obtains a sum above that which it paid out the excess must be handed to the claimant (COMP 7). As well as payments of compensation to insureds,[99] in certain circumstances the FSCS is obliged to secure continuity of insurance for insureds and may be permitted to assist an insurer that is facing financial problems (COMP 3.3.1–7). The FSCS does not apply to Lloyd's, which has its own arrangements for compensating members (COMP 1.5).

13. The Financial Ombudsman Scheme

If a claim is rejected or not settled to the satisfaction of the insured, the obvious recourse is litigation, but cost, time and probably a sense of fatalism are likely to deter all but the most determined. As noted above, the Insurance Ombudsman Bureau (IOB) was established in 1981 by a small number of leading insurers to provide a cheap, simple means of redress.[100] It was part of a more general enthusiasm for ombudsmen that began in the 1960s. Originally seen as a means of protecting citizens in their dealings with state agencies, they have now spread into all areas of consumer activity. In essence, the IOB dealt with

[98] Insolvency Act 1986, ss 1–7.

[99] On the time frame within which payment must be made, see COMP 9; on the limits on the amount payable, the method of payment and the calculation, see COMP 10–12.

[100] J Birds and C Graham, 'Complaints Mechanisms in the Financial Services Industry' (1988) 7 *Criminal Justice Quarterly* 313; A McGee, 'The Insurance Ombudsman and the Unfair Contract Terms Act 1977' (1992) 2 *Insurance Law & Practice* 86; P Rawlings and C Willett, 'Ombudsman Schemes in the United Kingdom's Financial Sector: the Insurance Ombudsman, the Banking Ombudsman and the Building Societies Ombudsman' (1994) 17 *Journal of Consumer Policy* 307; P Morris and R James, 'The Financial Ombudsman Service: A Brave New World in "Ombudsmanry"?' [2002] *PL* 640; PE Morris, 'The Financial Ombudsman Service and the Hunt Review: Continuing Evolution in Dispute Resolution' (2008) 8 *Journal of Business Law* 785. Other complaints mechanisms existed in the insurance industry: the Personal Insurance Arbitration Scheme operated by the Chartered Institute of Arbitrators; the Consumer Enquiries Department at Lloyd's, which passed unresolved complaints to the IOB; and the mechanisms created by individual firms and particular sectors of the industry.

complaints by private individuals against insurers who were members of the scheme. Its aim was to facilitate the settlement or withdrawal of a complaint by a variety of means, including making an award, which the insurer, but not the insured, was obliged to accept.[101] The IOB proved radical in its approach. It was required to consider the terms of the contract, relevant rules of law and principles of good insurance practice, including the Statements of Insurance Practice. However, the IOB tended to give priority to 'a fair and common sense conclusion' if it felt the result produced by the law was not appropriate. In other words, the IOB introduced notions of fairness and held insurers liable in situations where the courts would not have done. So, for instance, the IOB held insurers liable for the defaults of intermediaries in spite of the general rule that they are the agents of the insured; it relaxed the strictness of the duty of disclosure; and it introduced requirements of procedural fairness in, for example, the way insurers investigated claims.[102]

The various ombudsmen and other independent complaints arrangements that existed throughout the financial services industry were replaced by a unified, statutory scheme established by the FCA under Part XVI of the FSMA. This provides for a scheme 'under which certain disputes may be resolved quickly and with minimum formality by an independent person' (section 225), and it led to the establishment of the Financial Ombudsman Scheme (FOS). The scheme is funded by a combination of a levy on each authorised firm and a fee charged to firms linked to the number of complaints brought before the ombudsman (FEES 5). In 2003–04 the ombudsman dealt with more than 500,000 enquiries and just under 100,000 complaints were referred to adjudicators; by 2009–10 there were over 925,000 enquiries, of which more than 163,000 went to adjudicators. Since its establishment there have been two reviews of its work: the first, in 2004, was mainly focused on its complaints handling processes, while the second, the Hunt Review in 2008, was a lengthy and general review of the organisation and its operations.[103]

The FOS is regulated under the FSMA and the rules contained in DISP. It has two jurisdictions. The first is its compulsory jurisdiction, which covers those authorised firms that are obliged to participate in the scheme with regard to those complaints specified by the FCA (section 226). The second is the voluntary jurisdiction: if the activity does not come within the compulsory jurisdiction, a firm can voluntarily contract that the FOS will handle complaints relating to that activity (section 227). In the main, the procedures in relation to both types of jurisdiction are identical (DISP 3). The claim must be brought against a firm and relate to an activity that is subject to the compulsory or voluntary jurisdiction, so that the firm must have been authorised under the FSMA at the time of the relevant action, or it must have been a voluntary jurisdiction participant both at the time of the action and when the complaint is referred to the FOS. The complaint must be by an 'eligible complainant', defined as any of: a consumer;[104] a micro-enterprise (ie one that employs fewer than

[101] On the possibility of the insurer challenging the IOB through judicial review, see A McGee, 'Challenging the Decisions of the Insurance Ombudsman' (1994) 4 *Insurance Law & Practice* 43. Various challenges have been launched, eg *R (on the application of Green (t/a Green Denman & Co)) v Financial Ombudsman Service Ltd* [2003] EWHC 338 (Admin).

[102] Rawlings and Willett (n 100) 312–14.

[103] E Kempson, S Collard and N Moore, *Fair and Reasonable: An Assessment of the Financial Ombudsman Service* (Bristol, Personal Finance Research Centre, University of Bristol, 2004); Lord Hunt, *Opening Up, Reaching Out and Aiming High: An Agenda for Accessibility and Excellence in the Financial Ombudsman Service* (Report of the Independent Review of the Financial Ombudsman Service by the Rt Hon Lord Hunt of Wirral MBE) (2008).

[104] See *R (on the application of Bluefin Insurance Services Ltd) v FOS* [2014] EWHC 3413 (Admin), discussed in ch 4 below.

10 persons and has a turnover or balance sheet not exceeding £2 million); a charity with an annual income of less than £6.5 million; and a trust with a net asset value of less than £5 million (DISP 2.7.3). In 2019 the list of eligible persons was extended to any small business which is not a micro-enterprise (ie one that has an annual turnover of less that £6.5 million and either employs fewer than 50 persons or has a balance sheet of less than £5 million). The FOS will only consider a claim if the firm has made a final determination of its position as against the complainant and the complaint is made within six months of that determination (DISP 2.8).

The procedure for handling complaints is contained in DISP 3. The FOS may dismiss a complaint without investigation if it falls outside its jurisdiction (DISP 3.2). Summary rejection without consideration of the merits is also possible in a number of situations, namely where the claim: is frivolous or vexatious; has been or is being dealt with by another dispute resolution body entity; has been the subject of court proceedings with a decision on the merits; is the subject of court proceedings that have not been stayed; or is of a type which would – if dealt with – seriously impair the effective operation of the FOS (DISP 3.3, 3.4).[105] The FOS has said that if reasonable compensation has been offered, it will not launch an investigation simply to satisfy the complainant's desire for an explanation for the error.[106] In either case, the complainant has the right to make representations following the decision.

If an investigation is deemed to be necessary by the FOS, then, in line with the requirements in the FSMA, the FOS will aim to resolve complaints 'at the earliest possible stage and by whatever means appear to the FOS to be most appropriate, including mediation or investigation' (DISP 3.5.1), or reach a determination. The FOS may demand information from them, with the power to apply to the court if a demand is not satisfied (FSMA, sections 231–32). Both parties will be given an opportunity to make representations during those investigations. The practice of the FOS is initially to refer the matter to an investigator, who will produce a decision. If either party rejects the decision, and in the vast majority of cases the dispute is resolved at this stage, the matter will then be referred to an ombudsman for a final determination (DISP 3.5.4). Before arriving at a determination, the FOS must receive representations, but need not hold a hearing (DISP 3.5.5–7). The issues of the evidence that is admissible and the conclusions that can be drawn from it are largely left to the FOS. There is no requirement to follow judicial rules of evidence; indeed, there is a specific power to exclude evidence that a court might admit or include evidence that a court would not admit (DISP 3.5.8–12). The FOS must determine a complaint 'by reference to what is, in his opinion, fair and reasonable in all the circumstances of the case' (DISP 3.6.1; FSMA, section 228). This has led to the conclusion that the FOS is not bound by its own previous decisions, although a degree of certainty has its advantages and, as with the IOB, a rough jurisprudence is being constructed. It is not bound by the common law,[107] although it will take account of 'the relevant law, regulations, regulators' rules and guidance and standards, relevant codes of practice and, where appropriate, what he considers to have been good industry practice at the relevant time' (DISP 3.6.4).[108]

[105] The list was amended to comply with the EU's Consumer Disputes Directive, 2013/11/EU, as implemented by the Alternative Dispute Resolution for Consumer Disputes (Competent Authorities and Information) Regulations 2015, SI 2015/542.

[106] Case 41/3 (November 2004).

[107] *Clark v Argyle Consulting Ltd* 2011 SLT 180.

[108] The FOS may refer to non-statutory provisions that preceded statutory regulation: see http://tinyurl.com/4a7gomp. See FOS, *Ombudsman News* No 39 (August 2004); cases 31/3 (September 2003), 39/1 (August 2004), 39/2 (August 2004).

A determination may include an award of 'fair compensation', up to £350,000, raised from the initial £100,000 when the scheme was first implemented: the increased figure is accounted for by the inclusion of small businesses and also allows the FOS to deal with substantial property claims. A determination may also include a requirement that the firm take certain steps and costs may also be awarded to – but not against – the complainant, although such awards are likely to be rare (FSMA, sections 229, 230; DISP 3.7). The FOC cannot make a direction to take steps which has the effect of requiring a firm to pay more than the statutory cap of £350,000.[109] The reasoned determination must be notified to the parties, and the complainant (but not the firm) may accept or reject it within a prescribed time.[110] Rejection by the complainant means that neither party is bound by the determination (DISP 3.6.6). Determinations are to be published (FSMA, section 230A). Any determination is binding on the firm but not on the complainant, and the complainant is entitled to reject the decision of the FOS and to take the matter to court, where of course legal principle will be applicable.[111] However, rejecting a determination means it is of no effect whatsoever. By way of example, if the complainant is awarded compensation by the FOS but believes the sum to be inadequate, the complainant cannot simply go to court for an additional sum: the complainant must surrender the entire determination and hope that the court will be at least as generous as the FOS.

The FOS is subject to judicial review on two basic grounds: it acted without jurisdiction;[112] or it acted in breach of the rules of natural justice by failing to give a fair hearing.[113] While the courts will not challenge the substance of a determination, they have held consistently that if the FOS in its final ruling exercises its right to depart from strict legal principle,[114] it must give reasons for doing so.[115]

Clearly, the complaints brought before the FOS may reveal problems relating to individual firms or products, but they may also provide insights into the working of the regulatory system. The FCA and the FOS have, therefore, established a 'wider implications' procedure under which the two organisations meet and also liaise with trade and consumer bodies in situations where a case or a series of cases suggests that a change in regulation may be necessary. The obligation on the FOS to disclose information to the FCA was made statutory in 2013 by an amendment in the Financial Services Act 2012, inserting FSMA, section 232A.

The FOS publishes a regular newsletter, *Ombudsman News*, which sets out the latest thinking and summaries of the most important decisions. The FOS has also issued a series of technical notes on a range of topics. Since 2013, the individual decisions of the FOS have been published online in anonymised form, and although the FOS is not bound by precedent, it is possible to obtain indications of how the FOS is likely to respond to particular issues. By way of example: the FOS does not favour reliance on the technical defence

[109] *Bunney v Burns Anderson plc* [2007] EWHC 1240 (Ch).

[110] Failure to notify amounts to a rejection: FSMA, s 228(6), DISP 3.6.6(4); *Clark v Argyle Consulting Ltd* 2011 SLT 180.

[111] As in *Margate Theatre Royal Trust Ltd v White* [2005] EWHC 2171 (TCC), where the court concluded, contrary to the view of the FOS, that the claim by the insured under a public liability policy was covered by the policy.

[112] *R (on the application of Chancery (UK) LLP) v FOS* [2015] EWHC 407 (Admin).

[113] *R (on the application of Calland) v FOS* [2013] EWHC 1327 (Admin).

[114] *R (on the application of Heather Moor & Edgecomb Ltd) v FOS* [2008] EWCA Civ 642.

[115] *R (on the application of Aviva Life and Pensions (UK) Ltd) v FOS* [2017] EWHC 352 (Admin); *R (on the Application of Laura Critchley v Financial Ombudsman Service Ltd* [2019] EWHC 3036 (Admin).

of lack of insurable interest; before the abolition of the consumer's duty of disclosure by the Consumer Insurance (Disclosure and Representations) Act 2012 the FOS had in effect anticipated that legislation, and it continues to permit insurers to deny liability only in the clearest cases; the FOS has adopted a generous approach to policy interpretation, particularly where there is ambiguity or other lack of clarity; and failure by the insured to adhere to procedural requirements attached to claims against insurers may be excused in the absence of prejudice. As will be seen, the legislative reforms in the 2012 Act and again by the Insurance Act 2015 have done much to ensure that an insurer cannot seek a disproportionately harsh remedy for a relatively trivial breach of duty by the insured.

3

Insurance Intermediaries

1. Introduction

1.1. The Use of Agents in Insurance

This chapter sets out the basic rules of law applicable to agency relationships in the insurance context, by way of introduction to the specific issues arising in relation to agency that feature in subsequent chapters.

Agency refers to the relationship in which one person (the agent) acts for another (the principal) in effecting a transaction with another (the third party) whereby the agent is authorised to establish privity of contract between the principal and the third party. There is no statutory definition of agency, nor is there an all-embracing judicial definition, and for the purposes of the present text the terms 'agent' and 'intermediary' will be used interchangeably. As with the conduct of commerce generally, insurance transactions are conducted through the medium of intermediaries and as such they play a pivotal role in all aspects of insurance contract from formation through to claims.[1] The term 'insurance intermediary' is necessarily broad brush, but covers most importantly two classes of intermediary: employees and agents who carry out all of the functions of insurers; and brokers appointed by the insured to proffer advice, place insurance and assist with claims.

In *Harvest Trucking Co Ltd v Davis*,[2] Judge Diamond QC stated: 'A broker or other insurance intermediary is employed to act as a middle man between the person employing him – normally the person requiring insurance – on the one hand, and the proposed insurer or insurers on the other.' The regulatory principles affecting insurance intermediaries were discussed in chapter two, section 11 above. In outline, assisting in the administration and performance of a contract of insurance is a regulated activity for which authorisation by the Financial Conduct Authority (FCA) and the Prudential Regulatory Authority is required, although appointed representatives of insurers are exempt from that requirement and the insurers themselves are required to take responsibility for the acts and defaults of such agents. Brokers thus require their own authorisation and must comply with the Insurance: Conduct of Business sourcebook (ICOBS) in the *FCA Handbook*. Brokers wishing to

[1] See further C Henley and S Kemp, *The Law of Insurance Broking* (London, Sweet & Maxwell, 1995).
[2] [1991] 2 Lloyd's Rep 638.

place business at Lloyd's must be recognised by Lloyd's for that purpose and are subject to additional restrictions in the form of Lloyd's byelaws and a code of practice.

1.2. Authority of Agents

A principal is bound by the acts of an agent with respect to those matters over which the agent has authority from the principal. There are two broad types of authority: actual authority; and ostensible authority. In addition, the principal will be bound by acts of the agent carried out in the absence of authority but subsequently ratified by the principal. The fact that the agent has acted fraudulently and for the agent's own purposes does not affect the application of the rules relating to actual and ostensible authority.[3]

1.2.1. Actual and Ostensible Authority

An agent's actual authority will depend upon the agreement between the agent and the principal.[4] Where a principal has expressly authorised an agent to enter into a transaction or to act in a particular way (express authority), this is taken to include all those acts by the agent which are reasonably incidental and necessary to enable the agent to effect that transaction (implied authority).

The phrase 'ostensible authority'[5] refers to authority that the agent does not expressly or impliedly possess but nevertheless seems to do so. There are two distinct types of ostensible authority.

The first is usual authority, which consists of authority that an agent of the type and seniority in question would normally be expected to possess but in fact does not possess by reason of a restriction imposed by the principal. The third party is entitled to assume that usual authority exists unless the limitation is brought to the third party's attention.

The second is apparent authority, otherwise known as agency by estoppel, which arises where the agent is performing acts that an agent of that capacity would not normally be empowered to carry out but the agent has expressly or impliedly represented – held out – to the third party that the agent does in fact have authority to perform the act in question. The holding out must necessarily be by the principal and not by the agent. It has been said that apparent authority is the authority of an agent 'as it *appears* to others'.[6] Apparent authority was defined by Diplock LJ in *Freeman and Lockyer v Buckhurst Park Properties (Mangal) Ltd*[7] as the 'legal relationship between the principal and [third party] created by a representation made by the principal to the [third party], intended to be and in fact acted on by the [third party], that the agent has authority'.[8] At its root, apparent authority rests upon estoppel, so the representor (the principal) is estopped from asserting that he is not bound by the insurance contract effected by the agent.

[3] *Houldsworth v City of Glasgow Bank* (1880) 5 App Cas 317; *Lloyd v Grace Smith* [1912] AC 716.

[4] See the judgment of Diplock LJ in *Freeman and Lockyer v Buckhurst Park Properties (Mangal) Ltd* [1964] 2 QB 480.

[5] The cases and books are far from consistent in the terminology applied to this form of authority, but the concepts themselves are clear enough.

[6] *Hely-Hutchinson v Brayhead Ltd* [1968] 1 QB 549, 583 (Lord Denning).

[7] [1964] 2 QB 480.

[8] See also Lord Keith in *Armagas Ltd v Mundogas SA, The Ocean Frost* [1986] AC 717.

There are therefore two constituent elements to apparent authority: (a) a representation made by the principal; and (b) reliance upon that representation by the third party. The representation to the effect that the agent has authority can, of course, be made by words, but it generally arises from some form of conduct on the part of the principal as where, for example, the principal holds the agent out as entitled to act on his behalf. In either case, it must be made by a person possessing actual authority in the matter. The point was succinctly stated by Lord Denning MR in *Eagle Star Insurance Co Ltd v Spratt*,[9] a complex reinsurance decision in which the broker's knowledge of certain flaws in the execution of a policy was imputed to his principals: 'If you find conduct – standing by – of the principal, even though it is not communicated to the other party – and this conduct leads the other party to believe that the agent has authority, that is enough to bind the principal.'[10] Reliance upon the representation can be refuted by establishing that the third party had either actual or constructive knowledge of the agent's lack of authority.

1.2.2. Ratification[11]

A principal may ratify an act of an agent even though it was performed outside the scope of the agent's actual or apparent authority. For ratification to be effective the agent must have purported to act on behalf of a named[12] or identifiable[13] principal. Ratification is retroactive,[14] so that it relates back to the time when the contract was purported to be concluded by the agent. The effect of ratification is to place the principal in the same position as if he had been the original contracting party. Ratification requires knowledge of the circumstances surrounding the contract, together with some form of positive act by the principal. On that basis, an unauthorised policy taken out by the agent of the insured may afterwards be adopted by the insured.[15]

As will be seen in chapter seven, whether it is possible in non-marine insurance to ratify after a loss has occurred is a matter of some controversy. Although the decision in *Grover & Grover Ltd v Mathews*[16] is authority for the proposition that ratification is not possible after the occurrence of the loss where the principal has knowledge of the loss, nevertheless in *National Oilwell (UK) Ltd v Davy Offshore Ltd*[17] Colman J doubted whether he would have followed it. The judge saw no reason in principle why the marine insurance position, which permits ratification after a loss has taken place, should not be of general application in insurance law.

1.3. Rights and Duties in an Agency Relationship

The agency contract will set out the rights of an agent. The most important is the right to remuneration. In the insurance world, remuneration is generally earned in the form of

[9] [1971] 2 Lloyd's Rep 116.
[10] ibid 128.
[11] See ch 7 below, and the discussion of *National Oilwell (UK) Ltd v Davy Offshore Ltd* [1993] 2 Lloyd's Rep 582.
[12] *Re Tiedemann and Ledermann Frères* [1899] 2 QB 66; *Keighley, Maxsted & Co v Durant* [1901] AC 240.
[13] *Eastern Construction Co Ltd v National Trust Co Ltd and Schmidt* [1914] AC 197; *ING Re (UK) Ltd v R & V Versicherung* [2006] EWHC 1544 (Comm).
[14] *Bolton Partners v Lambert* (1888) 41 Ch D 295; *Presentaciones Musicales SA v Secunda* [1994] 2 All ER 737.
[15] *Lucena v Craufurd* (1808) 1 Taunt. 325; *Stirling v Vaughan* (1809) 11 East 619.
[16] [1910] 2 KB 401.
[17] [1993] 2 Lloyd's Rep 582.

commission, earned by proof that the agent's activities were the proximate cause of bringing a contract of insurance into existence. An agent will also normally be entitled to be indemnified for expenditure reasonably incurred by him on behalf of the principal.[18]

Although the duties of an agent are derived from contract, the duties are replicated by the general law. An agent's duties of care and skill arise in parallel in contract and in tort,[19] and both demand that the agent acts with the degree of care and skill reasonably to be expected of a person in the position of an agent of that type. Most importantly, the agent must exercise reasonable care to adhere to the principal's instructions. Although an action for breach of the duty to exercise reasonable care in the performance of a service can be brought in either contract or tort, the measure of damages is that for contract,[20] and there can be a deduction for contributory negligence where there is parallel liability.[21] Whether the principal sues in tort or in contract may nevertheless have practical implications because different rules on limitation of actions apply to the different causes of action. For contract, the six-year limitation period laid down by section 5 of the Limitation Act 1980 accrues when the breach occurs. The fact that damage is not suffered by the claimant until some later date does not extend the limitation period. If, on the other hand, the agent's breach gives rise to an action in negligence, under section 2 of the Limitation Act 1980 the cause of action accrues when damage is in fact sustained so that the limitation period starts to run at a later date in tort. The decision of the House of Lords in *Henderson v Merrett Syndicates Ltd*[22] affords a clear example of this logistical consideration. The claimants were Names in the Lloyd's insurance market and were members of syndicates managed by the defendant underwriters as agents. Having suffered considerable financial losses in respect of a number of policies underwritten by their syndicates, the claimants sued the defendants for the negligent mismanagement of their financial affairs. The action for breach of contract against those defendants with whom there was privity was time barred by virtue of the Limitation Act 1980. However, the action in negligence, which was founded upon the principle in *Hedley Byrne & Co Ltd v Heller & Partners*,[23] succeeded. The action in tort has the further limitation advantage that in cases where the breach of duty has not become apparent by the time of the expiry of the limitation period, there is a secondary 'discoverability' limitation period under section 11A of the 1980 Act[24] running for three years from the date on which the damage and the defendant's liability for it should have become known.

Equity treats an agent as a fiduciary, meaning that the agent must not allow personal interest and duty to the principal to come into conflict, and most importantly the agent must not make profits from opportunities arising from the agency relationship – and it is immaterial whether such profits come to the agent at the expense of the principal or whether they could not have been earned by the principal.[25]

[18] *Islamic Republic of Iran Shipping Lines v Zannis Compania Naviera SA (The Tzelepi)* [1991] 2 Lloyd's Rep 265.

[19] *Henderson v Merrett Syndicates* [1994] 3 All ER 506.

[20] *Wellesley Partnership LLP v Withers* [2015] EWCA Civ 1146.

[21] So held at first instance in *Forsikringsaktielskapet Vesta v Butcher* [1988] 1 All ER 19. This point was not pursued in the appeal proceedings, as to which see ch 17 below.

[22] [1994] 3 All ER 506.

[23] [1964] AC 465.

[24] Added by the Latent Damage Act 1986.

[25] *Keech v Sandford* (1726) Cas Temp King 61; *Bray v Ford* [1896] AC 44; *Boardman v Phipps* [1967] 2 AC 46; *Imageview Management Ltd v Jack* [2009] EWCA Civ 63, [2009] 2 All ER 666; *Wood v Commercial First Business Ltd* [2021] EWCA Civ 471.

2. The Insurer's Agents

An insurance company, as an artificial person, has to conduct business through its agents.[26] These will consist of employees of the insurer and also agents – which may be human or corporate – not in the insurer's employ but appointed to carry out various functions on behalf of the insurer. The use of agents by insurers has changed quite dramatically over the years. At one time insurers employed canvassing agents who visited households armed with blank proposal forms for various forms of cover for completion on the spot. Insurers also operated branch offices which could be visited by those seeking to place insurance. In the life industry in particular, premiums were collected by agents, who visited homes periodically (usually quarterly) for the purpose.

There are numerous decided cases on the scope of the authority of such agents, and in particular on the issue of whether there had been any holding out by insurers giving rise to ostensible authority. In *Zurich General Accident Liability Insurance Co Ltd v Rowberry*,[27] the insured instructed his brokers to arrange air travel insurance for his trip to France. The brokers erroneously notified the insurers that the destination was Paris. In fact, the insured was travelling to Nice. The insured disputed the insurer's claim for the premium, arguing that, due to mistake, there was never a contract between them. The Court of Appeal held that the insured was liable on the basis that his instructions to the brokers to arrange insurance cover on his behalf without specifically stating that Nice was his destination impliedly authorised them to nominate Paris as the entry point into France. Sir Raymond Evershed MR was of the view that:

> it is quite plain from the course which was adopted that the agents ... were authorised, from the beginning of the negotiations to the end, to negotiate on behalf of the principal [the insured] the precise form of policy to be issued in response to this proposal within, of course, the broad limits of the proposal terms. More precisely, I think it was clearly within the authority of the agents to nominate for the purposes of the policy, and if the policy so required, the airport in France to which and from [the insured] intended to travel.[28]

It is evident from this passage that an agent who is authorised to arrange insurance cover has implied authority to agree the content and scope of the policy.

The practices of the industry, combined with legislation prohibiting cold-calling and the growth of online placement, have been transformed since the 1970s. Branch offices for the most part no longer exist, and home visits no longer occur. Risks are accepted centrally, premiums are collected by direct debit and claims are handled centrally. In the light of these changes, little purpose is served by detailed discussion of the old agency authorities, as the examples they provide are no longer relevant.

The modern use of agents by insurers is far more complex. Much insurance is placed through websites that forward the details of proposers to insurers for quotations to be given. These heavily advertised websites, known as 'aggregators', are funded by commission paid by insurers, although a number of insurers have passed up the opportunity to

[26] See *Houghton v Northard, Lowe* [1928] AC 1, 18 (Lord Sumner).
[27] [1954] 2 Lloyd's Rep 55.
[28] ibid 57.

participate in aggregator sites, preferring direct sales. The legal status of aggregators has yet to be conclusively determined.[29] Other agents include: persons who have little or nothing to do with insurance generally but who provide insurance services incidental to their main business – travel agents, motor dealers, suppliers of electrical products and builders, to name just a few, may offer insurance as a part of the overall package; underwriting agents, who are appointed by insurers to write risks for them in return for commission; loss adjusters appointed by insurers to determine whether, and to what extent, a loss falls within the terms of the policy; companies appointed by insurers by way of outsourcing of administrative functions; and run-off agents employed by insurers no longer writing new business to settle all outstanding claims and to secure reinsurance recoveries in respect of them.

---

3. Insurance Brokers

3.1. The Incidence of a Broker's Agency

3.1.1. Brokers and Insurers

It is critical to ascertain whether the intermediary's principal is the insured or the insurer, as that will determine which of the parties is regarded as being in possession of information held by the intermediary, which of the parties is responsible for the acts or defaults of the intermediary and to which party the intermediary's duties are owed. It may be said in general terms that brokers (including Lloyd's brokers) are the agents of the insured, in that they are engaged by the insured to represent him or her in dealings with the insurer, while company representatives (canvassing agents, employees and tied agents) are the agents of the insurer. However, while that analysis is a good starting point, it may break down because the market practices of intermediaries – and in particular brokers operating in the commercial market – do not always reflect this distinction.

There are various situations in which a broker will be regarded as acting as the insurer's agent as well as an agent for the insured. The structure of the market indeed creates situations where dual agency is inevitable, and there is judicial recognition of the fact that a broker may need to perform functions for each party in order to fulfil the mandate to the insured; indeed, some cases have gone as far as describing a broker as a 'servant of the market'[30] or a 'common agent'.[31] As was said by Auld LJ In *HIH Casualty and General Insurance Co v JLT Risk Solutions*,[32] the role of a broker was 'notoriously anomalous for its inherent scope for engendering conflict of interest in the otherwise relatively tidy legal world of agency'. There is no objection in principle to a broker acting in a dual capacity where there is no conflict of interest involved, but where there is a potential conflict then it is necessary for the broker to obtain the full and informed consent of the insured as primary principal before doing so.[33]

[29] It was held in *InsuranceWide.Com Services Ltd v HM Revenue & Customs* [2010] EWCA Civ 422 that for tax purposes they are brokers acting for policyholders.

[30] *General Accident v Tanter, The Zephyr* [1984] 1 Lloyd's Rep 58.

[31] *JA Chapman & Co Ltd v Kadirga Denizcilik Ve Ticaret* [1998] Lloyd's Rep IR 377; *Heath Lambert Ltd v Sociedad de Corretaje de Seguros* [2004] Lloyd's Rep IR 905; *Goshawk Dedicated Ltd v Tyser & Co Ltd* [2007] Lloyd's Rep IR 224.

[32] [2007] EWCA Civ 710.

[33] *Excess Life Assurance Co Ltd v Fireman's Fund Insurance Co of Newark New Jersey* [1982] 2 Lloyd's Rep 599.

The formation of insurance contracts frequently involves a conflict of interest. Although it is the role of a broker in law to obey the insured's instructions by searching the market for cover, in practice brokers play a proactive rule in identifying new forms of business and drafting wording for adoption by insurers. It may well be, therefore, that when a client instructs a broker to obtain a policy of a given type, the broker at least prepares wording to be presented to insurers and may well have secured the insurer's agreement in advance that they will insure any client recommended by the broker.[34] Presentation of a proposal to insurers for cover in the London market will be accompanied by a pro forma Market Reform Contract, which sets out the terms of the insurance, for insurers to agree, modify or reject.

A broker may be given authority by insurers to accept proposals falling within agreed parameters. This is particularly common in the domestic motor market, where brokers are expressly or impliedly authorised to enter into interim insurance contracts and to issue cover notes pending full acceptance. The issue of implied authority was considered in *Stockton v Mason*,[35] where the insured, having exchanged his Ford Anglia for an MG Midget, instructed his broker to transfer his existing insurance to cover his new vehicle. The broker's clerk told him that everything would be all right and that the firm would make the necessary arrangements. The insured inferred that this meant that the same terms would apply. However, the new cover did not extend to the insured's son, who negligently caused an accident while driving the car with the result that damages amounting to £46,000 were awarded to the claimant. Reversing the county court's judgment, the Court of Appeal held that the insurers were liable because the broker had implied authority as their agent to enter into contracts of interim insurance. Lord Diplock observed:

> There must be every day thousands of cases, not only in motor insurance but in other forms of non-marine insurance, where persons wishing to become insured or wishing to transfer an insurance ring up their brokers and ask for cover or ask for fresh cover or ask to transfer the cover from an existing vehicle to another. In every case they rely upon the broker's statement that they are covered as constituting a contract binding upon the insurance company. In that sort of conversation, they are speaking, in the absence of any special circumstances, to the broker as agent for the insurance company, and the broker in dealing with the matter, is acting as agent for the insurance company and not as agent for the person wishing to have insurance. Of course, there may be exceptional cases. There was nothing exceptional about this.[36]

In the commercial market, the arrangements may go much further. It is very common at Lloyd's for a broker to be granted a binding authority, or 'binder', which authorises the broker to issue full policies on behalf of the insurers as long as they fall within specified financial limits and the policyholders meet the parameters laid down by the insurers.

The use of binding authorities on the face of things works for the benefit of the insured, as it means that the broker can effectively guarantee that insurance will be available to meet the insured's needs. However, the practice is not free from difficulties, because the broker will inevitably have some discretion in the making of underwriting decisions and there is a risk for the insurers that such decisions may favour the broker's client. The courts have

[34] *Forsikringsaktieselskapet Vesta v Butcher* [1989] 1 All ER 402, where both insurance and reinsurance had been prearranged.

[35] [1978] 2 Lloyd's Rep 430. See also *Woolcott v Excess Insurance Co* [1979] 1 Lloyd's Rep 231 (Court of Appeal), [1978] 1 Lloyd's Rep 633 (trial decision of the High Court); the retrial, ordered by the Court of Appeal, is reported at [1979] 2 Lloyd's Rep 210. See also *Aneco v Johnson & Higgins* [2000] Lloyd's Rep IR 12.

[36] ibid 432.

recognised that a potential conflict of interest exists, but they have refused to recognise that the broker owes a duty of care towards the insurer as that would conflict with the broker's primary duty to the assured to obtain insurance.[37]

A conflict of interest may arise also where a broker secures reinsurance for an insurer who requires such protection as a condition for acceptance of the risk. A broker who is seeking to place insurance for an insured with insurers and at the same time working to obtain reinsurance for those insurers is almost inevitably in a position of conflict of interest, by acting both for and against the insurers in respect of the same placement. The courts, while recognising the problem, have simply regarded the problem as one of the broker's own making and have treated the broker's primary duty as one of placement, owed to the assured in respect of the insurance and to the insurers in respect of the reinsurance.[38] Other matters that may give rise to conflicts of interest include broker remuneration and claims handling. These are considered in what follows.

3.1.2. Brokers and Third Parties

A broker may owe a duty of care to a third party if the broker has assumed responsibility to act on behalf of the third party.[39] That possibility will arise where the third party is known to be the intended assignee of the policy[40] or where the policy confers rights upon a third party that are enforceable by the third party under the Contracts (Rights of Third Parties) Act 1999.[41] There cannot be an assumption of responsibility to a third party who subsequently takes an assignment of the policy. More importantly, in the context of liability insurance, no duty of care is owed to a third party who is injured by the insured but who is unable to recover compensation by reason of the absence of enforceable insurance.[42] Where the insured is a company, and the shareholders of the company suffer loss in the form of diminution in the value of their investment by reason of the occurrence of an uninsured loss, the shareholders have no claim against the broker by reason of the bar on recovery for 'reflective loss'.[43] However, shareholders who have suffered loss over and above the loss of value may have a separate claim if such loss falls within the scope of the broker's duty. The sole shareholder in a company who has, to the knowledge of the broker, given personal guarantees of the company's debts may on that principle have a claim against the broker for loss suffered by the forced sale of personal assets to meet the guarantees.[44]

[37] *Empress Assurance Corp Ltd v Bowring & Co Ltd* (1905) 11 Com Cas 107; *Glasgow Assurance Corp Ltd v William Symondson & Co* (1911) 16 Com Cas 109; *Aneco v Johnson & Higgins* [2002] 1 Lloyd's Rep 157; *Sphere Drake v European International Underwriting* [2004] Lloyd's Rep IR 525; *Bonner v Cox Dedicated Corporate Member Ltd* [2006] Lloyd's Rep IR 385. But see *Morton Insurance Brokers Ltd v Sidhu* [2008] EWHC 417 (QB), where a motor insurance broker with authority to issue cover notes on the part of the insurers was held to be liable in damages to the insurers where an employee had issued cover notes backdated to before the date of accidents apparently falling within their scope.

[38] *Aneco Reinsurance Underwriting Ltd v Johnson & Higgins Ltd* [2002] Lloyd's Rep IR 91.

[39] See generally *Customs and Excise Commissioners v Barclays Bank* [2007] 1 AC 181.

[40] *Punjab National Bank v De Boinville* [1992] 3 All ER 104.

[41] *Crowson v HSBC Insurance Brokers* [2010] Lloyd's Rep IR 441.

[42] *Federation General Insurance Co v Knott Becker Scott* [1990] 1 Lloyd's Rep 98.

[43] *Johnson v Gore Wood & Co* [2002] 2 AC 1; *Sevilleja v Marex Financial Ltd* [2021] UKSC 31.

[44] Suggested in *Adelaide (SA) Pools & Spa Manufacturing and Installation Pty Ltd v Westcourt General Insurance Brokers Pty Ltd (No 2)* [2021] SASC 123.

3.2. Remuneration of Brokers

As has been noted earlier, an agent earns commission by arranging a contract between his principal and a third party. In some cases there will be a contract between the insured and the broker whereby the parties agree a fixed sum to be paid for the broker's services.[45] However, in other cases the application of the principle to insurance brokers creates something of an anomaly. Market practice is for the premium to be paid to the broker, and the broker then deducts commission and passes the net premium to the insurers. The question that arises here is, who pays the broker? It might be thought that the payment is by the insured: indeed, the equitable principle is that an agent may not take payment from any third party without his principal's full and informed consent.[46] However, market practice is to the contrary. The amount of commission is agreed between the broker and the insurer, and the cases are consistent that the broker is paid by the insurers for finding the business for them. The legal basis has been said to be either market custom or implied term,[47] a concept rejected by agency law generally.[48] Further, the law does not require the broker to disclose the amount of commission received from the insurers.

The anomalous rules applicable to brokers were confirmed by the Hong Kong Court of First Instance in *Hobbins v Royal Skandia Life Assurance Ltd*,[49] where the matter was given detailed analysis. The claimant instructed brokers to obtain life insurance linked to investments. The brokers stated that their commission would be paid by the insurers, although the amount was not disclosed. The return on the investments was poor, and the claimant sought to avoid the policy and recover his premiums by arguing that the brokers had in breach of their duty failed to disclose the amount of their commission and that their default rendered the policy void. Reyes J dismissed the action and held that the settled common law rule was that while the brokers were the agent of the insured, the brokers were paid by the insurers and there was no duty of disclosure in respect of the amount of commission. There are two important limits to this decision: commission that exceeds the normal market rate must be disclosed (a point not argued in *Hobbins*);[50] and ICOBS 4.3–7 require a broker to disclose the nature (but not the amount) of commission to a consumer client, and the amount of the commission to a commercial client on request.

If it is the case that a broker is paid by the insurers, and that commission is fully earned when the risk is placed, then it follows logically that the broker cannot owe any post-placement duties to the insured because there is no consideration for them. In *Grace v Leslie & Godwin Financial Services Ltd*,[51] discussed below, Clarke J simply dismissed that suggestion. Any potential difficulty was glossed over in *Carvill America Inc v Camperdown UK Ltd*,[52] in which the Court of Appeal held that the ability of the broker to claim commission from the insurers was based either on an agreement between the insured and the broker under which the insured was to pay gross premiums to the broker, or on an agreement between the insured and the insurers under which gross premiums would be paid to the reinsurers, who would then pay commission to the brokers. The remuneration rules have,

[45] As in *Absalom v TCRU Ltd* [2005] EWCA Civ 1586.
[46] *Wilson v Hurstanger* [2007] EWCA Civ 299.
[47] See, eg *Power v Butcher* (1829) 10 B & C 329; *Searle v AR Hales & Co Ltd* [1996] LRLR 68.
[48] *Accida Foundation v Simon C Dickinson Ltd* [2010] EWHC 3058 (Ch).
[49] [2012] HKCFI 10.
[50] See, eg *Baring v Stanton* (1876) 3 Ch D 502; *United Insurance Co of Libya v Aon Ltd* [2008] Lloyd's Rep IR 166.
[51] [1995] LRLR 472.
[52] [2006] Lloyd's Rep IR 1.

subject to the limits noted above, been permitted to stand and their incompatibility with ordinary equitable principles has been described as no more than a 'curiosity'.[53]

3.3. The Broker's Duties on Placing Insurance

3.3.1. Finding the Required Cover

The primary duty of the broker is to find a policy that suits the client's needs. In determining the scope of an agent's duty of care, the courts have paid heed to the codes of practice governing insurance intermediaries and the rules contained in ICOBS.[54] Almost every case that has examined the duties of a broker in placing insurance has sought to analyse the law in a series of propositions. There is no better exposition than that of Doyle J in the Supreme Court of South Australia in *Adelaide (SA) Pools & Spa Manufacturing and Installation Pty Ltd v Westcourt General Insurance Brokers Pty Ltd*.[55] His Honour's categorisation was as follows:

(a) An insurance broker, acting as the agent of the insured, owed a general duty to the insured concurrently in contract and in tort. While the precise content of the duty depended on the instructions given by the client to the broker, a contract between broker and client would generally include an implied term that the broker would exercise reasonable skill and care in the performance of his or her duties

(b) In general terms, satisfaction of this duty will require that the broker take reasonable steps to understand the nature and extent of the client's needs and instructions for insurance cover; to advise the client about the insurance cover available to meet those needs and instructions; and to arrange the insurance as instructed.

(c) What was required of a broker would depend upon the circumstances of the particular case. Considerations that would influence the steps required would include the level of commercial sophistication of the client; whether advice had been provided to the client in previous years; whether the broker had taken responsibility for a value or calculation, or had simply requested that the client provide the financial information necessary for that purpose; and whether the broker had reason to suspect that any of the information provided by the client was inaccurate.

(d) In determining what a reasonably careful insurance broker would have done in particular circumstances, expert evidence would ordinarily assist, and often be required. However, the expert evidence might not always be determinative of what was required of a competent insurance broker. And, consistently with this, particularly where the default relied upon was rudimentary in nature, such evidence might not be necessary.

(e) As a starting point, a broker had to take reasonable care to ascertain the client's needs. To do so, the broker would ordinarily be required to obtain some understanding of the client's business.

(f) Where there was a disparity in expertise between the broker and the client, it was the broker's responsibility to make appropriate inquiries of the client to ascertain their needs, rather than the client's responsibility to anticipate what the broker might need to know. In the case of a recurring retainer, the broker owed a duty to inquire about matters of which had not previously been the subject of inquiry.

[53] By Longmore LJ In *Absalom v TCRU Ltd* [2005] EWCA Civ 1586.
[54] See eg *Dunlop Haywards Ltd v Barbon Insurance Group Ltd* [2010] Lloyd's Rep IR 149.
[55] [2021] SASC 123.

(g) The process of obtaining instructions involved taking reasonable care to inform the client about the availability of the various forms of cover that might be suitable, and to then obtain instructions about the type and level of cover that the client wished to secure.
(h) A reasonably competent broker would understand the general principles of insurance law, and while not required to explain the law to the assured, the broker must highlight the 'legal pitfalls' where they might arise in effecting valid cover. Further, the broker should draw the client's attention to any onerous or unusual terms in the relevant policy, and explain the nature and effect of those terms.
(i) In the context of an Industrial Special Risks policy, the broker's obligation to advise in relation to the terms of the policy included an obligation to explain the meaning and significance of terms and concepts such as declared value, gross profit, uninsured working expenses, and under-insurance (or co-insurance).
(j) Ultimately, the insurance broker had to provide the client with advice and assistance to enable it to make an informed decision about its insurance requirements, and to give informed instructions to the broker about what insurance cover to procure on its behalf.
(k) However, the broker did not owe a general duty to prevent loss or risk of loss, nor to obtain cover that was 'bullet proof'. While the broker had to obtain a policy that was suitable for the purpose for which it was sought by the client, the appropriateness of the cover obtained would be informed by the client's instructions.
(l) Where a client had provided instructions which, on the broker's understanding, would leave the client at risk of being uninsured (or under-insured) if followed, it was the broker's duty to highlight and explain the consequences of putting those instructions into effect, and to confirm those instructions before acting upon them.

It is to be borne in mind that in the commercial insurance market many of the wordings are generated by brokers, and in such cases the duty is necessarily extended to making sure that the broker's own wording is suitable for the assured's needs.

There are numerous illustrations of these principles in the decided cases. In *O'Brien v Hughes-Gibb*,[56] brokers obtained insurance on the famous racehorse Shergar, but chose a policy that excluded kidnap even though such cover could have been obtained elsewhere in the market without an increase in premium. Shergar was taken and his fate has never been established, and it was widely believed that there had been an attempted kidnap even though no ransom demand was received. The test applied by the court was whether the brokers had acted in accordance with the standards expected of a reasonable broker operating in the market at the relevant time. The evidence showed that kidnap was not a major risk at the time, and that a reasonable broker would not have sought cover for it. Thus, there was no liability. It is important to note that the brokers were not in this case instructed to obtain kidnap insurance, and the case shows that it is the duty of a broker to consider the needs of the client over and above the actual instructions provided by the client.

In *Arbory Group Ltd v West Craven Insurance Services*,[57] the insured instructed brokers to obtain business interruption insurance, to protect against financial losses caused by the insured's inability to use its business premises if they suffered physical damage. The sum insured under a business interruption policy[58] rests upon the insured's valuation of its revenue and also an assessment of the duration of any period during which revenue might be lost (the indemnity period). The brokers failed to advise the insured as to the meaning of

[56] [1995] LRLR 90.
[57] [2007] Lloyd's Rep IR 491.
[58] This form of insurance is discussed in more detail in ch 18 below.

the various terms used in the wording, with the result that the premises were substantially underinsured. The brokers indeed admitted liability. A very similar case was *Adelaide (SA) Pools & Spa Manufacturing and Installation Pty Ltd v Westcourt General Insurance Brokers Pty Ltd*,[59] where the brokers had failed to advise the insured that it was necessary to provide an accurate valuation of revenue and also a proper assessment of the length of the indemnity period. These cases may be contrasted with *William Jackson & Sons Ltd v Oughtred & Harrison (Insurance) Ltd*,[60] where the shortfall was a result of the insured's own failure to obtain proper valuations for its business, the broker not being under a duty to undertake its own valuations, and *Dalamd Ltd v Butterworth Spengler Commercial Ltd*,[61] where the correct advice had been given to the insured as to the meaning of the various valuation terms used in the policy.

In *Horsell International Pty Ltd v Dive Two Pty Ltd*,[62] Dive Two was found liable for injuries caused to a fisherman when his vessel was hit by a dive vessel with six passengers aboard and navigated by Dive Two's owner. The claim against Dive Two was settled, and Dive Two sought indemnity from its liability insurers or, if the insurers were not liable under the policy, the brokers. The policy covered Dive Two for liability arising out if its 'scuba diving' business, although the purpose of the voyage on the day of the accident was a leisure cruise and not to transport divers. The policy was found not to cover the loss, but the New South Wales Court of Appeal held that the brokers faced default liability. The brokers had been instructed to obtain insurance for Dive Two's business, but a competent broker would have ensured that any insurance obtained was suitable for the client's needs. The brokers had accordingly been under a duty to determine whether the insured vessel was to be used for other purposes and to ensure that there was cover for such purposes. This case is of particular significance, in that the brokers operated a facility with the insurers for the coverage of business risks, and they had simply sought cover under the facility without making further inquiries.

Standard Life Assurance Ltd v Oak Dedicated Ltd[63] was a case in which the brokers failed to appreciate the significance of an alteration to the policy wording. The policy in this case was one of professional indemnity, with a limit of cover of £75 million and an excess of £25 million. The brokers, without checking the wording, assumed that the excess was in the aggregate, so that there was coverage when the total of all claims against the insured exceeded £25 million. However, the wording stated that the excess applied to 'each and every claim', meaning that there was coverage for any claim only where it exceeded £25 million. The claims against the insured were all relatively small and none were capable of coming close to £25 million. The brokers had thus procured a more or less worthless policy.

It has been stated in many of the cases that it is the duty of a broker to protect its client from litigation – a principle that applies to solicitors and other professionals, as well as insurance brokers. What that means in practice is that it does not suffice for the policy to cover the insured's needs as a matter of strict law; such coverage must be obvious and therefore not capable of giving rise to a dispute. The importance of this point can be seen from *Ground Gilbey Ltd v JLT UK Ltd*,[64] a case discussed below.

[59] [2021] SASC 123.
[60] [2002] Lloyd's Rep IR 230.
[61] [2018] EWHC 2558 (Comm).
[62] [2013] NSWCA 368.
[63] [2008] Lloyd's Rep IR 552.
[64] [2011] EWHC 124 (Comm).

3.3.2. Advice on Presentation of the Risk

Once the correct cover and the appropriate insurers have been identified, it is the broker's duty to advise the insured on how to present the risk. The insured's duty to make a fair presentation of the risk is discussed in chapter four, and it will there be seen that breach of that duty may confer upon the insurers the right to avoid the policy or at the very least to rewrite its terms. In consumer cases the duty is to avoid misrepresentation, whereas in commercial cases there is an additional obligation to disclose facts relevant to the risk whether or not questions are asked by the insurers.

The broker's duty in commercial cases extends to advising the insured of the duty to disclose all material facts and of the consequences of failing to do so. It is not sufficient merely to rely on generalised warnings and explanations contained in the documents. Rather, brokers must actively ensure that the insured knows about the entirety of the duty of disclosure, including what ought to be disclosed, and of the draconion consequences of a material non-disclosure or misrepresentation. In *Jones v Environcom Ltd (No 2)*,[65] the insured's business involved, amongst other things, recycling refrigerators. It was necessary to remove compressors, and in some cases this could be done only with the use of plasma guns. Those devices posed a risk of metal splatter and sparks, which could cause fires. A major fire occurred as the result of the use of a plasma gun, and the insurers avoided the policy on the ground that there had been non-disclosure of the use of plasma guns, of a series of small fires caused by such guns and of a fire shortly before the policy was renewed. The claim against the insurers was settled for £950,000, and the insured sought to recover the shortfall in its loss of some £6 million from its brokers. David Steel J dismissed the claim. He found that the brokers had been in breach of their duty to warn the insured of its duty of disclosure and it was not enough for the brokers to rely upon its written standard form explanations and warnings. Further, the brokers were also in breach of duty by failing to take adequate steps to elicit the information which required to be disclosed, and if it had done so the existence of the fires would have come to light. However, the breaches had not caused the insured's loss because had there been disclosure, the loss would not have been insurable at all or, if it was, then it would not have been insurable on terms and premium acceptable to the insured; and the insured had been in breach of its waste management licence, and that was a material fact which would have been relied upon by the insurers had other grounds for avoidance not existed. Further, had there been renewal, the policy would have demanded that the use of plasma guns cease, in which case there would have been no loss. The same point was made in *Synergy Health (UK) Ltd v CGU Insurance Plc*,[66] where the court held that the broker was under a duty to advise the insured of the scope of the duty of disclosure, here the fact that the insured premises did not have an intruder alarm. On the facts of the case the point did not arise, because the insurers were unable to show that the absence of the alarm would have affected their underwriting decision and so they had no defence.

Where the broker undertakes the task of presenting the risk to the insurers on behalf of the insured, the broker is under a duty to take reasonable care. The broker will thus face liability where information provided by the insured is disregarded or incorrectly presented. The burden of demonstrating that correct information was provided to the broker is borne

[65] [2010] EWHC 759 (Comm).

[66] [2010] EWHC 2583 (Comm), [2011] Lloyd's Rep IR 500. See also *Daland Ltd v Butterworth Spengler Commercial Ltd* [2019] PNLR 6.

by the insured. In *O'Connor v BDB Kirby & Co*,[67] the claimant arranged motor car insurance through the defendant broker. The proposal form was completed by the broker on the basis of answers supplied by the claimant, but it wrongly stated that the car was garaged when, in fact, it was parked on the street. The insurers avoided liability and the claimant sued the broker. It was held that the broker's duty was to take reasonable care in the circumstances and did not extend to guaranteeing the accuracy of the answers. In any case, there was no evidence as to how the mistake arose, and the claimant's failure to notice the inaccuracy when signing the form would have operated to break the chain of causation which flowed from the alleged negligence.

Each case must, of course, be taken on its facts, so where the insured does not have sight of the proposal form, the broker may be liable for any misrepresentations contained therein. In *Warren v Henry Sutton & Co*,[68] the claimant sought to add a friend to his policy as an additional driver for a touring holiday in France. The friend was represented as having a clean driving record, which was patently not the case. They were involved in an accident while on holiday and when the claimant sought indemnity the insurers avoided liability on the ground of misrepresentation. The claimant sued the brokers for damages, arguing that they had failed to ask about the friend's claims history. The Court of Appeal held that because the brokers had told the insurers in a telephone conversation that the friend had 'no accidents, convictions, or disabilities' without first confirming this with the claimant, they were liable. The majority of the court concluded that the misrepresentation arose as a result of the brokers' failure to ask the claimant the relevant questions.[69] In providing their services, the brokers were under a duty to make such enquiries as were necessary in the circumstances. Similarly, where a broker answers questions in a proposal form incorrectly but the relevant information falls within the broker's knowledge, the broker will be liable to place the insured in the same position he or she would have been in had the policy been valid.[70]

Non-disclosure by a broker also occurred in *McNealy v Pennine Insurance Co Ltd*.[71] The claimant, who was a property repairer and a part-time musician, instructed his brokers to effect comprehensive insurance on his motor car. The insurers offered low premium rates, but their underwriting instructions, of which the brokers were aware, contained a list of professions which were not acceptable and which included part-time musicians. The brokers stated the claimant's principal occupation but failed to check that he had a part-time occupation. When the claimant was involved in an accident, the insurers repudiated liability on the ground of non-disclosure. It was held that the brokers were liable to the claimant for the full amount of the claim. Waller LJ said that it was the duty of the broker

> to make as certain as he reasonably could that the [claimant] … came within the categories acceptable to the Pennine Insurance Co, and the only way in which he could properly do that, in my opinion, was to show him the list and probably go through it with him to make sure that the [claimant] understood that he had to be outside those particular risks.

[67] [1972] 1 QB 90. See also *First National Commercial Bank plc v Barnet Devanney (Harrow) Ltd* [1999] Lloyd's Rep IR 43.

[68] [1976] 2 Lloyd's Rep 276.

[69] Lord Denning MR dissented on the ground that the claimant was under a duty to disclose to the brokers the additional driver's record.

[70] *Dunbar v A & B Painters Ltd* [1986] 2 Lloyd's Rep 38.

[71] [1978] 2 Lloyd's Rep 18.

However, the Court of Appeal stressed that where the broker is not in possession of material facts and there are no special circumstances putting the broker on notice, there is no corresponding duty to warn the insured of his or her duty of disclosure.[72]

3.4. The Broker's Post-contractual Duties

The conceptual difficulty raised by the principle that a broker is paid by the insurers, namely that there is no consideration for any post-placement duties performed by the broker, has in practice been disregarded. It is now settled that brokers owe duties to the insured at two stages: when the policy is in operation; and when a claim arises.

3.4.1. The Operation of the Policy

Given that liability under the *Hedley Byrne* principle extends to the negligent performance of services, an agent who advises on the suitability of a particular policy should be able to explain its terms.[73] This may assume particular importance in relation to any conditions precedent to the insurer's liability. For example, in *JW Bollom & Co Ltd v Byas Mosley & Co Ltd*,[74] the insured, JWB, having suffered several false alarms, left the alarm to their premises switched off over a weekend. A fire occurred, causing some £8 million worth of damage. The insurers repudiated liability on the basis of a breach of condition precedent requiring the maintenance and use of the alarms. The claim was settled at £5 million. JWB successfully sued their brokers for £3 million, arguing that they had failed to take reasonable steps to bring the clauses to their, ie the insured's, attention.

In *Ground Gilbey Ltd v JLT UK Ltd*,[75] the insured brought a claim against the defendant broker, JLT, who had placed property insurance for Camden Market. There was a major fire after a portable heater (of a type using liquefied gas) set fire to some clothes on a stall. The use of such portable heaters had been identified by the insurers as posing a fire risk, and various risk improvement measures (RIMs) had been sent to JLT. The first of these was forwarded to the insured with the warning that the heaters should be removed immediately. However, the second RIM, which was sent to JLT in October 2007, was not passed to the insured. Nor had the broker advised the insured of the consequences of non-compliance with the required RIM. Further, the policy renewal schedule sent in April 2007 had included a Survey Condition stating that cover was conditional upon, amongst other things, satisfaction of all requested RIMs within the stipulated timescales. Again, this information was not passed to the insured by JLT. Rather, the broker sought to resolve the issue of the heaters by seeking the agreement of the insurers to the use of safer heaters. The fire occurred before any resolution had been reached. Following counsel's advice that the insurers may have a good defence on the basis of the non-compliance with the survey condition, the insured settled their claim for 70 per cent of the full value. It brought an action against JLT for the shortfall. Blair J held that because the broker knew that the heaters were being used, it should have appreciated that the insurance policy no longer clearly and indisputably met

[72] See also *Kapur v JW Francis & Co* [2000] Lloyd's Rep IR 361.
[73] *Harvest Trucking Co Ltd v Davis* [1991] 2 Lloyd's Rep 638.
[74] [2000] Lloyd's Rep IR 136.
[75] [2011] EWHC 124 (Comm).

the needs of the insureds. Taking a broad view of the duty, the judge found that JLT should have done more than merely forward the original RIMs, but should have advised their client that cover was at risk unless the heaters were removed or a safer alternative form of heating was agreed with the insurer. With respect to causation, JLT argued that even if they had informed the insured of the RIMs they would not have implemented them. Indeed, the judge expressed doubt as to whether the insured would have removed the heaters, but he agreed with the insured that 'if proper advice had been given indicating the urgency and importance of the matter, steps would have been taken to comply with the risk improvement measure'.[76]

The post-placement duties of brokers came to the fore in *HIH Casualty & General Insurance Ltd* v *JLT Risk Solutions Ltd*.[77] JLT designed insurance and reinsurance arrangements under which banks and financial institutions could invest in film production. The loans would be repaid from the profits generated by the films (known as a slate of films), although in the event that the films did not generate adequate profits the lenders would be indemnified by insurance. Not all of the films for which funding had been provided were made, and those that were made did not generate significant revenue. The reduced number of films had been adverted to in risk-management reports issued by a company, Flashpoint, which had been sent to JLT and then forwarded to HIH and the reinsurers. As a result of the reduction in film numbers the investors suffered massive losses, leading to payments by HIH which, in turn, sought to recover from the reinsurers. In earlier cases it was held that the reduction in the number of films being produced was a breach of warranty which gave the reinsurers a complete defence to the claim.[78] HIH therefore sought to recover from JLT for post-placement negligence. The trial judge held that JLT owed HIH a post-placement duty to warn them of the potential coverage issues which it had received from Flashpoint, and that they were in breach of that duty. However, the breach had not caused HIH loss. Langley J found that had HIH been alerted to the coverage issues it would have instructed JLT to seek the views of the reinsurers, but that would not have made any difference to the reinsurers' later rejection of liability. Further, even if the breach had caused HIH loss, HIH would have been contributorily negligent to the extent of 70 per cent: 20 per cent due to its failure to appreciate the risk to coverage on learning of the film reductions and 50 per cent in paying claims without first obtaining the agreement of the reinsurers to indemnify them.

The Court of Appeal affirmed the first instance decision in full. Auld LJ, who delivered the leading judgment (May LJ concurring), stated that where a broker devises, structures and establishes a complicated scheme of this sort, 'it is plainly a strong candidate for post-placement monitoring obligations of the sort alleged here'.[79] He agreed with Langley J that the facts made the case and the imposition of the post-placement duty unique. They relied on JLT's past practice of disseminating information through the risk-management reports about the production status and revenues of the films; that JLT was aware that the film reductions indicated in the risk-management reports represented a potential risk to the insurance and reinsurance coverage; and that HIH and the reinsurers may take different views on the risks. Longmore LJ took a wider view, commenting that:

> [A]n insurance broker who, after placing the risk, becomes aware of information which has a material and potentially deleterious effect on the insurance cover which he has placed is under an

[76] ibid [85].
[77] [2007] EWCA Civ 710.
[78] See *HIH v New Hampshire Insurance Co* [2001] 1 Lloyd's Rep 378; and [2001] 2 Lloyd's Rep 161, discussed in ch 7 below.
[79] [2007] EWCA Civ 0710, [61].

> obligation to act in his client's best interest by drawing it to the attention of his client and obtain his instructions in relation to it.[80]

He also agreed with Langley J's rejection of JLT's argument that its only duty in relation to post-placement information was to act 'as a mere postbox': 'Indeed, as between a lay client unversed in insurance matters and his insurance broker, I would think that the existence of such a duty should be comparatively uncontroversial.'[81] Accordingly, in Longmore LJ's view the duty will apply whenever the broker acquires information which may affect the coverage. This is a wide and far-reaching duty. It may be that the brokers will be compelled to include clauses in their contracts which exclude or limit this duty.[82]

3.4.2. Claims

In *Alexander Forbes Europe Ltd v SBJ Ltd*,[83] the action was brought by the claimants against their former insurance brokers, SBJ. The dispute arose out of pension mis-selling claims, and SBJ were held liable for failing to make the appropriate notification of the possibility of claims to the insurers under a professional indemnity policy.[84] David Mackie QC, sitting as a deputy High Court judge, found for the claimants. The defendant brokers had not been entitled to rely upon the supposed expertise of the claimants so as to lower their standard of care. The judge stated that: 'Brokers owe duties going beyond those of a post box. It was for the brokers to get a grip on the proposed notification, to appraise it and to ensure that the information was relayed to the right place in the correct form.'[85]

Claims handling can give rise to conflict issues. Megaw J in *Anglo-African Merchants Ltd v Bayley*[86] took a strict view of the duty of a broker. A claim made under a theft policy was met with the defence of non-disclosure. The insured's brokers had made their files available to the underwriters and their solicitors during the inquiry into the claim, but denied the insured's solicitors similar access. It was argued that in all matters relating to the placing of the risk, the broker was the agent of the insured, but that once a claim arose, the broker became the agent of the underwriters. Megaw J stressed, albeit obiter, that where an agent wishes to act for another principal, which on the facts of the case were the underwriters, the agent can only do so if he first obtains the fully informed consent of the insured. The judge concluded that 'in the absence of such express and fully informed consent it would be a breach of duty on the part of the insurance broker so to act'.[87]

The issue arose again in *North and South Trust v Berkeley*,[88] in which the insured demanded delivery up of an assessor's report from the broker. The underwriter, claiming that the information was confidential, petitioned for an injunction preventing the broker from releasing the report. Donaldson J questioned the propriety of the practice of Lloyd's,

[80] ibid [116].
[81] ibid [117].
[82] See also *Ground Gilbey Ltd v JLT UK Ltd* [2011] EWHC 124 (Comm).
[83] [2003] Lloyd's Rep IR 432.
[84] For the operation of notification under 'claims made' professional indemnity policies, see ch 15 below.
[85] ibid [32]. Notice to the broker, being the insured's agent, is not notice to the insurers unless the insurers have authorised that possibility: *Quadra Commodities SA v XL Insurance Company SE* [2022] EWHC 431 (Comm).
[86] [1970] 1 QB 311.
[87] ibid 323, applying the views of Scrutton LJ expressed in *Fullwood v Hurley* [1928] 1 KB 498, 502: 'No agent who has accepted an employment from one principal can in law accept an engagement inconsistent with his duty to the first principal … unless he makes the fullest disclosure to each principal of his interest, and obtains the consent of each principal to the double employment.'
[88] [1971] 1 WLR 470.

and of the insurance industry generally, of using brokers to instruct assessors to investigate a claim. Nevertheless, and somewhat curiously, the judge held that the contents of the assessors' report need not be disclosed to the insured. No doubt the learned judge was influenced by the fact that this practice was of common usage in the insurance industry, so neither the broker nor the underwriter knew that this arrangement was improper.[89] However, Donaldson J did go on to express surprise at the failure of the Committee of Lloyd's to change this practice in the light of Megaw J's criticisms expressed in *Bayley*. These criticisms were echoed by David Steel J in *Callaghan v Thompson*,[90] who confirmed that the broker remained the agent of the insured and was therefore in breach of the no-conflict rule by obtaining reports from loss adjusters on behalf of the underwriters.

Brokers at Lloyd's owe a continuing duty to the insured to retain all documentation used in placing the risk. In the event of a claim, that removes arguments as to what was and was not seen by the insurers when they accepted the risk for the purposes of determining whether the insurers have a defence based upon an unfair presentation of the risk.[91] But there are other important reasons as well. The point arose in a curious manner in *Grace v Leslie & Godwin Financial Services Ltd*,[92] a reinsurance case where the cover was placed many years before claims arose. At the time of placement, the brokers notified the reinsured of the identities of the reinsurers, but by the date of the loss the reinsured was unable to locate the information and the brokers had failed to keep their own records. This meant that it was impossible to identify the reinsurers against whom a claim could be made. Clarke J, having held that the brokers' commission included an element for claims handling, held that the brokers were under an implied duty to retain such information as was necessary for a claim to be made.

The anomalous role of brokers in this respect was highlighted in *Goshawk Dedicated Ltd v Tyser & Co Ltd*.[93] In this case the insurers had ceased underwriting and were in run-off, a process whereby the insurers remain in existence only to resolve outstanding claims so that the books can be closed.[94] The insurers requested the brokers to provide them with all placing and claims files so that the validity of present and future claims could be analysed. The brokers, fearing that there might be information adverse to the insureds' interests, refused the request and argued that the brokers were acting as the insureds' agents and could not make disclosure without their clients' consent. The Court of Appeal noted that it was market practice for insurers to rely upon brokers for placing and claims information, and held that to give effect to market practice and to allow brokers to process claims it was necessary to imply a term into the arrangements between insureds and brokers whereby the insureds gave a blanket authorisation to the brokers to provide insurers with all relevant information, thereby giving rise to an implied contract between brokers and insurers for the provision of information. The Court of Appeal regarded this analysis as preferable to the more cumbersome process whereby the insurers had to make the request to the insured, and the insured would then request the brokers to meet the request. One advantage of the Court

[89] For a detailed examination of the judge's reasoning, see BAK Rider, 'The Fiduciary and the Frying Pan' [1978] *Conveyancer* 114, 117–21. See also M Kay and D Yates, 'An Unremedied Breach of Fiduciary Duty' [1972] *MLR* 78.

[90] [2000] Lloyd's Rep IR 125.

[91] See ch 4 below.

[92] [1995] LRLR 472.

[93] [2007] Lloyd's Rep IR 224.

[94] Run-off business is commonly sold by insurers at a discount to run-off companies, whose profits are made by keeping the sums paid as low as possible under the price paid for the business.

of Appeal's approach of creating a direct duty owed by brokers to insurers was that if the information had been lost and could not be provided, the insured would not be responsible to the insurers for any prejudice suffered as a result.

Once a claim has been made out and the sums are required to be paid, it is the duty of the insurers to make payment to the insured. However, market practice in some forms of commercial insurance recognises that payment may be made to the broker. Under ICOBS, the risk of the broker's insolvency or default is borne by the insurers, which means that the insurers may be forced to pay twice if the sums are not paid over to the insured.

3.5. Placing and Producing Brokers

The complexities of the commercial insurance market are sometimes such that it is impossible for the broker instructed by the insured to secure the required cover. The broker (known as the 'producing broker') may therefore seek the assistance of another broker (known as the 'placing broker' to effect the placement. The use of placing brokers is of particular relevance at Lloyd's, where only accredited brokers are permitted to deal with Lloyd's syndicates. The producing broker alone has a claim against the insured for brokerage,[95] and it is then a matter for the sub-brokerage contract as to how the brokerage is to be divided between the producing and placing brokers, failing which the court will determine the division based upon the brokers' respective proportional contribution to placement.[96]

What, then, if something goes wrong somewhere along the brokerage chain? This may arise at the first step, where the insured's instructions to the producing broker are incorrectly conveyed to, or misunderstood by, the placing broker, with a resultant deficiency in cover. Equally, information provided by the insured to the producing broker in fulfilment of the duty of fair presentation may not reach the placing broker at all, or the placing broker may take the view that facts provided by the insured are not relevant to the insurance and accordingly are not disclosed. The view taken by English law is that an agent who delegates some or all of the agency duties to a sub-agent faces liability to the insured for the sub-agent's acts or omissions. By contrast, the sub-agent – who has no contractual relationship with the principal – does not owe a tortious duty to the principal unless the sub-agent has assumed personal responsibility to the principal. Applied to brokers, the default position is that: (a) the producing broker bears liability to the insured for the producing broker's own acts and omissions; (b) the producing broker bears liability to the insured for the placing broker's acts and omissions, not on the basis of vicarious liability but rather on the basis that the producing broker's duties are non-delegable;[97] (c) the placing broker does not owe a contractual or tortious duty of care to the insured unless there has been an assumption of responsibility – that will matter only if, for some reason, the insured cannot bring an action against the producing broker, eg by reason of exclusion or limitation provisions in the broking contract or by reason of the producing broker's insolvency; and (d) the placing broker owes a duty of care to the producing broker and so faces a claim for indemnity or contribution from the producing broker in respect of loss borne by the producing broker.

The general principle that responsibility is borne by the producing broker is illustrated by *Involnert Management Inc v Aprilgrange Ltd*.[98] The issue here was whether a placing

[95] *Prentis Donegan & Partners Ltd v Leeds & Leeds Co Inc* [1998] 2 Lloyd's Rep 326.

[96] *Absalom v TCRU Ltd* [2006] 2 Lloyd's Rep 129.

[97] *Involnert Management Inc v Aprilgrange Ltd* [2015] 2 Lloyd's Rep 289.

[98] [2015] 2 Lloyd's Rep 289.

broker owed a duty of care to the insured in the completion of the proposal form. It was held that the duty to ensure that the form was completed properly was that of the producing broker alone. The question in such cases thus becomes whether the producing broker has a claim for breach of the sub-agency contract, or for breach of a parallel duty of care in tort, against the placing broker and, if so, what proportion of the loss is to be borne by the placing broker.

The direct liability of the placing broker to the insured was discussed in *BP plc v Aon Ltd*.[99] BP entered into a contract with Aon Texas (AT), whereby AT was to operate an open cover subscribed to by a number of underwriters, with 'leading underwriters' administering the insurance on behalf of themselves and others, the 'following market' on the terms of a 'leading underwriter' provision agreed between them. Under the open cover, risks were to be declared by BP. AT delegated the declaration function to Aon London (AL), the placing brokers. AL proceeded to declare a series of risks to the leading underwriters, acting under the misapprehension that the leading underwriter clause in the open cover dispensed with the need for declarations to the following market. When the open cover expired at the end of June 2000, disputes arose between BP and the underwriters, and the point was taken by the following market that there had not been any valid declarations to them. The disputes were settled, although the following market did not accept liability for declarations not made to them. BP commenced proceedings against AT for breach of contract and AL for breach of a duty of care. The contract claim against AT was withdrawn on the basis of exclusion clauses, leaving BP with its claim in tort against AL (there being no contractual relationship between them). Colman J, having subjected the relevant authorities to detailed examination, held that AL owed a duty of care to BP and also to its co-insureds. The fact that BP had a contract with AT did not preclude a duty of care running in parallel with the contractual duty, and the law recognised that an agent could owe a duty of care to a third party who had a contract with his principal provided the agent voluntarily undertook liability to the third party. Colman J commented:

> In the context of the present case it is important to appreciate that, although the authorities on liability for negligent misstatements have, not surprisingly, concentrated on whether there has been sufficiently direct communication by the defendant to the claimant of an assumption of responsibility for the expert advice or special information or for the provision of professional services as in those passages from Lord Steyn's speech in *Williams v Natural Life*[100] ... it is clear from the authorities that the key question is whether the defendant's representation, judged objectively, is such as to amount to the assumption of a personal obligation as explicitly as if he were personally contractually binding himself to provide the advice, the information or the services.[101]

[99] [2006] Lloyd's Rep IR 577. See also *Dunlop Hawards (DHL) Ltd v Erinaceous Insurance Services Ltd* [2009] Lloyd's Rep IR 464, where the placing broker was actually appointed by the insured following a presentation to the insured by the placing broker.

[100] *Williams v Natural Life Health Foods Ltd* [1998] 1 WLR 830. Lord Steyn, reviewing the case law, noted (581) that: 'First, in *Henderson* it was settled that the assumption of responsibility principle enunciated in *Hedley Byrne & Co Ltd* v *Heller & Partners Ltd* is not confined to statements but may apply to any assumption of responsibility for the provision of services. The extended *Hedley Byrne* principle is the rationalisation or technique adopted by English law to provide a remedy for the recovery of damages in respect of economic loss caused by the negligent performance of services. Secondly, it was established that once a case is identified as falling within the extended *Hedley Byrne* principle, there is no need to embark on any further inquiry whether it is "fair, just and reasonable" to impose liability for economic loss. Thirdly, and applying *Hedley Byrne*, it was made clear that "reliance upon [the assumption of responsibility] by the other party will be necessary to establish a cause of action (because otherwise the negligence will have no causative effect)." Fourthly, it was held that the existence of a contractual duty of care between the parties does not preclude the concurrence of a tort duty in the same respect.'

[101] ibid [167].

On the facts of the case, Colman J was satisfied that AL had voluntarily assumed responsibility to BP to make valid declarations. He went on:

> There was adopted such a close relationship between Aon London and BP involving repeated direct contact between them that the substance of Aon's representation to BP was that Aon London was to perform such a crucial function in the process of effecting valid cover that in spite of the initial undertaking of Aon Texas to effect cover, Aon London was *independently* to be responsible for obtaining that cover. For this purpose it is clearly not necessary that there should have been express words to the effect that BP would have a right of action against Aon London. It would be enough if BP were entitled to infer from what was said and done that Aon London was to provide its professional services with regard to declarations and that, independently of Aon Texas or any other Aon entity, it could be relied upon by BP as undertaking responsibility to provide those services in accordance with the proper professional standards of an insurance broker on the London and European markets including Lloyd's.[102]

The relationship between the producing broker and the placing broker where things have gone wrong was discussed in *Dunlop Haywards Ltd v Barbon Insurance Group Ltd*.[103] The insured, a property consultant, instructed the producing broker to place liability insurance in the sum of £10 million for primary layer cover and a £10 million excess layer, on the same terms as their current expiring policy. The producing broker's instructions were deficient, and the placing broker obtained cover under which 'the indemnity provided by this policy is limited to liability arising from the insured's Commercial Property Management activities only'. The effect of this wording was to exclude coverage for liability for valuations, which formed a substantial part of the insured's business. The insured sought indemnification from the insurers for third party claims arising from negligent valuations, and the insurers declined to pay on the ground that the claims were outside the scope of the policy. Hamblen J held that both the producing and placing brokers had been in breach of duty for failing to obtain the correct cover. The producing broker's breach was obvious, and the placing broker's duties reflected those of the producing broker. The placing broker's duties were: to exercise reasonable care and skill in complying with the instructions given by the producing broker; to review the instructions given by the producing broker and to query them if they were unclear, illogical or absurd in the sense that they left the insured with serious gaps in protection; to review the terms of any quotations received from the insurers; to explain the terms of the proposed insurance; and to use reasonable skill and care to ensure that the terms of the policy reflected the instructions and were unambiguous so that there was no room for dispute as to coverage. On the facts of the present case, the placing broker was held to be in breach of duty by simply following instructions which clearly left the insured exposed to claims that formed the riskiest part of its business. Hamblen J held that the producing broker was entitled to a contribution from the placing broker, to be assessed at 20 per cent of the damages payable. *Dunlop Haywards* was a case where the deficiency in the instructions received by the placing broker was obvious. The position would clearly be different if the producing broker's instructions appear to be quite proper, that is, the placing broker is not responsible for ensuring that the producing broker has done its own job properly.

Tudor Jones II v Crowley Colosso Ltd[104] similarly involved a shortfall in cover. The insured, a US resident, purchased two islands in the Bahamas for development, including

[102] ibid [181].
[103] [2010] Lloyd's Rep IR 149. See also *Fisk v Brian Thornhill & Son* [2007] EWCA Civ 152.
[104] [1996] 2 Lloyd's Rep 619.

the construction of a marina. The insured instructed US producing brokers to obtain 'shovel to key' insurance covering the entire period from the beginning of work to its completion. The producing brokers were unable to find the required insurance, and instructed London placing brokers to try their luck in the London market. The placing brokers did obtain cover, but it did not extend to the entire works and terminated when individual parts of the works had been completed. The marina suffered significant damage in a hurricane before it had been completed. The producing broker settled the claim brought against it by the insured and sought a contribution from the placing broker. The court found that the appropriate apportionment of liability was as one-third for the producing broker and two-thirds for the placing broker. The former had been negligent in not giving clear instructions and in failing to query the meaning of the draft wording sent by the placing broker, but the latter had been negligent in failing to draw the producing broker's attention to the importance of the limitation.

3.6. Remedies and Defences

3.6.1. Damages

The primary remedy for breach of duty by a broker is damages assessed as for breach of contract, representing the sum that would have been recovered from the insurers had the broker acted with reasonable care and skill in carrying out the insured's instructions. Necessarily there is to be a deduction for any sum that would have been payable by way of additional premium for the desired coverage. The broker may also face damages for the legal and other costs incurred by the insured in unsuccessfully pursuing the insurers,[105] although in many cases the broker will be joined as co-defendant to the proceedings against the insurers so that a direct costs order may be made by the court in the event of findings that the insurers were not liable by reason of the broker's breach of duty. It is far from unknown for a broker to pay the claim and to take an assignment of the insured's rights against the insurers so that the action is brought directly by the broker.

It is possible to contemplate the situation in which the insured's business premises cannot be rebuilt by reason of a shortage of insurance proceeds or that the business becomes insolvent through loss of revenue, and the question then arises whether the broker is liable for such losses. There is no automatic bar to such recovery: the ruling in *Liesbosch Dredger v Edison, The Liesbosch*,[106] holding that a claimant's impecuniosity breaks the chain of causation between breach of duty and loss, was overruled by the House of Lords in *Lagden v O'Connor*.[107] However, it remains the case that 'in the case of negligent advice given by a professional adviser one looks to see what risk the duty was supposed to guard against and then looks to see whether the loss suffered represented the fruition of that risk'.[108] The starting point is that a broker assumes responsibility for securing insurance, but the duty

[105] *Seavision Investment SA v Evenett and Clarkson Puckle, The Tiburon* [1992] 2 Lloyd's Rep 26.

[106] [1933] AC 449.

[107] [2004] Lloyd's Rep IR 315. In both *Ramwade v WJ Emson & Co* [1987] R.TR 72 and *Verderame v Commercial Union Assurance Co Plc* [1992] B.CLC 793 consequential loss was held to be precluded on the ground that it had been caused by the assured's own parlous financial position, but those cases clearly cannot survive *Lagden v O'Connor*: see *Arbory Group Ltd v West Craven Insurance Services* [2007] Lloyd's Rep IR 491.

[108] *Manchester Building Society v Grant Thornton UK LLP* [2021] UKSC 20, [17], explaining *South Australia Asset Management Corp Respondents v York Montague Ltd* [1997] AC 191.

does not extend to consequential loss that might flow from a shortfall in coverage. That is indeed consistent with the common law principle that an insurer who fails to make timely payment bears no responsibility for the consequences suffered by an assured who is kept out of its money,[109] although, as will be seen in chapter 11, this rule has been reversed by statute, in section 13A of the Insurance Act 2015. The courts have recognised one exception, business interruption insurance, as the duty of the broker in securing such insurance is to protect the insured against business losses. In both *Arbory Group Ltd v West Craven Insurance Services*[110] and *Adelaide (SA) Pools & Spa Manufacturing and Installation Pty Ltd v Westcourt General Insurance Brokers Pty Ltd*,[111] it was accepted that the brokers were liable for loss of revenue, but only where that loss exceeded the shortfall in insurance as there would otherwise be 'double counting'. In both of these cases the loss of future business was less than the insurance shortfall and thus no additional damages were awarded.

Damages in excess of coverage shortfall were also awarded on the rather exceptional facts of *Aneco Reinsurance Underwriting Ltd v Johnson & Higgins*,[112] an application of the principle that damages are to be assessed by reference to the loss to which the duty applied. This case concerned retrocession, ie reinsurance taken out by a reinsurer, which had at the request of the brokers agreed to offer reinsurance to an insurer in the sum of $35 million but on the condition that the brokers secured retrocession of $11 million. The brokers failed to do so, with the result that the reinsurer faced liability of $35 million without any retrocession cover. It was held by the House of Lords that the brokers were liable for the full $35 million and not merely the shortfall of $11 million, their Lordships reasoning that, but for the brokers' negligence, the reinsurer would not have agreed to enter into the contract in the first place, so that the entire loss was attributable to the brokers' breach of duty.

3.6.2. Defences

Assuming that there has been a breach of duty by the broker leading to an absence of cover or inadequate cover, and that damages are on the face of things awardable, a number of full and partial defences may be open to the broker.

(1) The instructions given by the insured might have been incapable of being followed, eg because there was no available cover in the market or because the risk was illegal. A broker who has given incorrect advice to the insured on what matters need to be disclosed to the insurers will escape liability if it can be shown that the risk was uninsurable either at all or on the terms required by the insured. In most cases that defence will fail, as in *Standard Life Assurance Ltd v Oak Dedicated Ltd*,[113] where the evidence showed that the cover sought by the insured was available in the market. That may be contrasted with *Jones v Environcom Ltd (No 2)*,[114] where the risk was completely uninsurable. In most cases, however, it will be possible for the insured to point to ways in which the risk could have been made insurable. In *O&R Jewellers Ltd v Terry*,[115] one of the insured company's controllers had criminal

[109] *Sprung v Royal Insurance* [1999] Lloyd's Rep IR 111.

[110] [2007] Lloyd's Rep IR 491.

[111] [2021] SASC 123.

[112] [2001] UKHL 51.

[113] [2008] Lloyd's Rep IR 552. See also *Smith v Cologan* (1788) 2 TR 188n; *Eurokey Recycling Ltd v Giles Insurance Brokers Ltd* [2015] 2 All ER (Comm) 55; *ABN Amro Bank NV v Royal & Sun Alliance plc* [2021] EWHC 442 (Comm).

[114] [2010] EWHC 759 (Comm).

[115] [1999] Lloyd's Rep IR 436.

convictions that were not disclosed to the insurers, leading them to avoid the policy. The brokers were held to be liable for failing to advise that disclosure was required, and their argument that the convictions had made the risk uninsurable had discounted the possibility that means might have been found to sideline that particular individual: the court felt that the appropriate award was 30 per cent of the loss to represent the lost opportunity.

(2) The broker may be able to establish that, had the correct cover been obtainable, the insured would not have been prepared to pay the additional premium required to secure that cover. In the same way, a broker who has failed to draw the insured's attention to particular obligations in the policy may claim that the insured would have ignored any advice given by the broker as regards compliance with those obligations. In such cases the broker is able to establish that the breach of duty was not the proximate cause of the loss. The causation defence has been raised in many of these cases. An illustration is *Ground Gilbey Ltd v Jardine Lloyd Thompson UK Ltd*,[116] the facts of which were given earlier, where the broker was unable to satisfy the court that, had the use of fires been drawn to the insured's attention, the matter would not have been remedied.

(3) It is open to the broker to establish that the insurer would have an independent ground to deny liability to the insured unrelated to the broker's breach of duty. This defence requires the court to determine whether a reputable insurer would have relied upon the independent ground to deny liability. In *Fraser v BN Furman (Productions) Ltd*,[117] the Court of Appeal held a broker to be liable for failing to renew an employer's liability policy, dismissing the suggestion that the insurers would in any event have refused any claims because of the insured's breach of the policy obligation to take reasonable precautions to protect its employees: the Court of Appeal denied that the insured's conduct amounted to a breach of the clause,[118] but even if that was wrong a reputable insurer would not have taken that point so as to deny compensation to an injured employee. Even if the independent defence was one that by its nature might have been taken, the court will assess the percentage chance of that possibility and award the insured a proportional sum. In *Everett v Hogg, Robinson and Gardner Mountain (Insurance) Ltd*,[119] reinsurers relied upon a breach of the duty of fair presentation that was the fault of the broker but did not plead an independent breach of the same duty by the reinsured. The court's assessment was that had the only breach been that of the reinsured, then the loss would have been settled for about two-thirds, that sum being awarded against the broker. It was noted earlier that in *Jones v Environcom Ltd (No2)*[120] the court held that the broker's failure to advise the insured to disclose fires had not caused any loss, as the insured's separate failure to disclose that it was operating in breach of its waste management licence would have been relied upon by the insurers to avoid the policy.

(4) The insured has been guilty of contributory negligence. Brokers have sought to rely upon this defence where, by way of example, draft policy wording that was on its face inadequate was shown to the insured and approved. There was extreme reluctance to allow this defence to be taken before the passing of the Law Reform (Contributory Negligence) Act 1945, as the law at that time treated contributory negligence as an absolute defence. The effect of the 1945 Act is to permit apportionment, section 1(1) providing that:

> Where any person suffers damage as the result partly of his own fault and partly of the fault of any other person or persons, a claim in respect of that damage shall not be defeated by reason of the

[116] [2011] EWHC 124 (Comm).
[117] [1967] 3 All ER 57.
[118] On the principle that breach of a reasonable care clause is established only by recklessness, see ch 9 below.
[119] [1973] 2 Lloyd's Rep 217.
[120] [2010] EWHC 759 (Comm).

> fault of the person suffering the damage, but the damages recoverable in respect thereof shall be reduced to such extent as the court thinks just and equitable having regard to the claimant's share in the responsibility for that damage.

Even with the possibility of apportionment, the courts have reduced damages only in the clearest cases.[121] The principle here is that the broker is a professional hired to do a job and the insured is entitled to rely upon the broker's expertise.[122] As was said by Colman J in *National Insurance and Guarantee Corp Plc v Imperio Reinsurance Co UK Ltd*:[123]

> It is extremely difficult to envisage any factual situation arising out of a negligent breach of duty by a placing broker to his principal insured which it would be unconscionable for a representor or promisor insured to rely on his legal right to claim in respect of a breach of professional duty and where the insured has been at fault in representing his satisfaction with the cover which the broker has obtained.

In consumer cases in particular, there is little or no prospect of deduction.[124]

(5) The insured has failed to mitigate the loss. Mitigation may arise at two points. The first is prior to the loss, where the broker's breach of duty has become apparent but the insured has not taken any steps to procure alternative insurance. The second is following the loss, where the insured has not taken any steps to reduce harm flowing from the absence of insurance monies. This argument was raised in *Adelaide (SA) Pools & Spa Manufacturing and Installation Pty Ltd v Westcourt General Insurance Brokers Pty Ltd (No 2)*,[125] where the broker criticised the post-fire conduct of the insured in failing to take appropriate steps to raise funding to preserve the business. The court agreed that the insured's conduct was not free from criticism, but held that that was not to the degree necessary to break the chain of causation flowing from the broker's own breach.

(6) Brokers have also argued that the insured's loss was the result of a failure to pursue the insurers, and that had the insured done so there would have been full recovery. It was held in *Dalamd Ltd v Butterworth Spengler Commercial Ltd*[126] that the assured can, in the absence of proceedings against the insurers, recover from the broker if the insured can prove on the balance of probabilities that the insurers were not liable under the policy. That does not apply where the insured has separate insurance but has not sought to claim under it: the insured does not owe a duty to the broker to pursue other insurers, and in any event those insurers would have a claim against the broker by way of subrogation.[127] An alternative, and more likely, possibility is that the insured has secured a settlement with the insurers for less than the full amount of the loss and has sought the shortfall from the brokers. That was the scenario in *Ground Gilbey Ltd v Jardine Lloyd Thompson UK Ltd*.[128] JLT there argued that the settlement reached between insured and insurers was unreasonable in that the insurers had not at any stage terminated the cover and accordingly were as a matter of law liable for the full amount of the loss. Blair J found that the insured was keen to reach an early settlement, and that the insured's conduct was not unreasonable. The test was not whether

[121] *Synergy Health (UK) Ltd v CGU Insurance Plc* [2011] Lloyd's Rep IR 500.

[122] *Tudor Jones II v Crawley Colosso Ltd* [1996] 2 Lloyd's Rep 619; *GE Reinsurance Corp v New Hampshire Insurance Co* [2004] Lloyd's Rep IR 404; *Standard Life Assurance Ltd v Oak Dedicated Ltd* [2008] Lloyd's Rep IR 552; *Dunlop Haywards (DHL) Ltd v Barbon Insurance Group Ltd* 2010] Lloyd's Rep IR 149.

[123] [1999] Lloyd's Rep IR 249 (Colman J).

[124] *The Moonacre* [1992] 2 Lloyd's Rep 501.

[125] [2021] SASC 123.

[126] [2018] EWHC 2558 (Comm).

[127] *FNCB Ltd v Barnet Devanney (Harrow) Ltd* [1999] Lloyd's Rep IR 459.

[128] [2011] EWHC 124 (Comm).

the insurers had a good defence but whether, in all the circumstances, the settlement was one which reasonable commercial people might have made. Given that at the time of the settlement it was at least arguable that cover had been prejudiced, the insured's rights were 'uncertain or doubtful'.[129] Accordingly, notwithstanding that the settlement was 'towards the edge of the range which reasonable commercial people might have entered into',[130] JLT was therefore liable for the shortfall.

[129] ibid [105].
[130] ibid.

4

The Duty to Make a Fair Presentation of the Risk

1. Background

1.1. The Doctrine of Utmost Good Faith

This chapter is concerned primarily with the duty of the insured to make a fair presentation of the risk when seeking cover, and with the remedies available to insurers where there is a breach of that duty. The chapter also considers whether there is any reciprocal duty owed by insurers. The law has its origins in decisions reached in cases in the second half of the eighteenth century. At that time the only fully established class of insurance was marine. Fire insurance did not begin to develop until a decade after the Great Fire of London in 1666, and life insurance was in embryonic form and for the most part confined to mutual societies until late in the eighteenth century. The very many other classes of insurance so familiar today started to grow in the nineteenth century and for the most part did not give rise to litigation until much later. The duties discussed in this chapter thus have their origins in a time when there was a clear lack of symmetry in the information available to the insured and to the insurer. The laissez-faire approach of Victorian judges saw the extension of the early marine principles into all forms of insurance, and by the time of the codification of the law by sections 17–20 of the Marine Insurance Act 1906 the rules were entrenched. Those sections were regarded by the courts in the twentieth century as applying to all forms of insurance.[1]

[1] See eg *Cantiere Meccanico v Janson* [1912] 3 KB 452, 467 (Fletcher Moulton LJ); *Australia and New Zealand Bank Ltd v Colonial and Eagle Wharves Ltd* [1960] 2 Lloyd's Rep 241, 251 (McNair J); *Lambert v Co-operative Insurance Society* [1975] 2 Lloyd's Rep 485; *Container Transport International Inc v Oceanus Mutual Underwriting Association (Bermuda) Ltd* [1984] 1 Lloyd's Rep 476; *PCW Syndicates v PCW Reinsurers* [1996] 1 Lloyd's Rep 241. In *The Good Luck* [1988] 1 Lloyd's Rep 514, 546, Hobhouse J described the duty as 'an incident of the contract of insurance'.

The principle of fair presentation of the risk is derived from the duty of good faith. The feature that distinguishes insurance from other contracts as encapsulated in the good faith principle is the duty to disclose material facts in pre-contractual negotiations, in addition to the ordinary obligation applicable to all classes of contract not to make false statements in the pre-contractual negotiations. The root decision is that of Lord Mansfield CJ in *Carter v Boehm.*[2] The case concerned an insurance policy effected by the Governor of Sumatra, George Carter, against a French attack on Fort Marlborough. The insurers sought to avoid the contract when the insured claimed under the policy contending that he had failed to disclose the fort's weakness and the likelihood of it being attacked by the French. Although the defence failed on the ground that the matters not disclosed were well known in the London market, Lord Mansfield took the opportunity to explore the scope of the duty of disclosure borne by proposers of insurance. He stated:

> Insurance is a contract of speculation. The special facts upon which the contingent chance is to be computed lie most commonly in the knowledge of the assured only; the underwriter trusts to his representation, and proceeds upon confidence that he does not keep back any circumstance in his knowledge to mislead the underwriter into a belief that the circumstance does not exist … Although the suppression should happen through mistake, without any fraudulent intention, yet still the underwriter is deceived and the policy is void; because the *risque* run is really different from the *risque* understood and intended to be run at the time of the agreement … Good faith forbids either party, by concealing what he privately knows, to draw the other into a bargain from his ignorance of the fact, and his believing the contrary.[3]

On this reasoning, the deliberate failure to disclose facts which misled the insurer was a fraudulent concealment which renders the contract void for want of good faith. However, it is noteworthy that in this passage from his speech, Lord Mansfield went further by adding that even non-fraudulent suppression of material facts had the same result. The effect, therefore, is that a proposer was to bear a heavy burden of disclosure when completing a proposal form and when subsequently renewing the insurance contract. That was typically explained by virtue of the fact that insurers were wholly dependent upon the proposer providing full disclosure of all circumstances pertinent to the calculation of the risk underwritten by them.[4]

That said, it has been questioned whether such an onerous duty on the insured was actually envisaged by Lord Mansfield. It has been convincingly argued that this celebrated passage from Lord Mansfield's speech has been taken out of context, with the result that, read in isolation from the rest of his speech in the case, and indeed his views expressed in subsequent cases, a far stricter duty than was intended by him has been wrongly fashioned by successive English courts.[5] Professor Hasson contends that the effect of this lopsided reading of the judgment has been to distort the duty of disclosure so that it seems that

[2] (1766) 3 Burr 1905.

[3] ibid 1909. As pointed out by Lord Mustill in *Pan Atlantic Insurance Co v Pine Top Insurance Co* [1995] 1 AC 501, Lord Mansfield was attempting to introduce into English law a general principle of good faith. See also *Manifest Shipping Co Ltd v Uni-Polaris Shipping Co Ltd (The Star Sea)* [2001] 2 WLR 170, (Lord Hobhouse). That attempt was, of course, a failure.

[4] See further the judgment of Channell J in *Re Yager* (1912) 108 LT 28. The policy underlying the duty seems not to rest upon the need to prevent harm to the insurer but upon the need for a true and fair agreement whereby risk is transferred from one party (the proposer) to the other (the insurer). This objective depends on equality of information.

[5] See RA Hasson, 'The Doctrine of Uberrima Fides in Insurance Law: A Critical Evaluation' [1969] *MLR* 615; J Lowry, 'Redrawing the Parameters of Good Faith in Insurance Contracts' [2007] *Current Legal Problems* 338.

the insurer's role in the process is entirely passive. Yet, Lord Mansfield framed the duty in narrower terms so that the insured's duty of disclosure arose only with respect to facts that the insured 'privately knows, and the [insurer] is ignorant of, and has no reason to suspect'.[6] On the facts of *Carter v Boehm*, Lord Mansfield was of the view that:

> The underwriter knew the insurance was for the governor. He knew the governor must be acquainted with the state of the place. He knew the governor could not disclose it, consistently with his duty. He knew the governor, by insuring, apprehended, at least, the possibility of an attack. With this knowledge, without asking a question, he underwrote. By so doing, he took knowledge of the state of the place upon himself. It was a matter, as to which he might be informed in various ways: it was not a matter, within the private knowledge of the governor only.[7]

It is striking that throughout his judgments on the issue of non-disclosure Lord Mansfield referred only to 'good faith'. It was not until the middle of the nineteenth century that the courts sought to emphasise the duty by referring to it on a regular as one of 'utmost', 'perfect' or 'absolute' good faith, so that contracts of insurance were contracts *uberrima fides*. When the law was codified by the Marine Insurance Act 1906, section 17, headed 'Insurance is *uberrimae fidei*', provided that a contract of insurance is 'a contract based upon the duty of utmost good faith and, if the utmost good faith be not observed by either party, the contract may be avoided by the other party'. Section 17 did not, therefore, precisely mirror the language of Lord Mansfield's formulation, which drew a distinction between deliberate concealment and misrepresentation (bad faith) and innocent (good faith) mistaken non-disclosure.[8] Further, section 17 was – unlike the pre-1906 cases – not limited by its terms to pre-contractual disclosure by the insured, but rather extended to both pre-contractual and post-contractual disclosure by both parties. That largely unjustified extension from the 1980s onwards gave rise to a series of arguments as to the nature of the insurers' pre-contractual duty, the nature of the post-contractual duty of each of the parties and how sense could be made of those duties where the remedy was avoidance *ab initio* rather than breach of contract. It may be that the language of section 17 was never intended to have those consequences, given that it appeared in a group of sections which were concerned only with pre-contractual disclosure by the insured (section 18), pre-contractual disclosure by the insured's broker (section 19) and pre-contractual misrepresentation by the insured (section 20).

There is no longer much need in the present context to agonise over the scope and effects of section 17 of the 1906 Act. The Insurance Act 2015, section 14, amended section 17 of the 1906 Act by removing the remedy and reducing it to the bare statement that insurance is 'a contract based upon the duty of utmost good faith'. It is now largely a contractual matter, and is discussed in that context at various points in this book. By reason of the Insurance Act 2015, the duty of disclosure and the duty not to misrepresent are now divorced from utmost good faith, and take effect as the duty to make a fair presentation.

1.2. Fair Presentation: The Origins of the Modern Statutory Structure

The operation of sections 18–20 of the Marine Insurance Act 1906 proved to be unsatisfactory in a number of respects. First, the duty to disclose and not to misrepresent applied

[6] *Carter v Boehm* (1766) 3 Burr 1905, 1911.

[7] ibid 1915.

[8] For an examination of the late 18th- and 19th-century case law in which the notion of 'utmost good faith' appeared, see Lowry (n 5).

to 'material facts', with materiality to be assessed by reference to a hypothetical prudent insurer. The duty was broken if the fact withheld or misstated would have been of interest to a prudent insurer even though there would not have been any actual impact on the notional underwriting decision,[9] and it was not until the landmark 1995 decision of the House of Lords in *Pan Atlantic Insurance Co Ltd v Pine Top Insurance Co Ltd*[10] that the law recognised that an insurer had no remedy unless it could prove in addition to the objective test that, subjectively, its own underwriting decision would have been different had there been full disclosure. Secondly, the test of materiality disregarded the reasonableness or otherwise of the insured's own conduct and views. Thirdly, if a breach of duty could be shown, the entire policy could be avoided even though the material fact in question would have had only a minimal impact on the underwriting decision. Finally, there were no clear rules on how disclosure operated where intermediaries were used to present the risk.

By the 1970s it had become increasingly obvious that the law was unsuited to consumer contracts, as consumers were being required to fulfil a disclosure duty which was at worst unknown to them and at best uncertain in its scope in that the test for disclosure was materiality judged against the view of a prudent insurer. Even in commercial contracts the law was capable of disproportionate effects, with the entire policy being lost for a relatively trivial breach of duty. Limited reform was initially proposed by the Law Commission in 1980,[11] but the proposal to adopt a test for disclosure based on the view of a prudent insured was no more than a response to a suggested codification of insurance contract law by the European Commission. The move was buried once the European Commission abandoned this initiative.

In 2005 the English and Scottish Law Commissions undertook what was originally intended to be a root-and-branch review of insurance law, although that broad ambition was over time, and until the completion of the project in 2020, narrowed down to focus on particular aspects of the law. The key area was the operation of the principles applicable to disclosure and representation. The Commissions published two early issues papers, *Misrepresentation and Non-Disclosure* in September 2006 and *Intermediaries and Pre-Contract Information* in March 2007. Shortly afterwards a consultation paper, *Misrepresentation, Non-Disclosure and Breach of Warranty by the Assured*[12] was published. This key document foreshadowed the approach ultimately to be adopted, in proposing separate regimes for consumer insurances and business insurances. These documents were followed in April 2009 by another issues paper, *Micro-Businesses – Should Micro-Businesses Be Treated Like Consumers for the Purposes of Pre-Contractual Information and Unfair Terms?*, asking for views whether micro-businesses should be treated in the same way as consumers. Various attempts were made to define the term 'micro-business' by reference to turnover or the number of employees, or some combination thereof. Each of the options was problematic: a turnover figure was arbitrary and discriminated between existing and start-up businesses; and a solution based on employees raised issues as to the definition of an 'employee' and the appropriate number. The idea was abandoned, and later in 2009 the Law Commissions published firm proposals, including a draft Bill, for the reform of the law as it applied to consumers alone.[13]

[9] *Container Transport International Ltd v Oceanus Mutual Underwriting Association* [1984] 1 Lloyd's Rep 476.
[10] [1995] 1 AC 501.
[11] Law Commission, Working Paper No 70 (1979); Law Com No 104 (1980).
[12] Law Com CP No 182/Scot Law Com CP 134.
[13] *Consumer Insurance Law: Pre-contract Disclosure and Misrepresentation* (Cm 7758, 2009).

Those proposals were not controversial. Developments from the 1970s onwards had transformed the treatment of consumers by the insurance industry. The Unfair Contract Terms Act 1977, which regulates exclusion clauses in consumer and standard form commercial contracts, excluded insurance following representations by the insurance industry that exclusions from insurance policies go to the very risk written by insurers and so are not appropriately regulated by a general measure applicable to other forms of exclusion clause. Parliament was persuaded that any judicial supervision of exclusions from insurance coverage would amount to a rewriting of the policy. The industry, through the Association of British Insurers, responded with the adoption of two Statements of Insurance Practice, one long-term (life) and one general (non-life). These were both updated in 1986.[14] Paragraph 2(b) of the Statement of General Insurance Practice provided that an insurer would not repudiate a contract if the non-disclosed fact was one which 'a policyholder could not reasonably be expected to have disclosed' or where any misrepresentation by the insured is innocent. The Statement of Long-Term Insurance Practice was to similar effect. While the honest or innocent proposer therefore had nothing to fear, the Statements were probably not binding in law. The second development was the formation of the Insurance Ombudsman Bureau (IOB) in 1981 by a small group of insurers. The IOB was charged with the power to hear complaints by insurers and to determine their outcome in accordance with 'good insurance practice' rather than the strict law. Over time, the IOB developed a settled practice in relation to particular matters,[15] and effectively became the enforcement mechanism of the Statements of Practice. It also became more influential, and by the end of its two-decade life Lloyd's and most reputable insurance companies were members and agreed to abide by IOB rulings. The landscape changed significantly with the passing of the Financial Services and Markets Act 2000. What had previously been voluntary became compulsory. The IOB was merged with a number of other industry-operated ombudsmen operating in the financial services sector and given statutory status as a new body, the Financial Ombudsman Service. The Statements of Practice ceased to apply and were incorporated into the handbook of the regulator, the Financial Services Authority (FSA). The *FSA Handbook*'s first attempt to deal with the treatment of the utmost good faith doctrine by insurers was to be found in the Insurance Conduct of Business Rules 2005, replaced on 6 January 2008 by the FSA's Insurance: New Conduct of Business sourcebook (ICOBS).[16] ICOBS 8.1.1 incorporates the principal provision of the Statement of General Insurance Practice by providing that:

> A rejection of a consumer policyholder's claim is unreasonable, except where there is evidence of fraud, if it is for:
>
> (1) non-disclosure of a fact material to the risk which the policyholder could not reasonably be expected to have disclosed; or
>
> (2) non-negligent misrepresentation of a fact material to the risk.

The conclusion of the 2009 report and draft Bill was that a reform would simply bring the law into line with practice, but that it was preferable in the interests of certainty to adopt statutory principles rather than the unpublished discretionary decisions of the Financial

[14] For a thorough analysis of the 1986 Statements, see A Forte, 'The Revised Statements of Insurance Practice' [1986] *MLR* 754.

[15] The IOB's position on reasonable care clauses was adopted by the Court of Appeal in *Sofi v Prudential Assurance* [1993] 2 Lloyd's Rep 559.

[16] See ch 2 above.

Ombudsman Scheme (FOS).[17] The result was the Consumer Insurance (Disclosure and Representations) Act 2012, which came into force on 6 April 2013 and applies to all consumer insurance contracts, although not to small business contracts. Under the Act, consumer insurances were taken outside sections 18–20 of the Marine Insurance Act 1906, disclosure was abolished and the insurer was granted proportional remedies for misrepresentation only where the insured has acted unreasonably.

It initially proved to be more difficult for the Commissions to make out a case for reform of the law in the commercial market. In June 2012 the Commissions published a consultation paper, *Insurance Contract Law: The Business Insured's Duty of Disclosure and the Law of Warranties*.[18] That received broad consensus, and in July 2014 the Commissions published the report, *Business Disclosure; Warranties; Insurers' Remedies for Fraudulent Claims; and Late Payment*,[19] which included a draft Bill. The government accepted the report immediately, and the Insurance Bill 2014 was published days later. The measure passed into law as the Insurance Act 2015. This repealed sections 18–20 of the Marine Insurance Act 1906 and replaced them with a series of sections which retained significant parts of the old law while clarifying others (including the effect of non-disclosure by a broker) and introducing proportional remedies. There was an attempt in the legislation to draw a fair balance between the interests of both parties, and the concessions to the insured are counterbalanced by some concessions to the insurers. These are discussed in what follows. The 2015 Act came into force on 12 August 2016.

It is necessary to examine the commercial and consumer regimes separately.

2. Fair Presentation: Consumers

2.1. The Elements of the 2012 Act

2.1.1. Scope

The Consumer Insurance (Disclosure and Representations) Act 2012 is confined to 'consumer insurance contracts', defined by section 1 as meaning:

> a contract of insurance between –
>
> (a) an individual who enters into the contract wholly or mainly for purposes unrelated to the individual's trade, business or profession, and
>
> (b) a person who carries on the business of insurance and who becomes a party to the contract by way of that business (whether or not in accordance with permission for the purposes of the Financial Services and Markets Act 2000).

This definition is similar to that adopted under ICOBS, which defines a consumer as 'any natural person who is acting for purposes which are outside his trade or profession'. The ICOBS definition follows that used in the EU Directive on Distance Marketing of

[17] For a detailed examination of the position of the consumer-insured, see J Summer, *Insurance Law and the Financial Ombudsman Service* (London, Informa UK, 2010).

[18] Law Com CP No 204/Scot Law Com CP 155.

[19] Law Com No 353/Scot Law Com No 238 (Cm 8898) (LC 353).

Consumer Financial Services.[20] The main distinction between the definitions is that the 2012 Act includes mixed use policies where the main purpose is consumer. Under section 10 of the Act, insurers are prevented from contracting out of its provisions. A policy term, or a term in any other contract, is rendered void to the extent that it would put the consumer in a worse position than under the Act. The section demonstrates the eagerness of the Law Commissions to protect consumers by prohibiting insurers introducing elements of the old law via contract terms. Once a claim has arisen, the parties are not, under section 10, precluded from entering into a settlement contract.

In *R (on the application of Bluefin Insurance Services Ltd) v Financial Ombudsman Service Ltd*,[21] insurers were successful in overturning in judicial review proceedings a decision of the FOS holding that a company director who was the beneficiary of a directors' and officers' liability policy was a 'consumer' under the FOS definition so that there was jurisdiction to consider his complaint that the insurers had unfairly rejected his claim by reason of late notification. The court ruled that the FOS had incorrectly applied the definition.

2.1.2. Misrepresentation

The 2012 Act took the bold step of simply abolishing the duty of disclosure. The insured's common law duties and duties under the Marine Insurance Act 1906 are now replaced by a single unified duty, set out in section 2(2), 'to take reasonable care not to make a misrepresentation to the insurer'. Section 2(4) thus provides that 'The duty set out in subsection (2) replaces any duty relating to disclosure or representations by a consumer to an insurer which existed in the same circumstances before this Act applied'. The section 2(2) duty applies both on application for a new policy and on renewal of an existing policy. The Act does not seek to define the term 'misrepresentation', which remains a matter for the common law. However, section 2(3) provides that:

> (3) A failure by the consumer to comply with the insurer's request to confirm or amend particulars previously given is capable of being a misrepresentation for the purposes of this Act (whether or not it could be apart from this subsection).

There are three aspects to misrepresentation: did the insured know of the fact; did the insured appreciate that it was relevant to the application; and, if the insured knew of the fact, was reasonable care taken to state it accurately? Those three matters are not distinguished by the Act, with the result that the assured is required to take reasonable care in all of these respects.

The test of reasonable care is set out in section 3. The starting point in section 3(1) is that 'Whether or not a consumer has taken reasonable care not to make a misrepresentation is to be determined in the light of all the relevant circumstances'. Under section 3(3) 'the standard of care required is that of a reasonable consumer'. That means that the insured must have (a) acted reasonably in ascertaining the true position before he made his statement, (b) acted reasonably in considering whether or not it was relevant to the risk and (c) acted reasonably in his phraseology of the answers given (assuming that something more than a 'yes' or 'no was sought by the insurers. Point (a) is not intended to impose a duty upon the insured to undertake detailed investigations into the surrounding circumstances,

[20] Directive 2002/65/EU, Art 2(d).

[21] [2014] EWHC 3413 (Admin).

the position reached under the 1906 Act. Point (b) buries the 'prudent insurer' test applicable under the 1906 Act, so that the view of a prudent underwriter is completely irrelevant. Point (c) may involve an analysis of the manner in which the question was framed and the nature of the insured's response to it. Consumers are required to take reasonable care that their replies are accurate and complete. If consumers do provide insurers with information which was not asked for, they must also do so honestly and carefully.

If the insured has been dishonest, presumably either by ignoring the existence of a fact or by deliberately misstating a known fact, then under section 3(5) he is deemed to have shown a lack of reasonable care. Equally, if the insurer 'was, or ought to have been, aware of any particular characteristics or circumstances of the actual consumer, those are to be taken into account' (section 3(4)). Section 3(2) lists examples of things which may need to be taken into account in making a determination of reasonableness:

(a) the type of consumer insurance contract in question, and its target market,
(b) any relevant explanatory material or publicity produced or authorised by the insurer,
(c) how clear, and how specific, the insurer's questions were,
(d) whether or not an agent was acting for the consumer.

Example (c) counters the possibility of the duty being reintroduced by generalised questions such as 'Are there any other facts which you think we should know?' The Law Commissions favoured a test of validity for such questions along the lines of whether a reasonable consumer would understand that this question was asking about this particular information. The thinking here was that abolition of the disclosure duty might force insurers to ask the right questions in proposal forms. The Act does not require the insurer to ask specific questions, but section 3(2)(c) goes some way to ensuring that they do.

One further important change is made by section 6 of the Act. A representation made by the insured may not be converted into a warranty by means of a basis of the contract clause or by any other means. That means that the insurers may not sidestep the Act by requiring the insured to 'warrant' the truth of a statement. Warranties are discussed below in chapter eight, and it will there be seen that a warranty is an unconditional guarantee of the correctness of a statement, giving the insurers the right to treat the risk as not having attached, even though the statement was not material to the risk or had no inducing effect. In all cases the Act is to be applied.

2.1.3. Remedies

As long as the insured has complied with the section 2 duty of taking reasonable care, the insurers have no remedy against him. Remedies are available only if the insured has been guilty of a 'qualifying misrepresentation', defined by section 4 as having two elements:

(a) the consumer made the misrepresentation in breach of the duty set out in section 2(2), and
(b) the insurer shows that without the misrepresentation, that insurer would not have entered into the contract (or agreed to the variation) at all, or would have done so only on different terms.

Limb (b) reflects the position on inducement as laid down by *Pan Atlantic v Pine Top*. Limb (a) means that the insured has, in making a misrepresentation, acted deliberately, recklessly or carelessly (section 5(1)). A misrepresentation is deliberate or reckless if the consumer knew that it was untrue or misleading, or did not care whether or not it was untrue or misleading, and also knew that the matter to which the misrepresentation related was relevant to the insurer, or did not care whether or not it was relevant to the insurer (section 5(2)). The burden of proof here is on the insurers (section 5(4)), although it is to be presumed that the consumer had the knowledge of a reasonable consumer and that the consumer knew that a matter about which the insurer asked a clear and specific question was relevant to the insurer (section 5(5)). A misrepresentation which falls short of being deliberate or reckless, but which nevertheless was not made reasonably in accordance with section 2, is careless (section 5(3)).

The remedies for breach of duty are set out in schedule 1 to the Act. If a qualifying misrepresentation was deliberate or reckless, the insurers may avoid the contract and refuse all claims, and the premiums need not be returned except to the extent (if any) that it would be unfair to the consumer to retain them (schedule 1, paragraph 2).

With respect to careless misrepresentation, the parties are to be put back into the position that they would have been in but for the false statement. That depends upon how the insurers would have responded in the absence of misrepresentation. If the insurers would not have entered into the contract at all had the true position been stated, they are entitled to avoid the contract and refuse to pay claims, but they must return the premium (schedule 1, paragraph 5). If the insurers would have entered into the consumer insurance contract, but on different terms (excluding terms relating to the premium), the contract is to be treated as if it had been entered into on those different terms if the insurers so require (schedule 1, paragraph 6). If the insurers would have entered into the contract but only at an enhanced premium and a loss has occurred, a system of proportionality is adopted. The insured is able to recover that proportion of his loss which corresponds to the proportion of the proper premium actually paid (schedule 1, paragraphs 7 and 8). The Law Commissions noted that the principle of proportionality is used regularly by the FOS and should therefore not cause any difficulty.[22] If the insurers would have altered the terms and charged a higher premium, then the insurers are entitled to rely upon the altered terms as well as reducing the assured's claim proportionately.

In rare cases the insured's careless misrepresentation may be discovered before a claim has been made. In that situation the insurers may, under schedule 1, paragraph 9, terminate the contract by giving reasonable notice to the insured, or the insurers may simply inform the assured of the fact that he has made a careless misrepresentation, in which case the insured may himself give notice of termination. In either case, the premium is to be refunded. The insurers' right of termination does not extend to life insurance, and it does not relieve the insurers of the obligation to pay a claim which arises between notice and termination, although the apportionment principle applies to the claim.

In some cases deliberate or reckless misrepresentation is obvious, as in *Tesco Underwriting Ltd v Achunche*,[23] where the insured gave a false answer to a clear question relating to previous criminal convictions, so that the presumption in section 5(5) could be relied upon by them to avoid the policy. The same conclusion was reached in *Ageas Insurance Ltd v Stoodley*,[24] where the insured gave a negative response to an express question in a proposal for insurance on a motorhome that he had not made any claims in the previous five years when in fact in that period he had been involved in a collision and also in another accident

[22] In regard to negligent misrepresentation, the Law Commissions rejected a causal connection test on the ground that it was not practical.

[23] [2016] EWHC 3869 (QB).

[24] [2019] Lloyd's Rep IR 1.

in which two individuals were killed and the insured had been convicted of death by dangerous driving. A finding of deliberate or reckless misrepresentation was easily made.

However, proof of deliberate or reckless conduct is not always straightforward. In *Southern Rock Insurance Co Ltd v Hafeez*,[25] the insured's online application for a motor policy stated his address was in Giffnock, a town on the outskirts of Glasgow. The insurers sought a declaration of their right to avoid policy for deliberate or reckless misrepresentation, in that the insured's address was Glasgow itself, and that a far higher premium would have been charged had the correct information been provided. It was held that the insurers had not satisfied the statutory test: the insured had spent time at both addresses, so it could not be said that on any view the Giffnock address could not have been correct, and because the form had been completed online it was not possible to say whether the false statement had been made by the insured themself. The insurers in this case did not seek any remedy as an alternative to avoidance. It is to be borne in mind that even if the insurers think that they may not be able to prove deliberate or reckless misrepresentation they retain the right to avoid by showing that they would not have issued a policy had the truth been told. In *Jones v Zurich Insurance Plc*,[26] the insured, in applying for a travel policy covering personal effects, stated that he had not made any claims in the previous five years. That statement was false, as he had in that period recovered £15,000 for a diamond lost from his then girlfriend's ring. The insured then claimed for a watch valued at £195,000 lost on a skiing holiday. The insurers chose not to rely upon deliberate or reckless misstatement, and accordingly were held by the court to be unable to rely upon that argument in the absence of specific pleading even if the evidence pointed to deliberate or reckless conduct. However, the insurers were held to be able to avoid the policy by satisfying the court that the risk was not one that they would have been willing to accept.

Special provision is made where a policy has been varied and the variation has been induced by misrepresentation. In that situation the variation is to be severed, insofar as it can reasonably be treated separately, and the schedule then applies only to the variation. If severance is not possible, the entire contract becomes subject to the schedule (schedule 1, paragraphs 10–12).

2.1.4. Group Insurance

The 2012 Act reforms the consequences of misrepresentation in the context of group insurance. This form of cover is taken out, most commonly, by an employer as part of the employment benefits provided by the employer to the employees. The employer is the policyholder, and employees are declared to the policy when their employment commences; any benefits under the policy are generally payable directly to the employee or their dependants. When a declaration is made to the policy, the insurers may ask specific questions of the employee about the age and other relevant facts applicable to that employee, although often that information is channelled through the employer. The effect of section 7 of the 2012 Act is that any false statement may affect the employee being declared but does not affect the policy as a whole. Section 7(1) defines the type of group scheme to which it applies:

> (a) a contract of insurance is entered into by a person ('A') in order to provide cover for another person ('C'), or is varied or extended so as to do so,

[25] [2017] CSOH 127.
[26] [2021] EWHC 1320 (Comm).

(b) C is not a party to the contract,
(c) so far as the cover for C is concerned, the contract would have been a consumer insurance contract if entered into by C rather than by A, and
(d) C provided information directly or indirectly to the insurer before the contract was entered into, or before it was varied or extended to provide cover for C.

The provision is deliberately drafted in broad terms to cover an array of schemes so as to include insurance contracts which intend to provide cover to a person who is not a party to the contract but who would be a consumer if they had taken out the cover themselves. If the policy falls within this definition, any misrepresentation by or on behalf of one of the persons intending to benefit from the policy will be treated under the new proposed consumer regime (section 7(2)–(3)). Section 7(4) confirms that such a misrepresentation by one group member will have consequences for only that person and does not affect the rights of others. Section 7(5) makes it clear that the contractual arrangements between the policyholder and the insurers are unaffected. It should be emphasised that this section does not affect the policy itself: the policyholder is likely to be a business, so that insurers have their full range of rights against the policyholder if there was some breach of duty affecting the taking out of the policy itself.

2.1.5. Insurance on the Life of Another

Under section 8 of the 2012 Act, if a consumer policyholder takes out a policy on the life of another and the life assured is not a party to the contract, then any information provided by the life assured is to be treated as if it had been provided by the policyholder. The consumer regime will then apply to determine if the insurers have any rights where there has been misrepresentation. However, if the information sought relates to the state of mind, knowledge, circumstances or characteristics of the life assured, then any false statement is not to be treated as having been made by the policyholder, and the insurers will have to pay.

2.2. Intermediaries

Despite the exponential increase in the number of insurances placed online or by telephone, many consumer policies are channelled through insurance intermediaries. The abolition of the duty of disclosure for consumers has narrowed the range of issues that can arise from the use of an intermediary, and the most important question is whether a false statement made by an intermediary to the insurers is one made on behalf of the insured, in which case the rules relating to misrepresentation operate as if the statement was made by the insured. This produces the result that the state of mind of the intermediary rather than that of the insured is relevant in determining the remedy open to the insurers, which is somewhat curious, given that remedies under the 2012 Act are designed to reflect the insured's culpability. The scheme of the 2012 Act is that the insured bears the risk of the fraud or carelessness of the insured's own agent, the solution being indemnification from the agent. Accordingly, the law demands that it is necessary to determine whether the intermediary making the false statement was the agent of the insured or the agent of the insurers.

In the case of a broker, the answer is straightforward: the broker is the agent of the insured. In the case of an agent appointed by the insurers, the answer would on the face of things also appear to be straightforward: as long as no false statements were made by the insured to the agent, any falsities transmitted by the agent to the insurers cannot constitute misrepresentation that can be laid at the door of the insured. However, before the passing of the 2012 Act there was a line of complex and conflicting authority[27] concerning the situation where the proposal form was completed by the insurers' agent (generally one paid on commission) and then signed by the insured. One line of authority focused on the authority of the agent to receive information on behalf of the insurers, so that if the agent was aware of the true position but completed the proposal form incorrectly, the relevant information was deemed to be known by the insured. The leading authority to adopt that analysis was *Bawden v London, Edinburgh and Glasgow Assurance Co*,[28] where the insurer's agent completed the proposal form for accidental injury insurance on behalf of the proposer, who was illiterate and had lost an eye. The form stated that the applicant was free from any physical infirmity. This was patently untrue, and did not escape the agent's notice. The insured was later involved in an accident in which he lost his other eye. The Court of Appeal held that the agent's knowledge of the insured's condition at the time of the proposal was imputed to the insurer, with the result that the insured could claim under the policy.

However, the decision in *Bawden* was something of an outrider and the bulk of the later decisions adopted entirely different reasoning. In *Biggar v Rock Life Assurance Co*,[29] false answers were given to questions in the proposal form which was completed by the agent even though the insured had given him correct information. The insured failed to check the accuracy of the answers before signing the proposal form. It was held that the insurers were not liable. By signing the proposal form, the insured was taken to have adopted it. In *Newsholme Bros v Road Transport and General Insurance Co Ltd*,[30] a proposer for a motor insurance policy orally gave correct answers to questions relating to previous losses to the insurers' agent. The agent, who was not authorised to complete proposal forms, deliberately recorded untrue answers in the proposal form, which was then signed by the proposer warranting the truth of the statements contained therein. The Court of Appeal held that the agent's knowledge that the answers were false could not be imputed to the insurers. Scrutton LJ stated that:

> If the answers are untrue and [the agent] knows it, he is committing a fraud which prevents his knowledge being the knowledge of the insurance company. If the answers are untrue but he does not know it, I do not understand how he has any knowledge which can be imputed to the insurance company. In any case, I have great difficulty in understanding how a man who has signed, without reading it, a document which he knows to be a proposal for insurance, and which contains statements in fact untrue, and a promise that they are true and the basis of the contract, can escape from the consequences of his negligence by saying that the person he asked to fill it up for him is the agent of the person to whom the proposal is addressed.[31]

The decision in *Bawden* was confined to the situation where the insured had not instructed the agent to complete the proposal form.

[27] JE Adams, 'More Nails for the Coffin of "Transferred Agency"' [1999] *Journal of Business Law* 215; R Merkin, 'Transferred Agency in the Law of Insurance' (1983) 13 *Anglo-American Law Review* 33.

[28] [1892] 2 QB 534.

[29] [1902] 1 KB 516.

[30] [1929] All ER Rep 442. See also *Hazel v Whitlam* [2004] EWCA Civ 1600.

[31] ibid 451.

In the most recent case on the point, *Stone v Reliance Mutual Insurance Society Ltd*,[32] the insured was visited by an inspector employed by the insurers in order to reinstate a lapsed fire policy. The proposal form asked for details of lapsed policies and the insured's claims history. The inspector, who completed the form on the instructions of his employers, did not ask the insured for details, but answered incorrectly that there were none. The proposal form was signed by the insured's wife without reading it. Notwithstanding that the proposal form expressly stated that should it be completed by any person other than the insured, that person does so as agent of the insured,[33] the Court of Appeal, approving *Bawden*, held that the insurers could not avoid the policy. The decision is readily explainable on the basis of the inspector's actual and ostensible authority to complete proposal forms on behalf of prospective policyholders. Lord Denning MR, clearly influenced by the fact that the insurers could have discovered the true situation from their records of the insured, stated:

> No doubt it was Mrs Stone's mistake too. She ought to have read through the questions and answers before she signed the form: but she did not do so. Her mistake, however, was excusable, because she was of little education, and assumed that the agent would know all about previous policies and that there had been claims under them.[34]

The practice of insurers sending out commission agents with blank proposal forms has long ceased. The *Newsholme* problem was thus one that had largely disappeared before the 2012 Act was passed. The Law Commissions nevertheless chose to legislate so as to make sure that the point could not arise again. The Commissions subjected the *Newsholme* rule to detailed analysis.[35] They noted that the rule appeared to rest on two rationales: (1) that the agent ceased to act for the insurer as soon as he committed a fraud by entering information which he knew to be untrue; and (2) that the insured must be bound by their signature.[36] The Commissions were highly critical of each. Where the insurer's agent on his own initiative committed a fraud because he was anxious to earn the commission, the risk should not be borne by the insured. With respect to the signature issue, the Commissions concluded that an insured might sign a proposal form without checking it because they reasonably believed what the agent had told them and so the signature was not necessarily determinative. After consultation, the Commissions proposed to clarify the law by restating the agency relationship between the insurer, the consumer and the intermediary in a series of general principles to determine for which party the intermediary was acting.

The Law Commissions' conclusions were adopted by the 2012 Act. Sections 9 and 12(5) confirm that the normal principles of agency law apply where an intermediary assists a consumer in completing an application for insurance. Thus, the insured is bound by the

[32] [1972] 1 Lloyd's Rep 469.

[33] In *Facer v Vehicle and General Insurance Co Ltd* [1965] 1 Lloyd's Rep 113, the court viewed a similar clause stating that the agent is to be regarded as the insured's agent as conclusive of the issue. See also *M'Millan v Accident Insurance Co Ltd* 1907 SC 484.

[34] At 474.

[35] See eg the Issues Paper 3 *Intermediaries and Pre-Contract Information*, uk/lawcommission/docs/ICL3_Intermediaries_and_Pre-contract_Information.pdf, and the subsequent Policy Statement (March 2009), *Reforming Insurance Contract Law Policy Statement The Status of Intermediaries. For Whom Does an Intermediary Act in Transmitting Pre-contract Information from Consumer to Insurer?*

[36] Issues Paper 3, para 3.12.

misrepresentations of the assured's own agent, whereas the insurers are bound by the knowledge of their own agent so that misstatements by the agent are not the responsibility of the insured.

Schedule 2 of the Act sets out the rules for determining the status of agents. Paragraph 2 provides that an agent is to be treated as the agent of the insurer in each of the following cases:

(a) when the agent does something in the agent's capacity as the appointed representative of the insurer for the purposes of the Financial Services and Markets Act 2000;
(b) when the agent collects information from the consumer, if the insurer had given the agent express authority to do so as the insurer's agent; and
(c) when the agent enters into the contract as the insurer's agent, if the insurer had given the agent express authority to do so.

Explaining paragraph 2(a), the Law Commissions stressed in the 2009 report that 'the intermediary must be acting as the insurer's representative at the time of the action, and in connection with the cover in question'.[37] Paragraph 2(b) applies where the insurer has expressly told the intermediary to collect the information; implied authority is not included.[38] This may be in the terms of the agreement between the insurer and the intermediary. In circumstances where both consumer and insurer have a term to this effect in their contracts, the Law Commissions propose that the insurer's contract should be decisive.[39] Paragraph 2(c) is in line with the common law position. Where an intermediary acts outside of its authority, the insurer will still be bound unless the customer knew.[40]

By paragraph 3(1), in all other cases 'it is to be presumed that the agent is acting as the consumer's agent unless, in the light of all the relevant circumstances, it appears that the agent is acting as the insurer's agent'. Examples of factors which may tend to confirm that the agent is acting for the consumer are listed in paragraph 3(3):

(a) the agent undertakes to give impartial advice to the consumer;
(b) the agent undertakes to conduct a fair analysis of the market; and
(c) the consumer pays the agent a fee.

By contrast, paragraph 3(4) gives examples of factors that may tend to show that the agent is acting for the insurers:

(a) the agent places insurance of the type in question with only one of the insurers who provide insurance of that type;
(b) the agent is under a contractual obligation which has the effect of restricting the number of insurers with whom the agent places insurance of the type in question;
(c) the insurer provides insurance of the type in question through only a small proportion of the agents who deal in that type of insurance;
(d) the insurer permits the agent to use the insurer's name in providing the agent's services;
(e) the insurance in question is marketed under the name of the agent; and
(f) the insurer asks the agent to solicit the consumer's custom.

[37] *Consumer Insurance Law: Pre-contract Disclosure and Misrepresentation* (Cm 7758, 2009), para 8.37.
[38] ibid para 8.39.
[39] ibid para 8.37. This is because an insurer is assumed to know and understand the consequences of this declaration.
[40] ibid para 8.43.

3. Fair Presentation: Business Insurance

3.1. Scope of the Duty

The law on non-disclosure and misrepresentation has been entirely recast by the Insurance Act 2015. The Law Commissions' July 2014 report is the key explanatory document, and is referred to in this work as LC 353. The Act applies to any 'contract of insurance', a term that is not defined but is intended to include reinsurance and also the various facilities, such as open covers provided by brokers and other agents[41] whereby risks may be declared to a framework contract. By section 2(1) the legislation applies to non-consumer contracts only, including contracts made by small businesses, and by section 2(2) it applies also to variations to an existing policy during its currency. The 2015 Act, like the 1906 Act, draws a distinction between non-disclosure and misrepresentation, the former being concerned with the insured's duty to volunteer relevant information whereas the latter relates to the insured's duty to answer accurately questions that are raised by the insurer generally either in proposal forms or, in the commercial market, in face-to-face negotiations with a broker. There is nevertheless frequently no more than a fine line between the two and they are in some instances treated as different sides of the same coin by judges.[42] Further, section 3(1)–(2) of the 2015 Act uses the collective term 'duty of fair presentation' to encompass both non-disclosure and misrepresentation, and covers all written and oral information presented to the insurers leading up to the making of the contract (section 7(1)). The two concepts have much in common, notably the definition of facts that must be made known to the insurers and the remedies available for breach, but the difference is nevertheless important for the purposes of the 2015 Act, in that the insured's knowledge of the relevant facts, the independent knowledge of those facts by the insurers and the role of brokers are crucial elements in the scope of the duty of disclosure.

3.2. Non-disclosure

3.2.1. The Meaning of Non-disclosure

A fair presentation of the risk for disclosure purposes is one that satisfies two requirements. First, under section 3(3)(b), the disclosure must be 'in a manner which would be reasonably clear and accessible to a prudent insurer'. The primary target of this provision is 'data dumping', where a mass of information is provided to the insurers with the relevant information buried somewhere within it.[43]

[41] Discussed in ch 3 above.

[42] Indeed, in *HIH Casualty and General Insurance Co v Chase Manhattan Bank* [2003] Lloyd's Rep IR 230, the House of Lords noted that 'pure' non-disclosure is relatively rare. The fine distinction between non-disclosure and misrepresentation in insurance law is clearly and colourfully illustrated by Professor Clarke, who observes: 'If I describe the shandy that I have just bought you as lemonade, is that non-disclosure of part, the beer, or misrepresentation of the whole?' See M Clarke, 'Rescission: Inducements and Good Faith' [2004] *CLJ* 286, 288.

[43] LC 353, paras 7.41–7.45.

Secondly, by sections 3(3)(a) and 3(4), there must be disclosure either of (a) 'every material circumstance which the insured knows or ought to know' or (b) 'disclosure which gives the insurer sufficient information to put a prudent insurer on notice that it needs to make further enquiries for the purpose of revealing those material circumstances'. Head (a), full disclosure, is the default means of satisfying the duty.[44] The explanation of head (b) is best expressed by the Law Commissions themselves:

> even where a material circumstance is not itself disclosed, the proposer may have done enough to satisfy the duty of fair presentation if it has given the insurer sufficient 'signposts' which would lead a prudent insurer to make further inquiries which, when answered, would reveal material circumstances. This reflects the approach already taken by the courts in some cases. This [provision] is intended to ensure that insurers are engaged in the disclosure and fair presentation process. Insurers should not 'underwrite at claims stage', allowing questions to go unasked until a claim is received. If a prudent insurer, reviewing the disclosed information, would be prompted to ask further questions or to seek further information, a failure on the part of the actual insurer to do so should not prejudice the insured party at a later stage.[45]

As this paragraph points out, there is nothing actually new here because, where the insured has made limited disclosure in a way that it is obvious that there are further facts available, a failure by the insurers to ask follow-up questions is waiver, a rule preserved separately in section 3(5)(e), as discussed below.

The duty of disclosure does not extend to facts which diminish the risk (section 3(5)(a)). This provision appeared in the 1906 Act. Such facts are clearly material in that they would influence the prudent insurer and would impact upon the premium charged. However, the vulnerability of the insurer is not adversely affected where such facts are not disclosed. For example, in fire insurance it is not necessary to disclose that an extensive sprinkler system has been installed. Similarly, an insured need not disclose that comprehensive security measures have been installed to protect the subject matter of the insurance. The court will pay no heed to the argument that such measures suggest that the insured thought the insured vessel was at risk.[46]

3.2.2. The Insured's Knowledge

An insured can disclose only those circumstances known to or received by him or her – defined by section 7(2) as including any communication made or information provided to the insured. An insured cannot disclose what an insured does not know.[47] There are two forms of knowledge. The first is the insured's own knowledge. If the insured is an individual, this means the insured's actual knowledge (section 4(2)(a)), although this is expanded by section 6(1) to include 'not only actual knowledge, but also matters which the individual suspected, and of which the individual would have had knowledge but for deliberately refraining from confirming them or enquiring about them'. This is generally referred to as

[44] ibid para 7.39.
[45] ibid paras 7.37–7.38.
[46] *Decorum Investments Ltd v Atkin, The Elena G* [2002] Lloyd's Rep IR 450; *Johnson and Perrott Ltd v Holmes* [1925] 21 Ll L Rep 330.
[47] *Sealion Shipping Ltd v Valiant Insurance Co* [2012] EWCA Civ 1625; *Sea Glory Maritime Co v Al Sagr National Insurance Co, The Nancy* [2013] EWHC 2116 (Comm).

'blind-eye' knowledge, a term that came into widespread use following the Battle of Copenhagen in 1801, when Vice-Admiral Horatio Nelson was alleged to have put a telescope to his blind eye as a means of ignoring superior signals not to attack the French fleet. If the insured is a legal person – a company or a partnership – then the insured is treated by section 4(3)(a) as knowing what is known to one or more of the individuals who are part of the insured's senior management, defined by section 4(8)(c) as 'those individuals who play significant roles in the making of decisions about how the insured's activities are to be managed or organised'.[48] The legislation deliberately rejected a test based on the knowledge of directors, as it was thought that not all directors would be aware of matters affecting the insured whereas there might be other non-director managers who would have that information.[49] The knowledge of senior managers is expanded by section 6(1) to include their blind-eye knowledge. Irrespective of the individual or legal status of the insured, the knowledge of an individual also includes, by sections 6(6) and 6(7), what should reasonably have been revealed by a 'reasonable search' of information held within the insured's organisation by any other person to be insured under the policy or by any agent as long as the information is available to the insured (whether the search is conducted by making enquiries or by any other means).

The effect of this drafting is that the insured's duty is wider than one merely not to ignore the obvious, and includes an obligation to make a 'reasonable search'. The law before 2015 did not require any form of search.[50] The notion was explained by the Law Commissions as follows:[51]

> Conducting a reasonable search of information available to the insured is part of a good insurance placement process. The insurer is entitled to expect that the insured knows more about its operations than that which the directing mind and will or senior management happen to know, particularly in large, potentially multinational companies where the board members or equivalent could not generally be expected to have more than a high level, strategic overview.

Plainly, what constitutes a reasonable search will vary from organisation to organisation and as between different forms of risk. For example, a very extensive search may be required where the insured seeks to take out a global policy covering worldwide subsidiaries. The Law Commissions here commented that a reasonable search 'will depend on the size, nature and complexity of the business … the question should be judged objectively, by reference to a reasonable, prudent assured in that class'.[52]

What has to be disclosed is 'what should reasonably have been revealed' by a reasonable search, so it is arguable that if information is innocently or otherwise not provided to the insured by an employee the relevant information is nevertheless imputed to the insured. However, the Law Commissions have suggested that 'the insured should not be taken to

[48] This closely resembles the common law attribution principle as applied to companies: *Tesco Supermarkets Ltd v Nattrass* [1972] AC 153.

[49] The common law similarly recognised a flexible approach to imputation: *Meridian Global Funds Management Asia Ltd v Securities Commission* [1995] 2 AC 500.

[50] *Australia and New Zealand Bank Ltd v Colonial and Eagle Wharves Ltd Co plc* [1960] 2 Lloyd's Rep 241; *Economides v Commercial Union Assurance Co* [1998] QB 587.

[51] LC 353, para 8.78. The Law Commissions recognised that in a major organisation not even senior management would be in possession of all information relevant to insurers.

[52] ibid para 8.83.

have constructive knowledge of information which could not reasonably have been discovered, such as information which would have been withheld through negligence or fraud'.[53]

The second form of knowledge, which applies to both individual and corporate insureds, is that of any individual who is responsible for the insured's insurance (sections 4(2)(b) and 4(3)(b)). This concept is defined by section 4(8)(b) as an individual who 'participates on behalf of the insured in the process of procuring the insured's insurance (whether the individual does so as the insured's employee or agent, as an employee of the insured's agent or in any other capacity)'. An employee is defined by section 4(8)(a) as including any individual working for the agent in any capacity. Three classes of individual are caught by these sections:[54] employees and others working within the insured's organisation, other than senior managers, with responsibility for placing insurance; ad hoc agents, eg lawyers, banks or other institutions assisting the insured with placing insurance; and insurance brokers. As far as employees are concerned, pre-2015 Act law operated on the basis of the imputation to a company of the knowledge of any person empowered to receive information on its behalf. It may be that the 'reasonable search' concept reproduces much of the effect of the old law, but there is no longer any automatic imputation and the rather different question of whether the insured made all reasonable inquiries has to be asked. Turning to brokers, the 2015 Act repeals the old rule set out in section 19 of the 1906 Act that a broker placing insurance owed a duty to the insurers to make full disclosure of facts in the broker's possession[55] although the broker faced no liability to the insurers and instead the remedy was avoidance of the policy as against the insured. The 2015 Act now imputes the broker's knowledge to the insured,[56] and if there is a chain of producing and placing brokers, then the knowledge of the relevant individuals employed by those brokers will be imputed to the insured.[57] The change is one of form rather than substance, but the approach adopted by the 2015 Act removes the illogicality of a broker owing a duty to insurers for which they had no remedy against the broker: the broker's failure to disclose is the responsibility of the insured, but the insured may well have recourse against the broker, as described in chapter three.

There are two statutory exceptions to the imputation of knowledge to the insured from a person responsible for the insurance. First, by section 6(2), the common law rule in *Re Hampshire Land*[58] is preserved. The legal basis for the rule is somewhat obscure, but it has become taken to mean that an agent's own fraud is not imputed to the insured, because the insured could not reasonably be expected to discover such fraud.[59] Secondly, confidential information known to an employee of the insured's agent through a business relationship with a person not connected by the insurance is not imputed to the insured (section 4(4)–(5)). The primary purpose of this exception is to prevent imputation to the

[53] ibid para 8.86.

[54] ibid paras 8.61–8.65.

[55] The independence of the duty was confirmed by the House of Lords in *HIH Casualty & General Insurance Ltd v Chase Manhattan Bank* [2003] Lloyd's Rep IR 230.

[56] This confirms the common law rule that only the knowledge of the broker responsible for effecting insurance had to be disclosed: *Blackburn Low & Co v Vigors* (1887) 12 App Cas 531; *PCW Syndicates v PCW Insurers* [1996] 1 WLR 1136.

[57] LC 353, para 9.52.

[58] [1896] 2 Ch 743.

[59] *Societe Anonyme d'Intermediaires Luxembourgeois v Farex Gie* [1995] LRLR 116; *Group Josi Re v Walbrook Insurance Co Ltd* [1996] 1 All ER 791; *PCW Syndicates v PCW Insurers* [1996] 1 WLR 1136. See Watts, 'Imputed Knowledge in Agency Law – Excising the Fraud Exception' (2001) 117 *LQR* 300.

insured of market conditions known to the broker by reason of the broker's activities on the part of other clients.[60]

3.2.3. *The Insurers' Knowledge*

There is no duty to disclose circumstances known to the insurers. It was said in *Iron Trades Mutual Insurance Co Ltd v Companhia de Seguros Imperio*[61] that:

> The insurer is presumed … to be able to form his own judgment of the risk as it is presented to him … the proposer is under no duty to offer the insurer advice. The duty relates to facts not opinions. The duty is essentially a duty to make a fair presentation of the risk to the insurer.[62]

The issue was again picked up by Moore-Bick J in *Glencore International AG v Alpina Insurance Co Ltd*,[63] who stated that:

> The duty of disclosure requires the insured to place all material information fairly before the underwriter, but the underwriter must also play his part by listening carefully to what is said to him and cannot hold the insured responsible if by failing to do so he does not grasp the full implications of what he has been told.[64]

The common law principles have been codified by section 3(5) of the 2015 Act, which dispenses with disclosure of a circumstance in three situations.

First, the insurer knows it (section 3(5)(b)). For this purpose, section 5(1) states that

> an insurer knows something only if it is known to one or more of the individuals who participate on behalf of the insurer in the decision whether to take the risk, and if so on what terms (whether the individual does so as the insurer's employee or agent, as an employee of the insurer's agent or in any other capacity).

The section 6(1) definition of knowledge as including blind-eye knowledge is equally relevant here.

Secondly, the insurer ought to know it (section 3(5)(c)). The meaning of this provision is explained in section 5(2). An insurer ought to know something only if: (a) an employee or agent of the insurer knows it, and ought reasonably to have passed on the relevant information to an individual responsible for writing the risk; or (b) the relevant information is held by the insurer and is readily available to an individual responsible for writing the risk.

Thirdly, the insurer is presumed to know it (section 3(5)(d)). Presumed knowledge is defined in section 5(3) as consisting of: (a) things which are common knowledge; and (b) things which an insurer offering insurance of the class in question to insureds in the field of activity in question would reasonably be expected to know in the ordinary course of business. This is a little differently worded from the repealed provisions of section 18 of the Marine Insurance Act 1906, but no substantive change was intended.[65] Section 5(3)(a) is illustrated by *Carter v Boehm*. The point was explained by Lord Mansfield:

> The question therefore must always be whether there was, under all the circumstances at the time the policy was underwritten, a fair representation; or a concealment; fraudulent, if designed;

[60] LC 353, paras 9.41–9.46.
[61] [1991] 1 Re LR 213.
[62] ibid 224.
[63] [2004] 1 Lloyd's Rep 111.
[64] ibid 143, [122].
[65] LC 353, paras 10.57–10.63.

> or, though not designed, varying materially the object of the policy, and changing the risqué understood to be run. The underwriter at London, in May 1760, could judge much better at the probability of the contingency, than Governor Carter could at Fort Marlborough, in September 1759. He knew the success of the operations of the war in Europe. He knew what naval force the English and French had sent to the East Indies. He knew, from a comparison of that force, whether the sea was open to any such attempt by the French. He knew, or might know everything which was known at Fort Marlborough in September 1769, of the general state of affairs in the East Indies, or the particular conditions of Fort Marlborough, by the ship which brought the orders for the insurance. He knew that ship must have brought many letters to the East India Company; and, particularly, from the governor. He knew what probability there was of the Dutch committing or having committed hostilities.[66]

The operation of section 5(3)(b) may be shown by *Glencore International AG v Alpina Insurance Co Ltd*.[67] The insured, G, claimed against its insurers for the loss of stored crude oil. The policy covered all risks of loss, damage and transit, wherever the oil was located. G had provided the insurers with details of expected throughput of stored oil, but had omitted to do so for the policy year 1996–97. During late 1997 and early 1998, a storage operative misappropriated large quantities of G's oil and G's claim under the policy for US$250 million was rejected on the ground of non-disclosure and misrepresentation. It was held that an insurer who covers a commodity trader must be taken to know the whole range of circumstances affecting the business of the insured. Thus, the insurer must appreciate that market prices are volatile, that commodities are transported, placed in storage, subject to the forces of nature and can be dangerous. The insured's failure to give a throughput estimate for 1996–97 was a misrepresentation, but it had not induced the insurers to accept the risk because the quantity covered by the estimate was avery small percentage of the total risk. Moore-Bick J agreed with counsel's submission that:

> [W]hen an insurer is asked to write an open cover in favour of a commodity trader he must be taken to be aware of the whole range of circumstances that may arise in the course of carrying on a business of that kind. In the context of worldwide trading the range of circumstances likely to be encountered is inevitably very wide. That does not mean that the insured is under no duty of disclosure, of course, but it does mean that the range of circumstances that the prudent underwriter can be presumed to have in mind is very broad and that the insured's duty of disclosure, which extends only to matters which are unusual in the sense that they fall outside the contemplation of the reasonable underwriter familiar with the business of oil trading, is correspondingly limited.[68]

It should go without saying that an insurer should be aware of the terms of its own policies. That issue was discussed by Jacobs J in *ABN Amro Bank NV v Royal & Sun Alliance plc*[69] whether, in the renewal negotiations for a marine policy taken out by a bank insuring against loss of cargo over which it had security, the broker put forward an amendment which protected the bank in the event that the cargo had to be sold at a loss. The insurers asserted that they should have been informed of the addition of this provision, which provided far wider cover than was usually the case. The court ruled, basing its decision on market evidence, that there was no duty on a broker to disclose to the insurers the intended

[66] (1766) 3 Burr 1905.
[67] [2004] 1 Lloyd's Rep 111.
[68] ibid 132, [41].
[69] [2021] EWHC 442 (Comm).

meaning of a proposed policy term, and it was for the insurers to read and understand the provision for themselves.

3.2.4. Waiver of Disclosure by Insurers

There is no obligation to information which has been waived by the insurer (section 3(5)(e)). Waiver may take a variety of forms.

First, the policy may waive all disclosure, disclosure of specific types of information or disclosure of knowledge other than that held by a limited class of individuals.[70]

Secondly, the insurers may impliedly waive material facts by asking limited specific questions. For example, in *Revell v London General Insurance Co Ltd*,[71] it was held that where questions are directed towards specific motoring convictions the insurer can be taken to have waived disclosure of other convictions. In *R&R Developments Ltd v AXA Insurance UK plc*,[72] the insurers avoided the policy for non-disclosure on the ground that the insured had failed to disclose that one of its directors was a director of a company in administration at the date the proposal form was completed. The court held that the question by its terms did not ask about the insolvency of companies with which directors had been involved, but only about the insolvency of the directors themselves. Had the word 'involved' extended to companies, it would have been very wide and uncertain in meaning. Further, in asking about past losses, the question was concerned only with claims by individuals. On this ground, the judge concluded that the fact that a limited question relating to individual insolvency had been asked meant that disclosure of information as to corporate insolvency had been waived. He concluded that

> the defendant asked questions which were limited to the bankruptcy or an insolvency of the claimant and its directors. The claimant was therefore entitled to assume that the defendant was not interested in the financial position of other companies in which the directors were involved.[73]

Whether there is implied waiver depends upon the proper interpretation of the questions asked. In *Noblebright Ltd v Sirius International Corp*,[74] the question was whether the insured's business premises had suffered theft in excess of £10,000 at any time, or any smaller claims in the previous five years. No claims had been made, but the insured failed to disclose three incidents of attempted robbery in the previous five years. It was held that the express question did not relieve the insured from disclosing those matters. In *Sugar Hut Group v Great Lakes Reinsurance*,[75] the insured argued that the failure by the insurer to ask specific questions on the insured's trading history amounted to a waiver, as there were only two questions asking about his past trading and therefore the insurer purported that no other information was required. Burton J found that the answers to the questions in the proposal form indicated that the underwriters needed to enquire about further information. An insured could not rely on factors not being covered by the questions if the reality was

[70] *HIH Casualty & General Insurance v Chase Manhattan Bank* [2001] 1 Lloyd's Rep 30.

[71] (1934) 50 Ll L Rep 114. See also *O'Kane v Jones* [2005] Lloyd's Rep IR 174; *Cape Plc v Iron Trades Employers Insurance Association Ltd* [2004] Lloyds Rep IR 75.

[72] [2009] EWHC 2429 (Ch). See also *Doheny v New India Assurance Co* [2005] Lloyd's Rep IR 251; *Ristorante Ltd (t/a Bar Massimo) v Zurich Insurance Plc* [2021] EWHC 2538 (Ch).

[73] ibid [48].

[74] [2007] Lloyd's Rep IR 584.

[75] [2010] EWHC 2636 (Comm).

that they were not covered by the answers. The first decided case on the presentation provisions of the 2015 Act, *Young v Royal and Sun Alliance Insurance plc*,[76] has confirmed that the legislation has not altered the law on waiver. The claimant applied, through his broker, for insurance on commercial premises in Glasgow. The claimant affirmed the correctness of the statement in the online application form that 'no proposer, director or partner of the insured under the contract in question has ever been made bankrupt, insolvent, or subjected to such proceedings'. The presentation was confirmed by an email from the insurers stating that 'Insured has never … been declared bankrupt or insolvent … [or] had a liquidator appointed'. In fact, the claimant had in the previous five years been the director of four companies that had been dissolved after insolvent liquidation or had been placed into insolvent liquidation in the previous five years. Royal and Sun Alliance sought to avoid the policy on the ground of non-disclosure. The claimant argued that Royal and Sun Alliance had waived disclosure. The Inner House of the Court of Session held that the email confirmed the content of the declaration and was not designed to waive information.

The final form of waiver arises where the insured has been asked specific questions to which only limited answers have been given. If it is obvious from the answers that there is further information available, the onus is on the insurers to seek that information, failing which they will be treated as having waived it.[77] However, there can be waiver only where the insured's answers are obviously incomplete, as where the insured informs insurers that the insured vessel is carrying cargo without specifying its nature.[78] This issue was given detailed consideration by the Court of Appeal in *WISE (Underwriting Agency) Ltd v Grupo Nacional Provincial SA*,[79] where opposing views were expressed. The defendants, a Mexican insurer (Grupo Nacional Provincial, GNP), appealed to the Court of Appeal against a decision of Simon J that the claimants, WISE, the reinsurers, were entitled to avoid a reinsurance contract on the basis of non-disclosure. In essence, the facts were that P, a retailer of luxury goods in Cancun, Mexico, imported stock from Miami. The consignment in question was delivered to P's warehouse, where it was left outside overnight. The container was broken into and a number of cartons containing watches were stolen. The total value of the loss was US$817,797.00, of which US$700,390.00 represented the value of Rolex watches which made up part of the consignment. P had effected a goods in transit policy with GNP which, in turn, reinsured the risk ultimately through WISE. The slip presentation, which was in Spanish, referred to Rolex watches. However, the English translation prepared for the reinsurers referred, by mistake, to clocks. When GNP claimed under the reinsurance policy, the reinsurers sought to avoid it, arguing that the nature of the goods to be covered was misrepresented and that the presence of high-value brands of watches, together with the fact that regular shipments would be made, was not disclosed to them. GNP claimed that the reinsurers had impliedly waived the non-disclosure and, in the alternative, had affirmed the policy by giving 60 days' notice of its cancellation knowing of their right to avoid for non-disclosure. In terms of waiver, GNP argued that WISE knew that Cancun was a high-class resort; that the slip had originally been prepared in Spanish, with the consequent risk

[76] [2020] ScotCS CSIH_25.

[77] Of the many illustrations, see *Rendall v Combined Insurance Co of America* [2006] Lloyd's Rep IR 732.

[78] *Mann, MacNeal & Steeves v Capital & Counties Insurance Co* [1921] 2 KB 300. See also *New Hampshire Insurance Co v Oil Refineries Ltd* [2003] 1 Lloyd's Rep 368.

[79] [2004] EWCA (Civ) 962.

of imprecision in translation; that the shipment of goods from the USA to Mexico ought to have caused them to examine the risk closely; and that they knew that the goods included jewellery but failed to investigate its nature or the security arrangements for its shipment. GNP also argued that WISE had not been induced by the non-disclosure or misrepresentation. Longmore LJ, with whom Peter Gibson LJ agreed, held that there was no waiver of the duty of disclosure. Longmore LJ thought that:

> The doctrine of waiver … has therefore come to be invoked in cases where it can be said that, if an insurer does not ask an obvious question, he will have waived disclosure of any material fact which would have been revealed by the answer. That in turn lets in the concept of a prudent insurer since, if such a question would have been obvious to such insurer, the actual insurer cannot be heard to say that such question would not have been obvious to him.[80]

Longmore LJ therefore took the view that deciding whether there was waiver involved a twofold process. First, it had to be determined whether a material fact had not been disclosed. Secondly, it had to be established whether the insurer 'was put on inquiry by the disclosure of facts which would raise in the mind of the reasonable insurer at least the suspicion that there were other circumstances which would or might vitiate the presentation'.[81] On the facts he held that while there had been a material non-disclosure, there was nothing in the presentation of the risk that could be said to have raised the suspicion that Rolex watches were to be included in the consignment. Longmore LJ concluded by noting that:

> Mr Kealey's [counsel for the reinsures] argument in the present case has more than an echo of the submissions he made in *Marc Rich v Portman*, [1996] 1 Lloyd's Rep 430, 442. He there submitted that the insurer could and should have asked an (obvious) question about the loss experience of the assured; now he submits the insurer could and should have asked an (obvious) question about the unlikelihood of clocks being shipped to Cancun. I rejected the argument then and the Court of Appeal held I was right to have done so [1997] 1 Lloyd's Rep 225, 234. For my part I would reject it again.[82]

Rix LJ, dissenting on this issue, placed particular emphasis on the mutuality of the duty of utmost good faith, and stated that the only relevant question was whether the presentation was fair:

> Ultimately, it seems, the question is: Has the insurer been put fairly on inquiry about the existence of other material facts, which such inquiry would necessarily have revealed? The test has to be applied by reference to a reasonably careful insurer rather than the actual insurer, and not merely by reference to what such an insurer is told in the assured's actual presentation but also by reference to what he knows or ought to know … The reasonably careful underwriter is neither a detective on the one hand nor lacking in common-sense on the other hand. Mere possibilities will not put him on inquiry, and very little if anything can make up for non-disclosure of the unusual or special. Overriding all, however, is the notion of fairness, and that applies mutually to both parties, even if the presentation starts with the would-be assured.[83]

[80] ibid [108].
[81] ibid [111].
[82] ibid [117].
[83] ibid [64].

Applying this to the facts, Rix LJ concluded that a reasonably careful insurer would have been fairly put on inquiry, given what he knew from GNP's presentation and his general knowledge. He went on to state that:

> If the question is instead the overriding question: Is the ultimate assessment of GNP's presentation that it is unfair, or would it be unfair to allow the reinsurers a remedy of avoidance in such a case? I would answer that the presentation was fair, and that it would be unfair to allow reinsurers to take advantage of an error of translation in a case where, on the evidence, an exclusion of watches would seem to have been the obvious solution.[84]

For Rix LJ the duty of utmost good faith and, more particularly, its content insofar as it applied to insurers or reinsurers required them to play a proactive role in the disclosure process rather than relying solely upon the insured's presentation.[85] Subsequently, in *AXA Versicherung AG v Arab Insurance Group (BSC)*,[86] Males J confirmed that Rix LJ's dissenting view did not represent the law. It should be added that the reinsured was ultimately successful in *WISE* on another ground: Rix and Peter Gibson LJJ found that the reinsurers had affirmed the policy, notwithstanding the breach of the duty of disclosure, by giving notice of its cancellation and such notice was inconsistent with any claim to avoid the policy *ab initio*.[87]

3.3. Misrepresentation

The duty of fair presentation extends to misrepresentation. Section 9 of the 2015 Act, replicating section 6 of the 2012 Act for consumers, provides that a representation 'is not capable of being converted into a warranty by means of any provision of the non-consumer insurance contract … or of any other contract (and whether by declaring the representation to form the basis of the contract or otherwise)'. The restrictions imposed on insurers by the fair presentation rules cannot, therefore, be sidestepped by this device.

A fair presentation of the risk where statements are made is, under section 3(3)(c), one 'in which every material representation as to a matter of fact is substantially correct, and every material representation as to a matter of expectation or belief is made in good faith'. By section 7(5), 'a material representation is substantially correct if a prudent insurer would not consider the difference between what is represented and what is actually correct to be material'. These provisions replicate the common law as codified in the repealed section 20 of the 1906 Act. The test of substantial correctness has been held to mean that there will be a misrepresentation if the answer given by the insured is misleading. If, therefore, the insured states that a building is protected against fire by a sprinkler system, the fact that the system lacks a working pump and is inoperative renders the statement a false one.[88] Unlike the

[84] ibid [67].

[85] See (2004) 16(10) *Insurance Law Monthly*. See also *Synergy Health (UK) Ltd v CGU Insurance plc* [2010] EWHC 2583 (Comm).

[86] [2016] Lloyd's Rep IR 1.

[87] The majority found that the trial judge had overlooked an email which communicated in clear terms that WISE were cancelling the policy. Longmore LJ dissented on the basis that the judge's findings of fact could not be reversed.

[88] *Sirius International Insurance Corp v Oriental Assurance Corp* [1999] Lloyd's Rep IR 343. See also *Ansari v New India Assurance Ltd* [2009] EWCA Civ 93.

2012 Act, the 2015 Act says nothing about ambiguous questions by the insurers, although the common law recognises that the question to be asked is whether the insured's interpretation of the question was one that would chime with the views of a reasonable person in the insured's position.[89] Equally, the 2015 Act does not refer to the proper interpretation to be put on very general questions, although the common law recognises that the insurers cannot base misrepresentation on such questions. In *Connecticut Mutual Life Insurance Co of Hertford v Moore*,[90] the proposer for a life policy was asked the question: 'Have you had any other illness, local disease or personal injury?' The answer was no, but the insured had 12 years earlier suffered a partial fracture of the skull. The Privy Council held that this did not constitute misrepresentation, on the basis that insurers 'could not reasonably expect a man of mature age to recollect and disclose every illness, however slight, or every personal injury … It is manifest that this question must be read with some limitation and qualification to render it reasonable'.[91]

The legislation draws a distinction between statements of fact (which must be correct), statements of expectation or belief (which must be genuinely held) and statements of intention (which must when made reflect the insured's actual intention). Not every statement made by the insured or broker constitutes a representation. A distinction is drawn between statements that, viewed objectively, are capable of having some impact on the mind of the insurers and, to use the language of *Carlill v Carbolic Smokeball Co*,[92] are 'mere puffs'. It would be unusual in the commercial context for a pre-contractual statement to be regarded as falling outside the presentation of the risk, but that finding is possible where the statement is very general, eg where a reinsured stated that its construction insurance policyholders 'as a matter of principle maintained high standards'[93] or where the insured's premises are stated to 'have surveyed very well'.[94] The statement must also be one made either by the insured or an authorised agent: in *International Lottery Management Ltd v Dumas*,[95] the insurers were held to be unable to rely upon an independent legal opinion on the risks faced by an overseas business that they had instructed the insured to obtain.

Section 3(3) refers to statements of expectation, a category that encompasses the insured's future intentions. The good faith requirement here means that the intention must be honestly held. The focus is, therefore, on the insured's state of mind when the contract was made. It may well be that, after the policy has incepted, the insured acts in a different way, but there is only misrepresentation if that had been the insured's intention from the outset. By way of example, a statement by the insured that no explosives will be used in its mining operations will not be treated as misrepresentation if, after the contract is made, it becomes necessary for explosives to be used. The insurers' protection in such a case is to deal with the matter by an express policy term barring such use.

Statements of belief require further explanation. When a proposer represents his or her own belief, this is not a representation of 'fact' in the strict sense other than of the state of the proposer's mind. If the belief was not in fact held by him or her, an action for

[89] See *R&R Developments Ltd v Axa Insurance Ltd* [2009] EWHC 2429 (Ch).
[90] (1881) LR 6 App Cas 644.
[91] ibid 648.
[92] [1893] 1 QB 256.
[93] *Limit No 2 Ltd v Axa Versicherung AG* [2008] EWCA Civ 1231.
[94] *Zurich Insurance PLC v Niramax Group Ltd* [2021] EWCA Civ 590.
[95] [2002] Lloyd's Rep IR 237.

misrepresentation may lie.[96] Conversely, merely because the representor's belief turns out to be wrong will not, of itself, amount to an actionable misrepresentation.[97] In *Economides v Commercial Union Assurance Co plc*,[98] a key issue was whether or not an insured had to show reasonable grounds to support a representation of opinion. The insured, E, an 18-year-old student, had effected a household contents policy with the defendants in 1998. The total sum insured was £12,000 (index linked) and the maximum recoverable for valuables (as defined in the policy) was one-third of that amount. The proposal form which was completed and signed by him stated that the answers given were true to the best of his knowledge. At that time the answers given by the insured were true. In 1990 E's parents left Cyprus and came to live permanently in England. They moved in with him, bringing with them a considerable quantity of valuables, including jewellery worth some £30,000. E, now aged 21, saw some of the jewellery when his mother wore it, but showed little interest. However, his father, a retired police divisional commander, advised him to increase his contents policy by approximately £3000. The insured contacted the insurers and instructed them to increase cover to £16,000. The next renewal invitation stated that this was the sum insured. In 1991 E's flat was burgled and property worth some £31,000 was stolen, the bulk of which was the parents' valuables. When he claimed under the policy it became clear that the value of his parents' property was £30,970, which exceeded the sum insured. Further, the valuables in question exceeded one-third of the total sum insured or the total value of the contents, which was now estimated to be £40,000. The insurers avoided liability for misrepresentation. It was held by the Court of Appeal that a statement of belief, if given in good faith, does not need to be supported by reasonable grounds for that belief, but the existence or lack of reasonable grounds for such belief may be taken into account by the court in determining whether the representor has acted in good faith. Further, the duty on the insured, when representing the full contents value to be £16,000, was solely one of honesty.

At first instance, the judge found for the insurers on the basis that although E may have honestly believed his valuation to be correct, honesty was not enough in the absence of reasonable grounds on which he could have based the representation. The judge said: 'it would have been necessary for him to make substantially more inquiries than he did make before he could be said to have reasonable grounds for his belief'.[99] E's statement was therefore an actionable misrepresentation. Further, the trial judge went on to find that since E had been informed by his parents of the presence of the jewellery and silverware in the flat but had wilfully closed his eyes ('Nelsonian blindness') to the true nature and value of these items, the insurers were entitled to avoid the policy on the ground of non-disclosure. The judge was of the view that once these items were introduced into the flat by his parents, E should have made further inquiries, and such inquiries would have led him to the conclusion that material facts had not been disclosed.

[96] *Anderson v Pacific Fire and Marine Insurance Co* (1872) LR 7 CP 65, 69 (Willes J). In *Limit No 2 Ltd v AXA Versicherung AG* [2008] EWCA Civ 1231 the Court of Appeal held that a broker's misrepresentations as to the intention of the reinsured, which were unknown to the reinsured, entitled the reinsurer to avoid the policy. The representation that 'as a matter of principle they maintain high standards and would not normally underwrite construction risks unless the original deductible were at least £500,000 and preferably £1,000,000' was not a statement of opinion or belief, nor was it framed as a statement of expectation. It was construed as a representation of existing fact. Thus, the reinsurers could avoid the policy when it transpired that most of the risks written by the syndicates had deductibles smaller than the stated normal deductible figure.

[97] *Pawson v Watson* (1778) 2 Cowp 785, 788 (Lord Mansfield CJ).

[98] [1998] QB 587. See N Hird, 'How to Make a Drama Out of a Crisis' [1998] *Journal of Business Law* 279; HN Bennett, 'Statements of Fact and Statements of Belief in Insurance Contract Law and General Contract Law' [1998] *MLR* 886.

[99] At 641 (Mr Recorder Hockman QC), cited by Simon Brown LJ.

E appealed. The issue before the Court of Appeal was whether for the purposes of insurance law a representor had to show objectively reasonable grounds for his belief,[100] or whether honesty alone was sufficient. Simon Brown and Peter Gibson LJJ concluded that the duty on E when representing the full contents value to be £16,000 was, as set out in what is now section 7(3) of the 2015 Act, solely one of honesty:

> given that the appellant was at the time aged 21, given that the figure for the increase in cover was put forward by his father, and given that father was a retired senior police officer, inevitably better able than the appellant himself to put a valuation on the additional contents, there would seem to me every reason to accept the appellant's honesty.[101]

The standard therefore takes account of the level of skill or knowledge of the representor. That point is illustrated by *Kamidian v Holt*,[102] in which *Economides* was distinguished by reference to the context. The insured, K, claimed for damage to a Dr Metzger Egg Clock, which he alleged was a creation of Carl Fabergé. He bought the piece from Sotheby's at auction in November 1991. The piece was not described by Sotheby's as by Fabergé, but K asserted that he had recognised it as a Fabergé piece. In 2000 he loaned the Egg Clock for display at an exhibition in the USA. On arrival, it was found to have been damaged in transit. The Egg Clock had been insured as a Fabergé item under a valued policy in the sum of US$2.5 million. It was then returned to England, but was found to have suffered further damage on the return journey. K sought to recover repair and depreciation costs. The underwriters contended that K had made implied representations: (a) as to the provenance of the Egg Clock as a matter of fact, the representation being untrue because the Egg Clock was not by Fabergé; (b) as to the fact that the Egg Clock was generally accepted by the art world as being authentic, which on the facts was not the case; (c) as to the claimant's belief that it was generally accepted by the art world that the Egg Clock was an authentic Fabergé piece, a view that the claimant did not genuinely hold; and (d) as to the claimant's belief regarding the provenance of the Egg Clock, a view which the claimant did not genuinely hold. Tomlinson J upheld implied representation (b). He found that K knew that the piece was not generally accepted as being an authentic Fabergé, and therefore the implied representation to the underwriters that the clock was generally accepted by the art world as being a Fabergé was untrue. Accordingly, there had been a material misrepresentation and it had induced the underwriters to enter into the contract.

As in *Economides*, the proposal may simply require the insured to answer questions to the best of his or her knowledge of belief. In *Zeller v British Caymanian Insurance Co Ltd*,[103] Z, the insured, completed an application form for entry into his employer's group health insurance scheme. He was required to answer questions to the best of his knowledge and belief. In response to specific questions about his health, he disclosed a thyroid problem, but

[100] In so holding, the trial judge applied *Smith v Land & House Property Corp* (1884) 28 Ch D 7, 15 (Bowen LJ); *Brown v Raphael* [1958] Ch 636, 644 (Lord Evershed MR); *Credit Lyonnais Bank Nederland v Export Credit Guarantee Dept* [1996] 1 Lloyd's Rep 200; *Ionides v Pacific Fire and Marine Insurance Co* (1871) LR 6 QB 674; and *Highlands Insurance Co v Continental Insurance Co* [1987] 1 Lloyd's Rep 109.

[101] [1998] QB 587, 646 (Simon Brown LJ). Peter Gibson LJ, at 652–53, speaking of the identical provisions of the 1906 Act, stressed that: 'Once statute deems an honest representation as to a matter of belief to be true, I cannot see that there is scope for inquiry as to whether there were objectively reasonable grounds for that belief. Of course the absence of reasonable grounds for belief may point to the absence of good faith for that belief. But in a case such as the present where the bad faith of the plaintiff is not alleged, I can see no basis for the implication of a representation of reasonable grounds for belief.'

[102] [2008] EWHC 1483 (Comm).

[103] [2008] UKPC 4.

also stated that he was in good health. In answer to the question: 'Had any departure from good health *not* previously mentioned in any of the above questions for which treatment or advice may or may not have been sought?' Z answered 'No'. In fact, in consultations before the inception of the policy, Z had been diagnosed with a heart murmur, which ultimately led to him undergoing complicated and expensive heart surgery. Z therefore sought recovery from the insurers. Liability was denied on the basis that he had misrepresented the state of his health. The Privy Council held that the only question following *Economides* was whether the insured had honestly believed that he was in good health and the only duty on the insured was one of honesty.[104] Further, following *Joel v Law Union and Crown Insurance Company*,[105] Lord Bingham stated that

> the applicant is expected to exercise his judgment on what appears to him to be worth disclosing. He does not lose his cover if he fails to disclose a complaint which he thought to be trivial but which turns out later to be a symptom of some much more serious underlying condition.[106]

In looking at the question whether the insured should have disclosed the heart murmur 'as a departure of good health', the court stated that

> the answer must be 'Yes' if he so regarded them or should so obviously have so regarded them as to throw doubt on the truthfulness of a negative answer. The answer is 'No' if he genuinely did not know and honestly did not believe that they amounted to a departure from good health. On this point the evidence is clear: thyroidism and minor ailments apart, he honestly believed himself to be and to have been in excellent health.[107]

Accordingly, he was not guilty of non-disclosure or misrepresentation because he had answered questions completely and correctly to his best knowledge and belief.

3.4. Materiality and Inducement

3.4.1. Materiality

The duty of fair presentation applies to material facts. Section 7(3) provides the following definition: 'A circumstance or representation is material if it would influence the judgement of a prudent insurer in determining whether to take the risk and, if so, on what terms.' The prudent insurer test as developed by the courts in marine cases leading up to the passing of the 1906 Act was codified by that Act for the purposes of both non-disclosure and misrepresentation. That test was adopted by the courts in the nineteenth century by way of distinction from a test based on the subjective views of the insurer in question, as an objective approach was thought to be the best way of giving protection to the insured against the chosen insurer's possible idiosyncratic subjective views. Following the passing of the 1906 Act, the same test was applied also to other forms of insurance. In *Lambert v Co-operative Insurance Society*,[108] Cairns LJ stated:

> I see no reason why the rule should be different for fire or burglary or all risks insurance from that which has been laid down by statute for marine insurance … In providing by statute that the

[104] ibid [18].
[105] [1908] 2 KB 863.
[106] [2008] UKPC 4, [20].
[107] ibid.
[108] [1975] 2 Lloyd's Rep 485.

> test should be that of the insurer in marine insurance cases, I think that Parliament was doing no more than inserting in its code of marine insurance law what it regarded as the general rule of all insurance law.

There had been attempts by the courts to modify this requirement by substituting the test of the reasonable insured's opinion for that of the prudent insurer, as in *Joel v Law Union and Crown Insurance Co*,[109] where Fletcher Moulton LJ, when considering the measure of the insured's duty of disclosure, proceeded on the basis that: 'If a reasonable man would have recognised that the knowledge in question was material to disclose, it is no excuse that you did not recognise it.'[110] But that approach was not followed.[111]

The focus on the prudent insurer may have been in its origins motivated by a need to protect the insured, and early cases after the passing of the 1906 Act cautioned against any application of the test that imposed an unreasonable burden on the insured.[112] However, as the twentieth century wore on it became apparent that the prudent insurer test was capable of causing great injustice. This was highlighted by the decision of the Court of Appeal in *Container Transport International Inc v Oceanus Mutual Underwriting Association (Bermuda) Ltd* (*CTI*).[113] Adopting an approach plainly favouring insurers, the Court of Appeal held that an insured is bound to disclose those material facts which *might* influence the judgment of a prudent insurer in deciding whether to accept the risk or in setting the premium. Kerr LJ stressed that 'judgment' as used in section 18(2) should be given its *Oxford English Dictionary* definition so as to be construed as meaning 'the formation of an opinion'. Thus, to prove the materiality of an undisclosed circumstance, the particular insurer needs only to satisfy the court on a balance of probabilities that the 'judgment' (in the sense of formation of opinion) of a prudent insurer might have been influenced if the circumstance in question had been disclosed. Under this test, insurers are placed in a particularly strong position, for it is not necessary to prove that the 'influence' would have been decisive. The consequence was that all information (without taking into account what the reasonable insured considered relevant) will have to be disclosed on the basis that the prudent insurer might want to know it, even if, ultimately, it does not affect a prudent insurer's decision on whether to accept or reject the risk as offered and even if it was irrelevant to the insurer actually writing the risk.

The opportunity for a complete and authoritative review of the duty of disclosure came before the House of Lords in *Pan Atlantic Insurance Co Ltd v Pine Top Insurance Co.*[114] This was a complex reinsurance case in which one of the key issues was whether materiality

[109] [1908] 2 KB 863.

[110] ibid 718.

[111] See also *Lindenau v Desborough* (1828) 8 B & C 586, 592, in which Bayley J said: 'I think that in all cases of insurance, whether on ships, houses, or lives, the underwriter should be informed of every material circumstance within the knowledge of the assured; and that the proper question is, whether any particular circumstance was in fact material? and not whether the party believed it to be so. The contrary doctrine would lead to frequent suppression of information, and it would often be extremely difficult to show that the party neglecting to give information thought it material. But if it be held that all material facts must be disclosed, it will be in the interest of the assured to make a full and fair disclosure of all the information within their reach.' See further *London General Omnibus v Holloway* [1912] 2 KB 72, 86 Kennedy LJ; *Godfrey v Britannic Assurance Co Ltd* [1963] 2 Lloyd's Rep 515, 532.

[112] *Associated Oil Carriers Ltd v Union Insurance Society of Canton Ltd* [1917] 2 KB 184, where the Court rejected the suggestion that a prudent insurer would have regarded the German nationality of the insured vessel's charterer as a material fact at a time when there was not a state of hostility.

[113] [1984] 1 Lloyd's Rep 476.

[114] [1995] 1 AC 501. See NJ Hird, '*Pan Atlantic* – Yet More to Disclose' [1995] *Journal of Business Law* 608.

should be measured by reference to whether its 'influence' on the prudent insurer's judgment was 'decisive' or whether some lesser degree of impact would be sufficient. Lord Mustill (with whom Lords Goff and Slynn concurred, Lord Lloyd dissenting powerfully) could see no good reason for departing from the principle formulated by Lord Mansfield in *Carter v Boehm*, which had guided insurance law for more than two hundred years. Lord Mustill stated: 'I can see no room within [the principle] ... for a more lenient test expressed solely by reference to the decisive effect which the circumstance would have on the mind of the prudent underwriter.'[115] On the question of statutory interpretation, the majority view was that since Parliament had left the word 'influence' in section 18(2) unadorned by words such as *decisively* or *conclusively*, it must bear its ordinary meaning. His Lordship stated that 'this expression clearly denotes an effect on the thought processes of the insurer in weighing up the risk, quite different from words which might have been used but were not, such as influencing the insurer to *take* the risk'. The majority decision therefore was to reject the 'decisive influence' test, thereby leaving the insured in a highly vulnerable position.[116]

A further consequence of the *CTI* and *Pan Atlantic* analysis is that the objective state of mind of a prudent insurer is frequently to be assessed by the court on the basis of expert evidence of the particular type of insurance in question. Such evidence is admissible to assist the court in its determination of the prudent insurer's judgment where materiality is not obvious to the court.[117] The insurer itself is not precluded from giving evidence based upon its own reputation as a prudent insurer, and the insurer's own evidence may indeed be necessary where there is no other insurer in the market offering insurance on the same terms or using the same underwriting criteria.[118] The approach to be taken by the court towards expert evidence was considered by McCardie J in *Yorke v Yorkshire Insurance Co Ltd*,[119] who said:

> Expert evidence may frequently afford great assistance to the Court upon questions of novelty or doubt ... [but] Judges are always free to test and revise any form of expert testimony. It may be said, however ... in ... marine insurance cases ... expert evidence has usually been given by those actually engaged in the occupation of insurers ... But it must be pointed out that in questions of life insurance the matters at issue are usually physiological, medical, or neuropathic. The directors of insurance companies, however, are but rarely medical men ... The importance or otherwise of that which should be disclosed to a life insurance company may well be appreciated only by doctors or surgeons. Medical men may, therefore, often give a more useful opinion than the directors themselves as to what is or is not material and important.[120]

Expert evidence is, therefore, not conclusive and materiality remains one of fact for the judge based on the judge's assessment of the credibility of the evidence. In *Roselodge Ltd v Castle*,[121] the insurers rejected the claim of the claimants, who, as diamond merchants, had

[115] Lord Mustill went on to add that a circumstance may be material 'even though a full and accurate disclosure of it would not in itself have had a decisive effect on the prudent underwriter's decision whether to accept the risk and if so at what premium'.

[116] See J Birds and N Hird, 'Misrepresentation and Non-disclosure in Insurance Law: Identical Twins or Separate Issues?' [1996] *MLR* 285.

[117] *AC Ward & Son ltd v Catlin (Five) Ltd* [2010] Lloyd's Rep IR 695; *Brit UW Ltd v F & B Trenchless Solutions Ltd* [2016] Lloyd's Rep IR 69.

[118] That point was noted in *Drake Insurance Co v Provident Insurance Co* [2005] Lloyd's Rep IR 277.

[119] [1918–19] All ER Rep 877.

[120] ibid 881.

[121] [1966] 2 Lloyd's Rep 113. See also *Reynolds v Phoenix Assurance Co Ltd* [1978] 2 Lloyd's Rep 440.

insured diamonds against all risks. The insurers' defence was founded upon non-disclosure insofar that, first, the principal director of the insured company had been convicted of bribing a police officer in 1946 and, second, the insured's sales manager had been convicted of smuggling diamonds into the USA in 1956. According to one of the expert witnesses called by the insurer, a person who stole apples when aged 17 is much more likely to steal diamonds at the age of 67, even if he has led a blameless life for 50 years, than someone who has led a totally blameless life. This did not convince McNair J, who held that the 1946 conviction was not a material fact, it having 'no direct relation to trading as a diamond merchant'.[122] However, the judge did go on to hold that the 1956 smuggling conviction was a material fact.

As has been seen earlier in this chapter, the prudent insurer test has since been rejected by the 2012 Act in favour of a reasonable insured test for consumer insurance. The Law Commissions saw no need to make the same change for business insurance. There were two main considerations supporting that view: most commercial policies are placed through brokers, whose duty is to advise the client what information should be provided to insurers, and there is recourse against them if they fail in their duty; and there were sufficient other safeguards for insureds in the formulation of the duty in the 2015 Act and in particular the statutory codification of the *Pan Atlantic* decision giving recognition to the requirement for the inducement of the insurers in question.

3.4.2. Inducement

The 1906 Act referred to materiality only in terms of the influence on the judgment of a prudent insurer. It made no mention of whether the underwriting decision of the insurer who had written the risk would have been affected had there been a proper presentation of the risk. Until *Pan Atlantic*, that was the unchallenged position in the law. However, in *Pan Atlantic* the House of Lords unanimously held that the non-disclosure of a material fact, as with misrepresentation, must *induce* the particular insurer to enter into the contract.[123] In reaching this conclusion, their Lordships were clearly influenced by the argument that the 1906 Act codified the common law, and given that inducement was a requirement under the general law which provides for rescission of a contract, the Act must be taken as having the same effect. Accordingly, Lord Mustill stated that:

> I conclude that there is to be implied in the 1906 Act a qualification that a material misrepresentation will not entitle the underwriter to avoid the policy unless the misrepresentation induced the making of the contract, using 'induced' in the sense in which it is used in the general law of contract.[124]

The assimilation of non-disclosure with misrepresentation for the purposes of requiring inducement is curious. Inducement for the purposes of misrepresentation has always taken

[122] ibid 132.

[123] In essence, the House of Lords were injecting into the law on non-disclosure a requirement of causation analogous to the 'but for' test familiar to tort lawyers.

[124] Where there is a material misrepresentation, there is a rebuttable presumption of inducement: see *Redgrave v Hurd* (1882) 20 Ch D 1, 21; *Smith v Chadwick* (1884) 9 App Cas 187, 196. Lord Mustill went on to add that: 'As a matter of common sense, however, even where the underwriter is shown to have been careless in other respects the assured will have an uphill task in persuading the court that the withholding or misstatement of circumstances satisfying the test of materiality has made no difference.' See also *Svenska Handelsbanken v Sun Alliance and London Insurance plc* [1996] CLC 833.

an active form; in other words, silence cannot, without more, constitute misrepresentation.[125] However, Lord Mustill accepted that the proposition that non-disclosure must induce the contract might well have involved the House in making new law. Clearly, it did. Lord Goff, concurring, thought that the need to show inducement on the part of the actual insurer addresses the criticisms directed against the *CTI* decision. He reasoned that it was the absence of this requirement that prompted the call for the test of materiality to 'be hardened into the decisive influence test'.

The impact of *Pan Atlantic* was not immediately clear, and led some to suggest that the law had largely been left unaffected.[126] That was by reason of Lord Mustill's acceptance of a 'presumption of inducement', whereby proof of materiality by the insurer casts upon the insured the burden of proving that the insurer was not in fact induced by the non-disclosed fact. In other words, if the objective prudent insurer test was satisfied, then the burden shifted to the insured to show that the insurer itself would not have acted in the same way. Lord Lloyd, by contrast, regarded the presumption of inducement as a myth that had long since been exploded and that it remained incumbent on the insurer to prove that: a prudent underwriter would have been influenced by the insured's presentation of the risk; and the insurer itself would have acted differently with full disclosure. On Lord Lloyd's analysis, there was no link between the two limbs of the test. The initial objective prudent insurer test would strip out the insurer's own idiosyncrasies, leaving the matter to be determined by the insurer's actual response to information objectively regarded as material.

A line of cases immediately after *Pan Atlantic* pointed to the lack of judicial consensus on the nature of the inducement requirement. For example, in *Marc Rich & Co AG v Portman*,[127] Longmore J narrowed the scope of inducement so that it would only trigger where the insurers were unable, with good reason, to give evidence. The judge stressed that in cases where the court is in doubt, the defence of non-disclosure should fail because 'At the end of the day it is for the insurer to prove that the non-disclosure did induce the writing of the risk'.[128] In *Insurance Corporation of the Channel Islands v Royal Hotel Ltd*,[129] however, the presumption operated in favour of the insurers, notwithstanding that they did not give direct evidence to substantiate inducement.[130] But in *Assicurazioni Generali SpA v Arab Insurance Group (BSC)*,[131] the Court of Appeal took the view that although the non-disclosed or misrepresented fact need not be the sole inducement operating on the insurer,[132] it must be effective in *causing* the actual insurer to enter into the contract. Significantly, the majority of the court followed earlier decisions to the effect that the insurer must give evidence as to his state of mind. This, therefore, gives the insured the opportunity to

[125] See *Bell v Lever Bros Ltd* [1932] AC 161, 227 (Lord Atkin).

[126] A McGee, 'Utmost Good Faith in the Third Millennium' in D Feldman and F Meisel (eds), *Corporate and Commercial Law: Modern Developments* (London, Lloyd's of London Press Ltd, 1996) questions whether *Pine Top* really does fundamentally change the law to the extent assumed.

[127] [1996] 1 Lloyd's Rep 430. See also *Sirius v International Insurance Group Corp v Oriental Insurance Corp* [1999] Lloyd's Rep IR 343, where, in relation to misrepresentation, Longmore J also stressed that it is for the insurer to prove inducement. The judge did, however, recognise that the onus of proof is difficult to discharge.

[128] ibid 442.

[129] [1998] Lloyd's Rep IR 151.

[130] See also *Aneco Reinsurance Underwriting Ltd v Johnson & Higgins* [1998] 1 Lloyd's Rep 565; *International Management v Simmonds* [2004] Lloyd's Rep IR 247.

[131] [2003] 1 WLR 577.

[132] Following the decision in *St Paul Fire and Marine Insurance Co v McConnell Dowell Constructors Ltd* [1995] 2 Lloyd's Rep 116.

cross-examine the insurer with the view to demonstrating that he was not induced by the non-disclosed fact but would have entered into the contract on the same terms had there been full disclosure of all material facts. Clarke LJ, intending to lay down settled principles, summarised the position thus:

1. In order to be entitled to avoid a contract of insurance or reinsurance, an insurer … must prove on the balance of probabilities that he was induced to enter into the contract by a material non-disclosure or by a material misrepresentation.
2. There is no presumption of law that an insurer … is induced to enter in the contract by a material non-disclosure or misrepresentation.
3. The facts may, however, be such that it is to be inferred that the particular insurer … was so induced even in the absence from evidence from him.
4. In order to prove inducement the insurer or reinsurer must show that the non-disclosure or misrepresentation was an effective cause of his entering into the contract on the terms on which he did. He must therefore show at least that, but for the relevant non-disclosure or misrepresentation, he would not have entered into the contract on those terms. On the other hand, he does not have to show that it was the sole effective cause of his doing so.[133]

This ruling does not mean that the presumption of inducement has been excised entirely. It may still be necessary to resort to the presumption where, for example, the individual who underwrote the risk was for good reason unable to give evidence as to what he or she would have done had there been fair presentation.

The inducement principle was adopted by section 8(1) of the Insurance Act 2015 for commercial insurance:

> The insurer has a remedy against the insured for a breach of the duty of fair presentation only if the insurer shows that, but for the breach, the insurer –
>
> (a) would not have entered into the contract of insurance at all, or
> (b) would have done so only on different terms.

The inducement test means that insurers must establish that the non-disclosed or misrepresented fact was an effective cause, although not necessarily the only cause, of their agreement to underwrite the risk on the terms that they did. Specifically, the insurers are required to show that something different would have happened had there been a proper presentation of the risk. This is something of a hypothetical exercise, given that there was no proper presentation of the risk. The hypothesis of inducement is illustrated by *Drake Insurance plc v Provident Insurance plc*.[134] This was a motor insurance case. The insured had failed to disclose a speeding conviction and the insurer sought to avoid the policy on the basis that, taking an earlier accident that had been disclosed together with the non-disclosed conviction, it would have charged a higher premium. The majority of the Court of Appeal, Pill LJ dissenting, held that even if the conviction had been disclosed and the insurer sought to charge a higher premium, information would have come to light that the earlier accident had not been the insured's fault and this would have resulted in the premium being reduced to the normal level. Rix and Clarke LJJ thus took the view that in deciding whether the non-disclosed fact had induced the insurer to enter the contract, it is necessary to examine what

[133] [2003] 1 WLR 577, [64].
[134] [2004] Lloyd's Rep IR 277. See (2004) 16(2) *Insurance Law Monthly*.

would have happened had full disclosure been made. The court thus speculates as to what the position would have been had the fact been disclosed.[135]

The importance of adducing the underwriter's evidence to prove inducement was highlighted in *Lewis v Norwich Union Healthcare Ltd*,[136] in which the court had to decide whether a material statement induced the underwriter to enter into the insurance contract. The insured was issued with an income-protection health policy. The proposal form had been completed by his agent. The insured did not disclose a visit to his GP during which he complained of a stiff knee, although nothing untoward was found. Later, the insured suffered from incontinence and lower-back problems, and was forced to give up work. After finding that the non-disclosure was material, the court ruled that the insurers had not proved inducement. The judge placed importance on the failure of the underwriter who was responsible for writing the risk to give evidence, and stressed that inducement 'is not to do with what a hypothetical prudent underwriter would or would not have done. It focuses on the actual underwriter. The onus of proof is on the insurer.'[137] Further, the judge, following *Assicurazoni Generali SpA v Arab Bank*, reiterated the importance of the presumption that an insurer is not induced to enter into a contract. In the absence of evidence from the underwriter in question, the court was not satisfied, from the evidence of another underwriter and of the insurers' general practice, that the underwriter in question would have refused the risk or imposed an exclusion, particularly as it had been shown that the underwriter had not in other respects acted prudently.[138]

The court stated that had further enquiries been made, then, on the balance of probabilities, it would not have affected the terms of cover because nothing abnormal was found and there was no further evidence to suggest that had someone else examined him they would have found problems.[139] Clearly the court is engaging in a hypothetical process by stating that even if further enquiries had been made, it would not have affected cover.[140] In essence, the judge is speculating on the evidence, and deciding what the insurer would have done had it been in possession of the non-disclosed facts. Although the process stops short of that seen in *Drake*, it is nevertheless indicative of the approach now being taken in determining inducement for the purposes of non-disclosure. Judges are likely to decide what the position would have been had disclosure been made, and if they come to the conclusion that it would not have changed the underwriter's decision, there will clearly not be a finding of inducement. The *Lewis* decision demonstrates the importance of insurers laying

[135] See also *Bonner v Cox Dedicated Corporate Member* [2004] EWHC 2963 (Comm), where the court took account of the fact that, even with full disclosure, the countervailing market of the broker would have forced the insurers to accept the risk on unchanged terms. The same point was made by Cockerill J at first instance in *Niramax Group Ltd v Zurich Insurance Plc* [2020] EWHC 535 (Comm), although a suggestion to similar effect was rejected on the facts in *Berkshire Assets (West London) Ltd v Axa Insurance UK Plc* [2021] EWHC 2689 (Comm).

[136] [2009] EW Misc 2 (EWCC). See also *Laker Vent Engineering Ltd v Templeton* [2009] EWCA Civ 62. Here, the Court of Appeal confirmed that an insurer must produce evidence of materiality and inducement in order to avoid a policy for non-disclosure. With respect to the issue of materiality, the insurer called expert evidence from an underwriter with little experience in the industry of the insured. It was held that materiality had not been proven. Further, the insurer did not call for evidence from the actual underwriter as a means of demonstrating inducement. It was concluded, therefore, that the insurer had not established the point.

[137] *Lewis v Norwich Union Healthcare Ltd* [2009] EW Misc 2 (EWCC) [22].

[138] For example, by not awaiting the results of an allergy test before issuing the policy and not making enquiries about a newly disclosed course of injections.

[139] At [99].

[140] At [103].

down clear internal underwriting guidelines. Where such guidelines exist, it becomes much easier for the insurers to prove that, had there been a fair presentation of the risk, the guidelines would have been applied and the risk would have been either refused or at least accepted on terms less favourable to the insured. That was the position in *Berkshire Assets (West London) Ltd v Axa Insurance UK Plc*,[141] where the insurers were able to rely upon an internal Practice Note stating specifically that an insured who had an adverse claims history, past financial problems or a record of criminality would be turned down. On that basis, the insurers were held to have proved inducement justifying avoidance for the insured's failure to disclose the criminal convictions of a director. The converse proposition is also obviously true. It will be very difficult for insurers to establish inducement if it is shown that they had in the past accepted the risk will full knowledge of the matters not disclosed to them on renewal. That was the position in *Synergy Health (UK) Ltd v CGU Insurance Plc*,[142] where the insurers were unable to show that a false statement by the insured that an intruder alarm had been installed had induced them to renew a policy, given that in earlier years they had not insisted upon adherence to conditions imposed on the insured because they regarded the insured's management of risk as otherwise satisfactory.

Proving that something different would have happened is necessary for proof of inducement, but it is not sufficient. There has to be a causal link between the information misstated or withheld and the insurer's notional underwriting decision. In *Zurich Insurance PLC v Niramax Group Ltd*,[143] insurance on premises used by the insured in its waste collection and waste recycling business was taken out with Zurich in March 2015. In the preceding year the insurance had been placed with different insurers, who had imposed various special safety requirements as a condition of cover, but when the March 2015 policy was taken out the application stated in response to an express question that no other insurers had imposed special conditions. A standard premium was thus charged. The premises were damaged by fire in December 2015, and Zurich asserted the right to avoid the policy for misrepresentation. The evidence showed that if the question had been correctly answered then Zurich's underwriter would have referred the proposal to her superior and the outcome would have been that a higher premium would have been charged. That was because it would at that point have become apparent that the risk had been misclassified by the insurers so that a higher premium would have been attracted. There was no evidence that, but for the misclassification, the premium would have been increased. This was accordingly a case in which the change in terms was based not on the information misstated, but on the insurers' own error. There was on that basis no causal link between the insured's breach of duty and the notional underwriting decision.

The position on proving inducement is accordingly settled. The requirement is statutory, and to satisfy it the insurers must produce evidence and answer specific questions as to whether they were induced and show that something different would have happened had there been no breach of the duty of fair presentation. Failure to do so will lead to a finding that there is no remedy for any failure on the part of the insured.

[141] [2021] EWHC 2689 (Comm).
[142] [2010] EWHC 2583 (Comm). See also *Western Trading Ltd v Great Lakes Reinsurance (UK) Plc* [2015] Lloyd's Rep IR 561, affirmed *Great Lakes Reinsurance (UK) SE v Western Trading Ltd* [2016] EWCA Civ 1003.
[143] [2021] EWCA Civ 590.

3.5. Examples of Material Facts

3.5.1. General Definition

There is a great deal of authority on the matters that may constitute material facts. There are two broad heads of material facts. The first is 'moral hazard', which relates to the insured's financial affairs, claims history, previous refusals of cover and criminality. It was said by Blair J in *Sharon's Bakery (Europe) Ltd v AXA Insurance UK Plc*[144] that moral hazard was 'an increase in the likelihood of it being made to appear falsely that loss or damage had occurred falling within the scope of the policy' and that matters going to moral hazard involved conduct that was 'invariably dishonest'. Although most cases have exhibited dishonesty, the suggestion that dishonesty is required is not fully borne out by the cases. 'Moral hazard' and honesty are of particular significance for the insurance of jewellery and other valuable items, although plainly it is of less significance if the policy is against an entirely external loss such as war risk or natural catastrophe, where circumstances cannot be fabricated and where it may be more difficult to exaggerate loss. The second is 'physical hazard', referring to facts affecting the insured subject matter which increase the risk of its loss. Necessarily the physical hazard will vary as between different classes of insurance. The Insurance Act 2015 does not seek to provide any definition of its own, and is content in section 7(4) to provide possible illustrations:

(a) special or unusual facts relating to the risk,
(b) any particular concerns which led the insured to seek insurance cover for the risk,
(c) anything which those concerned with the class of insurance and field of activity in question would generally understand as being something that should be dealt with in a fair presentation of risks of the type in question.

3.5.2. Moral Hazard Generally

The state of an insured's finances is likely to be a material fact going to moral hazard, given that there are instances where an impecunious insured has brought about a loss in order to relieve cash flow problems at the expense of insurers. The materiality of an insured's financial history is obvious where the cover sought is business interruption insurance and property insurance.[145] There are commonly express questions on the insured's personal insolvencies in properties covering business premises and activities, and it was noted earlier in this chapter that such questions need to be framed with care if they are to catch the insured's involvement with insolvent businesses. The mere fact that the insured has been or is in arrears with his premiums on another policy is not necessarily a material fact. Late payment could be due to a number of reasons and was not sufficient to substantiate an allegation that he might lack the financial resources to maintain the subject matter of the policy (a vessel) in a satisfactory condition.[146]

[144] [2011] EWHC 210 (Comm). See also *Higherdelta Ltd v Covea Insurance Plc* [2017] CSOH 84.

[145] *James v CGU General Insurance plc* [2002] Lloyd's Rep IR 206. See also *McCormick v National Motor & Accident Insurance Union Ltd* (1934) 49 Ll L Rep 361; *Sugar Hut Group Ltd v Great Lakes Reinsurance (UK) Plc* [2010] EWHC 2636 (Comm).

[146] *North Star Shipping Ltd v Sphere Drake Insurance Plc* [2006] EWCA Civ 378; *O'Kane v Jones* [2004] Lloyd's Rep IR 389.

A further indication of financial problems, if not an intention to effect a fraud, concerns overvaluation of the insured subject matter. The general approach of the courts to overvaluation is that unless the excess is such as to constitute fraud there is no particular reason to intervene: very often, independent valuations are demanded by insurers; the insured will have paid a correspondingly high premium; and unless the parties have agreed that the insured is to recover the full insured value (under a valued policy, used typically in marine insurance[147]), the insured will only be able to recover actual loss irrespective of the maximum figure stated in the policy. Fraud may be established by the insurers where it is shown that the value placed upon the subject matter by the insured bore no reasonable relationship to the actual or perceived value of the subject matter, as in *Eagle Star Insurance Co Ltd v Games Video Co (GVC) SA, The Game Boy*,[148] where a vessel valued by the insured at US$1.8 million and insured for that sum proved to be worth no more than US$150,000 for scrap. An insured who has taken out multiple insurances on the same risk may also be regarded as a moral hazard risk. Double insurance is permissible,[149] and indeed was a necessary precaution in the days before insurers were subject to prudential regulation, but the existence of other insurance is potentially material and is generally the subject of an express question or a policy term which precludes recovery where some other insurance is in place.

In relation to claims history, the fact that the business of the insured may have substantially changed since the previous claims because, for example, the management has been replaced, or its place of business has been relocated and the workforce is different, will not necessarily excuse the non-disclosure. In *Marene Knitting Mills Pty Ltd v Greater Pacific General Insurance Ltd*,[150] Yeldham J commented that:

> It is clear that in asking whether 'the business' had any prior losses or claims for the purpose of determining the question of materiality of facts which were not disclosed … it is not necessary to have regard to the niceties of corporate structure.[151]

There are numerous examples from the decided cases where an insured has failed to disclose a prior refusal of cover. For example, in *Locker and Woolf Ltd v Western Australian Insurance Co Ltd*,[152] the insured was asked in the proposal form for fire insurance: 'Has this or any other insurance of yours been declined by any other company?' The insured answered 'No'. In fact, two years previously a proposal for motor insurance was refused by another company by reason of non-disclosure. A fire occurred and the insurers repudiated liability for non-disclosure of a material fact. It was held that they were entitled to do so. Slesser LJ stated:

> In my view, it is quite impossible in the present case to say that the non-disclosure of the fact that the person proposing to take out an insurance policy for fire has had a motor policy declined on the grounds of misrepresentation, untrue answers, and non-disclosure is not one which is very

[147] Valuation is conclusive in the absence of fraud: Marine Insurance Act 1906, s 27(3).

[148] [2004] Lloyd's Rep IR 867. See also *Involnert Management Inc v Aprilgrange Ltd* [2015] 2 Lloyd's Rep 289, where the point was made that every case turns on its facts.

[149] See ch 12.

[150] [1976] 2 Lloyd's 631. See also *Buse v Turner* (1815) 6 Taunt 338; *Rozanes v Bowen* (1928) 32 Ll L Rep 98, 102–03 (Scrutton LJ); *New Hampshire Insurance Co v Oil Refineries Ltd* [2002] 2 Lloyd's Rep 463.

[151] ibid 639, citing *Arterial Caravans Ltd v Yorkshire Insurance Co Ltd* [1973] 1 Lloyd's Rep 169, where it was held that the insured should have disclosed a previous claim for fire suffered by the enterprise in a former corporate guise.

[152] (1936) 54 Ll L Rep 211. See also *Glicksman v Lancashire & General Assurance Co* [1927] AC 139. This rule does not apply to marine insurance: see the first instance decision in *CTI v Oceanus Mutual Underwriting Association (Bermuda) Ltd* [1984] 1 Lloyd's Rep 476.

> material for the respondent insurance company to know. It is, in fact, a non-disclosure of the fact that the person who seeks to enter into the insurance has already been overtly discovered to be a person who tells untruths, conceals matters material … and was a highly undesirable person with whom to have any contractual relations whatever.[153]

Similarly, in *London Assurance v Mansel*,[154] the proposer for life insurance when answering the question on the proposal form: 'Has a proposal ever been made on your life at any other office or offices? If so, when?' failed to disclose that he had made proposals for life insurance to five insurance companies which had been declined although passed as fit by the companies' medical examiners. The insurers successfully repudiated liability on the ground of non-disclosure of a material fact. Previous claims under unrelated earlier policies may, depending upon the circumstances, also be material,[155] and previous fraudulent claims against other insurers must also be disclosed.[156]

3.5.3. Moral Hazard: The Insured's Criminal Record and Integrity

Facts relating to the integrity of the insured, such as his fraudulent conduct when effecting a policy, will obviously be material to the insurers in deciding whether to accept the proposal.[157] In *Insurance Corporation of the Channel Islands v Royal Hotel Ltd*,[158] a hotel owner falsified occupancy rates in order to obtain a bank loan and used the same documents to obtain business interruption insurance for an inflated sum. Mance J held that the insured's dishonesty was a material fact which would be taken into account by a prudent insurer.[159] The requirement of inducement was satisfied because it was unlikely that an insurer would insure the hotel had the conduct of its owners been known to it.[160] On the issue of inducement, the judge concluded:

> Looking at all the material before me, I am satisfied that all the underwriting personnel within ICCI and Mr Walpole as its managing director would have taken a serious view of Royal Hotel's conduct, and that ICCI would have been unlikely to offer renewal if it had known of such conduct before renewal … I also consider that this is the attitude which any reputable and experienced insurer (like the present insurers) would have been likely to adopt in the face of dishonest conduct such as Royal Hotel's here.[161]

[153] At 215.

[154] (1879) 11 Ch D 363.

[155] *Becker v Marshall* (1922) 11 Ll L Rep 114 (burglary claim material to a fire policy), but contrast *Ewer v National Employers' Mutual General Assurance Association Ltd* [1937] 2 All ER 193.

[156] *Parker v National Farmers Union Mutual Insurance Society Ltd* [2012] EWHC 2156 (Comm); *Joseph Fielding Properties (Blackpool) Ltd v Aviva Insurance Ltd* [2011] Lloyd's Rep IR 238; *Strive Shipping Corp v Hellenic Mutual War Risks Association* [2002] Lloyd's Rep IR 669.

[157] In *Locker & Wolf Ltd v Western Australian Insurance Co* (1936) 54 Ll L Rep 211, it was held that a previous refusal of motor insurance was a material fact which should have been disclosed in a proposal for fire insurance. Such a refusal related to the integrity of the insured.

[158] [1998] Lloyd's Rep IR 151.

[159] See also *Sharon's Bakery (Europe) Ltd v AXA Insurance UK plc* [2011] EWHC 210 (Comm), where the insured claimed for fire damage to its machinery. Before the loss occurred, the insured had obtained financing for the machinery, having supported its application with a false invoice. It was held that the false invoice was relied on by the insured as evidence of title and was, therefore, used for a dishonest purpose. This was a moral hazard which was material to the insurers' assessment and should have been disclosed.

[160] The insurers were, however, estopped from avoiding the policy, as to which see below.

[161] At 161. See also *James v CGU General Insurance plc* [2002] Lloyd's Rep IR 206, in which the fact that the insured, a garage owner, had defrauded customers and was in dispute with the Inland Revenue and the Customs and Excise Commissioners was held to be material to the insurers.

The question of moral hazard in relation to an insured's criminal history arose in *Lambert v Co-operative Insurance Society*.[162] The proposer effected an all risks insurance policy on her own and her husband's jewellery in April 1963. At that time she was not asked about previous criminal convictions and she did not disclose that her husband had been convicted some years earlier of receiving stolen cigarettes. The insurers issued the policy, which provided that it would be ipso facto void if there should be an omission to state any fact material for estimating the risk. The policy was renewed every year. In December 1971 the proposer's husband was again convicted of a criminal offence and sentenced to 15 months' imprisonment. This fact was not disclosed when the insured renewed her policy for the year 1972, and in April she claimed £311.00 for items of jewellery which had been lost. The insurers successfully repudiated the claim on the basis that the insured had failed to disclose a material fact relating to moral hazard at the time of applying for the original policy and at its subsequent renewals. Similarly, in *Schoolman v Hall*,[163] the insured, who effected a jeweller's block policy, had his claim for a burglary loss rejected by the insurers on the ground that he had failed to disclose his criminal record. Fifteen years prior to effecting the policy he had been convicted of larceny, robbery and receiving stolen goods. The court upheld the insurers' defence despite the fact that the insured's record related 'to a dim and remote past'.[164] In *March Cabaret Club & Casino Ltd v London Assurance*,[165] the insureds, a husband and wife, had effected a fire policy covering the premises of a club and restaurant owned by them. When the policy was renewed in April 1970 the husband failed to disclose that he had committed the offence of dishonestly handling stolen goods in June 1969, for which he was convicted at the Old Bailey in June 1970 and fined £2000. A fire occurred at the premises and the insurers successfully repudiated liability on the ground of non-disclosure of a material fact. May J observed that:

> Be it noted also that whereas there is a presumption that matters dealt with in a proposal form are material, there is no corresponding presumption that matters not so dealt with are not material. If any authority were required for that proposition one can find it in the case of *Schoolman v Hall*.[166]

The severe results which the sheer breadth of the insured's duty of disclosure is capable of producing can be seen from the decision in *Woolcott v Sun Alliance & London Insurance*.[167] The insured, who proposed a fire insurance policy on his house through the building society to which he was applying for a mortgage, did not disclose a robbery conviction he had received 12 years previously. Caulfield J held that the insurers could avoid the policy on the basis of moral hazard even though there appeared to be no connection between the insured's criminal conviction and the building's fire risk.

In *Norwich Union Insurance Ltd v Meisels*,[168] the judge adopted a more nuanced approach than has traditionally been the case. The insurers sought to avoid the policy on the grounds that the insured, M, had failed to disclose: (a) irregularities on the part of STPL, M's company, in the filing of accounts and returns with the Inland Revenue which had led

[162] [1975] 2 Lloyd's Rep 485.
[163] [1951] 1 Lloyd's Rep 139.
[164] ibid 143 (Asquith LJ). See also *Regina Fur Co v Bossom* [1951] 2 Lloyd's Rep 139; *Allden v Raven* [1983] 2 Lloyd's Rep 444.
[165] [2011] EWHC 210 (Comm).
[166] [1975] 1 Lloyd's Rep 169.
[167] [1978] 1 All ER 1253.
[168] [2007] Lloyd's Rep IR 69.

to the imposition of penalties; (b) the dissolution of a number of M's companies for failing to file accounts; (c) the insolvency of four of M's companies, with the Inland Revenue being a creditor in two of those cases; and (d) the use on the proposal form of an alias by M in respect of the property. Tugendhat J upheld the trial judge's view that none of these matters were material. He held that allegations of criminality were not necessarily material, and that materiality depended upon a combination of dishonesty, age and importance. He further held that if the insured had a good explanation for the allegations made against him ('exculpatory material'), then that was relevant both in determining whether the facts in question were material and also in determining whether the insurers would have been induced by the facts in question had they been disclosed (given that the insured would have had a good explanation and the insurers would then have disregarded the allegations). On the specific facts of the case, there was no allegation of dishonesty against M in respect of any of the matters in question (and indeed he had not been charged even with a regulatory offence), and given that the purpose of the insurers in requiring such information was to protect themselves against fraud by an insolvent insured, the facts could not be regarded as material. The judge concluded that:

> The test of materiality is by reference to what would influence the judgment of a prudent insurer. This is an objective test, and the characteristics to be imputed to a prudent insurer are in substance a matter for the courts to decide. There is room for a test of proportionality, having regard to the nature of the risk and the moral hazard under consideration. There may be things which are too old, or insufficiently serious to require disclosure, whether or not there is exculpatory material. And in cases where the information would be material and disclosable if there were no exculpatory material, the degree of conviction that the exculpatory material must carry, must depend on all the circumstances known to the insured.[169]

There is, however, an important exception to the duty to disclose a conviction. Section 4(3) of the Rehabilitation of Offenders Act 1974 relieves an insured of the duty to disclose a conviction which has become 'spent'. Convictions that carry custodial sentences of less than six months become spent after two years and those that carry sentences of between six months and two and a half years become spent after four years. A conviction which carries a sentence of two and a half years' and less than four years' imprisonment is spent after seven years, and a lengthier custodial sentence can never become spent. Where a conviction is 'spent', section 4(2) of the Act provides that any question in a proposal form regarding previous convictions is to be treated as not referring to such a conviction. However, section 7(3) of the Act confers discretion on the court to admit evidence as to spent convictions if the court is satisfied that 'justice cannot be done in the case except by admitting it'. In *Joseph Fielding Properties (Blackpool) Ltd v Aviva Insurance Ltd*,[170] the non-disclosure of a fraudulent claim against a previous insurer and the non-disclosure by the insured regarding previous non-disclosures/misrepresentations about unspent criminal convictions allowed the insurer to avoid the policy for non-disclosure. Interestingly, this was so even though the insured's convictions were spent at the time of entering into the current contract of insurance. The court held that 'the nature of the previous conviction was incidental to the breach of duty complained of',[171] so the making of the false statement had to be disclosed.

[169] ibid [25]. See also *Sharon's Bakery (Europe) Ltd v AXA Insurance UK plc* [2011] EWHC 210 (Comm).
[170] [2010] EWHC 2192 (QB).
[171] ibid [221].

3.5.4. Outstanding Charges and Allegations of Criminality

There has been some discussion in the authorities of the materiality of allegations of dishonesty which, in fact, are false. This may arise in particular where at the date of the policy there are outstanding criminal charges against the insured, or at least the insured is under some form of official investigation, but the insured is cleared after the policy has incepted. Forbes J in *Reynolds and Anderson v Phoenix Assurance Co Ltd*[172] denied that allegations were material, and ruled that:

> [T]he only occasion on which the allegation as an allegation must be disclosed is when it is not true. This appears to me to be a conclusion so devoid of any merit that I do not consider that a responsible insurer would adopt it and nor do I.[173]

That approach has been rejected in all other cases. The governing principle is that allegations of misconduct, as long as they have a solid base and are material to the risk, have to be disclosed even though they are not true and by the time of the trial have been proved not to be true. In *Brotherton v Aseguradoa Colseguros SA*,[174] Colombian media reports carried allegations of serious misconduct and related investigations involving the business activities of a senior employee of the insured bank. It was reported that he had been accused by the bank and government agencies of misappropriating the bank's assets. The bank was insured in Colombia under a bankers' blanket bond policy to provide cover against losses resulting from the fraud of employees. These reports had not been disclosed by the bank's Colombian insurers to their London reinsurers, and on discovering the reports they purported to avoid the reinsurance. In considering whether the reports were in principle material, Mance LJ drew a distinction between material intelligence that might ultimately be demonstrated as unfounded but which should nevertheless be disclosed and immaterial 'loose or idle rumours' which need not be disclosed by an insured or his agent. Counsel for the reinsurers had argued, inter alia, that materiality, at least in cases of moral hazard, must depend on the known existence of actual moral hazard rather than the possession of information which merely suggested the possibility of moral hazard. Mance LJ, however, rejected this contention on the basis that, as

> a matter of principle, and in the light of the authorities … it is difficult to see any reason why, if the evidence satisfies the court that a prudent underwriter would have regarded the information suggesting the possibility of moral hazard as material … that should not suffice.[175]

He concluded:

> I cannot see that the decision in *Pan Atlantic* that avoidance depends on inducement as well as materiality lends support to a conclusion that avoidance for non-disclosure of otherwise material information should depend upon the correctness of such information, to be ascertained if in issue by trial.[176]

[172] [1978] 2 Lloyd's Rep 440.

[173] ibid 460.

[174] [2003] EWCA Civ 705. See R Gay, 'Non-disclosure and Avoidance: Lies, Damned Lies, and "Intelligence"' [2004] *Lloyd's Maritime and Commercial Law Quarterly* 1.

[175] ibid [21]. In support of his reasoning, Mance LJ cited the following passage from Phillips J's judgment in *Inversiones Manria SA v Sphere Drake Insurance Co plc (The Dora)* [1989] 1 Ll R 69: 'When accepting a risk underwriters are properly influenced not merely by facts which, with hindsight, can be shown to have actually affected the risk but with facts that raise doubts about the risk.'

[176] ibid [28].

The issue of whether there had been non-disclosure of material facts was heard by Morison J.[177] He held that the media reports were, in fact, material on the basis that they did not have the appearance of 'gossip' but seemed to be reporting hard fact. Further, the reports were concerned with specific matters involving an identified individual. The judge also thought that it would be too extreme to conclude that everything reported in the newspapers was wrong.

The matter was again considered by the Court of Appeal in *North Star Shipping Ltd v Sphere Drake Insurance plc*.[178] A claim was made under a marine insurance policy for damage to a vessel caused by an explosion. The insurers avoided the policy on the grounds of non-disclosure of material facts. They relied on the insureds' failure to disclose that they were alleged to have committed fraud and were facing both criminal and civil proceedings, arguing that this information would have influenced the judgement of a prudent underwriter. The insurers contended that the allegations were material whether or not they were false. Waller LJ emphasised that the courts were attempting to strike the right balance between

> recognising first that there is something unjust in the notion that insurers can avoid a policy on the grounds of a suspicion as to the insured's probity flowing from an allegation which is in fact false, but second that it is difficult to gainsay an underwriter who gives evidence that an allegation of fraud would have an influence on his underwriting judgment if it was unknown at that time whether that allegation was true or false.[179]

He went on to recognise that the law in the area can be unjust and that

> if every false allegation of dishonesty must be disclosed in all types of insurance, that may place some insureds in the position of finding it difficult to obtain cover at all, and will certainly expose them to having the rates of premium increased unfairly.[180]

The Court of Appeal expressed considerable sympathy for Forbes J's views in *Reynolds and Anderson*, but felt constrained by authority to reject the contention which Waller LJ stated he otherwise 'might be tempted to follow'.[181] Waller LJ, noting that the orthodox test for material circumstance is 'one that would have an effect on the mind of the prudent insurer in estimating the risk', stressed that 'it is not necessary that it should have a decisive effect on his acceptance of the risk or the amount of premium to be paid'.[182] He concluded that it is only expert evidence which can determine the question of moral hazard and materiality.[183] Importantly, he did not agree with the statement that all allegations of fraud will be material, and so some allegations need not be disclosed:

> [I]t would seem to me that it must be possible to have a situation in which it is so clear that there is nothing in the allegation, such as an admission from the person who has made the allegation that he has made a terrible mistake as to identity, that the allegation no longer needs disclosing because it is no longer material.[184]

[177] [2003] Lloyd's Rep IR 762.
[178] [2006] EWCA Civ 378.
[179] ibid [4].
[180] ibid [17].
[181] ibid [18].
[182] ibid.
[183] ibid [19].
[184] ibid [35].

Nevertheless, the Court of Appeal held that the allegations in question were material and constituted a moral hazard. An allegation of fraud would affect the mind of a prudent underwriter, and so, even though the allegations turned out to be untrue, they needed to have been disclosed at the time of effecting the policy. These cases were followed in *Berkshire Assets (West London) Ltd v Axa Insurance UK Plc*,[185] a decision under the 2015 Act where the insured company did not disclose that a director faced criminal charges. It was held that the charges were material facts and that the insurers were entitled to avoid the policy because they had proved that had they been disclosed no policy would have been issued.

Given that charges, allegations and investigations are material facts, and given also that materiality has to be judged at the date on which the policy incepted,[186] the cases raise a further issue as to whether insurers are entitled to avoid the policy if it in fact proves to be the case that the insured was entirely innocent. In *Strive Shipping Corp v Hellenic Mutual War Risks Association (Bermuda) Ltd, The Grecia Express*,[187] insurers avoided a policy for failure by the insured to disclose a series of earlier losses each of which had occurred in somewhat curious circumstances. The court agreed that the losses were material, but at the trial he permitted the insured to adduce evidence which ultimately showed that on the balance of probabilities each of the losses was genuine. Colman J held on that basis that the insurers were not permitted to rely upon their avoidance, for two distinct reasons: an avoidance was always subject to be overturned by a court if found by matters proved at the trial to have been unjustified; and insurers were subject to a duty of utmost good faith which prevented them from relying upon their avoidance if it was inequitable to allow them to do so.

Each of these grounds was rejected by the Court of Appeal in *Brotherton v Aseguradora Colseguros SA (No 2)*.[188] Mance LJ rejected the first of Colman J's propositions in *Strive*, holding that the court has no role in permitting or refusing to permit avoidance, which was a self-help remedy. Mance LJ also roundly rejected the second reason put forward by Colman J. Mance LJ thought that it would be an 'unsound step' to introduce into English law a principle enabling an insured

> either not to disclose intelligence which a prudent insurer would regard as material or subsequently to resist avoidance by insisting on a trial, in circumstances where:
>
> (i) if insurers never found out about the intelligence, the insured would face no problem in recovering for any losses which arose – however directly relevant the intelligence was to the perils insured and (quite possibly) to the losses actually occurring; and
>
> (ii) if insurers found out about the intelligence, then (a) they would in the interests of their syndicate members or shareholders have normally to investigate its correctness, and (b) the insured would be entitled to put its insurers to the trouble, expense and (using the word deliberately) risk of expensive litigation, and perhaps force a settlement, in circumstances when insurers would never have been exposed to any of this, had the insured performed its prima facie duty to make timely disclosure.[189]

Shortly afterwards, a differently constituted Court of Appeal in *Drake Insurance plc v Provident Insurance plc*[190] gave further consideration to Colman J's utmost good faith suggestion.

[185] [2021] EWHC 2689 (Comm).
[186] *Seaman v Fonereau* (1743) 2 Stra 1183.
[187] [2002] 2 Lloyd's Rep 88.
[188] [2003] EWCA Civ 705.
[189] ibid [31].
[190] [2004] Lloyd's Rep IR 277.

It will be recalled that it was held that the non-disclosure did not induce the insurers to accept the risk and therefore they were not entitled to avoid the policy. Rix LJ observed that the doctrine of good faith should be capable of limiting the insurer's right to avoid in circumstances where that remedy, which has been described in recent years as draconian, would operate unfairly.[191] He went on to note that in recent years there appears to have been a realisation that in certain respects English insurance law has developed too stringently. Citing *Pan Atlantic*, Rix LJ stated that leading modern cases show that the courts are willing to find means to introduce safeguards and flexibilities which had not been appreciated before. Significantly, the judge felt inclined to say that it would not be in good faith to avoid a policy without first giving the insured an opportunity to address the reason for the avoidance.[192] By way of conclusion, he remarked that nowadays not all insurance contracts are made by those who engage in commerce and that the existence of widespread consumer insurance presents new problems: 'It may be necessary to give wider effect to the doctrine of good faith and recognize that its impact may demand that ultimately regard must be had to a concept of proportionality implicit in fair dealing.'[193] Both Rix and Clarke LJJ stated that insurers must not ignore facts which they know, or of which they have Nelsonian blindness. Pill LJ went further by requiring insurers to act in good faith and to make enquiries of the insured before taking the drastic step of avoiding the policy.

The effect of the authorities is, therefore, that an insurer, when determining whether to avoid a policy for breach of the duty of fair presentation respecting outstanding charges and allegations, owes a good faith duty to the insured to examine those allegations and not simply to take them at face value. That approach was recently confirmed in *Berkshire Assets (West London) Ltd v Axa Insurance UK Plc*,[194] where the court was at pains to note that the insurers' right to avoid had been exercised only after the insured had been given an opportunity to explain the matters withheld.

The amended version of section 17 of the Marine Insurance Act 2015, creating a general principle of utmost good faith but without specifying a remedy, gives some support for the wider approach in *Drake Insurance*. However, it may be that the changes to remedies in the Insurance Act 2015 and repeal of avoidance as an automatic right have greatly reduced the significance of the point.

3.5.5. Physical Hazard

Any fact which increases the risk of loss of the insured subject matter is said to relate to its physical hazard. For example, in life insurance, material facts will include the age, health, occupation and hobbies of the life insured. Needless to say, if the insured engages in dangerous pastimes such as skydiving this may be taken to increase the likelihood of accidental death and will need to be disclosed. With respect to buildings, material facts will include the age and condition of the building, the uses to which it is put, security arrangements and location, including activities on neighbouring land. Liability insurers wish to know the existence of past or potential claims against the insured. Motor insurance covers both first and third party risks, and insurers will typically want to know the nature of the insured

[191] ibid [87].
[192] ibid [92].
[193] ibid [89].
[194] [2021] EWHC 2689 (Comm).

vehicle, its average mileage, the identities and records of permitted drivers, and whether the vehicle is kept in a locked garage or parked in the road.

Physical hazard in life or health insurance encompasses a range of personal details: age; health; occupation and activities; and habits (smoking and drinking). Most policies will be consumer contracts and not subject to a duty of disclosure, so the very many old cases on the matter are largely redundant. At one time problems were caused where the insured was asked to give a factual statement as to health, but the modern tendency is to require questions only to the best of the insured's knowledge and belief. In *Joel v Law Union and Crown Insurance Co*,[195] Fletcher-Moulton LJ pointed out the problem that arose with life policies before the modern reforms:

> I will suppose that a man has, as is the case with almost all of us, occasionally had a headache. It may be that a particular one of these headaches would have told a brain specialist of hidden mischief, but to the man it was an ordinary headache indistinguishable from the rest. Now, no reasonable man would deem it material to tell an insurance company of all the casual headaches he had had in his life, and if he knew no more as to this particular headache, there would be no breach of his duty towards the insurance company in not disclosing it.

3.6. Duration of the Duty of Fair Presentation

3.6.1. Change of Circumstances before Contract

Section 21 of the Marine Insurance Act 1906, which is untouched by the 2015 Act, provides that 'A contract of marine insurance is deemed to be concluded when the proposal of the assured is accepted by the insurer, whether the policy be then issued or not'. Under section 3(1) of the Insurance Act 2015, the duty of fair presentation applies 'before a contract of insurance is entered into'. This means that the duty does not cease when negotiations come to an end but continues until the contract is made, although that may not necessarily be the date on which a policy is issued. The date on which a contract is made is discussed below in chapter five.

Where there is a change of circumstance between the submission of the proposal form and its formal acceptance, the insured must disclose the change to the insurer. For example, if a proposer falls ill after submitting a proposal for private medical insurance but fails to disclose this prior to acceptance, the insurers will be able to avoid the policy since an offer to provide insurance is generally made conditional upon there being no material change in the risk between the time when the offer was made and the time of acceptance.[196] Thus, in *Looker v Law Union and Rock Insurance Co Ltd*,[197] a policy for life assurance contained a clause which stipulated that 'The risk of the company will not commence until receipt of the first premium; and the directors meanwhile reserve the power to alter or withdraw the acceptance'. The insured fell ill after submitting his proposal but before cover had commenced and failed to give notice of his illness to the insurers. He sent a cheque for the first premium which was dishonoured, and died from pneumonia four days after the

[195] [1908] 2 KB 863. See also *Cook v Financial Insurance Co Ltd* [1998] 1 WLR 1765.

[196] *Canning v Farquhar* (1886) 16 QBD 727.

[197] [1928] 1 KB 554. See also *Assicurazioni Generali SpA v Arab Insurance Group (BSC)* [2003] Lloyd's Rep IR 131.

illness began. It was held that the insurers could avoid the policy since the duty of disclosure continued up until payment of the first premium. Acton J stated that 'that the acceptance is made in reliance upon the continued truth of the representations, and the proposer had failed to disclose the change in his state of health'.[198]

In the same way, if the insured has made representations to the insurers in the course of negotiations and they become untrue by reason of later events, section 7(6) of the Insurance Act 2015, re-enacting the 1906 Act, specifically provides that 'A representation may be withdrawn or corrected before the contract of insurance is entered into'.

3.6.2. Renewals

Non-life policies are periodic – normally annual – but in some situations, such as the insurance of construction projects, the duration may be much longer, even up to 10 years. A renewal constitutes a fresh contract, so the duty of fair presentation attaches on renewal. By contrast, life policies are continuous and are not renewed as such but remain in force until one or other of the parties terminates the contract or an event triggering payment occurs.

Where there is a renewal of a non-life policy, it is usual practice for the insurers to ask an express question about changes to the risk in the preceding period, but even in the absence of such a question the insured is under a duty to disclose to the insurers any material changes to the risk. The principle here is that the information disclosed on the taking out of a policy is to be regarded as accurate for renewal purposes unless the insured corrects it. In *Synergy Health (UK) Ltd v CGU Insurance plc*,[199] the insured brought an action against the insurers under the policy or, in the alternative, against the brokers for damages of breach of duty.[200] The insured provided laundry services to the NHS and insured its property against the risks of material damage and business interruption. A fire broke out at the premises and the insured claimed under the policy. The insurer sought to avoid the contract for material non-disclosure or misrepresentation. Before each renewal, the insured had completed a declaration of material facts form which stated that the insurance had been agreed on the basis that certain facts were true. The misrepresentation arose from a letter, in 2005, which was forwarded to the insurers, stating that an intruder alarm was installed on the insured premises. In fact, no such alarm was installed. The insurers alleged that this letter was a continuing material misrepresentation because it was never corrected or withdrawn prior to renewal. Flaux J held that there was a misrepresentation at renewal. By not correcting the misrepresentation, the insured had impliedly repeated it. However, the judge found that the insurers had not been induced to enter into the renewal and therefore could not avoid the policy. He noted that when assessing whether the insurer could have underwritten the risk, 'the question is necessarily a hypothetical one, since the court is seeking to establish what the underwriters would have done if full disclosure had been made, which by definition it was not'.[201] Accordingly, 'the court should approach with care and caution the evidence of the underwriters as to whether

[198] At 559.
[199] [2010] EWHC 2583. See also *Limit No 2 Ltd v Axa Versicherung AG* [2009] Lloyd's Rep IR 396.
[200] This is discussed in ch 3 above.
[201] ibid [185].

they were induced'.[202] In his reasoning, Flaux J cited the judgment of Colman J in *North Star Shipping v Sphere Drake Insurance Plc*:[203]

> In evaluating the underwriters' evidence it is important to keep firmly in mind that all their evidence is necessarily hypothetical and that hypothetical evidence by its very nature lends itself to exaggeration and embellishment in the interests of the party on whose behalf it is given. It is very easy for an underwriter to convince himself that he would have declined a risk or imposed special terms if given certain information. For this reason, such evidence has to be rigorously tested by reference to logical self-consistency, and to such independent evidence as may be available.

The judge concluded that 'the hypothetical full disclosure which is under consideration is such disclosure as would ordinarily be made on a fair presentation of the risk',[204] ie if disclosure had been made of all the material risks – in the present case that would be if the insurers knew the intruder alarm had not been installed. Flaux J found that the chief underwriter 'had not dealt in his witness statement with what his reaction would have been if the true position, of a series of errors rather than anything deliberate, had been disclosed to him'.[205] Although the chief underwriter had argued that he would have agreed cover subject to an alarm being installed, the judge believed he had to approach this statement with 'some scepticism'. He found that the underwriter regarded the insured as 'a well-managed risk'[206] and they would have attempted to retain the insured as a client, and upon disclosure would have been 'flexible' in reducing the premium.[207] The underwriter's agreement to renew the policy in 2007, despite allegations of misrepresentation and non-disclosure, was 'somewhat inconsistent with his assertion that if the true position had been disclosed to him prior to the 2006 renewal, he would have imposed a contractual condition'.[208] Taking these considerations as a whole, it was held that the insurers had not been induced by the material misrepresentation.

3.6.3. Change of Circumstances after Contract

Unless there is an express term to the contrary, the insured is under no duty to disclose a change of circumstance which occurs during the operation of the insurance contract.[209] The point was graphically made by Lord Pollock in *Baxendale v Harvey*,[210] who said:

> If a person who insures his life goes up in a balloon, that does not vitiate his policy ... A person who insures may light as many candles as he please in his house, though each additional candle increases the danger of setting the house on fire.[211]

In that case the insurers were held liable for loss resulting from the insured introducing onto the premises a steam engine used for grinding purposes. The insurers cannot,

[202] ibid [186].
[203] [2005] 2 Lloyd's Rep 76, [254].
[204] Ibid [187].
[205] ibid [194].
[206] ibid [197].
[207] ibid [198].
[208] ibid [202].
[209] *K/S Merc Skandia XXXXII v Certain Lloyd's Underwriters, The Mercandian Continent* [2001] Lloyd's Rep IR 802; *Manifest Shipping Co Ltd v Uni-Polaris Shipping Co Ltd, The Star Sea* [1997] 1 Lloyds Rep 360.
[210] (1859) H & N 449.
[211] ibid 452. See also *Commercial Union v The Niger Co Ltd* (1922) 13 Ll L Rep 75, 82, in which Lord Sumner said that a continuing duty of disclosure 'would turn what is an indispensable shield for the Underwriter into an engine of oppression against the insured'.

therefore, object if the insured changes its business operations to introduce more hazardous methods.[212]

There are two important limitations to this general principle. The first is that policy terms may either prohibit specific changes in the risk or at the very least require the insured to inform the insurers of a change so that they can review the terms of cover. In *Kausar v Eagle Star Insurance Co Ltd*,[213] a clause in the policy which stated 'You must tell us of any change of circumstances after the start of the insurance which increases the risk of injury or damage' was restrictively construed by Saville LJ so as not to impose a continuing duty of disclosure on the insured:

> [A]ll that this Condition does is to state the position as it would exist anyway as a matter of common law, namely that without the further agreement of the insurer, there would be no cover where the circumstances had so changed that it could properly be said by the insurers that the new situation was something which, on the true construction of the policy, they had not agreed to cover. The mere fact that the chances of an insured peril operating increase during the period of the cover would not, save possibly in most extreme of circumstances, enable the insurers properly to say this, since the insurance bargain is one where, in return for the premium, they take upon themselves the risk that an insured peril will operate.[214]

It has been argued that where a policy contains a cancellation clause giving the insurer the right of cancellation at any time, this has the effect of placing the insured under a continuing duty of disclosure. Such a view was roundly rejected by the Court of Appeal in *New Hampshire Insurance Co v MGN Ltd*,[215] in which Staughton LJ said: 'We should hesitate to enlarge the scope for oppression by establishing a duty to disclose throughout the period of a contract of insurance, merely because it contains (as is by no means uncommon) a right to cancellation for the insurer.'[216]

However, a duty to disclose a change of circumstances can arise by virtue of a so-called 'increase of risk' clause. Generally, such clauses, which are frequently found in fire policies, only operate to require disclosure of changes which are permanent in nature. In *Dobson v Sotheby*,[217] a barn was insured against fire and the policy stated that no fire or hazardous goods are to be kept on the premises. When the premises required tarring, a fire was lighted and a tar barrel was brought into the building. The tar boiled over and the premises were destroyed by the ensuing fire. Lord Tenterden CJ considered that:

> [T]he condition must be understood as forbidding only the habitual use of fire, or the ordinary deposit of hazardous goods, not their occasional introduction, as in this case, for a temporary purpose connected with the occupation of the premises. The common repairs of a building necessarily require the introduction of fire upon the premises.[218]

On that basis, an insured who brings into his house some device which by its nature is inherently dangerous, for example a blowtorch for the purpose of redecorating, will not need to notify the insurers unless a clause in the policy expressly imposes such a duty in relation

[212] *Pim v Reid* (1843) 6 M & G 1; *Shaw v Robberds* (1837) 6 A & E 75.
[213] [2000] Lloyd's Rep IR 154.
[214] ibid 159.
[215] [1999] Lloyd's Rep IR 459.
[216] ibid 61.
[217] (1827) M & M 90.
[218] ibid 923.

to temporary changes.[219] In *Ansari v New India Assurance Ltd*,[220] the claimant purchased commercial premises and leased them to a tenant. The claimant applied for insurance and described the tenant's business as 'wholesaling kitchenware'. He also gave a positive answer to the question: 'Are the premises protected by an automatic sprinkler installation?' The declaration on the form stated that the assured had answered questions to the best of his knowledge and belief. The subsequent policy provided in General Condition 2 stated that

> [t]his insurance shall cease to be in force if there is any material alteration to the Premises or Business or any material change in the facts stated in the Proposal Form or other facts supplied to the Insurer unless the Insurer agrees in writing to continue the insurance.

There was also a non-invalidation clause which provided that 'The interest of the freeholder … in this insurance shall not be prejudiced by any act or neglect whereby the risk of destruction or damage is increased without the authority or knowledge of the freeholder'.

The premises were badly damaged by fire, and subsequent investigations showed that the sprinkler system had been turned off and in any event there was no supply of water to the premises. It was also discovered that the tenant's business also consisted in selling large toys, including bicycles and small motor cycles. The insurers relied upon General Condition 2. It was held by the Court of Appeal, affirming the first instance decision of Patten J, that they were not liable. (1) The assured had stated that the sprinkler system protected the premises, a statement which was to be construed as meaning that the system was operative and not that it was merely installed. (2) There had been a material change in the facts stated about the sprinkler system. The test of materiality was not the wide one laid down for pre-contract disclosure, but was a narrower one which asked whether the alterations had a significant bearing on the risk. The clause, unlike that in *Kausar v Eagle Star Insurance Co Ltd*, did not reflect the common law rule that an insurer was discharged only if the risk was completely altered and not merely increased. (3) The assured was aware that the sprinkler had been turned off and thus could not rely on the 'non-invalidation' clause. (4) Mr Ansari had stated on the proposal form that the premises were occupied by a tenant whose business was the sale of kitchenware. There was no dispute that there had been a material change of use, in that scooters and mini-motorbikes were quite different from kitchenware.

The second limitation is that the law draws a distinction between a mere increase of risk (in the sense that a loss has become more likely), which does not impose any additional obligations on the insured, and change of risk (in the sense that the subject matter of the policy has completely altered), in which case the insurers are automatically discharged from liability as of the date of the change of risk. The distinction between the two concepts may be illustrated by two cases. In *Scottish Coal Co Ltd v Royal and Sun Alliance Plc*,[221] the insured mining company changed the means of extracting coal to one that increased the risk of a collapse. It was held that the risk had increased but that there was no change of risk because the activity remained that of mining. By contrast, in *Swiss Reinsurance Co v United India Insurance Co Ltd*,[222] a reinsurance case, insurers issued a construction all risks policy covering the building of a power plant. The contractors were not paid for their work, and walked off the site. Work was no longer able to continue, and the site was left unoccupied

[219] *Shaw v Robberds* (1832) 6 A & E 75; *Glen v Lewis* (1853) 8 Ex 607.
[220] [2009] EWCA Civ 93.
[221] [2008] Lloyd's Rep IR 718.
[222] [2005] Lloyd's Rep IR 341. See also *Cosford Union v Poor Law & Local Government Officers' Mutual Guarantee Association Ltd* (1910) 103 LT 463; *Hadenfayre Ltd v British National Insurance Ltd* [1984] 2 Lloyd's Rep 393.

but otherwise secured. A fire occurred. It was held that the policy had terminated automatically because the risk had been changed from a construction risk to one in respect of a site.

3.6.4. Open Covers and Declarations

An open cover is a framework contract under which the insurers agree in advance to accept risks of a given class and within stated financial limits. The facility is frequently one granted to a broker or other intermediary. Most open covers are obligatory from the point of view of the insurers. The position may be illustrated by reference to a cargo policy taken out by a shipowner or warehouse: all cargo entering into the custody or control of the insured may be declared to the policy, and if it is declared, then there is automatically insurance in place at an agreed premium based on value. The risk will attach when the declaration is made, although the premium will not be paid at that time but will be calculated when the insured or broker submits a periodic (eg monthly) list (often called a bordereau) listing the risks incepting in the previous period. The fact that the risk attaches at the outset means that if by oversight the insured fails to include a particular cargo in the bordereau and fails to pay the premium at the time, there is still insurance in place[223] unless the policy otherwise provides.[224] Some open covers are non-obligatory, so that the insurers reserve to themselves the right to reject individual declarations,[225] although that type of arrangement is comparatively rare.

A non-obligatory open cover is little more than a procedure whereby individual risks can be presented to the insurers so that each declaration operates as a contract of insurance in its own right and the duty of fair presentation attaches to each declaration. An obligatory open cover is rather more complex because the insurers have agreed upfront to accept any declaration that conforms to the terms of the open cover and there is no discretion either to refuse the risk or to accept it only on altered terms or a higher premium. There is for that reason no basis for a duty of fair presentation applicable to declarations.

3.7. Remedies for Breach of the Duty of Fair Presentation

3.7.1. The Statutory Remedies

The sole remedy for misrepresentation and non-disclosure at common law was avoidance of the policy. This was an all or nothing remedy, and was capable of operating disproportionately where the information in question would have made only a marginal difference to the underwriting of the risk. The insured was entitled to a return of premium on the basis of total failure of consideration, although under section 84(3)(a) of the 1906 Act the insurers could retain the premium if they could prove fraud. As has been seen earlier, at common law the court had no discretion to vary the relief. In *Brotherton v Aseguradora Colseguros SA*,[226] the Court of Appeal rejected the earlier reasoning of Colman J in *Strive Shipping*

[223] *Glencore International AG v Ryan, The Beursgracht* [2002] Lloyd's Rep IR 335.
[224] *JDA Co Ltd v AIG Insurance New Zealand Ltd* [2021] NZHC 2912, where the insured was required to nominate the scope of cover required, so the risk could not attach until that had occurred.
[225] As in *Societe Anonyme d'Intermediaires Luxembourgeois v Farex Gie* [1995] LRLR 116, a reinsurance case where the cover remained in place for 30 days pending a decision by the reinsurers.
[226] [2003] EWCA Civ 705.

Corp v Hellenic Mutual War Risks Association (Bermuda) Ltd, The Grecia Express[227] to the effect that avoidance is an equitable remedy that is discretionary. Mance LJ explained that the right to avoid was a self-help remedy that could be exercised without the court's authorisation. That analysis was subject to one possible exception in cases where, by the date of avoidance, the facts relied upon had been proved not to be material – a point discussed earlier – but the *Brotherton* analysis otherwise held good. There was an argument that, for misrepresentation, the court might exercise its general discretion in section 2(2) of the Misrepresentation Act 1967 to award damages in lieu of avoidance, although there was no decision to that effect. The prospects were limited: the section does not apply to non-disclosure; and in commercial cases at least the exercise of a discretion in favour of insureds would have undermined long-standing principles of insurance law.

The all-or-nothing approach attracted judicial criticism[228] and was rejected by the Law Commissions. The approach adopted in the 2015 Act is similar to that applicable to consumers in the 2012 Act. There is some curious drafting in the legislation which repeats, as in the 2012 Act, the concept of 'qualifying breach'.[229] The basic distinction under section 8(4) is between a deliberate or reckless breach and a breach that is not deliberate or reckless. A breach is deliberate or reckless if, by section 8(5), the insured knew that it was in breach of the duty of fair presentation or did not care whether or not it was in breach of that duty, the onus of proof being on the insurers (section 8(6)). The Law Commissions have explained that a deliberate breach encompasses, amongst other things, refraining from disclosing a circumstance which the insured knows to be relevant to the risk, engaging in data dumping so as to disguise the existence of material facts material, making false statements and giving a misleading impression by omission.[230] A reckless breach was not regarded as capable of precise definition, but includes a lack of interest in making a fair presentation or perhaps a complete disregard for the quality of the presentation.[231]

The remedies themselves are set out in schedule 1. In the case of deliberate or reckless breaches, the insurer may avoid the contract and is not required to return the premiums (paragraph 2). For all other breaches (paragraphs 3–5): (a) if the insurer would not have entered into the contract on any terms, the insurer may avoid the contract and refuse all claims, but must in that event return the premiums paid; (b) if the insurer would have entered into the contract but on different terms (other than terms relating to the premium), the contract is to be treated as if it had been entered into on those different terms if the insurer so requires; and (c) if the insurer would have entered into the contract (whether the terms relating to matters other than the premium would have been the same or different) but would have charged a higher premium, the insurer may reduce proportionately the amount to be paid on a claim by reference to the proportion of the loss represented by the premium actually paid measured against the premium that would have been paid without breach of duty. Equivalent principles are extended to variations.

While both the 2012 and 2015 Acts treat deliberate or reckless conduct in the same way, the 2015 Act treats innocent and careless misrepresentation or failure to disclose known

[227] [2002] 2 Lloyd's Rep 88.

[228] *Kausar v Eagle Star Insurance Co Ltd* [2000] Lloyd's Rep IR 154.

[229] In neither Act does the concept of 'qualifying breach' add anything to the principles in the legislation. Quite why it is there remains a curiosity.

[230] LC 353, para 11.43.

[231] ibid paras 11.44–11.46.

facts as giving rise to a remedy, whereas the 2012 Act is concerned only with careless misrepresentations. Innocence is an excuse for consumers but not for businesses.

3.7.2. Loss of Rights

Insurers may lose the right to rely upon breach of duty by waiver. There are two forms of waiver: waiver by affirmation and waiver by estoppel. They bear some common features, but there are some differences. Affirmation arises where the insurers have a conflicting choice of avoiding the policy or affirming its existence.[232] Once the election between those possibilities has been made and the position has been made clear to the insured, the insurers cannot change their mind. Estoppel arises where the insurers' conduct has induced the insured to believe that the insurers do not intend to avoid the contract and the insured has acted accordingly. Thus, affirmation must be communicated to the insured but, unlike estoppel, it is not necessary to prove that some representation by words or conduct was made by the insurers which was relied upon by the insured to his detriment.

3.7.3. Waiver by Affirmation

The most obvious example of waiver by affirmation is where the insurers expressly inform the insured that they are treating the policy as binding.[233] More problematic is the situation where the insurers have not specifically informed the insured that the policy has been affirmed but they have acted in a manner plainly inconsistent with any intention to avoid, eg issuing a formal policy document, making payment or accepting future premiums, as long as it is clear that those acts were not simply administrative and carried out automatically without being based on the insurers' knowledge of their rights.[234] The principle here is that an insurer with knowledge of its rights who seeks to rely upon the terms of the policy will be treated as having affirmed the policy by acting inconsistently with the right of avoidance: an insurer who purports to exercise a cancellation clause in a policy for breach of a term prohibiting the insured from securing a further policy on the same risk cannot later plead a right to avoid for the insured's failure to disclose that the premiums on the further policy had not been paid was a material fact.[235]

Waiver by affirmation may also be found where the insurers, faced with legal proceedings by the insured, rely upon coverage or other defences and do not seek to avoid until a late stage in the proceedings. In *Moore Large & Co Ltd v Hermes Credit & Guarantee plc*,[236] it was held that affirmation can occur where insurers have defended legal proceedings on the basis of coverage or terms of the policy knowing that a fair presentation defence might exist. On the facts, the insurers had sought to rely on the insured's breach of the disclosure duty at a late stage in the proceedings, having pleaded only that the policy did not cover the loss. Further, the insurers had the benefit of legal advice and it was held not to be open to them to argue that they were not bound by the tactical decisions of their legal advisers.

[232] *Bolton MBC v Municipal Mutual Insurance and Commercial Union Assurance* [2007] Lloyd's Rep IR 173.

[233] *Wing v Harvey* (1854) 5 De GM & G 265.

[234] *Morrison v Union Marine Insurance Co* (1872) LR 8 Ex 197; *Drake Insurance Co v Provident Insurance Co* [2004] Lloyd's Rep IR 277.

[235] *O'Kane v Jones* [2005] Lloyd's Rep IR 174; *Involnert Management Inc v Aprilgrange Ltd* [2015] 2 Lloyd's Rep 289.

[236] [2003] Lloyd's Rep IR 315. *ABN Amro Bank NV v Royal & Sun Alliance plc* [2021] EWHC 442 (Comm) had more or less the same facts.

Insurance Corporation of the Channel Islands v The Royal Hotel Ltd[237] is a paradigm case not only on the question of affirmation, but on the repercussions of tactical decisions taken during the litigation process. The insured hotel had been damaged in a series of fires and had to close in June 1992. Its owner claimed under two insurance policies effected with the claimant insurers, ICCI. The first policy covered material damage to the buildings and the second policy covered business interruption losses. The material damage policy contained an arbitration clause, and the claim under that policy went to arbitration. In 1994, while the arbitration proceedings were in progress, ICCI commenced judicial proceedings under the business interruption policy. In that action Mance J held[238] that the Royal Hotel had forfeited all benefit (some £950,000) under the business interruption policy because its director and company secretary had used fraudulent means to promote the hotel's occupancy rate so as to inflate the sums recoverable under the business interruption policy.

Having obtained that judgment, ICCI purported to avoid the material damage policy for non-disclosure of the fraud when the policy was taken out. Materiality and inducement were evidentially straightforward in the light of the insured's undisclosed moral hazard and the judge found in the insurers' favour on that point.[239] However, Mance J ruled that the right to avoid the material damage policy had been lost because the insurers had by their actions affirmed its validity. Mance J held that the evidence established that ICCI had first became aware of the insured's fraudulent conduct in 1993, but they had adopted the tactic of awaiting the outcome of the fraud proceedings under the business interruption policy before raising any right to avoid the material damage policy for breach of the duty of fair presentation. The tactical decision to participate in the material damage arbitration but not to plead any right to avoid despite knowledge of the insured's fraud amounted to affirmation of the material damage policy. ICCI was barred also by issue estoppel and abuse of process. It is instructive to examine in more detail Mance J's analysis of the elements of waiver by affirmation in reaching this conclusion.

Addressing the question of the knowledge required for affirmation, the judge noted that there had to be an informed choice to treat the contract as continuing despite its breach. He rejected counsel's argument that constructive knowledge was sufficient, viewing the authorities relied upon to support the proposition as cases on estoppel, rather than election. Mance J did accept, however, that determining the exact nature of someone's knowledge is a nebulous exercise:

> [K]nowledge is not to be equated with absolute certainty, itself an ultimately elusive concept. The impossibility of doubt which Descartes found only in the maxim 'I think, therefore I exist' is not the criterion of legal knowledge. For practical purposes, knowledge pre-supposes the truth of the matters known, and a firm belief in their truth, as well as sufficient justification for that belief in terms of experience, information and/or reasoning. The element of regression or circularity involved in this description indicates why knowledge is a jury question.[240]

Mance J ruled that the insurers had to be aware not just of the facts justifying avoidance, but also of the right of avoidance itself. However, where litigation was underway or in the offing and lawyers were involved, their knowledge of the legal position was imputed to the insurers.

[237] [1998] Lloyd's Rep IR 151.
[238] [1997] LRLR 20.
[239] The issues of moral hazard and non-disclosure arising from the facts of this decision are discussed above.
[240] [1998] Lloyd's Rep IR 151, 162.

The requirement that an unequivocal communication be made to the insured of the insurers' election not to avoid was also problematical in terms of determining what exactly the communication should evidence. The judge queried whether, on the one hand, it was sufficient that there was knowledge of the breach and a communication (by words or conduct) which demonstrated that an unequivocal choice had been made, or whether, on the other hand, the communication itself or the surrounding circumstances demonstrating such knowledge would suffice. On this issue Mance J concluded that for the purposes of affirmation the latter approach was correct:

> The communication itself or the circumstances must demonstrate objectively or unequivocally that the party affirming is making an informed choice. In the context of estoppel, where knowledge is not a pre-requisite (though reliance is), it is in contrast the appearance of choice with which the law is concerned.[241]

Therefore, the question whether there has been an unequivocal representation has to be considered in the light of the insured's knowledge about what the insurers actually knew. As such, where it is argued that a party's conduct amounts to an unequivocal representation, the impact such conduct has on the other party to the contract has to be objectively assessed. Mance J therefore posited that, in affirmation, as distinct from estoppel, the actual state of the other party's mind is not the test because affirmation 'depends on the objective manifestation of a choice'.[242] The difficulty lies with determining what knowledge can be objectively ascribed to the insured, for it is from his perspective that some choice has to be seen to have been exercised by the insurer. On the facts of the case, Mance J was of the opinion that where the choice lies between whether or not to avoid the policy on the ground of non-disclosure of material facts (ie the Royal Hotel's fraudulent conduct), it has to be determined how far a reasonable person in the insured's position would be aware of what matters were material to a prudent insurer and how, in the absence of such awareness, the reasonable person could regard any conduct of the insurers as unequivocal. Given the severity of the Royal Hotel's undisclosed conduct, it must have been clear and obvious to its director that his conduct would induce the contract. The insured must also have realised that the dishonest conduct in question had been discovered by the insurers if only on the basis of a common-sense consideration of the documents which had been supplied to them during the pre-trial proceedings in 1994.[243] On the evidence, the judge took the view that the insurers' solicitors became suspicious of the fraud during 1993 and were convinced of it by 1994 but decided on so-called 'tactical' grounds not to raise the issue of avoidance during the 1994 trial. For Mance J this therefore amounted to affirmation because 'they did for present purposes "know" the real position, however much Royal Hotel continued to brazen it out with implausible denials or evasions'.[244] The fact that the insured continued to deny dishonest conduct on their part, even during the earlier trial, did not preclude a finding that the insurers had the relevant knowledge and knew that the insured's denials were unsustainable.

Issues of waiver aside, on these unusual facts ICCI were caught by the principles of issue estoppel and abuse of process. The former is a rule of law whereby a legally binding decision

[241] Ibid, citing the judgment of Slade LJ in *Payman v Lanjani* [1985] Ch 457 in support of his finding.
[242] [1998] Lloyd's Rep IR 151, 163.
[243] ibid 174.
[244] ibid 171.

in earlier proceedings between the same parties on the same point cannot be reopened in later proceedings, and the latter – based on *Henderson v Henderson*[245] – is a procedural principle that confers upon the court the jurisdiction to refuse to hear a defence that could and should have been raised in earlier proceedings.

In *Scottish Coal Co Ltd v Royal and Sun Alliance Insurance plc*,[246] the insured made a claim under its policy which insured against risks arising from its mining activities. The insurers sought to avoid the claim on the ground of non-disclosure because the claimants had decided to engage in new mining techniques and had failed to disclose this change to the insurers. Following the decision in *ICCI*, it was held that the insurers had made an unequivocal election to affirm the contract. By March 2009 the underwriters knew that the insured had not disclosed its new plans which may have increased the risk under the policy; they failed to tell their risk inspector even though he advised them that he would want details of the new project and, despite their knowledge, the underwriters failed to enquire further to substantiate any other defences they had under the policy.[247] On 24 January 2001 the underwriters agreed to extend the policy without reserving any rights in relation to any earlier defences and they included, in the calculation of the premium, the losses which the insured had claimed for without suggesting that these were contested or inappropriate. Steel J said that 'against this background, it is difficult to categorise this extension, viewed objectively, as being other than an unequivocal election to affirm the contract'.[248]

The decision in *WISE* in relation to waiver is discussed above.[249] It will be recalled that the Court of Appeal, by a majority, held that GNP was entitled to recover. Although it was unanimously held that WISE had been induced by the presentation of the risk, Rix and Peter Gibson LJJ held that the reinsurers had affirmed the policy, notwithstanding the breach of the duty of disclosure, by giving notice of its cancellation, such notice being inconsistent with any claim to avoid the policy *ab initio*. Both judges took the view that the trial judge had overlooked correspondence which showed in unequivocal terms that WISE was cancelling the policy.[250] In the light of the authorities, the conditions that have to be satisfied by the insured in order to succeed in a plea of waiver by affirmation were set out by Simon J at first instance, as approved by the Court of Appeal:

(a) The insurer must have actual knowledge, rather than constructive knowledge, of the insured's breach of the duty of fair presentation.
(b) The insurer, either personally or through its legal advisers, must be aware of the existence of its legal rights. This point was articulated by Colman J in *Moore Large & Co Ltd v Hermes Credit & Guarantee Plc*,[251] where the insurers' decision not to rely upon avoidance until a late stage in the proceedings on the advice of their legal team gave rise to waiver, and that where lawyers were involved it was normally to be inferred that legal advice had been given. Leggatt J in *Involnert Management Inc v Aprilgrange Ltd*[252] was not satisfied that the requirement for

[245] (1843) 3 Hare 100. The principles were restated in *Virgin Atlantic Airways Ltd v Zodiac Seats UK Ltd* [2013] UKSC 46.
[246] [2008] Lloyd's Rep IR 718.
[247] ibid [92] and [93].
[248] ibid [94].
[249] [2004] EWCA (Civ) 962.
[250] Longmore LJ dissented on the basis that the judge's findings of fact could not be reversed.
[251] [2003] Lloyd's Rep IR 315.
[252] [2015] 2 Lloyd's Rep 289.

legal knowledge was necessary, but noted that the rulings on the relevance of the knowledge of legal advisers rendered the point largely immaterial.

(c) The insurer must have had a reasonable time to consider its options.

(d) There must have been an unequivocal and unconditional communication to the insured by words or conduct that the insurer had made an informed choice not to avoid the policy. A communication under a reservation of rights or without prejudice to existing rights is plainly not unconditional[253] and silence, even for a prolonged period, is not unequivocal.[254]

(e) The communication to the insured would have conveyed an intention to affirm to a reasonable person in the insured's position.[255]

3.7.4. Waiver by Estoppel

The elements of waiver by estoppel are stricter in the sense that the insured must have relied upon the insurers' representation in a detrimental fashion and the court must be satisfied that it would be inequitable for the insurers to be able to resile from their unequivocal representation[256] that there will be no avoidance. There can be estoppel even if the insurers had only constructive knowledge of the facts and were unaware of their legal rights, but the requirement that the insurers must be acting inequitably may operate in their favour in that regard.[257]

3.8. Contractual Arrangements Varying the Legal Position

We have seen that it is not possible for the parties to a consumer insurance contract to contract out of the protections conferred upon consumers. By contrast, business policies may restrict or indeed exclude in their entirety the unfair presentation rules, the only exception being section 9 of the 2015 Act, which prevents pre-contractual representations being converted into warranties. Various possibilities exist, including the bare statement that the contract takes effect as if the 2015 Act had not been passed, ranging to the modification of remedies so that there is always a right to avoid. Section 16 of the Insurance Act 2015 provides that any 'disadvantageous term' that puts the insured in a worse position than provided for by the Act is ineffective unless the transparency rules in section 17 are met. By section 17:

(1) In this section, 'the disadvantageous term' means such a term as is mentioned in section 16(2).

(2) The insurer must take sufficient steps to draw the disadvantageous term to the insured's attention before the contract is entered into or the variation agreed.

[253] *Callaghan & Hedges v Thompson* [2000] Lloyd's Rep IR 125; *Spriggs v Wessington Court School Ltd* [2004] EWHC 1432 (QB).

[254] *McCormick v National Motor & Accident Insurance Union* (1934) 40 Com Cas76; *Persimmon Homes Ltd v Great Lakes Reinsurance (UK) Plc* [2011] Lloyd's Rep IR 101; *Argo Systems FZE v Liberty Insurance PTE Ltd, London Special Risks Ltd* [2011] EWCA Civ 1572, where the insurers remained silent on the issue of avoidance for seven years.

[255] *Spriggs v Wessington Court School Ltd* [2005] EWHC 1432 (QB).

[256] *Orakpo v Barclays Insurance Services Ltd* [1995] LRLR 443.

[257] *Kammins Ballrooms Co Ltd v Zenith Investments (Torquay) Ltd* [1971] AC 850; *Motor Oil Hellas (Corinth) Refineries SA v Shipping Corp of India, The Kanchenjunga* [1990] 1 Lloyd's Rep 391; *Callaghan & Hedges v Thompson* [2000] Lloyd's Rep IR 125; *Kosmar Villa Holidays Plc v Trustees of Syndicate 1243* [2008] Lloyd's Rep IR 489; *Lexington Insurance Co v Multinacional de Seguros SA* [2009] Lloyd's Rep IR 1.

(3) The disadvantageous term must be clear and unambiguous as to its effect.
(4) In determining whether the requirements of subsections (2) and (3) have been met, the characteristics of insured persons of the kind in question, and the circumstances of the transaction, are to be taken into account.
(5) The insured may not rely on any failure on the part of the insurer to meet the requirements of subsection (2) if the insured (or its agent) had actual knowledge of the disadvantageous term when the contract was entered into or the variation agreed.

There is something of an ambiguity in these provisions. Take, for example, the situation in which the insurer offers a lower premium if the assured forgoes rights under the 2015 Act. Can that be said to be a 'disadvantageous term' which is subject to the section 17 requirements? There is no decision on the point to date.

It is, of course, entirely open to the parties to restrict the scope of the insured's duties or the remedies available to the insurers provided for in the Insurance Act. That was the position under the pre-existing law, as discussed at length by the House of Lords in *HIH Casualty & General Insurance Ltd v Chase Manhattan Bank*.[258] It was there confirmed that a clause which removed the duty of disclosure, and removed the right to avoid for non-disclosure or misrepresentation, was perfectly valid, with a possible limitation for fraudulent misrepresentation on the principle that if the contract was induced by fraud then the waiver of avoidance would itself have been induced by fraud. The clauses considered by the courts include:

(a) incontestability clauses used in life policies, whereby insurers agree that they will not avoid after the policy has been in force for a given period, eg five years;
(b) 'entire agreement' clauses, where the parties agree that only the matters appearing in the contract give rise to rights and liabilities, although it has been held that this cannot apply to misrepresentations because they do not form part of the contract;[259]
(c) clauses under which the policy is not to be regarded as voidable or cancellable – as held in *HIH*, this type of wording applies to innocent and negligent presentation of the risk, but probably not to fraud;
(d) waiver of remedies other than in cases of fraud, a provision held to require proof by the insurers of dishonesty on the part of the insured[260] and also preventing the insurers from relying on estoppel or alternative defences in order to deny liability for non-fraudulent presentation of the risk;[261] and
(e) waiver of remedies other than in cases where the insurers are satisfied that the breach of duty was free from fraud – this type of clause requires the insurers not to act capriciously or arbitrarily in assessing whether or not there was fraud, so that if the insurers determine from the outset that there was fraud and disregard any submissions by the insured to the contrary, they cannot rely upon the clause.[262]

[258] [2003] Lloyd's Rep IR 230. See also *Kingscroft Insurance Co Ltd v Nissan Fire & Marine Insurance Co Ltd* unreported 4 March 1996 QBD (Comm Ct), affirmed [1999] Lloyd's Rep IR 371.
[259] *Axa Sun Life Services Plc v Campbell Martin Ltd* [2011] EWCA Civ 133.
[260] *Mutual Energy Ltd v Starr Underwriting Agents Ltd* [2016] EWHC 590 (TCC).
[261] *ABN Amro Bank NV v Royal & Sun Alliance plc* [2021] EWCA Civ 1789.
[262] *UK Acorn Finance Ltd v Markel (UK) Ltd* [2020] EWHC 922 (Comm).

4. The Insurers' Duty of Fair Presentation

The fact that section 17 of the 1906 Act states that the duty of utmost good faith is borne by both parties to the contract, the insured and the insurer, has already been noted. The mutual nature of the specific duty of fair presentation was recognised by Lord Mansfield in *Carter v Boehm*,[263] when he stated that 'the policy would equally be void, against the underwriter, if he concealed; as, if he insured a ship on her voyage, which he privately knew to be arrived: and an action would lie to recover the premium'.[264] The 'arrived ship' illustration is the mirror image of the insured's duty, in that had the fact of arrival been disclosed to the insured then he would not have entered into the insurance contract. It follows that any information withheld or misstated by the insurers before the contract was entered into which would have influenced the insured's decision is material and has to be disclosed. However, any serious development of the law in this regard was hampered by the terms of section 17 of the 1906 Act, which, in its unamended form, gave rise only to the remedy of avoidance. It was of little value to an insured who had entered into a policy believing it to provide coverage when that proved not to be the case simply to recover their premiums. Other than in the exceptional circumstances set out by Lord Mansfield, where avoidance was an entirely appropriate remedy because there was no prospect of loss, the insurers' duty provided a right but no remedy.

In *Banque Financière de la Cité SA v Westgate Insurance Co Ltd*,[265] the courts were afforded the opportunity to consider the scope of the duty as it applies to insurers. This was a complex fraud perpetuated on the claimant bank. In outline, the bank was led to believe by its brokers and the insurers that it was fully insured against default on advances made to a borrower, whereas that was known by the insurers – through an employee – not to be the case. At first instance,[266] Steyn J reaffirmed the mutuality of the disclosure duty by holding that the insurers owed a duty of disclosure to the insured. Steyn J concluded that:

> In my judgment justice and policy considerations combine in requiring me to rule that in principle an insured can claim damages from an insurer arising from loss suffered by the insured as a result of a breach of the obligation of the utmost good faith by the insurer.[267]

The Court of Appeal and the House of Lords affirmed this element of the trial judge's decision, but reversed his finding that the remedy against the insurer for breach was damages, confining it to avoidance of the contract and return of the premiums only on the basis that the court's power to grant relief arose from its equitable jurisdiction. The test to be applied in determining materiality from the insurers perspective was, in Steyn J's opinion, whether 'good faith and fair dealing require disclosure' to the insured.[268] However, the Court of

[263] (1766) 3 Burr 1905, 1909.

[264] See also the judgment of Rix LJ in *WISE (Underwriting Agency) Ltd v Grupo Nacional Provincial SA* [2004] EWCA (Civ) 942; T Yeo, 'Of Reciprocity and Remedies: Duty of Disclosure in Insurance Contracts' (1991) 11 *Legal Studies* 131.

[265] [1990] 1 QB 665, CA, [1991] 2 AC 249, HL.

[266] Sub nom *Banque Keyser Ullman SA v Skandia Insurance Co* [1987] 1 Lloyd's Rep 69.

[267] ibid 96.

[268] ibid 94.

Appeal, notably Slade LJ, criticised this formulation as being far too broad and vague as a test for determining the existence of the duty which might arise 'even in the absence of any dishonest or unfair intent'.[269] For Slade LJ, the insurer's duty of disclosure should

> extend to disclosing facts known to him which are material either to the nature of the risk sought to be covered or the recoverability of a claim under the policy which a prudent insured would take into account in deciding whether to place the risk for which he seeks cover with that insurer.[270]

The House of Lords approved Slade LJ's reasoning in this respect. It is unfortunate that the opportunity for a thorough and authoritative assessment of the insurers' duty of good faith was not taken up.

The narrow approach adopted by the Court of Appeal in *Westgate* towards the insurers' duty of good faith was applied in *Aldrich v Norwich Union Life Insurance Co Ltd*.[271] Norwich Union had sold certain 'property backed guarantee plans' to Lloyd's names whereby guarantees were given in respect of their liabilities. Calls by Lloyd's exhausted the guarantees and Norwich Union sought to enforce the security provided by the names. The security included the assignment of endowment and life policies to the insurer. The Court of Appeal upheld the striking out of claims that Norwich Union had failed to disclose its knowledge that the syndicates to which the names belonged were likely to incur substantial losses. It was held that there was no obligation on Norwich Union to disclose matters relating to the risk of losses at Lloyd's because that particular risk was not covered by the endowment and life policies; the only issue material to such policies related to the insureds' (ie the Names') lives. One possible modification of these cases was suggested by Rix LJ in *Sherdley v Nordea Life & Pension SA*,[272] where, in the period when the policy was being negotiated, the insurers altered the choice of law and jurisdiction provisions in the terms but did not inform the insured of the changes. In the event nothing turned on the point, but Rix LJ commented that it was contrary to the principle of utmost good faith for an insurer to act in that way, and that in appropriate circumstances the insurer might be estopped from relying upon the altered terms.

The English and Scottish Law Commissions recognised that sole remedy of avoidance available under section 17 of the 1906 Act was of little practical benefit to a policyholder in this situation, and took the view that the law should recognise a mutual and properly enforceable duty of good faith. However, the Insurance Act 2015 in its amendment of section 17 stopped short of conferring a remedy in damages of the type contemplated by Steyn J. The section merely repealed the words setting out the remedy, leaving it to the courts to determine exactly how a general principle of utmost good faith should operate. It may be that *Sherdley* is an illustration of exactly how section 17 as amended might operate in the present context. The meaning of section 17 generally is discussed below in chapter eight.

[269] [1990] 1 QB 665, 772.
[270] ibid.
[271] [2000] Lloyd's Rep IR 1.
[272] [2012] EWCA Civ 88.

5

Formation of the Insurance Contract

1. The Making of the Contract

1.1. Offer and Acceptance

Although special rules apply to insurance contracts, such as the requirement for insurable interest and the duty of fair presentation, they otherwise share much common ground with other types of contracts. Indeed, many of the early cases establishing general rules of contract law were decisions on insurance policies. The test of whether an agreement exists and what are its terms is objective: in other words, even though the judges speak about the parties' intention, this intention is discovered not by attempting to understand what the parties themselves believed they had done, but by the appearance of their words and actions. For an insurance contract, as with any contract, there must be agreement between the parties on the principal terms,[1] which necessarily includes the risk to be covered, the insured subject matter, the duration of the cover, the premium – although it may suffice that there is an objective means of calculating premium if it is not fixed at the outset – and the benefit due in the event of a covered loss. At the root of the courts' approach to contract is the desire to facilitate rather than obstruct agreements, at least where commercial parties are involved and especially where they acted as though a contract existed:

> Where … there is a clear intent to create legal relations and the transaction or transactions are clearly of a commercial character, English law is perfectly ready to recognize the contractual relations that the parties so clearly intend and will not frustrate them on account of some difficulty of analysis.[2]

Some reinsurance contracts provide that disputes under the agreement are to be referred to arbitration and that the agreement itself is to be 'interpreted as an honourable engagement rather than as a legal obligation'. In the absence of an arbitration clause, this type of

[1] *Allis-Chalmers Co v Fidelity and Deposit Company of Maryland* (1916) 114 LT 433; *Murfitt v Royal Insurance Co* (1922) 38 TLR 334, 336 (McCardie J); *Kirby v Cosindit Societa per Azioni* [1969] 1 Lloyd's Rep 75.

[2] *General Accident Fire and Life Assurance Corpn Ltd v Tanter, The Zephyr* [1984] 1 Lloyd's Rep 58, 72 (Hobhouse J).

provision runs the risk of the contract being held void for uncertainty. However, since the passing of the Arbitration Act 1996, section 46, it has been permissible for the parties to agree that the arbitrators can decide the dispute in accordance with principles other than legal principles, and even before the Act the courts had managed to uphold the contract by holding that the words did no more than relieve the arbitrators from adhering to strict rules of construction.[3]

To determine whether an agreement has been concluded, the courts always look for an offer and a matching acceptance. In insurance, the offer will usually be made by the prospective insured completing a proposal form or other application – via a broker or an aggregator website – and sending it to the insurers.[4] The proposer will almost certainly not be aware of the detailed terms of the insurer's standard wording other than those that are subject to regulatory pre-contractual disclosure requirements, and the law recognises that an offer is made on the insurer's standard terms whether or not the insured are aware of them.[5] An offer continues until it is accepted or rejected by the offeree, a reasonable period of time has passed or it has been revoked by the offeror prior to acceptance.[6] Clearly, there can be no acceptance if the offeree is unaware of the existence of the offer since the parties could hardly be said to have come to an agreement.[7] The acceptance must match the offer and be unconditional, otherwise it may be regarded as a counter-offer, which will be a rejection of the original offer and will begin the whole process over again. It is important to distinguish a counter-offer from a mere inquiry about the terms of the offer, which does not amount to a rejection.[8] This distinction is not easily made and will depend on the particular circumstances. The negotiations for a commercial policy may be protracted and consist of a variety of exchanges by email, telephone and drafts.[9] Even in the consumer context, where in response to a proposal by the prospective insured the insurer sends out a policy that includes a term of which the prospective insured was previously unaware, this might constitute a counter-offer.[10] On the other hand, where the insurer responds with a policy in standard form, then as long as it is not inconsistent with the proposal, it may be held to be a valid acceptance even though it includes terms not expressly communicated, if the insured could reasonably be expected to know that there would be such terms.

Generally, the acceptance of the offer must be communicated to the offeror, unless the offeror waives this requirement.[11] It may be possible to infer acceptance from conduct, such as where the insured pays, or the insurers accept, the premium.[12] If the offer is made by the

[3] *Home Insurance Co and St Paul Fire and Marine Insurance Co v ADAS* [1983] 2 Lloyd's Rep 675; *Eagle Star Insurance Co v Yuval Insurance Co* [1978] 1 Lloyd's Rep 357.

[4] *Rust v Abbey Life Insurance Co Ltd* [1979] 2 Lloyd's Rep 334.

[5] *General Accident Insurance Corp v Cronk* (1901) 17 TLR 233; *Super Chem Products Ltd v American Life and General Insurance Co* [2004] Lloyd's Rep IR 446; *US Trading Ltd v Axa Insurance Co Ltd* [2010] Lloyd's Rep IR 505.

[6] The parties may have entered a separate contract under which the offeror is obliged to keep the offer open for a period of time.

[7] *Taylor v Allon* [1966] 1 QB 304.

[8] *Hyde v Wrench* (1840) 3 Beav 334; *Stevenson v McLean* (1880) 5 QBD 346.

[9] See the facts of *Landel Pty Ltd v Insurance Australia Ltd* [2021] QSC 247.

[10] *Canning v Farquhar* (1886) 16 QBD 727, 733 (Lindley LJ), but see the different analyses of the issues presented by Lord Esher MR and Lopes LJ.

[11] *Carlill v Carbolic Smoke Ball Co* [1893] 1 QB 256, 262 (Lindley LJ); *Brinkibon Ltd v Stahag Stahl und Stahlwarenhandelsgesellschaft mbH* [1983] 2 AC 34, 41 (Lord Wilberforce) and 48 (Lord Brandon). But see A Barron, 'Acceptance by Silence and Insurance Contracts' [2009] *Journal of Business Law* 633.

[12] *Canning v Farquhar* (1886) 16 QBD 727, 731 (Lord Esher MR).

insurer, the communication of an acceptance to a third party, such as a broker, is insufficient unless the broker is the agent of the insurer, which is not usually the case in the absence of special arrangements. Where the insurers offer to renew an annual motor policy by issuing a cover note that extends the old policy, the motorist can be deemed to have accepted by driving on the basis of that offer.[13] In *Rust v Abbey Life Assurance Co*,[14] Rust, having been given advice both by the insurers and by her own advisors, completed a proposal form and sent it to the insurance company. This action was treated by the Court of Appeal as an offer that the insurers accepted by sending out a policy, so the parties were bound. However, the court went on to say that, even if the insurer's action in sending out the policy was merely a counter-offer because it included terms not previously seen by Rust, her delay in taking seven months to object to those terms amounted to an acceptance. The court was not saying that silence amounts to an acceptance – it is a general rule that it does not[15] – but merely that acceptance can, in appropriate circumstances, be inferred from conduct. In view of the context of this case and in particular the extensive advice Rust had received, it was 'an inevitable inference from the conduct of the plaintiff in doing and saying nothing for seven months that she accepted the policy as a valid contract between herself and the first defendants'.[16] A case in which the insurers were bound in spite of not having communicated acceptance is *Roberts v Security Co Ltd*.[17] Roberts completed a proposal form for burglary insurance, which stated that he agreed to the usual terms applying. Subsequently, the company completed and sealed a policy, but did not deliver it to Roberts. He then suffered a loss through a burglary. The Court of Appeal held the insurers liable since their act of writing the policy signified acceptance even though they had not notified this fact to Roberts.

It is a general principle of contract law that once an offer has been accepted and an agreement formed neither party may unilaterally withdraw.[18] The contract may, of course, give the parties the right to cancel the contract. Where a policy contains a term allowing cancellation by the insurer, it will usually also provide for a portion of the premium to be repaid to the insured. There is old authority to the effect that the breadth of such clauses is not a matter in which the courts will interfere: so a clause giving the insurer an unfettered right to cancel will be enforced.[19] However, at least in consumer insurance contracts, such a term might be deemed unfair, and therefore not binding under the provisions of the Consumer Rights Act 2015. The insured also has certain statutory rights to cancel an insurance contract, which are independent of that contract.

It is common for an agreement on insurance to specify that either the contract is not binding or, alternatively, that the contract is binding but the risk does not commence, until a specified requirement is met, such as the payment of the premium or the completion of a satisfactory medical examination. In *Canning v Farquhar*,[20] between completing the

[13] *Taylor v Allon* [1966] 1 QB 304.

[14] [1979] 2 Lloyd's Rep 334.

[15] *Felthouse v Bindley* (1862) 11 CBNS 869; *De Mezey v Milwaukee Mechanics' Insurance Co* [1945] 12 ILR 122 (Alberta).

[16] Per Brandon LJ, 340.

[17] [1897] 1 QB 111.

[18] AH Hudson, 'Retraction of Letters of Acceptance' (1966) 82 *LQR* 169. There are situations in which one of the parties can avoid an insurance contract: for instance, as has been seen above, a failure by the insured to make a fair presentation of the risk may entitle the insurers to treat the contract as void: see ch 4.

[19] *Sun Fire Office v Hart* (1889) 14 App Cas 98.

[20] (1886) 16 QBD 727. See also *Harrington v Pearl Life Assurance Co* 30 Times LR 613; *Looker v Law and Union Rock Co Ltd* [1928] 1 KB 554; *British Credit Trust Holdings v UK Insurance Ltd* [2004] 1 All ER (Comm) 444; *Pilkington United Kingdom Ltd v CGU Insurance plc* [2004] Lloyd's Rep IR 891.

proposal form for life assurance and his agent tendering the first premium, Canning fell from a cliff and sustained an injury from which he later died. The Court of Appeal held that the insurers were not liable. Lord Esher MR and Lopes LJ decided that the offer was made when the premium was tendered and what came before that time was merely pre-contractual negotiation. Since this represents the majority opinion, it is the ratio decidendi of the case, but Lindley LJ reached the same conclusion by a different method. While he agreed that what went on before the tendering of the premium did not amount to a binding contract, he believed it was important since only by referring to what the other judges called negotiations could the terms of the contract be determined. He regarded the offer by the insurers as represented by the proposal plus the extra terms, such as the amount of the premium, which were mentioned later. That offer had been made on the basis of a statement in the proposal that Canning was in good health and since this was no longer true at the time the premium was tendered, the offer had lapsed and could no longer be accepted. On this analysis, if Canning's health had not changed, acceptance would have been by the prospective insured tendering the premium and not by the insurers accepting it since the offer by the insurers must be capable of acceptance by the prospective insured and this can only be the case if the act of acceptance is tendering the premium.[21]

A condition precedent may prevent the contract from coming into existence; or it may suspend either or both parties' obligations to perform, in whole or in part, until the condition is met; and it may also be that one or both parties is not allowed to withdraw. There may or may not be an obligation on one of the parties to fulfil the condition, so that failure to do so may or may not amount to a breach. Whether a term is a condition precedent and its effect depends on the intention of the parties so merely labelling it as a 'condition precedent' is not conclusive. A condition subsequent, on the other hand, is where the contract comes into existence and both parties must perform as agreed, but their obligations terminate on the happening of a specified event. Finally, as will be seen later in the discussion of claims, the policy may stipulate conditions precedent to recovery: the insured may be required to do certain things before the liability of the insurer is triggered, such as inform the insurer of the loss within a particular period of time. But this merely affects the liability of the insurer and not the formation of the contract.

The other point to make is that the formation of the insurance contract is affected by regulatory provisions made under the Financial Services and Markets Act 2000: 'A firm must take reasonable steps to ensure a customer is given appropriate information about a policy in good time and in a comprehensible form so that the customer can make an informed decision about the arrangements proposed.'[22] This will apply to new contracts and renewals.

[21] In some jurisdictions there are presumptions concerning the formation of the contract and the payment of the premium: in Alberta, for example, the policy will bind where it has been delivered irrespective of whether the premium has been paid (Insurance Act, RSA 1980, s 208(1); *McDowell v Wawanesa Mutual Insurance Co* 102 DLR (3d) 561 (Alberta)); in the USA, the courts in most states impose liability on the insurer where the insured has completed a proposal and paid the premium and there has been an unreasonable delay by the insurer in responding (J Lowry and P Rawlings, *Insurance Law: Cases and Materials* (Oxford, Hart Publishing, 2004) 236–38). See also *Elite Builders Ltd v Maritime Life Assurance Company* [1984] ILR 1-1798 (British Columbia); and in Australia, the Insurance Contracts Act 1984 (Cth), s 75.

[22] ICOBS, 6.1.5. See A Barron, 'Acceptance by Silence and Insurance Contracts' [2009] *Journal of Business Law* 633.

1.2. Commencement of the Risk

The date on which the contract of insurance is made and the date on which the risk commences are not necessarily the same. There is normally a gap between the date on which the offer and acceptance coincide, giving rise to a binding contract, and the date on which the risk commences so that the insurers face liability. The policy will normally specify a commencement date, but in some cases there will be a condition that has to be satisfied before the risk commences. That may be the date on which the premium is paid, although premiums these days are generally paid in instalments and so this form of provision is less common. In marine or buildings insurance, there may be inspection conditions and other requirements imposed upon the insured. It is important to remember that the duty of fair presentation comes to an end when the contract is made and not when the risk commences. Marine policies may be written on a time (day to day) or voyage (place to place) basis: policies on cargo are overwhelmingly in the form of voyage covers, commencing when the goods are first moved in a warehouse at the port of origin until safely stowed in the warehouse at the port of destination, so that loading and unloading risks are covered.[23] Voyage policies are also used for goods being transported by road, rail and air.

Leaving aside the special case of voyage policies, the policy will specify a commencement date and a termination date. If a policy runs, for example, from 1 January 2022 to 1 January 2023, if both days are included, then the policy actually runs for a year and a day. The presumption is that the start date is excluded, which is suggested by the word 'from', but that the policy is in force for the day specified as the termination date, although the policy may make the position clear by stating which dates are included or excluded, or by providing that both days are included in the coverage.[24] The default position is demonstrated by *Cartwright v McCormack*,[25] where a motor policy came into effect at 11.45 am on 2 December and was stated to be in force for 15 days from the date of commencement of the risk. An accident occurred at 5.45 pm on 17 December. The Court of Appeal held that there was coverage, in that the words 'date of commencement' excluded the first day so that the risk incepted at midnight on 2 December. This possibility gave rise to an interesting dispute in *QBE Insurance (International) Ltd v Allianz Australia Ltd*.[26] QBE issued a property policy for the period '4 September 2009 at 4 pm to 4 September 2010 at 4 pm'. The cover was renewed with Allianz under a policy stating that the 'effective date' was 4 September 2010. A loss by earthquake occurred at 4:35 am on 4 September. QBE was plainly liable for the claim, but asserted that Allianz was also liable with effect from the start of 4 September 2010 and sought to recover a proportionate part of the payment from Allianz under the contribution principle applicable where there are two policies in place covering the same loss, as discussed in chapter 12 below. The New Zealand Court of Appeal held that, construed objectively, the intentions of the parties to the Allianz contract was to provide successive cover but not overlapping cover, so the Allianz policy was to be construed as incepting at 4 pm on 4 September 2010 and therefore was not in place at the time of the earthquake.

[23] Institute Cargo Clauses 2009, cl 10.
[24] *Heinrich Hirdes GmbH v Edmunds, The Kiel* [1991] 2 Lloyd's Rep 546.
[25] [1963] 1 All ER 1.
[26] [2018] NZCA 239.

1.3. Renewals and Extensions

Where an insurance is for a limited period – and that is the case for the vast majority of non-life policies – and the parties choose to renew the cover at the expiration of that period, they enter a fresh contract on the same or different terms. As was seen in chapter four, the duty of fair presentation of the risk reattaches on renewal. A renewal must be distinguished from an extension in which the contract permits the parties to extend the period for which it operates. In a renewal, unless new terms have been incorporated into the new policy, the old terms will apply.[27] That distinction may be blurred by the use of 'automatic renewal' clauses, the effect of which is that the policy is automatically renewed on the renewal date unless one or other of the parties has given notice of termination,[28] and although it is almost certainly the case that the duty of fair presentation revives the duty that may be ousted by a clause providing for automatic renewal on unchanged terms.[29] It was also noted in chapter four that life policies are single contracts that do not renew but continue until the occurrence of the insured event, be it the death of the life insured or the expiry of a given period at the end of which the policy benefits are paid. This does not amount to a new contract, so the duty of disclosure does not revive.

There is no substance to the commonly held belief that cover automatically continues for a period after a policy has expired; furthermore, there is no obligation on the insurer to issue a notice to the effect that the cover is about to expire, even if it would seem to be good business practice for them to do so.[30] A contract of insurance can expressly allow days of grace for payment during which cover will continue. This is common in contracts of life assurance, where what is at issue is not the renewal of the contract but the continuation of the existing policy subject to cancellation in the event of the premium not being paid. If a loss should occur within the days of grace, the insured will be able to recover, although the premium must still be paid. Where a term of the contract allows days of grace and states that the policy will remain in force for a specified period 'from the date upon which the last premium became due', that period runs from the date when the premium was due and not from the end of the days of grace.[31]

1.4. Insurance Contracts in the Subscription Market

Consumer policies are generally subscribed to by a single insurer. Large commercial risks, including marine and reinsurance risks, are normally spread amongst a number of insurers, each subscribing for a proportion of the risk. Subscribing insurers may be insurance companies, Lloyd's syndicates[32] or a combination of the two.

[27] *Great North-Eastern Railway v Avon Insurance plc* [2001] 2 All ER (Comm) 526; *Axa Corporate Solutions SA v National Westminster Bank* [2010] EWHC 1915 (Comm).

[28] *Kirby v Cosindit* [1969] 1 Lloyd's Rep 75.

[29] *Arash Shipping Enterprises Co Ltd v Groupama Transport* [2011] EWCA Civ 620.

[30] *Mobil Pty Ltd v FM Insurance Ltd* (1986) 4 ANZ Ins Cas 60-718 (NSW). There are, however, certain regulatory requirements with respect to notification about a policy that is due to expire: see ch 2 above.

[31] *McKenna v City Life Assurance Co* [1919] 2 KB 491.

[32] Cresswell J provides a useful outline of the history and operation of Lloyd's in *Society of Lloyd's v Clementson* [1997] LRLR 175.

The manner in which a large commercial risk is placed in the London market has undergone important changes. The established practice, which dated back to the eighteenth century, was for a broker, acting as agent of the assured, to prepare a summary proposal, known as a slip, which would then be passed round potential subscribing insurers. Any insurer who wished to subscribe would 'scratch' (ie stamp and sign) the slip for a given percentage and thereby become bound to that percentage. The slip would continue to be submitted to successive insurers until the broker obtained the required level of cover. Thereafter, a formal policy wording would be issued on behalf of the market. Although the system lasted for well over 200 years, it was not free from difficulties. In the first place, market practice was slack, and very often no formal policy wording would be issued at all: that meant that the only evidence of a complex contract would be a short document, the slip, which contained little or no detail. If the slip was lost, there was no evidence at all as to the identity of the subscribers or the terms of cover.[33] Secondly, it was unclear, and indeed doubtful, whether a slip satisfied the requirements for a policy document imposed by section 22 of the Marine Insurance Act 1906, discussed below. Thirdly, the resolution of discrepancies between the slip and the policy was a matter of some complexity, and the courts could do no better than to say that whether the slip or policy prevailed or whether the slip could be used to rectify the policy in the event of any difference between them was a matter of fact to be determined in every case.[34]

The fear of the London market was that the lack of transparency in contract terms was a disincentive to potential assureds, and in 2001 a voluntary system – London Market Principles (LMP) – was adopted. Under this scheme, policy wordings would be issued in a standard form as soon as the slip was fully subscribed. In the event, the LMP were not widely followed, and this led the then regulator, the Financial Services Authority, to warn the market that unless something was done on a voluntary basis, then regulatory action would follow. The outcome was the adoption in 2008 of the Market Reform Contract (MRC). Under the MRC system, the broker is required to prepare the policy wording before the risk is presented. Accordingly, insurers are no longer presented with a slip. Instead, they receive the full policy wording, and they scratch not the slip but the policy itself. This overcomes the absence of wording, and it also minimises the possible argument that something other than what is contained in the policy was agreed between the broker and the insurers.[35] Thereafter, full policy documentation must be provided to the insured. It should be stressed that the MRC does not dictate the actual terms of cover; it merely requires that such terms exist from the outset. It remains the practice in the market for brokers to test the water by preparing quotation documents as a preliminary to circulating the MRC, so it remains necessary to determine whether any particular document is a formal offer or merely a request for a quotation. Insurers may for their part scratch the MRC conditionally only, for example subject to the receipt from the insured of a satisfactory proposal form or the answers to specific questions, so that they have the right to refuse cover if the further information provided is not satisfactory to them.[36]

[33] *Grace v Leslie & Godwin Financil Services Ltd* [1995] LRLR 472.

[34] *HIH Casualty and General Insurance v New Hampshire Insurance* [2001] 2 Lloyd's Rep 161.

[35] The process is described in *AIG Europe SA v John Wood Group PLC* [2022] EWCA Civ 781. See also the September 2018 'Principles and Guidance' issued by the London market: CC-COP-Sept-2018.pdf (lmg.london).

[36] *Involnert Management Inc v Aprilgrange Ltd* [2015] EWHC 2225 (Comm).

The change in documentation has not, however, altered the procedure for placing risks. The broker will, as before, in the first instance approach an underwriter who specialises in the particular risk. If the underwriter wishes to take a proportion of the risk, the underwriter will scratch it accordingly, subject to any necessary amendments to what has been proposed by the broker. This underwriter will generally, although not necessarily, take on the role of 'leading underwriter' in accordance with the usual 'leading underwriter clause' in the MRC, which allows this underwriter to negotiate amendments, and possibly even settle claims on behalf of all subscribing insurers.[37] Having obtained an initial scratch, the broker will continue round the market, presenting the MRC to other insurers, and the expertise of the leading underwriter in the particular field of insurance may make it easier for the broker to persuade others to subscribe. Once the MRC is fully subscribed, it will come into force on the day, or on the event (eg payment of the premium), specified in it.

One problem that arises from the practice of the London market involves the number of contracts that have been formed. Is there a single contract to which all those underwriters who subscribe to the MRC are parties, or are there separate contracts with each underwriter? If there are several contracts relating to the same risk, each underwriter could negotiate different terms, and if a claim were made, the underwriters would not be required to take a common position: 'some may contest it, some may compromise it and others may decide to pay in full'.[38] These 'absurd consequences' led Donaldson J to take the view that the contract was not concluded until the slip (now the MRC) was fully subscribed.[39] The Court of Appeal, however, was less convinced of their absurdity and rejected his approach.[40] The Court held that a contract exists once the agreement is scratched by the underwriter, and therefore each such subscription amounts to a separate contract.[41] A contract (or contracts) exists even where the MRC never becomes fully subscribed. The market does recognise the difficulty of having each underwriter negotiating different terms and, in practice, this does not happen, particularly in view of the willingness to defer to the lead underwriter's expertise. Indeed, it is common to include in the MRC 'the leading underwriter clause', referred to above.

If the MRC is over-subscribed, ie the underwriters taken together have agreed to cover more than the size of the risk, their liability (and the premium due to each underwriter), by a custom recognised by the courts by way of exception to the general rule, will be reduced

[37] *Roadworks (1952) Ltd v JR Charman* [1994] 2 Lloyd's Rep 99; *American International Marine Agency of New York v Dandridge* [2005] EWHC 829 (Comm). It is unclear whether the leading underwriter is the agent of the other insurers or whether the actions of the leading underwriter simply operate as a 'trigger' which operates to bind them automatically to what the leading underwriter has agreed. The latter view seems preferable, in that it prevents the following underwriters for seeking relief for breach of the agency agreement, although that does not necessarily mean that the leading underwriter does not owe a duty of care: those points were made by Teare J in *San Evans Maritime Inc v Aigaion Insurance Co SA* [2014] EWHC 163 (Comm).

[38] *General Reinsurance Corporation v Forsakringsaktiebolaget Fennia Patria* [1983] QB 856, 864 (Kerr LJ).

[39] *Jaglom v Excess Insurance Co Ltd* [1972] 2 QB 251, 257.

[40] *General Reinsurance Corporation v Forsakringsaktiebolaget Fennia Patria*, 866 (Kerr LJ). See also the Court of Appeal's rejection of the different approach to this problem by Staughton J at first instance. He argued that, while there was a contract at the time of scratching, the custom of the market gave the broker the right to cancel up to the time when the slip was fully subscribed. The Court of Appeal recognised that, while underwriters might well allow a broker to cancel in order to maintain the good business relations, the broker has no legal right to require them to do so.

[41] *Touche Ross & Co v Baker* [1992] 2 Lloyd's Rep 207; *Royal & Sun Alliance Insurance plc v Textainer Group Holdings Ltd* [2021] EWHC 2102 (Comm).

in the proportion that their part of the risk bears to the whole.[42] This means that at the point of the subscription it will not be clear what is the underwriter's share of the risk or premium. The broker can approach the underwriters with an estimate as to the likely size of the over-subscription ('a signing indication') and hence the final percentage of the risk which each underwriter will bear, although the broker is probably not liable if the indicated level of signing down is not obtained.[43] The obverse of over-subscription is where the broker fails to obtain complete cover. This does not entitle the insured (or, of course, the underwriter) to cancel the contracts already agreed between the broker and the underwriters who have scratched the MRC, although the underwriters might not resist such a request from the broker since they may take the view that to do so would undermine the goodwill between brokers and underwriters on which the market depends.[44]

There is also the problem that statements made by the insured's broker to the leading underwriter will not be actionable as misrepresentations by later underwriters because, while statements made by the broker may have induced the leading underwriter to enter the contract, this will not have been the case with those subsequent underwriters.[45]

1.5. Formalities

There is no general rule at common law requiring insurance contracts to be written.[46] Suggestions in *Hampton v Toxteth Co-operative Provident Society Ltd*[47] that a contract of insurance required the existence of a written policy should be treated as confined to the special circumstances of that case, which concerned a statutory provision – long since repealed – that precluded regulation of contracts not embodied in a policy. An insurance contract may be formed orally and 'can be made in informal, colloquial language'.[48] The contract is indeed made when offer and acceptance coincide, and in the modern era of face-to-face electronic communication there may well be nothing written at that point. Invariably, however, the agreement will be followed by proper policy wording, and we have seen earlier in this chapter that business placed in the London subscription market must be in the form of a written document containing the terms of cover submitted by the broker and signed and stamped by the insurers.

Leaving aside industry practice, in the case of some types of insurance a written policy or written evidence of the existence of a contract is necessary, although the provisions are of some antiquity. The Life Assurance Act 1774 states that 'it shall not be lawful' to make any life policy without inserting the name of the person who is to benefit, which suggests

[42] *General Reinsurance Corporation v Forsakringsaktiebolaget Fennia Patria* [1983] QB 856; *Ionides and Chapeaurouge v Pacific Fire and Marine Insurance Co* (1871) LR 6 QB 674, 684–85 (Blackburn J); *Morrison v Universal Marine Insurance Co* (1872) LR 8 Ex 40, 45 and (1873) LR 8 Ex 197, 199; *Eagle Star Insurance Co Ltd v Spratt* [1971] 2 Lloyd's Rep 116; Marine Insurance Act 1906, s 21.

[43] *General Accident Fire and Life Assce Corpn v Tanter, The Zephyr* [1984] 1 Lloyd's Rep 58.

[44] *General Reinsurance Corporation v Forsakringsaktiebolaget Fennia Patria* [1983] QB 856, 874 (Slade LJ). A broker who is unsure whether there is sufficient interest in the market may circulate a quotation slip, which is not an offer, but may reveal any difficulties and will, for instance, enable the broker to adjust the terms of the slip.

[45] *General Accident Fire and Life Assce Corpn v Tanter, The Zephyr* [1984] 1 Lloyd's Rep 58.

[46] *Murfitt v Royal Insurance Co Ltd* (1921–22) 38 TLR 334, 335 (McCardie J).

[47] [1915] 1 Ch 72. See also *Hall D'Ath v British Provident Association for Hospital and Additional Services* (1932) 48 TLR 240.

[48] *Stockton v Mason and the Vehicle and General Insurance Co Ltd and Arthur Edward (Insurance) Ltd* [1978] 2 Lloyd's Rep 430, 432.

that a written document is required (section 2).[49] This supplements the prohibition on insurance on lives without interest in the 1774 Act and is discussed in chapter six below. The 1774 Act does not apply to other classes of insurance,[50] and the only other statutory formality applicable to property policies is found in the Marine Insurance Act 1788, under which the name of the insured or agent must be inserted into a policy on goods or merchandise. The Act has long been redundant. By sections 22 and 23 of the Marine Insurance Act 1906 a marine insurance contract is inadmissible unless embodied in a policy. The English and Scottish Law Commissions examined this requirement in Issues Paper 9, published in October 2010. They argued that section 22 is out of date because it originates from the imposition of stamp duty in 1795 and was designed to prevent the parties from agreeing insurance contracts without paying tax. As stamp duty was abolished in 1970, they argued that its original justification has disappeared, and it has the potential to cause problems for insureds and for recent contract certainty initiatives. The paper concluded that there should be no special formality requirements, meaning that section 22 should be repealed, bringing it in line with normal contract rules that apply to non-marine insurance. That proposal was not implemented in the Insurance Act 2015. In practice it is of no significance, and leaving it on the statute book does no harm.

In relation to some other types of insurance, it may be a criminal offence not to have a particular document, but such a failure does not necessarily affect the enforceability of the contract itself. The insurance contract which is mandatory under the Employers' Liability (Compulsory Insurance) Act 1969 does not have to be written, but a certificate of insurance must be issued by the insurers and displayed by the insured (section 4). That Act also refers to the employer insuring 'under one or more approved policies' (section 1), which might suggest the need for a document, although probably the word 'policies' is simply used as a synonym for contract of insurance. It is an offence under the Road Traffic Act 1988 to use a motor vehicle unless it is covered by 'a policy of insurance', and 'a policy' will have no effect for the purposes of the Act until the insurers have delivered to the insured 'a certificate of insurance' in a particular form.[51] Moreover, a motorist commits an offence by failing to produce such a certificate when required to do so by a police officer.[52]

2. Temporary Cover

It often happens that, pending the writing of a policy or a decision over renewal, the insurers will offer to provide temporary cover for a short period during which decisions are to be made. Such temporary cover amounts to a contract of insurance and is particularly

[49] The assumption that the word 'policy' means a written document is commonplace: *Hall D'Ath v British Provident Association for Hospital and Additional Services* (1932) 48 TLR 240. However, it has been held that the word 'policy' includes any insurance contract, whether written or not: *Re Norwich Equitable Fire Assurance Society Royal Insurance Co's Claim* (1887) 57 LT 241, 246 (Kay J).

[50] *Mark Rowlands Ltd v Berni Inns Ltd* [1985] 3 All ER 473; *Siu v Eastern Insurance Co Ltd* [1994] 1 All ER 213.

[51] Road Traffic Act 1988, ss 143, 145 and 147. If for some reason the policy is voidable, there is no offence of driving without insurance since the policy is valid until it is avoided: *Goodbarne v Buck* [1940] 1 KB 771. See ch 13 below.

[52] Road Traffic Act 1988, s 165.

common in those areas of insurance where the law requires some form of documentary evidence of cover, such as is the case with motor insurance under the Road Traffic Act 1988.[53] Insurers commonly authorise brokers to enter into provisional contracts, and where such an arrangement exists the broker will be agent for both parties and will have express authority to bind the insurers.[54]

The normal analysis of contract formation applies: the offer will have been made by the prospective insured, usually through the completion of a proposal form, and acceptance is by the insurer offering temporary cover. In the case of a renewal, the insurers may allow the insured a period during which cover is maintained so that if the insured renews – or indeed obtains cover elsewhere – there is no gap in coverage, a matter particularly important for activities where insurance is compulsory against potential liabilities In this situation, the insurer makes the offer to renew cover for the interim period pending agreement on a fresh contract, and it is the insured that has the choice to accept or refuse this offer.[55] Once the formal policy is issued, the temporary cover terminates. Where the insurers decide during the currency of the temporary cover not to take on the risk, then the cover notice expires when they notify the insured of this decision and the note will usually be issued on terms entitling its cancellation.[56] The cover note will state the period during which it provides cover and it will cease to operate once that period has passed, whether or not another cover note or a full policy has been issued.

Whether what seems to be a cover note does, in fact, amount to a contract of insurance depends on it fulfilling the normal requirements for a contract: it is possible that the note is merely a receipt for money paid in advance and that there is no insurance until the company has properly considered the proposal. The case of the loquacious motorist, *Taylor v Allon*,[57] provides a salutary illustration of the contractual significance of the cover note, and in particular demonstrates that when issued by the insurer the note merely amounts to an offer which crystallises into a contract only if accepted by the prospective insured. A motorist was convicted of driving a car while not insured. His old insurance policy had expired on 5 April and the insurers sent a cover note to provide insurance for 15 days. On 16 April the motorist obtained cover with a different company. Unfortunately, he had been stopped by the police the day before. He not only failed to produce the cover note, but told the police he was negotiating a change of insurers and that he did not realise the old policy had expired. The court upheld his conviction for driving without insurance. The cover note amounted to an offer to extend the insurance period, which he had not accepted merely by driving. There was, therefore, no insurance contract and he was guilty of the offence charged. It is implicit in this case that by issuing the cover note the insurers are making an offer the acceptance of which does not have to be communicated. The motorist must still accept the offer, although the act of acceptance need only be such as would lead a reasonable person to infer that it had been accepted,[58]

[53] See ch 13 below.

[54] *Stockton v Mason and the Vehicle and General Insurance Co Ltd and Arthur Edward (Insurance) Ltd* [1978] 2 Lloyd's Rep 430, 431.

[55] This arrangement is commonplace in motor vehicle liability insurance, where the insurer will issue a cover note for a brief period pending a decision on renewal because otherwise the motorist would commit an offence under the Road Traffic Act 1988 in continuing to drive without insurance.

[56] *Stockton v Mason and the Vehicle and General Insurance Co Ltd and Arthur Edward (Insurance) Ltd* 1978] 2 Lloyd's Rep 430, 431 (Lord Diplock).

[57] [1966] 1 QB 304.

[58] *Carlill v Carbolic Smoke Ball Co* [1893] 1 QB 256.

which might be simply driving in reliance on the offer. The offer in the renewal notice will lapse by the end of the expiration of the period specified, or earlier if either the insurer communicates their withdrawal of the offer[59] or the insured rejects the offer.[60]

Temporary cover may also be offered conditionally on the payment of premium. In *Danbol Pty Ltd v Swiss Re International Se*,[61] insurance on business premises was in place up to 24 August 2018. The insurers decided not to renew the cover, as they regarded the storage of gas bottles on the premises as too great a risk. Negotiations continued, and on the day of expiry the insurers emailed the insured maintaining their refusal to renew but adding 'given the time-frame we will offer 14 days extension to assist with placement', the quoted premium being $3506.06. A loss occurred on 30 August 2018, but at that time no premium had been paid. The Court of Appeal of Victoria held that there was no temporary cover: a condition for payment of the premium had been imposed, but it had not been satisfied by the insured and so the offer had not been accepted.

In non-consumer contracts, the insured is under the duty of fair presentation up to the point at which the insurers agree to issue the cover note following a proposal by the insured,[62] or, in the case of a cover note sent by insurers to extend existing cover, within a reasonable period of time after receipt.[63] The cover note will not amount to a contract unless there is agreement on the material terms (risk, duration of cover, premium). It will be subject to such terms as were notified at the time it was made and any loss which occurs while it is in operation will be dealt with under its terms rather than those of any later, permanent policy, even where that policy purports to have retrospective effect.[64] If the cover note is issued following the expiration of a policy, the presumption will be that the cover is on the same terms as the old policy.[65] Where the cover note mentions terms or refers to another document which is accessible to the insured and in which terms are listed, then those terms will apply. There is likely to be no problem if the insured has completed a proposal form since that form or the accompanying literature will usually mention the terms upon which the insurers undertake insurance business. In addition, as has been seen, there are strong authorities suggesting that the insurer's standard terms will be implied, unless a contrary intention can be shown or those terms are not reasonably available for inspection.[66] On the other side is the decision in *Re Coleman's Depositories Ltd and Life & Health Assurance Association*.[67] An employer completed a proposal form for insurance to cover liability to employees injured at work and a cover note was issued on 28 December. A policy was issued on 3 January which purported

[59] *Maguire v AMP Fire & General Insurance Co Ltd* (1982) ANZ Ins Cas 60-470 (New Zealand).

[60] The motorist in *Taylor v Allon* had not rejected the offer since, although he was negotiating cover with another company, at the time he was stopped he had not entered into another contract and might, therefore, have become aware of and decided to take up the offer contained in the cover note. Nevertheless, this does not help him because he had not accepted the offer in the cover note, and therefore there was no contract based on its terms. In *China Ping An Insurance (Hong Kong) Co Ltd v Tsang Fung Yin* [2012] HKCFI 390 the Hong Kong Court of First Instance found a contract on very similar facts, and *Taylor v Allon* was simply not referred to in the judgment.

[61] [2020] VSCA 274.

[62] *Mayne Nickless v Pegler* [1974] 1 NSWLR 228.

[63] *Marene Knitting Mills v Greater Pacific General Insurance Ltd* [1976] 2 Lloyd's Rep 631.

[64] *Re Coleman's Depositories Ltd and Life & Health Assurance Association* [1907] 2 KB 798.

[65] *Stockton v Mason and the Vehicle and General Insurance Co Ltd and Arthur Edward (Insurance) Ltd* [1978] 2 Lloyd's Rep 430, 431 (Lord Diplock).

[66] *General Accident Insurance Co v Cronk* (1901) 17 TLR 233; MA Clarke, 'Notice of Contractual Terms' (1976) 35 *CLJ* 51.

[67] [1907] 2 KB 798; also *Neil v The South East Lancashire Insurance Co Ltd* 1932 SC 35.

to be effective from 1 January. This was delivered to the employer on 9 January. The policy required the employer to notify the insurer immediately after an employee was injured at work, but this term had not been mentioned when the cover note was issued. The relevant accident occurred on 2 January. It was held that because the insured was unaware of the term until 9 January, it did not apply to this accident. The decision seems curious and could present problems were it not for the fact that insurers have adopted the practice of expressly referring to their usual policy terms in the cover note, much as a railway company refers to its standard terms and leaves it up to the traveller to enquire as to what they are.

---

3. Premium

3.1. Payment of the Premium

Each party to an insurance contract must provide consideration: normally,[68] the insured agrees to pay a premium and the insurers promise to provide a benefit in the event of a loss arising that falls within the terms of the policy. The premium will be set by the insurers at a level that attracts business, but that also both reflects the risk of a claim by this insured and, across the business as a whole, is likely to result in a profit.[69] The premium will be payable either in a single sum or, more typically, by instalments on credit terms. Even where the premium is payable by instalments, it is still a single premium for the entire period, so that if the risk is terminated the outstanding instalments will still have to be paid on the principle that the risk is not divisible unless the parties have agreed to the contrary.[70]

The premium is an important aspect of the agreement, and if one has not been agreed by the parties this may indicate that they have not concluded a contract. Where an 'agreement' for insurance on building work specified 'a reasonable premium', it was held that there was no contract since 'it cannot be said that there is a sum which can be defined and described as being undisputed'.[71] Yet, the failure to set the amount of the premium may not be fatal. In the case of a normal risk, such as involved in burglary insurance or motor vehicle liability, the amount of the premium is set according to the insurer's usual tariff. Indeed, the Marine Insurance Act 1906, section 31(1) recognises the common practice of effecting marine insurance at a premium 'to be arranged' (generally shortened to TBA). If the parties never specify what that premium is, then 'a reasonable premium is payable', which means one calculated at the prevailing market rate. The issue of premium calculation may arise where the risk terminates but the insurers have by means of a 'held covered' clause agreed to continue the insurance subject to payment of a further premium. The Marine Insurance Act 1906, section 31(2) allows the parties to provide for an additional premium in such circumstances, and if no additional premium is agreed, then a reasonable premium will be payable.

[68] But not always. In 'after the event' insurance, which is taken out by a claimant to fund litigation, no premium is paid at the outset. If the claimant wins, the premium is paid by the defendant by way of costs. If the claimant loses, the premium is absorbed by the insurers.

[69] Insurers do not, of course, simply rely on premium income to meet their obligations. Premium income is invested and insurers also pass on risk through reinsurance contracts (on which see ch 17 below).

[70] *JA Chapman & Co Ltd v Kadirga Denizcilik ve Tikaret AS* [1998] Lloyd's Rep IR 377.

[71] *Kirby v Cosindit Societa per Azioni* [1969] 1 Lloyd's Rep 75, 79 (Megaw J).

However, that is conditional on the risk being insurable: if agreement cannot be reached and there is no market rate, then the held covered clause cannot operate.[72]

The premium will usually be a payment of money,[73] but can take almost any form as long as there is, in the words of Lush J when speaking of consideration more broadly,[74] 'some right, interest, profit, or benefit accruing to the one party, or some forbearance, detriment, loss, or responsibility given, suffered, or undertaken by the other'. For instance, the Marine Insurance Act 1906, section 85(2) recognises mutual marine insurance agreements under which shipowner members do not pay a premium but pay an initial sum and then agree to contribute by way of 'calls' to losses suffered by fellow members as and when they occur.[75]

Offers of 'free insurance' have sometimes been made by a variety of businesses, from credit card issuers to newspapers and car retailers, as a way of enticing potential customers to buy products or as a means of acquiring marketing information about customers.[76] In such cases, even though there is no premium in the form of money, it is not usually difficult to discover consideration. For instance, an agreement to provide insurance might be collateral to an agreement to open a credit card account: in exchange for the promise to provide insurance, the consumer promises to enter into the main agreement. *Imperial Tobacco Ltd v Attorney-General*,[77] while not on the issue of insurance, gives some indication of the willingness of the courts to surmount this problem of consideration in appropriate cases. Purchasers of a certain brand of cigarettes obtained the chance of winning a cash prize, and the House of Lords ruled that, although no extra was charged for the cigarettes, there was consideration for the chance:

> [W]here a person buys two things for one price, it is impossible to say that he had paid only for one of them and not for the other. The fact that he could have bought one of the things at the same price as he paid for both, is in my view immaterial.[78]

In *Fuji Finance Inc v Aetna Life Insurance Co Ltd*,[79] Nicholls V-C expressed the view that if there were no attempts to link the amount of the premium to the risk this might indicate that the agreement was not an insurance contract. This might exclude 'free insurance' offers, since even if it is possible to find consideration it will not be based on an actuarial calculation. It seems better to use the lack of a link between the consideration and the risk as an indicator rather than as conclusive evidence that there is no insurance contract, and to be

[72] *Liberian Insurance Agency Inc v Mosse* [1977] 2 Lloyd's Rep 560.

[73] *Lion Mutual Marine Insurance Association Ltd v Tucker* (1883) 12 QBD 176, 187 (Brett MR).

[74] *Currie v Misa* (1875) LR Ex 153, 162.

[75] Such agreements historically played an important role in providing protection and indemnity cover (P&I cover) for ships in circumstances where it was difficult to obtain insurance from commercial insurers at reasonable rates. Nowadays, P&I clubs provide cover for shipowners' liabilities, in particular crew injury, cargo claims and pollution liabilities. Some P&I clubs specialise in war risks cover. See *The Standard Steamship Owners' Protection and Indemnity Association (Bermuda) Ltd v Gann* [1992] 2 Lloyd's Rep 528; HN Bennett, *The Law of Marine Insurance* (Oxford, Clarendon Press, 2006); T Coghlin, 'Protection and Indemnity Clubs' [1984] *Lloyd's Maritime and Commercial Law Quarterly* 403; M Tilley, 'The Origin and Development of the Mutual Shipowners' Protection & Indemnity Associations' (1986) 17 *Journal of Money Laundering Control* 261; M Tilley, 'Protection and Indemnity Club Rules and Direct Actions by Third Parties' (1986) 17 *Journal of Money Laundering Control* 427.

[76] In view of the regulatory restrictions on those who may offer insurance (see ch 2 above), such offers will be made under authority granted by an authorised insurer.

[77] [1981] AC 718.

[78] ibid 739 (Viscount Dilhorne).

[79] [1995] Ch 122. The decision was reversed on appeal, but the issue discussed here was not mentioned: [1997] Ch 173.

fair this seems to have been what Nicholls V-C was himself suggesting. In *Nelson and Co v Board of Trade*,[80] Nelson, a firm of tea merchants, offered an annuity for life to customers who were widowed (the offer was only open to women) and who could establish a record of tea purchases from the company. The customers did not pay a premium, and the funds for the annuity came out of the company's general profits. There was no policy – only a card on which purchases were recorded – but the court found no difficulty in concluding that this was insurance business. However, the issue of the premium was not specifically raised. That case was not followed by the Court of Appeal in *Hampton v Toxteth Co-operative Provident Society Limited*.[81] The society ran a general shop and advertised the offer of 'free life assurance'. Death benefits proportionate to a member's expenditure were to be paid out of what was called an 'Insurance Fund'. The majority of the judges took the view that the lack of either a policy or a premium and the apparent power the society had to stop allocating money to the fund showed that this was not life insurance but merely an allocation of the society's profits that could be terminated at any time.[82]

At common law, payment of the premium to a broker is not payment to the insurer unless the policy otherwise provides, although this principle has been reversed by the *FCA Handbook*, Client Assets (CASS) 5.2.1 stating that there is a deemed receipt by the insurers. In the unique context of marine insurance, the obligation to pay the premium rests on the broker and not the insured, and that is the case whether or not the insured has first paid the broker,[83] so the broker carries the risk that the premium is not paid by the insured.[84] In July 2010 the English and Scottish Law Commissions published Issues Paper 8, titled *The Broker's Liability for Premiums: Should Section 53 Be Reformed?*[85] They highlighted that the rule that the premium under a marine policy is to be paid by the broker and not by the insured has its origins in eighteenth-century market practice and had created a number of legal and practical difficulties. The Law Commissions concluded that the default position should be that insureds be liable for the premium for the cover from which they benefit and the broker only be liable if it has expressly assumed such liability. That reform was not adopted in the Insurance Act 2015 and section 53 continues to operate.

3.2. Effect of Non-payment of Premium

The consequences of non-payment of the premium are determined primarily by the policy itself. In some cases it may be specified that the contract does not come into existence, or

[80] (1901) 84 LT 564.

[81] [1915] 1 Ch 721, although see the strong dissenting judgment by Phillimore LJ, who mentioned the case, as did counsel.

[82] Lord Cozens-Hardy MR did refer to the use of the words 'free insurance' in the society's advertising as 'inaccurate, misleading, and highly improper': [1915] 2 Ch 721, 733. It is worth noting that the case concerned whether the company's offer brought it within the terms of the Assurance Companies Act 1909, which regulated insurance and which only applied if a policy had been issued (s 1). See also *Hall D'Ath v British Provident Association for Hospital and Additional Services* (1932) 48 TLR 240. The decisions discussed in the text turn on their particular facts and the issues would now be affected by the regulatory legislation (see ch 2 above).

[83] Marine Insurance Act 1906, s 53(1); *Carvill America Incorp v Camperdown UK* [2005] EWCA Civ 645.

[84] For that reason the policy may confer the right to cancel upon a broker who is not indemnified for the payment by the insured.

[85] A Tettenborn, 'Section 53 of the Marine Insurance Act 1906 – an Exercise in Streamlining?' [2013] *Lloyd's Maritime and Commercial Law Quarterly* 401.

alternatively the contract is made but the risk does not attach unless the premium – or the first instalment of the premium – has been paid. Assuming that the risk has attached but no payment is made, the insurers may bring an action for the premium, but that would be most unusual, particularly in consumer cases. That nevertheless did occur in *Clydesdale Financial Services Ltd v Smailes*,[86] although the action was dismissed insofar as the risk had not attached. The insured, a firm of solicitors, brought personal injury claims for clients on a contingency fee basis, and funded their activities by bank loans. The firm took out financial guarantee insurance which made payment in the event that a client claim was defeated so that no fee became payable. Some 839 policies were issued, but no premiums were paid. It was held that the insurers could recover the premiums only on nine of the policies because for the remaining 830 policies loans had not been taken out and so the risk had not attached.

More commonly, the policy will provide that no claim is to be paid unless the premium has been received, although an express provision to that effect is required as the common law position is that payment of the premium and payment of the loss are independent obligations subject only to a right of set-off in respect of the unpaid premium from the sum due from the insurers.[87] The policy term may be more extreme and provide for forfeiture of the policy or all benefits under the policy in the event of non-payment. However, where the policy merely sets out a given time by which premiums have to be paid, the insured's failure to meet the date will not automatically amount to a forfeiture of the policy: that can happen only if the policy provides that payment by the due date is 'of the essence'. If time is not of the essence, then the insured is in breach of contract but that breach is not regarded as repudiatory and forfeiture is possible only after the insurers have given notice to the insured that they require payment within a specified further period and payment has still not been made.[88]

3.3. Return of Premium

The rules on return of premium were determined by a series of marine cases at the end of the eighteenth century, as codified in section 84 of the Marine Insurance Act 1906. The starting point is that the premium is earned only when the insurers first come on risk, so that if the risk never attaches, the insurers have to return any premium on the basis of total failure of consideration.[89] The premium will be repayable where the insurers avoid the contract because of a breach of the duty of fair presentation of the risk,[90] or where there is a mistake of fact or law which renders the contract void, as, for instance, would be the case if both parties entered into a life insurance contract in the mistaken belief that the insured life was alive.[91]

[86] [2009] EWHC 3190 (Ch).
[87] *Lake v Reinsurance Corp Ltd* 1967 (3) SA 124 (South Africa).
[88] *Fenton Insurance Co Ltd v Gothaer Versicherungsbank Wag* [1991] 1 Lloyd's Rep 172; *Figre Ltd v Mander* [1999] Lloyd's Rep IR 193.
[89] *Stevenson v Snow* (1761) 3 Burr 1237, 1240; *Tyrie v Fletcher* (1774) 2 Cowp 666; s 84(1) of the 1906 Act. The principle applies to all forms of insurance: *Clydesdale Financial Services Ltd v Smailes* [2009] EWHC 3190 (Ch).
[90] On these issues, see ch 4 above.
[91] See below.

However, again consistently with the principle of total failure of consideration, if the risk has attached for any time at all, the insurers potentially face liability under the policy and the premium has been fully earned. Apportionment on a time on risk basis has not been recognised by the common law. Thus, as soon as the risk has attached, no part of it is returnable even if the policy comes to an end a day later. There are two important exceptions to this general rule. First, the policy may by its terms be apportionable as between different risks, although that is a comparatively rare possibility. In *Swiss Reinsurance Co v United India Insurance Co Ltd*,[92] the reinsurance policy in question was on construction risks associated with the building of a power plant. As is usually the case, under construction all risks policies there was separate cover for the period of construction itself and for a 12-month maintenance period running from the date of the handover of the works to the client. The premiums for these periods had been calculated separately and simply aggregated. The construction work was halted and the policy was held by the court to have lapsed. The reinsured was plainly unable to recover the premium for the construction period, but argued that the premium was to be apportioned between the building and maintenance period and that, as the latter had not commenced, the premium was to that extent recoverable. Morison J disagreed, holding that there was a single policy and that it was inappropriate to apportion the premium even though it might have been calculated on that basis. The second possibility, which is commonly found in motor policies at least, is that there is to be a pro rata refund of premium (minus expenses) if the policy is cancelled early, eg because the insured has sold the insured vehicle. The possibility of agreement to that effect is recognised by section 93 of the Marine Insurance Act 1906.

---

4. Mistake

4.1. Effect of Mistake on the Contract

What happens if one or both of the parties are mistaken about some aspect of the agreement? In broad terms, contract law will not intervene unless the mistake has been induced by a false statement by one of the parties. What is otherwise required for judicial intervention is a mistake that demonstrates that there was never any real agreement, or that the fundamental assumption upon which the insurance was based was false.[93] In such cases the purported agreement is of no effect and the court will order the return of any premium paid.[94]

The fact that one party to a contract realises that the other party is mistaken does not by itself impose a duty to point out that mistake, unless failing to do so would be a breach of the duty of disclosure, or there is an element of misrepresentation or fraud in the concealment.[95] In *The Prince of Wales, &c Association v Palmer*,[96] evidence was brought

[92] [2005] Lloyd's Rep IR 341.

[93] *Great Peace Shipping Ltd v Tsavliris Salvage (International) Ltd, The Great Peace* [2002] 4 All ER 689.

[94] *Fowler v The Scottish Equitable Life Insurance Society and Ritchie* (1858) 28 LJ Ch 225.

[95] *Container Transport International Inc and Reliance Group Inc v Oceanus Mutual Underwriting Association (Bermuda) Ltd* [1984] 1 Lloyd's Rep 476, 512 (Parker LJ).

[96] (1855) 25 Beav 605.

to show that William Palmer had induced his brother, Walter, to take out a life insurance policy on his own life with the intention of later persuading Walter to assign the benefit of that policy to William and then, in the rather understated words of Romilly MR, 'precipitating, by his own act, the period at which those insurances were to become claims on the insurance offices'. William was later accused by a coroner's jury of murdering Walter, but was never convicted of that crime, although he was hanged for the murder of John Parsons Cobb. In an action on the policy on Walter's life, the court concluded that the contract had been entered into for fraudulent purposes and was, therefore, void.[97]

It may be that there is genuine agreement and no misunderstanding between the parties, but they share a mistaken belief about the existence of a particular state of affairs which is fundamental to the contract: that the person whose life is being insured is alive, the ship is afloat or the house is standing when, in fact, she is dead, the ship is at the bottom of the sea and the house is a pile of ashes.[98] In *Pritchard v Merchants' and Tradesmen's Mutual Life Assurance Society*,[99] the insurers accepted the renewal of an annual life insurance policy without requiring proof of the good health of the insured life, although the terms of the agreement allowed them to demand it. Neither the insurers nor the person renewing the policy was aware that the insured life had already died. The court held that the payment of the premium and its acceptance were founded on a mistake. The court reasoned that the continued good health of the insured life must have been regarded by the parties as central to the contract, otherwise it would have been pointless to mention it.[100] Similarly, in *Scott v Coulson*,[101] the sale of a life assurance contract was void for mistake because both parties wrongly believed the person whose life was the subject of the contract was still alive. In *Strickland v Turner*,[102] a contract for the sale of an annuity on the life a man who, unknown to both parties, was already dead was held to be void because there was a total failure of consideration, the purchaser having received nothing in exchange for the price paid. A more recent example may be found in the decision of the New Zealand High Court in *ECH Holdings Ltd v Vero Insurance New Zealand Ltd.*[103] Here, the insured's building had been badly damaged in the Canterbury earthquakes in 2010 and 2011. The insured renewed the insurance for a further three years, at which point the claim was finally settled on the basis that the building had been rendered a total loss by the earthquakes so that the renewals were of no benefit to the insured. The Court held that the premiums paid under the renewal contracts should be returned to the insured on the basis of total failure of consideration, although somewhat inexplicably the Court did not go further and rule that the renewals were void for fundamental mistake. Lesser mistakes that do not affect the operability of the policy will not suffice. In *O'Kane v Jones*,[104] the insured's agent obtained a hull policy in the

[97] This must be distinguished from the more common situation where the life insurance policy was entered into without the intention of murdering the insured life and claiming. In that case, the contract is valid but unenforceable by the murderer. In the *Palmer* case, the contract was void *ab initio* for fraud.

[98] *Galloway v Galloway* (1914) 30 TLR 531; *McRae v Commonwealth Disposals Commission* (1951) 84 CLR 377. See ch 9 below.

[99] (1858) 3 CB (NS) 622.

[100] The contract obliged the insurer to accept the renewal if the premium was paid within 30 days. If the premium was paid outside that period but within three months, the insurance might be revived 'on satisfactory proof of health'. Payment arrived two days outside the 30-day period.

[101] [1903] 2 Ch 249.

[102] (1852) 7 Exch 208.

[103] [2021] NZHC 3104.

[104] [2005] Lloyd's Rep IR 174.

mistaken belief that an existing policy had been cancelled for non-payment of the premiums. It was held that the second policy was not void for mistake, that the insured had two valid policies and that the insured was entitled to bring a claim under either of the policies up to the full amount of its loss. The significance of the point was that the insurers under the second policy were liable for a contribution claim from the first insurers who had duly paid the loss. Double insurance and contribution are discussed in chapter 12 below.

Mistake as to the identity of the person with whom a contract is being made has always caused difficulty. The key is that the person asking for relief must show that the intention to contract with a particular person and no other, and that the person with whom the alleged contract was made was not that person. From the point of view of the insurer, the identity of the insured is nearly always important as it goes to moral hazard, although there are situations where the insurers are content to insure any person meeting a given description, eg where an open cover has been issued to the insured. From the point of view of the insured, the identity of the insurer may be less important. In the old case of *Mackie v The European Assurance Society*,[105] which bears little resemblance to the modern form of contracting but is nevertheless a useful illustration of the legal principle, the insured did not realise that the agent, through whom he was arranging insurance and who had previously dealt with one insurer, was now dealing with a different insurer. The court refused to hold the contract void for mistake since the insured intended to obtain insurance through this agent and that is what happened. The identity of the insurer was regarded as irrelevant, or at best a secondary matter.

4.2. Rectification

The courts possess an equitable jurisdiction to rectify a policy where it does not conform to the intentions of the parties. The leading authority on rectification, the decision of the Court of Appeal in *FSHC Group Holdings Ltd v GLAS Trust Corporation Ltd*,[106] allows rectification in two situations. The first is where the parties have in the course of negotiations reached agreement on a particular point, but when the contract is reduced to writing it is inconsistent with, or does not include, that agreed point. The test here is objective, based upon what a reasonable person would have taken the earlier negotiations between the parties to mean. In *Markel Bermuda Ltd v Caesars Entertainment Inc*,[107] the problem arose by oversight. The parties had for some years contracted on standard terms, which included a US law and jurisdiction provision, but the policies had always by endorsement deleted that provision and replaced it with a choice of New York law and arbitration in London.[108] The endorsement was omitted in the final version of the contract, leading the insured to assert that judicial proceedings of the policy could be commenced in the USA. Bryan J, describing the omission as a 'cock up', held that the policy should be rectified. Other errors that may be rectified in this way are clerical mistakes, for instance an incorrect spelling of the name of the insured, an erroneous recording of a car's registration plate or a particular

[105] (1869) 21 LT 102.
[106] [2019] EWCA Civ 1361.
[107] [2021] EWHC 1931 (Comm).
[108] This is the standard 'Bermuda Form' arbitration clause, the effect of which is to prevent either the English or New York courts from reviewing any award on the ground of error of law.

business activity described as being undertaken by A Ltd when A Ltd has been taken over by B Ltd.[109]

The second form of rectification arises where the parties had in the course of negotiations developed a common understanding falling short of agreement as to the terms of the policy. For example, it was held in *GLAS* that the test for rectification was subjective, so that a party who had believed one thing at the time but subsequently asserted another after the contract would be constrained by equity from going back on the common assumption.

The fact that the contract contains a mistake is not sufficient to justify rectification. The equitable remedy is designed to correct errors in transcription or failures to implement common understandings, not to correct errors made by one party who has misunderstood the effect of what has been written. The point is perfectly illustrated by an Australian test case on insurance coverage for COVID-19 losses, HDI Global Specialty SE v Wonkana No 3 Pty Ltd.[110] The policy here, issued in 2019, covered the insured for business interruption losses resulting from an outbreak of infectious disease. There was, however, an exclusion for diseases listed in the Quarantine Act 1908 to be subject to the imposition of quarantine. The 1908 Act had been repealed by the Biosecurity Act 2015 and a new regime had been put in place, and a declaration for COVID-19 was made under the 2015 Act. The insurers contended that reference to the 1908 Act should be treated as applicable to the 2015 Act. The New South Wales Court of Appeal disagreed. Whatever the reason for the naming of the wrong Act, although probably a simple mistake, there had been no agreement or common understanding that the 2015 Act should have been mentioned in the policy. This was a case where the policy said precisely what the insurers intended it to say, and rectification was not available.[111]

---

5. Illegality

The courts will refuse to enforce an insurance contract the making of which is banned by legislation or which has as its purpose the commission of a crime or tort. That is the case even if the parties were not aware of the illegality: a policy designed to cover property in an alien enemy[112] or the profits expected from an illegal drugs deal would be

[109] *Nittan (UK) Ltd v Solent Steel Fabrication Ltd Trading as Sargrove Automation and Cornhill Insurance Co Ltd* [1981] 1 Lloyd's Rep 633, 637 (Lord Denning MR) and 639 (Brightman LJ).

[110] [2020] NSWCA 296, followed in *Swiss Re International SE v LCA Marrickville Pty Ltd* [2021] FCA 1206; there was no appeal on this point, [2022] FCAFC 17.

[111] These cases were distinguished in *Certain Underwriters at Lloyd's of London v Dural 24/7 Pty Ltd* [2022] FCA 206, where the policy additionally provided that 'References to a statute law also includes all its amendments or replacements'. The court held that the 2015 Act was the replacement for the 1908 Act, and accordingly the listing of COVID-19 under the 2015 Act operated as a listing under the 1908 Act for the purposes of the policy so that there was no cover.

[112] *Janson v Driefontein Consolidated Mines Ltd* [1902] AC 484, 499 (Lord Davey). Although there is no modern authority on the effect that an external event such as a war has on a contract of insurance when the policyholder subsequently becomes an enemy alien, this point has been touched upon, in a narrower sense, in *Islamic Republic of Iran Shipping Lines v Steamship Mutual Underwriting Association (Bermuda) Ltd* [2010] EWHC 2661, where the issue was whether UK government regulations, which restricted dealing with particular bodies other than for limited purposes, operated to render illegal, or to frustrate, a P&I club insurance. The outcome turned on the proper construction of the regulations.

illegal and unenforceable.[113] An insurance policy will also be void and illegal if the insured does not have an insurable interest and the policy falls within the Life Assurance Act 1774.[114] In such circumstances any premium paid cannot be recovered.[115] If an insurance contract is made by a person, in the course of carrying on insurance business, who has not obtained authorisation under the Financial Services and Markets Act 2000, the contract is unenforceable against the insured and the insured is entitled to recover any premium paid, although it will be enforceable if the 'insurer' is authorised to carry on a regulated activity but is not authorised to undertake insurance business.[116]

A contrast should be drawn between a statutory ban on contracting and a statutory requirement that has not been complied with by the insured. Some pieces of legislation can be regarded as purely regulatory, so that failure to comply may attract a fine but the insurance itself is unaffected. An old illustration of the point relates to the requirement for crew to be given written contracts of employment: failure to provide such contracts did not render illegal an insurance on the voyage.[117] In the same way, overloading a vessel does not render void a contract of carriage.[118] In every case it is necessary to examine the legislation to ascertain Parliament's intention.

Is it permissible to insure property that the insured has acquired in an unlawful fashion? In *Bird v Appleton*,[119] the insured cargo had been purchased using funds obtained from unlawfully selling another cargo, but the court was clearly of the view that the origin of the purchase price of property was not relevant to its insurance. In *Geismar v Sun Alliance and London Insurance Ltd*,[120] a claim was made on a theft policy after jewellery was stolen. The jewellery had been smuggled into the country and was, therefore, liable to confiscation, but the authorities would have had no claim on any insurance money. The court held that even though theft and not confiscation was the cause of the loss, the insurers were not liable: 'if the contract of insurance purports to cover property which the law forbids him to have, then the contract is directly connected with the illegal act and is unenforceable'.[121] In contrast to this is the decision of the Court of Appeal in *Euro-Diam Ltd v Bathurst*.[122] A wholesaler of diamonds insured an export shipment to West Germany and was allowed to claim on the policy when the jewels were stolen after their arrival in that country. The wholesaler had misrepresented their value to the German customs so that the importer might avoid tax, although, unlike in *Geismar*, there had been no misrepresentation to the insurers. In addition to this act of smuggling, the transaction was illegal under West German law. The court held that the right to possess goods will be enforced even if the owner acquired them by virtue of an illegal contract, so long as it is not necessary to use the illegal contract to establish the claim.[123] The principle in *Bird v Appleton* was here applied.

[113] More often the insurance is not taken out for an unlawful purpose but the loss sustained involves a criminal act by the insured, and the issue is whether or not the insurer is liable. This is discussed in ch 10 below.

[114] s 4(1); see ch 6 below.

[115] *Harse v Pearl Life Assurance* [1904] 1 KB 559.

[116] See ch 2 above.

[117] *Redmond v Smith* (1844) 7 Man & G 457.

[118] *St John Shipping Corp v Joseph Rank Ltd* [1957] 1 QB 267. See also *21st Century Logistic Solutions Ltd v Madysen* [2004] EWHC 231 (QB) (VAT fraud did not render illegal a contract of sale).

[119] (1800) 8 TR 562.

[120] [1978] 1 QB 383.

[121] ibid 394 (Talbot J).

[122] [1987] 2 WLR 517.

[123] See *Bowmakers Ltd v Barnet Instruments Ltd* [1945] KB 65; *Tinsley v Morgan* [1994] 1 AC 340, 375 (Lord Browne-Wilkinson).

6

Insurable Interest

1. History and Legal Framework[1]

At common law there was no general prohibition on wagering contracts in general,[2] at least in the absence of some overriding public policy consideration affecting the subject matter of the wager such as corruption[3] and the threat of physical violence or other harm to the community.[4] As far as insurance was concerned, there was a series of cases in which insurance taken out on the vessels of others were struck down, not because of their wagering propensity but because the parties had agreed that interest in the subject matter was needed by the insured in order to recover.[5] That barrier was overcome by the use of wording in the policy making it clear that interest was not required, eg 'policy proof of interest'. However, a series of legislative measures were introduced in the eighteenth and nineteenth centuries which clamped down on gambling in general and insurance without interest in particular: as was seen in chapter one, the line between insurance and gambling is in most cases the existence or otherwise of insurable interest.[6] There were three main triggers for this change in approach: the perceived moral evils inherent in wagering, which have rendered many

[1] F Arnold-Dwyer, *Insurable Interest and the Law* (London, Routledge, 2020).

[2] *Pope v St Leger* (1693) 1 Salk 344; *Assevieda v Cambridge* (1710) 10 Mod 77; *Harman v Van Hatton* (1716) 2 Vern 717; *De Paiba v Ludlow* (1721) 1 Comyns 361; *Dean v Decker* (1746) 2 Str 1250. See also *Craufurd v Hunter* (1798) 8 TR 13, 23 (Lord Kenyon CJ), 25 (Grose J).

[3] *Foster v Thackeray* (1781) 1 TR 57; *Atherfold v Beard* (1788) 2 TR 610.

[4] *Allen v Rescous* 83 ER 505; *Walker v Derwent* unreported 1747; *Jones v Randall* (1774) 1 Cowp 37; *Hartley v Rice* (1808) 10 East 22; *Gilbert v Sykes* (1812) 16 East 150; *Burn v Taylor* (1823) R & M 28.

[5] *Whittingham v Thornburgh* (1690) 2 Vern 206; *Martin v Sitwell* (1691) 1 Show 156; *Goddard v Garrett* (1692) 2 Vern 269; *Le Pypre v Farr* (1716) 2 Vern 716.

[6] In *Carlill v Carbolic Smoke Ball Co* [1892] 2 QB 484, 490–91, Hawkins J defined a wagering contract as 'one by which two persons, professing to hold opposite views touching the issue of a future uncertain event, mutually agree that, dependent upon the determination of that event, one shall win from the other, and that other shall pay or hand over to him, a sum of money or other stake; neither of the contracting parties having any other interest in that contract than the sum or stake he will so win or lose, there being no other real consideration for the making of such contract by either of the parties'. This definition was approved by the Court of Appeal in *Ellesmere v Wallace* [1929] 2 Ch 1, 24, 36, 48–49. See also *Newbury International Ltd v Reliance National Insurance Co Ltd and Tyser Special Risks Ltd* [1994] 1 Lloyd's Rep 83.

destitute; the concern that those who lack interest in the subject matter of the insurance might be tempted to bring about the loss in order to gain the proceeds of the policy, a particular problem when the nation relied upon vessels for trade and for use as privateers in time of war; and the impact on the insurance market itself, devoting essential funds to those who never intended to own or repair vessels.[7]

The complex statutory structure may be outlined as follows. The earliest measure was the Marine Insurance Act 1745, which rendered void marine policies without interest, or those which provided that the policy itself was to be conclusive proof of interest or those made 'interest or no interest'. The preamble of the 1745 Act stated:

> Whereas it hath been found by Experience, that the making Assurances, Interest or no Interest, or without further Proof of Interest than the Policy, hath been productive of many pernicious Practices, whereby great Numbers of Ships, with their Cargoes, have either been fraudulently lost and destroyed …

The statutory prohibition on gambling was extended by the Life Assurance Act 1774, otherwise known as the Gambling Act 1774. This Act demands the insured to have insurable interest at the date of the policy (section 1), requires the insertion in the policy of the names of all interested persons (section 2) and precludes recovery of any sum beyond the value of the insured's interest (section 3). The 1774 Act excluded insurances on 'ships, goods and merchandises' (section 4). A general prohibition on gambling in general was introduced by the Gaming Act 1845, section 18 of which rendered wagers unenforceable, and this also caught insurance contracts insofar as they fell outside the 1745 and 1774 Acts. The 1745 Act was repealed and re-enacted in more expansive form by the Marine Insurance Act 1906, to take account of the numerous decisions on insurable interest in the nineteenth century determining the meaning of 'interest', a term that had been left undefined by the 1745 Act. This was supplemented by the Marine Insurance (Gambling Policies) Act 1909, which criminalises marine insurance without interest. Section 18 of the Gaming Act 1845 was repealed by the Gambling Act 2005, a measure which removed many of the earlier restrictions on various forms of gambling and replaced them with a complex regulatory structure.

Independently of insurable interest and gambling legislation, the common law recognises that insurance contracts are of indemnity. That means that the insured cannot recover more than the amount of its own interest. There are important exceptions. Valued policies, used primarily in the marine market, allow the parties to fix a conclusive value on the insured subject matter, to be used as the basis of the measure of recovery: this is recognised by section 27 of the Marine Insurance Act 1906. Agency and other arrangements involving third parties may permit an insured to recover the value of the third party's interest. Most importantly, there is no indemnity principle for life insurance, because it is not possible to measure the value of a life, and so life policies are written on an agreed value basis.

The resulting current structure, a combination of legislation and common law principles, is as follows. The Marine Insurance Act 1906, as supplemented by the 1909 Act, lay down the requirements for insurable interest in marine insurance. The Life Assurance

[7] In *Feasey v Sun Life Assurance Co of Canada* [2002] Lloyd's Rep IR 835, Langley J expressed the view that gambling through insurance undermines the security of the insurer, and it may have been this factor which led to the 18th-century legislation prohibiting insurance without interest. See also J Lowry and P Rawlings, 'Rethinking Insurable Interest' and commentary by Lord Mance in S Worthington (ed), *Commercial Law & Commercial Practice* (Oxford, Hart Publishing, 2003).

Act 1774 imposes a ban on insurance without interest for life and other insurances other than policies on ships, goods and merchandises. There is no specific legislation for other forms of insurance, including buildings insurance, and the repeal of the Gaming Act 1845 by the Gambling Act 2005 appears to have removed insurance from the sphere of the gambling legislation. Section 335(1) of the 2005 Act states that 'The fact that the contract relates to gambling shall not prevent its enforcement'. On the face of things, this validates gambling by insurance, but other provisions of the Act prevent that possibility. Section 3 of the 2005 Act defines gambling as 'gaming, betting or participating in a lottery'. Of those, only 'betting' is potentially relevant to insurance, but the definition of 'betting' in section 9 refers to 'the likelihood of anything occurring or not occurring' and it is far from obvious that insurance can be so categorised. That point aside, section 10 of the 2005 Act excludes from the definition of gambling any activity regulated by section 22 of the Financial Services and Markets Act 2000, and of course insurance is such an activity. The better view is that the 2005 Act leaves the legal position unaffected. The outcome is that the common law applies to policies falling outside the 1774 and 1906 Acts. That means, most importantly for such policies, that the principle of indemnity demands that the insured can recover no more than its actual loss. As will be seen in the rest of this chapter, there is considerable uncertainty on exactly what interests satisfy the 1774 and 1906 Act, there is inconsistency in certain key areas between the 1774 and 1906 Acts (including the timing of interest) and there remain doubts as to how the legislation applies to insurances other than marine and life. Although the English and Scottish Law Commissions examined insurable interest in some detail in the course of their review of insurance law between 2006 and 2018, their ultimate proposals for reform were limited and in any event have not been implemented. So the complex jigsaw of rules remains in place.

This chapter begins with a discussion of insurable interest in lives. It then considers insurable interest in property. It is convenient in the latter section to consider marine and non-marine insurance side by side rather than entirely separately. There are some differences between the two in respect of the timing of interest, but the key question – the meaning of insurable interest – is common to both marine and non-marine insurance, and it is more logical to examine the authorities in one place.

---

2. Insurable Interest in Lives: The Life Assurance Act 1774[8]

2.1. Effects of the 1774 Act

Section 1 of the 1774 Act, having stated that the measure was targeted at a 'mischievous kind of gaming', provides that:

> From and after the passing of this Act no insurance shall be made by any person or persons, bodies politick or corporate, on the life or lives of any person or persons, or on any event or events whatsoever, wherein the person or persons for whose use, benefit, or on whose account such policy or policies shall be made, shall have no interest, or by way of gaming or wagering; and that every

[8] R Merkin, 'Gambling by Insurance – A Study of the Life Assurance Act 1774' (1980) 9 *Anglo-American Law Review* 331.

> insurance made contrary to the true intention and meaning hereof shall be null and void to all intents and purposes whatsoever'.

The phrase 'or other event of events whatsoever', which is used also in the section 2 requirement for the names of all interested parties to be inserted into the policy, has given rise to considerable judicial debate over the precise scope of the 1774 Act. While it is unclear whether the statute applies to real property insurance and liability insurance, modern case law suggests that it does not. In *Mark Rowlands Ltd v Berni Inns Ltd*,[9] the insurer argued that the insured's tenant could not benefit from a building's fire insurance because he was not named in the policy, as required by section 2 of the Act. Kerr LJ expressed the opinion that to give the phrase 'or other event or events' contained in section 2 their literal meaning, so as to hold that the Act applies to indemnity insurance, would create 'havoc in much of our insurance law'.[10] He therefore concluded that 'this ancient statute was not intended to apply, and does not apply, to indemnity insurance, but only to insurance which provides for the payment of a specified sum on the happening of an insured event'.[11] In a similar vein, in *Siu Yin Kwan v Eastern Insurance Ltd*,[12] Lord Lloyd of Berwick stated that:

> section 2 must take colour from the short title and preamble to section 1. By no stretch of the imagination could indemnity insurance be described as a 'mischievous kind of gaming'. Their Lordships are entitled to give section 2 a meaning which corresponds with the obvious legislative intent.[13]

The view expressed by Lord Denning MR in *Re King, Robinson v Gray*[14] that the 1774 Act did apply to buildings insurance was dismissed by Lord Lloyd on the bases that it was obiter, it was not reflected in the judgments of the other two members of the court and the point was not argued. In any case, with respect to insurance on real property, it should be borne in mind that the principle of indemnity operates to prevent a person who lacks insurable interest from recovering under the policy. The position thus seems to be that the 1774 Act is confined to life policies.

Section 1 states that 'no insurance shall be made' without insurable interest. Section 2, discussed below, which requires the name of the insured person to be inserted into the policy, states that 'It shall not be lawful' for a policy to be made unless that requirement is fulfilled. There is a clear distinction between the wording of the two sections, and at first sight it might be thought that a breach of section 1 renders the policy void whereas section 2 adds the additional sanction of illegality. The difference is that if the policy is void, then neither party has rights under it but there is a total failure of consideration that allows the insured to recover any premiums paid; however, if the policy is illegal, then the common law precludes the court from restoring any benefits and the premiums are thus forfeited. In *Harse v Pearl Life Assurance Co*,[15] the Court of Appeal construed the wording of section 1

[9] [1986] QB 211.
[10] At 227.
[11] ibid.
[12] [1994] 2 AC 199.
[13] ibid 224. See also *Dalby v India and London Life Assurance Co* (1854) 15 CB 365, 387 (Parker B); *Tattersall v Drysdale* [1935] 2 KB 174, 181 (Goddard J). *cf* the approach taken by Manning J in *Davjoyda Estates Ltd v National Insurance Co of New Zealand* (1967) 65 S R (NSW) 381, 428.
[14] [1963] Ch 459, 485.
[15] [1904] 1 KB 558.

as giving rise to illegality and thus giving rise to a forfeiture of premiums. There followed a series of decisions in which the courts fashioned exceptions to the rule that sums paid under an illegal contract are forfeited, including timely repentance by the insured, misrepresentation by the insurer and mistake. Those cases are of historical interest only following the ruling of the majority of the Supreme Court in *Patel v Mirza*,[16] where the general prohibition on restitution of benefits conferred under an illegal contract was replaced with a test which balances the purpose of the illegality, the requirements of public policy and proportionality. There is no authority as to how the test would apply to illegality under the 1774 Act.

2.2. Time When Interest Must Be Shown

Section 3 of the Act goes on to state that 'no greater sum shall be recovered or received from the insurer or insurers than the amount of value of the interest of the insured in such life'. Taking the literal reading of section 1 and section 3 together, it might appear that the interest of the insured would have to be satisfied both at the time of effecting the policy and at the time of the loss, as with indemnity insurance generally.[17] The question of when insurable interest has to be shown received a definitive answer in *Dalby v The India and London Life Assurance Co.*[18] The life of the Duke of Cambridge had been insured with the claimant's company, Anchor Life, for £3000 under four policies. Anchor reinsured the risk with the defendants. When the insured subsequently cancelled the life policies, Anchor nevertheless maintained the reinsurance policy until the duke's death, at which time the Anchor sought payment. The defendants refused to pay on the basis that Anchor's interest in the duke's life ceased when the insured cancelled the policies. However, the court held that the requirement of insurable interest imposed by the 1774 Act must be shown to exist at the date of effecting the policy only and that life could not be equated with indemnity insurance. Parke B construed section 3 of the 1774 Act as merely requiring the insured to 'value his interest at its true amount when he makes the contract'.[19] The judge opined that to hold to the contrary would result in the injustice of the insured paying a fixed premium over the term of the policy, only to find that he could recover some uncertain sum which depended on the value of his interest at the time of the death.[20]

The decision in *Dalby* has not escaped criticism.[21] Taking the facts of the case itself, it is evident that the mischief which the 1774 Act was designed to address is undermined by the finding that insurable interest on death is not required. Indeed, once the insured cancelled his policies on the Duke of Cambridge's life, it is difficult to see what possible interest Anchor had in the duke's life. It is certain that the company did not suffer a loss when he died because it was no longer bound to pay insurance monies to the insured. In this respect,

[16] [2016] UKSC 42.

[17] As was held in *Godsall v Boldero* (1807) 9 East 72.

[18] (1854) 15 CB 365.

[19] ibid 404. It is noteworthy that in *Feasey v Sun Life Life Assurance Corporation of Canada* [2003] EWCA Civ 885, [73] Waller LJ, citing *Dalby*, confirmed that: 'In a life policy the date at which the insurable interest must exist is the date of the taking out of the policy. Furthermore, that is the date for valuing the insurable interest.' *Feasey* is a significant decision and is considered in greater detail below.

[20] ibid 403.

[21] See, eg Merkin (n 8).

it can be seen that *Dalby* apparently has the effect of legitimising gaming. This also arises in the context of, for example, a creditor who insures the amount of a debt owing to him at the time when the insurance is effected but who continues to maintain the policy on the debtor's life after the loan has been repaid. Again, *Dalby* permits an employer who has obtained a 'keyman' policy on an employee to keep paying the premiums even after the employment has terminated. Nevertheless, the practical justification for *Dalby* lies in the fact that insurance is commonly used as a vehicle for investment and saving, and as such it has been said that 'it is desirable to give life policies the ordinary characteristics of property'.[22]

2.3. Defining Insurable Interest in Life Policies

There is no definition of insurable interest in the 1774 Act. However, the obvious inference to be drawn from the wording of section 3, confining the insured to recovering the value of the interest insured, is that there must be a financial or pecuniary interest. It was confirmed by the Court of Appeal in *Feasey v Sun Life Assurance Corp of Canada*[23] that the test is not simply whether the insured is wagering. While a wager would fall foul of the 1774 Act, it did not follow that the absence of any intention to wager operated to take a policy outside the Act. What is required, therefore, is an insurable interest.

2.3.1. Own Life and Spouse Policies

In two categories of life insurance insurable interest is conclusively presumed to exist, and section 3 of the Life Assurance Act 1774 is disapplied so that there is no upper limit on the sum insured. The two exceptions are: (i) policies on the insured's own life where the insurance is for the insured's own benefit;[24] and (ii) policies on the life of a spouse. The rationale underlying the presumption that spouses possess an unlimited insurable interest in their respective lives[25] was explained by Farwell J, who said in *Griffiths v Fleming*[26] that 'a husband is no more likely to indulge in "mischievous gaming" on his wife's life than a wife on her husband's'. Section 253 of the Civil Partnerships Act 2004 extends the common law presumption in favour of 'spouses' to civil partners of the same sex. There is no authority on cohabiting couples, and while it is the case that there is no conclusive presumption in favour of insurable interest, a mutual pecuniary interest would normally be obvious.

2.3.2. Other Family Relationships

Subject to the exception of spouses, the general rule is that the proposer for life insurance must have some pecuniary interest in the insured life and, by analogy with the principle of indemnity in section 3, the sum recoverable is limited to the extent the loss is capable of being quantified. With respect to family relationships, the requirement of insurable interest can have

[22] *Grigsby v Russell* 222 US 149 (1911) (Holmes J). See, eg *Fuji Finance Inc v Aetna Life Insurance Ltd* [1997] Ch 173.
[23] [2003] EWCA Civ 885.
[24] *Wainright v Bland* (1836) 1 M & W 32; *M'Farlane v Royal London Friendly Society* (1886) 2 TLR 755, DC.
[25] For a wife's interest in her husband's life, see *Reed v Royal Exchange Assurance Co* (1795) Peake Add Cas 70, in which Lord Kenyon CJ said at 70 that 'it must be presumed that every wife had an interest in the life of her husband'. For a husband's interest in his wife's life, see *Griffiths v Fleming* [1909] 1 KB 805; *Murphy v Murphy* [2004] Lloyd's Rep IR 744.
[26] [1909] 1 KB 805.

particularly harsh consequences. For example, it is settled that an adult child does not have an insurable in the life of a parent. In *Harse v Pearl Life Assurance Co*,[27] the claimant effected two life policies on the life of his mother, who lived with him as his housekeeper and to whom he paid an allowance. The claimant's father was alive but, being paralysed, he did not work and would therefore be unable to meet the funeral expenses of his wife in the event of her predeceasing him. One of the policies stated that it was to cover funeral expenses. Upon discovering that the policies were void for want of insurable interest, there being no obligation on a child to bury his parent,[28] the claimant sued for the recovery of the premiums paid by him, which now amounted to more than the original sum assured. It was held by the Court of Appeal that the claimant's lack of insurable interest rendered the policy illegal.

Whether a minor has an interest in the lives of his parents is doubtful because there is no common law obligation on a parent to maintain a child.[29] However, such an obligation may arise by virtue of a maintenance order compelling a parent to support a child, in which case insurable interest will exist. In practice, the principle that a child has no insurable interest in the life of its parents is generally circumvented by a parent taking insurance on his or her own life and ensuring that it is expressed to be for the benefit of the child.[30] As with cohabitees, it would seem sensible for the law to recognise that a minor has an insurable interest qua dependant in the life of a parent.[31]

Although it is common practice for parents to insure the lives of their children,[32] at law a parent lacks insurable interest because no financial loss results from the child's death. In *Halford v Kymer*,[33] a father effected a policy on the life of his son, which named himself as beneficiary should the son die before attaining the age of 21 years. In holding that the father lacked insurable interest, the court rejected the father's contention that he had a financial interest in his son's life because he expected his son to reimburse him the costs of maintenance and education at some future time. Bayley J, construing the relevant provision in the Life Assurance Act 1774, was emphatic in his rejection of the father's claim:

> It is enacted by the third section, 'That no greater sum shall be recovered than the amount of the value of the interest of the insured in the life or lives.' Now, what was the amount or the value of the interest of the party insuring in this case? Not one farthing certainly. It has been said that there are numerous instances in which a father has effected an insurance on the life of his son. If a father, wishing to give his son some property to dispose of, make an insurance on his son's life in his (the son's) name, not for his (the father's) own benefit, but for the benefit of his son, there is no law to prevent his doing so; but that is a transaction quite different from the present; and if a notion prevails that such an insurance as the one in question is valid, the sooner it is corrected the better.[34]

[27] [1904] 1 KB 558.

[28] [1903] 2 KB 92. The Court of Appeal proceeded on the basis that the trial judge's finding on the point was correct. See also *Howard v Refuge Friendly Society* (1886) 54 LT 644, 646 (Matthew LJ).

[29] *Bazeley v Forder* (1868) LR 3 QB 559, 565 (Lord Cockburn CJ); *Stopher v NAB* [1955] 1 QB 486, 495 (Lord Goddard CJ).

[30] See the Married Women's Property Act 1882, s 11, considered in ch 7 below.

[31] The Fatal Accidents Act 1976 extends the definition of 'dependent child' of the deceased to include a posthumous child.

[32] The obvious example being holiday insurance, although such a policy may be viewed as a contract for necessaries entered into by the parent as agent for the child. See further Lord Wilberforce's speech in *Woodar Investment Development Ltd v Wimpey Construction UK Ltd* [1980] 1 All ER 571.

[33] (1830) 10 B & C 724.

[34] ibid 729. Yet, given the paucity of case law on such family policies, it would seem that insurers rarely raise the point of lack of insurable interest by way of defence to a claim.

At odds with the case law considered above is the decision in *Barnes v London, Edinburgh & Glasgow Life Insurance Co Ltd*,[35] in which the Court of Appeal held that a person who had undertaken to care for her infant stepsister had an insurable interest in her life to the extent of securing 'the repayment of the expenses incurred'.[36] The decision has been doubted,[37] and is unlikely to be followed by a future court.

2.3.3. The Employer–Employee Relationship

An employer may have an insurable interest in the life of an employee and, conversely, an employee may have an insurable interest in the life of his employer. In practice, policies are taken out only on key personnel. Calculating the value of the interest can be a relatively simple exercise in the straightforward employer–employee situation. The starting point is generally the contract of employment between the parties, so that where an employee is employed on a contract terminable by notice, the court will ascertain the value of the length of the notice period to the insured/employer.[38] It is always open to either party to prove additional interest if the contract provides for other forms of benefit, and most 'keyman' policies are for an agreed value based on the worth of the employee to the business.[39]

An employee who is working under a fixed term contract has an insurable interest in the employer's life up to the value of the wages to be paid during that term, although this type of policy would now be exceptional in the extreme. In *Hebdon v West*,[40] Hebdon, a bank clerk, was employed for seven years under a fixed term contract at a salary of £600.00 per annum. The bank had also lent him £4700 and the managing partner, Pedder, had promised him that the debt need not be repaid during his, Pedder's, lifetime. At a time when his contract had approximately five years to run, Hebdon insured Pedder's life through two life companies, one policy being for £5000 and the other for £2500. After six years Pedder died and the employment was terminated. Hebdon received £5000 under the first policy but when the second insurers refused his claim, he sued. The first insurers had not raised the point that the value of the policy exceeded the salary due to Hebdon over the entire term. Further, as insurable interest in life policies must be found to exist at the date when the policy is effected, not at the date of the loss, they could not in any case raise the point that his employment contract had only one year left to run at the date of the death (a quantifiable loss of salary of only £600.00). However, with respect to the second life policy, Wightman J held that the promise made by Pedder not to call in the debt was gratuitous and therefore non-enforceable. This had the effect that since Hebdon's insurable interest had been amply satisfied by the first policy, he therefore lacked the requisite insurable interest to enforce the second policy. Wightman J, considering the effect of the 1774 Act, said:

> We assume, then, that the plaintiff had a pecuniary interest in the life of Pedder to the extent of £2,500 at the time he effected the policy with the defendant's office. If that be so, the question then

[35] [1891] 1 QB 864.
[36] ibid 866 (Lord Coleridge CJ).
[37] See *Griffiths v Fleming* [1909] 1 KB 805; *Harse v Pearl Life Assurance Co* [1904] 1 KB 558.
[38] *Simcock v Scottish Imperial Insurance Co* (1902) 10 SLT 286.
[39] *Fuji Finance Ltd v Aetna Insurance Co Ltd* 1996] 4 All ER 608. Older authorities support the restrictive view that an employer's interest does not extend to the estimated loss to the business caused by the employee's death: see *Simcock v Scottish Imperial Ins Co* (1902) 10 SLT 286; *Turner & Co v Scottish Provident Institution* (1896) 34 SLT 146 (involving a commercial agent rather than an employee).
[40] (1863) 3 B & S 579.

> arises whether payment, after the death of Pedder, of £5,000 by another life insurance company … is a bar to the plaintiff's claim … Looking to the declared object of the legislature … it was intended by the third section of the Act that the insured should in no case recover or receive from the insurers (whether upon one policy or many) more than the insurable interest which the person making the insurance had at the time he insured the life.[41]

The judgment is illuminating insofar as the judge proceeds on the basis that the effect of section 3 of the Act is to treat life policies as contracts of indemnity, the sole distinction being the time when insurable interest must exist. However, the strict orthodoxy of quantifying the pecuniary interest of the insured by reference to the terms of the employment contract is often ignored by the courts. This is apparent where, for example, the death of an employee would have serious implications for the profits and asset value of a business, and so the court will have regard to consequential losses ensuing from the death.[42]

In *Feasey v Sun Life Assurance Corporation of Canada*,[43] the generous approach to insurable interest under the 1774 Act was confirmed. Steamship, a protection and indemnity club, insured the liabilities of its shipowner members under a policy with Syndicate 957 at Lloyd's for personal injury or death suffered by their employees on board a vessel or offshore rig. Syndicate 957 reinsured its liability with Sun Life and Phoenix. Steamship's policy in its original form provided a straightforward indemnity to shipowners for liabilities incurred by them. However, a change in Lloyd's rules made it impossible for that form of reinsurance cover to be granted, and it was changed so that it reflected, as closely as possible, Steamship's overall exposure to claims over a three-year period. That was done by allocating a fixed sum to every death or injury suffered on board, whether or not the member was actually liable in damages for the incident. The reinsurance thus ceased to be one on pure liability but rather became one whereby Steamship insured the lives of the employees of its members. A dispute arose between the syndicate and its own reinsurers, the latter arguing that Steamship had no insurable interest in the lives and well-being of employees so that the policy was rendered illegal by the Life Assurance Act 1774, section 1. By way of alternative, the reinsurers argued that, contrary to section 3 of the Act, Steamship was seeking to claim more than the value of any insurable interest it had. Both the first instance judge[44] and the majority of the Court of Appeal held that Steamship did possess a pecuniary interest in the losses covered by the policy and that its interest was capable of being ascertained when the policy was entered into. As a matter of construction, the insurance was found to be one to pay fixed sums on the happening of certain events and, as such, it therefore fell within section 1 of the Act. Waller LJ stated that:

> It is sufficient under section 5 of the Marine Insurance Act for a person interested in a marine adventure to stand in a 'legal or equitable relation to the adventure.' That is intended to be a broad concept … In a policy on life or lives the court should be searching for the same broad concept … It may be that on an insurance of a specific identified life, it will be difficult to establish a 'legal or equitable' relation without a pecuniary liability recognised by law arising on the death of that particular person. There is however no authority which deals with a policy on many lives and over a substantial period and where it can be seen that a pecuniary liability will arise by reference to those lives and the intention is to cover that legal liability … The interest in policies falling within

[41] ibid 589–91.
[42] This, at least, can be deduced from *Fuji Finance v Aetna Life Insurance Co* 1996] 4 All ER 608.
[43] [2003] EWCA Civ 885.
[44] [2002] Lloyd's Rep IR 835.

> section 1 of the 1774 Act must exist at the time of entry into the policy, and be capable of pecuniary evaluation at that time.[45]

Rejecting the alternative contention of the reinsurers based upon section 3 of the Act, the Court of Appeal held that they had failed to demonstrate that Steamship was seeking to recover a sum exceeding the value of its interest as at the date of the contract. As will be seen below, *Feasey* has much wider implications for insurable interest generally.

Partners have an insurable interest in each other's lives up to the amount of capital or other loss which might, in the event of the death or retirement of a partner, be suffered by remaining partners.[46]

2.3.4. Creditor and Debtor Insurance

A secured creditor has an insurable interest in the life of a debtor.[47] Such interest will ensue even after the debt has been paid because, as has been seen, the requirement of insurable interest need only be shown at the time when the life policy is effected and so a creditor can recover the whole sum insured even if the debtor dies after repaying the debt.[48] The value of the creditor's interest is the amount of the debt, including interest payments. A debtor may have insurable interest in the life of a creditor where the latter has made a binding promise not to call in the debt: an expectation that the debt will not be called in does not suffice.[49]

2.4. Naming the Insured in the Policy Document

The Life Assurance Act 1774, section 2 provides that:

> It shall not be lawful to make any policy or policies on the life or lives of any person or persons, or other event or events, without inserting in such policy or policies the person or persons' name or names interested therein, or on whose account such policy is so made or underwrote.

Section 2 is designed to prevent avoidance of section 1 of the Act requiring insurable interest by precluding a person with interest in the policy from taking out the insurance in his or her own name but in reality for the benefit of another person. Sections 1 and 2 are to that extent symbiotic. At its simplest level, the mischief which section 2 is designed to prevent is the situation where, for example, X appears to effect an insurance policy on a life in which she has an insurable interest, but in reality the contract is for the benefit of Y, who lacks insurable interest. The object of the Act is not to prevent Y ultimately benefiting from X's policy, since X may apply the proceeds of such policy in any way she pleases. Rather, it is to ensure that if Y is to gain immediate benefit, then Y's name must appear in the policy from the outset and, if the policy is to be valid, Y must have an insurable interest when the policy is effected.[50] The issue of whether the name of the true insured is declared in the policy is

[45] [2003] EWCA Civ 885, [97].
[46] *Griffiths v Fleming* [1909] 1 KB 805.
[47] *Godsall v Boldero* (1807) 9 East 72.
[48] *Dalby v The India and London Life Assurance Co* (1854) 15 CB 365.
[49] *Henson v Blackwell* (1845) 4 Hare 434.
[50] See *Shilling v Accidental Death Insurance Co* (1857) 2 H & N 42, in which the premiums on a policy taken out by a father on his own life were in fact paid by his son, the beneficiary. It was held that the insurance was the son's, and since he lacked insurance interest, the policy was null and void by virtue of s 1 of the 1774 Act.

resolved by enquiring whether the contract 'is really and substantially intended for the benefit' of that named person.[51] This is amply illustrated by the decision in *Wainwright v Bland*.[52] The insured, Miss Abercromby, effected a policy on her own life in her own name. This was done on the advice of Wainwright, the claimant, with whom she lived. Previously she had taken out a number of other life policies, two of which had been assigned to Wainwright just before her death. On the evidence, it was apparent that the insured could not afford the premiums herself but had paid them with money supplied by the claimant. It is evident that the court was suspicious that the insured had been murdered by the claimant, and the jury decided that the policy was invalid. In addressing the jury, Lord Abinger CB said:

> [T]he question in this case is, who was the party really and truly effecting the insurance? Was it the policy of Miss Abercromby? Or was it substantially the policy of Wainwright the [claimant], he using her name for the purposes of his own? If you think it was the policy of Miss Abercromby, effected by her for her own benefit, her representative is entitled to put it in force; and it would be no answer to say that she had no funds of her own to pay the premiums; Wainwright might lend her the money for that purpose, and the policy still continue to be her own. But, on the other hand, if, looking to all the strange facts which have been proved before you, you come to the conclusion that the policy was, in reality, effected to Wainwright; that he merely used her name, himself finding the money, and meaning (by way of assignment, or by bequest, or in some other way), to have the benefit of it himself; then I am of opinion such a transaction would be a fraudulent evasion of the [Life Assurance Act] and that your verdict should be for the defendants.[53]

Section 2 has proved to serve little practical purpose, particularly since often it will be the insured's next of kin who benefits from the insurance and there is no requirement that their names should be specified in the policy. The conundrum created by the section 2 requirement can be seen by returning to the example postulated above. Even if Y's name is declared in the policy, this alone will not render the policy valid because, in any case, Y lacks the requisite insurable interest. If, on the other hand, Y does have insurable interest in X's life, it should not matter that her name does not appear in the policy because the object of the Act (to prohibit 'a mischievous kind of gaming') is not violated. If there is an infringement of section 2, then there is all but inevitably an infringement of section 1 unless the name has been omitted by oversight, in which case the illegality sanction is draconian in the extreme. The decision in *Evans v Bignold*[54] serves to illustrate the point clearly. Mr Evans approached the trustees of his father-in-law's estate and asked them to advance him £200.00, which was the amount due to his wife under the terms of her father's will when she reached 21 years. In case she died before then, a surety was found to secure repayment of the advance, and the surety required Mr Evans to take out a life policy on Mrs Evans's life. The policy was, however, effected in her name. She did attain 21 years and so repayment of the advance was not required. Nevertheless, the policy continued and, when she died, her administrator (Mr Evans) sought to claim on the policy. The court was forced to decide that since the policy had originally been taken out for the benefit of Mr Evans and his name did not appear on the policy, it was unlawful and unenforceable. Since Mr Evans, as Mrs Evans's husband, had an insurable interest in her life, section 2 of the Act operated to defeat a policy which did not involve any element of gaming.

[51] *M'Farlane v Royal London Friendly Society* (1886) 2 TLR 755, 756 (Pollock B).
[52] (1835) 1 Mood & R 481.
[53] ibid 486–87.
[54] (1869) 4 LR QB 622.

Most importantly, there is nothing in the Act that precludes the holder of a policy from assigning that policy to a third party without interest.[55] The only constraint on assignment arises where the policy was taken out with the intention of assigning it to that party, but such a policy falls foul of section 1 and section 2 is not required. That point was made by Pollock CB in *M'Farlane v Royal London Friendly Society*:[56]

> 'There is nothing to prevent any person from insuring his own life a hundred times … provided it is bona fide an insurance on his own life, and at the time, for his benefit, and … there is nothing to prevent him from dealing with such policies by assigning them to some-one else … even though at the time he effected the policies he had the intention of so dealing with them … But if ab initio the policy effected in the name of A is really and substantially intended for the benefit of B and B only … that is within the evil and mischief of [the 1774 Act].

Section 2, as well as achieving nothing, has posed a series of difficulties. One of the first to emerge was its operation in respect of group policies, for example those effected by an employer or a trade union in respect of employees. This is because it is unclear from the outset exactly who will, from time to time, fall within the group. That potential problem in this situation was averted by section 50 of the Insurance Companies Act 1973, which disapplies section 2 of the 1774 Act, provided that the class of persons covered by the policy is identifiable with reasonable certainty. However, other issues arise, as where policies are taken out as part of a family trust arrangement and the beneficiaries cannot at the outset be identified.

2.5. Proposals for Reform

The English and Scottish Law Commissions considered the operation of the Life Assurance Act 1774 at length. In an issues paper published in January 2008,[57] a number of problems were identified. The Law Commissions argued that: (i) the law was difficult to analyse; (ii) the boundary between life and liability insurance was blurred; (iii) it could be difficult to obtain insurance because cohabitants and other family members could not insure each other's lives; (iv) technicalities, such as section 2 of the 1774 Act, could be used to avoid policies; (v) employers were potentially unduly limited in the amount for which they could insure the lives of employees; (vi) insurance on an open-ended debt was uncertain; (vii) the issue of moral hazard or gambling was no longer relevant in the light of changes to the gambling legislation; (viii) the validity of policies covering the interests of more than one person was at risk; and (ix) the remedy for breach was unclear.[58]

The issues paper was followed in December 2011 by a consultation paper, *Reform of Insurance Law*.[59] This rejected any suggestion that the UK should follow Australia and New Zealand in repealing the 1774 Act and instead argued that insurable interest remained important in distinguishing between gambling and insurance. Instead, a more modest set of

[55] *Goshawk Dedicated Ltd v Tyser & Co Ltd* [2007] Lloyd's Rep IR 224.

[56] (1886) 2 TLR 755, 756. See also *Brewster v National Life Insurance Society* (1892) 8 TLR 648. In each of these cases the court did not find an initial intention to assign.

[57] The Law Commission Issues Paper 4, *Insurable Interest*.

[58] ibid para 1.15 and Part 4.

[59] Law Com CP No 201/Scot Law Com CP 152.

reform proposals were put forward. Those proposals were, after consultation, refined and included in a draft Insurable Interest Bill published in April 2016. That Bill was, again after consultation, modified. The most recent proposals are to be found in the Insurable Interest Bill 2018, which at time of writing is awaiting enactment, although the prospects of that happening are at the moment remote. The impact of the 2018 Bill as regards life insurance is as follows.

The Life Assurance Act 1774 is to be repealed and replaced. The legislation is to apply to 'life-related insurance', defined as a contract of insurance under which the insured event is the death, injury, ill-health or incapacity of an individual, or the life of an individual continuing. A life-related insurance contract is void unless, at the time the insured enters into it, the assured has an insurable interest, although the sanction for an absence of insurable interest is no longer to be illegality but merely voidness so that any premiums paid may be recoverable. As may be seen from the above discussion, the effect of section 1 of the 1774 Act as modified by *Patel v Mirza* is thereby retained. Where the Bill would effect an important change is in the definition of insurable interest, namely 'a reasonable prospect that the assured will suffer economic loss if the insured event occurs'. The Bill offers a non-exhaustive list of circumstances where there is insurable interest, including policies taken out by a person: on his or her own life; on the spouse, civil partner or cohabitee of the insured; on the life of a person who is, or is treated as, the insured's child or grandchild; on the life of a member of a pension or other group scheme administered by the insured; and for the benefit of a third person. This would expand the traditionally recognised ambit of insurable interest, although it arguably does little more than recognise the more expansive approach in *Feasey*. The Bill also repeals the unsatisfactory naming requirement in section 2 of the 1774 Act, and replaces it with a broader provision allowing identification by a class or description, including who later fall within the relevant class or description at a future date.

---

3. Insurable Interest in Marine and Property Insurance

3.1. The Requirement for Insurable Interest

Section 4(1) of the Marine Insurance Act 1906, which re-enacts the effect of the 1745 Act, states that 'Every contract of marine insurance by way of gaming or wagering is void'. Section 4(2) then defines a gaming or wagering contract as one:

> (a) where the assured has not an insurable interest as defined by this Act, and the contract is entered into with no expectation of acquiring such an interest; or
> (b) where the policy is made 'interest or no interest', or 'without further proof of interest than the policy itself, or without benefit of salvage to the insurer', or subject to any like term:
>
> Provided that, where there is no possibility of salvage, a policy may be effected without benefit of salvage to the insurer.

This section applies when the policy incepts and demands that the insured is not wagering or gambling at that date. Section 4(2)(a) is satisfied in two situations. First, the insured has an insurable interest at the date the contract is made: the definition of insurable interest is discussed below. If there is such an interest, then plainly the insured cannot be described as gaming or wagering, although the subsection says nothing about the amount of insurable interest, and it suffices that some interest exists even though it falls short of the sum insured under the policy. It is only where the overvaluation is excessive to the point that it is fraudulent that the law steps in to treat the insured as gaming or wagering.[60] Secondly, the insured does not have insurable interest but does have an expectation of acquiring an insurable interest at a later date: this would apply, for example, to an insured who intended to purchase a cargo and who has insured in anticipation of doing so. Section 4(2)(b) repeats the provisions of the 1745 Act whereby 'ppi' (policy proof of interest) policies are banned, and that is the case even though there is actually valid insurable interest.[61] The words 'without benefit of salvage' in a policy are another clear indication that interest is being dispensed with: as will be seen in chapter 17, an insurer who pays for a total loss is entitled to take whatever remains of the insured subject matter by way of salvage, but that plainly cannot happen if the insured person is not the owner of the insured subject matter. The only exception is set out in the proviso, where salvage is not possible. Section 6 of the 1906 Act codifies the principle of indemnity, providing that the insured must demonstrate an insurable interest at the date of the loss.

Turning to non-marine insurance, on the assumption that the Life Assurance Act 1774 is confined to life insurance, there is no legislative requirement for insurable interest. There is one old buildings insurance decision, *Sadlers Co v Badcock*,[62] which is often cited to support the view that the common law required insurable interest at the inception of the contract, but that was an obiter statement and the case itself decided the obvious point that a tenant whose lease had come to an end had no further interest in the property and had no valid claim for a later loss by fire. The point has never been repeated. The only insurable interest requirement is therefore that imposed by the indemnity principle: at the date of the loss, the insured must have suffered a loss in order to make a claim.[63]

3.2. The Definition of Insurable Interest

3.2.1. General Definition

The classic definition of insurable interest in property insurance was formulated by Lord Eldon LC in *Lucena v Craufurd*.[64] This case, arising out of the French Revolutionary Wars, concerned the right of Crown Commissioners to insure vessels belonging to the Dutch Republic that had been taken into protective custody by the Commissioners to prevent them falling into French hands and had been lost while being transported to England. The insurance was upheld on the basis that the Commissioners were acting under the authority of the Crown and the implied right to take all necessary measures to protect the vessels, including insuring them. However, the Court rejected the suggestion that the Commissioners had the right to insure in their own names. While it was the case that once the vessels had arrived in England they had a right of possession, there was until arrival no more than a mere expectation – in the form of a contingent right of possession – that interest would

[60] *Glafki Shipping Co SA v Pinios Shipping Co, The Maria (No 2)* [1984] 1 Lloyd's Rep 660.

[61] *John Edwards and Co v Motor Union Insurance Co Ltd* [1922] 2 KB 249.

[62] (1743) 2 Atk 554.

[63] *Sparkes v Marshall* (1836) 2 Bing NC 761; *Howard v Lancashire Insurance Co* (1885) 11 SCR 92.

[64] (1806) 2 Bos & Pul (NR) 269. This case is discussed in detail in R Merkin, *Marine Insurance: A Legal History* (Cheltenham, Edward Elgar, 2021) 6-039–6-059.

be obtained. Lord Eldon stated that insurable interest existed where there was 'a right in property, or a right derivable out of some contract about the property, which in either case may be lost upon some contingency affecting the possession or enjoyment of the party'.[65] Accordingly, the insured had to possess some present legally enforceable right, whether legal or equitable, or a contractual right, to the insured property. A mere expectation did not suffice. Lord Eldon justified a restrictive definition of insurable interest on the basis that it was necessary to ensure certainty and to avoid illusory insurance. His Lordship was, of course, concerned to ascertain the limits on who could insure. Taking the facts of *Lucena v Craufurd*, which centred on ships lost at sea, Lord Eldon said:

> If moral certainty be a ground of insurable interest, there are hundreds, perhaps thousands, who would be entitled to insure. First the dock company, then the dock-master, then the warehouse-keeper, then the porter, then every other person who to a moral certainty would have any thing to do with the property, and of course get something by it.[66]

By contrast, Lawrence J took a wider view:

> Interest does not necessarily imply a right to the whole or part of a thing … but having some relation to or concern in the subject of insurance, which relation or concern, by the happening of the perils insured against, may be so affected as to produce a damage, detriment or other prejudice to the person insuring … To be interested in the preservation of a thing, is to be so circumstanced with respect to it as to have benefit from its existence, prejudice from its destruction.

Lord Eldon's view was incorporated into the definition of insurable interest in section 5 of the Marine Insurance Act 1906. By section 5(1), 'every person has an insurable interest who is interested in a marine adventure', and section 5(2) provides that

> In particular a person is interested in a marine adventure where he stands in any legal or equitable relation to the adventure or to any insurable property at risk therein, in consequence of which he may benefit by the safety or due arrival of insurable property, or may be prejudiced by its loss, or damage thereto, or by the detention thereof, or may incur liability in respect thereof.

While this definition is confined to marine policies, it provides a useful insight into the requirement of insurable interest in insurance law generally. Of particular note in this respect is the reference in section 5(2) to the insured standing in a 'legal or equitable relation' to the property at risk, so that where the insured will be prejudiced by the loss or damage of the insured property, the requirement of insurable interest will be established. In summary, insurable interest in property is satisfied where the insured has some proprietary, contractual or possessory interest in it.[67] This will, for example, exclude a beneficiary under a will and also an intestate's next of kin, for although 'there is no man who will deny that such an heir at law has a moral certainty of succeeding to the estate; yet the law will not allow that he has any interest, or any thing more than a mere expectation'.[68]

[65] ibid 321.

[66] ibid.

[67] In this respect, a proprietary interest encompasses an equitable interest in property even if the interest is not one which would found an action in negligence in respect of the damage to the property or goods in question: *Leigh & Sillavan v Aliakmon Shipping Co Ltd, The Aliakmon* [1986] 1 AC 785, 812 (Lord Brandon).

[68] *Lucena v Craufurd* (1806) 2 Bos & Pul (NR) 269, 325. But note that a person who finds property and keeps it acquires an insurable interest in it even though a third party may have better title: *Marks v Hamiliton* (1852) 7 Exch 323.

The narrow approach adopted by Lord Eldon's definition is starkly illustrated by *Macaura v Northern Assurance Co Ltd*,[69] in which the insured, Macaura, was the only shareholder in a limited company which owned a substantial quantity of timber, much of which was stored on his land. Two weeks after effecting insurance policies with several companies in his own name, the timber was destroyed by fire. A claim brought by Macaura on the policies was disallowed on the ground that he lacked insurable interest in the timber.[70] Lord Sumner, proceeding on the basis that neither the company's debt to the insured nor his shares were exposed to fire, observed:

> the fact that he was virtually the company's only creditor, while the timber is its only asset, seems to me to make no difference ... he was directly prejudiced by the paucity of the company's assets, not by the fire.[71]

His Lordship stated that the insured 'stood in no "legal or equitable relation to" the timber at all. He had no "concern in" the subject insured. His relation was to the company, not to its goods.'[72] As a gratuitous bailee he was not liable for the timber and therefore an interest could not be based on bailment. As an unsecured creditor of the company by virtue of his shareholding, he could not insure the company's property in the absence of some security over it.[73] The guiding principle in *Macaura* is pivoted upon the separate legal personality accorded to companies, so that a company is, in law, an entity distinct from its members. It was the company which owned the timber and therefore had a proprietary interest in it, not its shareholder. The fact that the timber was in his possession did not give him a proprietary interest.

It may be that *Macaura* and the narrow approach adopted in that case are no longer good law. In *Feasey* it was pointed out by Waller LJ that the opening words of section 5(2) of the 1906 Act – 'in particular' – are of some significance, as they make it clear that the section 5(2) definition is not exhaustive. It was held in *Feasey* that property policies are, depending on their proper construction, potentially of three types: (1) policies on the property itself; (2) policies on wider interests in the property; and (3) non-pecuniary interests, such as a right to possession coupled with a right of enjoyment. Category (1) consists of straightforward property policies where the subject matter itself is insured against loss or damage. Category (2) is concerned with insurance not of the subject matter, but of the adventure relating to it. The leading authority is *Wilson v Jones*,[74] where a policy was taken out on an undersea transatlantic cable intended to provide a telegraphic link between Britain and the USA. The cable snapped and the scheme was temporarily abandoned. The insured was an investor in the scheme, and he claimed under the policy. It was held by the court that the policy was not against damage to the cable itself (and the assured plainly had no interest in the cable) but rather against the failure of the scheme and the loss of the investment. On that basis, the insured was able to recover. *Wilson* was distinguished in

[69] [1925] AC 619. See also the American case of *Farmers' Mutual Insurance Co v New Holland Turnpike Road Co* (1888) 122 Pa 37, in which it was held that a turnpike company that insured a bridge spanning a stream and which linked two sections of the company's road lacked insurable interest in the bridge because the company had no legal or equitable interest in it.

[70] It is impossible to resist the conclusion that the defence was taken only because of a strong suspicion of fraud.

[71] ibid 630.

[72] ibid.

[73] On this point, see also *Moran, Galloway & Co v Uzielli* [1905] 2 KB 555.

[74] (1867) LR 2 Exch 139.

Quadra Commodities SA v XL Insurance Company SE,[75] where the policy was against loss of or damage to a cargo of grain in storage. The insured had paid for the grain but it had not been delivered. In the light of suggestions that the grain had never existed, the insured relied upon *Wilson* to argue that the policy was not on the grain – which, if it had never existed, could obviously not have been lost[76] – but rather on the adventure in the form of the success of the storage operation. Butcher J held that the policy properly construed was against physical loss only, but he also found that the grain had existed and it had been fraudulently sold to multiple purchasers, including the insured. On that basis, the insured was able to establish insurable interest in the grain by virtue of payment and by virtue of its right to possession, points discussed below.

Category (3) is exemplified by the decision of Colman J in *Sharp v Sphere Drake Insurance Ltd, The Moonacre*,[77] where the sole shareholder in a company was held to have an insurable interest in a yacht purchased by the company, as the yacht was intended for his use and a power of attorney had been granted to him in respect of it. Category (3) was also successfully relied upon in *Quadra*. By paying for the grain, the insured had established its right to possess the grain, and that was sufficient to found an insurable interest: it was irrelevant that there were competing buyers also able to establish rights to possession.

3.2.2. Sales of Real Property

English law recognises a distinction between the making of a contract of sale for land and the execution of the contract by conveyance. Until such time as the conveyance of land is completed and the purchase price has been paid, both the vendor and the purchaser have insurable interest in the land and any buildings included in the contract. The vendor's interest is based on ownership of the property, and the purchaser's interest rests upon the principle that the risk is transferred when the contract is made so that even if the property is destroyed or damaged the full price must be paid. The vendor's interest was discussed in *Collingridge v Corporation of Royal Exchange Assurance Association*.[78] The insured, who had effected a fire insurance policy in respect of his premises, was served with a compulsory purchase order by the Metropolitan Board of Works. While a draft conveyance was being prepared, the premises were destroyed by fire. It was held that the insured's claim was valid because at the time of his loss he had not divested himself of his insurable interest in the property. Mellor J, rejecting the insurers contention that the insured could not claim under the policy, said:

> I cannot see on what grounds the plaintiff, being as he is an unpaid vendor, and having possession and right to possession, can be held disentitled to sue … the insurance company cannot in any event be released from a contract of which the terms are clear, and which there has been nothing to invalidate.[79]

The vendor's policy is purely for the vendor's benefit. If the vendor has insured the property and it is damaged, the vendor's insurers, having paid the claim, are entitled to be

[75] [2022] EWHC 431 (Comm).
[76] See ch 12 below.
[77] [1992] 2 Lloyd's Rep 501.
[78] (1877) 37 LT 525.
[79] ibid 527.

subrogated to the vendor's contractual right to recover the purchase price.[80] The purchaser must accordingly take out his or her own policy if the risk of having to pay the full purchase price, irrespective of what has happened to the property between contract and conveyance, is to be averted.

That creates the unfortunate situation in which the same property has to be insured by both parties. There was an attempt to overcome this problem by statute. Section 47(1) of the Law of Property Act 1925 provides that any insurance proceeds received by the vendor are 'on completion of the contract, be held or receivable by the vendor on behalf of the purchaser and paid by the vendor to the purchaser'. However, the conditions imposed upon the operation of this principle by section 47(2), including the consent of the insurers, mean that the section rarely applies. The practical solution adopted by the market is for property policies to state that, if the subject matter is sold and damaged before conveyance, the insurance proceeds shall be payable to the purchaser unless the purchaser has obtained insurance in his or her own right.[81]

3.2.3. Sale of Goods

Contracts for the sale of goods similarly recognise the separate concepts of risk and property (ownership). However, unlike contracts for the sale of land, the general rule for contracts for the sale of goods is that risk follows ownership.[82] The making of a contract of sale may operate to transfer both risk[83] and property to the buyer, which will be the case where the goods are identified, do not form part of a bulk of identical goods and there are no contractual conditions preventing the passing of risk and property, eg the payment of the price or delivery. International sale contracts are characterised by the passing of risk when the goods are shipped but property not passing until payment has been received. The buyer will have insurable interest if property alone has passed, because the buyer has become the owner. Similarly, the buyer will have insurable interest if the risk alone has passed, since if they are lost the buyer will be liable to pay the contract price.[84] It has also been held that a buyer who has paid for the goods but who has neither property nor risk may still insure the goods against loss or damage.[85] Property and risk in goods forming part of a bulk may pass to the buyer in the limited circumstances set out in section 20A of the Sale of Goods Act 1979, namely, where there is a sale of a specified quantity of goods from an identified bulk and the buyer has paid the price, the buyer becomes an owner in common of the bulk.[86]

A seller who has agreed to sell goods on the basis that title remains with him until the price has been paid has an insurable interest in goods based upon both ownership and the

[80] *Castellain v Preston* (1883) 11 QBD 380.

[81] The wording may be seen in *National Farmers Union Mutual Insurance Society Ltd v HSBC Insurance (UK) Ltd* [2010] EWHC 773 (Comm).

[82] Sale of Goods Act 1979, s 17.

[83] For the presumptions as to the passing of risk, see s 18 of the Sale of Goods Act 1979.

[84] Sale of Goods Act 1979, s 20. See *Stock v Inglis* (1885) LR 10 App Cas 263; *Anderson v Morice* (1875) 10 C P 609.

[85] *Quadra Commodities SA v XL Insurance Company SE* [2022] EWHC 431 (Comm).

[86] However, under the definition in s 81 of the 1979 Act, the bulk must consist of a collection of goods in a defined space or area, and if the bulk is not in a single place, then the buyer cannot become common owner of the bulk under s 20A even though the price has been paid: *Quadra Commodities SA v XL Insurance Company SE* [2022] EWHC 431 (Comm).

risk of loss falling upon the seller. Similarly, an unpaid seller in possession of the goods or, if parted with possession, one who has exercised the right of stoppage in transit will have insurable interest by virtue of possession as security for the purchase price.[87]

3.2.4. Bailment

A bailee is simply a person in possession of property belonging to another. Bailment is normally contractual, as where goods are stored in a warehouse, although it may be voluntary. In all cases, subject to contract, the bailee will owe to the bailor a duty of care in respect of the goods, and therefore has an insurable interest in respect of any liability to the bailor. The bailee also has a right to insure against loss of profits,[88] eg storage charges, if the goods are damaged while in the bailee's possession. The common law has gone a step further and recognised that a bailee is entitled to insure for the full value of the goods – which is likely to be a sum greater than the amount of the bailee's liability, which may be limited by contract – but the bailee must hold the proceeds for the benefit of the bailor. Whether the policy covers the bailee's liability or the value of the goods is a matter of its proper construction. In *Waters v Monarch Fire and Life Assurance* Co,[89] the claimants were flour merchants, warehousemen and wharfingers whose warehouse was destroyed by an accidental fire, together with goods in it of which they were bailees. They had taken out two policies of insurance covering, under one, 'goods in trust or on commission therein' and, under the other, 'property of the assured or held by them in trust or on commission'. It was held that, as a matter of construction, the policies covered goods of third parties of which the claimants were bailees. Lord Campbell CJ, construing the words 'goods in trust', said:

> I think that means goods with which the assured were entrusted; not goods held in trust in the strict technical sense, so that there was only an equitable obligation on the assured enforceable by a subpoena in Chancery, but goods with which they were entrusted in the ordinary sense of the word.[90]

The policies therefore covered not just the claimants' 'personal interest' in the goods, but all damage and loss. Crompton J said: 'the parties meant to insure those goods with which the claimants were entrusted, and in every part of which they had an interest, both in respect of their lien and in respect of their responsibility to their bailors'.[91] Having recovered the full value of the merchandise, the insureds, having deducted a sum reflecting their own interest, held the excess on trust for the owners of the goods.

The decision in *Waters* was followed in *Tomlinson (Hauliers) Ltd v Hepburn*.[92] The claimants, who were road haulage carriers, insured a consignment of cigarettes in respect of which they had contracted with the manufacturer to transport. The cigarettes were stolen without any fault or liability on the part of the claimants. The insurers repudiated the claim on the ground that, in the absence of any liability on the part of the claimants, there was no loss in respect of which they required indemnification. The House of Lords construed

[87] See the Sale of Goods Act 1979, ss 41 and 44–46.
[88] *Maurice v Goldsborough Mort & Co* [1939] AC 452.
[89] (1856) 5 El & Bl 870. See also *London & North-Western Ry v Glyn* (1859) 1 E & E 652.
[90] ibid 880.
[91] ibid 882.
[92] [1966] AC 451.

the contract as insurance on goods and held that the claimants, as bailees, had an insurable interest. The claimants could, therefore, retain any insurance monies covering their own loss (which on the facts of the present case was none), holding the balance on trust for the manufacturer. Lord Pearce noted that:

> The bailee of goods ... has a right to sue for conversion, holding in trust for the owner such damages as represent the owner's interest ... It would seem irrational ... if he could not also insure for their full value. Both those who have the legal title and those who have a right to possession have an insurable interest ... There seems, therefore, no reason in principle why they should not be entitled to insure for the whole value and recover it. They must, however (like [claimants] in actions of trover or negligence), hold in trust for the other parties interested so much of the moneys recovered as is attributable to the other interests.[93]

The approach taken by the House of Lords is premised upon commercial convenience.[94] It prevents multiplicity of insurances on the same property and avoids the need to inquire into the nature and extent of the interests of the different parties.[95]

However, whether the insured is entitled to recover for all the goods in his possession is a question which depends upon the construction of the policy in question. In *Ramco (UK) Ltd v International Insurance Co of Hanover Ltd*,[96] fire destroyed industrial premises occupied by the insured. The all risks policy covered buildings, content and stock. The terms 'contents' and 'stock' were defined as 'property of the Insured or held by the Insured in trust for which the Insured is responsible'. The insurers admitted liability in respect of property owned by the claimants but, because some of the goods that were damaged or destroyed were bailed to the insureds, they disputed the amount recoverable. The question for the Court of Appeal was whether the addition of the words 'for which he is responsible' restricts the insurers' liability to those goods damaged in a way which imposes liability on the bailee, but not otherwise.[97] The insurers argued that case law had long recognised that the addition of these words carried that meaning and that the court should not disturb that understanding.[98] In effect, the contention was that the phrase 'for which he is responsible' excluded the application of *Waters*. Andrew Smith J found in favour of the insurers,

[93] ibid 477.

[94] See the speech of Lord Pearce in ibid; see also the speech of Lord Reid in the same decision (467), who cited with approval the statement of Lord Campbell CJ in *Waters v Monarch Life and Fire Assurance Co* (1856) 5 El & Bl 870, 881: 'It would be most inconvenient in business if a wharfinger could not, his own cost, keep up a floating policy for the benefit of his customers.'

[95] *Ebsworth v Alliance Marine Insurance Co* (1873) LR 8 CP 596, 612 (Lord Bovill CJ). But note the view expressed by Waller LJ in *Ramco (UK) Ltd v International Insurance Co of Hanover Ltd* [2004] EWCA Civ 675, [32]: 'The principles established by *Waters* were highly convenient principles, but constituted an exception to the equally ancient common law principle that normally a claimant cannot sue for loss which he has not himself suffered; this was particularly striking where the cause of action was contractual (as a claim on an insurance policy always will be) since it appears inconsistent with the doctrine of privity of contract to enable a goods-owner to recover his loss when he is not a party to the contract. There is thus something of an anomaly in allowing a bailee to recover for a loss he has not suffered ... The anomaly is much less striking now that the Contracts (Rights of Third Parties) Act 1999 is on the statute book. But enabling a party to a contract to recover for a loss he has not suffered or enabling a goods-owner to recover pursuant to a contract to which he is not a party is still the exception rather than the rule; the 'exception' established in *Waters* should not itself be extended beyond its proper limits without good reason and no such reason exists in the present case.'

[96] ibid.

[97] The Court of Appeal was not required to consider whether, if cover was so restricted, the amount recoverable was limited to the insured's liability.

[98] See, eg *North British & Mercantile Insurance Co v Moffat* (1871) LR 7 CP 25; *Engel v Lancashire & General Assurance Co Ltd* (1925) 21 Ll L Rep 327.

holding that the term 'responsible' referred to those goods in respect of which the insureds were legally liable. The Court of Appeal agreed. Waller LJ explained that:

> If a form of words has been in use for 80 years which describes one sort of insurance rather than the other, it would be meddlesome for this court to decide that the selected form of words do not achieve their intended purpose, unless there were some real reason for supposing that the form of words is unsatisfactory in practice. The fact that the form of words is the subject-matter of a previous decision of this court is a compelling reason why the courts should not depart from that settled meaning.[99]

3.2.5. Marine Insurance: Specific Cases

Sections 7–13 of the Marine Insurance Act 1906 set out a series of specific situations in which insurable interest is taken to exist. Some of the sections are now redundant, others merely illustrate the above principles. Section 7 provides that defeasible and contingent interests are insurable. This catches the situations: (a) where the insured has interest but that interest may be defeated by later events, eg where the insured is in possession of property to which another has a better claim;[100] and (b) where the insured genuinely anticipates obtaining interest in subject matter, although if interest is not obtained by the time of loss then the principle of indemnity precludes recover. Section 8 states that partial interests are insurable, and that would include, for example, a security interest over property. Section 9, concerning reinsurance, is discussed in chapter 18 below. Section 10 confers upon the lender of money on bottomry or respondentia an insurable interest in the loan. These concepts are now obsolete, but until the middle of the nineteenth century were widely used. In essence, the master of a vessel was impliedly authorised by the owner to grant security over the vessel (bottomry) or its cargo (respondentia) in order to obtain funds to effect repairs to the vessel so that it could continue its voyage. The lender would recover the loan only if the vessel arrived safely at its destination. Hence, lenders were permitted to insure against the risk that the vessel would not complete the voyage by reason of an insured peril. Section 11 allows the master and crew to take out insurance against loss of wages. Until the law was changed by legislation in the middle of the nineteenth century, wages were earned only if the vessel completed its voyage and freight was earned by the shipowner ('freight is the mother of wages'), and wages were not insurable because that removed the crew's incentive to bring the vessel home. The abolition of the freight rule by the Merchant Shipping Act 1854, entitling the crew to wages come what may, undermined the ban on insuring wages, and the point was codified by section 11: this provision is now redundant. Section 12 is concerned with the situation where freight is paid by the cargo owner to the shipowner in advance of the voyage, on terms that the freight is not returnable if the vessel is prevented from completing the voyage: the cargo owner may therefore insure the non-returnable advance freight. Section 13 allows an insured who insures for the benefit of another person the right to insure the insurance paid by him. Finally, section 14 states that where the vessel is mortgaged, the mortgagor has an insurable interest in the full value of the vessel and the

[99] *Ramco (UK) Ltd v International Insurance Co of Hanover Ltd* [2004] EWCA Civ 675, [32].

[100] As in *Geismar v Sun Alliance and London Assurance Ltd* [1978] 1 QB 383, where an insured who had smuggled jewellery into England in circumstances where it was liable to be forfeited to the customs authorities was nevertheless held to have insurable interest in it, although the insured's claim was defeated on public policy grounds, as discussed in ch 5 above.

mortgagee has an insurable interest in the amount of the sum advanced under the mortgage: that reflects the law in relation to ordinary mortgages as well as maritime mortgages.

3.3. Towards a Broader Test of 'Factual Expectation'

The old restrictive approach to insurable interest has not escaped judicial criticism in England, nor has it found favour with academics or in other common law jurisdictions.[101] For example, Lord Eldon's reasoning was emphatically rejected by Wilson J in *Constitution Insurance Company of Canada v Kosmopoulos*,[102] in which the Canadian Supreme Court adopted the more liberal 'factual expectation' test propounded by Lawrence J in *Lucena v Craufurd*.[103] Put simply, under this test a moral certainty of profit or loss is sufficient to constitute insurable interest. Thus, on very similar facts to *Macaura*,[104] the insured was able to recover under the policies on the basis that as a sole shareholder of the company he 'was so placed with respect to the assets of the business as to have benefit from their existence and prejudice from their destruction. He had a moral certainty of advantage or benefit from those assets but for the fire.' Addressing the concern of Lord Eldon that a broader definition of insurable interest would lead to an increase of liability of insurers upon the occurrence of a single insured event owing to an increased number of policies covering the same risk, Wilson J said:

> But insurance companies have always faced the difficult task of calculating their total potential liability arising upon the occurrence of an insured event in order to judge whether to make a particular policy or class of policies and to calculate the appropriate premium to be charged. It is not for this Court to substitute its judgment for the sound business judgment and actuarial expertise of insurance companies by holding that a certain class of policies should not be made because it will result in too much insurance. I would have thought that a stronger argument could be made that there is too little insurance. Why should the porter in Lord Eldon's example not be able to obtain insurance against the possibility of being temporarily out of work as a result of the sinking of ships? … A broadening of the concept of insurable interest would, it seems to me, allow for the creation of more socially beneficial insurance policies than is the case at present with no increase in risk to the insurer. I therefore find both of Lord Eldon's reasons for adopting a restrictive approach to insurable interest unpersuasive.[105]

The broader 'factual expectation' test has been followed in many American states. For example, paragraph 3401 of Article 34 of the New York Insurance Law defines insurable interest as including 'any lawful or substantial economic interest in the safety or preservation of property from loss, destruction or pecuniary damage'. The Wisconsin Insurance Code has gone further by dispensing with the requirement of an insurable interest for the validity of

[101] In *Stock v Inglis* (1885) LR 10 App Cas 263, Lord Brett MR noted that it is 'merely a technical objection … which has no real merit … as between the assured and the insurer'. More recently, see the comments of Waller LJ in *Feasey v Sun Life Assurance Corporation of Canada* [2003] EWCA Civ 885. For criticism, see AJ Campbell, 'Some Aspects of Insurable Interest' (1949) 27 *Canadian Bar Review* 1; RA Hasson, 'Reform of the Law Relating to Insurable Interest in Property – Some Thoughts on *Chadwick v Gibraltar General Insurance*' (1983–84) 8 *Canadian Business Law Journal* 114; Lowry and Rawlings (n 7). For the implications for insurance law of the Gambling Act 2005, see J Davey, 'The Reform of Gambling and the Future of Insurance Law' [2004] *Legal Studies* 507.

[102] (1987) 1 SCR 2.

[103] (1806) 2 Bos & Pul (NR) 269.

[104] [1925] AC 619.

[105] ibid 17.

an insurance policy. In New Zealand, the Insurance Law Reform Act 1985, section 7(1) abolishes the requirement of insurable interest in the case of life insurance, and all contracts of indemnity insurance and similar measures have been adopted in Australia in the Insurance Contracts Act 1984, sections 16–18.

It is plain from the more recent English decisions that a wider and more liberal approach is being taken to the question of insurable interest. As already noted, section 5(2) of the 1906 Act is not expressed in exhaustive terms and it has been possible for the courts to expand the definition. In *Mark Rowlands Ltd v Berni Inns Ltd*,[106] the Court of Appeal adopted and approved the definition propounded by Lawrence J in *Lucena v Craufurd*,[107] despite the fact that Lord Eldon's formulation of insurable interest formed the backdrop to the House of Lords decision in *Macaura*.[108] More recently, the issue has emerged in the context of insurers' rights of subrogation. Simply put, on paying a claim in full, the insurer takes on the rights of action which the insured would have had: in effect, the insurer steps into the shoes of the insured, as discussed below in chapter 13. This means that the insurer can, for instance, sue the tortfeasor responsible for the loss. However, the tortfeasor can use all the defences that would have been available against an action brought by the insured, and the insurer will have no action where the loss is caused by the insured.[109]

This is of particular importance in insurance policies relating to construction contracts, in which the head contractor is commonly required by the contract to insure the project for their own benefit and that of the subcontractors. The issue then comes down to whether the subcontractor has an insurable interest which will grant immunity against the insurers' subrogation rights. In *Petrofina (UK) v Magnaload Ltd*,[110] Lloyd J held that each of the individual subcontractors on a construction site had an insurable interest in the entire works despite the fact that they were working only on limited parts of the site, their interest arising not from any ownership or possession, but from the fact that, in the event of negligence, they would face liability for any part of the works damaged or destroyed. Although the subcontractors had no property interest in the works in progress, they had an insurable interest in the continued existence of those works. In so finding, the judge drew the analogy of the insurable interest possessed by a bailee in goods bailed to him. Accordingly, it was possible for a policy covering the entire works to be taken out on a co-insurance basis by the head contractor and all subcontractors. Lloyd J reasoned that to hold to the contrary would result in commercial inconvenience as each subcontractor would need

> to take out his own separate policy. This would mean, at the very least, extra paperwork; at worst it could lead to overlapping claims and cross claims in the event of an accident. Furthermore … the cost of insuring his liability might in the case of a small sub-contractor, be uneconomic.[111]

The judge therefore held that the subcontractor's insurable interest lay in a 'pervasive' interest in the entire property. In the absence of any English decision directly on the point,

[106] [1986] QB 211.
[107] (1806) 2 Bos & Pul (NR) 269.
[108] [1925] AC 619.
[109] *Simpson v Thompson* (1877) 3 App Cas 279.
[110] [1983] 2 Lloyd's Rep 91. See also *Sharp v Sphere Drake Insurance Ltd, The Moonacre* [1992] 2 Lloyd's Rep 501; J Birds, 'Insurable Interests' in N Palmer and E McKendrick (eds), *Interests in Goods* (London, LLP, 1998) ch 4.
[111] *Petrofina (UK) v Magnaload Ltd* [1983] 2 Lloyd's Rep 91, 96–97. In *Hopewell Project Management Ltd v Ewbank Preece Ltd* [1998] 1 Lloyd's Rep 448 it was held that the term 'contractor' or 'subcontractor' in a contractor's all risk policy did not encompass those who gave advice in a professional capacity, which on the facts of the case were those who provided advisory engineering services in respect of the installation of gas turbines.

Lloyd J turned to the decision of the Supreme Court of Canada in *Commonwealth Construction Co Ltd v Imperial Oil Ltd*, in which de Grandpre J stated:

> On any construction site, and especially when the building being erected is a complex chemical plant, there is ever present the possibility of damage by one tradesman to the property of another and to the construction as a whole … By recognising in all tradesmen an insurable interest based on that very real possibility, which itself has its source in the contractual arrangements opening the doors of the job site to the tradesman, the Courts would apply to the construction field the principle expressed so long ago in the area of bailment. Thus all the parties whose joint efforts have one common goal, eg the completion of the construction, would be spared the necessity of fighting between themselves should an accident occur involving the possible responsibility of one of them.[112]

This approach was adopted by Colman J in *National Oilwell Ltd v Davy Offshore (UK) Ltd*,[113] in holding that the suppliers of a subsea well head completion system for a floating oil production facility were co-insured's under the contractors' all risks policy. The judge dismissed the contention that there cannot be an insurable interest based merely on potential liability arising from the existence of a contract between the insured and the owner of property. He held that an insurable interest could be found in 'the insured's proximate physical relationship to the property in question'.[114] Citing Lloyd J's judgment in *Petrofina*, Colman J said:

> There is, in my judgment, in particular no reason in principle why such a supplier should not, and every commercial reason why he should, be able to insure against loss of or damage to property involved in the common project not owned by him and not in his possession. The argument that because he has no possessory or proprietary interest in the property he can have no insurable interest in it and that his potential liability in respect of loss of or damage to it is insufficient to found such an insurable interest is in my judgment misconceived.[115]

The Court of Appeal tentatively approved of the more expansive approach to the issue of insurable interest in *Glengate-KG Properties Ltd v Norwich Union Fire Insurance Society Ltd*.[116] The court had to consider the meaning of the phrase 'the interest of the insured' in a policy covering the owner of a building against consequential loss following a fire or other insured peril. The issue for the court was whether the insured could recover for the loss of architects' drawings which were, at the time of the loss, owned by the architects, even though the insured might eventually have acquired them. It was held that the insured had an insurable interest in the drawings despite his lack of proprietary interest in them. Although

[112] (1976) 69 DLR (3d) 558, 561.

[113] [1993] 2 Lloyd's Rep 582.

[114] ibid 611. See also *Stone Vickers Ltd v Appledore Ferguson Shipbuilders Ltd* [1991] 2 Lloyd's Rep 288, 301, in which Colman J (sitting then as Mr Anthony Colman QC, a deputy judge of the High Court) stated that a risk of being 'materially adversely affected by loss of or damage to' the contract works 'by reason of the incidence of any of the perils insured against' was capable of amounting to 'a sufficient [insurable] interest in the whole contract works' (reversed by the Court of Appeal on another ground without the issue of insurable interest being considered [1992] 2 Lloyd's Rep 578). In *Hopewell Project Management Ltd v Ewbank Preece Ltd* 1998] 1 Lloyd's Rep 448, 456, Mr Recorder Jackson QC, applying *National Oilwell UK Ltd*, stated that had the defendant contractors satisfied the definition of 'insured' contained in the policy, 'the fact that the defendants were carrying out the professional services on site, and the fact that the defendants might incur legal liability for negligently causing damage to the contract works, gave the defendants an insurable interest in the contract works'.

[115] ibid.

[116] [1996] 1 Lloyd's Rep 614.

the court saw his insurable interest as being in respect of consequential loss rather than in the actual drawings themselves, nevertheless Auld LJ and Sir Iain Glidewell, citing *Mark Rowlands Ltd v Berni Inns Ltd*, expressed the view that the insured could have insured the drawings on the basis of Lawrence J's 'factual expectation' test.[117] While not the primary issue in these cases, the definition of insurable interest was nevertheless decisive in determining the rights and obligations of the parties. This line of authority can therefore be seen as amounting to some recognition by the English courts of the broader conception of interest adopted in Canada and elsewhere. However, some limit was placed upon this trend by the Court of Appeal in *Deepak Fertilisers & Petrochemical Corporation v Davy McKee (London) Ltd and ICI Chemicals and Polymers Ltd*.[118] The court did accept the broad conception of insurable interest in finding that a subcontractor in a building contract possessed an insurable interest in the entire works during construction. This was because of the economic disadvantage which would be suffered if, in the event of the structure being damaged or destroyed, they lost the opportunity to complete the work and receive remuneration. However, the court stressed that once the work had been completed, such interest came to an end.

The litigation arose out of the construction for Deepak of a methanol plant in India which exploded a few months after it was commissioned. There was a 'marine-cum-erection' policy under which contractors and subcontractors were named as co-assureds. The subcontractors included Davy McKee, a firm of consulting engineers, and ICI, who had provided expertise and technology. The critical question was whether the co-assureds had an insurable interest and were therefore immune from an action brought by Deepak's insurers exercising subrogation rights. At first instance, Rix J rejected the insurers' contention that the decisions in *Petrofina* and *National Oilwell Ltd* pointed to the cessation of insurable interest after completion of the works and concluded that Davy and ICI possessed the requisite interest so long as they were arguably responsible for damage to it. Since it was the insurer's case that Davy and ICI bore responsibility for the explosion even though it happened after completion of the plant, Rix J felt that they should 'in principle ... be entitled to insure against their potential liability'.[119] In his view, the question relating to any temporal limitation on a contractor's insurable interest had not arisen in the earlier case law, but he saw no reason why an architect, technical designer or constructor should not be able to insure against liability for damage due to their fault, even though it occurred after completion of the structure.

The Court of Appeal, reversing the judge's decision, held that the insurable interests of the co-assureds ceased immediately upon completion of the works and did not continue thereafter merely because they could be exposed to potential liability at some future time. It followed that any damage to the plant after it was commissioned that was attributable to the fault of Davy could not be regarded as covered by the insurance policy. The insurers, therefore, could sue Davy. Stuart-Smith LJ stated that once the works were complete:

> Davy would only suffer disadvantage if the damage to or destruction of the property or structure was the result of their breach of contract or duty of care. In order to protect the contractor and

[117] ibid 623–24 and 625–26, respectively.

[118] [1999] 1 Lloyd's Rep 387. See also *Tyco Fire & Integrated solutions (UK) Ltd v Rolls-Royce Motor Cars Ltd* [2008] 1 CLC 625. See further AT Olubajo, 'Pervasive Insurable Interest: A Reappraisal' [2004] *Construction Law Journal* 45.

[119] [1998] 2 Lloyd's Rep 139, 158.

> sub-contractors against the risk of disadvantage by reason of damage or destruction of the property or structure resulting from their breach of contract or duty, they would, in accordance with normal practice take out liability insurance, or, in the case of architects, professional indemnity insurance … what they cannot do is persist in maintaining an insurance of the property or structure itself.[120]

Significantly, he did concede that the trial judge had been correct in stating that an architect, technical designer or contractor can participate in insurance under an all risks policy because if the project were not completed due to the occurrence of an insured risk they would lose remuneration. Stuart-Smith LJ thereby adds further authority to the line of decisions beginning with *Petrofina*.[121] However, he took the view that an all risks policy on a building project is property insurance. The contractor and subcontractors have insurable interests because they may suffer economic loss if building work ceases. Once the construction is completed, the contractors no longer have such an interest in the property and must effect a separate policy to cover any potential liability for their own negligence or breach of contract which results in damage to the building arising after completion. This maintains the distinction between property and liability insurance, which, it has been argued,[122] was undermined by the decisions in *Stone Vickers* and *National Oilwell*. Indeed, on this point it was seen above that Waller LJ in *Feasey* was of the same mind.

The issue was revisited by the Court of Appeal in *Co-operative Retail Services Ltd v Taylor Young Partnership*.[123] The action arose as a consequence of a fire occurring on a construction site owned by the claimants, Co-operative Retail Services Ltd (CRS). The main contractor was Wimpey (W), the architects were Taylor Young Partnership (TYP), the electrical engineers were Hoare Lea & Partners (HLP) and the electrical subcontractors, who worked on the building's generator system, were Hall Electrical (H). H entered into a warranty with CRS and W in which H undertook to exercise all reasonable skill. CRS claimed that the fire was caused by negligence or breach of contract on the part of TYP and HLP. TYP and HLP argued that the fire was caused by breaches of the main contract by W and breaches of warranty by H, and they therefore sought contribution from them under the Civil Liability (Contribution) Act 1978. Both the trial judge and Brooke LJ referred extensively to *National Oilwell* and *Petrofina*, placing particular emphasis on Lloyd J's use of the *Commonwealth Construction* case and the notion of pervasive interest (although the decision was upheld by the House of Lords, reference was not made to this point).[124] Brooke LJ accepted that CRS's insurers, acting through subrogation, could not pursue W or H because they were named as co-insureds under CRS's policy,[125] and consequently they were not liable to contribute to TYP and HLP because, as co-insureds, they were not 'other person[s] liable in respect of the same damage (whether jointly with him or otherwise)' under section 1(1) of the 1978 Act.

We saw above in relation to life policies that the Court of Appeal in *Feasey* advocated a more flexible approach towards the determination of insurable interest. The point was

[120] [1999] 1 Lloyd's Rep 387, 399.

[121] Stuart-Smith LJ (ibid) observed: 'Davy undoubtedly had an insurable interest in the plant under construction and on which they were working because they might lose the opportunity to do the work and to be remunerated for it if the property or structure were damaged or destroyed by any of the "all risks", such as fire or flood.'

[122] See J Birds [2002] *Journal of Business Law* 351.

[123] [2001] Lloyd's Rep IR 122.

[124] [2002] UKHL 17.

[125] See *Simpson v Thompson* (1877) 3 App Cas 279.

made that the court also took the opportunity to consider the requirement in the round and expressed views on the determination of insurable interest in property insurance. Waller LJ categorised the construction cases considered above and in *Sharp v Sphere Drake, The Moonacre*[126] as 'policies in which the court has recognised interests which are not even strictly pecuniary'.[127] Having reviewed the case law, he went on to summarise the authorities in the following terms:

> The principles which I would suggest one gets from the authorities are as follows: (1) It is from the terms of the policy that the subject of the insurance must be ascertained; (2) It is from all the surrounding circumstances that the nature of an insured's insurable interest must discovered; (3) There is no hard and fast rule that because the nature of an insurable interest relates to a liability to compensate for loss, that insurable interest could only be covered by a liability policy rather than a policy insuring property or life or indeed properties or lives; (4) The question whether a policy embraces the insurable interest intended to be recovered is a question of construction. The subject or terms of the policy may be so specific as to force a court to hold that the policy has failed to cover the insurable interest, but a court will be reluctant so to hold. (5) It is not a requirement of property insurance that the insured must have a 'legal or equitable' interest in the property as those terms might normally be understood. It is sufficient for a sub-contractor to have a contract that relates to the property and a potential liability for damage to the property to have an insurable interest in the property.[128]

The observations of Waller LJ on the position in property insurance are, strictly speaking, obiter. Nevertheless, they serve to reinforce the view that an overly strict test of insurable interest is out of line with current commercial practices. As such, it is noteworthy that the unease on the part of certain judges towards the requirement is by no means a modern phenomenon.[129] As indicated above, the courts have long been ill disposed towards allowing lack of insurable interest to be pleaded where insurers are fully cognisant of the risk covered by the policy.[130] This can be seen in *The Capricorn*,[131] in which Mance J observed that:

> [T]he present policy is not on its face one which the parties made for other than ordinary business reasons; it does not bear the hallmarks of wagering or the like. If underwriters make a contract in deliberate terms which covers their assured in respect of a specific situation, a Court is likely to hesitate before accepting a defence of lack of insurable interest.

[126] [1992] 2 Lloyd's Rep 501.

[127] ibid [90].

[128] ibid [97].

[129] It should be noted that in *Feasey* Ward LJ, dissenting, reasoned that the House of Lords' decisions in *Lucena v Crauford* and *Macaura v Northern Assurance* were binding and had to be followed.

[130] In this respect, the position of insurers is safeguarded by the duty of fair presentation: see ch 4. See *Feasey v Sun Life Assurance Co of Canada* [2003] EWCA Civ 885, in which Langley J, considering the rationale underlying the Life Assurance Act 1774, observed that 'in the early 19th century the law of disclosure had not been developed to provide the protection to insurers which it does today'.

[131] *Cepheus Shipping Corporation v Guardian Royal Exchange Assurance plc, The Capricorn* [1995] 1 Lloyd's Rep 622, 641. Some 110 years earlier, Lord Brett MR had observed that 'it is the duty of a Court always to lean in favour of an insurable interest, if possible, for it seems to me that after underwriters have received the premium, the objection that there was no insurable interest is often, as nearly as possible, a technical objection, and one which has no real merit, certainly not between the assured and the insurer': *Stock v Inglis* (1885) LR 10 App Cas 263. See also *Feasey v Sun Life Assurance Corporation of Canada* [2003] EWCA Civ 885, [6], where Waller LJ stated: 'It is not attractive to contemplate that where insurers have carefully crafted a policy which was intended to be enforceable [that] … a point on insurable interest could arise.' See further the report of the Australian Law Reform Commission, *Insurance Contracts*, No 20 (1982) ch 5; ALRC Discussion Paper No 63, *Review of the Marine Insurance Act 1909*, ch 7. In different context, but to the same effect, see *Cleaver v Mutual Reserve Fund Life Association* [1892] 1 QB 147, 151 (Lord Brett MR); *Saunders v Edwards* [1987] 1 WLR 1116, 1134 (Bingham LJ).

The insistence on requiring insurable interest, whatever definition is adopted, harks back to a time when policy issues dictated that this should be a precondition to the validity of the insurance contract. Once those policy arguments are removed, the justification for the requirement disappears.[132] It is arguable that the principle of indemnity, which prohibits recovery to those who cannot establish proof of loss, is in itself sufficient to render the requirement redundant. The English and Scottish Law Commissions, having considered the matter at length, ultimately concluded in their 2018 draft Bill that substantial changes were not required. The draft Bill proposed minor changes to marine insurance, most importantly the repeal of the criminal sanction for insuring without interest in the Marine Insurance (Gambling Policies) Act 1909. For non-marine insurance, the Law Commissions proposed no changes to the law.

Perhaps the last word should be left to HH Judge Mackie QC in *Western Trading Ltd v Great Lakes Reinsurance (UK) Plc*,[133] a case in which a variety of defences to a claim were put forward, including that the occupier of a building responsible for its maintenance had no insurable interest in it. That defence was unreservedly rejected:

> It has in the past been unusual for insurers to raise questions of insurable interest except in the context of fraud. This is an issue which, judging by the materials generated when taking the risk, the [insurers] neither took an interest in (nor alerted [the assured] to the perceived importance of) until the claim came in. There is nothing in the proposal forms or other correspondence to alert a broker or potential customer of [the insurers] and its subsidiaries that it should consider the issue closely, and perhaps take legal and accountancy advice, before entering into a policy with them.

[132] On this, see the comments of the Australian Law Reform Commission, *Insurance Contracts*, 5; *Review of the Marine Insurance Act 1909*, para 11.24.

[133] [2015] EWHC 103 (QB). The decision was upheld in *Great Lakes Reinsurance (UK) SE v Western Trading Ltd* [2016] EWCA Civ 1003 without reference to this point.

7

Third Party Rights

1. Third Parties and Insurance

The question to be addressed in this chapter is whether a person who is not an original party to a policy of insurance can acquire rights under the policy. There are obvious legal obstacles to a claim by a third party. The first is the common law doctrine of privity of contract, and although privity has ceased to be an automatic bar following the passing of the Contracts (Rights of Third Parties) Act 1999, that Act can be excluded by contract. The second is an absence of consideration moving from the third party to the insurers. Thirdly, there may be insurable interest issues, in that a policy that purports to confer benefit on a third party will be ineffective if the third party cannot suffer any loss insured by the policy. That was the position in *Cruise and Maritime Services International Ltd v Navigators Underwriting Agency Ltd, The Marco Polo*,[1] where a liability policy taken out by the charter of a vessel was held not to protect an intermediary even though the intermediary was identified as an insured person. As a matter of the general law, that can happen in one of two ways: the policy may be taken out for the benefit of a third party; and there may be an assignment of the policy or its proceeds to a third party. This chapter is concerned with those two matters. There are other possibilities discussed elsewhere in this book. The Third Parties (Rights against Insurers) Act 2010 confers rights of action under liability policies in favour of third parties suffering losses at the hands of any insured person.[2] The victim of a motor accident has a direct claim against the negligent driver's insurers under the Road Traffic Act 1988 and the European Communities (Rights against Insurers) Regulations 2002.[3] The Fires Prevention (Metropolis) Act 1774, section 83 provides that any 'person interested' in a building can require the insurer to reinstate following damage irrespective of whether such a person is a party to the contract of insurance.[4] A policy may also confer a negative benefit on a third party, in the form of immunity from a subrogation claim by the insurers.[5]

[1] [2017] EWHC 843 (Comm).
[2] See ch 15 below.
[3] SI 2002/3061; ch 14 below.
[4] See ch 12 below.
[5] See ch 13 below.

This chapter considers the circumstances in which a third party may derive rights under an insurance policy to which he or she is not a party. On the assumption that such rights have been acquired, a further question is the nature and scope of those rights where the effect of the arrangements is to create co-insurance as between the insured and third parties.

---

2. Insuring on Behalf of Another Person

2.1. Agency

2.1.1. Ordinary Agency Principles

Where an agency relationship can be shown to exist, the agent may sue on the insurance contract in his own name on behalf of the principal.[6] With respect to the principal, the position was succinctly stated in *Lloyd's v Harper*[7] by Lush LJ: 'It is true that the [third party principal] has a right, if he pleases, to take action himself and sue upon the contract made by the broker for him, for he is a principal party to the contract.'[8] The primary insured under a policy may contract as agent for third parties and thereby bring them within the scope of the cover as co-insureds. Agency will be created if three conditions are satisfied. First, the insured must be authorised by the third party to effect insurance on the third party's behalf. Secondly, the insured must have intended to effect insurance as agent for the third party. If the insured is authorised by the third party to procure insurance, or – as is commonly the case – the insured is required by contract with the third party to procure insurance, then it is straightforward to find that the insured intended to insure for the third party.[9] Thirdly, the policy by its terms covers the third party's interests. The mere fact that a policy can be construed as extending to a third party does not suffice: unless the third party had appointed the insured as agent, or has ratified the insured's action in taking out the policy, the third party cannot claim the benefit of the insurance.[10] Agency is widely used in insurance. To take two common examples, a parent company may insure on behalf of itself and its subsidiaries and a building contractor may insure on behalf of itself and all subcontractors.

The requirements for agency are illustrated by *Williams v Baltic Insurance Association of London Ltd*.[11] The claimant effected a motor policy on his car which covered liability to third parties for personal injuries caused by the use of the vehicle. The policy also contained a clause (clause 2) which stated that the insurers would indemnify the insured against

> all sums for which the insured (or any licensed personal friend or relative of the insured while driving the car with the insured's general knowledge and consent) shall become legally liable in compensation for loss of life or accidental bodily injury caused to any person.

[6] See the speech of Lord Campbell CJ in *Waters v Monarch Life and Fire Assurance Co* (1856) 5 El & Bl 870, 881; *Cochran & Son v Leckie's Trustee* (1906) 8 F (Ct Sess) 975. As to an unnamed insured, see *Provincial Insurance Co of Canada v Leduc* (1874) LR 6 PC 224, 244 (Sir Barnes Peacock).

[7] (1880) 16 Ch D 290.

[8] ibid 321.

[9] *National Oilwell v Davy Offshore* [1993] 2 Lloyd's Rep 582.

[10] *Rugby Football Union v Clark Smith Partnership Ltd* [2022] EWHC 965 (TCC).

[11] [1924] 2 KB 282.

The claimant's sister, while driving the car with his consent, was involved in an accident which resulted in her being liable to pay damages for injuries caused to third parties. The issue question which arose for Roche J's determination was whether the claimant could be indemnified on his sister's behalf. Construing clause 2 of the policy, it was plain to the judge that it was expressed to cover precisely the situation which arose on the facts of the case. On this point, Roche J using language which resonates with that of agency principles, concluded that:

> The [claimant] is the insured in the sense that he is the person who effected the insurance, but it is an insurance for himself and the other persons mentioned in cl. 2, and, accordingly, the company's contract is to indemnify all such persons in the event of those things happening against which the insurance is effected.

On this basis, the third party as principal could enforce the contract effected by her agent, her brother. *Vandepitte v Preferred Accident Insurance Corporation of New York*[12] has facts analogous to *Williams v Baltic* insofar as the insured had contracted with the insurers for an indemnity against third party risks and the policy provided that the indemnity should extend to any person driving the insured's car with his consent. Vandepitte (V), the third party, had obtained judgment against the insured's daughter (B) for personal injuries caused by her negligence while driving the insured's car with his permission. V sued the insurers to recover the amount of the unsatisfied judgment on the basis that B was insured against liability by virtue of her father's policy.[13] Counsel for V argued that because the policy extended the indemnity against third party risks to those driving the vehicle with the insured's permission and because B habitually did so, it can be inferred that the father effected the policy upon her behalf as well as his own. By leaving the defence of the action to the insurers as required by the policy, this could be taken as ratification by B of the contract. Lord Wright, delivering the opinion of the Privy Council, held that the policy did not extend to cover the liability of the insured's daughter. The contracting party was B's father and he had not effected the policy as agent for B, who was completely unaware of having entered into a contract of insurance and, as such, no agency could be inferred. It should here be noted that this precise question has been addressed by what is now section 148(7) of the Road Traffic Act 1988, under which

> a person issuing a policy of insurance under section 145 of this Act shall be liable to indemnify the persons or classes of persons specified in the policy in respect of any liability which the policy purports to cover in the case of those persons or classes of persons.[14]

A recent New Zealand case further illustrates the operation of the agency rules. In *HHR Christchurch NTL Ltd v Crystal Imports Ltd*,[15] Crystal was the owner of the Warner's Hotel in Cathedral Square, Christchurch, and had leased the building to tenants on terms that the tenants were permitted, but not required, to effect buildings insurance covering Crystal. The insurance stated, by way of 'noting' that Crystal was an 'interested party … for its respective rights and interests'. The tenants informed Crystal that such insurance was in place, and Crystal therefore chose not to renew its own policy. Crystal claimed against the

[12] [1933] AC 70.
[13] Note that in *Williams* it was the insured who sued on the policy, not the third party as here.
[14] See ch 14 below.
[15] [2015] NZCA 283.

insurers following serious earthquake damage to the hotel. The New Zealand Court of Appeal held that Crystal had no claim under the policy: although the tenants had been authorised to insure on Crystal's behalf, there was no evidence that it had intended to do so, and in any event the policy wording was not sufficient to extend coverage to Crystal. *HHR* is an important decision on the effect of 'noting' a third party's interest on a policy. Noting is a common practice, although the limited English authority that exists is to the effect that noting does not have the effect of bringing the noted party within the terms of the cover.[16] *HHR* confirms that noting gives a false sense of security and does not create co-insurance.

2.1.2. Undisclosed Principal

The law of agency recognises that a third party is entitled to take the benefit of a contract made on his behalf by an authorised agent even if the existence of the third party has not been disclosed. The general position was stated by Lord Denning MR in *Teheran-Europe Co Ltd v ST Belton Tractors) Ltd*,[17] where he said:

> A person may enter into a contract through an agent whom he has actually authorized to enter into the contract on his behalf–.where an agent has such actual authority and enters into a contract with another party intending to do so on behalf of his principal, it matters not whether he discloses to the other party the identity of his principal, or even that he is contracting on behalf of a principal at all, if the other party is willing or leads the agent to believe that he is willing to treat as a party to the contract anyone on whose behalf the agent may have been authorized to contract. In the case of an ordinary contract, such willingness of the other party may be assumed by the agent unless either the other party manifests his unwillingness or there are other circumstances which should lead the agent to realize that the other party was not so willing.[18]

The doctrine of undisclosed principal was adopted by Colman J in *National Oilwell Ltd v Davy Offshore (UK) Ltd*,[19] in considering whether the suppliers, NOW, as co-insureds could make a direct claim under a contractors' all risks policy taken out by its customer DOL. The learned judge stated that NOW could establish privity of contract with the insurers by establishing that they were the undisclosed or unnamed principals of DOL, subject to establishing that at the time of effecting the policy DOL intended to effect insurance cover on behalf of NOW.[20] Reviewing the earlier authorities,[21] Colman J held that where at the time the insurance contract was concluded the principal insured or other contracting party had express or implied actual authority to make the contract so as to bind some other party as co-insured and intended to bind that other party, the latter may enforce the policy as the undisclosed principal and co-insured irrespective of whether the policy described a class of co-insured of which he or she was or became a member. The judge went on to explain that evidence of the requisite intention may be provided by the terms of the policy document,

[16] *First National Commercial Bank Plc v Barnet Devanney (Harrow) Ltd* [1999] Lloyd's Rep IR 43, reversed on other grounds and without reference to this point [1999] Lloyd's Rep IR 459.

[17] [1968] 2 QB 545.

[18] ibid 555.

[19] [1993] 2 Lloyd's Rep 582.

[20] ibid 597.

[21] Principally, *Boston Fruit Co v British and Foreign Marine Insurance Co* [1905] 1 KB 637; *Graham Joint Stock Shipping Co v Merchants Marine Insurance Co* [1924] AC 294; and the Court of Appeal's decision in *Stone Vickers Ltd v Appledore Ferguson Shipbuilders Ltd* [1992] 2 Lloyd's Rep 578.

by the terms of any contract between the principal insured or other contracting party and the alleged co-assured, or by any other admissible material showing what was subjectively intended by the principal.

In *Siu Yin Kwan v Eastern Insurance Co Ltd*,[22] the Privy Council took the opportunity to subject the third party principal's rights to detailed consideration. The central issue in the case, which concerned employers' liability insurance effected by shipping agents on behalf of shipowners, was the insurers' contention that non-marine insurance contracts were so personal that the doctrine of undisclosed principal did not apply to them. The Privy Council rejected their argument, holding that the doctrine was of general application. That finding raised the further question that in insurance contracts the identity of the insured is a material fact to the assessment of the risk and that failure to disclose the agency arrangement was a breach of the duty of fair presentation. The Privy Council held on this point that in a case where the insurance was being taken out by a known agent on behalf of a principal, and the insurers agreed to insure, the identity of the principal was plainly a matter of indifference and could not be regarded as material to the risks insured against, ie employers' liability.[23] The questions in the proposal form were completed fully as if they referred to the shipowners and the policy document did not exclude, either expressly or impliedly, the rights of the shipowners to sue as undisclosed principal.

These decisions were distinguished in *Talbot Underwriting Ltd v Nausch Hogan & Murray, The Jascon 5*.[24] The barge *Jascon 5*, which was owned by CPL, was sent to Singapore for repair and refurbishment by S. The contract stated that S would indemnify CPL for all claims for damage to the vessel and would insure against those risks. CPL for its part was required to take out a builder's all risks policy, which was to cover the interests of S. The all risks policy named CPL and its 'Subsidiary, Affiliates, Associated and Interrelated Companies and/or Joint Ventures as may be required as their respective rights and interest may appear' as the insured. Further, the policy also stated that it extended to the 'Assured, interest of Mortgagees (and Notices of Assignment in respect thereof), Loss Payees, Additional Assureds and Waivers of Subrogation as may be required'. CPL did not inform the insurers that S was intended to be a co-insured under the policy. The vessel was flooded while undergoing repairs and S claimed on the insurance. This was rejected by the insurers on the basis that S was not an insured under the policy. In relation to the issues surrounding undisclosed principal, the Court of Appeal held that S could not claim under the policy. Moore-Bick LJ, who gave leading judgment, reviewed the principles laid down in *Siu Yiu*, and noted that the key question was 'whether the terms of the contract or the circumstances surrounding it were such as to make it clear that the insurers were willing to contract only with the person or persons identified as the assureds in the slip'.[25] The judge went on to say:

> The mere identification, whether by name or description, of certain persons as assureds cannot be sufficient of itself to demonstrate an unwillingness on the part of the insurer to contract with any other person. If it were otherwise, the principles under discussion would have no application

[22] [1994] 1 All ER 213.

[23] *cf* an existing motor insurance policy, about which Sir Wilfred Greene MR said in *Peters v General Accident Fire & Life Assurance Corp Ltd* [1938] 2 All ER 267, 269: '[A] contract of that kind is in its very nature not assignable … That appears to me to be altering *in toto* the character of the risk.'

[24] [2006] Lloyd's Rep IR 531.

[25] ibid [26].

> at all to contracts of insurance. Each case must therefore be decided by reference to the terms of the contract under consideration and the circumstances in which it came to be made, though no doubt due regard should be had to the warning of Lord Lloyd in *Siu Yin Kwan v Eastern Insurance Co Ltd* that if the courts are too ready to construe written contracts as contradicting the right of an undisclosed principal to intervene it would go far to destroy the beneficial assumption in commercial cases to which Diplock LJ referred in *Teheran-Europe Co Ltd v ST Belton (Tractors) Ltd*.[26]

With these considerations in mind, Moore-Bick LJ, agreeing with Cooke J at first instance, thought that the omission of S as a category of insureds on the slip was 'striking, particularly when it is borne in mind that their inclusion as co-assureds would have a significant effect on the insurers' rights of subrogation and therefore on the risk'.[27] Although the doctrine of undisclosed principal could apply only where the policy properly construed was capable of extending to the interests of the undisclosed principal, the judge thought that the wording of the policy in the present case was limited to specific classes of insured. Moore-Bick LJ commented, obiter, that if the court was wrong on the undisclosed principal point and S was an undisclosed principal, the existence of S as an intended principal was a material fact which ought to have been disclosed to the insurers. He stated that:

> The fact that the law generally recognises the right of an undisclosed principal to sue and be sued on a contract does not relieve the nominal insured from the duty to make full disclosure of all material circumstances in each case, including any which may relate to his undisclosed principal. That is essential to ensure a fair presentation of the risk to the insurer.[28]

Although he recognised that in most cases the identity of the undisclosed principal does not matter, in the present case it was material to the risk, because if S was a co-insured it would limit the insurers' subrogation's rights.[29] The undisclosed principal doctrine could not, therefore, operate if the insurers had no indication that the insured was acting for a third party as well as himself.

2.1.3. *Ratification*

Where an agent enters into a contract on behalf of his principal but without authority, the principal is permitted to ratify the unauthorised act and to adopt the contract. Ratification applies to insurance in the same way as any other contract. There are a number of conditions for ratification. First, the principal must at the time the contract was made have been of full capacity and entitled to enter the contract in his or her own right. This principle is derived from decisions to the effect that a contract made on behalf of a company not formed until after the contract has been made cannot be ratified by the company.[30] Secondly, the principal must be identified: it is a long-standing rule that an undisclosed principal cannot ratify a contract.[31] Thirdly, the agent must have intended to contract on behalf of the principal, a test satisfied in insurance cases where the agent is authorised or required

[26] ibid [27].
[27] ibid [35].
[28] ibid [43].
[29] ibid [41].
[30] *Natal Land Co v Pauline Syndicate* [1904] AC 120.
[31] *Keighley, Maxsted & Co v Durant* [1901] AC 240.

to procure insurance on behalf of the principal. Ratification was analysed by Colman J in *National Oilwell Ltd v Davy Offshore (UK) Ltd*:[32]

> Where at the time when the contract of insurance was made the principal [insured] or other contracting party had no actual authority to bind the other party to the contract of insurance, but the policy is expressed to insure not only the principal [insured] but also a class of others who are not identified in that policy, a party who at the time when the policy was effected could have been ascertained to qualify as a member of that class can *ratify and sue* on the policy as co-assured if at that time it was intended by the principal [insured] or other contracting party to create privity of contract with the insurers on behalf of that particular party. (emphasis added)[33]

The judge went on to explain that evidence of the requisite intention may be provided by the terms of the policy document, by the terms of any contract between the principal insured or other contracting party and the alleged co-assured, or by any other admissible material showing what was subjectively intended by the principal.

Ratification places the insured in the same position he would have been in had the agent's acts been authorised from the outset. As to the time when ratification must take place, the law seems far from settled. In marine insurance, ratification can take place after the occurrence of the loss.[34] On the other hand, with respect to non-marine insurance, it was held in *Grover & Grover Ltd v Mathews*[35] that a non-marine policy cannot be ratified after the occurrence of the loss if at the time of the ratification the insured has knowledge of the loss. Hamilton J observed that the marine insurance exception 'was an anomalous rule which it was not, for business reasons, desirable to extend'.[36] The learned judge did not go on to explain what the 'business reasons' were. The decision in *Grover* can be criticised as being wrong in principle, particularly in the light that it has long been settled that ratification has a retroactive effect on the insurance contract.[37] Indeed, in *National Oilwell*, Colman J stated, by way of dicta, that had it been necessary for him to decide the point, he would not have followed *Grover* but would have held that NOW could ratify with knowledge of an insured loss, notwithstanding the insurance was non-marine. The judge noted that Canadian,[38] American and Australian courts have all permitted ratification of non-marine policies after the loss has occurred to the knowledge of the ratifying party. He therefore concluded that:

> I can see neither legal principle nor commercial reason why the English Courts should not take the same approach. A rule which has worked perfectly well for over a century for marine insurance can be expected to work equally well for non-marine. It is undesirable that different rules should apply to the two classes of insurance and in the absence of binding or compelling authority to the contrary the English courts should take a different view on a question of principle in insurance law from the views already established in other common law jurisdictions.[39]

It is suggested that Colman J's view is correct for it accords with principle, and the decision in *Grover* should not be followed by a future court when called upon to decide the issue.

[32] [1993] 2 Lloyd's Rep 582.
[33] ibid 596–97.
[34] *Williams v North China Insurance Co* (1876) 1 CPD 757. See the Marine Insurance Act 1906, s 86.
[35] [1910] 2 KB 401.
[36] ibid 404.
[37] *Bolton Partners v Lambert* (1888) 41 Ch D 295.
[38] See, eg *Spencer v Continental Insurance Co* [1945] 4 DLR 593.
[39] [1993] 2 Lloyd's Rep 582, 608. *cf Portavon Cinema Co Ltd v Price and Century Insurance Co Ltd* [1939] 4 All ER 601, 607, in which Branson J professed to not having 'the boldness of youth' to refuse to follow *Grover*.

2.2. Trusts

2.2.1. Creating a Trust

The notion that a contracting party may enter into the contract as a trustee for another, so that the other has a beneficial interest in the contract, was recognised by the House of Lords in *Les Affreteurs Reunis v Walford*,[40] where it was held that the charterer of a vessel had acted as trustee for the shipbrokers in contracting with the shipowners so that the broker could enforce a term in the charter under which the broker was to receive commission. The notion of implying a trust into a commercial contract has since that case found little favour, and in *Vandepitte v Preferred Accident Insurance Corporation of New York*[41] the alternative argument that the insured intended to create a beneficial interest was summarily rejected, Lord Wright stating that in the absence of an unambiguous declaration, the courts were reluctant to imply a trust because 'serious duties and obligations rest on any person claiming to be insured, which necessarily involve consent and privity of contract'.[42]

It is possible for an employer to create a trust of a group life policy on the lives of employees. The leading case is *Bowskill v Dawson*,[43] where a company established a scheme under which the trustee effected a life policy for the company's employees. Construing the terms of the particular scheme pertaining to the 'rights' and 'claims' of the employees or their legal representatives, the Court of Appeal held that they were beneficiaries under a voluntary trust. The court noted that they had more than mere expectancies. The scheme conferred upon the employees legally enforceable rights which entitled them as beneficiaries to call upon the trustees to perform the trusts of the deed under which they benefited. Romer LJ observed that: 'Indeed, it may well be that, had the insurance company refused to pay and the trustees declined to sue, the defendants themselves could have sued the [insurance] company adding the trustees as defendants.'[44]

On the other hand, in *Green v Russell*,[45] where an employer effected a group accident policy on behalf of his employees named in the schedule to the policy, Romer LJ found that a trust had not been created. The terms of the policy permitted the employer to surrender it and receive back a proportionate sum of the premium. He therefore retained absolute ownership of the policy and was not bound to maintain the insurance.

The English and Scottish Law Commissions examined the position of group schemes.[46] They recognised two main problems with the current law governing insurable interests in group insurance. First, it is unclear how insurable interest is to be found in group life or critical illness insurance schemes. Second, the employee's entitlements under a group scheme arise by virtue of their contract of employment. While employers have a clear insurable interest in a contractual liability, it is less clear that they have insurable interest in the lives of their employees for such large amounts.[47] Although the Commissions recognised the need for reform, they did not put forward any particular recommendations. The law remains unreformed.

[40] [1919] AC 801.
[41] [1933] AC 70.
[42] ibid 81.
[43] [1955] 1 QB 13. See s 50 of the Insurance Companies Act 1973.
[44] ibid 28.
[45] [1959] 2 QB 226.
[46] The Law Commission Issues Paper 4, *Insurable Interest*, para 7.81.
[47] ibid para 7.83.

Trusts remain important in the context of life insurance. A life insured may create an express trust of the benefit of the policy in favour of a third party, often a son or daughter, and by so doing will avoid the requirement of insurable interest in the child's life. The effect of the insured declaring that he holds the proceeds of the policy on trust for a third party is that on the insured's death or the date of the policy's maturity, the insurers will make payment direct to the beneficiary rather than to the insured's personal representatives. In this way, the insurance monies do not form part of the deceased's estate for the purposes of inheritance tax, nor will they be subject to the claims of the insured's creditors. However, an insured who creates a trust will be precluded from varying its terms without obtaining the consent of the beneficiary.[48] He will also be bound to act responsibly when considering the interests of the beneficiary. Thus, the trustee/insured may lose the right to assign or surrender the policy unless such a course of action is in the best interests of the beneficiary.[49] The third party beneficiary can enforce the policy through the trustee and may only enforce it directly if he becomes the legal owner. If the trustee fails to pay the insurance monies to the beneficiary, he can sue the trustee for it.

For an express trust to be completely constituted there must be: (i) trust property, which in the case of life insurance is the benefit of the policy; (ii) identifiable beneficiaries; and (iii) a clear and unequivocal declaration that the insured intents to create a trust.[50] In accordance with the maxim that equity looks to the intent rather than the form, no particular form of language is necessary to create a trust. However, it is not sufficient if the policy merely states that it is for the benefit of a particular third party,[51] or that the proceeds of the policy should be paid to the third party.[52] Yet the court will endeavour to find a duly constituted trust. In *Re Webb, Barclays Bank Ltd v Webb*,[53] a father effected policies on the lives of his two children. The proposal form stated that he was the 'grantee' and that the insurance was effected 'on behalf of and for the benefit of the person therein named as the life assured', ie the child. The respective policies provided that on the child's death at or after attaining 21 years of age, the proceeds would be paid to his representatives and, on each child's twenty-first birthday, the father's interest in the policy would cease. Up until then, the father had power to surrender the policies, assign them and recover the premiums should the child die before reaching 21 years. The policies also stated that should the father, having paid all the premiums, die before the child's twenty-first birthday, the policies would continue in force until the child reached 21 years. The father did in fact die before the children reached the specified age. The issue before the court was whether the policies belonged to his estate or to the children. Farwell J, stressing that 'the whole question … depends upon the construction of the particular policy',[54] held that the father had created a trust in favour of the children. In his reasoning, the judge found that it was material that the policies provided that the father's interest would cease when the children reached 21 and that the insurance monies

[48] *Re Schebsman* [1944] Ch 83.

[49] *Re Equitable Life Assurance Society of US Policy and Mitchell* (1911) 27 TLR 213.

[50] See, eg *Jones v Lock* (1865) 1 Ch App 25. In *Milroy v Lord* (1862) 4 De G F & J 264, 274 Turner LJ stated that: 'In order to render a voluntary settlement valid and effectual, the settlor must have done everything which according to the nature of the property comprised in the settlement was necessary to be done in order to render the settlement binding upon him. He may, of course do this by … [declaring] that he himself holds it on trust for [the purposes of the settlement].'

[51] *Re Foster's Policy* [1966] 1 WLR 222, 227 (Plowman J).

[52] *Cleaver v Mutual Reserve Fund Life Assurance* [1892] 1 QB 147, 152 (Lord Esher MR).

[53] [1941] Ch 225.

[54] ibid 234.

were not payable until the children reached that age. Accordingly, the children and not the father possessed the beneficial interest in the policies.

2.2.2. *Married Women's Property Act 1882*

To avoid life insurance monies being swallowed up by the debts of a deceased spouse's estate, the Married Women's Property Act 1882 (MWPA) allows for the creation of a statutory family trust, thereby avoiding the necessity of executing a trust deed. The statutory trust ensures that on the death of a married insured, the policy monies will be paid direct to the surviving spouse (and/or children) and will not form part of the deceased's estate. Thus, if the deceased is bankrupt at the time of death, the creditors cannot look to the proceeds of a life policy written under the MWPA for payment of the insured's debts, provided, of course, that the trust was not created with the intention of defrauding the creditors.[55] Section 11 of the MWPA provides that a policy effected by a married man or woman on his or her own life and which is expressed to be for the benefit of the survivor or his or her children, or for the benefit of the surviving spouse and children together, shall create a trust if favour of them.[56] The monies payable under such a policy will not form part of the insured's estate and will not therefore be subject to his or her debts. In addition to pure life policies, the statutory trust can also be applied to policies limited to accidental death and to endowment insurance which carry an element of life cover.[57] The Civil Partnerships Act 2004 seeks to ensure that parties in a same-sex relationship are treated in the same way as married couples. Section 70 of the 2004 Act extends the operation of section 11 of the MWPA to civil partners.

The purpose of this provision is to protect the insured's immediate dependants, ie spouse and/or children, although it has been held that it is not necessary for the beneficiary to prove actual dependency either at the time when the policy was effected or at the time of the insured's death.[58] All that need be shown is that the beneficiary falls within the qualifying relationship of spouse or child, including an adopted child. While a future spouse or child also qualifies, the section does not extend to cohabitees. The obvious effect of section 11 is to make the insured a trustee of the policy, the consequence being that he is under a duty to administer it in the best interests of the beneficiaries. Thus, a decision to surrender the policy must be made in the interests of the beneficiaries and any surrender value will be held on trust for them.[59]

If the policy document specifically identifies the spouse or child(ren), then the named beneficiaries acquire an immediate vested interest in the insurance. In *Cousins v Sun Life*

[55] Insolvency Act 1986, ss 423–25.

[56] A joint life policy effected by spouses may create two separate policies, both of which may fall within the scope of s 11: *Re S (deceased)* [1996] 1 WLR 235 applying *Griffiths v Fleming* [1909] 1 KB 805, 817–19 (Farwell and Kennedy LJJ). Note the reservations expressed by Robert Walker LJ in *Rooney v Cardona* (*The Times*, 4 March 1999), in which his Lordship said that had he been called upon to consider the issue he would have taken the view that 'the court was not bound to apply the views expressed by two members of the court in *Griffiths v Fleming* in relation to a policy which they regarded as a mistaken amalgamation of two separate contracts. The policy with which the court was concerned made no reference to s 11 of the 1882 Act. It was not expressed to be effected for the benefit of Mr Cardona or Mrs Cardona.' In the absence of any evidence as to separate proposal forms, the judge would have been disposed to think that it was not within s 11 of the 1882 Act.

[57] *Re Ioakimidis Policy Trusts* [1925] Ch 403.

[58] *Re Browne's Policy* [1903] 1 Ch 188, 190 (Kekewich J).

[59] *Re Fleetwood's Policy* [1926] Ch 48.

Assurance Society,[60] the Court of Appeal refused to grant the insured a declaration that he had sole beneficial interest in the policy by virtue of his wife, who had been named in the policy, having predeceased him. It was held that the insurance monies belonged to his late wife's estate even though the insured had remarried. If, on the other hand, the policy does not specifically name the beneficiaries but merely refers, for example, to 'my wife' or 'to my children', the beneficiaries will have a contingent interest so that only those who satisfy that description at the time of the insured's death will benefit. If there is more than one beneficiary, they will benefit in equal shares as joint tenants unless the policy, the insured's will or a deed provides to the contrary.[61] The share of any contingent beneficiary who predeceases the insured will be shared among the survivors.[62] If the purposes of the trust fail, a resulting trust arises in favour of the life insured and his estate. Should the insured divorce, the court has the power to vary any settlement, including insurance, made on the parties to the marriage.[63]

2.3. Contracts (Rights of Third Parties) Act 1999

Much of the law on agency and trusts has been overtaken by the terms of the Contracts (Rights of Third Parties) Act 1999. The broad effect of the legislation is to allow a third party to derive rights from an insurance policy issued to the insured. If that is to happen, the following requirements must be satisfied. First, there must be some contractual provision conferring a benefit on the third party in respect of one or more terms. The contract must either expressly provide that the third party may enforce a term (section 1(1)(a)) or it must purport to confer a benefit upon the third party as long as the contract properly construed shows an intention that the third party could enforce the term (sections 1(1)(b) and 1(2)). Secondly, the third party must be identified by name or class (section 1(3)). The policy may, for example, provide cover to the insured's subsidiaries, affiliates or contractors, and – unlike the position at common law – parties identified in this way are protected even though they were not appointed (or in the case of a company, not even formed) at the date of the contract. The class must necessarily be a limited one and the benefit must be expressly conferred upon a member of that class: the Act does not, for example, apply to a liability policy which provides that the insured is entitled to an indemnity for claims made by third parties – the class is too wide, and the benefits are at best indirect.[64] Thirdly, the rights of the third party are, under sections 1(4) and 3, subject to the terms of the insurance policy, so that the third party is in precisely the same position as the insured. Any defences that could have been pleaded against the insured are available against the third party unless there is some express waiver provision. Finally, the insurers cannot be called upon to pay twice: by section 5, the insurers are protected against double liability in that any payment to the insured or to the third party reduces the sum due under the policy. Equally, a settlement between the insurers and the insured binds the third party.

[60] [1933] 1 Ch 126.
[61] *Re Browne's Policy* [1903] 1 Ch 188.
[62] *Re Seyton* (1887) 34 Ch D 511.
[63] Matrimonial Causes Act 1973, s 24; Matrimonial Proceedings and Property Act 1970, s 27.
[64] The necessary protection for third party claimants is conferred by the Third Parties (Rights against Insurers) Act 2010: see ch 15 below.

As already noted, the Act is subject to contract, and it is common to find blanket exclusions of the Act in insurance policies, and in such cases the pre-existing law remains relevant. However, although section 4 preserves the effect of the common law and equitable exceptions to privity, it is unlikely that agency or any of the other devices used to circumvent the privity doctrine would confer greater rights than those available under the Act.

3. The Rights of Co-insureds

3.1. The Nature of Co-insurance[65]

This chapter has thus far discussed the manner in which the coverage of a policy taken out by an insured can be extended to a named or identifiable third party. Where there is more than one insured, the result is that there is co-insurance, which is a collective term for two quite different contractual relationships. The first is joint insurance, which only applies if the parties covered by the policy have the same interest in the insured property, the best (and possibly only) example being co-ownership, as in the case of matrimonial property and partnership. The second is composite insurance, where the parties have different interests in the insured subject matter. A non-exhaustive list, taken from the decided cases, includes: parent and subsidiary companies; contractor and subcontractor; lessor and lessee; mortgagor and mortgagee; owner and charterer of a vessel; cohabitees; and company directors. Care should be taken with terminology. Some forms of composite insurance are referred to as 'joint names', a phrase commonly found in the construction industry, where the practice is for all contractors and subcontractors to be insured under a single policy. This does not mean that the policy is 'joint' in the sense that the policyholders hold the same interest in the insured subject matter, because they do not; rather, it is composite in the sense that the policy contains all of their names.

The distinction between joint and composite insurance is crucial. Under a joint policy the interests of the co-insureds are indivisible, so that although there are two or more parties, there is a single policy for all of them. That means that the rights of the joint insureds stand and fall together. If one joint insured has failed to make a fair presentation of the risk or broken a term of the policy, the insurers' remedies are available against each of the joint insureds, so that no one joint insured can be in a better position than the others. Innocent joint insureds will thus bear the consequences of any breach of duty by the guilty joint insured. By contrast, composite insurance consists of a bundle of rights separable as between each of the composite insureds, so that the acts or defaults of one composite insured do not affect the rights of other composite insureds and the sum insured will be recoverable separately by each co-insured insofar as each has suffered loss.[66] There is some debate as to whether a composite insurance arrangement consists of a bundle of separate bilateral contracts between the insurer and each individual composite insured or whether there is just one policy that confers separate rights on each of the co-insureds. The courts have not been consistent in their terminology, and in the vast majority of cases the point is

[65] P MacDonald Eggers, 'For One or For All: Joint and Composite Insurance Policies' (2017) 130(2) *BILA J* 1.
[66] *Corbin & King Ltd v AXA Insurance UK Plc* [2022] EWHC 409 (Comm).

of no practical relevance. However, it mattered in *New Zealand Fire Service Commission v Insurance Brokers Association of New Zealand Inc & Vero New Zealand Ltd*,[67] where a property and business interruption policy was obtained by the New Zealand Ports Collective, consisting of eight separate port authorities. The total aggregate sum insured was NZ$250 million for fire damage, a figure something below the actual value of the insured subject matter. Under New Zealand law a levy was imposed on the premiums payable under fire policies, with the proceeds allocated to the funding of the New Zealand Fire Service. The levy was based upon the value of the insured subject matter. The Ports Collective argued that there was a single contract of insurance and that the levy should be calculated by reference to the aggregate sum insured, because no more than that amount could ever be recovered under the policy. The Supreme Court agreed with the Fire Service that there were eight different contracts, one with each composite insured, and that the levy was to be calculated by adding together the maximum potential coverage available to each of the co-insureds even though that sum was substantially greater than NZ$250 million. The case turned upon its facts, but it is apparent that it raises a presumption that a composite insurance arrangement constitutes a bundle of separate contracts rather than a single contract conferring distinct individual rights. The weight of English authority supports the bundle of contracts analysis.[68]

While, therefore, a composite policy insures separate interests, a further question is whether joint interests can be insured under a composite policy. This point has arisen in particular in the context of matrimonial policies, the question being whether the misconduct or breach of duty by one spouse prevents recovery by the other. The view adopted in England is that husband and wife policies are, in the absence of express words of severance, to be construed as joint rather than composite, so that the innocent spouse can have no better rights than the guilty spouse.[69] By contrast, in New Zealand the courts have in some cases construed matrimonial policies as composite, thereby protecting the innocent spouse.[70]

3.2. The Rights of the Parties under Co-insurance Arrangements

3.2.1. Insurable Interest and Measure of Indemnity

In the case of a joint policy, there is only one insured sum and it must be paid to the insureds jointly. A composite policy, by contrast, consists of persons with different insurable interests in the insured subject matter. This caused particular difficulties with construction insurance, as it is not immediately obvious what insurable interest a subcontractor responsible for only a small part of an overall construction project can possess in the works as a whole. The problem has been overcome, as discussed in chapter six, by recognition of 'pervasive' insurable interest, whereby each co-insured engaged on the project has an insurable interest in the entire works and as an insured person thus has immunity against subrogation claims in the

[67] [2015] NZSC 59.
[68] See, most recently, *Corbin & King Ltd v AXA Insurance UK Plc* [2022] EWHC 409 (Comm).
[69] *Direct Line v Khan* [2002] Lloyd's Rep IR 364.
[70] *Maulder v National Insurance Co of New Zealand Ltd* [1993] 2 NZLR 351; *Gate v Sun Alliance Insurance Ltd* [1995] LRLR 385.

event that damage is caused by their negligence. Where a loss has occurred under a composite policy, it was held in *General Accident Fire and Life Assurance Corp Ltd v Midland Bank Ltd*[71] – seemingly the first case to use the phrase 'composite insurance' – that, in the absence of contrary wording, each composite insured has a separate claim for its own loss and that the insurers must make payment on that basis. In that case, following a fire, loss was suffered by the tenant alone, although separate cheques were issued by the insurers to the tenant, the landlord and the mortgagee of the premises, and both the landlord and the mortgagee transferred their cheques to the tenant. On discovering that the tenant's claim was fraudulent, the insurers sought restitution from the landlord and the mortgagee. The Court of Appeal dismissed the action, holding that the claim was that of the tenant alone and the insurers' claim could only be against the tenant.

3.2.2. Breach of the Duty of Fair Presentation

The issue that arises in co-insurance arrangements is whether non-disclosure or misrepresentation on the part of one co-insured will entitle the insurer to avoid the contract as against all parties (ie including the innocent co-insureds) or merely against the guilty co-insured. In the case of a joint policy, the rights of all will be lost by reason of breach of duty by any of the joint insureds. The position is different for composite insurance. This is apparent from cases involving composite insurance procured by the owner of the insured subject matter covering the mortgagee of the property as co-insured: breach of duty by the owner does not affect the rights of the mortgagee.[72]

The same principle applies to liability policies. In *Arab Bank plc v Zurich Insurance Co*,[73] Browne was the managing director of John D Wood Commercial Ltd, an incorporated firm of professional estate agents and valuers. He was at all material times a substantial shareholder in the company. Browne prepared valuations for banks which were fraudulently high in that the valuation figures were deliberately or recklessly provided and did not represent the open market value of the properties: the figures were in each case grossly in excess of the true open market value and/or recent sale price. On occasions he was assisted by another director and (relatively minor) shareholder, Pitts. The company received the fees. The other directors of the company were innocent and free of any fraudulent conduct or intent to deceive. The claimants, Arab Bank and Banque Bruxelles Lambert SA, obtained judgments against the company in negligence and when the company went into liquidation they sought to enforce those judgments directly against the company's underwriters, Zurich, under what is now the Third Parties (Rights against Insurers) Act 2010. Zurich argued that Browne's fraud relieved them from liability. The indemnity insurance in question had been effected in August 1990. Browne had completed the proposal but, despite an express question, withheld information as to potential claims and the insurers denied liability. Rix J held that composite policies should be viewed as a bundle of separate contracts between the insurers and the co-insureds: dishonesty by one co-insured did not therefore permit the insurers to avoid the policy against all the other parties. It is to be noted that the decision would have

[71] [1940] 2 KB 388.

[72] *Woolcott v Sun Alliance and London Insurance Ltd* [1978] 1 Lloyd's Rep 629; *Parker v National Farmers Union Mutual Insurance Society Ltd* [2013] Lloyd's Rep IR 253.

[73] [1999] 1 Lloyd's Rep 262. See also *Brit Syndicates v Italaudit SpA* [2008] Lloyd's Rep IR 601.

been the same if Rix J had construed the policy as a single contract but conferring separate rights on each composite insured.

The issue has also arisen in the context of groups of companies. The question here is whether breach of the duty of fair presentation by one insured company in a group will necessarily entitle the insurers to exercise remedies against other companies in the group. In *New Hampshire Insurance Co v MGN Ltd*,[74] fidelity insurance policies were issued to companies in a group controlled by Robert Maxwell. He dishonestly transferred assets from some of the companies and used them to benefit the financial position of others. When claims on the policies were made by the companies for losses suffered as a result of these transfers, the insurers repudiated liability on the basis that breach of the duty of fair presentation by one company in the group corrupted all the insured companies in that group. The Court of Appeal held that the companies had separate interests to insure and not a joint interest in the same property, a fact that must have been known to the insurers, given the companies' different business activities. Staughton LJ said that 'all the contracts of insurance were composite in nature, there being more than one insured and each being insured separately'.[75] Accordingly, the breach of duty by one of the insured companies did not entitle the insurers to avoid the policies of the others.

3.2.3. Breach of Other Duties

Deliberate or reckless conduct in respect of the subject matter, or a fraudulent claim, by one joint assured will defeat the rights of the others, as is shown by the husband and wife fraudulent claims case *Direct Line v Khan*.[76] By contrast, if the policy is composite, the rights of the innocent co-insured are protected. In *Samuel & Co Ltd v Dumas*,[77] the insured shipowner scuttled his vessel and a claim was made by the mortgagee bank also insured under the policy. The House of Lords held that in principle the conduct of the owner did not defeat the bank's claim, although there was no recovery on the distinct ground that scuttling was not a risk covered by the policy and so there had not been an insured loss.

4. Assignment

4.1. Forms of Assignment

A third party may acquire rights against the insurers by way of assignment. Two forms of assignment are possible: assignment of the policy, so that the assignee takes over the role of insured under the policy; and assignment of the right to recover under the policy, so that the insured remains the contracting party and it is simply the case that the insurance monies

[74] [1997] LRLR 24.

[75] ibid 57. In support of its decision, the Court of Appeal cited *P Samuel & Co Ltd v Dumas* [1924] AC 431, where the insured parties were a shipowner and the mortgagee of the vessel.

[76] [2002] Lloyd's Rep IR 364.

[77] [1924] AC 431.

are to be paid to the third party. A sale of the insured subject matter to the third party does not operate to transfer to the third party either the policy itself or any benefits under the policy[78] and indeed such a sale may bring an end to the insurance because the insured no longer has an insurable interest and thus will be unable to recover in the event of a loss. It has been held that the sale of a motor vehicle puts an end to the seller's insurance on the vehicle,[79] although if the policy offers cover to the insured while driving any vehicle then the policy remains in place to that extent.[80]

4.2. Assignment of the Policy

A contract of insurance is a chose in action and in principle a chose in action is assignable at law. The machinery for the legal assignment of a contract is set out in section 136 of the Law of Property Act 1925. As long as the assignment is in writing and notice is given to the debtor, then the assignee obtains legal title. However, section 136 does not affect the underlying principles as to whether or not a chose in action can be assigned, it merely sets out how an assignment may be effected. In particular, section 136 does not overturn the equitable rule that contracts imposing personal obligations cannot be assigned. The rules applicable to assignment vary as between classes of policy.

Life policies have, despite the provisions of the Life Assurance Act 1774, been regarded as assignable since the rulings in *Dalby v The India and London Life Assurance Co*[81] and *M'Farlane v Royal London Friendly Society*[82] that insurable interest is required only at the inception of the policy and not at any later date, and that assignment is lawful as long as the policy is not a colourable device whereby the policy is taken out by the insured but always with the intention that it should be assigned to a third party without interest. Life policies are regarded as investment contracts whose value includes any sale value, and are freely assignable other than in the unlikely event that there is a contractual prohibition on assignment.[83] In recognition of the importance of assignability, the Policies of Assurance Act 1867 was passed to allow the insured to pass legal title to the policy to a third party if the prescribed statutory form of assignment was used. At the time, legal assignments of choses in action in general were not permitted, and assignments took effect only in equity so that the assignee was not able to bring proceedings on the policy in his or her own name. The 1867 Act rapidly became redundant in the light of the Judicature Act 1875, which permitted assignment of choses in action, a measure re-enacted as section 136 of the 1925 Act. If there is a dispute as to the ownership of a policy, the insurers may pay the money into court under the Life Assurance Companies (Payment into Court) Act 1896 and the matter can be resolved judicially.

[78] *Rayner v Preston* (1881) 18 Ch D 1. The principle is codified in s 15 of the Marine Insurance Act 1906.

[79] See, eg *Rogerson v Scottish Automobile Insurance* [1931] 1 All ER Rep 606; *Tattersall v Drysdale* [1935] 2 KB 174; *Peters v General Accident Fire and Life Assurance Corp* (1937) 60 Ll L Rep 311; *Boss v Kingston* [1962] 1 Lloyd's Rep 431.

[80] *Dodson v Peter H Dodson Insurance Services* [2001] Lloyd's Rep IR 278.

[81] (1854) 15 CB 365. See ch 6 above.

[82] (1886) 2 TLR 755, 756. See also *Brewster v National Life Insurance Society* (1892) 8 TLR 648. In each of these cases the court did not find an initial intention to assign.

[83] *Re Turcan* (1888) 40 Ch D 5.

Marine policies are also assignable. By section 50(1) of the Marine Insurance Act 1906 'A marine policy is assignable unless it contains terms expressly prohibiting assignment. It may be assigned either before or after loss.' This section reflects the commercial operation of contracts for the sale of cargo. Cost, Insurance and Freight (CIF) sale contracts operate on the basis that the seller procures insurance for the cargo and then assigns the cover to the purchaser as soon as the cargo is shipped so that the risk is transferred to the buyer. If, therefore, the cargo is damaged on its voyage, the buyer remains liable for the purchase price but has a valid insurance claim. Although section 50 was based on practice relating to cargo, it extends to all marine policies, including those on vessels where different considerations apply. In practice, the standard wordings for hull policies require the consent of the insurers for the assignment of the policy to the purchaser of the vessel. Under section 50(2) of the 1906 Act, where there has been an assignment of the entirety of the insured's interest in the policy,[84] the assignee may sue in the assignee's own name.

All other policies are not assignable in equity, as they are regarded as contracts for the performance of personal obligations. As has already been seen, the identity of the insured is a key factor in the insurers' assessment of the risk, particularly where moral hazard issues may be raised, and assignment could easily sidestep the underwriting process. If there is to be a valid assignment, the consent of the insurers is required, and even with consent it is necessary for the policy to be assigned at the same time as the subject matter to which it relates. We have already seen that if the subject matter is sold the policy is not automatically assigned with it, and that the policy lapses for want of insurable interest so that it cannot later be assigned. Conversely, if the policy is assigned in advance of the subject matter, the assignee has no insurable interest, and so if there is a loss, then neither the original insured nor the assignee can recover.

Where there is a valid assignment, the general rule that assignment is subject to equities is applicable. This means that the assignee cannot be in any better position than the original insured. Any defences that the insurers would have had against the insured prior to assignment, eg a remedy for breach of the duty of fair presentation or breach of condition, is equally available against the assignee.

4.3. Assignment of the Proceeds of the Policy

The right to receive payment for a claim under an insurance policy is a chose in action and is assignable at law using the machinery set out in section 136 of the Law of Property Act 1925. There must, however, be an existing claim: any attempt to assign the benefits of a future claim cannot take effect at law because there is no more than a contingency. The right to payment, unlike the policy itself, is not regarded as a personal right, so the proceeds of claims under all forms of policy can be assigned and the consent of the insurers is not required. The insured remains the policyholder and the only effect of an assignment is that the policy monies otherwise due to the insured are to be paid to the third party. As with policy assignments, the assignee takes subject to equities.

[84] As to which, see *Raiffeisen Zentralbank Osterreich AG v Five Star General Trading* [2001] Lloyd's Rep IR 460, holding that if any part of the benefit is retained by the insured, then the assignee cannot rely upon this provision.

It is to be stressed that, in contrast to the position where the policy is assigned, the insured remains the policyholder and the indemnity payable is calculated by reference to the policyholder's own loss. That creates a potential difficulty where the insured has suffered a loss and assigns the claim to the assignee in return for payment. The courts will treat the payment as reducing the insured's loss, which means that the sum recoverable from the insurers by the assignee will be net of the sum received by the insured from the assignee.[85] That point is discussed in more detail in chapter 19 below.

[85] *Colonia Versicherung AG v Amoco Oil Co* [1997] 1 Lloyd's Rep 261.

8

The Terms of the Insurance Contract

1. The Classification of Terms of Insurance Contracts

1.1. The Perspective of the General Law of Contract

This chapter is concerned with the obligations of the parties to a contract of insurance as set out in the contractual terms. Although insurance contracts are generally subject to the ordinary common law rules applicable to the classification of terms and the consequences of their breach, insurance contracts have in some respects developed their own peculiar features.

The common law of contract proceeds on the basis that not all obligations created by an agreement are of equal significance or importance to the parties. The orthodox classification of contractual terms categorises such obligations as either 'conditions' on the one hand, or 'warranties' on the other. A condition is an essential term of the contract and is fundamental in nature. The effect of its breach is to entitle the innocent party to terminate the contract and sue for damages. The word 'condition' may also carry a different meaning insofar as such a term may be either a condition precedent or a condition subsequent. A condition precedent is a term 'which must be fulfilled before any contract is concluded at all'.[1] In this sense it has been described as a precondition, 'something which must happen or be done before the agreement can take effect'.[2] Although the contract crystallises as soon as the parties conclude their agreement, if the contingent event does not occur, the contract does not become operative.[3] A condition precedent is not restricted to the situation where the contract provides for a third party to perform some specified act, but may also arise where one of the contracting parties themselves is required to carry out some act.[4] A condition subsequent, by contrast, operates to bring an existing contract to an end upon the occurrence of a stipulated event.[5]

[1] *Trans Trust SPRL v Danubian Trading Co Ltd* [1952] 2 QB 297, 304 (Denning LJ).

[2] *L Schuler AG v Wickman Machine Tool Sales Ltd* [1974] AC 235, 250 (Lord Reid). See also *Marten v Whale* [1917] 2 KB 480.

[3] *Pym v Campbell* (1856) 6 E & B 370.

[4] *Aberfoyle Plantations Ltd v Cheng* [1960] AC 115 (PC); *Trans Trust SPRL v Danubian Trading Co Ltd* [1960] AC 115 (PC).

[5] *Head v Tattersall* (1871) LR 7 Exch 7; *Thompson v Asda-MFIGroup plc* [1988] Ch 241; *Gyllenhammer & Partners v Sour Brodogradevna* [1989] 2 Lloyd's Rep 403; *Brown v Knowlsey* [1986] IRLR 102. See LS Sealy, '"Risk" in the Law of Sale' [1973] *CLJ* 225.

A warranty is a subsidiary promise, the breach of which entitles the innocent party to damages only and not to terminate the contract. The distinction between the two is initially a matter of form, in that the courts will accept the parties' own agreement as to whether a term is a condition or a warranty. If there is no explicit label attached to a term by the parties, the courts will make the determination for themselves. In *Glaholm v Hays*,[6] the court stated that a term is a condition if the 'performance of the stipulation [went] to the very root … of the contract'. In *Wallis, Son & Wells v Pratt and Haynes*,[7] Fletcher Moulton LJ observed that:

> But from a very early period of our law it has been recognised that … [contractual] obligations are not all of equal importance. There are some which go so directly to the substance of the contract or, in other words, are so essential to its very nature that their non-performance may fairly be considered by the other party as a substantial failure to perform the contract at all. On the other hand, there are other obligations which, though they must be performed, are not so vital that a failure to perform them goes to the substance of the contract.

In determining the nature of a term which has been broken, the courts continue to have regard to the consequences of the breach. Thus, the fact that the effects of the breach are not significant may lead the court to hold that the term is not a condition.[8]

The rigidity of the distinction between – and of the consequences of breach of – conditions and warranties has in the general law led to the emergence of a third category, namely innominate or intermediate terms.[9] Where the term is unclassified by the parties, the innominate label entitles the court to look at the substance of the term in order to ascertain whether its breach has had serious or trivial consequences for the performance of the contract. If the breach is serious, the innocent party may treat itself as discharged as for a breach of condition, but if the breach is trivial, then the innocent party will be entitled only to damages (which may be nominal) representing the actual loss suffered. Whether a party may terminate the contract in the event of breach of an innominate term thus lies within the discretion of the court.[10] In this way, innominate terms operate as a flexible device whereby termination is made to depend upon the court's view of the seriousness of the consequences flowing from the breach. Nevertheless, the classification of contractual terms as major obligations (conditions) or minor obligations (warranties) has withstood the rigours of judicial challenge and continues to represent the orthodoxy.

1.2. Classification of Terms

A survey of the marine insurance cases leading up to the passing of the Marine Insurance Act 1906 shows that 'conditions' were not used. The obligations of the insured were set out in 'warranties', used in the general sense of 'promises'. If a warranty was not complied with, the insurers were not on risk. Warranties were of three broad types: (1) warranties which defined the risk run by the insurers, eg warranted free of capture and seizure and warranted that there would be no recovery for small cargo losses – such warranties were in

[6] (1841) 2 Man & G 257, 268.
[7] [1910] 2 KB 1003, 1012.
[8] *State Trading Corporation of India v M Golodetz Ltd* [1989] 2 Lloyd's Rep 277.
[9] See, eg *Hong Kong Fir Shipping Co Ltd v Kawasaki Kisen Kaisha Ltd* [1962] 2 QB 26, 70 (Diplock LJ); *Cehave NV v Bremer Handelsgesellschaft mbH, The Hansa Nord* [1976] QB 44.
[10] *Cehave NV v Bremer Handelsgesellschaft mbH, The Hansa Nord* [1976] QB 44.

effect exclusion clauses; (2) warranties given by the insured as to the nature of the insured risk as presented to the insurers, so that if there was a misrepresentation then there would be breach of warranty and the risk would not attach. The advantage of the use of warranties in this context was that insurers were spared the need to show that the elements of misrepresentation had been satisfied, in particular that the matter misstated was material to the risk: all that had to be shown was falsity; and (3) warranties in the form of promises as to the manner in which the voyage would be conducted: these related to matters such as sailing with a naval convoy in time of war and carrying sufficient guns to repel pirates or other enemies, and the courts adopted an implied warranty that the vessel was be fit for the voyage to be undertaken. The advantage of this type of warranty – best described as 'continuing' – for insurers was that there was no need for them to prove that there was any causal connection between the breach of term and the loss. Breach was sufficient to bring the cover to an automatic end.

In the second half of the nineteenth century onwards, new forms of drafting were adopted. Type (1) warranties largely fell into disuse in marine insurance and have never featured in other classes of policy. Type (2) warranties, by contrast, were adopted for life and property insurance by the use of 'basis of the contract' clauses whereby the insured undertook on the proposal or other application that all of the answers given to the insurers were accurate. It became accepted that a basis clause converted all answers into warranties, so that if any answer – material or not, inducing the insurers or not – was false, the risk simply did not incept. Such warranties were particularly damaging where the insured was answering questions about factual matters that in many cases could not be known, eg the state of the insured's health. The use of type (3) warranties became widespread in all forms of insurance, giving rise to the possibility that minor and non-causative breaches discharged the insurers from all liability under the policy. The common law relating to warranties was codified in sections 33–35 of the Marine Insurance Act 1906. In addition, insurers adopted a range of conditions precedent that had to be satisfied before cover or liability would attach, and various conditions subsequent governing the insured's conduct during the currency of the policy. By the turn of the twenty-first century, policies of all kinds included basis of the contract clauses, continuing warranties, conditions precedent and conditions subsequent. The effect of a breach of a policy term rested not upon the substance of the breach or the harm done to the insurers, but rather upon the manner in which the term was classified because classification determined the consequences of breach irrespective of the merits.

The common law classification of policy terms holds good under the Insurance Act 2015. However, the underlying theme of the changes in the law introduced by the Act is in many cases to replace form with substance, so that the effect of breach is determined not by the nature of the clause, but rather by the consequences for the insurers of the breach. Thus, the law has not altered the manner in which terms are classified, but it has altered the consequences flowing from that classification. The Act makes two important changes: breaches of warranty suspend rather than terminate the risk; and breach of policy terms irrelevant to the loss in question cannot be relied upon by the insurers.[11] The classification of policy terms and the common law, and now statutory consequences of breach, may be summarised as follows.

(a) *Conditions precedent to the attachment of cover*. These relate to things to be done by the insured, or events that must occur, for the risk to attach. At common law, if the

[11] Other than in consumer cases, it is possible for insurers to contract out of these provisions, although any exclusion must be transparent within the meaning of s 17, as discussed in ch 4 above.

condition is not met, there is no cover under the policy. Such conditions are unaffected by the Insurance Act 2015.

(b) *Conditions precedent to liability*. Such a condition arises after the contract is made and refers to something to be done or not done by the insured if a claim is to be made under the policy. A condition precedent can range at one extreme from security arrangements for a building to the obligation to provide claims information at a particular time and in particular form. Conditions which are concerned with reducing the risk of loss are subject to section 11 of the Insurance Act 2015, under which there has to be some connection between the breach of the condition and the circumstances of the loss. The broad effect of section 11 is to prevent reliance by the insurers on risk conditions irrelevant to the loss. However, section 11 does not apply to conditions which are entirely unrelated to the risk, eg conditions relating to claims. The common law continues to apply to them.

(c) *Contract terms not stated to be conditions precedent*. If a term is not stated to be a condition precedent and is broken, the effect of breach is at common law to be determined in accordance with ordinary contractual principles. Most such terms will be treated by the courts as innominate so that the insurers' remedies depend upon the seriousness of the breach. Even if the breach is serious, where the term relates to the risk itself section 11 of the Insurance Act 2015 requires some form of connection between the breach and the loss for the insurers to have any remedy.

(d) *Pre-contractual warranties and basis of the contract clauses*. At common law, if a warranted statement is false, the risk does not attach irrespective of materiality and inducement. Basis and similar clauses have been deprived of effect by section 6 of the Consumer Insurance (Disclosure and Representations) Act 2012 for consumers and by section 9 of the Insurance Act 2015 for businesses. As noted in chapter four, all pre-contractual statements are to be assessed as representations and thus subject to the rules on materiality, inducement and proportional remedies.

(e) *Post-contractual warranties*. If a warranty is broken, at common law the risk is terminated with effect from the date of the breach, and that remains the case even if the breach is corrected. That position is altered by the Insurance Act 2015 in two respects. First, by section 10, a breach of warranty merely suspends the risk, so that if there is no breach of warranty at the time of the loss, then the insurers are liable. Secondly, by section 11, even if there is a breach of warranty at the time of loss, there has to be a connection between the breach and the loss before the insurers have any remedy.

(f) *Suspensory provisions*. Some warranties and conditions are expressed to be suspensory only, so that while the insured is in breach there is no cover. As seen in point (e) above, this is now the statutory approach to all warranties.

This rather complex framework and the issues arising from it are discussed in detail in the rest of this chapter.

---

2. Conditions

2.1. Conditions Precedent to the Risk

A condition precedent to the risk is a term whose content has to be satisfied before the insurers can face liability under the policy. At one time it was common for payment of the premium to be a condition precedent to cover, but the use of direct debit and other payment mechanisms has largely led to the demise of that particular provision. Examples of other conditions that may be imposed on the inception of cover include the inspection of a vessel to ensure seaworthiness and the implementation of safety or security premises for insured premises. The Insurance Act 2015 does not apply to pre-risk conditions: if the risk has not attached, then there is simply no cover in place.

2.2. Conditions Precedent to Liability

A condition precedent to liability assumes that the risk has attached, and is one that requires compliance by the insured in order for a valid claim to be made. If the insured fails to comply with the term, there is no actionable breach of contract as such; rather, the insured has failed to satisfy the requirements for a claim to be made. The claim will thus be lost but the policy will continue as before: both past and any future claims are unaffected, and there is no question of the insurers claiming damages because they have not faced liability and have not suffered any loss. Conditions precedent may be procedural clauses or substantive risk clauses. Procedural clauses set out, amongst other things, the duty to notify actual or potential losses and to provide financial and other information following a loss. They may relate also to matters such as payment of the premium. In *Kazakstan Wool Processors (Europe) Ltd v Nederlandsche Credietverzekering Maatschappij NV*,[12] the policy contained a term, Article 13, to the effect that in the event of any breach of condition precedent the insurers would have the right to retain any premium paid and give written notice terminating the policy. The insured was required to submit monthly trading terms, upon which premiums were to be calculated. The assured was in breach of this provision. The insurers argued that Article 13 entitled them to deny liability for all claims, including those that had been met when the insureds were in compliance. They therefore requested the return of an earlier payment. The insured argued, on the other hand, that it was unreasonable to construe Article 13 as permitting the insurers to avoid liability retrospectively in respect of risks that had attached prior to the breaches. The Court of Appeal rejected the insurers' contention. Peter Gibson LJ said:

> I can accept that all liability under the policy does not include liabilities which have crystallised and been paid. It is inappropriate to refer to terminating such a liability. Indeed it may be questioned whether it is a liability at all once it has been discharged. I can also accept that if a liability has accrued unconditionally, for example if the insurer has delayed payment after it became due, it will not be caught by the termination. It cannot have been contemplated that the insurer could benefit from its own breach. But it is hard to see how all future or contingent liabilities under the policy are not terminated on the plain wording of the clause.[13]

Procedural clauses of these types are not caught by section 11 of the Insurance Act 2015 because they have nothing to do with the risk. Subject to the rules on waiver, non-compliance is fatal to a successful claim. In principle, the Consumer Rights Act 2015 could apply to strike down a condition precedent that created a significant imbalance in the rights of the parties, but in *Parker v National Farmers Union Mutual Insurance Society Ltd*[14] it was held that the predecessor legislation to the 2015 Act – the Unfair Terms in Consumer Contracts

[12] [2000] Lloyd's Rep IR 371.
[13] ibid 380.
[14] [2012] EWHC 2156 (Comm).

Regulations 1999 – did not prevent the enforcement of claims provisions in that it could not be said that a requirement on the insured to comply with claims provisions, coupled with an implied obligation on the insurers to act reasonably in handling a claim, created a significant imbalance in the parties' rights.

Substantive risk clauses, by contrast, are concerned directly with the possibility of loss and measures required to reduce that possibility. They cover matters such as the obligation to follow the insurers' instructions on security (eg to maintain burglar alarms and sprinkler systems) or, in a motor policy, to maintain the vehicle in a roadworthy condition or to use it for specified purposes only. Failure by the insured to comply is, at common law, an absolute defence to any claim, subject to waiver, and now to the effect of section 11 of the Insurance Act 2015, both of which are discussed below.

2.3. Terms Not Expressed to Be Conditions Precedent

There is a dramatic contrast between the breach of a condition precedent and the breach of a term not expressed to be a condition precedent, even though they cover precisely the same substantive or procedural issues and the only difference between the two is in the terminology describing the status of the clause. Terms that are not conditions precedent are governed by common law rules. It is only where the term can be regarded from the outset as one that goes to the root of the insurance contract that any breach can be regarded as repudiatory, thereby giving the insurers the right to terminate the policy for breach. It will generally not be possible for a term to be regarded as fundamental in this respect. There is only one reported example of a policy term being found to be one to be classified as a common law condition: in *Svenska Handelsbanken v Sun Alliance & London Insurance Plc*,[15] it was held that a bank's contractual obligation, under a policy on loss caused by bad debts, to maintain ordinary lending criteria was fundamental to the policy so that unusual forms of lending amounted to a repudiation of the policy.

The practice of the courts when faced with unclassified terms, particularly with claims provisions, is to treat those terms as 'innominate' rather than 'conditions' in the ordinary contractual sense, thereby giving the insurers the right to treat a breach as repudiatory only where the breach goes to the root of the policy. The matter was first considered in *Alfred McAlpine plc v BAI (Run-Off) Ltd*,[16] where the Court of Appeal enlisted this terminology in order to classify a notice of loss clause, condition 1(a), which required the insured to give notice of a claim under the policy 'as soon as possible'. Waller LJ ruled that condition 1(a) was not so fundamental that its breach amounted to a repudiation of the whole contract. However, Waller LJ, citing the judgment of Giles J in *Trans-Pacific Insurance Co (Australia) Ltd v Grand Union Insurance Co Ltd*,[17] suggested that it was necessary to assess the effect of a breach of a condition not on the policy as a whole but on the claim itself, and that if the insured's breach caused severe prejudice to the insurers in their handling of the claim then the claim itself could be regarded as repudiated. The policy itself would thus remain in place but the insurers could refuse to pay the claim. However, in *Friends Provident Life & Pensions Ltd v Sirius*,[18] the Court of Appeal (Waller LJ unsurprisingly dissenting) rejected

[15] [1996] 1 Lloyd's Rep 519.
[16] [2000] Lloyd's Rep IR 352. For criticism of the decision, see J Davey [2001] *Journal of Business Law* 179.
[17] (1989) 18 NSWLR 675.
[18] [2005] Lloyd's Rep IR 135.

the possibility of 'partial repudiation' with its consequence that a breach of an innominate term in a policy might enable an insurer to defeat a claim. In *Friends Provident* the term in question was also a claims notification clause.[19] Mance LJ, delivering the leading judgment, held that Waller LJ's views in *BAI* were not binding because they were obiter.[20] Agreeing with Moore-Bick J's finding that the clause in question was an innominate term, he rejected the trial judge's conclusion based on *Alfred McAlpine* that breach of such a clause, if sufficiently serious, would entitle the insurers to avoid liability for the claim. Mance LJ stated that there was no reason for the court to construct 'a new doctrine of partial repudiatory breach'. A sufficiently serious breach of an innominate term could only ever lead to the discharge of the entire policy, not a particular claim.

If, as is almost inevitably the case, the breach of an innominate term is insufficiently serious to justify repudiation of the policy, insurers are left with the option of seeking damages for breach of contract. In practice, such a claim will rarely be worth pursuing because in most cases it will be difficult for the insurers to prove any loss, so damages will be nominal, although if loss can be proved then the insurers will be entitled to set off any loss from the sums payable under the policy. Where the breach is of a claims condition, the insurers' claim will be for loss of opportunity to investigate the claim properly and thereby to rely upon a possible defence.

2.4. Distinguishing Conditions Precedent and Other Terms

It is apparent that there is a dramatic difference between the consequences of the breach of a condition precedent (automatic inability to recover) and the consequences of a breach of an innominate condition (a right to recover other than to the extent that the insured's breach has caused loss to the insurers). It thus becomes vital to determine whether a policy term is a condition precedent or an innominate term. Given that breach of a condition precedent can easily produce disproportionately harsh effects where the breach is technical and has not inflicted any loss on the insurers, there is a consistent line of authority for the proposition that clear wording is needed to create a condition precedent. What is required is 'conditionality'.

This can be achieved by an express description of a term as a 'condition precedent', and the courts will not go behind that designation unless it is plainly not possible in practice for the term to operate in that way, eg where a policy against loss by employee fraud (fidelity insurance) requires criminal proceedings to be commenced against the employee as that is not necessarily a matter that can be controlled by the insured.[21] Other forms of wording can achieve conditionality, including phrases like 'unless' and 'provided that'.

It is increasingly common for policies to contain a general statement that all terms are conditions precedent or that the insurers are not liable unless there has been compliance with all policy terms. Such provisions are generally taken at face value, a point illustrated recently by *Arch Insurance (UK) Ltd v McCullough*,[22] where the insured's public policy said that 'observance of the terms of this [insurance] relating to anything to be done or complied

[19] See ch 11 below.

[20] For the same reason, Mance LJ also rejected Longmore LJ's approval of *BAI* expressed in *The Mercandian Continent* [2001] EWCA Civ 1275.

[21] *London Guarantee v Fearnley* (1886) 5 App Cas 911.

[22] [2021] EWHC 2798 (Comm).

with by the insured is a condition to any liability of the company' and the insured's claim for indemnity was lost by failing to give timely notice of an accident occurring at his motor cycle track for which proceedings were brought by the injured victim. There are some cases which indicate that it is permissible for a court to go through the list of 'deemed' conditions precedent to determine which of them is sufficiently serious to justify being treated as a condition precedent. That occurred in *Re Bradley and Essex and Suffolk Accident Indemnity Society*,[23] where an obligation under an employers' liability policy for the employer to maintain a wages book was held not appropriate to be a condition precedent to claims, as the sole purpose of the requirement was to enable the insurers to calculate the premium based on potential loss of earnings claims. It may be that such cases are no longer reliable. In *Denso Manufacturing UK Ltd v Great Lakes Reinsurance (UK) Plc*,[24] it was held that a general clause operated to convert an obligation in a litigation costs policy (after the event) to co-operate with the insurers into a condition precedent. Although that provision was clearly of great importance to the insurers, so there could not have been any real dispute that it was an appropriate condition precedent, Cockerill J commented that 'the hostility to conditions precedent manifested in *Re Bradley* has been somewhat moderated over the years'.[25] Any obvious ambiguity in a general clause will, however, be construed against the insurers. By way of example, if a policy gives a list of conditions, some of which provide that breach permits the insurers to deny liability and others of which are silent, and there is additionally a general clause deeming all terms to be conditions precedent to liability, the court may well be justified in holding that the general clause is of no effect.[26]

2.5. Breach of Condition

2.5.1. *Construction of Conditions*

Whether there has been a breach of a condition is a matter of its construction. Illustrations of the position in respect of claims conditions are given in chapter 11 below. The burden of proving breach is borne by the insurers. There are numerous authorities on the construction of risk and claims conditions, and they show that the courts were, even without the assistance of legislation, able in the case of ambiguity or uncertainty to avoid disproportionate or draconian effects. The condition precedent in *Sugar Hut Group Ltd v Great Lakes Reinsurance (UK) Plc*[27] required that 'all waste or refuse outside the Buildings is stored in (a) non-combustible lidded and lockable containers or (b) metal skips'. The insured stored waste in strong plastic bins, and the insurers denied liability for a fire on the basis that limb (a) implied the use of metal only. That argument was rejected, the court pointing out that if that had been the intention then it could easily have been made express and that the reference to metal in (b) strongly suggested that (a) was not subject to that limitation. In *Cornhill Insurance v DE Stamp Felt Roofing*,[28] roofing contractors obtained a liability policy which

[23] [1912] 1 KB 415.
[24] [2017] EWHC 391 (Comm).
[25] ibid para 25.
[26] That was the suggestion in *Aspen Insurance UK Ltd v Pectel Ltd* [2009] Lloyd's Rep IR 440.
[27] [2010] EWHC 2636 (Comm).
[28] [2002] Lloyd's Rep IR 648. See also *US Trading Ltd v Axa Insurance Co Ltd* [2010] Lloyd's Rep IR 505. Contrast *Bonner Williams v Peter Lindsay Leisure Ltd* [2001] 1 All ER (Comm) 1140, where no instructions had been given to employees.

imposed a condition precedent that they 'shall have arranged' for fire precautions to be put in place. The contractors were held not to be in breach in circumstances where instructions had been given to employees but they had been disregarded. The courts have also been wary of 'pay to be paid' terms in property policies, under which the insured is required to fund the cost of repairs as a condition of recovery from the insurers. As will be seen in chapter 10, such clauses have been construed as meaning that the insured is entitled to an indemnity when entering into a contract for the effecting of repairs and thereby incurring liability for payment but without actual payment having been made. Similar clauses are used in liability policies and reinsurance contracts, as discussed in chapters 15 and 18 below.

2.5.2. Waiver of Breach of Condition

A breach of condition may be waived by the insurers. As discussed in detail in chapter three, English law recognises two forms of waiver: waiver by affirmation; and waiver by estoppel.

Waiver by affirmation arises where the insurers have an option either to rely upon the breach or to disregard it, and once they have taken a step on either road and unequivocally communicated that to the insured, they cannot withdraw. For example, in *Lickiss v Milestone Motor Policies at Lloyd's*,[29] a motorcyclist claimed an indemnity from the insurers in respect of damages he was required to pay to a third party arising from an accident caused by the insured's negligence in which he damaged a taxicab. The policy contained a condition which provided that 'full particulars' should be communicated to the insurance company 'as soon as possible after the occurrence of any accident … and shall forward immediately any … notice of intended prosecution'. The accident occurred on 17 May 1964 and the insured received a notice of intended prosecution, but did not inform his insurers. In the meantime, the insurers received a letter from the police, dated 18 June, notifying them of the proceedings. By letter dated 23 June, the insurers wrote to the insured, explaining that:

> We understand that proceedings are being taken against you on 2 July … It would be appreciated if you would let us know why you have not notified us of these proceedings since we will wish to arrange your defence.

Subsequently, the insurers denied liability on the basis that the insured was in breach of condition in not notifying them of the intended prosecution. It was held by the Court of Appeal that the letter of 23 June constituted a waiver by the insurers of the insured's breach. Waiver by estoppel is a narrower concept, requiring an unequivocal representation by the insurers that they do not intend to rely upon a defence, a representation that is relied upon by the insured in circumstances that it would be inequitable for the insurers to resile from their stated position.

There has been much discussion surrounding the consequences of a breach of a condition precedent, and, in particular, whether the insurer can elect to waive, or can be estopped from exercising, its rights following the breach of a notification clause. These were the main issues in *Kosmar Villa Holidays v Trustees of Syndicate*.[30] In August 2002, James Evans was on holiday with friends at an apartment in Corfu, which had been hired through Kosmar Villa Holidays plc. Early one morning, while it was still dark, he decided to dive

[29] [1966] 2 Lloyd's Rep 1.

[30] [2008] EWCA Civ 147. See J Lowry and P Rawlings, 'Conditions Precedent in Insurance Contracts' [2009] *Journal of Business Law* 275; J Lowry and P Rawlings, 'Claims and Conditions Precedent to Liability' [2008] *Journal of Business Law* 179.

into the shallow end of the swimming pool at the apartments. His head struck the bottom of the pool, fracturing his spine and resulting in partial tetraplegia. He brought a claim in negligence against Kosmar, and the trial judge held Kosmar liable subject to a reduction in the compensation on account of the claimant's contributory negligence. That decision was overturned by the Court of Appeal, which concluded there was no breach of duty by Kosmar, or, if there had been a breach, it was not the cause of the injury.[31] Kosmar subsequently sought to recover the costs it had incurred in defending this action from its insurers, Euclidian, under a combined liability policy. At the time the action against the underwriters started, it was commonly believed that there was liability to Evans. It was only when the claim against Kosmar was taken to the Court of Appeal that it became clear there was no such liability and the only issue was costs. The difficulty facing Kosmar was General Condition (GC) 7(1), which required that: 'The Insured shall immediately after the occurrence of any Injury or Damage give notice in writing with full particulars thereof to insurers'. In addition, GC 7(2) stated that:

> Upon receipt by or on behalf of the Insured of notice … of an intention by any person or body to make a claim against the Insured or of any allegation of negligence which might give rise to such a claim or on the discovery of any such act of negligence, the Insured shall notify insurers as soon as practicable.

It was common ground between the parties that GC 7(1) was a condition precedent to Euclidian's liability and that Kosmar had not observed the notice requirement. The point at issue was whether or not Euclidian had waived this breach or were estopped from raising it as a defence to the claim. The injury to Mr Evans had occurred on 22 August 2002, but Kosmar did not notify Euclidian until 4 September 2003. Euclidian immediately requested, and Kosmar supplied, further information about the incident. In one communication, on 17 September 2003, Euclidian outlined its strategy, which was not to deny liability for negligence at that stage, but to wait until all the evidence was gathered and then present it to Mr Evans in the expectation that he would recognise the hopeless nature of his claim. Shortly after this, Euclidian asked Mr Evans's solicitors to 'note our interest in this matter and ensure that all future correspondence is sent direct to us'. It was not until September 30 that Euclidian expressly required an explanation from Kosmar for its failure to comply with GC 7(1), and stated that, while continuing to deal with the claim by Mr Evans, 'we must reserve our position until such time as you have replied and we have had the opportunity to consider your comments'. On 21 October, Euclidian repudiated liability. Kosmar brought an action against Euclidian for recovery of its costs.

The Court of Appeal overturned the first instance decision that there had been waiver by affirmation. Rix LJ, referring to the judgment of Lord Diplock in *Kammins Ballrooms Co Ltd v Zenith Investments (Torquay) Ltd*[32] discussing the difference between waiver by election and waiver by estoppel, put the matter in this way:

> 'Waiver' is a word sometimes used loosely to describe a number of different legal grounds on which a person may be debarred from asserting a substantive right which he once possessed or from raising a particular defence to a claim against him which would otherwise be available to him. We are not concerned in the instant appeal with the first type of waiver. This arises in a situation where a person is entitled to alternative rights inconsistent with one another. If he has

[31] See *Evans v Kosmar Villa Holiday plc* [2006] EWHC 3417 (Comm); overturned on appeal [2008] 1 WLR 297 (CA).

[32] [1971] AC 850.

> knowledge of the facts which give rise in law to these alternative rights and acts in a manner which is consistent only with his having chosen to rely on one of them, the law holds him to his choice even though he was unaware that this would be the legal consequence of what he did. He is sometimes said to have 'waived' the alternative right … but this is better categorised as 'election' rather than as 'waiver' … The second type of waiver which debars a person from raising a particular defence to a claim against him, arises when he either agrees with the claimant not to raise that particular defence or so conducts himself as to be estopped from raising it … The ordinary principles of estoppel apply to it.

Rix LJ also cited Lord Goff's speech in *Motor Oil Hellas (Corinth) Refineries SA v Shipping Corp of India, The Kanchenjunga.*[33] Lord Goff contrasted election with equitable estoppel, which occurs where a person unequivocally represents that he or she does not intend to enforce certain rights and the other party acts in reliance upon that representation, so that it becomes inequitable for the representor to enforce the rights. There are similarities between election and equitable estoppel in that both require an unequivocal representation, but there are also important differences. Election requires an informed choice, it does not require reliance by the other party and it is irrevocable. Estoppel does not require an informed choice by the representor and it only suspends rights (although, in practice, this may have the same effect as if it were irrevocable). While the party making an election is choosing whether or not to exercise a right that has arisen, the representation in equitable estoppel is a promise not to enforce legal rights in the future. Rix LJ preferred the view that election involved the exercise of a right, while estoppel was a representation that rights would not be enforced, rather than the approach of Lord Diplock, who distinguished between rights, which were the subject of election, and defences, which were the subject of estoppel.[34]

Before the Court of Appeal, Euclidian argued that the breach automatically discharged its liability.[35] This meant that it was not open to Kosmar to argue that Euclidian subsequently made its election to affirm the contract.[36] Rix LJ agreed, holding that following the breach of GC 7(1), Euclidian was not required to make an election as to whether to reject or to accept the claim. In the event that he was wrong and the doctrine of election did apply, Rix LJ took the view that the correspondence from Euclidian in September did not constitute an unequivocal communication of waiver of the need for compliance with GC 7(1), or an acceptance of liability. Euclidian had made it clear from the outset that it was not in a position to decide on the liability for Mr Evans's injury until it had more information from Kosmar, which meant it had not accepted its liability for such a claim. In addition, the inquiries about the reasons for the delay in notification, which had not been answered, meant Kosmar could not realistically have believed that Euclidian had waived compliance with the clause. In his view, it was not necessary for an insurer expressly to reserve its rights in order to maintain them in circumstances where there has been no unequivocal communication of a waiver. He agreed that the insurer should be allowed a reasonable period of time within which to reserve its rights, if otherwise there would be an unequivocal communication of a waiver. He also said that in determining what constituted a reasonable time, consideration should be given to the delay in reporting the claim. Unfortunately, Rix LJ did not explain why a delay should affect the meaning of reasonable time: a long delay may

[33] [1990] 1 Lloyd's Rep 391.

[34] ibid [66]; M Clarke, *The Law of Insurance Contracts*, 4th edn (LLP Professional Publishing, 2002) para 26-4A2.

[35] As has been seen, under s 33(3) of the Marine Insurance Act 1906, if a warranty is not complied with, then, subject to contrary agreement, 'the insurer is discharged from liability as from the date of the breach of warranty'.

[36] *Kosmar Villa Holidays* [2008] EWCA Civ 147, [40].

disincline the insurers to waive their rights or may make it a lengthier process, but it does not, in itself, justify extending the time that would otherwise be reasonably necessary to make the election. More importantly, Rix LJ went on to lament the fact that, having raised all of these issues, Gross J failed to give them any weight. He pointed out that the operation of the insurance market means that insurers often forgo their strict legal rights, as they did in earlier claims made by Kosmar, and the law should not discourage this practice by imposing on insurers strict and unreasonable deadlines.

Having concluded that this situation did not fall within the realms of the doctrine of election, Rix LJ said that Euclidian was not prevented from denying the claim by estoppel because there had been no representation by the insurer, or, alternatively, if there had been a representation, Kosmar's efforts in compiling information for Euclidian did not constitute reliance or detriment sufficient to make it inequitable for Euclidian to rely on Kosmar's breach.

Further, the Court of Appeal refuted the idea that the method of claims handling after the meeting constituted estoppel by convention and so prevented enforcement of GC 7(1). There was no common assumption or consistent representation that Euclidian would deal with each claim in any way other than on a case-by-case basis. Rix LJ pointed out that, in any event, the expectation after the meeting remained that a claim as serious as that of Mr Evans would be notified immediately. In sum, the failure to enforce the condition precedent in one case did not prevent Euclidian from insisting on its observance in other cases.[37]

2.6. Section 11 of the Insurance Act 2015

2.6.1. Background to Reform

The Law Commissions accepted at an early stage in their post-2006 deliberations that it would be appropriate in the interests of fairness to adopt measures to prevent insurers from relying upon irrelevant breaches of condition in order to deny liability. It was regarded as wrong that an insured who failed to install a burglar alarm could lose a claim for loss by fire, when the breach had no possible connection to the loss. The Law Commissions considered two overseas models. Section 11 of the Insurance Law Reform Act 1977 in New Zealand states that:

> Where –
>
> (a) by the provisions of a contract of insurance the circumstances in which the insurer is bound to indemnify the insured against loss are so defined as to exclude or limit the liability of the insurer to indemnify the insured on the happening of certain events or on the existence of certain circumstances; and
>
> (b) in the view of the court or arbitrator determining the claim of the insured the liability of the insurer has been so defined because the happening of such events or the existence of such circumstances was in the view of the insurer likely to increase the risk of such loss occurring, –
>
> the insured shall not be disentitled to be indemnified by the insurer by reason only of such provisions of the contract of insurance if the insured proves on the balance of probability that the loss

[37] Gross J, at first instance, said that evidence that this insurer had previously ignored a term in a policy held by another insured did not mean it was estopped from relying on that term in the present policy, and, without evidence of trade usage (of which there was none), the mere fact that in other contracts between other parties notification clauses were not generally insisted on did not raise an estoppel in relation to the policy in this case.

> in respect of which the insured seeks to be indemnified was not caused or contributed to by the happening of such events or the existence of such circumstances.

This measure was replicated by section 54 of the Insurance Contracts Act 1984 (Australia). This applies where, under the policy, an act by the insured or some other person permits the insurers to refuse to pay a claim. The section then provides that:

> (2) … where the act could reasonably be regarded as being capable of causing or contributing to a loss in respect of which insurance cover is provided by the contract, the insurer may refuse to pay the claim.
>
> (3) Where the insured proves that no part of the loss that gave rise to the claim was caused by the act, the insurer may not refuse to pay the claim by reason only of the act.
>
> (4) Where the insured proves that some part of the loss that gave rise to the claim was not caused by the act, the insurer may not refuse to pay the claim, so far as it concerns that part of the loss, by reason only of the act.

Each of these measures specifically adopts a causation test, so that the insurers only have a defence to the extent that the loss was caused by the insured's breach of contract. The English and Scottish Law Commissions, at an early stage in their post-2006 deliberations, accepted from an early stage that amendment along these lines was necessary to avoid the unfairness of, for example, an insured who had in breach of contract failed to install a burglar alarm losing a fire claim entirely unrelated to the breach. However, the insurance market strongly opposed the introduction of a causation test, as that was thought to give rise to uncertainty, and the Law Commissions sought to find an alternative formulation.[38] After a number of attempts, a form of wording was finally settled at the end of 2014 while the Insurance Bill 2014 was progressing through Parliament. This was accompanied by an explanation in the form of a *Stakeholder Note*. The provision finally adopted, section 11 of the Insurance Act 2015,[39] which is entirely free of any reference to causation, is as follows:

> (1) This section applies to a term (express or implied) of a contract of insurance, other than a term defining the risk as a whole, if compliance with it would tend to reduce the risk of one or more of the following –
> (a) loss of a particular kind,
> (b) loss at a particular location,
> (c) loss at a particular time.
>
> (2) If a loss occurs, and the term has not been complied with, the insurer may not rely on the non-compliance to exclude, limit or discharge its liability under the contract for the loss if the insured satisfies subsection (3).
>
> (3) The insured satisfies this subsection if it shows that the non-compliance with the term could not have increased the risk of the loss which actually occurred in the circumstances in which it occurred.

There is no authority on the meaning of this section. Unsurprisingly, insurers have been unwilling to test the section in the courts, for fear of an adverse precedent. Exclusion clauses have also been widely adopted in business insurance policies to contract out of the section.

[38] Law Com CP No 204/Scot Law Com CP 155; Law Com CP No 353/Scot Law Com CP 238 (LC 353); *Business Disclosure; Warranties; Insurers' Remedies for Fraudulent Claims; and Late Payment* (Cm 8898, 2014); Law Commissions, *Stakeholder Note: Terms Not Relevant to the Actual Loss* (December 2014).

[39] B Soyer, 'Risk Control Clauses in Insurance Law: Law Reform and the Future' (2016) 75 *CLJ* 109; M Clarke, 'The Future of Warranties and Other Related Terms in Contracts of Insurance' in M Clarke and B Soyer (eds), *The Insurance Act 2015* (London, Routledge, 2017) 54–59; B Rix, 'Conclusion: General Reflections on the Law Reform' in ibid 117–19; R Merkin and O Gurses, 'Insurance Contracts after the Insurance Act' (2016) 132 *LQR* 445.

However, assuming that section 11 applies, the following paragraphs consider its terms. There is little relevant guidance from the Law Commissions on the impact of the changes made by the final version of the measure.

2.6.2. *Scope*

The section applies to any contract term however it is classified, so conditions and warranties alike are within its scope. The term must be of a type such that compliance with it would tend to reduce the risk of losses of the specified types. This is plainly an objective test,[40] based on the practical operation of the term, and, unlike the New Zealand measure, the section is not concerned with the insurers' subjective intentions in adopting the term, although in practice the two are unlikely to differ. It would seem to suffice that the term addresses any part of a possible loss. The loss referred to would seem to be that of the insured and not that of the insurers. This is a crucial point. The insured's loss is that resulting from an insured peril, whereas the insurers' loss is having to pay a claim. On the former interpretation, the only terms that are caught by section 11 are those relating to occurrence of an insured peril. On the latter interpretation, any term affecting the insurers' liability for the claim – encompassing notification and co-operation clauses – would be within the provision. The Law Commissions plainly did not intend section 11 to encompass post-loss breaches, a point obvious from every illustration of the operation of the section set out in its various reports. Further, the wider meaning of loss is inconsistent with the three types of loss set out in section 11(1) – kind, location and time – and also inconsistent with section 11(2), which refers to 'liability under the contract for the loss'.

Given that section 11(1) extends only to what may be classed as 'risk' clauses, the risk that the term tends to diminish is one of loss of a particular kind, at a particular location or at a particular time. The Law Commissions have conceded that these phrases do not have a clear meaning.[41] Loss of a particular kind could mean a generic form of loss, such as burglary, or it could mean a specific type of burglary. By way of example, a requirement to fit a particular form of lock to a door could mean burglary via that door or it could mean burglary generally: if section 11(1) refers only to the tendency to reduce the risk of loss through that locked door, then the insurers could rely upon that clause even if the burglary took place by breaking a window: it would fall outside section 11 because compliance did not tend to reduce the risk of burglary generally. Loss at a particular location was intended to refer to a specific set of premises rather than a broad geographical area, so it could be argued that a clause prohibiting the insured from using a vehicle outside the UK is outside section 11. Loss at a particular time is also problematic, and seems to be limited to clauses such as those requiring the employment of a night watchman outside working hours.

2.6.3. *Defining the Risk as a Whole*[42]

This phrase was added to the final version of section 11 as presented to Parliament, so there is no guidance on its meaning. Its apparent purpose was to preclude the use of terms setting out the types of risk covered by the policy. For example: the coverage of a motor policy may

[40] LC 353, paras 18.14–18.16.
[41] ibid para 18.49.
[42] O Gurses, 'Section11 of the Insurance Act 2015: When Does a Term Define the Risk as a Whole in an Insurance Contract? Balancing the Interest of the Assured and Insurer' [2020] *Journal of Business Law* 184.

be confined to social, domestic or pleasure purposes so that business losses fall outside the risk as defined; a professional liability policy may be limited to claims against the insured arising from specified business activities; and university premises may be insured only for losses arising from educational activities. The Law Commissions in the December 2014 *Stakeholder Note* gave four illustrations: the uses to which property is put; the geographical limits of the policy; the class of vessel being insured; and the minimum age, qualifications and characteristics of an insured person.

The difficulty with the limitation is that it is possible to draft any exclusion in terms of risk definition. Take a policy stating that the insured premises must be fitted with a burglar alarm: that is a risk clause within section 11 in that it is concerned with loss of a particular kind. However, redraft the policy to provide that it applies only to a building fitted with a burglar alarm. The risk as a whole is a building with a burglar alarm, so if the alarm is not fitted, then the risk definition has not been satisfied and section 11 has no application. It is apparent, therefore, that section 11 must address substance and not form.[43] The same issue has arisen in both New Zealand and Australia under their respective pieces of legislation, although the 'risk as a whole' limitation is not statutory but has been implied by the courts to recognise that policies cannot be treated as providing unlimited cover. The test adopted in Australia is to ask whether the term in question constitutes 'a restriction or limitation which must necessarily be acknowledged in the making of a claim, having regard to the type of insurance contract under which that claim is made'.[44] If it does, the term defines the risk. The Australian courts have held that an exclusion in a motor policy for accidents occurring while insured vehicles were being driven by drivers who had not obtained minimum scores in personality tests,[45] a requirement that a vessel had to clear customs[46] and a restriction in a liability policy removing cover for 'injury to any person who normally lives with you'[47] were not risk defining. By contrast, limitations in a policy against the use of a vessel outside Australian waters,[48] on the use of a vehicle more than 450 km from the insured's base[49] and respect of bad debts on the classes of debt insured[50] were risk defining. There are similar decisions in New Zealand holding that an exclusion from a public liability policy for the use of farm buildings for any other purpose constituted a risk defining clause,[51] as did a limitation in a professional indemnity policy to liabilities arising from investment activities.[52]

2.6.4. *Effect of Non-compliance*

Assuming that the term in question is within section 11 and does not define the risk as a whole, section 11(3) prevents reliance by the insurers if the insured 'shows that the non-compliance with the term could not have increased the risk of the loss which actually occurred in the circumstances in which it occurred'. The Law Commissions' stated intention was to avoid a causation test, which focused on the question whether the insured's conduct did in fact cause or contribute to the loss, and instead to ask whether the insured's

[43] A point made in Australia in *Pantaenius Australia Pty Ltd v Watkins Syndicate 0457 at Lloyd's* [2016] FCA 1.
[44] *Maxwell v Highway Hauliers Pty Ltd* [2014] HCA 33, [23].
[45] ibid.
[46] *Pantaenius Australia Pty Ltd v Watkins Syndicate 0457 at Lloyd's* [2016] FCA 1.
[47] *Allianz Australia Insurance Co v Inglis* [2016] WASCA 25.
[48] ibid.
[49] *Stapleton v NTI Ltd* [2002] QDC 204.
[50] *Prepaid Services Pty Ltd v Atradius Credit Insurance NV* [2012] NSWCA 252.
[51] *Nelson Forests v Three Tuis* [2010] NZHC 2178.
[52] *Hall v FP North Ltd* (2010) ANZ Ins Cas 61-631.

failure to comply could have increased the risk of the loss that actually occurred whether or not that failure actually did so. The distinction is between conduct that did contribute to the loss and conduct that, viewed objectively, might have contributed to the loss. It is far from certain whether the Law Commissions have in fact achieved their objective; indeed, much of the evidence given to the House of Lords' Committee responsible for passing the Insurance Bill asserted that causation remained at the heart of the provision. Some cases are straightforward: failure to comply with a burglar alarm requirement for an insured building will not exempt the insurers from a claim for damage caused by fire or by a collision with the building by a motor vehicle or aircraft. Compliance could not have affected the outcome. However, where there is some connection between the term and the loss, matters are more complex, and there is little clarification from the Law Commissions themselves in the *Stakeholder* note. They put forward the example of a motor policy containing a roadworthiness term. The vehicle has a defective headlight and skids on black ice, giving rise to an accident. The Law Commissions' view was that the insured could not rely upon section 11(3). If the headlight had been working, then the risk of the loss that had occurred would not have been increased. The analysis is, however, problematic. Section 11(3) focuses attention on 'the loss which actually occurred in the circumstances in which it occurred'. It is arguable that even if the headlight had been working, black ice could not have been seen or, even if it had been, a skid could not have been prevented. The question posed by the concentration on the actual loss and its circumstances thus becomes, what actually happened? That is, arguably, pure causation.

It is of interest to speculate how section 11 would apply to the facts of *New Zealand Insurance v Harris*.[53] The insured's tractor was insured against loss or damage other than when it was 'let out on hire'. The tractor was hired to a third party, and it was destroyed by fire on the third party's premises. The New Zealand court held that the exclusion was not operative under the 1977 Act, in that there was an insufficient causal link between the breach of policy term and the fire, and that 'refined analysis in terms of metaphysical inquiries into causation should be eschewed'. On the assumption that the term did not define the risk as a whole so as to be excluded from section 11, under section 11(3) it would surely have been easy for the insured to show that 'non-compliance with the term could not have increased the risk of the loss which actually occurred in the circumstances in which it occurred' (ie fire), in that hiring the tractor had no connection with the loss that actually occurred even though, had it not been lent, the loss would not have occurred.

3. Insurance Warranties[54]

3.1. The Nature of Warranties

3.1.1. The Meaning of the Word 'Warranty'

It was noted earlier in this chapter that warranties in the form of basis of the contract clauses guaranteeing the truth of representations are, as a result of section 6 of Consumer

[53] [1990] 1 NZLR 10.

[54] Soyer, 'Risk Control Clauses' (n 39); B Soyer, *Warranties in Marine Insurance* (3rd edn 2017); D Owen, *The Law of Insurance Warranties* (2021); J Lowry and R Edmunds, 'The Reform of Insurance Warranties: Looking Beyond the Past' in PS Davies and M Raczynska (eds), *Contents of Commercial Contracts* (London, Bloomsbury, 2020) ch 19.

Insurance (Disclosure and Representations) Act 2010 and section 9 of the Insurance Act 2015, no longer permissible in either consumer or business contracts. Contracting out is not permitted in either case. It remains to consider the effect of warranties that impose obligations on the insured or restrictions on the insured's conduct as codified by sections 33–35 of the Marine Insurance Act 1906. Such warranties may be termed 'promissory'. By section 33(1),

> [a] warranty … means a promissory warranty, that is to say, a warranty by which the assured undertakes that some particular thing shall or shall not be done, or that some condition shall be fulfilled, or whereby he affirms or negatives the existence of a particular state of facts.

This broad definition encompasses a series of quite different promises: (a) that at the date of the contract a particular state of affairs does or does not exist; (b) that during the currency of the policy the state of affairs will continue to exist, or will not come into existence; (c) that at the date of the contract the insured has or has not acted in a particular way; (d) that during the currency of the policy the insured will or will not act in a specified way; (e) that at the date of the contract the insured intends to act or to refrain from acting in a specified way; and (f) that at the date of the policy the insured held a particular belief. Promises (a), (c), (e) and (f) relate to the date of the contract and require only that the promise was then accurate. Promises (b) and (d), by contrast, relate to the future. The distinction is of great importance. At common law, a promise of the former type must be satisfied on inception, failing which the risk does not attach and there can be no future liability. Once the risk has attached, however, the policy is unaffected if the promise ceases to be true thereafter. By contrast, at common law, a promise of the latter type must be adhered to throughout the currency of the policy, and if it ceases to be true then the risk determines automatically.

The common law approach to warranties is rigid; a warranty must be exactly complied with; there is no requirement for a warranty to be material to the risk; the automatic termination principle means there is no need for any causal link between the breach of warranty and the loss; and even if the breach of warranty has been remedied by the date of the loss, the insurers remain off risk – in other words, a breach of warranty cannot be remedied. There may well have been justification for this approach in the early days of marine insurance, when losses occurred in remote parts of the world, leaving few if any survivors able to given evidence as to the cause of the loss, so it made sense to render breach sufficient to justify discharging the insurers from liability. However, that justification has long ceased to be supportable, and the law was transformed by the Insurance Act 2015. Section 10 has largely abolished the automatic termination rule and replaced it with the principle that the risk is suspended during any period of breach. Even if a loss occurs at a time when the risk is suspended, section 11 – discussed earlier – allows an insurer to rely upon the breach only if there is some link between the breach and the loss. As a result of these changes, it is likely that the use of warranties is likely to diminish, and where warranties are included in policies, they are for the most part to be treated as ordinary contract terms. However, for the reasons explained below, sections 10 and 11 will not be applicable to all warranties, and aspects of warranties other than those relating to remedies for breach are unaffected by the 2015 Act, so it is necessary to consider the current legal status of warranties.

3.1.2. Creation of Warranties

Warranties may be express or implied (Marine Insurance Act 1906, section 33(2)). There are two warranties implied by the common law as codified by the Marine Insurance Act:

the warranty of seaworthiness for marine voyage policies in section 39(1) and the warranty of legality in section 41. Both are discussed in chapter 17 below. All other marine, and all non-marine, warranties have to be express. Section 35 provides that:

> (1) An express warranty may be in any form of words from which the intention to warrant is to be inferred.
> (2) An express warranty must be included in, or written upon, the policy, or must be contained in some document incorporated by reference into the policy

The purpose of section 33(2) is to ensure that the insured is aware of what is being warranted. As is specified by section 35(1), it is not necessary for any form of words to be used in order to create a warranty. The use or absence of the word 'warranty' is therefore not conclusive, although it is plainly of some significance. Provided due care has been taken in describing the nature of a term, that is likely to be decisive. In *Virk v Gan Life Holdings plc*,[55] Potter LJ explained that:

> In relation to the exercise of construction to be undertaken by the court, the question of 'labelling' is influential rather than decisive, particularly if the label … has been applied to a number of terms of differing type and practical importance. On the other hand, if care and logic appear to have been applied in the attachment of the label to one term but not to another, the label (or absence of it) is likely to be decisive.[56]

It was observed by Lord Blackburn in *Thomson v Weems*[57] that:

> In policies of marine insurance I think it is settled by authority that any statement of fact bearing upon the risk introduced into the written policy is, by whatever words and in whatever place, to be construed as a warranty, and prima facie, at least that the compliance with that warranty is a condition precedent to the attaching of the risk. I think that on the balance of the authority the general principles of insurance law apply to all insurances, whether marine, life or fire.[58]

While there is no particular formula, nevertheless the language creating a warranty must be unequivocal, showing clearly that it is the intention of the parties that the term in question is viewed by them as fundamental to the contract.[59] In *HIH Casualty and General Insurance Ltd v New Hampshire Insurance Co*,[60] the issue was whether a term in the policy which stated that six films would be made was a warranty. Rix LJ laid down three tests for deciding the nature of a term:

> In my judgment, once the six film term is established as a term of the insurance or reinsurance contract, the grounds for holding it to be a warranty are very strong. It is a question of construction, and the presence or absence of the word 'warranty' or 'warranted' is not conclusive. One test is whether it is a term which goes to the root of the transaction; a second, whether it is descriptive of or bears materially on the risk of loss; a third, whether damages would be an unsatisfactory or inadequate remedy. As Lord Justice Bowen said in *Barnard v Faber*, [1893] 1 QB 340 at p 344: 'A term as regards the risk must be a condition.' Otherwise the insurer is merely left to a

[55] [2000] Lloyd's Rep IR 159.

[56] ibid 165.

[57] (1884) 9 App Cas 671.

[58] ibid 684. See also *Barnard v Faber* [1893] 1 QB 340, 343–34 (Bowen LJ); *Svenska Handelsbanken v Sun Alliance and London Insurance plc* [1996] CLC 833, 876 (Rix J).

[59] See, eg the speech of Viscount Finlay in *Dawsons Ltd v Bonnin* [1922] 2 AC 413 (HL), 428; see also Lord Blackburn in *Thomson v Weems* (1884) 9 App Cas 671, 682. See further *CTN Cash & Carry Ltd v General Accident plc* [1989] 1 Lloyd's Rep 299; the judgment of Morland J in *Kler Knitwear Ltd v Lombard General Insurance Co Ltd* [2000] Lloyd's Rep IR 47.

[60] [2001] 2 Lloyd's Rep 161.

> cross-claim in a matter which goes to the risk itself, which is unbusinesslike ... In the present case, the six film term would seem to answer all three tests. It is a fundamental term, for even if only one film were omitted, the revenues are likely to be immediately reduced.[61]

This approach was applied by the Court of Appeal in *Toomey (of Syndicate 2021) v Banco Vitalicio de Espana SA de Seguros y Reasseguros*.[62] The defendants, Spanish insurers, insured a Spanish first-division football club, Atletico de Madrid, against loss of income should the club be relegated. The club had been required to effect such insurance by Audivisual (AV), which had exclusive rights to televise the club's home matches. AV had paid the club advances, a percentage of which, subject to certain conditions, was returnable in the event of relegation. The insurance policy provided security to AV for its exposure under promissory notes in the sum of Pts 2.9 billion. The insurers reinsured the risk with a number of reinsurers in London. At the end of the 1999–2000 season the club was relegated to the second division. The defendants paid the loss, but the reinsurers refused to pay on the reinsurance on the basis that there was a material misrepresentation in the draft slip relating to the nature of the direct policy. At first instance, it was held to be a valued policy and not, as represented, an indemnity policy. The reinsurers' exposure was therefore greater than appeared. Toulson J also held that the description in the slip of the policy was a warranty and that there was breach. The Court of Appeal agreed on both issues. With respect to the warranty issue, the Court held, applying the tests formulated by Rix LJ in *HIH*, that a term may be a warranty even though it is not expressed as such provided it goes to the root of the transaction and bears materially on the risk of loss and if damages would not be an adequate remedy. On the facts, these conditions were satisfied.

3.2. Construction of Warranties

3.2.1. Present and Continuing Warranties

It was noted above that a present warranty must be complied with at the date of the contract whereas a continuing warranty must be complied with throughout the policy. The distinction between the two is thus crucial, but not always obvious. In determining whether, as a question of construction, a warranty relates to the future, the courts have regard not only to the purpose of the warranty, but to the purpose of the policy itself. Thus, in *Hair v Prudential Assurance Co Ltd*,[63] Woolf J held that a warranty in a fire policy that the insured premises were occupied could not be construed as amounting to a continuing obligation but rather as 'an indication of the state of affairs which existed at the time that the answers were given [and as such] they did not amount to a warranty that no change would occur'.[64] There are numerous contrasting cases. In *Beauchamp v National Mutual Indemnity Insurance Co*,[65] the proposal form asked 'Are any explosives used in your business?' The insured answered that there were none. This was correct at the time it was made but the insured, a builder, did subsequently use explosives when, for the first time in his business, he was contracted to demolish a building. It was held, as a matter of construction, that the question and its

[61] ibid 182, [101].
[62] [2004] EWCA Civ 622. See also *International Management Group v Simmonds* [2004] Lloyd's Rep IR 247.
[63] [1983] 2 Lloyd's Rep 667.
[64] ibid 672.
[65] [1937] 3 All ER 19.

answer related to the future. Similarly, in *Hales v Reliance Fire and Accident Insurance Co*,[66] a question in the proposal form asked 'Are any inflammable oils or goods used or kept on the premises?' The insured answered 'Lighter fuel'. It was held that the question and answer were a warranty as to the existence of the fact at the time of the proposal and also during the currency of the risk. Accordingly, there was a breach when the insured took delivery of a quantity of fireworks 17 days prior to 5 November. McNair J accepted that warranties in fire and burglary policies as to the condition of the premises and precautions taken to prevent loss will prima facie be construed as continuing, otherwise such warranties will be of little value to the insurers.[67] But this view is now open to question in the light of Saville LJ's interpretation of *Hales* in the recent decision in *Hussain v Brown*.[68] His Lordship took the view (based on decided cases,[69] and doubting the approach of McNair J in *Hales*) that questions contained in proposal forms which are constructed in the present tense cannot be taken to import warranties as to the future. Saville LJ stated that:

> [T]here is no special principle of insurance law requiring answers in proposal forms to be read, *prima facie* or otherwise, as importing promises to the future. Whether or not they do depends upon ordinary rules of construction, namely consideration of the words the parties have used in the light of the context in which they have used them and (where the words admit of more than one meaning) selection of that meaning which seems most closely to correspond with the presumed intentions of the parties.[70]

The futurity of a warranty must therefore be manifestly apparent from the words used, and the tense in which the question is framed will be the material factor. In *Kennedy v Smith and Ansvar Ins Co Ltd*,[71] the insured warranted in a proposal for motor insurance that 'I am a total abstainer from alcoholic drinks', which was true at the time it was made. However, after a cricket match, the insured drank a small quantity of beer on an empty stomach. He then drove himself and two friends home. His vehicle was involved in an accident and his two passengers were killed. He sought an indemnity from his insurers for the delictual damages he was liable to pay, but the insurers refused the claim on the basis that a continuing warranty had been broken. It was held that the warranty related to the past and was not promissory as to the future. Construing the term *contra proferentem*, the Lord President said that:

> The statement does not require to be given a future promissory content to make it intelligible. It is quite intelligible if it is read literally for no doubt the risk during the period of insurance is reduced if at the outset the proposer is a total abstainer since it may reasonably be hoped that he is unlikely to abandon his principles. It would have been simple to include in the statement if this had been intended, that the insured shall continue to be a total abstainer for the period of the insurance.

[66] [1960] 2 Lloyd's Rep 391.

[67] ibid 395. See further, J Birds, 'Warranties in Insurance Proposal Forms' [1977] *Journal of Business Law* 231, 236–38.

[68] [1996] 1 Lloyd's Rep 627, noted by N Hird [1996] *Journal of Business Law* 404.

[69] *Weber & Berger v Employers' Liability Assurance Corporation* (1926) 24 Lloyd's Rep 15; *Woolfall & Rimmer v Moyle* [1942] 1 KB 66.

[70] [1996] 1 Lloyd's Rep 627, 629. It is noteworthy, at least in terms of gaining some insight into contemporary judicial thinking, that Saville LJ (630) went on to stress that 'it must be remembered that a continuing warranty is a draconian term. As I have noted, the breach of such a warranty produces an automatic cancellation of the cover, and the fact that a loss may have no connection at all with that breach is simply irrelevant. In my view, if underwriters want such protection, then it is up to them to stipulate for it in clear terms.' See also *Kirkbride v Donner* [1974] 1 Lloyd's Rep 549.

[71] 1976 SLT 110. See also *Woolfall & Rimmer v Moyle* [1942] 1 KB 66.

> No such statement was, however, included and in my opinion is not, without undue straining of the language used, to be implied.[72]

In *Ansari v New India Assurance Ltd*,[73] the court had to decide whether an affirmative answer to the question 'Are the premises protected by an automatic sprinkler installation?' was tantamount to importing a continuing warranty to the contract. The insured held commercial property owners' insurance with New India. A fire broke out on the property and the insured claimed. New India denied liability, relying on General Condition 2 of the contract, which stated:

> This insurance shall cease to be in force if there is any material alteration to the Premises or Business or any material change in the facts stated in the Proposal Form or other facts supplied to the Insurer unless the Insurer agrees in writing to continue the insurance.

It was argued there had been a material alteration when the sprinkler system was not operative. The insured contended that the answer in the proposal form did not state that the sprinkler system was working nor would continue to be working. The Court of Appeal, affirming the judgment of Pattern J, stated that the proposal form contained a statement that the premises were protected by an automatic sprinkler system. Moore-Bick LJ explained that:

> Where an automatic sprinkler system has been installed in a building it forms an integral part of the building and moreover is one which (unlike an intruder alarm) is intended to function permanently, in the sense of being constantly ready to operate in the event of a fire without the need for human intervention.[74]

The court distinguished *Hussain v Brown*:

> [I]in that case it would have been difficult to read the warranty that the premises were fitted with an intruder alarm as containing by implication a continuing warranty that it would be maintained and put into operation whenever the premises were left unattended. Apart from anything else, such an interpretation could lead to a complete loss of cover as a result of a simple act of negligence on the part of the insured or his employees in failing to set the alarm.[75]

Moore-Bick LJ rejected the insured's appeal and construction of the policy because

> to construe the completed form as meaning no more than that they were fitted with an automatic sprinkler system which might or might not be functioning would be contrary to common sense. Apart from anything else, it would give little or no effect to the word 'protected'.[76]

Where the insured is an individual (ie a consumer) as opposed to a business entity, warranties of opinion or belief are commonly encountered in proposal forms. The effect of this type of term is that the insured warrants that the answers given in the proposal form are true to the best of his belief and knowledge. The insured must exercise due care when completing the proposal form.[77] In contrast with warranties of fact, a warranty of opinion will only be broken if the insured is dishonest or reckless. For example, in *Confederation Life*

[72] ibid 117.
[73] [2009] EWCA Civ 93.
[74] ibid [25].
[75] ibid [27].
[76] ibid [28].
[77] *Huddleston v RACV Insurance Property Ltd* [1975] VR 683. See Birds (n 67).

Assn v Miller,[78] the insured warranted in a life policy that to the best of his knowledge and belief he had suffered no serious injury. Gwynne J held that this would be untrue only if the answer given was wilfully false.

Further, householders who insure possessions against theft or other loss are frequently required to estimate and warrant the value of specific items. Where this is the case, it has been held that the value of a possession, a stamp collection, is a matter of opinion, so that, provided the insured gave a bona fide estimate, the warranty would not be broken where a subsequent expert valuation showed the original estimate to be too low.[79]

3.2.2. The Obligations Imposed by Warranties

Section 33(3) provides that 'A warranty, as above defined, is a condition which must be exactly complied with, whether it be material to the risk or not'. The strict compliance requirement is double edged in that the insured must comply exactly with the terms of the warranty[80] even though the inability to comply is outside the insured's control, eg inability to obtain a licence from a third party,[81] but strict compliance suffices even if the purpose of the warranty is defeated: that emerges from one of the earliest cases, *Hide v Bruce*,[82] where a warranty requiring a vessel to be armed with 20 guns was held not to have been broken even though 60 crew were required to man that number of guns but the crew numbered only 25.[83] A more modern example is *Sea Glory Maritime Co v Al Sagr National Insurance Co, The Nancy*,[84] where the warranty 'Vessel International Safety Management Compliant' imposed a continuing obligation to ensure that the vessel held the specified Document of Compliance but did not go further to require compliance with every provision of the Safety Management Code. The absence of any need for materiality is demonstrated by *Dawsons Ltd v Bonnin*,[85] where the owner of a taxi warranted that it was garaged in Glasgow. That was an inadvertent misstatement, the taxi in fact being garaged in a farm outside Glasgow. The House of Lords held that there was a breach of warranty even though the taxi was at lower risk at its actual location.

The draconian consequences of a breach of warranty have led the courts to be cautious of interpretation overgenerous to insurers. The point has been made judicially that questions 'framed in a slovenly way' are 'mere traps' and will be strictly construed against the insurers who seek to rely on them.[86] In *Re Bradley and Essex and Suffolk Accident Indemnity Society*,[87] Farwell LJ surveyed the relevant authorities and stressed that:

> It is especially incumbent on insurance companies to make clear, both in their proposal forms and in their policies, the conditions which are precedent to their liability to pay, for such conditions

[78] (1887) 14 SCR 330. See further *Gerling-Konzern General Insurance Co v Polygram Holdings and Metropolitan Entertainment In* [1998] 2 Lloyd's Rep 544, in which the insured was required to make enquiries of certain employees in regular contact with the life-insured.

[79] *Timms v FAI Insurances Ltd* (1976) 12 ALR 506.

[80] It is uncertain whether there is a *de minimis* exception. There are statements to that effect, eg *Sugar Hut Group Ltd v Great Lakes Reinsurance (UK) Plc* [2011] Lloyd's Rep IR 198, but no decided case on the point.

[81] *International Management Group (UK) Ltd v Simmonds* [2004] Lloyd's Rep IR 247.

[82] (1783) 3 Doug KB 213.

[83] The Court appears to have been influenced by the fact that the ship was in a foreign port and recruitment was all but impossible, but later cases have made it clear that compliance problems are irrelevant to the questions of interpretation and breach.

[84] [2013] EWHC 2116 (Comm).

[85] [1922] AC 413.

[86] *Zurich General Accident and Liability Insurance Co Ltd v Morrison* [1942] 2 KB 53, 57–58 (Lord Greene MR).

[87] [1912] 1 KB 415.

> have the same effect as forfeiture clauses, and may inflict loss and injury to the assured and those claiming under him out of all proportion to any damage that could possibly accrue to the company from non-observance or non-performance of the conditions. Accordingly, it has been established that the doctrine that policies are to be construed '*contra proferentes*' applies strongly against the company.[88]

There are numerous examples of the courts adopting a restrictive approach to interpretation. In *AC Ward & Son Ltd v Caitlin (Five) Ltd*,[89] the insured's theft policy contained two clauses described as warranties, which were related to security. The first stated that:

> It is warranted that … the whole of the protections provided for the safety of the insured property shall be maintained in good order throughout the currency of this insurance and that they shall be in full and effective operation at all times … All defects occurring in any protections must be promptly remedied.

The second clause stated that:

> It is warranted that … the burglar alarm system shall have been put into full and effective operation at all times when the Insured's premises are closed for business, and at all other appropriate times, including when the said premises are left unattended.

At the time of the loss, neither of these provisions was being complied with. At first instance, HHJ Mackie QC held that the insurers were not entitled to summary judgment based on breach of these terms. He found that the terms were warranties and not, as the insurers had argued, conditions that merely suspended coverage for any period of non-compliance. That meant that the terms were to be given the narrow construction appropriate to draconian clauses such as warranties. Further, the terms were not to be construed as unconditional statements that there was no recovery if security protection or burglar alarms were not working. Instead, they were to be construed as meaning that the insured was under a duty to remedy defects promptly, so that there was no recovery only if the defects were or ought to have been known to the insured and had not been remedied. The Court of Appeal dismissed the appeal, holding that the insurers' interpretation of the warranties were draconian and that the more unreasonable or draconian the effects of insurance terms were, the clearer and more specific they had to be. In *Pratt v Aigaion Insurance Co SA, The Resolute*,[90] a policy on a small fishing vessel with a crew of three stated 'Warranted Owner and/or Owner's experienced skipper on board and in charge at all times and one experienced crew member'. The vessel was lost by fire when moored and with no crew aboard. The Court of Appeal expressed the view that the warranty was inappropriate to a vessel of this type, and had probably been cut and pasted from a policy designed for a larger vessel. The Court held that the purpose of the warranty was to guard against negligent navigation, and that the words 'at all times' were to be construed as meaning at all times when the vessel was at sea. The

[88] ibid 430. See also *Kennedy v Smith and Ansvar Insurance Co Ltd* 1976 SLT 110, 116–17, in which the Lord President stated that 'if insurers seek to limit their liability under a policy by relying upon an alleged undertaking as to the future prepared by them and accepted by an insured, the language they use must be such that the terms of the alleged undertaking and its scope are clearly and unambiguously expressed or plainly implied, and … any such alleged undertaking will be construed, *in dubio, contra preferentem*'. See further *Notman v Anchor Assurance Co* (1858) 4 CB NS 476, 481 (Lord Cockburn CJ); *Fowkes v Manchester and London Life Assurance and Loan Association* (1863) 3 B & S 917, 929 (Blackburn J); *Cook v Financial Insurance Co Ltd* [1998] 1 WLR 1765, 1771 (Lord Lloyd of Berwick); *John A Pike (Butchers) Ltd v Independent Insurance Co Ltd* [1998] LRLR 410.

[89] [2009] EWCA Civ 1098.

[90] [2004] Lloyd's Rep IR 149.

impossibility of a three-man crew complying with the warranty featured large in the Court of Appeal's reasoning.[91]

Nevertheless, an insured cannot rely upon an apparent ambiguity where to a reasonable person the meaning would be clear. In this situation the court will follow the basic rule of interpreting the words reasonably. Thus, where an insured warrants that he has not suffered any illnesses of consequence when in fact he had attempted suicide by way of an overdose and was, as a result, critically ill, the court will construe the word 'illness' in a fair business-like manner so that the effects of the overdose would be covered by the term.[92] A marine example is *Amlin Corporate Member Ltd v Oriental Assurance Corp*,[93] the warranty there precluding the vessel from departing a sheltered port if there was a typhoon or storm warning at that port. The court rejected the insured's contention that the warranty applied only where the warning itself prohibited sailing. In *Argo Systems FZE v Liberty Insurance Pte Ltd*,[94] a breach of a warranty occurred before the inception of the insurance policy. The policy was incepted to cover the insured's floating casino to be towed from the US Gulf to India. The tow contract was in standard form and included a term under which that the tug owner was not to be liable for any loss sustained during the tow. The policy, which was governed by English law, contained a warranty stating: 'no release, waivers or "hold harmless" given to Tug'. The vessel sank during the voyage and the insurers, having obtained a copy of the Towcon, declined cover on the grounds that the insured had breached the insurance contract. The insured argued that it was contrary to the orthodox rules of construction to construe the warranty so that the policy was worthless as soon as it was entered into as it would produce 'commercially absurd' results.[95] They argued that there was an implied condition that the 'hold-harmless' warranty would not apply where they entered a contract on standard terms, that it was standard practice to limit liability in this context and, further, if the warranty was valid, it only applied to different terms, not the one included in the agreement. In construing the warranty, HHJ Mackie QC agreed with the insurers. The insurers argued that construing the term in the way they contended was not commercially absurd, that there was no room for implying any terms as this was unnecessary and that standard term contracts can be amended.[96] The judge said:

> [A]s I see it in construing the policy of insurance I cannot impress upon Liberty [the insurer] both knowledge of the standard form and also a willingness to accept that the wording of the explicit warranty it has required should be read subject to that form. It was for Argo, or its advisers, to ensure that the policy of insurance it took out was consistent with the towing contract it had entered into.[97]

[91] See also *Elafonissos Fishing and Shipping Co v Aigaion Insurance Co SA* [2012] EWHC 1512 (Comm). Contrast *Brownsville Holdings Ltd v Adamjee Insurance Co Ltd, The Milasan* [2000] 2 Lloyd's Rep 458 (warranty that 'professional skippers and crew in charge at all times') and *GE Frankona Reinsurance Ltd v CMM Trust No 1400, The Newfoundland Explorer* [2006] 1 Lloyd's Rep IR 704 (the vessel warranted 'fully crewed at all times'), in each of which the warranties were held to have been broken, in the latter case in the absence of circumstances rendering compliance impossible.

[92] *Yorke v Yorkshire Insurance* [1918] 1 KB 662. See also *Kumar v Life Assurance Corporation of India* [1974] 1 Lloyd's Rep 147, in which the insured warranted that she had never had an operation. Kerr J held that a caesarean delivery must, as a matter of ordinary and technical usage, be taken to be an 'operation'.

[93] [2014] EWCA Civ 1135, [2014] 2 Lloyd's Rep 561. See also *Vlasons Shipping Inc v Neuchatel Swiss General insurance Co Ltd, The Aquarius Bright* [2002] VSC 509.

[94] [2011] EWHC 301 (Comm).

[95] ibid [18].

[96] ibid [21].

[97] ibid [22]. The judge's ruling that the breach of warranty had been waived was reversed on appeal, *Liberty Insurance PTE Ltd v Argo Systems FZE* [20111] EWCA Civ 1572.

The same principle underlies *Bluebon Ltd v Ageas (UK) Ltd*,[98] in which there was a warranty in a policy taken out by a hotel stating 'electrical installation be inspected and tested every five years' by an approved contractor. The hotel contended that the next inspection was due within five years from the date of the policy, but the court ruled instead that the next inspection was due within five years from the date of the last inspection. The hotel's interpretation would have rendered the warranty all but meaningless, in that the five years would run from the date of each annual renewal and so would never have been required. The court went on to hold that failure to inspect did not take effect as a full warranty, but merely suspended the risk from the date of breach up to the point at which an inspection had taken place.

3.2.3. Severability

It is common practice for insurers to subdivide the policy document into separate schedules, each of which will relate to different types of risk put on cover. Some policies have a general section applying to all schedules and containing warranties of various types. However, other policies have separate warranties in each schedule. Where the latter is the case, the question arises whether each schedule will be construed in isolation from the rest of the policy document of which it forms an integral part. If the policy is construed as a whole, without its schedules being treated as distinct, then a breach of warranty contained in one schedule will enable the insurers to repudiate the contract even though the particular risk in question is covered by another schedule in the policy altogether. Typically, insurers argue that where there is a single policy any breach of warranty discharges them from liability, notwithstanding the fact that the policy is multi-sectioned. However, the Court of Appeal has recently held that this is not necessarily the case. In *Printpak v AGF Insurance Ltd*,[99] the insured had effected a commercial inclusive policy which covered various types of risk for loss and damage in the event of a fire at the insured's print factory. When the insured claimed for fire loss, the insurer repudiated liability, alleging arson, and also arguing that it was discharged from liability because the fire had started while the burglar alarm had been switched off during building work, in breach of a warranty requiring the alarm to be fully operational whenever the building was closed. It was held by the Court of Appeal that while the policy should be viewed as a single contract, nevertheless it was not a seamless document. The particular policy comprised separate schedules, each dealing with a different type of risk and having different section endorsements. The section dealing with cover against theft contained the alarm warranty as an endorsement. Given that the schedules described the endorsements as 'section endorsements' and that they were 'operative only as stated in the policy schedule', the court took the view that these words limited the warranties to the individual sections. It therefore concluded that a breach of warranty in one section did not operate to invalidate cover under the other self-standing sections. The insurers were therefore held liable in respect of the fire claim. Hirst LJ explained that:

> [I]t does not follow from the fact that the policy is a single contract that it is to be treated as a seamless contractual instrument. On the contrary, in the present case, its whole structure is based on its division into sections ... The commercial inclusive endorsements are all stated in terms to be 'operative only as stated in the policy schedules'. In my judgment those words explicitly write the warranty into the relevant section in which it appears and not into the others.[100]

[98] [2017] EWHC 3301 (Comm).

[99] [1999] Lloyd's Rep IR 542. See J Davey [1999] *Journal of Business Law* 580. *cf James v CGU Insurance plc* [2002] Lloyd's Rep IR 206.

[100] ibid 546.

The divisibility issue arises also where there are co-insureds. The general principle here is that, irrespective of whether co-insurance is regarded as a group of separate contracts contained in a single document or one contract but with numerous different parties,[101] warranties apply separately to each co-insured. That was held to be the position in *Arab Bank v Zurich Insurance Co*,[102] where the managing director of a company who applied for a professional liability policy for the benefit of himself and other directors warranted that to the best of his knowledge there were no pending claims. That statement was false. Rix J held, applying the separate contracts principle, that the innocent directors were not in breach of warranty and were entitled to recover.

---

4. Consequences of Breach of Warranty

4.1. The Common Law and the Codification

Section 33(3) of the Marine Insurance Act 1906, codifying the common law, stated that if a warranty was not complied with then 'the insurer is discharged from liability as from the date of the breach of warranty, but without prejudice to any liability incurred by him before that date'. It was at one time suggested that these words meant that non-compliance with a warranty was repudiatory breach of contract, which, in accordance with ordinary contractual principles, conferred upon the insurer the right to treat the policy as at an end by giving notice to the insured. That construction was rejected by the House of Lords in *Bank of Nova Scotia v Hellenic Mutual War Risks Association, The Good Luck*.[103] The facts of the case are complex but, put simply, the owner of the ship, the *Good Luck*, insured it with the defendant association and effected a mortgage on the vessel through the claimant bank, to which the benefit of the insurance was assigned. The defendants undertook to notify the assignee bank promptly in the event that 'the association ceases to insure' the vessel. In breach of warranty, the ship sailed into the Arabian Gulf, where on 6 June 1982 it was hit by Iraqi missiles, which resulted in it being a constructive total loss. Both parties knew of the attack on the ship but the defendants, having discovered the breach of warranty, failed to notify the bank. In the meantime, the bank, believing that the loss was covered by insurance, made further advances to the shipowners. However, such further loans would not have been made had the bank been advised that the insurance had ceased. The bank sued the Association for damages in respect of its breach of undertaking. Lord Goff of Chieveley, delivering the principal speech,[104] took as the starting point of his analysis of the consequences of a breach of warranty the wording of section 33(3) of the Marine Insurance Act 1906. In his view, the words were unequivocal and showed that 'discharge of the insurer from liability is automatic and is not dependent upon any decision by the insurer to treat the contract or the insurance as at an end'.[105] Going on to cite Lord Blackburn in *Thomson v Weems*,[106] Lord Goff drew the distinction between conditions as fundamental terms of a contract and

[101] See the discussion in ch 7.
[102] [1999] 1 Lloyd's Rep 262.
[103] [1991] 3 All ER 1.
[104] Lord Bridge, Lord Brandon, Lord Oliver and Lord Lowry concurring.
[105] [1992] 1 AC 233, 262.
[106] (1884) 9 App Cas 671.

conditions precedent, noting that compliance with an insurance warranty is a condition precedent to the attaching of the risk.[107] He stressed that if an insured is in breach of a promissory warranty, the effect is to discharge the insurer from liability 'as from the date of the breach, for the simple reason that fulfilment of the warranty is a condition precedent to the liability of the insurer'.[108] Lord Goff reasoned that this conclusion was in accord with the rationale of insurance warranties, namely 'that the insurer only accepts the risk provided the warranty is fulfilled'.[109] His Lordship continued by pointing out that a promissory warranty was in effect a promissory condition precedent, non-fulfilment of which would prevent the contract from coming into existence. Thus, since the insurer's liability was discharged from the date of the breach and the contract was not avoided *ab initio*, the result is that the insured's obligations, eg to pay a premium, might survive the insurer's discharge from liability.[110]

The question whether breach of warranty also resulted in automatic discharge from liability in non-marine insurance was not addressed by the House of Lords. However, in *HIH Casualty and General Insurance Ltd v New Hampshire Insurance Co*,[111] Rix LJ proceeded on the basis that it did:

> it is well established that a breach of warranty produces an automatic discharge of a contract of insurance from the moment of breach [citing *The Good Luck*] … Once this is appreciated, it becomes readily understandable that, if a promissory warranty is not complied with, the insurer is discharged from liability as from the date of the breach of warranty, for the simple reason that fulfilment of the warranty is a condition precedent to the liability of the insurer. This moreover reflects the fact that the rationale of warranties in insurance law is that the insurer only accepts the risk provided that the warranty is fulfilled. This is entirely understandable; and it follows that the immediate effect of a breach of a promissory warranty is to discharge the insurer from liability as from the date of the breach.[112]

The automatic termination principle necessarily meant that once a loss occurred the insurers were not required to prove any causal link between the breach and the loss. A breach of warranty could occur long before the loss itself, so that there would be no insurance in place when the loss occurred and thus no basis for a causation requirement. Further, the common law, as codified by section 34(2) of the 1906 Act, stated that: 'Where a warranty is broken, the assured cannot avail himself of the defence that the breach has been remedied, and the warranty complied with, before loss.' The principle is illustrated by *Quebec Marine Insurance Co v Commercial Bank of Canada*,[113] in which, contrary to the implied warranty of seaworthiness, the insured vessel's boiler was defective. The boiler was repaired, and

[107] See, eg *Gerling Konzern General Insurance Co v Polygram Holdings Inc* [1998] 2 Lloyd's Rep 544.

[108] [1992] 1 AC 233, 262–63. The burden of proof is on the insurer who alleges that there has been a breach of warranty or condition, *Barrett v Jermy* (1849) 3 Ex 535, 542 (Parke B).

[109] ibid 263.

[110] Non-fulfilment of a condition precedent at the time when the insurance contract is concluded prevents it taking effect because 'there is in reality no contract', *Newcastle Fire Insurance Co v Macmorran & Co* (1815) 3 Dow 255, 259 (Lord Eldon). Liability will be repudiated by the insurers by virtue of the breach of warranty, which will therefore constitute 'a good defence' to the insured's claim: ibid 264 (Lord Goff). See also *Unipac (Scotland) Ltd v Aegon Insurance Co (UK) Ltd* [1999] Lloyd's Rep IR 502.

[111] [2001] 2 Lloyd's Rep 161.

[112] ibid 184–85, [122]. See also *HIH Casualty and General Insurance Ltd v AXA Corporate Solutions* [2002] Lloyd's Rep IR 325 (Jules Sher QC). Note the curious consequences that can result from automatic termination. For example, if the insured is late in paying the premium, the risk discharges but the premium still has to be paid: see *Chapman v Kadirga* [1998] Lloyd's Rep IR 377.

[113] (1870) LR 3 PC 234.

thereafter the vessel was lost by unrelated sea perils. The Privy Council ruled that the breach of warranty brought an end to the risk, and the risk was not reinstated by the remedial action taken in respect of the breach of warranty.

4.2. Suspensory Conditions

Some policies have used, in place of warranties, suspensory provisions under which the risk is suspended for any period during which the insured is not in compliance with a warranty but the risk reattaches when the breach has been remedied. As we have just seen, the common law rejected that approach, but even in the absence of an express suspensory clause the courts had in some cases construed terms that on their face appeared to be warranties as being merely suspensory. In *Provincial Insurance v Morgan*,[114] the proposer for a motor policy stated in the proposal form that the lorry to be insured was to be used for delivering coal. The insured warranted the truth of his answers and the proposal form was made the basis of the contract. At the time of the accident, the lorry was carrying coal, although earlier that day it had been used to carry timber. The insured's claim was repudiated by the insurers, who argued that there had been a breach of warranty. It was held by the House of Lords that the statement in the proposal form did not amount to a warranty but was merely descriptive of the risk insured. Lord Russell stated that the insured's statements could be read as nothing more than mere statements of 'intentions as to the use of the vehicle and the goods to be carried in it'.[115]

Farr v Motor Traders' Mutual Insurance Society[116] provides a clear illustration of the point. The claimant, answering a question in the proposal form which contained a basis of contract clause, stated that the insured taxicabs were only driven in one shift per 24 hours. This was true at the time the statement was made. However, when one of the two cabs was off the road for repairs, the other was driven in two shifts during the day. Subsequently, when the repairs were completed and the two cabs were being driven in only one shift, one of them was involved in an accident and the insured claimed. The insurers argued that the policy was void for breach of warranty. It was held that the claimant's answer was merely descriptive of risk and was not a promissory warranty. Although cover was suspended during the time when the vehicle was driven in two shifts, cover had resumed at the time of the accident so that the insurers were liable.

In motor insurance effected for non-business use, the policy typically restricts cover to when the vehicle is being used for 'social, domestic and pleasure' purposes only; the effect of such a clause is to suspend cover should the insured use the vehicle for some other purpose which has a business element.[117] When considering whether the insured's use of a vehicle at the time of the loss was for 'social, domestic and pleasure purposes', the court will examine the true purpose of the journey to determine whether cover was suspended. Thus, in *Seddon v Binions*,[118] Roskill LJ observed that the court should look at the 'essential or predominant character' of the insured's use at the time of the loss.[119] In a similar vein, Megaw LJ looked to 'the primary purpose' of the relevant journey to see whether it could 'properly or fairly

[114] [1933] AC 240.
[115] ibid 278.
[116] [1920] 3 KB 669.
[117] *Wood v General Accident Fire and Life Assurance Corporation Ltd* (1948) 82 Ll L Rep 77.
[118] [1978] 1 Lloyd's Rep 381. See *Caple v Sewell* [2002] Lloyd's Rep IR 627.
[119] ibid 385.

be described as use for social, domestic and pleasure purposes'.[120] If the essential character of the journey was of a business nature, the loss would not be covered. Where insurance cover for a motor vehicle is restricted, for example, to when it is being used for 'social, domestic and pleasure purposes *and* for the business of the insured' and at the time of the loss the vehicle is being used by the insured's work colleague on their employer's business, the insured will not be covered. The words 'for the business of the insured' restricts cover to the insured's business use only, not that of her colleague.[121] But where the insured, as a courtesy, gives a lift to someone who was carrying on some business, the insured's use of the vehicle would nevertheless continue to be social even though the passenger was assisted in carrying on his business by receiving that lift.[122]

It seems that, as with the law of contract generally, the nature of a particular term is always a question of law based on the court's construction of the wording used, no doubt taking account of the consequences of the breach.[123] In *De Maurier (Jewels) Ltd Bastion Insurance Co*,[124] an all risks policy contained a 'warranty' that the insured's vehicles would be fitted with approved locks and alarm systems. The insured suffered two losses. When the first loss occurred, the locks were not of the required type, but by the time of the second loss there was compliance with the term. The insurers denied liability on the basis, inter alia, that the policy was voidable *ab initio* for breach of a promissory warranty, and was avoided by them two days after the second loss. However, during the course of the trial the insurers admitted liability in respect of the second loss. It was held by Donaldson J that, as a matter of construction of the so-called 'warranty', it was merely a term describing the risk, so that the insurers were not liable for the first loss, the policy being suspended by the breach, but were right to admit liability for the second loss. In *CTN Cash & Carry v General Accident*,[125] the court took the opportunity to again lay down explicit guidelines to the construction of contractual terms. A burglary insurance policy effected by the insureds on their cash and carry depots contained the term that: 'It is warranted that the secure cash kiosk shall be attended and locked at all times during business hours'. It was held that the clause was not a warranty but a term descriptive of risk. Macpherson J, having reviewed the authorities,[126] defined a warranty as a term which goes to the root of the contract, the breach of which therefore entitles the insurers to avoid liability under the policy. The fact that the insurers used the word 'warranty' was not sufficient to convert the term into one which is so fundamental to the contract that it goes to its root.[127]

In *Kler Knitwear Ltd v Lombard General Insurance Co Ltd*,[128] the judge adopted the phrase 'suspensive condition' to describe the effect of a term in the policy which was stipulated to be a warranty. The insured, a hosiery and knitwear company with premises in Leicester, effected a policy with the defendants which contained, inter alia, the following sprinkler installations warranty:

> It is warranted that within 30 days of renewal 1998 the sprinkler installations at the Jellicoe Rd/Gough Rd/Spalding Rd locations must be inspected by a LPC approved sprinkler engineer

[120] ibid 386.
[121] *Passmore v Vulcan Boiler & General Insurance Co Ltd* (1936) 54 Ll L Rep 92.
[122] ibid 94 (Du Parcq J).
[123] See *Wallis, Son & Wells v Pratt and Haynes* [1910] 2 KB 1003.
[124] [1967] 2 Lloyd's Rep 550.
[125] [1989] 1 Lloyd's Rep 299.
[126] Citing, in particular, from the judgment of Bankes LJ in *Roberts v Anglo Saxon Insurance Co* [1927] KB 590.
[127] In *Roberts v Anglo Saxon Insurance Co* (1926) 26 Ll L Rep 154, 157, MacKinnon J stated that 'nothing turns upon the use of the word 'warranted' [which is] always used with the greatest ambiguity in a policy'.
[128] [2000] Lloyd's Rep IR 47.

> with all necessary rectification work commissioned within 14 days of the inspection report being received.

The sprinkler installations were not inspected within the required 30 days of renewal, but rather about 60 days after. The insured premises at Jellicoe Road were damaged by a storm and the claimant sought to recover under the policy for his losses arising from damage to raw materials and finished goods and from disruption of the business. The insurers rejected the claim on the basis that the sprinkler inspection clause is a true contractual warranty. Morland J, citing Saville LJ in *Hussain v Brown*,[129] came to 'the clear and unhesitating conclusion' that the so-called 'warranty' was, on its true construction, merely a suspensive condition. However, the decision is open to doubt. General Condition 2 of the policy provided that:

> [E]very Warranty to which this Insurance or any Section thereof is or may be made subject shall from the time the Warranty attaches apply and continue to be in force during the whole currency of this Insurance and non-compliance with any such Warranty; whether it increases the risk or not, or whether it be material or not to a claim, shall be a bar to any claim in respect of such property or item, provided that whenever this Insurance is renewed a claim in respect of Damage occurring during the renewal period shall not be barred by reason of a Warranty not having been complied with at any time before the commencement of such period.

It thus ascribed a label to the term, and it stated when the warranty attached and the consequences of breach.[130] Given that this was a commercial contract, one is left wondering what else the insurers needed to do to achieve their purpose.

In *Sugar Hut Group v Great Lakes Reinsurance*,[131] Burton J discussed the construction of insurance warranties. The insureds operated four nightclubs. In September 2009 a fire broke which caused substantial damage to one of the clubs and they sought indemnity under the policy. The insurers denied the claim on a number of grounds, including breach of two warranties.[132] The first was a frying and cooking equipment warranty (requiring that ducting be kept free from combustible materials and inspected 'at least once every 6 months'). Burton J rejected the argument by the insured that the duct should be checked every six months starting from the date of inception of the policy. Instead, as a matter of business efficacy, the inspection should be every six months since the last inspection. There had therefore been a breach. The judge held that the part referring to six-monthly inspections could be regarded as a suspensive condition. Unlike the position for ordinary warranties, where the breach of a suspensive condition is repaired, the insurer will be back on risk. However, in this case the inspection was not just late, it had not taken place by the time of the fire, and hence cover was in any event suspended as at the date of the damage.[133] There was also a breach of the combustible materials part of the warranty, and Burton J rejected an argument that this should be treated as *de minimis*. He could find no case law to support the argument that the *de minimis* concept applied to breaches of insurance warranties.[134] Further, this was a warranty as to a state of affairs. The second warranty related to a burglar alarm warranty (requiring a NACOSS Central Monitoring Station Alarm be installed and operational). Burton J held this to be a true warranty

[129] [1996] 1 Lloyd's Rep 627.
[130] See, eg *Virk v Gan Life Holdings plc* [2000] Lloyd's Rep IR 159.
[131] [2010] EWHC 2636 (Comm).
[132] The other grounds were non-disclosure and reliance on a condition precedent.
[133] [2010] EWHC 2636 (Comm), [42].
[134] ibid [44].

which, on the facts, had been breached.[135] The slip contained a term that cover was subject to a satisfactory survey and the carrying out of necessary risk improvements. The judge held that these obligations survived into the policy and/or that, contrary to any general presumption, the policy did not supersede the obligations in the slip. Compliance with a risk improvement notice was a suspensory condition. Since the fire took place before the work was carried out, there was no cover in place at the date of the damage. Interestingly, though it would not have helped the insured on the facts, the judge severed elements of the warranties relating to fortnightly cleaning and specialist cleansing every six months, and construed them as suspensive conditions.[136] Accordingly, Burton J was able to dissect what purported to be a self-contained warranty into different terms, each having different consequences.

A decision to similar effect, *Bluebon Ltd v Ageas (UK) Ltd*,[137] was discussed above. The approach of the courts has not, however, been consistent: it was seen earlier in this chapter that the suspensory interpretation was rejected in *AC Ward & Son Ltd v Caitlin (Five) Ltd.*[138]

4.3. Statutory Reform

The unique features of warranties as recognised by the common law have long been the subject of criticism. The use of warranties was condemned by the Law Reform Committee in 1957 and again by the Law Commissions in 1980,[139] the latter proposing that warranties should be confined to matters material to the risk and that the automatic termination rule should be repealed. The law was not, however, altered. In *Forsikringsaktieselskapet Vesta v Butcher*,[140] a reinsurance case discussed in chapter 18 below, Lord Griffiths described the absence of the need for a causal connection between breach and loss as 'one of the less attractive features of English insurance law'.[141] It was left to the English and Scottish Law Commissions to conduct a thorough review. An early issues paper in November 2006[142] suggested the adoption of a causal link between breach and loss, a suggestion reproduced in modified form by consultation papers published in 2007.[143] After a good deal of further consultation, the Law Commissions finally proposed in their July 2014 consultation papers[144] the removal of the automatic termination remedy for breach and its replacement with one of suspension. The changes are set out in section 10 of the Insurance Act 2015, which modifies section 33(3) and repeals section 34 of the Marine Insurance Act 1906:

> (1) Any rule of law that breach of a warranty (express or implied) in a contract of insurance results in the discharge of the insurer's liability under the contract is abolished.

[135] ibid [49].
[136] ibid [46].
[137] [2017] EWHC 3301 (Comm).
[138] [2009] EWCA Civ 1098.
[139] *Insurance Law: Non-Disclosure and Breach of Warranty* (Law Com No 104, 1980).
[140] [1989] 1 All ER 402.
[141] ibid 406.
[142] Issues Paper 2, *Warranties*.
[143] *Insurance Contract Law: Misrepresentation, Non-Disclosure and Breach of Warranty by the Insured* (Law Com CP No 182/Scot Law Com CP 134, 2007).
[144] LC 353.

(2) An insurer has no liability under a contract of insurance in respect of any loss occurring, or attributable to something happening, after a warranty (express or implied) in the contract has been breached but before the breach has been remedied.
(3) But subsection (2) does not apply if –
  (a) because of a change of circumstances, the warranty ceases to be applicable to the circumstances of the contract,
  (b) compliance with the warranty is rendered unlawful by any subsequent law, or
  (c) the insurer waives the breach of warranty.
(4) Subsection (2) does not affect the liability of the insurer in respect of losses occurring, or attributable to something happening
  (a) before the breach of warranty, or
  (b) if the breach can be remedied, after it has been remedied.
(5) For the purposes of this section, a breach of warranty is to be taken as remedied.
  (a) in a case falling within subsection (6), if the risk to which the warranty relates later becomes essentially the same as that originally contemplated by the parties,
  (b) in any other case, if the insured ceases to be in breach of the warranty.
(6) A case falls within this subsection if.
  (a) the warranty in question requires that by an ascertainable time something is to be done (or not done), or a condition is to be fulfilled, or something is (or is not) to be the case, and
  (b) that requirement is not complied with.

Section 10(1) repeals the automatic termination rule previously set out in section 33(3) of the 1906 Act. In its place, by section 10(2), an insurer has no liability in respect of any loss occurring at a time when the insured was in breach of warranty. The risk is thus suspended for the period of breach, but the warranty is by section 10(4) ineffective if the loss occurred before the breach of warranty or after the breach of warranty has been remedied. The legislation thus permits a breach of warranty to be remedied, and section 10(5) provides that a breach of warranty is to be taken as remedied in two situations: (a) where the warranty requires something to be done or not done, or a condition is fulfilled, and after the remedial steps have been taken by the insured the risk has become essentially the same as that originally contemplated by the parties (sections 10(5)(a) and 10(6)); or (b) in any other case, if the insured has ceased to be in breach of warranty. Thus, the insurer has no liability only if the loss occurs before the breach has been rectified. This suggests that there can be no recovery if there is a loss at the time of breach, but in fact the Act provides otherwise. Section 11(4) of the Act states that section 11 can apply in addition to section 10. The apparent intention of section 11(4), derived from the Law Commissions' reports and accepted by all commentators, is that in the period of breach the insurer may face liability if the insured can bring himself or herself within section 11 by showing that, in the words of section 11(3), 'the non-compliance with the term could not have increased the risk of the loss which actually occurred in the circumstances in which it occurred'. The drafting of section 10(2), stating that 'an insurer has no liability' in the period of breach, is accordingly highly misleading, and it would have been better to state expressly that 'subject to section 11, an insurer has no liability' in the period of breach.

The effect of the provisions is thus as follows. (1) If the loss occurs before there is any breach of the warranty, the warranty is to be disregarded. (2) If the loss occurs at a time when the insured was in breach of remedy, the insurers are not liable unless the insured can bring himself or herself within section 11 so that there is no connection between the breach and the loss. It should be remembered that section 11 does not apply to a term that defines the risk as a whole, and warranties were originally designed as terms that defined the risk run by the insurers. However, the label 'warranty' does not remove the effect of section 11(3): all depends upon the nature of the term whatever it is called. The operation of section 11(3) was considered earlier in this chapter. (3) If the loss occurs after a breach of warranty has been remedied, the insurers cannot rely upon the breach of warranty. The most important limitation on section 10 is that it is not clear that a breach of remedy can always be remedied. If a warranty requires a specified state of affairs to exist at the date of the policy, then it is arguable that the breach cannot be remedied, as that would require the remedy to have retroactive effect. There is on that basis an argument that the marine implied warranty of seaworthiness for voyage policies set out in section 39(1), which requires the vessel to seaworthy at the commencement of the voyage, is outside section 10. The point is discussed below.

Section 10(3), re-enacting the earlier law, prevents an insurer from relying upon a breach of warranty in three cases: the warranty has ceased to be applicable in the circumstances; compliance would be rendered unlawful by any subsequent law; or the breach has been waived. Of those, only waiver is of real significance. Waiver can arise at two stages: before the loss, where the insurers have indicated that they will not rely upon any future breach; and after the loss, when the insurers have indicated that they will not rely upon an actual breach. The former is relatively unusual and is illustrated by *Samuel & Co Ltd v Dumas*,[145] where a warranty given by the insured that other insurance would not be effected was held to have been waived by the insurers by subscribing to a policy banned by the warranty. As for post-breach waiver, before the passing of the 2015 Act the position was the same as for waiver of conditions precedent, discussed earlier in this chapter. Because the effect of a breach of warranty is to prevent liability from arising, there is no option conferred upon the insurers so that there could not be waiver by affirmation. The only available form of waiver was thus waiver by estoppel, requiring an unequivocal representation by the insurers that they intend not to rely upon the breach, relied upon by the insured to its detriment in a fashion that would make it inequitable for the insurers to change their mind. The narrowness of this form of waiver was demonstrated by *Liberty Insurance Pte Ltd v Argo Systems FZE*.[146] As was seen above, the insured in that case was held to be in breach of a warranty against relinquishing its rights against any third party with whom a towage contract was concluded. There was no appeal against that finding, and the sole issue on appeal was whether the insurers had waived their right to rely upon the breach. The claim had first been rejected on other grounds in 2003, subject to an overall reservation of rights, it had not been referred to in proceedings brought by the insured in the USA and it was not until 2008, when English proceedings were commenced, that the insurers first raised the breach of this warranty. The evidence showed that the insurers had been aware of the breach but had chosen not to rely upon it until the English proceedings were issued. The Court of Appeal held that there was no estoppel on the facts: the original rejection letter preserved all defences; the failure by the insurers to refer to the matter in the US proceedings did not constitute an unequivocal representation of any sort; and the decision of the insurers to delay for some seven years before raising the point again could not be construed as an unequivocal representation not to raise the defence.

[145] [1924] AC 431.
[146] [2011] EWCA Civ 1572.

The question is, therefore, whether section 10 of the 2015 Act has changed the law. The point is not specifically addressed, as section 10(3) simply refers to loss of rights by waiver. Although there is no authority on the point, the better view appears to be that there is no change in the law. Section 10(2) states that 'an insurer has no liability' where there is a breach of warranty, and that strongly implies that the breach automatically suspends the risk (subject to the insured proving that the breach can be disregarded under section 11). If there is no option, then there cannot be a waiver by affirmation and the only remaining possibility is waiver by estoppel.

9

Construing the Terms of the Insurance Contract

1. The Intentions of the Parties

1.1. The Approach of the English Courts

The underlying principle of English law in the interpretation of any contract is that its terms must be construed in accordance with the intentions of the parties. The manner in which the intentions of the parties are to be ascertained is these days restated in virtually every decision on contract interpretation. The law is found in a series of decisions of the House of Lords and the Supreme Court.[1] It is possible to subject the various judgments to minute analysis, and that inevitably reveals differences of nuance, emphasis and expression, but, as was said by Coulson J in *HSM Offshore BV v Aker Offshore Partner Ltd*:[2]

> Although some practitioners and legal commentators with nothing better to do have sought to exploit certain fine linguistic differences between the various judgments, in my view they all point in the same general direction. What matters is the objective meaning of the language, to be derived from the natural or usual meaning of the words used, when seen against the background/context of the contract; where there are rival interpretations, one test is to consider which interpretation is more consistent with business common sense.

The key points to be derived from the plethora of cases are the following. First, the test is purely objective, based upon the interpretation that would be understood by a reasonable person with some knowledge of the commercial context. The objective approach is justified on the ground that permitting evidence of subjective intent would give rise to the production of a mass of conflicting evidence that may be subjected to a great degree of hindsight.

[1] *Charter Reinsurance Co Ltd v Fagan* [1996] 3 All ER 46; *Investors Compensation Scheme Ltd v West Bromwich Building Society* [1998] 1 WLR 896; *Chartbrook Ltd v Persimmon Homes Ltd* [2009] UKHL 38; *Rainy Sky SA v Kookmin Bank* [2011] UKSC 50; *Arnold v Britton* [2017] UKSC 24; *Wood v Capita Insurance Services Ltd* [2017] AC 1173; B Eder, 'The Construction of Shipping and Marine Insurance Contracts: Why Is It So Difficult?' [2016] *Lloyd's Maritime and Commercial Law Quarterly* 220.

[2] [2017] EWHC 2979 (TCC), [165].

Secondly, in construing words and phrases, it is necessary to have regard to the factual matrix, the term used by Lord Hoffmann in *Investors Compensation Scheme Ltd v West Bromwich Building Society*[3] and meaning, in his words, 'absolutely anything which would have affected the way in which the language of the document would have been understood by a reasonable man'. Thirdly, the literal meaning of words should be adopted, and the court will be slow to depart from that meaning simply because the contract has worked out badly for one of the parties, so that interpretation is not a retroactive process. Fourthly, if there are rival interpretations, that most consistent with commercial sense should be adopted. Finally, it should not be assumed that the parties have erred in their drafting unless the outcome is plainly absurd.

Although the court's task is to determine the meaning of a contract, it 'cannot either re-write contracts or impose on parties to them what the Court may think would have been a reasonable contract'.[4] Its role is to determine the intention of the parties:

> When one speaks of the intention of the parties to the contract, one is speaking objectively – the parties cannot themselves give direct evidence of what their intention was – and what must be ascertained is what is to be taken as the intention which reasonable people would have had if placed in the situation of the parties. Similarly when one is speaking of aim, or object, or commercial purpose, one is speaking objectively of what reasonable persons would have in mind in the situation of the parties.[5]

Lord Hoffmann observed that construing a contract is 'not a game with words. It is an attempt to discover what a reasonable person would have understood the parties to mean.'[6] In *Investors Compensation Scheme Ltd v West Bromwich Building Society*,[7] he said:

> Interpretation is the ascertainment of the meaning which the document would convey to a reasonable person having all the background knowledge which would reasonably have been available to the parties in the situation in which they were at the time of the contract.

But he also remarked that where a detailed analysis of the words in a commercial contract led to a conclusion that flouted 'business common sense', 'it must be made to yield to business common sense'. Later, in *Chartbrook Ltd v Persimmon Homes Ltd*,[8] Lord Hoffmann said that where a term of the contract is ambiguous,

> the process of interpretation does not require one to formulate some alternative form of words which approximates as closely to that of the parties. It is to decide what a reasonable person would have understood the parties to have meant by using the language which they did.[9]

Sir Anthony Clarke summarised these principles in *Pratt v Aigaion Insurance Co SA*[10] by saying that 'any clause in a contract must be construed having regard to its context within the contract, which must in turn be set in its surrounding circumstances or factual matrix', and adding that 'the more unreasonable the result, the more unlikely it is that

[3] [1998] 1 WLR 896.
[4] *Sinochem International Oil (London) Co Ltd v Mobil Sales and Supply Corpn* [2000] 1 Lloyd's Rep 339 (Mance LJ).
[5] *Reardon Smith Line Ltd v Yngvar Hansen-Tangen* [1976] 1 WLR 989, 996 (Lord Wilberforce).
[6] *Jumbo King Ltd v Faithful Properties Ltd* FACV000007/1999 (Hong Kong).
[7] [1998] 1 WLR 896.
[8] [2009] UKHL 38.
[9] See also *King v Brandywine Reinsurance (UK) Ltd* [2004] EWHC 1033 (Comm); *Re Sigma Finance Corp (in administrative receivership)* [2009] UKSC 2.
[10] [2008] EWCA Civ 1314, [9]. See ch 8 above.

the parties can have intended it, and if they do intend it the more necessary it is that they should make their meaning clear'.[11]

In *Financial Conduct Authority v Arch Insurance*,[12] the joint judgment of Lords Hamblen and Leggatt applied those principles in the insurance context:

> The core principle is that an insurance policy, like any other contract, must be interpreted objectively by asking what a reasonable person, with all the background knowledge which would reasonably have been available to the parties when they entered into the contract, would have understood the language of the contract to mean. Evidence about what the parties subjectively intended or understood the contract to mean is not relevant to the court's task … In the case of an insurance policy of the present kind, sold principally to SMEs, the person to whom the document should be taken to be addressed is not a pedantic lawyer who will subject the entire policy wording to a minute textual analysis … It is an ordinary policyholder who, on entering into the contract, is taken to have read through the policy conscientiously in order to understand what cover they were getting.

The references to a reasonable person with background knowledge mean also that it is necessary to give effect to understandings in the market. There may be customary understandings in the market to which effect should be given. Custom was important in the eighteenth and nineteenth centuries, when there was little relevant authority on words and phrases, and the evidence of merchants was crucial. These days it is far more difficult for the parties to establish a custom that would alter the apparent meaning of words, but if the evidence is that there was a market understanding that was both universally understood and applied, and was reasonable as between the parties, then the courts will give effect to it. It was on that basis that in *Gard Marine & Energy Ltd v Tunnicliffe*[13] David Steel J ruled that there was an established practice in the energy insurance market for excesses to be scaled down by reference to the proportion of the insured's interest in the insured subject matter so that a failure to refer to scaling in a reinsurance contract did not preclude a finding that a proper interpretation required scaling.

Where there has been a series of judicial rulings on particular wordings, it is to be assumed that the insurance industry is aware of those rulings and has adapted contractual drafting accordingly. As seen in chapter six, in *Ramco (UK) Ltd v International Insurance Co of Hannover Ltd*[14] the Court of Appeal held that the phrase 'goods held in trust or commission or for which he is responsible' was to be construed as permitting a bailee to insure for the full value of the goods despite having only a limited interest in them, as that had been the consistent holding in a series of earlier cases. The principle clearly cannot be applied if the cases do not speak with one voice. Confronted by contradictory views in the cases as to the meaning of 'accident', Mustill LJ, in *De Souza v Home and Overseas Insurance Co Ltd*,[15] thought it 'better to withdraw a little from the authorities to the former ground of *this* policy and *these* facts, and to look critically at each authority to see whether it really leads inexorably to a solution of our present problem'.[16] In his view, the curious

[11] ibid [12].

[12] [2021] UKSC 1. This approach was adopted by Cockerill J in *Corbin & King Ltd v AXA Insurance UK Plc* [2022] EWHC 409 (Comm).

[13] [2011] EWHC 1658 (Comm).

[14] [2004] Lloyd's Rep IR 606. This decision was applied in a sequel action against brokers, *Ramco Ltd v Weller Russell & Laws Insurance Brokers Ltd* [2009] Lloyd's Rep IR 27.

[15] [1995] LRLR 453.

[16] ibid 456.

state of the case law had obliged the judge at first instance to reach a conclusion that did not conform to a common-sense understanding of the word:

> The cases, regarded simply as decisions, are difficult if not impossible to reconcile. Some of them would, I believe, be regarded by at least some lawyers as wrong. Others would perhaps be differently decided in today's social context, and even at the time it is plain that the Judges were not all of a like mind. In many instances I venture to detect, not a chain of reasoning leading inexorably to a conclusion, but the intuitive choice of a solution, followed by efforts to rationalize it. Again, as reported case succeeds reported case even finer distinctions of language are drawn: sometimes so fine that, approaching them with all the respect due to their authors I find them either impossible to understand, or to reconcile with statements by other judges worthy of equal respect.[17]

It has been suggested that where certain words are used in similar policies across the industry, it makes sense to presume that those words have the same meaning.[18] This has much to recommend it where the wording of different policies is the same; otherwise it is sensible to regard earlier decisions as, at best, constituting 'valuable and helpful guidance',[19] and to recognise that 'Authorities may determine the principles of construction, but a decision upon one form of words is no authority upon the construction of another form of words',[20] or where the language used to describe the same peril differs between different policies.[21]

1.2. Pre-contractual Negotiations: The Exclusionary Rule

The factual matrix as formulated by Lord Hoffmann specifically excludes evidence of previous negotiations between the parties because, at that point, they were not in agreement.[22] In *Chartbrook v Persimmon*,[23] Lord Hoffmann said that, while this exclusion could result in parties being bound by terms which a reasonable person would not have intended, it 'may be justified in the more general interest of economy and predictability in obtaining advice and adjudicating disputes'; but, along with Baroness Hale, he suggested the Law Commission conduct an empirical study into the effects of admitting pre-contractual material. That exercise has yet to be carried out. The most important practical consequence of the exclusionary rule in the context of insurance is that it is not permissible for an insurer to give evidence of the manner in which premiums were calculated so as to demonstrate the intended scope of cover or the meaning of an exclusion. The point is illustrated by *Ted Baker Plc v Axa Insurance UK Ltd*,[24] where the commercial

[17] ibid 455–56. On the construction of 'accident' policies, see chs 10 and 16 below.

[18] *Dino Services Ltd v Prudential Assurance Co Ltd* [1989] 1 Lloyd's Rep 379, 382 (Kerr LJ). This case provides an interesting illustration of the dilemma: in construing 'by forcible and violent means', the Court of Appeal held itself bound by precedent when construing 'forcible', but there was no precedent with regard to the word 'violent'. See also *John Reilly v National Insurance and Guarantee Corporation Ltd* [2008] EWCA Civ 1460; *AC Ward & Son v Catlin (Five) Ltd* [2009] EWHC 3122 (Comm).

[19] *Tate Gallery (Trustees) v Duffy Construction Ltd (No 1)* [2007] EWHC 361 (TCC).

[20] *In re an Arbitration between Coleman's Depositories Ltd, and The Life and Health Assurance Association* [1907] 2 KB 798, 812 (Buckley LJ).

[21] *Pratt v Aigaion Insurance Co SA* [2008] EWCA Civ 1314.

[22] *Prenn v Simmonds* [1971] 2 All ER 237; *MSC Mediterranean Shipping Co SA v Polish Ocean Lines, The Tychy (No 2)* [2001] 2 Lloyd's Rep 403.

[23] [2009] UKHL 38.

[24] [2012] EWHC 1406 (Comm). See also *Margate Theatre Royal Trust Ltd v White* [2006] Lloyd's Rep IR 93.

policy offered by the insurers was in sections, and it was open to the insured to buy for additional premium specific additional forms of cover as specified in those sections. The insured decided not to purchase fidelity insurance, protecting against theft by employees. Thefts did occur, and the insured relied upon ordinary theft coverage, which was insured under the policy. Eder J held that all that mattered was the proper construction of the word 'theft', which included theft by any person, including an employee, and it was not material that the insurers had priced the policy on the assumption that employee theft was insured only if additional fidelity cover had been purchased.

As seen in chapter five, there is an important exception to the exclusionary rule where it is contended that the written contract contains a mistake. If it is alleged that the mistake is one of transcription, in that what was objectively actually agreed by the parties has not been reduced to writing, then the policy can be rectified. If the allegation that the parties' subjective common assumptions have not been properly recorded, then rectification is also possible. The latter form of rectification is the only exception to the objective approach of the courts to the interpretation of contracts.

1.3. The Post-contractual Conduct of the Parties

It is not permissible to examine the post-contractual conduct of the parties in order to ascertain how the contract should be construed. The meaning of a contract is to be determined at the date it is made, otherwise 'A contract meant one thing the day it was signed but, by reason of subsequent events, meant something different a month or a year later'.[25] The focus on the meaning of words at the time the contract was made creates difficulties where it is necessary to decide whether the policy covers matters that could not have then been known. A policy exclusion for the lung disease pneumoconiosis was held not to apply to the lung disease mesothelioma as the latter had not been diagnosed as a separate condition until after the policy had been taken out.[26] A policy providing coverage for business interruption due to the official imposition of 'sanitary arrangements' was held not to include the social distancing requirements laid down during the COVID-19 pandemic because that concept had not been known when the policy was taken out.[27]

There are two situations in which the post-contractual conduct of the parties may be relevant. First, as was said by Longmore LJ in *Great North-East Railway Ltd v Avon Insurance*:[28]

> If the question is whether a term was incorporated into a contract, the subsequent conduct of the parties may be very relevant to the inquiry whether such a term was or was not agreed … [S]ubmissions to the contrary were, with respect, a misapplication of the principle that the subsequent conduct of the parties cannot be relied on as an aid to the construction of the contract.

Secondly, post-contract conduct may amount to a variation of the contract, or at least give rise to an estoppel by convention, which precludes a party from relying upon the original terms.

[25] *Whitworth Street Estates (Manchester) Ltd v James Miller & Partners Ltd* [1970] AC 583, 603.
[26] *Cape Plc v Iron Trades Employers Insurance Association Ltd* [2004] Lloyd's Rep IR 75; *T&N Ltd v Royal & Sun Alliance Plc* [2004] Lloyd's Rep IR 106.
[27] *Brushfield Ltd v Arachas Corporate Brokers Ltd* [2021] IEHC 263.
[28] [2001] EWCA Civ 780, [29].

1.4. *Contra Proferentem*

Contra proferentem is a principle of construction that has in the past been widely applied by the English courts. It was pointed out in *Youell v Bland Welch (No 1)*[29] that there are two quite separate rules here: in the case of ambiguity, words should be construed against the contracting party who put them forward; and exclusion clauses should be construed narrowly so as not to undermine the parties' contractual obligations. The *contra proferentem* principle means that the ambiguous words will be construed in favour of the insured since it is the insurers who draw up the contract: 'It is extremely important with reference to insurance, that there should be a tendency to hold for the assured than for the company, where any ambiguity arises upon the face of the policy.'[30] In *Tektrol Ltd v International Insurance Co of Hannover Ltd*,[31] Buxton LJ noted that where there was difficulty in determining the circumstances in which an exclusion clause applied, 'it is at least a relevant factor in such an enquiry to recall that the insurers indeed could have made things much clearer in their own favour if that was indeed their intention when they drew the policy'. Examples of *contra proferentem* in operation are legion. In *English v Western Insurance Co*,[32] it was held that an exclusion in a motor policy for any 'member of the assured's household' referred only to a household of which he was head rather than one to which he belonged, so his sister was covered. In *Pratt v Aigaion Insurance Co SA*,[33] discussed in chapter eight, the Court of Appeal held that the words 'at all times' in a crewing warranty in a marine policy were ambiguous and referred only to times when the vessel was at sea. *Contra proferentem* applies also to questions asked of the insured by the insurers in the placement process: the line of cases discussed in chapter four, beginning with *R&R Developments Ltd v AXA Insurance UK Plc*,[34] concerning the insolvency of the insured, again illustrate the point. In consumer contracts the *contra proferentem* principle has been given statutory effect by section 69 of the Consumer Rights Act 2015, under which 'If a term in a consumer contract … could have different meanings, the meaning that is most favourable to the consumer is to prevail'.

However, *contra proferentem* has important limitations, and it is probably fair to say that since the introduction of consumer protection legislation, and in particular statutory controls over exclusion clauses, the need for a *contra proferentem* doctrine is far less pressing. Indeed, it has recently been said by Lord Mance in a published arbitration award on business interruption insurance[35] that *contra proferentem* is a principle of last resort. The following points may be noted.

First, in the commercial insurance market many standard form and bespoke wordings used in policies are those prepared by brokers. Thus, in *Youell v Bland Welch (No 1)*,[36] if the wording has been put forward by the broker to the insurer and accepted by the

[29] [1992] 2 Lloyd's Rep 127.

[30] *Fitton v Accidental Death Insurance Co* (1864) 17 CB (NS) 122, 134–35 (Willes J).

[31] [2005] EWCA Civ 845, [8].

[32] [1940] 2 KB 156.

[33] [2008] EWCA Civ 1314.

[34] [2010] 2 All ER (Comm) 527.

[35] *Various Policyholders v China Taiping Insurance (UK) Co Ltd* 10 September 2021, an approach adopted by the Australian Federal Court in *LCA Marrickville Pty Ltd v Swiss Re International SE* [2022] FCAFC 17. See ch 19 below.

[36] [1992] 2 Lloyd's Rep 127.

insurer, there is no basis for construing the words against the insurer,[37] so that if the issue is the proper construction of an exclusion clause the two limbs of *contra proferentem* are self-cancelling: it was held in that case that there was no basis for construing an express 48-month limit for reinsurance coverage as unlimited in order to match the underlying insurance.

Secondly, the court will approach a document with the expectation that there are no ambiguities rather than with the intention of seeking them out, and the *contra proferentem* rule cannot be used unless there is ambiguity.[38] The general principle is that if the words have a clear meaning, the courts will give effect to that meaning even though this leads to a consequence which seems unreasonable,[39] although 'the more unreasonable the result the more unlikely it is that the parties can have intended it, and if they do intend it the more necessary it is that they shall make that intention abundantly clear'.[40] In *McGeown v Direct Travel Insurance*,[41] the insured took out holiday insurance that covered 'a permanent physical disability which prevents you from doing any paid work (if you are not in paid work, we will provide the same cover for any permanent disability which prevents you from doing all your usual activities) – £50,000'. The insured, who was not in paid work, suffered an injury which prevented her from horse riding. At first instance, it was held that the clause was ambiguous and the claimant was, therefore, entitled to the benefit of the *contra proferentem* principle, so that the ambiguity should be resolved in her favour. The Court of Appeal overturned this decision. It held that the court should not seek ambiguity and that, in this case, there was no ambiguity when the clause was construed within the context of the contract as a whole. Other clauses set down a maximum for various types of loss and the amount recoverable depended on the amount of the loss. This clause, however, provided a large lump-sum payment. Looked at against this background, it cannot have been the intention of the contract to provide the payment of £50,000 for anything but the most serious of injuries. Turning to the wording of the clause itself, the Court took the view that, since someone in work would have to be prevented from being able to do any paid work, it was appropriate to construe the second part of the clause as requiring that the disability suffered must constitute a substantial intrusion into the insured's usual activities and it was not sufficient merely to show that she could no longer pursue one particular activity.

Thirdly, exclusion clauses in insurance policies are somewhat different in nature from other contractual exclusions. As a matter of principle an insurer must be able to balance the risk covered against the premium charged, and one means by which this can be achieved is through an exclusion clause. In theory, the broader the exclusion clause the lower the risk to the insurer and, therefore, the lower the premium, and an insured who wants better cover must pay a higher premium. In construing the exclusion clause, the English courts will, in line with general principles of contract, not assess the adequacy of the consideration (that is, the premium) and so cannot properly determine whether the insurer has written a broad exclusion clause because the premium is set at a very low level. The fact that an insurance

[37] Although in *Swiss Re International Se v LCA Marrickville Pty Ltd* [2021] FCA 1206 Jagot J in the Federal Court of Australia took a different approach, preferring the view that even if the words were broker-drafted, they were ultimately proffered by the insurers. This point was not referred to on appeal, *LCA Marrickville Pty Ltd v Swiss Re International SE* [2022] FCAFC 17.

[38] *Cole v Accident Ins Co* (1889) 5 TLR 736, 737.

[39] *Joel v Law Union and Crown Insurance Co* [1908] 2 KB 863.

[40] *L Schuler AG v Wickman Machine Tool Sales Ltd* [1974] AC 235, 251 (Lord Reid). See also *Forsikringsaktieselskapet Vesta v Butcher* [1989] AC 852, 910 (Lord Lowry).

[41] [2003] EWCA Civ 1606.

exclusion is not one designed to remove contractual liability that would otherwise exist, but rather determines what cover has actually been bought by the insured, has been recognised by statute,[42] which excludes insurance exclusions from judicial scrutiny, and also by the courts. Peter Macdonald Eggers QC in *Crowden v QBE Insurance (Europe) Ltd*[43] put the matter in this way:

> an exclusion clause in an insurance policy is not designed to exclude, restrict or limit a primary liability on the part of the insurer; instead, it is intended to define the risk which the insurer is prepared to accept by way of the insurance contract. Further, the exclusion clause in an insurance policy does not ordinarily operate to deprive the insured of rights which existed prior to or but for the cover afforded by the Policy.

1.5. Reasonable Expectations of the Insured

It is important to emphasise that the English focus on commercial common sense is not the same as the principle of interpretation that has found favour in the USA in particular, namely the reasonable expectations of the insured. According to the Restatement, Contracts (2d), only if there is ambiguity will the court adopt the meaning that 'operates against the party who supplies the words'.[44] Many states have, however, taken a slightly different approach. In California, for instance, the Civil Code states that if there is ambiguity the term 'must be interpreted in the sense in which the promisor believed, at the time of making it, that the promisee understood it'.[45] If this fails to resolve the uncertainty, the term will 'be interpreted most strongly against the party who caused the uncertainty to exist'.[46] In applying these provisions, the California courts have adopted a presumption in favour of coverage, and they have also said that they will 'generally interpret the coverage clauses of insurance policies broadly, in order to protect the objectively reasonable expectations of the insured', because the insurer typically drafts the policy, 'leaving the insured little or no meaningful opportunity or ability to bargain for modifications'.[47]

There have, however, been even more radical developments in some jurisdictions. In an important essay published in 1970, Professor Keeton argued that in many US jurisdictions the courts construe insurance contracts according to the reasonable expectations of the insured even if there is no ambiguity. He suggested that this approach was adopted where there was unconscionability (using that word in a fairly broad sense) in the conduct of the insurer or detrimental reliance by the insured. Unconscionable conduct might be present, for instance, where a policy provided very little cover in light of the size of the premium, or where the policyholder had little opportunity to examine the policy and discover a clause that in clear terms limited cover. Keeton saw this approach as justified on a number of grounds.

[42] The Unfair Contract Terms Act 1977 excludes insurance contracts from being tested by reference to reasonableness. See also the discussion of the Consumer Rights Act 2015 below.

[43] [2017] EWHC 2597 (Comm), citing the judgments of Lords Hodge and Toulson in *Impact Funding Solutions Ltd v Barrington Support Services Ltd* [2016] UKSC 57. For confirmation, see *Doorway Capital Ltd v American International Group UK Ltd* [2022] EWHC 182 (Comm).

[44] Restatement, Contracts (2d) §206. See, eg *JA Brundage Plumbing and Roto-Rooter Inc v Massachusetts Bay Insurance Co* 818 F Supp 553 (NY 1993).

[45] California Civil Code, §1649.

[46] ibid §1654.

[47] *AIU Insurance Co v Superior Court* 51 Cal3d 808, 822 (Calif 1990). See also *Montrose Chemical Corp v Admiral Insurance Co* 42 Cal Rptr2d 324 (Calif 1995).

First, he regarded policy documents as usually very long and complex documents, which, as insurers knew, policyholders rarely read, and which most would not be able to understand in any event. He did, however, acknowledge that insurers were beginning to meet this objection by writing policies in plain language. Secondly, policyholders, he asserted, were often not able to see the policy until after the contract, and this contributed to the disinclination of the policyholder to read the document. Thirdly, he thought that in many situations it was appropriate to protect the reasonable expectations of the insured because it would be unconscionable to allow the insurer to enforce limitations in coverage. Fourthly, he believed it appropriate to protect the reasonable expectations of the policyholder where they arose as a result of the marketing practices of the insurer (or of the insurance industry as a whole), and in particular where the marketing made it appear that broader cover was being provided than was the case. Finally, he took the view that the reasonable expectations of the insured should be protected where they emerged from the way the insurer characterised coverage in the documentation by, for example, using words such as 'comprehensive cover plan' or placing a broad statement about the coverage in large print at the start of the policy and then limiting that statement in smaller print later on.[48] These justifications indicate the conditions under which, in Keeton's view, many courts would examine the reasonable expectations of the insured. He was not suggesting that the insurance policy be ignored, although he was arguing that its terms should only apply if they met the reasonable expectations of the insured, and that those expectations be defined in the light of matters such as the marketing strategy used by the insurer for that policy, the format of the document, the language in which its terms were expressed, the access of the insured to the policy terms at the time of the contract and the actual knowledge of the insured.

Reviewing the US case law is of little assistance, because it is clear that English law has firmly rejected the expectations of the insured test[49] and the English courts are indeed reluctant to hear argument based on US insurance cases because of their number and their pro-insured tendency. English law does not permit departure from the words used unless it is clear that something has gone wrong, and purposive interpretation is necessary only where the outcome would otherwise not make commercial sense. A clear example of the latter is the approach to 'reasonable care' clauses, which are construed as requiring no more than an absence of reckless or deliberate conduct as otherwise the indemnity provided by the insurers would in many cases be meaningless.[50] In *Cornish v The Accident Insurance Company*,[51] a clause in a policy covering accidental death or injury purported to exclude liability where the accident was caused 'by exposure of the insured to obvious risk of injury'. The Court of Appeal took the view that since the purpose of the policy was to provide cover for accidental death or injury, it 'must not be construed so as to defeat that object, nor so as to render it practically illusory'.[52] Taken literally, the clause would exclude from cover someone who is injured crossing the street, even if that person took reasonable care. 'Such a result is so

[48] RE Keeton, 'Insurance Law Rights at Variance with Policy Provisions' (1970) 83 *Harvard Law Review* 961; RE Keeton and AI Widiss, *Insurance Law: A Guide to Fundamental Principles, Legal Doctrines and Commercial Practices* (St Paul, West Publishing, 1988) 627–46. See also the essays on this topic collected in (1998) 5 *Connecticut Insurance Law Journal*.

[49] *Zagora Management Ltd v Zurich Insurance Plc* [2019] EWHC 140 (TCC). For the same view in Australia, see *LCA Marrickville Pty Ltd v Swiss Re International SE* [2022] FCAFC 17.

[50] See ch 10 below.

[51] (1883) 23 QBD 453. Also *Paine v Catlins* [2004] EWHC 3054 (TCCC); *Tektrol Ltd v International Insurance Co of Hannover Ltd* [2005] EWCA Civ 845.

[52] ibid 456 (Lindley LJ).

manifestly contrary to the real intention of the parties that a construction which leads to it ought to be rejected'.[53] The Court of Appeal, therefore, concluded that 'a literal construction is inadmissible, and some qualification must be put on the words used'.[54] Tuckey J indeed observed in *Amey Properties Ltd v Cornhill Insurance plc*[55] that

> the Courts have adopted different approaches to the construction of the words of exclusion clauses depending upon the nature of the policies in which they appear and in particular whether to give a wide construction would be repugnant to the whole purpose for which the policy was taken out.[56]

In *Arch Insurance*, discussed above, the Supreme Court held that a business interruption policy should be construed in accordance with the understanding of a typical business seeking such cover rather than in a pedantic legal fashion, but the point there being made was that understanding was the relevant factual matrix test for this form of cover. That is far from saying that the insured's reasonable expectations are to prevail in every case.

---

2. Specific Rules of Construction

2.1. Words with Established Meaning

If a technical word has been used by the parties, it will normally be given its technical meaning. That may have results that could not have been contemplated by an ordinary policyholder. Thus, an 'explosion' means a physical or chemical reaction, and not simply the fracturing of an engine casing caused by an internal component breaking off.[57] The technical rule applies with particular force where the term is one that has a clear legal meaning. Where the phrase 'liable as damages' appeared in a policy, it was argued that the general principles of construction should be applied and these would take into account that reasonable parties could not be expected to have knowledge of the full implications of the Riot (Damages) Act 1886[58] since this depended on reading cases on the legislation and, possibly, its long history. Longmore LJ rejected this argument, saying:

> A technical phrase has been used and it must be interpreted in its technical sense without regard to reasonably available background knowledge. If, therefore, the phrase 'legally liable to pay as damages' has connotations which a reasonably experienced layman might not appreciate or if the phrase leads to an inquiry which only a lawyer or a historian would be qualified to conduct, the concept of limiting this inquiry to background knowledge reasonably available to an insurance broker or an insurer must necessarily fade into the background.[59]

[53] ibid. See also *Morley and Morley v United Friendly Insurance plc* [1993] 1 WLR 996; ch 16 below.

[54] *Cornish v The Accident Insurance Company* (1883) 23 QBD 453. For a recent illustration of the application of this principle, see *Allianz Marine Aviation (France) v GE Frankona Reinsurance Ltd London* [2005] EWHC 101 (Comm).

[55] [1996] LRLR 259.

[56] ibid 264. See *Blackburn Rovers Football & Athletic Club plc v Avon Insurance plc* [2005] EWCA Civ 423.

[57] *Commonwealth Smelting v Guardian Royal Exchange* [1984] 2 Lloyd's Rep 608; *Aegis Electrical and Gas International Services Co Ltd v Continental Casualty Co* [2008] Lloyd's Rep IR 17.

[58] Now the Riot Compensation Act 2015: see ch 16 below.

[59] *Bedfordshire Police Authority v Constable* [2009] EWCA Civ 64, [18].

An exclusion in property policy for 'riot' was construed in accordance with the legal definition of that term – a noisy gathering – even though the effect was to exclude a straightforward robbery.[60] Similarly, 'theft' is usually defined according to its meaning in the Theft Act.[61] Although there is logic in this approach, it may produce unexpected results,[62] given that theft is both wider and narrower than most people might think: defrauding an insured by enticing her to hand over property in return for a forged cheque amounts to theft because there is no genuine consent to parting with possession,[63] whereas taking a car for joyriding is not theft because there is no intention to permanently deprive the insured of possession.

There are important exceptions to the application of technical meaning. A strict legal analysis will not be appropriate where the risk is not located in the UK. In *Wooldridge v Canelhas Comercio Importacao e Exportacao Ltd*,[64] the claimant ran a wholesale jewellery business in São Paulo. Its stock of jewellery was insured under a policy which, in a clause headed 'Hold-Up or Robbery', excluded liability in respect of loss by 'robbery' when the premises were open for business or when any employee was present at the premises. English law was the governing law of the contract. Members of the managing director's family were kidnapped and the managing director was told that in order to get them back he had to go to the premises and obtain all the emeralds in stock. He went to the premises, got his staff to fill two bags with emeralds and then made the exchange with the kidnappers. The insurers denied liability on the ground that 'robbery' according to its legal meaning involved the taking of property using violence and this was what had occurred. The Court of Appeal held the insurers liable. Mance LJ observed that it was not appropriate to apply the strict English or Brazilian definition of robbery; instead, the court should construe the clause within the context of the policy as a whole and interpret it according to the view that would be taken by 'ordinary commercial men'. He concluded that the clause was designed to exclude loss where the premises were open for business and the theft was effected by violence directed at the staff, so that there had to be a connection between the theft and the violence to staff in the shop. Here, there was no violence against the managing director or the staff, and even though there was duress, this came from the kidnapping of the family members, which was a different type of risk. While Mance LJ firmly rooted this approach to the meaning of 'robbery' in English construction principles, there was older authority for his view, as he briefly acknowledged. In *Algemeene Bankvereeniging v Langton*,[65] where an English policy covered property in Belgium, Maugham LJ had said:

> [I]t is quite wrong in principle to construe the words … 'fire, burglary, theft, robbery, or hold-up' as if those words could only be construed in a technical sense according to English law. The Belgian bank, of course, do not know what the precise technical meaning, for instance, of the word 'larceny' is, if the word 'larceny' had been used, in England, and I imagine it is equally true to say that very few commercial men in this country are fully aware of the fact that in order entirely

[60] *London and Lancashire Fire Insurance Co Ltd v Bolands Ltd* [1924] AC 836: see ch 16 below.

[61] *Grundy (Teddington) Ltd v Fulton* [1981] 2 Lloyd's Rep 661 (affirmed [1983] 1 Lloyd's Rep 1); R Leng, 'The Scope of "Theft" in Insurance' (1991) 1 *Insurance Law & Practice* 16; A McGee, '"Forcible and Violent" Means of Entry' (1991) 1 *Insurance Law & Practice* 36.

[62] For a slightly different critique, see M Wasik, 'Definitions of Crime in Insurance Contracts' [1986] *Journal of Business Law* 45.

[63] *Dobson v General Accident Fire and Life Assurance Corporation plc* [1989] 2 Lloyd's Rep 549.

[64] [2004] EWCA Civ 984.

[65] (1935) 51 Ll L Rep 275.

> to apprehend the meaning of that word, you must go through more than 100 closely printed pages of 'Archbold on Criminal Pleading, Evidence and Practice', and consult certainly more than 100 decisions going back for over 100 years. I am content with this, that in my opinion, the phrase 'lost, destroyed, or otherwise made away with by fire, burglary, theft, robbery or hold-up, whether with or without violence, and whether from within or without', is a phrase which has to be construed as ordinary commercial men would construe it, or rather would understand it.

He noted that 'ordinary commercial men' would recognise that the offence leading to the loss would occur in Belgium and, therefore, that the words should be construed in light of the fact that the investigation and any prosecution would be undertaken under Belgian law. In any case, as Maugham LJ observed, the clause itself did not appear to have been intended to be understood in a technical way because of its use of non-legal words, such as 'made away with' and 'hold-up'. It is submitted that the conclusion in both cases is further supported by the fact that, since the parties were in England and Brazil in one policy and in England and Belgium in the other, and the inquiries into the crime would take place in, respectively, Brazil and Belgium, there cannot have been an intention to apply a technical meaning drawn from the criminal law of one particular country.

Reliance on the legal meaning of a term may also be inappropriate where it is clear from the context that it was not being used in a technical sense. An additional reason for the ruling in *Algemeene* was that the policy also covered property 'made away with', which obviously had no legal meaning and whose inclusion demonstrated that the policy was not to be construed in strict technical terms.

2.2. Context

The overall context in which a word or phrase is used may demonstrate that its ordinary or technical meaning was not intended by the parties. In perhaps the leading case on context, *Charter Reinsurance Co Ltd v Fagan*,[66] the House of Lords held that the requirement for recovery by the reinsured, that it 'shall actually have paid' its policyholders, was held by the House of Lords to mean that it sufficed that the reinsured's liability had been established and quantified. The purpose of the reinsurance had been to ensure that the reinsured was not left without funds, and the entirety of the policy demonstrated that it was written on a liability rather than payment basis. Lord Hoffmann noted also that the term was ambiguous, in that if an item was purchased on deferred payment terms, then, strictly speaking, the purchaser could on the day of purchase properly say that the price actually paid was nothing. The fact that a policy is compulsory under legislation means that it should be construed as giving the cover required by that legislation;[67] the same applies where the policy is specifically taken out to insure against contractual liability, it being appropriate to give the contract and the policy the same meaning.[68]

Context may be relevant in the rather narrower sense of the *ejusdem generis* rule, whereby a word contained in a list takes its meaning from the other terms in the list. In *Young v Sun Alliance*,[69] four inches of water percolated upwards into the insured's bathroom from

[66] [1996] 3 All ER 46. See generally ch 18 below.

[67] *Charlton v Fisher* [2001] Lloyd's Rep IR 387, holding that the word 'accident' in the Road Traffic Act 1988 encompassed deliberate acts: see ch 14 below.

[68] *Oakapple Homes (Glossop) Ltd v DTR (2009) Ltd* [2007] EWHC 2555 (Comm).

[69] [1976] 2 Lloyd's Rep 189.

an underground water source. The insured's policy, which insured against 'storm, tempest, flood', was held not to respond to the loss: although what had occurred might colloquially have been referred to as flood, the conjunction of that word with storm and tempest required some event that was sudden, violent or abnormal and not merely a gentle accumulation of water. This principle is of particular importance where the relevant provision lists a series of specific risks and concludes with a generality. The insured was the beneficiary of this approach in *King v Travellers' Insurance Association*,[70] where the policy excluded the loss of 'jewellery, watches, field-glasses, cameras and other fragile or specially valuable articles'. The court held that the insured had a claim for loss of a fur coat as such an item, although valuable, did not possess the quality of fragility common to the enumerated items. The same analysis was applied in marine insurance to the Lloyd's SG clause in use for 200 years until 1983, which listed a series of maritime and war perils and concluded with the words 'all other perils': the courts consistently ruled that those general words took their meaning from the preceding list so that, most importantly, the words did not extend to mechanical breakdown.[71] The point is more difficult where there is only a single word followed by a generality, an issue which has arisen in business interruption policies, where the Australian courts have ruled that the general concluding words in the term 'conflagration or other catastrophe' did not encompass financial losses resulting from COVID-19, given the physical nature of 'conflagration'.[72]

2.3. Validity

It is a general principle of contract law that the courts will give such meaning to ambiguous words as renders the instrument valid rather than void or of no effect. In terms of legality, there is a line of authority holding that an arbitration clause is to be treated as governed by English law if it would be unlawful if found to be governed by another law,[73] and in terms of enforceability the English courts will be reluctant to hold obscure wording in a policy to be void for uncertainty.[74]

2.4. Superfluous Words

At one time there was a judicial tendency to give effect to every word and phrase in a policy. The modern practice of drafting often includes an element of 'scissors and pasting', so that clauses used in earlier contracts are simply added to the wording of a new contract. That gives rise to possible irrelevance, as where the term relates to an entirely different form of cover as a property form using the word 'premises' is used to insure a marine risk,[75] and inconsistency, as where a choice of jurisdiction clause is added to a contract that contains

[70] (1931) 48 TLR 53.
[71] See ch 18 below.
[72] See ch 19 below, where other illustrations are given.
[73] *SulAmérica Cia Nacional de Seguros SA v Enesa Engenharia SA* [2012] EWCA Civ 638.
[74] *Charman v New Cap Reinsurance* [2004] Lloyd's Rep IR 373.
[75] *Beacon Life v Gibb* (1862) 1 Moo PCNS 73, the court ruling that a prohibition on keeping gunpowder on the premises extended to storage on a vessel.

an arbitration clause[76] or where two distinct but overlapping obligations have been applied to the same peril.[77]

The approach of the courts has mellowed to some extent over time, in recognition of the pitfalls of drafting practices. Again this is an issue that has come to the fore in COVID-19 litigation. In *Financial Conduct Authority v Arch Insurance*,[78] the lengthy policy document issued to the insured covered on page 38 loss of business 'following … any occurrence of [an infectious disease] within a radius of 25 miles of the Premises …', but there was an exclusion on page 93 for 'loss or damage due to contamination pollution soot deposition impairment with dust chemical precipitation adulteration poisoning impurity epidemic and disease'. What was given with the one hand was on the face of things taken away with the other. The Supreme Court refused to countenance that possibility, and held that a reasonable person reading the policy as a whole would not have understood the basic cover to have been removed by a general clause much further on in the document: 'loss or Damage due to contamination pollution soot deposition impairment with dust chemical precipitation adulteration poisoning impurity epidemic and disease'. There is no longer a strict presumption that every word must be given effect.

2.5. The Format of the Policy

Modern policies written in plain English often use explanatory provisions, headings, different colours, different sizes of text and boxes. This format may be attractive, but raises the question whether equal weight is to be given to the various statements as to cover, exclusions and the duties of the insured. A recent New Zealand decision, *Sleight v Beckia Holdings Ltd*,[79] is illustrative of the point. An information box stated that 'This section explains when we'll repair or rebuild the home and when we'll pay you cash for your loss, if we accept your claim', and the wording then provided that in the event of damage the insurers would pay 'the cost of repairing or rebuilding the home to a condition as similar as possible to when it was new, using current materials and methods'. The insured argued that the information box made it clear that the insurers had agreed to rebuild rather than merely pay the cost of rebuilding. The court was unimpressed by the inconsistency, but ruled that the policy wording took priority and that the information box was relevant only if there was an ambiguity in the policy. In other words, the information box could resolve ambiguities but could not create them. It is also practice for insurance to be in the form of a standard policy booklet to which is appended a schedule setting out details of the risk, the amount of premium and specific additional terms. It is settled that the two documents are of equal weight and are to be read together.[80]

[76] The courts typically give primacy to the arbitration clause and confine the jurisdiction clause to enforcement of the award: *Axa Re v Ace Global Markets Ltd* [2006] EWHC 216 (Comm).

[77] *Milton Furniture Ltd v Brit Insurance Ltd* [2015] EWCA Civ 671, where the court gave independent effect to two conditions requiring burglar alarms, one applicable in all cases and one applicable only when the premises were unoccupied.

[78] [2021] UKSC 1.

[79] [2020] NZHC 2851.

[80] *Standard Life Assurance Ltd v Oak Dedicated Ltd* [2008] Lloyd's Rep IR 552; *Spire Healthcare Ltd v Royal & Sun Alliance Insurance Plc* [2018] EWCA Civ 317.

3. Consumer Rights Act 2015

As already noted, the control of exclusion clauses in the Unfair Contract Terms Act 1977 does not extend to insurance contracts, because insurance exclusions are of a rather different nature from ordinary contractual exclusions. However, the Consumer Rights Act 2015, replacing the Unfair Terms in Consumer Contracts Regulations 1999,[81] does not exempt insurance contracts. The general effect of the 2015 Act is to impose a fairness test for the enforceability of terms in consumer contracts. The Act applies to any contract between a trader and a consumer (section 61(1)). The general rule set out in section 62(1) is that an unfair term of a consumer contract is not binding on the consumer, the test being whether, 'contrary to the requirement of good faith, it causes a significant imbalance in the parties' rights and obligations under the contract to the detriment of the consumer' (section 62(4)). 'Significant imbalance' has been defined as arising where a term was so weighted in favour of the supplier as to tilt the parties' rights and obligations under the contract significantly in his favour, and 'good faith' has been held to mean fair and open dealing by the use of terms that were expressed fully, clearly and legibly, free of concealed pitfalls or traps.[82] Fairness is to be determined by taking into account the nature of the subject matter of the contract, and by reference to all the circumstances existing when the term was agreed and to all of the other terms of the contract (section 62(5)). If a term is unfair and cannot be enforced, the rest of the contract continues so far as is practicable (section 67).

By way of guidance, schedule 2 contains an indicative and non-exhaustive list of terms that may be regarded as unfair (section 63(1)). The schedule lists 20 terms, but in transposing them to the insurance context the following terms are likely to be regarded as unfair: permitting the insurer to terminate the policy at any time; forfeiture of the premium if the policy is terminated; any term not reasonably accessible to the insured prior to the making of the contract; transferring the agency of an intermediary from the insurer to the insured; and restriction of the insured's right of access to the courts, eg by a reduced period for the issue of proceedings.

The most difficult aspect of the Act is the exclusion set out in section 64(1). A term may not be assessed for fairness to the extent that: (a) it specifies the main subject matter of the contract; or (b) assessment would require comparison of the appropriateness of the price payable under the contract with the service provided. The purpose of section 64(1) is to prevent a court from rewriting the consumer contract and the price paid under it, so that in the context of insurance the insured cannot challenge the scope of cover offered, the extent of any exclusions from cover and the premium paid under the policy. It is thus only ancillary terms, eg notice of loss or co-operation requirements, that are likely to fall within the Act. There is an important modification in section 64(2), namely that a term is excluded by section 64(1) only if it is 'transparent' (expressed in plain, intelligible language and legible (section 64(3)) and 'prominent' (brought to the insured's attention in such a way that a reasonably well-informed, observant and circumspect insured would be aware of it (section 64(4)–(5)).

[81] SI 1999/2083. The Regulations implemented Council Directive 93/113 on Unfair Contract Terms.

[82] *Director General of Fair Trading v First National Bank Plc* [2002] 1 AC 481, decided under the earlier Regulations.

4. Utmost Good Faith

Some mention should here be made of section 17 of the Marine Insurance Act 1906 as amended by the Insurance Act 2015.[83] It was noted in chapter four that section 17 in its original form imposed a bilateral and continuing duty of utmost good faith and that the only remedy was avoidance. The remedy demonstrates that the true purpose of section 17 was to state a general principle applicable to pre-contractual presentation of the risk, spelt out in more detail in sections 18–20, but its broad wording led the courts to conclude that it might operate post-contractually. However, any development was hampered by the avoidance remedy, which was of little use to an insured who complained that the policy did not reflect his needs, and indeed was incongruous where the insured was in breach of a post-contractual obligation and the insurers sought to avoid the policy *ab initio*.

The effect of the Insurance Act 2015 was to sever section 17 from pre-contractual duties, so that utmost good faith is now a stand-alone concept. Further, the removal of the avoidance remedy potentially opens the door to a closer judicial examination of the post-contract conduct of the parties. The English and Scottish Law Commissions, in recommending the amendment of section 17,[84] took the view that it would thereby become an 'interpretative principle', thereby suggesting that utmost good faith is not a freestanding concept but rather operates where there is an express policy term and in some way affects the interpretation of a term. The operation of section 17 in the context of claims, where it probably has its greatest impact, is examined in chapter 11 below, but perhaps a few words should here be said about how section 17 might impact future interpretation of insurance contracts.

Some guidance may be obtained from Australia, where utmost good faith takes effect as an implied contractual term under section 13 of the Insurance Contract Act 1984 (Cth). The leading authority on the meaning of section 13, *CGU Insurance Ltd v AMP Financial Planning Pty Ltd*,[85] determined that the test for utmost good faith was not dishonesty but rather commercial fair dealing, so that each party is required to take into account the interests of the other. The key provision for current purposes is section 14(1) of the 1984 Act, which provides that 'If reliance by a party to a contract of insurance on a provision of the contract would be to fail to act with the utmost good faith, the party may not rely on the provision'. By section 14(3),

> in deciding whether reliance by an insurer on a provision of the contract of insurance would be to fail to act with the utmost good faith, the court shall have regard to any notification of the provision that was given to the insured …

Perhaps surprisingly, very little use has been made of section 14. The leading authority is *Australian Associated Motor Insurers Ltd v Ellis*,[86] a motor case where the insured was

[83] K Lewins, 'Going Walkabout with Australian Insurance Law: The Australian Experience of Reforming Utmost Good Faith' [2013] *Journal of Business Law* 1; B Soyer and A Tettenborn, 'Mapping (Utmost) Good Faith in Insurance Law – Future Conditional?' (2016) 132 *LQR* 618; M Hemsworth, 'The Fate of "Good Faith" in Insurance Contracts' [2018] *Lloyd's Maritime and Commercial Law Quarterly* 143.

[84] Law Com CP No 353/Scot Law Com CP 238, para 30.22.

[85] [2007] HCA 36.

[86] (1990) 54 SASR 61.

under a duty to inform the insurers of any modifications to the insured vehicle, failing which the insurers would not face liability. Reliance on the clause was held to be contrary to good faith, because the consequences of breach had not been specifically made known to the insured even though the relevant information was on the application form and in the policy itself. Later cases have cast doubt upon *Ellis*, notably *Re Zurich Australian Insurance Ltd*,[87] where it was said of *Ellis* that the duty to act honestly had been 'elevated to an obligation in an insurer to coddle its insured and to allow idiosyncratic judicial solicitude to replace principle'. The 'interpretative' role of the amended version of section 17 of the Marine Insurance Act 1906 is, in the light of this analysis, open to some doubt, and it may be that section 17 is simply *contra proferentem* on steroids. It was suggested in *Hammer Waste Pty Ltd v QBE Mercantile Mutual Ltd*[88] that the 1984 Act prevented insurers from relying upon ambiguous terms, and if they chose to do so and were defeated in judicial proceedings they might be ordered to pay costs on an indemnity rather than standard basis.

[87] [1999] 2 Qd R 203.
[88] [2002] NSWSC 1006.

10

Causation

1. Proximate Cause Rule

The insured, who puts forward a claim, must show that it is more probable than not that the loss was proximately caused by one of the perils which the insurers contracted to cover.[1] To take a simple example, if the policy covers loss of goods by fire, the insured must show that, on the balance of probabilities, fire caused the loss, and obviously there is no claim if the goods were lost by some other event falling outside the cover offered by the policy. But what if the fire is caused by the insured carelessly tossing away a cigarette, or by an act of arson committed by a third person or by the insured? What if the goods are damaged not by the fire which has broken out in the warehouse, but by smoke, by part of the building in which they are kept collapsing as a result of the fire or by the water used by firefighters to extinguish it? What if the goods are moved from a burning building into the street to save them and are damaged by rain or are stolen? The question is, what loss have the insurers agreed to cover? If the fire has reduced the security of the warehouse and, as a result, thieves are able to enter and steal the goods, the cause of the loss is theft, not fire. The result is the same if the goods are removed from a burning building and placed on the pavement from where they are stolen.[2] When a building, which was insured against fire, was damaged by a mob drawn to a fire in an adjacent property, the cause of the loss was the action of the mob, not the fire.[3] On the other hand, a theft policy did cover the loss when a shop was burgled

[1] *Glowrange v CGU Insurance plc* [2001] EWHC 523 (Comm), [14], (Colman J). On causation in general, see HLA Hart and T Honore, *Causation in the Law* (Oxford, Clarendon Press, 1985); JM Culp, 'Causation, Economists, and the Dinosaur: A Response to Professor Dray' (1986) 49(3) *Law and Contemporary Problems* 23. On causation in insurance law, see AL Parks, 'Marine Insurance: Proximate Cause' (1979) 10 *Journal of Money Laundering Control* 519; P Muchlinski, 'Causation and Proof of Loss in Marine Insurance' in FD Rose (ed), *New Foundations for Insurance Law: Current Legal Problems* (London, Stevens & Sons, 1987); M Clarke, 'Insurance: The Proximate Cause in English Law' [1981] *CLJ* 284; J Lowry and P Rawlings, 'Proximate Causation in Insurance Law' (2005) 68 *MLR* 310; M Song, 'Revisiting Concurrent Causation and Principles in English Insurance Law: A Legal Fiction?' [2021] *Journal of Business Law* 457.

[2] *Marsden v City and County Insurance Co* (1865) LR 1 CP 232. In practice, insurers have not contested such claims because of the fear that to do so would encourage the insured to leave goods in burning buildings.

[3] ibid.

during an air raid because, although loss 'occasioned by hostilities' was an excepted peril, the cause was theft and the air raid merely made the burglars' task easier.[4]

The first question is, therefore, what peril have the insurers agreed to cover, which leads us back to the contract; the second question is, was the loss caused by that peril? The focus in this chapter is on identifying the cause for the purposes of insurance law. Causation is also a crucial element in tort law and criminal law, and although there are statements that the principles are universal, it might be thought that there are important distinctions. As was pointed out by the Australian Federal Court in *LCA Marrickville Pty Ltd v Swiss Re International SE*:[5]

> [I]n the law of tort and in the criminal law it is concerned with the attribution of personal liability or culpability for a personal act. In both, the boundaries are set by public policy. In insurance, the principles of causation … are concerned with whether an insurer is obliged to provide indemnity pursuant to the bargain between it and the insured … it is apt to keep in mind that, it is by the policy's terms that the insurer stakes its money against an actuarially assessed risk that an insured peril will be the proximate cause of the insured's loss. This requires a different causal analysis from that applied in relation to the assessment of a person's culpability for an act … the causation requirement is narrower.

The search for a proximate cause can lead through a long chain of events: the death of a pedestrian might be said to have been caused by the negligence of the motorist who ran her down, or by her decision to cross the road at that moment. Indeed, the enquiry could go even further: 'it seems to me to be impracticable to go back to cause upon cause, which would lead us back ultimately to the birth of person, for if he had never been born the accident would not have happened'.[6] As Blackburn J pointed out in a marine insurance case, a loss typically occurs as the result of a series of events:

> The ship perished because she went ashore on the coast of Yorkshire. The cause of her going ashore was partly that it was thick weather and she was making for Hull in distress, and partly that she was unmanageable because full of water. The cause of that cause, viz, her being in distress and full of water, was, that when she laboured in the rolling sea she made water; and the cause of her making water was, that when she left London she was not in so strong and staunch a state as she ought to have been.[7]

As will be seen later, the parties may agree in the policy on the test for determining causation, but where they have not, general principles have been formulated by the judiciary. In an early case, Willes J said, 'you are not to trouble yourself with distant causes, or to go into a metaphysical distinction between causes efficient and material and causes final; but you are to look exclusively to the proximate and immediate cause of the loss'.[8] This idea of proximity was later incorporated in the Marine Insurance Act 1906, section 55(1):

> Subject to the provisions of this Act, and unless the policy otherwise provides, the insurer is liable for any loss proximately caused by a peril insured against, but, subject as aforesaid, he is not liable for any loss which is not proximately caused by a peril insured against.[9]

[4] *Winicofsky v Army and Navy General Assurance Assocn Ltd* (1919) 88 LJKB 1111.

[5] [2022] FCAFC 17.

[6] *Lawrence v The Accidental Insurance Co Ltd* (1881) 7 QBD 216, 221 (Watkin Williams J); *Coxe v Employers' Liability Assurance Corpn Ltd* [1916] 2 KB 629, 634 (Scrutton J).

[7] *Dudgeon v Pembroke* (1874) LR 9 QB 581, 595.

[8] *Ionides v The Universal Marine Insurance Co* (1863) 14 CB (NS) 259, 289.

[9] It is worth noting the use of the phrase 'unless the policy otherwise provides', since it reinforces the importance of seeing whether the parties have agreed on a definition of causation which differs from that laid down in the section.

In other words, the operative cause in insurance law is the proximate cause of the loss. This gives little assistance in determining cases, and some of the Victorian decisions simply looked for the event that was closest in time to the occurrence of the loss. When Mr Lawrence was killed by a train after an epileptic seizure had led to him falling from the platform at Waterloo Station, the court decided that his death was caused not by the seizure, but by the train. It was, therefore, an accident and covered by a personal accident policy.[10] This might be seen as merely choosing the latest cause, but the decision can be justified on other grounds.[11] To say that the proximate cause is the last in time may merely be to assert that the cause that is closest in time to the loss is likely to be regarded as having a greater impact than other causes in the chain of events that lead to the loss. In 1918 Lord Shaw declared that: 'To treat proximate cause as if it was the cause which is proximate in time is ... out of the question. The cause which is truly proximate is that which is proximate in efficiency.'[12] Lord Greene MR observed that ultimately this issue 'is really a matter for the common sense and intelligence of the ordinary man',[13] and Lord Denning MR referred to 'the effective or dominant cause of the occurrence, or, as it is sometimes put, what is in substance the cause, even though it is more remote in point of time, such cause to be determined by common sense'.[14] Lord Mance has suggested that the use of the last cause in time in the Victorian cases might explain the strict approach taken to warranties:

> If the only relevant cause is the last cause in time, then a prior breach of a simple contractual obligation regarding fitness could have been regarded as irrelevant. Hence, the development of the concept of a warranty which, if broken, automatically discharged from liability for loss or damage, irrespective of how such loss or damage was in law to be regarded as caused.[15]

In *Reischer v Borwick*,[16] a marine policy covered a ship against damage caused by a collision but not by perils of the sea. After the ship was holed in a collision, a temporary repair was effected so that it could be towed into a harbour. However, the motion through the

[10] *Lawrence v The Accidental Insurance Co Ltd* (1881) 7 QBD 216. See also *Winspear v The Accident Insurance Co Ltd* (1880) 6 QBD 42, where the insurer was held liable when Mr Winspear had a seizure and drowned in the river Rea at Edgbaston. Some US jurisdictions have adopted a test which, while defined in terms of proximate cause, is determined by looking for the last cause in time: *Bird v St Paul Fire & Marine Insurance Co* 120 NE 86 (1918); *Queen Insurance Co v Globe & Rutgers Fire Insurance Co* 263 US 487; *Pan American World Airways, Inc v Aetna Casualty & Surety Corp* 505 F2d 989 (1974). But see the analysis in *Continental Insurance Co v Arkwright Mutual Insurance Co* 102 F3d 30 (1996).

[11] The seizure caused him to fall, but it did not cause his death – after all, he might have fallen away from the track or onto the track when no train was entering the station.

[12] *Leyland Shipping Co Ltd v Norwich Union Fire Insurance Society Ltd* [1918] AC 350, 369. In *Pink v Fleming* (1890) 25 QBD 396, 397, Lord Esher MR distinguished between marine policies, where the court would look simply for 'the last cause', and non-marine policies, where it would be prepared to go back further and look for the 'efficient cause'. But see *Reischer v Borwick* [1894] 2 QB 548 (particularly at 552 (Lindley LJ)), where the court, while apparently agreeing with Lord Esher, did not apply the distinction in practice. The House of Lords rejected Lord Esher's distinction and approved of *Reischer* in *Leyland Shipping*. For endorsement of *Leyland*, see *Syarikat Takaful Malaysia Berhad v Global Process Systems Inc, The Cendor MOPU* [2011] UKSC 5.

[13] *Athel Line Ltd v Liverpool & London War Risks Insurance Association Ltd* [1946] 1 KB 117, 122.

[14] *Gray v Barr, Prudential Assurance Co Ltd (Third Party)* [1971] 2 QB 554, 567. See *Wayne Tank and Pump Co Ltd v Employers' Liability Assurance Corpn Ltd* [1974] QB 57, 67 (Lord Denning MR). Lord Wright, in *Yorkshire Dale SS Co Ltd v Minister of War Transport* [1942] AC 691, 706, said: 'Causation is to be understood as the man in the street, and not as either the scientist or the metaphysician, would understand it.' In 1917, Lord Sumner had argued that: 'Proximate cause is not a device to avoid the trouble of discovering the real cause or the "common-sense cause"': *Becker, Gray and Co v London Assurance Corpn* [1918] AC 101, 112. See also *Tate Gallery (Trustees) v Duffy Construction Ltd* [2007] Lloyd's Rep IR 758, [43], where Jackson J observed that 'causation tends to coincide with commonsense'.

[15] *The Cendor MOPU* [2011] UKSC 5, [56].

[16] [1894] 2 QB 548.

sea caused by the towing led the hole to reopen and the ship sank. Even though in terms of time it might be said that the loss resulted from the motion of the sea, which was not covered, the Court of Appeal held that the proximate cause of the loss was the collision. In *Leyland Shipping Co Ltd v Norwich Union Fire Insurance Society Ltd*,[17] the *Ikaria* was insured against loss from perils of the sea but not from war. During the First World War, the ship was hit by a torpedo, which blew a hole in its side and damaged the bulkheads. It was towed into a safe harbour. While anchored, a gale blew up, causing the ship to bump against the harbour wall. The harbour authorities, fearing it might sink and block access, ordered the ship's removal into open sea, where it grounded at each low tide. After two days of this buffeting, the bulkheads failed and the ship sank. Even though the ship would probably have been safe had it stayed in the harbour, the House of Lords took the view that the proximate cause of the loss was the torpedo. The impact of the torpedo meant it was reasonably certain that seawater would flow into the ship and this is what happened, even if the extent of the damage caused might not have been expected. In *The Cendor MOPU*,[18] the Supreme Court emphasised that section 55(1) of the Marine Insurance Act 1906 required the court's inquiry to be based on fact and common-sense principles, and reaffirmed the principle that the proximate cause is the cause which is proximate in efficiency.[19] In this case[20] the insurance related to an offshore oil-drilling platform during a towage voyage from the USA to Malaysia. The policy covered all risks, except loss 'caused by inherent vice or nature of the subject matter insured', which reflected the wording of section 55(2)(c) of Marine Insurance Act 1906. Mid-voyage, one leg of the rig broke, and the next day the other two legs broke. The question was whether the loss had been caused by perils of the sea, which were covered, or inherent vice of the rig, which was not. As the insurers knew, there were stress cracks in the legs before the voyage and, indeed, the insurers required the rig to be checked mid-voyage. The weather encountered had been such as might have been reasonably expected during such a voyage. The Supreme Court held the insurer liable. The proximate cause of the loss was the perils of the sea, namely, a wave that caught the first leg in such a way as to cause it to break, which, in turn, led to stress on the other legs and their failure. Lord Mance concluded a comprehensive discussion of the distinction between inherent vice and perils of the sea by saying that the insurer will only avoid liability by showing that the loss arose from 'inherent characteristics or defects in a hull or cargo leading to it causing loss or damage to itself … without any fortuitous external accident or casualty'.[21] The loss was caused not by some inherent defect in the rig itself, but by a wave hitting the leg in such a way as to break it. Thus, if it is established that a peril covered by the contract was the proximate cause of the loss, the insurer will be liable for all the consequences that flow naturally from this peril: as Malcolm Clarke has put it, the full extent of the loss 'will be recoverable, even though such extent was no more than not unlikely to occur at the time of the peril'.[22]

There is probably little point in examining in detail the numerous cases in which causation has been discussed, as each turns on its facts and there is rarely a point of law involved. However, in very general terms, it is possible to divide the cases into three categories. The

[17] [1918] AC 350.
[18] [2011] UKSC 5.
[19] ibid [18].
[20] For further details, see ch 17 below.
[21] ibid [81].
[22] Clarke above n 1, 289.

first category consists of cases where a peril has administered a 'death blow', in that a loss is thereafter inevitable and the only uncertainty is the precise event that is going to give rise to that loss. In other words, the ultimate loss is simply the consequence of the occurrence of the peril. *Leyland Shipping Co Ltd v Norwich Union Fire Insurance Society Ltd* illustrates that possibility, as does *Sealion Shipping Ltd v Valiant Insurance Co*,[23] where an initial mechanical breakdown was held to be the proximate cause of two further breakdowns so that they were to be treated as just one occurrence. Secondly, there are cases where a peril has put the subject matter at greater risk of loss, eg where a vessel runs aground and the cargo is looted. It has been held that such a loss is one by perils of the sea rather than theft,[24] but the cases are inconsistent on this underlying issue, as may be seen from the personal injury decisions typified by that of Mr Lawrence, already discussed. Thirdly, the insured may seek to take evasive action in order to prevent a peril from occurring: in general terms, as long as the action is taken 'in the teeth of the peril',[25] then the chain of causation is not broken, but if the action is precipitate – as where a vessel chooses a route replete with natural hazards in order to avoid an enemy – then it may be that the cause of the loss is marine rather than war risks.

As a final matter, it is necessary to address the burden of proof. It is up to the insured to establish on a balance of probabilities that the loss was proximately caused by an insured peril.[26] If the insured does this, the burden of proof shifts to the insurers to show that another explanation was more probable: where a ship is insured against fire, then if the insured shows that the loss was caused by fire, the insurers must demonstrate, on a balance of probabilities, that fire was not the proximate cause of the loss, or that the fire was caused by an excepted peril.[27] If the insurers allege that the loss was caused deliberately by the insured or by someone else with the insured's connivance, particularly if that act was a criminal offence, the degree of proof required will be 'commensurate with the gravity of the allegation made'. That burden will not be discharged 'if the evidence fails to exclude a substantial, as opposed to a fanciful or remote, possibility that the loss was accidental'.[28]

2. Agreements to Alter the Rule of Causation

Although the proximate cause rule has sometimes been called a rule of law,[29] it is merely a term that is implied into the insurance contract as representing 'the real meaning of the parties'.[30] It is accordingly open to the parties to oust the proximate cause principle. The policy may seek to widen the causal requirement for a peril to be operative so that if it

[23] [2012] EWHC 50 (Comm).
[24] *Bondrett v Hentigg* (1816) Holt NP 149.
[25] See the discussion later in this chapter; see also the analysis of suing and labouring in ch 17 below.
[26] *Foreign Marine Insurance Co Ltd v Gaunt* [1921] 2 AC 41; *Rhesa Shipping Co SA v Edmunds, The Popi M* [1985] 2 All ER 712, discussed in ch 17 below.
[27] *Slattery v Mance* [1962] 1 QB 676.
[28] *National Justice Compania Naviera SA v Prudential Assurance Co Ltd, The Ikarian Reefer* [1995] 1 Lloyd's Rep 455, 459 (Stuart-Smith LJ).
[29] *Leyland Shipping Co Ltd v Norwich Union Fire Insurance Society Ltd* [1917] 1 KB 873, 892 (Scrutton LJ).
[30] *Becker, Gray and Co v London Assurance Corpn* [1918] AC 101, 112 (Lord Sumner). See also *Reischer v Borwick* [1894] 2 QB 548, 550 (Lindley LJ); *Leyland Shipping Co Ltd v Norwich Union Fire Insurance Society Ltd* [1918] AC 350, 369 and 370 (Lord Shaw); Marine Insurance Act 1906, s 55(1).

plays any part in the loss then it is insured or excluded, as the case may be, and equally the causal effect may be narrowed so that unless the peril is the sole cause of the loss then it cannot operate as an insured or excluded peril, as the case may be. A series of cases from the late nineteenth and early twentieth centuries involving accident policies provides an interesting illustration of attempts by insurers to alter the test of causation by restricting the causal scope of the insured peril or by expanding the causative scope of exclusions. It seems clear that the aim of the companies in writing the causation clauses in these policies was to exclude liability where injury or death was linked to some cause other than the accident, and certainly they disputed liability in these cases on the basis that this was what the policies had done.

Turning first to clauses limiting the causal scope of the insured peril, in Mr Lawrence's case,[31] the policy rendered the insurers liable 'where such accidental injury is the direct and sole cause of death … but it does not insure in case of death … arising from fits'. The court regarded 'direct and sole cause' as simply a restatement of the proximate cause rule. In *Fitton v Accidental Death Insurance Co*,[32] a policy insured against death resulting from various accidental injuries, but specified that the injury must be 'the direct and sole cause of death' and excluded liability for death arising from, among other things, hernia 'or any other disease or cause arising within the system of the insured before or at the time or following such accidental injury (whether causing death … directly or jointly with such accidental injury)'. The insured suffered an accidental fall that led to a strangulated hernia which, in turn, resulted in his death. The insurers were held liable because the policy exempted them 'only where the hernia arises within the system' and not where it was caused by the accident.[33] Similarly, in *Isitt v Railway Passengers Assurance Co*,[34] the insurers were liable under a policy that only covered death from 'the effects' of an accidental injury. The insured suffered an accidental injury and he was confined to bed. However, the injury was so painful that he was unable to bear the weight of any bed clothing. This led him to contract pneumonia, from which he died. Willes J thought an appropriate direction to the jury would be:

> Do you think that the circumstances leading up to the death, including the cold which caused pneumonia, were the reasonable and natural consequences of the injury and of the conditions under which the assured had to live in consequence of the injury? If you find that no foreign cause intervened and that nothing happened except what was reasonably to be expected under the circumstances, you may and ought to find that the death resulted 'from the effects of the injury' within the meaning of the policy.[35]

[31] (1881) 7 QBD 216.
[32] (1864) 17 CB (NS) 122.
[33] ibid 134 (Vaughan Williams LJ).
[34] (1889) 22 QBD 504.
[35] ibid 512–13. In *Smith v Cornhill Insurance Co Ltd*, a motor policy included cover for the death of the insured caused by an accident while riding in the car. The insured crashed the car into a ravine and, as a result, she sustained brain damage. In a state of semi-consciousness, she left the car, wandered around and stumbled into a stream. As a result of entering the water, she had a heart attack and died. The shock would have been harmless but for her other injuries. The insurers were held liable, even though the judge thought that the death was not the natural or probable consequence of the accident, because 'the causation of events, each one the result of the preceding event, lead back to the accident': [1938] Ll L Rep 122, 130 (Atkinson J). This does not seem a useful technique for determining the operative cause; indeed, it merely returns us to the problems discussed at the beginning of this chapter. Anyway, the same result would surely have been achieved by applying more orthodox principles.

In an attempt to avoid these types of decisions, accident insurers reworded their policies to cover injury or death only where the accident was:

> the direct or proximate cause thereof, but not where the direct or proximate cause thereof is disease or other intervening cause, even although the disease or other intervening cause may itself have been aggravated by such accident, or have been due to weakness or exhaustion consequent thereon, or the death accelerated thereby.

Such a policy came before the Court of Appeal after Mr Etherington fell during a hunting expedition, became soaked, caught pneumonia and died. The Court decided that the insurers had not avoided the *Isitt* decision with the new clause. This conclusion seems to have been influenced by the view that not to hold the insurers liable would make it difficult to establish a claim, unless the insured died at the time the accident occurred, and that would make such policies of very limited utility. Vaughan Williams LJ, noting the insurer's intention to avoid the consequences of *Isitt*, said, 'though that may have been the desire of the company, they have not had what I may call the commercial courage to express as plainly as they might have done what their counsel says they intended to express'. He added:

> When the disease or other cause is dependent on the accident, I think it is right to say that the term 'direct or proximate cause' covers in such a case not only the immediate result of the accident, but also all those things which may fairly be considered as results usually attendant upon the particular accident in question.[36]

Vaughan Williams LJ can be seen as having fallen back on the proximate cause rule either because the clause was ambiguous or because he applied the principle of construction that avoids the literal meaning of a clause which would render the cover afforded by the policy illusory.

The cases are not, however, fully consistent. In *Jason v Batten*,[37] the term 'any Accident bodily injury resulting in and being – independently of all other causes – the exclusive direct and immediate cause of the ... injury or disablement' excluded liability where a motorist, who had a narrowed coronary artery, sustained a severe coronary thrombosis when a car accident caused a blood clot to form which blocked that artery. It was held that if he had not had the narrowed artery, he would not have had a coronary thrombosis. The accident brought forward that thrombosis, but the court found that he would have suffered an attack within three years in any event. So, while the accident advanced the thrombosis by causing the blood clot to form, it was not 'independently of all other causes the exclusive ... cause'

[36] *In the Matter of an Arbitration between Etherington and the Lancashire and Yorkshire Accident Insurance Co* [1909] 1 KB 591, 598 (Vaughan Williams LJ). See also *Mardorf v Accident Insurance Co* [1903] 1 KB 584. The insurers in another case did, however, escape liability. In *Smith v Accident Insurance Co* (1870) LR 5 Exch 302, the policy excluded death arising from, among other things, erysipelas 'arising within the system of the insured before or at the time of or following such accidental injury'. Mr Smith accidentally cut his foot, the result of which erysipelas set in and he died. The insurers were held not to be liable. Cleasby B took the view that the clause had been inserted so that where there was a supervening cause it would not be necessary to determine whether death had been caused by a disease that arose independently, or as a result, of the injury. The majority also distinguished *Fitton* on the ground that the wording of the clause was different. Dissenting, Kelly CB could find no such difference and argued that the clause only exempted the insurers where the disease arose independently of the injury. This approach seems not only preferable, but to have been adopted by the courts in the later personal accident cases. *Smith* was not referred to in *Etherington* and, while mentioned by counsel in *Mardorf*, was not referred to in the judgments.

[37] [1969] 1 Lloyd's Rep 281.

of the thrombosis. Moreover, the thrombosis was 'directly or indirectly' caused by a pre-existing condition, namely the narrowed artery. If, however, the accident had activated a condition that was latent and that, but for the accident, would have remained so, the insurers would have been liable.[38]

The accident policy in *Coxe v Employers' Liability Assurance Corpn Ltd*[39] concerned not an insured peril with a narrow causative scope, but rather an exclusion with an expanded causative scope. The clause here excluded liability for death 'indirectly caused by, arising from, or traceable to' war. As part of his duties during the First World War, Captain Ewing was required to inspect sentries on a railway line that was poorly lit because of air raids and to which access was forbidden to civilians. He was hit and killed by a train. While Scrutton J took the view that the train was the proximate cause, the use in the contract of the word 'indirectly' obliged him to determine whether the loss had been indirectly caused by an excluded peril. The war had placed Ewing in a position of special danger and, therefore, was the indirect cause of his death, so the claim was refused. However, as Scrutton J pointed out, a line must be drawn somewhere. Presumably, the decision would have been different if Ewing had been standing on a platform waiting for a troop train and had died in the same way as Lawrence. In these circumstances the clause would not have excluded the insurer's liability because the war would have been merely a part of the background to the accident and not one of its causes, direct or indirect: he might not have been on the platform but for the war, however, the war did not pose the danger from which he died. The need for a limit was picked up by Cooke J in *ARC Capital Partners Ltd v Brit Syndicates Ltd*.[40] This case concerned a professional indemnity policy which covered claims made against the insured in the period October 2013 to October 2014 but excluding 'any claim and or claims arising from or in any way involving any act, error or omission committed or alleged to have been committed prior to 5th June 2009'.[41] Cooke J noted that the *Coxe* decision gave a wider scope to the exclusion than proximate cause wording, but he ruled that historical matters were not encompassed even by this wording. Accordingly, acts of negligence committed after that date were covered even though they related to contracts entered into in 2008.

There are various other means by which policies seek to vary the proximate cause test, and numerous – often inconsistent, depending upon the context – authorities on their meaning. It is useful to bear in mind the warning of the Supreme Court in *Financial Conduct Authority v Arch Insurance*[42] that 'it is rare for the test of causation to turn on such nuances'. Terms such as 'arising from', 'resulting from', 'attributable to' and 'in connection with' are generally regarded as adopting the ordinary proximate cause test. The cases on the words 'arising out of' are at odds,[43] as are those on 'consequences of'.[44]

[38] *Fidelity and Casualty Co of New York v Mitchell* [1917] AC 592.

[39] [1916] 2 KB 629. See also *Blackburn Rovers Football & Athletic Club plc v Avon Insurance plc* [2005] EWCA Civ 423.

[40] [2016] EWHC 141 (Comm).

[41] The 'retroactive date'. See ch 15 below.

[42] [2021] UKSC 1, [162].

[43] *Sutherland Professional Funding Ltd v Bakewells* [2011] EWHC 2658 (Comm) (proximate cause); *Kajima UK Engineering Ltd v Underwriter Insurance Co Ltd* [2008] Lloyd's Rep IR 391 (wider than proximate cause).

[44] *Ionides v Universal Marine Insurance Association* (1863) 14 CBNS 259 (proximate cause); *XL Insurance Co SE v BNY Trust Company of Australia Ltd* [2019] NSWCA 215 (wider than proximate cause).

3. Concurrent Causes[45]

3.1. The Nature of Concurrent Causes

It has long been the view that if there are two or more contributory causes to a loss, it is the duty of the court to identify one of those causes as the proximate cause. That was the view of the majority of the Court of Appeal in *Reischer v Borwick*,[46] repeated by Lord Dunedin in the *Leyland Shipping* case.[47] However, it is not until relatively recently that the courts have given much thought to the possibility of there being more than one proximate cause. In 1974, in the root decision on concurrent causes, *Wayne Tank and Pump Co Ltd v Employers' Liability Assurance Corpn Ltd*,[48] Cairns LJ suggested the judges 'should [not] strain to find a dominant cause'.[49] It is now recognised that there may be concurrent causes of a loss. First, two separate events may occur, each of which, taken alone, would have caused the loss. Secondly, the loss may be the result of a sequence of events each of was dependent upon the other, ie interdependent causes. The difficulty in insurance cases arises where one of the causes is an insured peril but the other is not within the scope of cover.

3.2. Interdependent Concurrent Causes

The cases have for the most part been concerned with interdependent causes. On the assumption that the two causes cannot be separated in terms of proximity, the courts have drawn a distinction between two situations: one peril is insured and the other is not insured; and one peril is insured and the other is excluded. In the former situation, the insured is entitled to recover. That is because the loss is proximately caused by an insured peril, and the uninsured peril can be disregarded. In *JJ Lloyd Instruments Ltd v Northern Star Insurance Co Ltd, The Miss Jay Jay*,[50] the Court of Appeal held that a ship, *The Miss Jay Jay*, had been lost as the result of a combination of two events: the adverse condition of the sea and defects in the boat's design of which the insured was unaware. The insurance policy covered loss by adverse sea conditions, but did not mention loss by a design fault. Clearly, if the design fault had been the sole cause, there would have been no liability on the policy, but here the insurers were held liable. Slade LJ said:

> As there were no relevant exclusions or warranties in this policy the fact that there may have been another proximate cause did not call for specified mention since proof of a peril which was within the policy was enough to entitle the plaintiffs to judgment.

The actual decision of the Court of Appeal cannot stand with the later ruling of the Supreme Court in *The Cendor MOPU*,[51] which held that in marine cases where

45 J Lowry and P Rawlings, 'Proximate Causation in Insurance Law' (2005) 68 *MLR* 310.
46 [1894] 2 QB 548.
47 [1918] AC 350, 353 and 371. See also *Board of Trade v Hain Steamship Co Ltd* [1929] AC 534, 541.
48 [1974] QB 57.
49 [1916] 2 KB 629.
50 [1987] 1 Lloyd's Rep 32.
51 [2011] UKSC 5.

unseaworthiness is alleged there can be only one proximate cause, which is either a peril of the sea or unseaworthiness; the two cannot operate concurrently. It is either one or the other, so that a finding that the vessel was unseaworthy is another way of stating that there was no peril of the seas.[52] That had been the view of Mustill J at first instance in *Miss Jay Jay*, and it was approved by the Supreme Court. However, the principle established by the Court of Appeal in *Miss Jay Jay* holds good and has indeed been affirmed as a correct statement of the law in later cases.

The second situation arises where there are two causes, one of which is covered by the policy, while the other falls within the terms of an exception clause. In this situation there is a conflict between the insuring clause and the exclusion clause, and it is now settled that the exclusion clause prevails. In *Wayne Tank and Pump Co Ltd v Employers' Liability Assurance Corpn Ltd*,[53] Wayne installed equipment to store and convey liquid wax in a factory. Subsequently, the factory burnt down as the result of two negligent actions by Wayne: the first was to supply plastic pipe – defective because the thermostat did not work – to convey hot wax; and the second was to switch on the equipment and leave it unattended. The question before the Court of Appeal was whether the liability for the losses caused by Wayne's negligence was covered by a public liability policy. That policy's principal clause stated that the insurers 'will indemnify the Insured against all sums which the Insured shall become legally liable to pay as damages consequent upon … damage to property as a result of accidents as described in the Schedule'. There was an exception for 'damage caused by the nature or conditions of any goods or the containers thereof sold or supplied by or on behalf of the insured'. The Court of Appeal held that 'goods' included the pipe and thermostat. Lord Denning MR and Roskill LJ concluded that the proximate cause of the loss was the defective piping and thermostat and, therefore, the exclusion clause meant the insurers were not liable. They went on to say that even if there were two proximate causes – the defective installation, which was within the terms of the policy, and the defective goods, which was not – the insurers were not liable because having 'stipulated for freedom [from the excepted risk], the only way of giving effect to it is by exempting them altogether'.[54] Cairns LJ preferred this second approach.

Is this second approach right? It has been followed in other common law jurisdictions,[55] although the courts in California have taken a different view. In *State Farm Mutual Auto Ins Co v Partridge*,[56] the insured accidentally shot and injured his friend. The court decided there had been two acts of negligence by the insured: filing down the trigger mechanism on his gun to create a 'hair trigger' and driving with the gun in his hand while his friend sat in the passenger seat. Without both of these separate actions the injury would not have happened. The problem was that the policy rendered the insurer liable if the cause was the negligence with regard to the hair trigger, but not if the cause was negligent driving. The court held that where there were two proximate causes and one was covered, the insurer was liable irrespective of the fact that the policy excluded liability for the other cause.

[52] See ch 17 below.

[53] [1974] QB 57.

[54] ibid 67 (Lord Denning MR).

[55] *AMI Insurance Ltd v Legg* [2017] NZCA 321.

[56] 10 Cal3d 102 (1973). See also *Waseca Mutual Ins Co v Noska*, 331 NW2d 917 (1983); *US Fidelity & Guaranty Co v State Farm Mutual Automobile Ins Co* 437 NE2d 663 (1982); *LeJeune v Allstate Ins Co* 365 So2d 471 (La, 1978); *Houser v Gilbert*, 389 NW2d 626 (1986); *Lawver v Boling* 238 NW2d 514 (1976); *Scottsdale Ins Co v Van Nguyen* 763 P2d 540 (1988); *Unigard Mutual Ins Co v Abbott*, 732 F2d 1414 (1984).

In their book, *Insurance Law*,[57] Keeton and Widiss suggest that decisions like *Partridge* show that, 'when there are several distinct or distinguishable factors which contribute to a loss, a persuasive case can be made for the proposition that courts will apply the causation theory that will relate the loss to a covered peril'.[58] They see this as an aspect of the way courts construe policies in light of the reasonable expectations of the insured:[59]

> In many instances, decisions on causation questions involving insurance policy terms are best understood as manifestations of the judicial inclination to favor coverage either by construing ambiguous policy provisions against an insurer or by protecting the reasonable expectations of an insured.[60]

This idea has never achieved wide acceptance in the USA and the courts tend only to look at the reasonable expectations of the insured where there is ambiguity in the contract.[61] However, in relation to exception clauses, US courts generally appear to take the view that 'exclusionary clauses are interpreted narrowly, whereas clauses identifying coverage are interpreted broadly',[62] and do seem relatively easily persuaded that there is ambiguity in an exception clause.

The decision in *Partridge* suggests that the *Wayne* approach is not self-explanatory. It is possible to argue in favour of *Wayne* that the exclusion clause in an insurance contract is central to the bargain between the parties if only because it is a key factor in determining the level of premium charged; therefore, the insurer should not be held liable in any case where one proximate cause falls within that clause. On the other hand, one might say that the application of the exception is unclear and, therefore, should be construed against the insurer. This would lead to the same result as was reached in *Partridge*. Further, the Canadian courts have determined that in the event of concurrent causes, one insured and one excluded, the exclusion is to be given priority only where the policy clearly so provides: on that basis, it was held in *Derksen v 539938 Ontario Ltd*[63] that a liability policy covering bodily injury but excluding liability insured under a motor policy responded where the injury was inflicted by a motor vehicle.

3.3. Independent Concurrent Causes

A loss can be the result of independent concurrent causes where two entirely unrelated events affect the insured subject matter. Tort law has long applied the 'but for' test to this situation, asking whether Peril A would have caused a loss but for the occurrence of Peril B. However, the but for test has its limitations. One much quoted example is where a person is shot simultaneously but independently by two hunters.[64] In such a case, it cannot be said that Hunter A's act was the proximate cause of the injury, because the victim would

[57] RE Keeton and AI Widiss, *Insurance Law: A Guide to Fundamental Principles, Legal Doctrines, and Commercial Practice* (St Paul, West Publishing, 1988).

[58] ibid 557.

[59] See ch 9 above.

[60] Keeton and Widiss (n 57) 559.

[61] *Montrose Chemical Corp v Admiral Ins Co* 42 Cal Rptr2d 324 (1995).

[62] *Garvey v State Farm Fire and Casualty Co* 257 Cal Rptr 292, 298 (1989).

[63] [2001] SCC 72. See also *Weeks v Aviva Canada Inc* 2006] NSSC 83; *Canadian Maritime Engineering Ltd v Intact Insurance Co* 2019 NSSC 328.

[64] The facts of *Cook v Lewis* [1951] SCR 830.

have been injured by Hunter B. In that type of situation, unless the causes are regarded as concurrent and each is regarded as the proximate cause, neither of the tortfeasors would face liability because it could not be said that the acts of either of them resulted in the injury. Applied to insurance, the difficulty becomes that one of the perils may be insured and the other uninsured or excluded. It was thus suggested by Allsop CJ in *McCarthy v St Paul International Insurance Co Ltd*[65] that the correct approach is to construe the policy to determine whether it was contemplated that the existence of an independent uninsured cause of loss would defeat a claim for loss caused by an insured peril. The English courts, in the line of mesothelioma cases beginning with *Fairchild v Glenhaven Funeral Services Ltd*,[66] have recognised that where it is impossible to determine which of two or more tortious acts was the proximate cause of a loss, causation principles should be set aside and each of the wrongdoers should face full liability, and Lord Mance in *Employers' Liability Insurance Trigger Litigation, BAI (Run Off) Ltd v Durham*[67] rejected the 'but for' test in such cases.

It is more likely to be the case that two independent concurrent losses have a common source, and in that situation there is every reason for the courts to be more generous to the insured in that stripping out related but uninsured causes from the analysis is perhaps more justifiable than stripping out causes completely divorced from the insured peril.[68] That was the position in *Orient-Express Hotels Ltd v Assicurazioni Generali SpA*,[69] discussed in more detail in chapter 19 below, where financial loss to a New Orleans hotel in the 2005 hurricanes was caused concurrently by material damage to the hotel (an insured peril) and the closure of the city (an uninsured peril). The judge, applying the 'but for' test, concluded that the loss would have been suffered even if there had been no damage to the hotel and the policy therefore did not respond. That conclusion was rejected by the Supreme Court in *Financial Conduct Authority v Arch Insurance*,[70] where financial losses in the COVID-19 pandemic were concurrently caused by local outbreaks (an insured peril) and outbreaks throughout the UK (an uninsured peril). The Supreme Court ruled that as long as the other perils were uninsured (as opposed to excluded), then the insured peril should not be deprived of its causative effect even though, when measured against the uninsured causes, the impact would have been relatively small.

4. The Conduct of the Insured

4.1. Evasive Action Taken by the Insured[71]

It is not unusual for an insured to take action which, although aimed at reducing the loss for which the insurers would be liable, leads to damage. This does not necessarily break the

[65] (2007) 157 FCR 402.

[66] [2002] UKHL 22. See ch 19 below.

[67] [2012] UKSC 14. See also *Kuwait Airways Corporation v Iraqi Airways Co (Nos 4 and 5)* [2002] AC 883; *Petroleo Brasileiro SA v ENE Kos 1 Ltd, The MT Kos* [2012] UKSC 17.

[68] That point was made by the full federal court in *LCA Marrickville Pty Ltd v Swiss Re International SE* [2022] FCAFC 17.

[69] [2010] EWHC 1186 (Comm).

[70] [2021] UKSC 1.

[71] MJ Mustill, 'Fault and Marine Losses' [1988] *Lloyd's Maritime and Commercial Law Quarterly* 310; P Todd, 'Mitigation, Causation and Policy' [2014] *Lloyd's Maritime and Commercial Law Quarterly* 481.

chain of causation. Indeed, the consequence of finding that it did might not suit insurers since it could discourage action to reduce loss: an insured might not pour water on goods to put out a fire if doing so affected a claim on a fire policy. The issue is one of causation. In *Canada Rice Mills Ltd v Union Marine and General Insurance Co*,[72] the captain of the *Segundo* closed the ventilators in the cargo hold to prevent seawater entering during rough weather and this resulted in the insured cargo of rice being damaged through overheating. The Privy Council took the view that, although seawater did not touch the cargo, the loss was caused by the rough sea, and therefore the insurers were liable on a policy that covered loss by perils of the sea: Lord Wright called the action of the ship's master 'such a mere matter of routine seamanship necessitated by the peril that the damage can be regarded as the direct result of the peril'.[73] In other words, like the orders issued by the harbour authorities in *Leyland Shipping*, his action did not break the effect of the perils of the sea. Where the action taken by the insured is designed to protect the insured property from a peril covered by the policy, the test is: 'Is it a fear of something that will happen in the future or has the peril already happened and is it so imminent that it is immediately necessary to avert the danger by action?'[74] Fire insurers were held liable when a fire broke out near the insured goods and the port authorities decided to throw some of the goods into the sea and douse the rest with water to prevent the fire spreading.[75] In another such case the judge said

> I have found that fire did not actually break out, but it is reasonably certain that it would have broken out, and the condition of things was such that there was an actual existing state of peril of fire, and not merely a fear of fire.[76]

However, there will be cases where evasive action taken by the insured is too remote from the insured peril. Such a case was *Becker, Gray and Co v London Assurance Corpn*.[77] A voyage was abandoned because of the fear of capture, but here the House of Lords ruled that this loss was caused by the captain's voluntary decision since the threat was not imminent. According to Lord Sumner, 'mere apprehension that a restraint of princes will come into operation'[78] is not sufficient; the abandonment has to be caused by an actual or imminent threat.

In the case of marine policies, the Marine Insurance Act 1906, section 78(4) places the insured under an obligation to take such action to avert or to minimise loss from an insured peril as the prudent uninsured person would have taken, and where there is a suing and labouring clause (which is inevitably the case) there is a corresponding duty on the insurers to indemnify the insured for costs reasonably incurred in seeking to prevent or mitigate

[72] [1941] AC 55.

[73] ibid 70.

[74] *Symington & Co v Union Insurance Society of Canton Ltd* (1928) 139 LT 386, 390 (Scrutton LJ). See also *Stanley v Western Insurance Co* (1868) LR 3 Ex Ch 71, 74 (Kelly CB); *In the Matter of an Arbitration between Etherington and the Lancashire and Yorkshire Accident Insurance Co* [1909] 1 KB 591, 599 (Vaughan Williams LJ); *Joseph Watson and Son Ltd v Firemen's Fund Insurance Co of San Francisco* [1922] 2 KB 355, 359 (Rowlatt J); *Canadian Rice Mills Ltd v Union Marine and General Insurance Co Ltd* [1941] AC 55, 71 (Lord Wright). See also *Butler v Wildman* (1820) 3 B & Ald 398, where a similar principle was applied in the case of goods thrown overboard to prevent them from falling into enemy hands (although see the doubts expressed about the decision by Lord Sumner in *Becker, Gray and Co v London Assurance Corpn* [1918] AC 101, 116).

[75] *Symington & Co v Union Insurance Society of Canton Ltd* (1928) 139 LT 386.

[76] *The Knight of St Michael* [1898] P 30, 34 (Gorrell Barnes J). But see H Bennett, 'Causation in the Law of Marine Insurance: Evolution and Codification of the Proximate Cause Doctrine' in D Rhidian Thomas (ed), *The Modern Law of Marine Insurance* (London, LLP, 1996).

[77] [1918] AC 101. See also *PMB Australia Ltd v MMI General Insurance Ltd* [2002] QCA 361.

[78] *Becker, Gray and Co v London Assurance Corpn* [1918] AC 101, 114.

a loss in addition to any loss actually suffered. These provisions are discussed in detail in chapter 17, where it is pointed out that section 78(4) was in error in drawing from the cases decided up to the date of the codification in 1906 that such a duty existed. Later cases have construed section 78(4) as meaning that it is limited to rare situations where negligence or misconduct breaks the chain of causation. No requirement equivalent to section 78(4) is implied into non-marine policies, although an insured who unreasonably fails to mitigate their loss may be unable to claim for the additional loss in the unlikely event that a court determines that the additional loss was proximately caused by the insured's failure because the chain of causation from the original cause has been broken.[79] The absence of any duty to mitigate was confirmed in the context of first party policies in *City Tailors Ltd v Evans*,[80] where the insured was held to be able to recover the full amount if its loss of profits even though it had failed to mitigate the loss by acquiring new premises. Again, in *All Leisure Holidays Ltd v Europaische Reiseversicherung AG*[81] the insured under a travel policy was entitled to recover the costs of a cancelled cruise and was under no obligation to accept the offer of an alternative cruise. The same principle has been applied to liability policies. In *Yorkshire Water Services Ltd v Sun Alliance & London Insurance plc*,[82] sewage escaped from a sewage works owned by Yorkshire Water Services (YWS). To reduce the likelihood of damage to neighbouring property and, therefore, of claims against YWS, the company undertook works costing £4 million. YWS claimed that it had been under a duty to mitigate its loss and accordingly there was a corresponding duty on the insurers to pay the mitigation costs under a public liability policy, which provided cover against 'legal liability for damages' and 'all other costs and expenses in relation to any matter which may form the subject of a claim'. The Court of Appeal took the view that the insurer was only required to indemnify YWS for sums due as compensation to third parties and not costs incurred by YWS in carrying out work on its own property. The suggestion that a term should be implied into the policy rendering the insurers liable for reasonable expenditure on work undertaken to alleviate loss was rejected, the Court pointing out that it would be difficult to assess what was reasonable: if the potential liability were a claim for compensation of £300,000 from the owner of neighbouring property, would it be reasonable to require the insurers to meet the sum of £4 million paid for the works? This would become even more difficult if the damage to the neighbouring property had not been quantified. In the end, however, the case rested on the issue of what the insurer had agreed to cover.

Although the Australian courts have followed the English approach in rejecting the existence of a duty to mitigate,[83] they have taken a different view on the question of whether an insured who chooses to mitigate is entitled to recover the costs of doing so, although the decisions have turned on the proper construction of the insuring clauses in question. In *Guardian Assurance Co Ltd v Underwood Construcitons Pty Ltd*,[84] the insured, under a

[79] *British Westinghouse Electric Co Ltd v Underground Electric Rys Co of London* [1912] AC 673, 689 (Viscount Haldane LC); *England v Guardian Insurance Ltd* [2000] Lloyd's Rep IR 404; *Linelevel Ltd v Powszechny Zaklad Ubezpieczen SA, The Nore Challenger* [2005] 2 Lloyd's Rep 534.

[80] (1921) 91 LJKB 379.

[81] [2011] EWHC 2629 (Comm).

[82] [1997] 2 Lloyd's Rep 21. See also *Pilkington United Kingdom Ltd v CGU Insurance Plc* [2004] Lloyd's Rep IR 891, where the insured was held to be unable to recover the cost of replacing defective glass panels in the roof of Waterloo Station even though there was a risk that they might fall and cause injuries for which the insurers would have faced liability.

[83] *AFG Insurances Ltd v City of Brighton* (1972) 126 CLR 655; *EK Nominees Pty Ltd v Indemnity Corp Pty Ltd* (1990) 6 ANZ Ins Cas 61-008.

[84] (1974) 48 ALJR 307.

contractor's all risks policy, was held to be entitled to recover the costs of remedial action after its excavation activities had caused rockfalls that threatened buildings adjoining the site. The court's view was that there had been damage to those buildings, in the form of a threat to their physical integrity, and so the measures fell within the insuring clause. In *EJ Hampson Syndicate 1204 v Mining Technologies Australia Pty Ltd*,[85] the insured equipment, which had been trapped underground following a mine collapse, was rescued by the insured at considerable expense (although the cost was less than half the value of the equipment). Davies JA noted that the policy contained a clause that excluded liability for loss to property which could have been avoided by the insured exercising reasonable care; therefore, he implied a term allowing the recovery of expenditure incurred by the insured in exercising such reasonable care. McPherson JA, on the other hand, did not regard it as necessary to decide whether there was an implied term because the insured could recover under a clause permitting repair of the insured property and he took the view that retrieving the equipment amounted to repair. In *PMB Australia Ltd v MMI General Insurance Ltd*,[86] the implied term approach was rejected. There the policy covered losses incurred through business interruption when an outbreak of salmonella stopped the manufacture of peanut butter; however, the clause was held not to cover expenditure incurred to alter the factory in order to prevent future outbreaks, and therefore future losses. The case may, however, be explained on the basis that there was no imminent peril and it could not therefore be said that the expenditure had been incurred to avert a threatened loss.

A contractual or other right to recover mitigation costs is not subject to apportionment simply because mitigation steps were in the insured's interest and some other benefit was derived from them. The ransom payment made by the insured in *Royal Boskalis Westminster NV v Mountain*[87] not only freed the insured vessels, but also secured the release of crew who were not insured under the policy. No deduction was ordered to reflect the fact that the insured's act had conferred uninsured benefits, and that

> provided that expenses can reasonably be said to have been incurred for the preservation of property, it does not seem … either sound in principle or desirable that the assured should be penalised if they were sufficiently concerned for lives at risk to have been concerned to save not only their property but also those lives.

In *Ace European Group v Standard Life Assurance Ltd*,[88] the insured's professional indemnity policy conferred a right to recover 'costs or expenses reasonably and necessarily incurred by the Assured in taking action to avoid a third party claim'. An investment fund operated by the insured dramatically decreased in value and, facing claims by third party investors, substantial sums were paid into the fund by the insured to restore its value.

This action generated confidence in the fund. The amount of the payment was claimed from the insurers, and their attempt to reduce the mitigation costs payable by them on the basis that the payment had the dual purpose of preventing claims and restoring the insured's reputation was firmly rejected both on principle and also because no satisfactory method of calculating apportionment could be suggested.

[85] [1999] 1 Qd R 60.
[86] [2002] QCA 361.
[87] [1997] 2 All ER 929.
[88] [2012] EWCA Civ 1713.

4.2. Public Policy

4.2.1. Deliberate Intention to Cause Loss

A criminal act may well be one deliberately carried out by the insured with the purpose of bringing about the loss. In that case, criminality has no independent relevance: an insured who deliberately brings about his own loss – whether or not the act was a criminal one – cannot recover from the insurers on the principle that insurance is against fortuities and not certainties. In *Beresford v Royal Insurance Co*,[89] a man burdened by huge debts committed suicide. The insurers were not held liable on a life policy. Even though there was a clause which only excluded liability if suicide occurred within a year of the policy commencing and the death was outside that period, the House of Lords decided that, since at that time suicide was a crime, public policy would not allow recovery.[90] However, an alternative ground for the decision was that the insured had committed a deliberate act giving rise to the loss, and the insurers were discharged also on that basis.

> On ordinary principles of insurance law an assured cannot by his own deliberate act cause the event upon which the insurance is payable. The insurers have not agreed to pay on that happening. The fire assured cannot recover if he intentionally burns down his house, nor the marine assured if he scuttles his ship, nor the life assured if he deliberately ends his own life. This is not the result of public policy, but of the correct construction of the contract.[91]

The passing of the Suicide Act 1961 has removed the illegality defence, and the insurers would on the same facts now face liability by the terms of the policy.

So, although criminality and deliberately inflicted loss may go hand in hand, the consequences of criminality alone are relevant where the insured's unlawful act, though deliberate, was not intended to cause loss. The principle is enshrined in the Marine Insurance Act 1906, section 55(2)(a), under which 'The insurer is not liable for any loss attributable to the wilful misconduct of the assured'. The act in question must amount to wilful misconduct. In *Porter v Zurich Insurance Co*,[92] Mr Porter, while suffering from a persistent delusional disorder, attempted to commit suicide by setting his home on fire. Midway through his attempt, he changed his mind and escaped, but the house and its contents were damaged. Mr Porter's claim was rejected by his insurers. Coulson J remarked that it was 'trite law' that public policy prevented recovery where loss had been intentionally caused by the assured's criminal act, such as in this case.[93] He did, however, recognise that Mr Porter could recover if he had been insane, which would require proof 'on the balance of probabilities, that they were insane, within the meaning of the M'Naghten Rules, at the time of the fire'.[94] Therefore, the

[89] [1938] AC 586.

[90] The inclusion of such a clause would not make the whole contract void *ab initio* because it could be severed from the rest of the contract. The Lords chose not to follow a decision of the US Supreme Court in which it was held that, although a term not allowing a claim in the event of suicide would be implied into a life policy, where the policy mentioned the issue by, for instance, providing for payment if the suicide occurred after a certain period, there was no general principle to prevent payment, and it was up to each state to legislate, if it chose, to preclude payment: *Northwestern Mutual Life Insurance Co v Johnson* (1920) 254 US 96. See also *Moore and Kettle v Woolsey and Knill* (1854) 4 E & B 243, 254–55 (Lord Campbell CJ).

[91] *Beresford v Royal Insurance Co Ltd*, [1938] AC 586, 595 (Lord Atkin).

[92] [2009] EWHC 376 (QB).

[93] ibid [9].

[94] ibid [17].

appropriate test was whether Mr Porter did not know 'the nature and quality of the act he was doing; or if he did know it, that he did not know that he was doing what was wrong'.[95] Coulson J found that Mr Porter was not insane. He had a delusional disorder, which meant that he knew what he was doing and that it was wrong.[96]

The policy itself may restrict recovery where there has been a deliberate act by the insured. The meaning of this type of wording was discussed by the Supreme Court in *Burnett v International Insurance Company of Hanover Ltd*,[97] where it was held that an act is deliberate only if the consequences of the act were intended. The insured in this case was a security company which provided doormen to enforce security at clubs operated by the insured's clients. The policy excluded the insurers' liability for deliberate acts. An employee of the insured was involved in an altercation with an inebriated customer, the unfortunate consequence of which was the death of the customer. The doorman was prosecuted for murder but was acquitted on the jury's finding that he had not intended to kill, and the conviction was for manslaughter only. The Supreme Court held that a deliberate act was not simply one that was intentionally carried out but rather was one that required an intention to injure. If that intention was present, then any form of injury was to be regarded as deliberate, but if there was no intention to injure then the act was not deliberate even though it was voluntary in a physical sense.

4.2.2. Loss Not Intended

The most difficult question is whether an insured who has committed a criminal act unintentionally leading to the loss is barred from recovering under the policy. The policy may itself deal with the matter. There may be an obligation to comply with legislation, failing which there is no recovery. Some clauses are absolute in their effect, others are triggered only where the assured has failed to exercise reasonable care[98] to comply with legislation.[99] An alternative form of wording excludes the liability of the insurers if the insured has committed a criminal act. This type of wording has been construed narrowly, applying only where the insured had consciously been guilty of wrongdoing.[100]

As a preliminary point, it should be emphasised that if the contract is lawful in its formation, in that it is not contrary to legislation and does not have as its objective the achievement of an unlawful purpose,[101] then an unlawful act by the insured does not render the contract illegal as formed. The contract is valid, and the issue becomes whether the insured's conduct precludes a claim.[102] That is a matter of public policy, expressed in the maxim *ex turpi causa*

[95] ibid [23].

[96] In *Beresford* Lord Atkin added that where the person who committed suicide was insane at the time the insurers might be held liable 'if one premises that the insanity in question prevents the act from being in law the act of the assured' (ibid). But where the policy specifically excludes liability for insane as well as sane suicide, there will be no claim: *Ellinger & Co v Mutual Life Insurance Co of New York* [1905] 1 KB 31.

[97] [2021] UKSC 12.

[98] As will be seen below, this refers to reckless rather than purely negligent conduct.

[99] The cases on this point all come from Australia, and the authorities are reviewed in *Noori v Majestic Plumbing Services Pty Ltd* [2021] VSC 63, where the policy was construed as imposing only a reasonable care obligation to comply with legislation.

[100] *Marcell Beller Ltd v Hayden* [1978] QB 694.

[101] As to which, see ch 5 above.

[102] This is a principle of ordinary contract law: *Ashmore, Benson, Pease & Co Ltd v Dawson Ltd* [1973] 2 All ER 856.

non oritur action (an action does not arise from a dishonourable cause). It has been said that to allow someone to profit from their crime would remove 'those restraints operating on the minds of men against the commission of crimes, namely, the interest we have in the welfare and prosperity of our connexions'.[103] It is unrealistic to suppose that someone who is not deterred from committing a crime by the possibility of being punished will be deterred by the prospect of being refused a claim under an insurance policy.[104] Furthermore, such goals would seem more appropriately the province of the criminal law. In his important essay on public policy, Shand suggested that it has never been the purpose of contract law 'to regulate the conduct of the community at large by altering or invalidating the rights and obligations of individual parties'. Nevertheless, he went on to admit that 'deterrence has become a firmly established factor in the application of public policy to contract law'.[105] The other justification for intervention is that the courts will not lend the legal process to enforcing a claim based on the criminal act of the insured because 'no system of jurisprudence can with reason include amongst the rights which it enforces rights directly resulting to the person asserting them from the crime of that person',[106] and 'The human mind revolts at the very idea that any other doctrine could be possible in our system of jurisprudence'.[107]

The court will not, however, refuse a claim merely because there has been some incidental illegal act.[108] In the root case, *Richardson v Mellish*,[109] the defendant's vessel was chartered to the East India Company, and the claimant agreed to resign the captaincy in favour of the defendant's nephew and in return for the captaincy of another vessel owned by the defendant that had been chartered to the Company. The claimant's action for reinstatement following the death of the defendant's nephew was resisted on a number of grounds, including that the arrangement was equivalent to the unlawful sale of a public office. The court found no illegality, and Burrough J made the following classic statement:

> I, for one, protest … against arguing too strongly upon public policy; – it is a very unruly horse, and when once you get astride it you never know where it will carry you. It may lead you from the sound law. It is never argued at all but when other points fail.

Diplock LJ has commented that whether the court will refuse to assert a right, even in favour of someone who has committed an antisocial act, will depend on the nature of that act and the nature of the right.[110] Further, there must be a causal connection between the crime and the loss, otherwise the motorist who deliberately drove a car without an MOT certificate would have no claim if a camera were stolen from that car. Moreover, the principle of public policy that denies the criminal's claim must be set against another principle

[103] *Amicable Society for a Perpetual Life Assurance Office v James Bolland, Joseph Hare and Matthias Koops Knight* (1830) 4 Bligh (NS) 194, 211.

[104] *Hardy v Motor Insurers' Bureau* [1964] QB 745, 770 (Diplock LJ).

[105] JG Shand, 'Unblinkering the Unruly Horse: Public Policy in the Law of Contract' (1972) 30 *CLJ* 144, 154–55. Indeed, the tendency is growing to use the civil law to control anti-social behaviour (for example, local authorities obtaining injunctions against tenants in public housing who are accused of racist threats) or to obtain damages from those who have not been convicted by a criminal court. See also M Clarke, 'Insurance of Wilful Misconduct: The Court as Keeper of the Public Conscience' (1996) 7 *Insurance Law Journal* 173.

[106] *Cleaver v Mutual Reserve Fund Life Association* [1892] 1 QB 147, 156 (Fry LJ).

[107] *In the Estate of Cunigunda (otherwise Cora) Crippen, Deceased* [1911] P 108, 112 (Evans P). See also *Holman v Johnson* (1775) 1 Cowp 341, 343.

[108] *Saunders v Edwards* [1987] 1 WLR 1116, 1134 (Bingham LJ).

[109] (1844) 7 Man & G 457.

[110] *Hardy v Motor Insurers' Bureau*, [1964] QB 745, 767–68.

that requires people to perform their contractual obligations. Lord Esher MR summed up the predicament:

> No doubt there is a rule that, if a contract be made contrary to public policy, performance cannot be enforced either at law or in equity; but when people vouch that rule to excuse themselves from the performance of a contract, in respect of which they have received the full consideration, and when all that remains to be done under the contract is for them to pay money, the application of the rule ought to be narrowly watched, and ought not to be carried a step further than the protection of the public requires.[111]

A boundary must, therefore, be drawn between an unenforceable and an enforceable claim where the insured has committed a deliberate and criminal act. When a solicitor suffered a loss as the result of entering into a champertous contract he was unable to claim under his policy because he had deliberately entered into the illegal contract and the fact that he did not realise it was a criminal offence to do so was irrelevant.[112] Similarly, someone who is fined for a criminal act will not be able to recover the fine from an insurer.[113] After Henry Fauntleroy was hanged in 1824 for forging a Bank of England note, his estate was unable to claim on a life policy that he had taken out nine years before, even though it can hardly be supposed that he committed the forgery with the intention of being convicted and hanged.[114]

The scope of public policy has been the subject of much judicial debate. Some courts, notably the Court of Appeal in *Euro-Diam v Bathurst*, adopted a 'public conscience' test. The House of Lords in *Tinsley v Milligan*[115] disapproved of that analysis, and by a majority opted for a formal approach which asked whether the claimant was required to rely upon the illegality. After a series of conflicting Supreme Court decisions,[116] a nine-member Supreme Court panel was assembled to hear the appeal in *Patel v Mirza*.[117] The claimant in this case sought to recover £620,000 paid to the defendant, to be used to purchase shares based on the defendant's inside information. In the event the purchase did not go ahead, and the claimant sought a return of his payment. The claim was allowed, but the Supreme Court divided 6:3 on the reasons for that result. The majority view, exemplified by Lord Toulson, was that a threefold test was to be applied: what was the underlying purpose of the prohibition; would denial of the claim have any impact on public policy;[118] and was denial of the claim a proportional response to the illegality, taking into account the extent to which the claimant would have to rely upon his own illegal act to substantiate the claim? The minority – the powerful trio of Lords Mance, Clarke and Sumption – favoured a more rigid analysis based upon the link between the illegality and the claim, and strongly expressed concerns about adopting an approach which was largely discretionary.

[111] *Cleaver v Mutual Reserve Fund Life Association* [1892] 1 QB 147, 151.

[112] *Haseldine v Hosken* [1933] 1 KB 822.

[113] By analogy with *Safeway Stores Ltd v Twigger* [2011] 1 Lloyd's Rep 462.

[114] *Amicable Society for a Perpetual Life Assurance Office v Bolland* (1830) 4 Bligh (NS) 194. For a similar approach in the USA, see *Millen v John Hancock Mutual Life Insurance Co* 13 NE2d 950 (1938), although contrast *Weeks v New York Life Insurance Co* 122 SE 586 (1924) and *John Hancock Mutual Life Insurance Co v Tarrence* 244 F2d 86 (1957).

[115] [1993] 3 All ER 65.

[116] *Hounga v Allan* [2014] UKSC 47; *Les Laboratoires Servier v Apotex Inc* [2015] AC 430; *Jetivi SA v Bilta (UK) Ltd* [2015] UKSC 23.

[117] [2017] AC 467.

[118] This may be an important consideration in liability insurance cases, where the loser of the claim is denied is the insured's third party victim rather than the insured himself.

4.3. Deliberate Killing

4.3.1. The Forfeiture Rule

The forfeiture rule is 'the rule of public policy which in certain circumstances precludes a person who has unlawfully killed another from acquiring a benefit in consequence of the killing'.[119] The operation of the principle that a criminal must not be allowed to benefit from the crime can be seen in those spousal murder cases where the murderer is the beneficiary under a policy on the victim's life.[120] After Dr Crippen was hanged in 1910 for the murder of his wife, his estate was not allowed to claim as the beneficiary of a life policy on her life.[121] Unlike *Prince of Wales Association v Palmer*,[122] where the life policy was void because it had been entered into so that Palmer could collect by murdering the insured life, in *Crippen* the contract was valid but could not be enforced by either Crippen or his estate.[123] On the other hand, a beneficiary under a life policy, who has neither committed nor connived in the criminal act that caused the death of the insured life, will be able to recover, as where a husband was the beneficiary under a policy on his wife's life and his wife was killed while she was deliberately setting fire to a house.[124] Indeed, the fact that the murderer is the first named beneficiary, and therefore cannot enforce a claim, does not mean that another beneficiary cannot. The rule does not make the policy void, it merely makes it unenforceable by the criminal.[125] After Florence Maybrick was convicted of the murder of her husband, James,[126] a claim under a policy on his life was refused by the insurers on the ground that she should not be allowed to benefit from her crime. The court agreed, but did not see why the insurers should avoid liability and ordered that Florence's claim be ignored, which meant that under the terms of the policy the proceeds went to James's estate.[127] Using this approach, *Beresford* would have been decided differently if the beneficiary had not been the suicide's own estate.[128] In cases like *Crippen*, it was a legal fiction that enabled the insurers to avoid paying while allowing them to keep the premiums, namely that Crippen's personal representatives were treated as being Crippen himself. In reality, of course, it would not have been Crippen who enjoyed the proceeds of the life policies but his beneficiaries.[129] On the other hand, it can be argued that, while the offender does not benefit, they should not be

[119] Forfeiture Act 1982, s 1(1).

[120] B Kingree and L Turner, 'Life Insurance as Motive for Murder' (1994) 29 *Tort and Insurance Law Journal* 761.

[121] *In the Estate of Cunigunda (otherwise Cora) Crippen, Deceased* [1911] P 108, 112 (Evans P).

[122] (1855) 25 Beav 605.

[123] See also *Davitt v Titcumb* [1990] Ch 110; *Mackender v Feldia AG* [1967] 2 QB 590, 599 (Lord Denning MR).

[124] *Brown v American International Life Co* 778 F Supp 912 (1991).

[125] *Mackender v Feldia AG* [1967] 2 QB 590, 599 (Lord Denning MR). This passage was cited with approval by the Supreme Court of Canada in *Oldfield v Transamerica Life Insurance Co of Canada* 210 DLR (4th) 1 (2002).

[126] James Maybrick is one of the many men suggested to be the Whitechapel Murderer (Jack the Ripper).

[127] *Cleaver v Mutual Reserve Fund Life Association* [1892] 1 QB 147. Florence Maybrick was also precluded from taking as a beneficiary of James's estate. An American case did apply the *Cleaver* idea to allow a claim where a person was killed by the police during the commission of a serious felony and the beneficiary under a life policy was the insured's mother, although this approach has been rejected in other states: *Davis v Boston Mutual Life Insurance Company* 351 NE 2d 207 (1976); *Murphy v Culhane* [1977] QB 94.

[128] In *Beresford v Royal Insurance Co Ltd* [1938] AC 586, 605, Lord Atkin reserved his opinion on whether 'third parties who have bona fide acquired rights for value under such policies' would have an enforceable claim. See *Moore v Woolsey* (1854) 4 El & Bl 243.

[129] *Prudential Life Insurance Co v Goldstein* 43 F Supp 765, 767.

able to direct who should. This view was pressed by Lord Macmillan in *Beresford v Royal Insurance Co Ltd*:[130]

> To enforce payment in favour of the assured's representative would be to give him a benefit, namely, of having by his last and criminal act provided for his relatives or creditors. And no criminal can be allowed to benefit in any way by his crime.

In any event, this 'fiction' continues to prevent recovery.[131]

The forfeiture rule will apply not just where the claimant under a policy has been convicted of a murder, which led to the loss, but where diminished responsibility or provocation was successfully pleaded,[132] or where the defendant was not punished but was confined under the Mental Health Act,[133] although there is room for doubt as to whether it would apply where the defendant was found to be criminally insane under the Criminal Procedure (Insanity) Act 1964, section 1.[134] In *Dunbar v Plant*,[135] where the Court of Appeal extended the rule to the criminal complicity involved in a suicide pact,[136] Mummery LJ said:

> It is sufficient that a serious crime has been committed deliberately and intentionally ... The essence of the principle of public policy is that (a) no person shall take a benefit resulting from a crime committed by him or her resulting in the death of the victim and (b) the nature of the crime determines the application of the principle. On that view the important point is that the crime that had fatal consequences was committed with a guilty mind (deliberately and intentionally). The particular means used to commit the crime (whether violent or non-violent) are not a necessary ingredient of the rule. There may be cases in which violence has been used deliberately without an intention to bring about the unlawful fatal consequences. Those cases will attract the application of the forfeiture rule. It does not follow, however, that when death has been brought about by a deliberate and intentional, but non-violent, act (eg poison or gas) the rule is inapplicable.[137]

Indeed, there may be no crime in the sense of a criminal conviction for the rule to operate. Lord Lane CJ was of the opinion that, 'in each case it is not the label which the law applies to the crime but the nature of the crime itself which will dictate whether public policy demands the court to drive the applicant from the seat of justice'.[138]

4.3.2. Forfeiture Act 1982

A number of consequences flow from the forfeiture rule that might be regarded as undesirable. For instance, a wife who, after a long history of suffering abuse, kills her violent husband will be prevented from recovering under a policy on his life,[139] as would a wife who helps her terminally ill husband to commit suicide. Parliament has, therefore, introduced

[130] [1938] AC 586, 605.

[131] *Hardy v Motor Insurers' Bureau* [1964] QB 745, 767 (Diplock LJ). See generally N Enonchong, *Illegal Transactions* (London, Lloyd's of London Press, 1998) 205–52; Shand (n 105) 160.

[132] *In re S, decd* [1996] 1 WLR 235.

[133] *Re Giles* [1972] Ch 544, 552 (Pennycuick V-C); *Dalton v Latham* 2003 WL 18023075, (9) (Patten J).

[134] *Dalton v Latham* [2003] EWHC 796 (Ch).

[135] [1997] 4 All ER 289.

[136] Suicide Act 1961, s 2(1).

[137] [1997] 4 All ER 289.

[138] *R v Chief National Insurance Commissioner, ex parte Connor* [1981] QB 758, 765 (Lord Lane CJ). Although this was a case on entitlement to the widow's allowance under the Social Security Act 1975, the principle applies more generally: *Gray v Barr, Prudential Assurance Co Ltd (Third Party)* [1971] 2 QB 554.

[139] For a different approach in the USA, see *Calaway v Southern Farm Bureau Life Insurance Co Inc* 619 SW2d 301 (1981).

flexibility into the application of the rule. Under the Forfeiture Act 1982,[140] unless the offender has been convicted of murder (section 5), the court can modify the rule if, having regard to the conduct of the offender and the victim and other material circumstances, 'the justice of the case requires' it (section 2(2)). The procedure is that once the court has decided the forfeiture rule applies, it will consider matters such as an offender's moral culpability, the financial position of an offender[141] and any provocation.[142]

Since the Act the judges have struggled to define the level of culpability required to disqualify an offender. It was held in *Re H (Deceased)*[143] that the use of the Act to modify the rule might be appropriate even where someone was convicted of manslaughter on the grounds of diminished responsibility if the killing had not involved 'deliberate, intentional and unlawful violence or threats of violence'.[144] Yet, this seems out of line with other opinions on the rule, and, as Patten J has recently remarked, Parliament could have excluded the application of the rule where there was diminished responsibility, but chose not to do so.[145] *Re H (Deceased)* was also doubted by Judge Kolbert in *Jones v Roberts*,[146] on the ground that *Royse v Royse*,[147] a decision of the Court of Appeal that was on all fours with the facts in *Re H*, had not been cited. He also thought that allowing someone who had been convicted of manslaughter on the grounds of diminished responsibility to benefit from their crime involved reshaping public policy to such an extent that it could only be undertaken by a higher court. Finally, Judge Kolbert said that battering someone to death with a hammer (as Jones did) was a deliberate, intentional and unlawful act of violence in spite of the finding of diminished responsibility. In *Dunbar v Plant*,[148] the Court of Appeal took a more liberal view in relation to complicity in a suicide pact. Phillips LJ said that, while the forfeiture rule applied to a killing in such circumstances, since the Director of Public Prosecutions had clearly not thought it in the public interest to permit a prosecution under the Suicide Act 1961 (section 2(4)), the court should use its discretion under the Forfeiture Act. Moreover, he thought that it would be wrong to punish the survivor of a suicide pact by application of the rule where it was a rational decision, as where it involved an elderly couple both suffering from an incurable disease, or 'the product of an irrational depression or desperation'. In neither situation would the public interest be served by applying the forfeiture rule and, therefore, total relief under the Forfeiture Act should be given.[149]

4.3.3. Deliberate Killing and Liability Insurance

In *Gray v Barr*,[150] Mr Barr, suspecting that his wife had restarted a love affair with Mr Gray, burst into the latter's house brandishing a shotgun. He fired into the ceiling, then made his

[140] The Act was introduced following *R v Chief National Insurance Commissioner, ex parte Connor* [1981] QB 758; P Larkin, 'The Rule of Forfeiture and Bereavement Benefits' (2004) 11 *Journal of Social Security Law* 59. The Act applies only to the acquisition of certain types of property interest and, therefore, not to liability insurance (s 2(1)).

[141] *In re K, decd* [1985] Ch 85, 96.

[142] See also *Re S, decd* [1996] 1 WLR 235.

[143] [1990] 1 FLR 441.

[144] ibid 447 (Peter Gibson J).

[145] *Dalton v Latham* 2003 WL 18023075.

[146] [1995] 2 FLR 422. See also *Re S, decd* [1996] 1 WLR 235.

[147] [1984] 3 WLR 784.

[148] [1997] 4 All ER 289.

[149] ibid 1285. Phillips LJ recognised that some suicide pacts might involve such culpability as would require the application of the rule: he hinted, for instance, that a pact prompted by one person who was afraid of the consequences of a theft which he had committed might prompt the application of the rule.

[150] [1971] 2 QB 554. *Gray v Barr* is a case which, while being given a thorough pounding by academics, has been admired and, what is more to the point, followed by the judiciary in England and abroad. See JA Jolowicz,

way towards Gray, who, doubtless fearing for his life, tried to grapple the gun away from Barr. During the struggle the gun went off and Gray was killed. Barr was acquitted of murder and manslaughter, but was sued by Gray's wife. On the question of whether Barr's liability for Gray's death was covered by a third party liability policy, which responded only to 'accidents', the Court of Appeal acknowledged that such policies were designed to cover death caused by the insured's negligence, but nevertheless denied the claim. Lord Denning MR offered two approaches. First, he said that if the shooting had been deliberate there would be no cover. He contrasted the facts of this case with the situation where someone out hunting unintentionally shot another person dead: that, he said, would be an accident within the terms of the policy, even if there had been such gross negligence as to lead to a conviction for manslaughter, because there had been no deliberate act directed at the person killed. In the present case, however, while the immediate cause of death was the second, unintentional shot, it could not be separated from the deliberate act of entering Gray's house with a loaded gun: 'The whole tragic sequence flows inexorably from that act.'[151] In summary, it seems that Lord Denning required there to have been a deliberate act aimed at the person killed, which act was so closely linked to the act that led to the death to make the two actions into one event. As an alternative, Lord Denning said that a civil court was not bound by the verdict of the criminal court: in Denning's view, Barr was guilty of manslaughter, and because 'his conduct is wilful and culpable, he is not entitled to recover'.[152] Phillimore LJ also thought that the two shots could not be separated. The wilful act of going into the house with the shotgun may have led to an unexpected and unintended result, but it was one which could reasonably have been anticipated and it was, therefore, not an accident. He added that 'the true question is whether people would commonly agree with Mr Barr if after describing all the circumstances as they occurred he went on to say: "It was an accident." I confess that I would not.'[153] Yet, Phillimore LJ need not have looked very far to find someone who differed with him on that view. Salmon LJ separated the two shots and concluded that the death was an accident because it occurred as the result of the second, unintended shot. But he went on to say that there was an implied term in the contract that precluded recovery where an accident occurred in the course of the insured threatening unlawful violence with a loaded gun. If, in the alternative, there was no such implied term, he would still deny the claim on the ground of public policy: 'Crimes of violence, particularly when committed with loaded guns, are amongst the worse curses of this age. It is very much in the public interest that they should be deterred.'[154]

There are some problems with this case, not least of which is the lack of a clear ratio decidendi. Nevertheless, the decision would seem to be authority for the view that the court will look at the nature of the insured's act and decide if there was a deliberate criminal act directed at another person who is thereby killed, regardless of whether violence was

'Liability Insurance – Manslaughter – Public Policy' [1970] *CLJ* 194; JG Fleming, 'Insurance for the Criminal' (1971) 34 *MLR* 176; Shand (n 105). For a critical discussion of the impact of the case in Canada, where it has been cited with approval in the Supreme Court, see RA Hasson, 'The Supreme Court of Canada and the Law of Insurance 1975' (1976) 14 *Osgoode Hall Law Journal* 769, 776–78. See also RB Wuehler, 'Rethink Insurance's Public Policy Exclusion: California's Befuddled Attempt to Apply an Undefined Rule and a Call for Reform' (2001) 49 *University of California at Los Angeles Law Review* 651.

[151] See [1971] 2 QB 554, 567.

[152] ibid 568.

[153] ibid 585.

[154] ibid 581. It is hard to disagree with Salmon LJ's opinion of guns, although, if viewed in terms of death and injury caused by the motor car, it could be said to be a much greater 'curse of this age'.

involved or there was any criminal conviction.[155] Geoffrey Lane J provided a useful method of distinguishing between different types of manslaughter, which returns us to the issue of the deliberate nature of the act:

> The logical test, in my judgment, is whether the person seeking the indemnity was guilty of deliberate, intentional and unlawful violence, or threats of violence. If he was, and death resulted therefrom, then, however unintended the final death of the victim may have been, the court should not entertain a claim for indemnity.[156]

This oft-quoted definition should be amended in the light of Mummery LJ's remarks about the stipulation that there must be violence or the threat of violence. The question remains as to whether the act must be directed at the person whose death occurs: what if A threatens B with a gun and during the ensuing struggle the gun is accidentally fired, killing C? Although statements in *Gray v Barr* seem to suggest the act must be directed at the person killed, it seems clear that they should not be read so narrowly and, indeed, it is not part of Geoffrey Lane J's test.

The word 'accident' in a liability policy is to be determined from the point of view of the insured, not from the point of view of the victim or even the actual perpetrator of the act. In *Burnett v International Insurance Company of Hannover*,[157] the killing of a drunken customer by a security guard was held to be accidental from the point of view of the insured, the security guard's employer. In the absence of any complicity or orders on the part of the insured, what had happened was from the point of view of the insured an accident. For this purpose, an accident means loss arising other than from a deliberately incurred or courted risk, so that if the harm was not intended, then it is accidental.[158]

4.3.4. Motor Manslaughter

In spite of the lack of a general principle in insurance law in favour of ensuring that third parties receive compensation, when someone is killed or injured by a motorist the courts have seemed to focus on this objective to the exclusion of the issues that so exercised the Court of Appeal in *Gray v Barr*.[159] In *Tinline v White Cross Insurance Association Ltd*,[160] a speeding motorist killed one pedestrian and injured two others as they were crossing Shaftesbury Avenue in London's West End. He was convicted of manslaughter involving gross or reckless negligence. In litigation over the liability of his insurers, Bailhache J remarked that: 'Speaking generally, it is true to say that it is against public policy to indemnify a man against the consequences of a crime which he knowingly commits.'[161] However, a motor

[155] This proposition fits in with cases in which the issue has been whether a claimant could obtain redress through the civil courts in connection with a felony where there had been no prosecution, such as *Ex parte Ball, In re Shepherd* (1879) 10 Ch D 667 and *Midland Insurance Co v Smith* (1891) 6 QBD 561, 576, in which Watkin Williams J said: 'it seems clear to me that the prosecution of the felon is not an absolute condition precedent to the accruing of the cause of action'. Leaving aside the role of jury equity in criminal trials, the assessment of whether there has been a crime will, in civil proceedings and on the balance of probabilities, be making such a conclusion more likely.

[156] [1970] 2 QB 626, 640. See *In re K, decd* [1985] Ch 85.

[157] [2021] UKSC 12.

[158] See the lengthy discussion of the possible tests for 'accident' in *Matton Developments Pty Ltd v CGU Insurance Ltd (No 2)* [2016] QCA 208.

[159] [1971] 2 QB 554. It is worth recalling that a distinction exists in criminal law where the degree of negligence required to convict a motorist of manslaughter is much higher than that required to convict someone accused of manslaughter involving a weapon: compare *R v Andrews* [1937] AC 576 with *R v Larkin* [1943] KB 174.

[160] [1921] 3 KB 327.

[161] ibid 332.

policy covering liability to third parties must include 'negligence whether slight or great'.[162] Therefore, the insurers were liable on the policy. It is difficult to reconcile such decisions with *Gray v Barr*. Barr did not intend to kill any more than did the motorist in *Tinline*, and both Barr and the motorist committed deliberate and criminal acts which led to the deaths. The key distinction could be that in *Tinline* the deliberate act that caused death was not directed at anyone in the way that Barr's act of entering the house with a gun had been directed at Gray. Yet, this seems not to assist us with two cases where motorists directed their cars at people just as surely as Barr directed his gun (more so, perhaps). In *Hardy v Motor Insurers' Bureau*,[163] where the driver was convicted of wounding with intent to commit grievous bodily harm, and in *Gardner v Moore*,[164] where the driver was convicted of maliciously inflicting grievous bodily harm, the Court of Appeal and the House of Lords respectively decided that, although the deliberate and criminal nature of such acts meant that an insured driver, who had already paid damages to the victim, could not claim an indemnity from the insurers, if the victim could not recover compensation from the driver, the driver's insurers were liable, or the Motor Insurers' Bureau was where the driver was not insured or could not be traced.[165] Indeed, the victim in such cases would be able to claim directly against the insurer under the provisions of the Road Traffic Act 1988. Diplock LJ, in a judgment later approved by the House of Lords in *Gardner v Moore*, suggested that:

> The court has to weigh the gravity of the anti-social act and the extent to which it will be encouraged by enforcing the right sought to be asserted against the social harm which will be caused if the right is not enforced.[166]

In the same case, Lord Denning MR said:

> If the motorist is guilty of a crime involving a wicked and deliberate intent, and he is made to pay damages to an injured person, he is not entitled to recover on the policy. But if he does not pay the damages, then the injured third party can recover against the insurers under s.207 of the Road Traffic Act 1960; for it is a liability which the motorist under the statute was required to cover. The injured third party is not affected by the disability which attached to the motorist himself … The policy of insurance which a motorist is required by statute to take out must cover any liability which may be incurred by him arising out of the use of the vehicle by him. It must, I think, be wide enough to cover, in general terms, any use by him of the vehicle, be it an innocent use or a criminal use, or be it a murderous use or a playful use.

These cases can only be distinguished from *Gray v Barr* on public policy grounds. But what public policy goals are achieved by the distinction which the courts make? When the judges in *Gray* said that Barr's action was dangerous, they must have meant it was dangerous for third parties like Gray. They did not consider it more important to provide protection for those third parties other than to use the case to point out what was already obvious – that waving shotguns about is dangerous. Moreover, by not holding the insurers liable to indemnify the miscreant, they made the victim pay for a lesson which is unlikely to have any impact.[167] The idea that the decision in *Gray* would deter husbands from using guns to

[162] ibid 332. *James v British General Insurance Co Ltd* [1927] 2 KB 311.
[163] [1964] QB 745.
[164] [1984] AC 548.
[165] See ch 14 below.
[166] [1984] AC 548. See also *Geismar v Sun Alliance and London Insurance Ltd* [1978] 1 QB 383, 390 (Talbot J).
[167] Whether Mrs Barr received compensation from Gray is irrelevant to the argument, as in most cases tortfeasors are unlikely to be able to afford to pay.

threaten those whom they believed to be their spouses' lovers seems fanciful. Even ignoring the likelihood that *Gray* is not widely known, it is unlikely that the husband who is so much out of control as to contemplate shooting the lover will be brought back to his senses by an insurance policy. As for the broader consideration that the law must not be used to indemnify people for their criminal actions, this has not outweighed the wish to compensate the victims of malicious motorists. What is the difference between someone, who has a licence to own a shotgun, waving that gun in someone's face and a licensed motorist driving on the pavement? Both are illegal ways of conducting oneself, and Parliament has chosen to control them by a combination of licensing provisions and criminal offences. It seems better for the judges to leave the matter of deterring and punishing criminal behaviour to the criminal courts, and in a civil action to focus on the narrower issues between the parties, that is, the question of the victim's compensation, as they have done with injuries caused by motorists.[168] On the other hand, why should the wrongdoer be indemnified by the insurer for the consequences of their wrongdoing and is consideration of the plight of the victim relevant? Whatever sympathy we may feel for victims of criminal or tortious acts, there is no principle of public policy which requires a third party (the insurers) to compensate them (by indemnifying the insured) in circumstances not provided for in the contract of insurance. The victims of motorists have been made relevant by the intervention of legislation. The Road Traffic Act 1988 not only requires motorists to have a certain level of cover against third party liability, but gives the third party rights to pursue a claim against the insurers directly and restricts the ability of the insurers to limit their liability to third parties.[169] The significance of the legislation is illustrated by the Court of Appeal's decision in *Charlton v Fisher*.[170] A driver deliberately – although without an intention of causing injury – steered into another car in a car park. This caused injury to a person in the other car, but because the incident took place on private land the Road Traffic Act 1988 did not apply and the driver's insurer was held not to be liable because the injury was the result of a deliberate criminal act.

4.4. The Relevance of the Insured's Negligence

The early marine cases on crew negligence laid down the principle that negligence leading to loss by an insured peril – fire,[171] or a peril of the seas[172] – was to be disregarded and the proximate cause of the loss was to be treated as the insured peril. The cases were codified by the Marine Insurance Act 1906, section 55(2)(a), which provides that, 'unless the policy provides, [the insurer] is liable for any loss proximately caused by a

[168] See *Hardy v Motor Insurers' Bureau* [1964] QB 745, 769–70 (Diplock LJ). This returns us to arguments that were rehearsed earlier in the chapter, where it was seen that, on occasion, the civil courts do see deterrence as part of their function.

[169] However, even before the introduction of compulsory third party liability insurance in 1930, the courts were seeking to protect victims of motorists: *Tinline v White Cross Insurance Association Ltd* [1921] 3 KB 327. That the distinction does not rest simply on this issue of insurance is also suggested by the notion that the courts may apply the forfeiture rule less rigorously in motor manslaughter cases: *Jones v Roberts* [1995] 2 FLR 422, 425 (Judge Kolbert).

[170] [2002] QB 578. See ch 14 for further discussion of this case.

[171] *Busk v Royal Exchange Assurance Co* (1818) 2 B & Ad 73.

[172] *Trinder Anderson & Co v Thames and Mersey Insurance Co* [1898] 2 QB 114.

peril insured against, even though the loss would not have happened but for the misconduct or negligence of the master or crew'. Negligence is therefore not a 'peril' as such, but rather is a contributory factor to the manner in which an insured peril has occurred. The same principle has been applied to property policies. In *Harris v Poland*,[173] the insured lit a fire in the fireplace, forgetting that she had previously hidden her jewellery there. The court decided that, while her actions were probably negligent, she did not act intentionally, and the insurers were therefore liable under a policy which covered 'loss or damage by fire'.

Most policies these days contain a requirement that the insured takes 'reasonable care to avoid loss'. Such clauses were first found in liability policies, and it is apparent that an attempt to exclude negligence makes no sense because the policy covers liability to a third party and that depends on the insured having been negligent.[174] In a case on an employer's liability policy, it was held that the insurers were liable in spite of the presence of such a clause unless the conduct was reckless, which required the insured to have acted

> with actual recognition … that a danger exists, and not caring whether or not it is averted. The purpose of the condition is to ensure that the insured will not, because he is covered against loss by the policy refrain from taking precautions which he knows ought to be taken.[175]

The application of reasonable care provisions to first party property cover was first tested in *Sofi v Prudential Assurance Co Ltd*.[176] A theft policy required the insured to 'take all reasonable steps to safeguard any property insured'. The insured locked jewellery worth £42,035 in the glove compartment of his car and then left the car in a car park at Dover Castle for 15 minutes. During this time the jewels were stolen. The insurers were liable because it could not be shown that the insured had acted recklessly in thinking that the jewels were safer in the car.[177] The Court focused on the fact that the policy covered both third party liabilities and first party cover, and the meaning afforded to the reasonable care clause in the liability section of the policy could not vary in the property section. However, since the decision in *Sofi* there has been a consistent line of authority holding that a reasonable care clause has the same meaning of recklessness, in liability, hybrid and pure property policies. The test for recklessness is subjective, the questions being whether the insured was aware of the risk and deliberately courted that risk.

There has been a finding of recklessness in a small number of cases. In *Gunns v Par Insurance Brokers*,[178] the insurer was not held liable because the insured's conduct was reckless. The insured, a jeweller, went away for the weekend, leaving valuables in a safe, which the insurers had previously declared to be unsatisfactory, and without activating the alarm

[173] [1941] 1 KB 462.

[174] *Tinline v White Cross Insurance Association Ltd* [1921] 3 KB 327, 330 (Bailhache J). See also *Shaw v Robberds, Hawkes and Stone* (1837) 6 Ad & E 75, 84 (Lord Denman CJ); Marine Insurance Act 1906, s 55(2)(a). See the discussion in ch 10 above of *Cornish v Accident Insurance Company* (1883) 23 QBD 453.

[175] *Fraser v BN Furman (Productions) Ltd* [1967] 1 WLR 898, 906 (Diplock LJ).

[176] [1993] 2 Lloyd's Rep 559. See the comment of the Insurance Ombudsman Bureau (IOB) on this case: *Annual Report 1993*, cited in P Hart (ed), *Digest of Annual Reports and Bulletins* (London, IOB, 1999). Prior to *Sofi*, the IOB had taken a view of such clauses that was more favourable to insurers than was taken by the Court of Appeal. On clauses excluding liability where the driver leaves the ignition key in the car, see *Hayward v Norwich Union Insurance Ltd* [2001] 1 All ER (Comm) 545.

[177] The insurers' suspicions were raised because this was not the first time that the same property had been stolen. Fraud was not pleaded, however.

[178] [1997] 1 Lloyd's Rep 173.

system. In addition, shortly before the theft, he had reported a suspicion that he was being followed. In *Devco Holder Ltd v Legal and General Assurance Society Ltd*,[179] the insured was held to have acted recklessly by leaving the keys in the ignition of his unlocked Ferrari. In *Lambert v Keymood Ltd*,[180] the insured's conduct in lighting bonfires near to buildings was held to be reckless given that there had been warnings to the insured as to the dangers of this conduct.

[179] [1993] 2 Lloyd's Rep 567.
[180] [1999] Lloyd's Rep IR 80.

11

Claims Procedure

1. Claims

It was seen in chapter eight above that a policy may contain a range of claims conditions, and these are generally expressed to be conditions precedent. Such conditions must be strictly complied with by the insured when claiming payment to cover an insured loss. Looked at another way, these terms may be described as conditions precedent to the liability of the insurers so that in the event of a breach the insurers' liability does not attach. Whether or not there has been a breach of such a condition is a question of construction, and in construing the particular term the court will have regard to its purpose.[1] Insurers typically argue that these clauses are important for a number of reasons: they allow insurers to investigate claims as soon as possible; they enable them to minimise any future potential losses which may arise; and they provide certainty as to what other claims (including third party claims) may be in the pipeline. Conditions precedent to recovery generally lay down requirements as to the requisite notice to be given to the insurers in the event of a loss; the particulars of the loss to be furnished by the insured; and, in the event of a dispute arising between the parties, that settlement should be by way of arbitration.

1.1. Determining the Nature of Claims Conditions

Recent case law points to an insured-friendly approach being adopted by the courts towards the determination of the nature of a claims condition. In chapter eight we saw that in *Alfred McAlpine plc v BAI (Run-Off) Ltd*,[2] the Court of Appeal, importing the terminology of 'innominate terms' from the general law of contract, classified a notification clause – condition 1(a) in the policy, which required the insured to give notice of a claim under the policy 'as soon as possible' – as a term which fell short of a condition precedent. However,

[1] *Stoneham v Ocean, Railway and General Accident Insurance Co* (1887) 19 QBD 237, 239 (Mathew J). See also *Welsh v Royal Exchange Assurance* [1939] 1 KB 294. A claims condition does not amount to a forfeiture clause and so the courts do not have equitable jurisdiction to relieve the insured of his obligation to comply: *Diab v Regent Insurance Co Ltd* [2006] UKPC 29.

[2] [2000] Lloyd's Rep IR 352.

it is noteworthy that the clause in question was not described as a condition precedent, unlike other terms in the policy. Waller LJ explained that the term was not so fundamental that its breach amounted to a repudiation of the whole contract. It lacked the quality of 'essentiality':

> Condition 1(a) is … an innominate term. Breach of it, however serious, would be unlikely to amount to a repudiation of the whole contract of insurance. Furthermore, it is not a term the breach of which, or any breach of which, would entitle the insurer not to pay the claim because that would simply make it a condition precedent. But, in my view, a breach which demonstrated an intention not to continue to make a claim, or which has very serious consequences for BAI, should be such as to entitle BAI to defeat the claim. If a term is a condition precedent to liability, any breach defeats liability but does not lead to a repudiation of the whole contract. I see no reason why although a term is not a condition precedent so that any breach defeats liability, it cannot be construed as a term where a serious breach defeats liability.[3]

In support of his conclusion, the judge cited *Trans-Pacific Insurance Co (Australia) Ltd v Grand Union Insurance Co Ltd*,[4] where the Supreme Court of New South Wales took the view that a notice clause could not have the 'quality of essentiality such that any breach thereof entitled [the insurer] to terminate the contract'. As has been seen, this view was also taken by the majority of the Court of Appeal in *Friends Provident v Sirius International Insurance Corporation*.[5] It therefore appears settled that claims conditions not expressed to be conditions precedent are viewed as innominate terms. The rights of insurers will depend upon whether the insured's conduct is such as to amount to the repudiation of the policy as a whole or upon whether the breach is minor enough in nature so that the appropriate remedy lies in damages. In *Friends Provident*, Waller LJ observed that repudiation of the policy is likely to arise only 'in extreme circumstances', such as where there has been 'consistent breach over a number of claims'.[6]

1.2. Notice of Loss

Notification clauses are of three broad types: fixed term; immediate; and as soon as possible or practicable. Under the first type, the policy will require notification within a fixed time period following the occurrence of the insured peril or of an event that may give rise to a claim. At one time these provisions were construed strictly. In *Cassel v Lancashire & Yorkshire Insurance Co*,[7] the insured was involved in a canoeing accident, but his injuries were latent for some eight months. His claim under an accident policy failed because he had not complied with the 14-day notice period specified in the policy. In *Diab v Regent Insurance Co Ltd*,[8] however, Lord Scott expressed the view that, in the general law of contract, time was not of the essence and it probably sufficed if the insurers received sufficient notice to be

[3] ibid [34].

[4] (1990) 6 ANZ Ins Cas 60-949.

[5] [2006] Lloyd's Rep IR 45e. See J Lowry and P Rawlings, 'Conditions Precedent in Insurance Contracts' [2009] *Journal of Business Law* 275; J Lowry and P Rawlings, 'Claims and Conditions Precedent to liability' [2008] *Journal of Business Law* 179.

[6] It has been held that the insured's fraud in his breach of the term will not render the breach repudiatory: see *K/S Merc-Skandia XXXXII v Certain Lloyd's Underwriters* [2000] Lloyd's Rep IR 694.

[7] (1885) 1 TLR 495. For an extreme example, see *Adamson & Sons v Liverpool & London & Globe Insurance Co Ltd* [1953] 2 Lloyd's Rep 355.

[8] [2006] UKPC 29.

able to investigate the claim. It might be thought that the classification of a notice clause as a condition precedent might be sufficient to make time of the essence, but the point is probably not of great significance in that fixed term clauses have fallen into disuse. 'Immediate' clauses have not been taken at their word but have instead been construed as requiring notice as soon as possible or practicable.

The approach of the courts to such clauses depends upon the nature of the policy and also whether timely notification was something that could be controlled by the insured. In *Verelst's Administratrix v Motor Union Insurance Co*,[9] a motor policy contained a condition which provided that in the event of a loss 'the insured or the insured's personal representative ... shall give notice ... to the ... company of such loss as soon as possible after it has come to the knowledge of the insured or the insured's personal representative'. While visiting India, the insured was killed in a motoring accident. Her administratrix did not know of the insurance company with which the insured had effected cover until nearly a year after the accident had occurred, when she came across the policy while sorting out old papers belonging to the insured. The insurers sought to repudiate liability for breach of the notice requirement. It was held that the administratrix could recover. Roche J construed the clause to mean 'as soon as possible to the legal representative under the existing circumstances which prevailed and applied'.[10] The question of knowledge is of particular importance in liability insurance, and is discussed in chapter 15 in that context. It suffices to note here that it is not fully resolved whether the test is objective (would a reasonable person have known of the facts), subjective (did the insured actually know the facts) or hybrid (would a reasonable person in the insured's position have known the facts). In practice there is likely to be little difference in outcome whichever test is used.[11]

A contrasting decision is *Aspen Insurance UK Ltd v Pectel Ltd*,[12] where the insured, a specialised construction contractor with expertise in the removal of asbestos, was insured under a combined liability policy with a 'retroactive date' of 11 February 2004 so that only acts of negligence occurring after that date were insured. Condition 4 set out the claims procedure, and condition 4(a) required the insured to give immediate written notice to brokers of: '(i) any occurrence which may give rise to indemnity under this insurance'. Condition 13, entitled 'Observance', went on to state that 'The liability of Underwriters shall be conditional on ... The Assured paying in full the premium demanded and observing the terms and conditions of this insurance'. On 9 February 2004 the insured commenced preparatory work on the South Tunnel of BT's Deep Level Tunnel Facility in Manchester, and work on the North Tunnel was commenced on 22 March 2004. A fire occurred in South Tunnel on the morning of 29 March 2004. The insurers were not notified of the fire until 22 March 2007. Teare J held, in a trial on preliminary issues, that the insurers were not liable. The retroactive clause did not provide a defence. While it was the case that work on the South Tunnel had commenced on 9 February 2004, the fire arose in the North Tunnel only. The claims condition required immediate notification of any occurrence which may give rise to indemnity: that meant notification 'with all reasonable speed considering the circumstances of the case' of any occurrence in respect of which there was a real as opposed to a fanciful risk of the underwriters having to indemnify the insured, and in determining

[9] (1950) 21 Ll L Rep 227.

[10] ibid 229.

[11] A point made by Longmore LJ in *Faraday Reinsurance Co Ltd v Howden North America Inc* [2012] EWCA Civ 980.

[12] [2008] EWHC 2804 (Comm).

whether there was such a risk, the court was to apply an objective test, taking into account the knowledge that the insured possessed in order to determine the extent to which the insured was aware of, and hence capable of notifying, occurrences which may give rise to an indemnity. On the facts, notification should have been made immediately, or at the very latest by November 2004, when it was clear that the materials used by the assured were under investigation. Compliance was a condition precedent to liability, as the commercial purpose of the condition was to allow the insurers to receive early notification of any event which could give rise to a claim. Teare J further held that: (a) a breach of the condition did not affect the policy as a whole, but only the claim in question; and (b) the effect of condition 13 was not necessarily to require all conditions to be treated as conditions precedent, but condition 4(a) was appropriately regarded as a condition precedent.

In liability insurance, the policy will normally require the insured to give notice to the insurers of the occurrence of circumstances events 'likely to give rise to a claim'.[13]

In commercial policies, written notice is normally required, often via the brokers,[14] and such notice must be 'sufficiently clear and unambiguous that it leaves the reasonable recipient in no reasonable doubt that the assured is by the communication purporting to give notice'.[15] In consumer cases, it is increasingly common for insurers to accept oral telephone notifications. It is not necessary for the notice to be given personally by the insured. It has been held that where the police have communicated notice of the loss to the insurers, the insured is relieved from the duty of notifying them personally, even if personal notification is expressly required by the policy, because 'it would be a futile thing to require the [insured] himself to give them the self-same information. The law never compels a person to do that which is useless and unnecessary.'[16]

Breach of a notification provision is fatal to a claim where the provision is a condition precedent. If the clause is not so classified, the insured has a valid claim despite late notification and the insurers' remedy is generally restricted to damages provided they can show loss. In *Friends Provident*, Waller LJ thought that the possibility of a claim for damages was 'illusory', while the majority of the Court of Appeal thought that the calculation of damages would be possible, such as where the insurers' subrogation rights have been lost. However, in cases where there has been late notification to liability insurers of a third party claim which might or might not have been successfully defended, both Mance LJ and Sir William Aldous admitted that damages would be purely speculative. Damages were sought in *Milton Keynes BC v Nulty*,[17] where the insured electrician failed to inform his liability insurers of a fire at local authority premises where he had been working. The insurers did not become aware of the fire until the following year, by which time the insured had died and proceedings were brought directly against the insurers by the local authority (standing in the shoes of the insured) on the basis that the fire had been caused by the insured's negligence in discarding a lit cigarette end. The insured's failure to notify meant that it had not been

[13] See ch 15 below for the operation of liability policies.

[14] In the absence of any authorisation given to the broker by the insurers to receive notice for them, notice to the broker alone is ineffective: *Quadra Commodities SA v XL Insurance Company SE* [2022] EWHC 431 (Comm).

[15] Gloster J at first instance in *HLB Kidsons v Lloyd's Underwriters* [2008] Lloyd's Rep IR 237, applied in *Kajima UK Engineering Ltd v Underwriter Insurance Co Ltd* [2008] Lloyd's Rep IR 391.

[16] *Barrett Bros (Taxis) Ltd v Davies (Lickiss and Milestone Motor Policies at Lloyd's, Third Parties)* [1966] 2 Lloyd's Rep 1, 5 (Lord Denning MR). The decision was questioned obiter in *AXA Insurance UK Plc v Thermonex Ltd* [2012] EWHC B10 (Mercantile), but in the context of a liability policy where notice was given by the claimant against the insured.

[17] [2011] EWHC 2847 (TCC). The point did not arise on appeal, [2013] EWCA Civ 15.

possible for the insurers to undertake a contemporaneous investigation of the causes of the fire, and they asserted that but for the breach they might have been able to demonstrate that the fire had been the result of one or more causes not relating to the insured's conduct, eg a fault in the building's electrical system or intrusion by thieves. The court thought that the prospects of success were unlikely, but deducted an admittedly unscientific 15 per cent by way of damages for breach of contract from the sum awarded.

1.3. Particulars of the Loss and Co-operation Clauses

In addition to notification, the insured will generally be under a duty to submit particulars of the loss to the insurers and generally to co-operate with the insurers in the handling of the claim. What is required will depend upon the nature of the policy, but it should be borne in mind that if the clause is framed as a condition precedent then any failure to comply will defeat the claim, whereas if the clause is not framed as a condition precedent then breach will not preclude recovery but the insurers can recover damages for breach if they can prove loss by reason of the breach. As with conditions relating to notice periods, terms in a consumer contract which stipulate the required particulars to be supplied to the insurers as proof of the loss will need to satisfy the Consumer Rights Act 2015. However, that may be relatively easy in the light of *Parker v National Farmers Union Mutual Insurance Society Ltd*,[18] where it was held that the obligations under a co-operation clause are generally justifiable in order to allow the insurers to process a claim properly and that in any event the insured is protected by ICOBS 8, under which insurers must act reasonably in dealing with claims.

In a first party cover for property or other damage, the insured's duty is to provide sufficient detail to enable the insurers 'to form a judgment as to whether or not he has sustained a loss'.[19] A condition that 'full particulars' of the loss must be given has been defined as meaning 'the best particulars which the assured can reasonably give'.[20]

The question whether an insurance company can claim damages for breach of a claims co-operation clause not framed as a condition precedent was discussed in *Porter v Zurich Insurance Co*,[21] where P insured his house and possessions with Zurich for 12 months from 12 September 2000. The policy excluded loss caused by 'any wilful or malicious act by a member of the family'. The policy also contained a claims co-operation clause following a loss. P suffered from a persistent delusional disorder. On 27 March 2001 he had been drinking heavily, and decided to commit suicide by setting fire to his house. Having set a fire, he changed his mind and escaped, but the house was seriously damaged. The house had to be boarded up, but in the following months there were three thefts of possessions from it. Claims were made for the fire damage and also for the thefts. The insurers relied upon public policy and the 'wilful act' exclusion to defeat the fire claim. With respect to the theft claims, they relied upon P's failure to co-operate with loss adjusters as a result of his failure to produce documents and also refusing to allow access to the house. Coulson J held that the insurers were not liable for the fire claim. An insured could not at common law recover for a loss deliberately caused by his own criminal act, or under the policy for his

[18] [2012] EWHC 2156 (Comm).
[19] *Mason v Harvey* (1853) 8 Exch 819, 820–21 (Pollock CB).
[20] ibid.
[21] [2009] EWHC 376 (QB).

own wilful act, if he had intended to cause the loss or if he acted with reckless disregard to the consequences of his actions. The insured could nevertheless recover if he could prove insanity within the legal test laid down by the M'Naghten Rules,[22] namely that he was so insane that he was not legally responsible for his actions. That test had not been satisfied on the facts: the insured knew exactly what he was doing. The theft claims could go ahead to a hearing on quantum. Although the insured was in clear breach of the claims co-operation clause, the insurers had not shown that those breaches caused any loss recoverable by way of damages. The insurers had merely alleged that some of the goods claimed to have been stolen were also said to have been fire damaged for the purposes of the fire claim, but such duplication did not give any automatic defence. The insurers had to prove actual loss flowing from the failure to co-operate.

In liability insurance the duty will typically be more extensive, given that the insurers will be required to ascertain whether the insured has incurred any liability to the third party and to defend any proceedings. Co-operation provisions frequently found in liability insurance policies[23] will require the insured to co-operate by, for example, undertaking not to settle with a third party, or by undertaking not to take any other steps which may prejudice the insurers' position. A common example is a clause prohibiting the insured from admitting liability to a third party. Breach of the insured's duty to co-operate will, if expressed as a condition precedent to liability, defeat the claim.[24] In *Shinedean Ltd v Alldown Demolition (London) Ltd*,[25] ADL was employed as contractors by Shinedean to carry out demolition and excavation work at a residential property in 2002. In doing so, a neighbour's wall partially collapsed. Shinedean satisfied the claim for damages from the neighbour and then brought proceedings against ADL for the increased costs of their development. Shinedean obtained a default judgment against ADL, who had gone into liquidation, in 2004. In the same proceedings, the claimants also claimed against the contractors' insurers, declaring that they were entitled to an indemnity under the contractors' indemnity insurance policy pursuant to what is now the Third Parties (Rights against Insurers) Act 2010. There was a requirement, in ADL's insurance policy with Axa, that the insured must deliver to them all such proofs and information relating to the claim as might reasonably be required and to tender all necessary information and assistance to enable Axa to settle or resist a claim. It took more than two years for the contractors to supply Axa with the relevant information. The question for the courts was whether the insurers were entitled to deny that indemnity, on the basis that the contractors had failed to provide them with information within a reasonable time.

At first instance,[26] it was held that since the insurers had not suffered any material prejudice on account of the delay, then it could be regarded that the information was given within a reasonable time, therefore meaning that the insurers were obliged to indemnify. On appeal, May LJ, in upholding the insurers' appeal, stated that there was no absolute principle which included or excluded material prejudice as a consideration that was relevant to the determination of a 'reasonable time'. Instead, he advocated a broader test:

> [E]ach case turns on its own facts but there is no determinative principle that a duty on the insured to provide relevant information within a reasonable time will not be broken if, in the end, it turns

[22] See *M'Naghten's Case* (1843) 10 Cl & Fin 200.
[23] See *AIG Europe (Ireland) Ltd v Faraday Capital Ltd* [2006] EWHC 2707 (Comm).
[24] *London Guarantee Co v Fearnley* (1880) 5 App Cas 911.
[25] [2006] EWCA Civ 939.
[26] [2005] EWHC (Comm) 2319.

> out there is no prejudice to insurers. Insurers are entitled to know where they stand, and under this policy Axa were entitled to receive the information in good time, whether they were in the end prejudiced by failure to achieve this or not.[27]

Thus, it was easy for May LJ to conclude that to have provided the relevant information nearly two and a half years late, particularly when it was available much earlier, was 'obviously unreasonably late'.[28]

The duty of utmost good faith is of no assistance to insurers in this context. In *K/S Merc-Scandia XXXXII v Certain Lloyd's Underwriters, The Mercandian Continent*,[29] the insured boat builder, based in Trinidad, faced a claim by the purchaser of a defective vessel. One of the insured's employees entered into an ad hoc agreement with the purchaser for any proceedings to be brought in the English courts. The insured received information – which was incorrect, as it turned out – that proceedings in Trinidad might lead to a lower damages award, and he forged a letter which predated the jurisdiction agreement under which the authority of any employee to negotiate with the purchaser was removed. The letter was relied upon by the insurers to contest the jurisdiction of the English courts over the dispute, which, but for the agreement, would not have been available to the purchaser. The insurers were held not to be able to refuse to indemnify the insured despite their wasted efforts in contesting jurisdiction. There was a co-operation clause, but it was not a condition precedent and so the only remedy was damages, and while it was possible that the insurers could have proved loss on the facts, no claim for damages had been made. The alternative claim was for breach of the duty of utmost good faith under the then unamended version of section 17 of the Marine Insurance Act 1906, where the only remedy for breach of the duty was avoidance of the contract. Longmore LJ felt that it was necessary to construe section 17 consistently with the contract itself, and ruled that the remedy of avoidance was available to the insurers only where they also had a right to treat the policy as repudiated for breach: in other words, the right to terminate for breach and the right to avoid were alternative remedies and the latter was not available in the absence of the former. As a claims clause was innominate, and the breach was not repudiatory, there was no right to avoid. It should be added that the removal of the avoidance remedy from section 17 of the 1906 Act by section 14 of the Insurance Act 2015 has removed the alternative right to avoid, and the redesignation of section 17 as an interpretative provision means that it now has nothing to add to the insurers' rights in this regard.

1.4. Waiver of Breach of Condition

Breach of claims conditions, in the same way as breach of all other conditions, can be waived by the insurers, although if the clause is in the form of a condition precedent then breach automatically discharges the insurers and their liability will be reinstated only if the insured can make good the elements of estoppel.[30] A particular question arising with claims clauses is whether an insurer who has denied liability for a claim by reason of, for example, breach of the duty of fair presentation or on coverage grounds thereby discharges

[27] ibid [21].
[28] ibid.
[29] [2001] Lloyd's Rep IR 802. See also *Agapitos v Agnew, The Aegeon* [2002] Lloyd's Rep 42, discussed below. See HY Yeo, 'Post-Contractual Good Faith – Change in Judicial Attitude?' [2003] *MLR* 425.
[30] See ch 8 above.

the insured from its obligations to comply with claims provisions. Thus, the insured is able to rebut the insurers' defence, but can the insurers then rely upon failure to comply with the claims clause? The English courts have taken what might be thought to be the rather harsh view that denying liability does not amount to an unequivocal representation that, if liability is subsequently established, claims obligations will not be relied upon. That approach was adopted by the Privy Council in *Diab Regent Insurance Co Ltd*,[31] where the defence taken by the insurers but later abandoned was that the claim was fraudulent, and in *Lexington Insurance Co v Multinacional de Seguros SA*,[32] where reinsurers were held to be able to rely upon a failure to co-operate in the form of a settlement by the reinsured without their permission even though the reinsurers had earlier refused to provide indemnity. By contrast, in *Ted Baker Plc v Axa Insurance UK Plc (No 2)*,[33] the insurers denied liability for theft of clothes by an employee of the insured, on the ground that the insured had not insured against fidelity losses. In earlier proceedings[34] it was held that general coverage for theft in the policy encompassed fidelity – a good illustration of the principle that coverage is determined by an objective interpretation of the policy and not by reference to the insurers' subjective views as to what cover had been paid for by the premium[35] – and in the second action the insurers relied upon breach of co-operation provisions following their denial of liability. The Court of Appeal, reversing Eder J, on this point held that the facts of the case had given rise to a 'duty to speak' on the part of the insurers independently of the duty of utmost good faith, although Christopher Clarke LJ was provisionally of the view that the duty to speak might be of enhanced importance in insurance cases.[36] Nevertheless, the lesson for insureds is that even if the insurers deny liability, it is sensible to treat that denial as a nullity and to adhere to claims obligations in pursuing the insurers.

1.5. Arbitration Clauses

It is very common for commercial insurance contracts and reinsurances to provide for the resolution of disputes in arbitration. It is often said that arbitration is cheaper and speedier than litigation, although in practice this is often untrue in that: the parties must pay the arbitrators as well as arrange the venue; the pool of arbitrators able to resolve complex disputes is limited, so there may be considerable delay in assembling an appropriate tribunal (typically of three members); and there is greater scope for the parties to arbitration than litigation to use procedural devices to delay the process and to challenge the ultimate award. The main advantage of arbitration for the parties is that the proceedings and the award are private and confidential, so that no precedent is set on policy wordings and the business secrets of the insured can remain so. The use of arbitration has indeed often been criticised for depriving the common law of authority on points of law that frequently arise.

Arbitration clauses in consumer and small business policies were considered by the Law Reform Committee in 1957, and its report[37] concluded that insurers were placed

[31] [2006] UKPC 29.
[32] [2008] EWHC 1170 (Comm).
[33] [2017] EWCA Civ 4097.
[34] *Ted Baker Plc v Axa Insurance UK Ltd* [2012] EWHC 1406 (Comm).
[35] See ch 9 above.
[36] All of this was to no avail on the facts: the insured's claim was dismissed on the basis that each of the thefts was below the excess imposed by the policy so there was no recovery.
[37] *Fifth Report on Conditions and Exceptions in Insurance Policies* (Cmnd 62, 1957).

at considerable advantage in that legal aid was unavailable. The Association of British Insurers and Lloyd's announced that their members would not enforce arbitration clauses in cases where the insured indicated a desire to have the issue of liability, as opposed to *quantum*, determined by a court. That remains the position for many small business policies. Consumer arbitration clauses are now governed by sections 89–91 of the Arbitration Act 1996. These provisions bring arbitration clauses within the ambit of the Consumer Rights Act 2015, and the effect is that an arbitration clause is automatically unfair and void if the sum claimed is less than £5000[38] and in other cases the clause may be void if it causes a significant imbalance in the rights of the parties.[39] In practice, arbitration clauses are not included in consumer contracts.

An issue that arises with respect to an arbitration clause contained in an insurance contract is the question of its validity where it is claimed that the policy is vitiated as a result of, for example, non-disclosure or lack of insurable interest. An arbitration clause is, by virtue of section 7 of the Arbitration Act 1996, an independent undertaking in its own right, so that as long as the dispute falls within the scope of the clause, it is irrelevant whether the insurer has relied upon any defence challenging the existence of the contract of insurance. At one time there was doubt as to the position where the insurer sought to rely upon a fraudulent claim. In *Super Chem Products Ltd v American Life and General Insurance Co Ltd*,[40] the issue was whether the insurers could require compliance with the claims clauses in the policy while, at the same time, alleging fraud. The insured had a material damage and business interruption policy. The factory in question was damaged by fire and the insurers pleaded, inter alia, arson. They also sought to rely on the insured's failure to commence proceedings within 12 months as stipulated by the policy. The Privy Council held that the plea of arson did not amount to a repudiation of the policy. In so holding, the board overruled the much criticised dicta of Viscount Haldane LC in *Jureidini v National British and Irish Millers Insurance Co Ltd*,[41] to the effect that an insurer who repudiates liability on the basis of fraud and arson cannot 'insist on a subordinate term of the contract still being enforced'.[42] It is now clear, in the light of *Super Chem*, that an allegation by the insurers that the insured has been guilty of a fraudulent claim does not prevent them from relying upon the arbitration clause.[43]

2. The Insurers' Duties in Handling Claims

It has already been noted that ICOBS 8 requires insurers to act reasonably in handling claims and in reaching any decision to deny liability. Independently of ICOBS, the common

[38] Unfair Arbitration Agreements (Specified Amount) Order 1999, SI 1999/2167.

[39] See *Mylcrist Builders Ltd v Buck* [2008] EWHC 2172 (TCC).

[40] [2004] Lloyd's Rep IR 446 (PC). Noted by D Friedmann [2004] *LQR* 407.

[41] [1915] AC 499.

[42] ibid 505. Lord Steyn in *Super Chem* was at pains to align the insurance law position with that of the general law of contract. See also *Port Jackson Stevedoring Pty Ltd v Salmond and Spraggon (Australia) Pty Ltd* [1981] 1 WLR 138 (PC).

[43] In *Diab v Regent Insurance Co Ltd* [2006] UKPC 29, the Privy Council rejected the argument that a denial of liability for fraud had the effect of waiver of compliance with notification clauses, or at least operated as an estoppel against the insurers. Such denial did not constitute either an election being made not to rely on the notice clause or an unequivocal representation that it would not so rely.

law has recognised that any contracting party with a discretion under the contract cannot exercise that discretion in an arbitrary or capricious fashion. That principle, long before its final articulation by the Supreme Court in *Braganza v BP Shipping Ltd*,[44] had been applied in insurance cases, and although there is no clear authority on the point, it is very likely that the principle has been reinforced by the duty of utmost good faith imposed by section 17 of the Marine Insurance Act 1906.[45]

There are two groups of cases where the discretions may be conferred. The first is the policy provision whereby the insured must submit such proofs of loss and other documents as demanded by the insurers. Early cases holding that the discretion was absolute[46] are probably no longer reliable, and more recent cases have decided that the insurers cannot deny information unreasonably.[47] That will be the case if what is sought is irrelevant to the claim itself or if they have in some way indicated that they would not require information that is later demanded. The latter possibility arose in *Widefree Ltd v Brit Insurance Ltd*.[48] The claimant operated a jeweller's shop in Hatton Garden, and held a policy against 'loss or damage from any cause whatsoever'. The policy excluded 'Property Insured found to be missing at stockholding where the Insured is unable to prove the date and circumstances of any loss' and it also contained a claims co-operation clause in the following terms:

> The Insured shall in case of a loss or damage and as condition precedent to any right of indemnification in respect thereof give to the Insurers such information and evidence as to the property lost or damaged as the Insurers may reasonably require and as may be in the Insured's power.

On 9 October 2008, two Arab women came into the shop, but left without buying anything. On 22 October 2008, Mr Abrahams discovered that a ring worth about £100,000 was missing: this came to light when he wished to show the ring to another customer. The claimant believed that the ring had been stolen by the two women. There were five CCTV cameras in operation in the shop on 9 October 2008, but only Camera 2 showed the incident which gave rise to suspicions of theft by the women. The police advised Mr and Mrs Abrahams that Camera 2 was the only relevant camera, and to have the footage from Camera 2 downloaded to DVD. Loss adjusters visited the shop on 6 November 2008 and asked to see the Camera 2 footage. Thereafter the footage on the other cameras was wiped. The insurers denied liability on the grounds of the unexpected loss exclusion and breach of the claims co-operation clause in that the insured had not retained the CCTV footage from all five cameras. The defences were dismissed. Peter Leaver QC held that the insured had proved on the balance of probabilities that there had been a theft on 9 October 2008. Further, the clause had not been triggered because the loss had not been found at stockholding, but rather in response to a request by a customer. He further found that there was no breach of the claims co-operation clause. It was the duty of the insured not to destroy evidence which might reasonably be required by the insurers, but the insurers had not asked for CCTV footage other than from Camera 2, and after the visit on 6 October 2008 it was reasonable for

[44] [2015] UKSC 17.

[45] That was suggested in two reinsurance cases, *Gan Insurance Co Ltd v Tai Ping Insurance Co Ltd (Nos 2 and 3)* [2001] Lloyd's Rep IR 667 and *Eagle Star Insurance Co Ltd v Cresswell* [2004] EWCA Civ 602, discussed in ch 18 below. For the position in Australia, where there is an implied term of utmost good faith, see *Baulderstone Hornibrook Engineering Pty Ltd v Gordian Runoff Ltd* [2006] NSWSC 223, where it was asserted that any policy discretion must be exercised honestly, bona fide and reasonably.

[46] eg *Welch v Royal Exchange Assurance* [1939] 1 KB 294.

[47] *Moore v Woolsey* (1854) 8 E & B 243; *Napier v UNUM Ltd* [1996] 2 Lloyd's Rep 550; *Quinn Direct Insurance Ltd v The Law Society of England and Wales* [2009] EWHC 2588 (Ch).

[48] [2010] All ER 14.

the insured to have wiped the other cameras. The clause was triggered by a request from the insurers, and in the absence of any request it could not be said that the insured had failed to comply. A similar and more recent decision from Australia, *Diamond World Jewellers Pty Ltd v Catlin Australia Pty Ltd*,[49] something of a comedy of errors, makes the same point. The insured's jewellery store was raided by a number of youths, who threatened the staff into handing over the contents of locked cabinets and themselves broke open glass cabinets. One of the thieves cut himself in the process, so that he could easily be traced by DNA, but much of the jewellery was dropped by the thieves in effecting their escape. The thieves were drug users, doubtless contributing to their incompetence. The insurers demanded records of what had been stolen, even though they were aware that the insured's record-keeping was poor and that the information would not be readily obtainable. To make matters worse, the insured's broker had inexplicably advised the insured to clean up the premises, to melt down jewellery recovered after the robbery and to effect repairs before the insurers had been given an opportunity to examine the scene for themselves. Both parties were held to have been in breach of their duties of utmost good faith on those facts, although in the event the insured was able to recover for loss that it could prove had been suffered and was denied recovery for alleged loss that could not be proved.

The second group of cases where a discretion may be in play is where the insurers have a discretion in evaluating the information provided to them. This is particularly important in claims under accident policies for total and permanent disablement (TPD), which often provide that the insurers must be satisfied that there is TPD. The Australian and New Zealand courts have ruled that the insurers' assessment must be carried out fairly, and that although the court could not substitute its own commercial judgement for that of the insurers, the court would at least ensure that the insurers had reached their decision by reference to relevant considerations and had disregarded matters unconnected to the merits of the claim.[50]

3. Fraudulent Claims by the Insured

The law on fraudulent claims has been transformed by two developments, one common law and one statutory. The common development, in the form of the decision of the Supreme Court in *Versloot Dredging BV v HDI Gerling Industrie Versicherung AG*,[51] has been a reclassification – and narrowing – of the forms of conduct that amount to fraudulent claims. The second, sections 12 and 13 of the Insurance Act 2015, has clarified a complex mass of common law authorities as to the remedies open to an insurer following the making of a fraudulent claim.[52]

[49] [2021] NSWSC 1431.

[50] *MetLife Insurance Ltd v Sandstrom* [2021] NSWCA 123; *Van Der Noll v Sovereign Assurance Co Ltd* [2013] NZHC 3051.

[51] [2016] UKSC 45.

[52] R Aikens, 'When Is a "Fraudulent Claim" only a "Collateral Lie"?' [2017] *Lloyd's Maritime and Commercial Law Quarterly* 339; P Rawlings and J Lowry, 'Insurance Fraud and the Role of the Civil Law' (2017) 80 *MLR* 525; L Zhao, 'Fraudulent Claims and Good Faith in Insurance Law' (2018) 24 *Journal of International Maritime Law* 131; E Katsampouka, 'Exemplary Damages and Insurance Fraud' (2019) 135 *LQR* 380; J Tarr, 'Grappling with Fraudulent Insurance Claims and "Collateral Lies"' [2019] *Journal of Business Law* 43; K Richards, 'Time's Up for Wholly Fraudulent Insurance Claims: The Case for New Statutory Remedies' [2020] *Journal of Business Law* 580.

3.1. What Is a Fraudulent Claim?

3.1.1. The Meaning of 'Fraud'[53]

A statement in a claim is fraudulent if the insured either knew it to be false or else was reckless as to its truth.[54] Dishonesty is required; mere carelessness will not suffice. Dishonesty was defined by Lord Hutton in *Twinsectra v Yardley*[55] in terms accepted for the purposes of insurance by Eder J in *Aviva Insurance Ltd v Brown*.[56] Dishonesty involves both objective and subjective elements, and requires proof that the insured's conduct was dishonest by the ordinary standards of reasonable and honest people (objective) and that the insured realised that by those standards his conduct was dishonest (subjective). The onus of proof is on the insurers. The test is the balance of probabilities and not reasonable doubt but, given the nature of the allegation, the courts demand more cogent evidence than would otherwise be required in civil cases.[57]

3.1.2. The Meaning of 'Claim'

A claim is simply a demand for payment. Whether or not a claim is fraudulent is to be assessed at the date the claim was made: as will be seen below, as a result of the *Versloot* case, if a claim is genuine it does not become fraudulent if the insured subsequently seeks to prove the claim by presenting false evidence. In *Direct Line Insurance plc v Fox*,[58] the defendant's property policy contained the typical fraudulent claims clause: 'If any claim or part of a claim is made fraudulently or falsely, the policy shall become void and all benefit under this policy will be forfeited.' The insured suffered a fire at his house, and was paid some £32,000 in respect of damage to contents and on finding alternative accommodation pending rebuilding work. On 7 June 2007 he reached agreement with insurers, under which he agreed to accept the sum of £46,524.50 in full settlement and discharge of all claims for the buildings: an initial payment of £42,412.00 was to be paid, followed by a final payment of £4112.50 for VAT subject to the defendant providing invoices demonstrating the outlay for VAT. The defendant subsequently submitted an invoice from a builder, which showed that VAT had been paid. Further investigation showed that the invoice had probably been forged and that the work had not been carried out by that builder. The insurers sought to recover all sums paid by them under the policy, in reliance on the fraudulent claims clause. The court ruled that they were unable to do so, on the ground that the insured had not made a fraudulent claim at all. The settlement agreement resolved the claim and replaced it with a new agreement: there was no challenge to the validity of the agreement, and all that had happened was that the insured had failed to produce valid evidence that he had paid VAT, so that the only consequence was that he could not recover the sum payable for VAT. If that was wrong, then the court rejected the insured's alternative arguments that fraud could be retracted – the court's view was that fraud could not be retracted, but even if that was

[53] There is a statutory definition of fraud in s 2 of the Fraud Act 2006, relevant for the purposes of the criminal law only, although it similarly refers to dishonesty designed to make a gain.

[54] *Derry v Peek* (1889) 14 App Cas 337, 371 (Lord Herschell). See also *Lek v Mathews* (1927) 29 Ll L Rep 141. See further *Manifest Shipping Co Ltd v Uni-Polaris Shipping Co Ltd, The Star Sea* [2001] UKHL 1, [102] and [111].

[55] [2002] 2 AC 164. See also *Ivey v Genting Casinos Ltd* [2017] UKSC 67.

[56] [2011] EWHC 362 (QB).

[57] *Hornal v Neuberger Products Ltd* [1957] 1 QB 247.

[58] [2009] EWHC 386 (QB).

wrong, any retraction in the present case was after the fraud had been discovered; and the fraud clause was void under the Unfair Terms in Consumer Contracts Regulations 1999 (now the Consumer Rights Act 2015) – the court held that the clause did not operate to avoid the policy *ab initio* but merely precluded recovery for losses occurring after the fraud, so that it reflected the common law.

The position under liability policies is more complex. The trigger for a claim under a liability policy is proof that the insured has established and quantified his liability to a third party. Any communications between the insured and the insurers up to that point are not part of the claim that later follows. This may be seen from *K/S Merc-Skandia*, the facts of which were given above, where the fraud took place before the insured's liability to the third party had been established and quantified. There was no plea of fraudulent claim in that case, and the Court of Appeal noted that the insurers' decision not to rely on utmost good faith was correct.

It follows from the reasoning in *Fox* that if a fraudulent claim is made, it does not cease to be fraudulent if the lie subsequently unravels in the course of the claim being pursued.[59] It is not clear whether a genuine repentance of fraud affects the position, but to date the cases have involved the fraud being uncovered rather than voluntarily admitted. It is not necessary for the insurers to prove that fraud had any inducing effect on them in their handling of the claim. However, if the insurers were aware that the claim was to some extent fraudulent but they nevertheless chose to continue to process the claim, then they may be prevented from pleading fraud at a later date. Awareness of fraud may arise in particular where the claim is on its face obviously false. That was the position in *Danepoint Ltd v Allied Underwriting Insurance Ltd*,[60] where the insured's premises, a block of some 13 flats, were damaged by fire. The insured claimed for reinstatement costs together with loss of rent. With respect to the reinstatement costs, these were agreed at £83,000, subject to inspection by the insurer's loss adjusters. The work was to be carried out by a third party builder, Titchfield Construction. The insurers paid £25,000 on account and then received interim invoices totalling £60,000 from a different builder, Gulf Falcon. In fact, at the time the invoices were received, only around £7500 of work had been completed. The judge thought that the invoices 'were wholly over-stated and stood at the very edge of credibility', but he concluded that they could be disregarded: the judge noted that the loss adjuster was required by the settlement agreement to inspect the works periodically to ensure that the project was being carried out, so, 'by inference, that he could ensure that any further interim payments were properly justified'. However, the claim for loss of rent was fraudulent: the claimant had asserted that all tenants had vacated the property immediately following the fire on 13 June 2001, but the evidence showed that most of the flats remained occupied thereafter. As there was only one claim with two heads of loss, the entire claim fell for fraud.

3.1.3. Classes of Fraudulent Claim

There are four recognised classes of fraudulent claim which set out the types of conduct giving rise to fraudulent claims, taken from the judgment of Mance LJ in Mance LJ in *Agapitos v Agnew*.[61]

[59] *Stemson v AMP General (NZ) Ltd* [2006] Lloyd's Rep IR 852.
[60] [2006] Lloyd's Rep IR 690.
[61] [2002] Lloyd's Rep IR 573.

First, 'the assured had suffered no loss at all or the loss was self-inflicted'. The former type is found in numerous cases, perhaps the most intriguing being *Patel v Windsor Life Assurance Co Ltd*,[62] where the life of an individual had been insured by the claimant under a number of policies. It was asserted that the life insured had died in India, but there was sufficient evidence to persuade the court that the death and cremation certificates had been forged, and there was a strong suggestion that the life insured had never in fact existed. There are also many authorities on claims where deliberate destruction has been asserted, the vast majority relating to sunk ships[63] and burned buildings.[64] The courts here have followed expert evidence on the indicia of fraud, including such forensics as may be available and also the financial position of the insured. If the evidence is finely balanced, the presence or absence of a motive may be determinative.[65]

Secondly, 'the assured's loss was less than had been claimed'. Exaggerated loss is perhaps the most common class of fraud, and the principle here is that the insured will lose the entire claim as there would otherwise be no incentive for the insured to be honest. In *AXA General Insurance Ltd v Gottlieb*,[66] Mance LJ had occasion to consider whether, under the common law rule relating to fraudulent claims, an insurer could recover interim payments made prior to any fraud in respect of genuine losses incurred on the claim to which the subsequent fraud related. The submission of the insured's counsel to the effect that where a genuine right to indemnity has both arisen and been the subject of a payment made prior to any fraud committed in respect of the same claim, there was no conceptual basis for requiring the insured to repay the sums received. Mance LJ stated that:

> If a later fraud forfeits a genuine claim which has already accrued but not been paid, the obvious conceptual basis is that the *whole* claim is forfeit … If the whole claim is forfeit, then the fact that sums have been advanced towards it is of itself no answer to their recovery.[67]

The effect of counsel's argument would be to result in the anomaly that forfeiture of the whole claim should be restricted to the whole of the outstanding claim only: in other words, to any part that remains unpaid as at the date of the fraud. Mance LJ explained that the rationale of the rule relating to fraudulent claims is that an insured should not expect that, should the fraud fail, he will lose nothing. The court should not, therefore, undermine the prophylactic policy of the common law rule by holding that forfeiture should not apply to a part of a claim which is otherwise honest. Accordingly, it was held that the effect of the common law is to forfeit the whole of the fraudulent claim so that the consideration for any interim payments made on that claim fails. Such sums are thus recoverable by the insurers irrespective of whether they were paid prior to the fraud. It was seen in *Danepoint Ltd* above that the constituent elements of a single claim are not to be separated out, so that a fraudulent claim affecting one part of the alleged loss taints the entire claim without any consideration of proportionality, without any consideration of proportionality: in *Yeganeh v Zurich Insurance*,[68] the insured's house was damaged in a fire leading to a genuine claim

[62] [2008] Lloyd's Rep IR 359.

[63] Most recently, *Kairos Shipping v ENKA Co LLC, The Atlantik Confidence* [2016] EWHC 2412 (Admlty); *Suez Fortune Investments Ltd v Talbot Underwriting Ltd, The Brilliante Virtuoso* [2019] EWHC 2599 (Comm).

[64] Most recently, *James v CGU Insurance* [2002] Lloyd's Rep IR 20; Cook v Sirius International Insurance Corporation Australian Branch [2021] NSWCA 192.

[65] *Yeganeh v Zurich Plc* [2010] EWHC 1185 (QB), remitted [2011] EWCA Civ 398 for further evidence.

[66] [2005] EWCA Civ 115. Keene and Pill LJJ concurred.

[67] ibid [27], citing *Galloway v Guardian Royal Exchange (UK) Ltd* [1999] Lloyd's Rep IR 209 and *Direct Line Insurance v Khan*, [2002] Lloyd's Rep IR 364 (considered below).

[68] ibid.

for £270,000, but the insured claimed fraudulently the sum of £12,465 for Armani suits that were said to be in the bedroom at the time of the fire. The entire claim was held to have been tainted by the fraud.

An insured who overclaims for lost or damaged property is not necessarily fraudulent: the insured may wrongly assume that compensation is available for sentimental as well as market value; the subject matter may be unique and not capable of objective valuation; and the insured may take the view that the insurers are likely to offer a sum far less than the actual value of the subject matter and therefore inflates the claim by way of bargaining. In *Ewer v National Employers' Mutual General Insurance Association*,[69] the claimant claimed the current cost price of new items of furniture to replace his second-hand items which had been destroyed by fire. Mackinnon J, although describing the claim as preposterous, held that no deception was perpetuated. He said:

> I do not think [the claimant] was doing that in any way a fraudulent claim, but as a figure to start off with as a bargaining figure. We have been told that the defendant company wanted to see invoices. The invoices, of course, would show what the articles cost. As the [claimant] could not produce the invoices showing what the articles cost, I think he did the best he could in substituting for it ... The [claimant] knew the claim would be discussed, and probably drastically criticised, by the assessors: he had been asked for invoices, and he started the bargaining with them by putting down the cost price of these articles as if they were new.

While over-valuation is not therefore in itself sufficient to establish fraud, a grossly exaggerated claim of the true value of the loss will raise a presumption of fraud.[70] Such indulgence as displayed by MacKinnon J towards 'preposterously' exaggerated claims was not so readily accepted by Hoffmann LJ in *Orakpo v Barclays Insurance Services*,[71] although he did explain that:

> In cases where nothing is misrepresented or concealed, and the loss adjuster is in a good a position to form a view of the validity of the claim as the insured, it will be a legitimate reason that the insured was merely putting forward a starting figure for negotiation.[72]

The degree of overvaluation may also be important, in that the court may disregard a *de minimis* percentage exaggeration[73] although a small percentage exaggeration may be treated as fraudulent where the sums concerned are large.[74]

Thirdly, 'the assured believed at the time of his claim that he had suffered a loss, but, having subsequently discovered that he had suffered no loss at all or a loss smaller than that claimed for, failed to correct the false information'.

Fourthly, 'the assured had suffered a loss but had suppressed a defence known to him which might be available to insurers'. This was the position in *Agapitos v Agnew*[75] itself, where the insured carried out welding work on a vessel in breach of a contractual warranty restricting hot works. The insured's attempt to disguise the breach of warranty rendered the claim fraudulent.

[69] (1937) 157 LT 16.

[70] *Goulstone v Royal Insurance Co* (1858) 1 F& F 276; *Central Bank of India v Guardian Assurance Co* (1936) 54 Ll L Rep 247; *Orakpo v Barclays Insurance Services* [1995] LRLR 433. 450 (Staughton LJ).

[71] [1995] LRLR 433.

[72] ibid 451. In *Central Bank of India v Guardian Assurance Co* (1936) 54 Ll L Rep 247, a claim for some 100 times the true value of the loss was held to be fraudulent.

[73] *Tonkin v UK Insurance Ltd* [2007] Lloyd's Rep IR 283.

[74] *Galloway v Guardian Royal Exchange (UK) Ltd* [1999] LRLR 209.

[75] [2002] Lloyd's Rep IR 573.

3.1.4. Fraudulent Means or Devices

Mance LJ's fifth category in *Agapitos* was that 'the assured had furthered a genuine claim by the use of "fraudulent means or devices"'. Until the *Versloot* decision, the cases were consistent that an insured who had suffered a genuine loss but who sought to embroider the evidence as to how the loss occurred was guilty of fraud. In *Agapitos*, Mance LJ ruled that a genuine loss was to be treated as the subject of a fraudulent claim if the insured resorted to falsehoods in order to boost his prospects of recovery: 'a fraudulent claim exists where the insured claims, knowing that he has suffered no loss, or only a lesser loss than that which he claims (or is reckless as to whether this is the case)'.[76] A fraudulent device, however, is 'used if the insured believes that he has suffered the loss claimed, but seeks to improve or embellish the facts surrounding the claim, by some lie'.[77] The question which Mance LJ focused upon was whether a genuine claim could become fraudulent because it was made fraudulently and whether, in consequence, the duty of utmost good faith was broken. He thought that an acceptable solution would be to 'treat the use of a fraudulent device as a sub-species of making a fraudulent claim' and to treat as relevant for this purpose:

> [A]ny lie, directly related to the claim to which the fraudulent device relates, which is intended to improve the insured's prospects of obtaining a settlement or winning the case, and which would, if believed, tend, objectively, prior to any final determination at trial of the parties' rights, to yield a not insignificant improvement in the insured's prospects – whether they be prospects of obtaining a settlement, or a better settlement, or of winning at trial.

Further, the Court of Appeal also went on to hold that once litigation between the insurers and the insured has commenced, the consequences of making a fraudulent claim or promoting a claim with fraudulent devices are superseded by the procedural rules governing civil litigation.

The fraudulent means or devices principle was applied in a series of first instance decisions. In *Sharon's Bakery (Europe) Ltd v AXA Insurance UK Plc*,[78] where machinery belonging to the insured was damaged by fire, the insured had no document of title to the subject matter and used a forged invoice to show its purchase. It was held, obiter,[79] that the claim was fraudulent even though it was not suggested that the invoice was greater than the purchase price or that the sum sought by the insured was exaggerated. The limits of the principle were shown in *Aviva Insurance Ltd v Brown*,[80] where a proportionality element was introduced. The insured in that case claimed for the cost of renting alternative accommodation following a fire, and sought to expedite recovery from the insurers by claiming falsely that the landlord was demanding payment of the rent: Eder J felt that the lie was insufficiently serious to justify a finding that the claim was fraudulent, although there was a finding of fraud on the separate ground that the insured had sought to recover rental payments made by him when in fact the property was indirectly in his ownership.

In *Versloot*,[81] the Supreme Court by a majority overturned these cases and ruled that the use of lies to support a genuine claim did not constitute fraud, and that English law

[76] ibid [30].

[77] ibid.

[78] [2011] EWHC 210 (Comm).

[79] The insurers were held to be entitled to avoid the policy for non-disclosure of the fraudulent use of the invoice to secure a bank loan.

[80] [2011] EWHC 362 (QB).

[81] [2016] UKSC 45. J Alexander and D Brinkman, 'Versloot and the Insurance Act 2015' [2019] *Lloyd's Maritime and Commercial Law Quarterly* 11.

did not recognise the concept of fraudulent means or devices. The engines on the insured vessel were irreparably damaged and became a constructive total following a sequence of events by the crew: negligence in failing to close the sea inlet valve of the emergency fire pumps led to an ingress of water into a pipe, which froze and then defrosted and cracked. Water reached the engine room, but the bulkheads had negligently been left unsealed and the pumps could not cope with the volume of water. Solicitors for the insurers were charged with investigation of the loss, and they were informed by an employee of the vessel's managers that he had been told by the crew that a bilge alarm warning of the ingress of water had sounded but heavy weather had prevented the crew from taking any action. The statement was untrue but had been made to pre-empt any suggestion that the vessel had not been properly maintained. It is to be emphasised that the bilge alarm made no difference to the loss, so this was a case where the only fraud related to a largely irrelevant statement as to what had actually occurred. The majority of the Supreme Court found for the insured. Lord Sumption, giving the leading majority judgment, held that 'collateral lies' did not amount to a fraudulent claim, and that the characterising element of a fraudulent claim was that the insured was attempting to obtain something to which he was not entitled. While it was the case that insurers might have been put to unnecessary expense in investigating the truth or otherwise of the insured's version of events, that did not justify a refusal of the claim. Lord Mance unsurprisingly dissented, with the support of much of the insurance industry, whose view of such matters is that all fraud should be treated in the same way.

3.1.5. Co-insurance

A further issue that has arisen is the position with respect to co-insurance where a fraudulent claim is made by one insured but not the other. There is an important distinction between joint insurance (indivisible interest) and composite insurance (divisible interest).[82] The position where a fraudulent claim is made by a joint co-assured was considered in *Direct Line Insurance plc v Khan.*[83] The home of the co-insureds, Mr and Mrs Khan, was destroyed by fire. Mr Khan made a claim, supported with forged documents, for rent he allegedly paid for alternative accommodation. In fact, no such rent was paid because he owned the alternative accommodation himself. The claim was held to be fraudulent, and the insurers recovered all monies they had paid in respect of reinstating the damaged house, replacing its contents and the payment of rent. The trial judge rejected the argument that Mrs Khan was the sole policyholder and rejected the argument that she should be able to recover on the basis that the fraud had been committed by her husband without her knowledge. Arden LJ, dismissing her appeal, held that in joint insurance the effect of a fraudulent claim advanced by one co-insured is fatal to the claim of the other co-insureds even though they may be entirely innocent.

However, in composite insurance, where more than one interest is covered in a policy, each insured has a separate contract with the insurers and the fraud of one insured will not prejudice the claims of another in respect of the same loss.[84]

[82] See ch 7 above.

[83] [2002] Lloyd's Rep IR 364.

[84] *P Samuel & Co v Dumas* [1924] AC 431; *Arab Bank plc v Zurich Insurance Co* [1999] 1 Lloyd's Rep 262.

3.2. The Consequences of a Fraudulent Claim

3.2.1. Effect of the Insurance Act 2015 on a Fraudulent Claimant

The common law was in a somewhat confused state as to the basis for the rule that a fraudulent claim permitted the insurers to deny liability. The earliest authority, *Britton v Royal Insurance Co*,[85] involved an express clause providing that in the event of a fraudulent claim all benefit under the policy would be forfeited, and Willes J commented obiter that this wording – standard in fire policies of the time – was 'in accordance with legal principle and sound policy'. The phrase is nevertheless one replete with ambiguity, and a century later the courts began to toy with the notion that a fraudulent claim was breach of the duty of utmost good faith justifying *ab initio* avoidance[86] and thereby nullifying any valid claims made before the fraud. The confusion is best exemplified by *Orakpo v Barclays Insurance Services Ltd*,[87] where the members of the Court of Appeal variously suggested that the remedy was avoidance (Sir Roger Parker), termination for repudiation (Hoffmann LJ) or enforceability to the extent that the claim was valid (Sir Christopher Staughton). However, subsequently, in *Axa General Insurance v Gottleib*,[88] the Court of Appeal rejected the argument that a fraudulent claim was a breach of section 17 of the Marine Insurance Act 1906 and held that if there was fraud it operated prospectively from the date of the fraud and not retrospectively so as to defeat accrued rights. What remained unclear was whether a fraudulent claim simply provided a defence to the claim itself, on the principle that a person may not benefit from his own wrong, or whether it amounted to a repudiation of the policy so that the insurers could terminate the policy for breach as from the date of the fraud and also claim damages for breach.[89]

The appropriate remedy was discussed at length by the Law Commissions in an issues paper published in July 2010 and a further document, *Reform of Insurance Law*, published in December 2011.[90] The Law Commissions' final proposals were published in July 2014[91] along with a draft Bill, and were enacted as sections 12 and 13 of the Insurance Act 2015. The former provision in full is as follows:

> (1) If the insured makes a fraudulent claim under a contract of insurance –
> (a) the insurer is not liable to pay the claim,
> (b) the insurer may recover from the insured any sums paid by the insurer to the insured in respect of the claim, and
> (c) in addition, the insurer may by notice to the insured treat the contract has having been terminated with effect from the time of the fraudulent act.
> (2) If the insurer does treat the contract as having been terminated –
> (a) it may refuse all liability to the insured under the contract in respect of a relevant event occurring after the time of the fraudulent act, and
> (b) it need not return any of the premiums paid under the contract.

[85] (1866) 4 F & F 905, 909. See also *Worsley v Wood* (1796) 6 TR 710; *Goulstone v Royal Insurance* (1858) 1 F & F 276; *Norton v Royal Insurance* (1885) 1 TLR 460.
[86] *Black King Shipping v Massie, The Litsion Pride* [1985] 1 Lloyd's Rep 437; *Continental Illinois National Bank of Chicago v Alliance Assurance Co Ltd, The Captain Panagos* [1986] 2 Lloyd's Rep 470.
[87] [1995] LRLR 433.
[88] [2005] Lloyd's Rep IR 369.
[89] Damages were held not to be available in *London Assurance v Clare* (1937) 57 Ll L Rep 254, but the contrary was assumed in *Parker v National Farmers Union Mutual Insurance Society Ltd* [2012] EWHC 2156 (Comm).
[90] Law Com CP No 201/Scot Law Com CP 152.
[91] Law Com CP No 353/Scot Law Com CP 238.

(3) Treating a contract as having been terminated under this section does not affect the rights and obligations of the parties to the contract with respect to a relevant event occurring before the time of the fraudulent act.
(4) In subsections (2)(a) and (3), 'relevant event' refers to whatever gives rise to the insurer's liability under the contract (and includes, for example, the occurrence of a loss, the making of a claim, or the notification of a potential claim, depending on how the contract is written).

Section 12 does not define fraud and leaves the matter to the common law, as recommended by the Law Commissions. Assuming that there has been fraud, subsection (1) gives the insurers the right to reject the claim and to recover any sums paid under it, and additionally to treat the contract as terminated with effect from the date of the fraudulent act. If that option is exercised, then by subsection (2) the insurers can treat the entire premium as forfeited and they do not face liability for a loss occurring after the date of termination. However, by subsections (3) and (4), if a 'relevant event' in the form of a different loss had occurred before the date of the fraud, then the insurers remain liable for that loss despite the fact that the loss is not substantiated until after the policy has been terminated. The Law Commissions gave a helpful example of the operation of section 12 in relation to property insurance.[92] Assume a fire in January, a flood in February and a burglary in April, and assume also a fraudulent claim in March in respect of the fire and termination of the policy in May, when the fraud is discovered. Under section 12: the termination dates back to March; the fire claim is tainted by fraud and cannot be recovered; the flood claim can be made because the event occurred before termination; and the burglary claim is invalid because the policy was terminated retroactively in March and there was no policy in force when the burglary took place.

In the case of a liability policy where the trigger is the notification of a claim, or circumstances that may result in a claim, against the insured, notification before the date of termination preserves the claim. That is the effect of the definition of 'relevant event' in subsection (4).

It is likely that in most cases the insurers will exercise their option to terminate the policy as well as refuse to pay the claim. They are not, however, permitted to terminate other policies held by the insured.[93] An insurer who chooses not to terminate and simply pays the claim remains liable under the policy for future claims. The Act is silent on the unresolved question as to whether damages are awardable for breach of contract whether or not the policy is terminated.

3.2.2. Beneficiaries and Co-insureds

Separate provision is made in section 13 of the 2015 Act for group insurance, namely the situation where an employer or other organisation takes out a policy providing cover for a group of beneficiaries who are not themselves contracting parties and a fraudulent claim is made by one of the beneficiaries. The result is that the fraudulent beneficiary is treated as if he was an insured person and is subject to the principles in section 12, but the policy itself cannot be terminated and the rights of other beneficiaries are unaffected. However, the Act does not affect the position where there is co-insurance.

[92] ibid paras 23.57 and 23.58.
[93] That more drastic remedy is offered in Australia by the Insurance Contracts Act 1984, s 56.

3.2.3. Express Fraudulent Claims Clauses

Sections 15 and 16 of the Insurance Act 2015 set out the extent to which the parties can contract out of the provisions of sections 12 and 13. The remedies for fraudulent claims cannot be excluded in consumer contracts, but contracting out is permitted in relation to non-consumer contracts if the relevant clause meets the transparency requirements, namely that it is clear and brought to the insured's attention. In a pre-Act case, *Joseph Fielding Properties (Blackpool) Ltd v Aviva Insurance Ltd*,[94] the insured claimed an indemnity of over £2 million against the insurer in respect of a fire which had occurred on the insured property. The insurer defended the claim on a number of grounds, one of them being that during the currency of the policy the insured had made a fraudulent claim regarding drain damage. The insured had paid £6700 to a contractor for drainage repairs but had claimed £9870. Further, Aviva sought to rely on a fraudulent claims clause, Condition 7 of the policy, which stated:

> We will at our option avoid the policy from the inception of this insurance or from the date of the claim or alleged claim or avoid the claim
>
> (a) if a claim made by you or anyone acting on your behalf to obtain a policy benefit is fraudulent or intentionally exaggerated, whether ultimately material or not or
>
> (b) a false declaration or statement is made or fraudulent device put forward in support of a claim.

The court found that the insured had behaved fraudulently, that the sum contained in the invoice was fraudulently exaggerated, and this was, therefore, within the meaning of Condition 7. This type of clause would now be permissible only if the transparency requirements were satisfied.

It is to be emphasised that the contracting out rules apply only to matters governed by the 2015 Act, so there is nothing to prevent the insurers from laying down a wider definition of fraud than is recognised by the common law by encompassing fraudulent means and devices. For example, the Act does not touch provisions such as clause 45.3 of the International Hull Clauses 2003, one of the sets of clauses in use in the marine insurance market.[95] This states that it is a condition precedent to the liability of the insurers that the insured has not at any stage prior to the commencement of legal proceedings knowingly or recklessly misled or attempted to mislead the insurers 'in the proper consideration of a claim or the settlement thereof by relying on any evidence which is false'.

4. Fraudulent Claims by Third Parties

Liability insurers face an additional fraud hazard in the form of claims by third parties against the insured. These will typically take the form of exaggerated claims for personal injuries allegedly suffered at the hands of the insured, normally at work or on the roads. This matter was not addressed by the law until the passing of section 57 of the Criminal Justice and Courts Act 2015. Up to that point, the position was that the court could not strike out an exaggerated claim and the victim was entitled to recover a sum representing

[94] [2010] EWHC 2192 (QB).
[95] See ch 17 above.

his actual injuries, with the remainder being disallowed. However, in *Fairclough Homes Ltd v Summers*,[96] the Supreme Court imposed important limits on the victim's rights: the existence of fraud undermined the victim's credibility, which made it much harder to prove actual loss; there would be a costs penalty in that the victim would be ordered to pay full 'indemnity' rather than 'standard' costs, thereby probably leaving the victim worse off; interest would be reduced; the court could give permission for contempt of court proceedings to be brought; and a recommendation could be made to the Director of Public Prosecutions or the Crown Prosecution Service for a criminal prosecution.

All of this has been superseded by section 57. The section applies where the court reaches a finding of 'fundamental dishonesty', in which case the claim may be dismissed in its entirety unless it is satisfied that the claimant would suffer 'substantial injustice'. Costs may also be awarded against the claimant and there are potential follow-up criminal proceedings. The cases on section 57 have adopted a three-stop approach: (a) is there dishonesty, as determined in accordance with the common law objective/subjective test; (b) is the dishonesty fundamental, the test being whether the fraud has substantially affected all or a part of the presentation of the claim as where injury is feigned or greatly exaggerated; and (c) would depriving the claimant of all compensation give rise to 'substantial injustice' affecting more than simply the loss of damages?[97]

One major area of contention has proved to be 'whiplash' claims by victims of motor accidents: whiplash takes the form of injury to the soft tissue of the neck or back, but there is rarely any external evidence of such injury. To stem the flow of such claims, the Whiplash Injury Regulations,[98] which came into force on 31 May 2021, lay down fixed sums for pain and suffering from the injury, depending upon its likely duration, rising from £240 to £4215, although additional sums may be sought for loss of earnings and other expenses. If the total claim is for less than £5000, it must be made through the online Official Injury Claim portal, and, most importantly, legal fees are not recoverable in portal claims even if the claim succeeds.

5. Limitation Periods

By section 5 of the Limitation Act 1980, proceedings must be issued for an action on a contract within six years from the date on which the cause of action accrued. English law has accepted the principle that a claim under an insurance policy is one for breach of contract for unliquidated damages[99] in that the obligation of the insurers is to hold the insured harmless, and so the action accrues at the date of the occurrence of the insured peril. The dates on which the insured makes a claim under the policy, the insurers deny a claim under the policy and the loss can be measured are all immaterial to the accrual of the cause of action.[100] The relevant insured peril for the purposes of liability insurance is the

[96] [2012] UKSC 26.

[97] Of the numerous illustrations, see *London Organising Committee of the Olympic and Paralympic Games v Sinfield* [2018] EWHC 51 (QB); *Elgamal v Westminster City Council* [2021] EWHC 2510 (QB).

[98] SI 2021/642, made under the Civil Liability Act 2018.

[99] For the implications of this rule for damages for late payment, see ch 12 below.

[100] *Callaghan v Dominion Insurance Co* [1997] 2 Lloyd's Rep 541 (property insurance); *Chandris v Argo Insurance Co Ltd* [1963] 2 Lloyd's Rep 64 (marine insurance); *Bann Carraig Ltd v Great Lakes Reinsurance (UK) PLC* [2021]

date on which the liability of the insured to the third party is established and quantified.[101] It is permissible for policies to alter the date of the accrual of action, eg by requiring that proceedings be commenced within a fixed period from the date of the loss, although this wording is rarely, if ever, seen in the modern market. Policy terms that postpone the right of recovery by the insured, eg conditions precedent requiring the reinstatement of buildings or payment of third party claims, do not affect the limitation period.

The Limitation Act does not bar contract claims after the expiry of six years, but merely gives the defendant a defence to the claim. It is therefore open to insurers to waive the limitation period, and this commonly happens where settlement negotiations are ongoing when the limitation period is about to expire. The parties will normally enter into a 'standstill agreement' whereby time is frozen. In the absence of a standstill agreement, the insurers may lose the right to rely upon the limitation period on the application of ordinary principles of waiver and estoppel, but something more than silence on the issue is required.[102]

6. Settlements

If there is a dispute between the insured and the insurers as to liability or quantum, the matter will usually be resolved short of litigation or arbitration by a settlement agreement. The law encourages settlements and has accepted that, by surrendering their respective rights to pursue the dispute in legal proceedings, each party has provided consideration for the agreement. A settlement is thus a binding contract which replaces the policy, so any later dispute is one arising under the settlement and not the insurance. The effect is that if the insurers refuse to pay under the settlement, the insured cannot treat the settlement as repudiated and revert to a claim under the policy: the action has to be for breach of the settlement agreement.[103]

A settlement agreement is not a contract that attracts the duty of fair presentation, so neither side is required to disclose material facts to the other.[104] However, a misrepresentation[105] or undue influence[106] may render a settlement contract voidable. There is also some authority for the proposition that a settlement can be overturned for 'sharp practice',[107] and one possible example is secret payments made to the insured's agent.[108] In a New Zealand Court of Appeal decision, *Southern Response Earthquake Services Ltd v Dodds*,[109] it was found that the insurers had been guilty of misrepresentation by sending to the insured a redacted version of an expert report which referred only to rebuild costs of

NIQB 63 (business interruption insurance); *Mulchrone v Swiss Life (UK) Plc* [2006] Lloyd's Rep IR 339 (life insurance).

[101] *K/S Merc-Scandia XXXXII v Certain Lloyd's Underwriters, The Mercandian Continent* [2001] Lloyd's Rep IR 802.

[102] *Ace Insurance SA-NV v Seechurn* [2002] Lloyd's Rep IR 489; *Fortisbank SA v Trenwick International Ltd* [2005] Lloyd's Rep IR 464.

[103] *Korea Foreign Insurance Co v Omne Re SA* [1999] Lloyd's Rep IR 509.

[104] See generally *Bell v Lever Bros* [1932] AC 161.

[105] *Saunders v Ford Motor Co* [1970] 1 Lloyd's Rep 379.

[106] *Horry v Tate & Lyle Ltd* [1982] 2 Lloyd's Rep 416.

[107] *Bank of Credit and Commerce International v Ali* [2001] 1 All ER 961.

[108] See *Taylor v Walker* [1958] 1 Lloyd's Rep 490.

[109] [2020] NZCA 395.

$895,937.78 and omitted the report's further conclusion that a further sum of $253,028.80 would be necessary to cover administration, demolition and debris removal costs. There was no intent to deceive the insured, as the case law at the time denied liability for such costs, which was why they were not referred to. Thereafter judicial decisions concluded that such costs were recoverable. The court regarded the insurers as having made a misrepresentation and allowed the insured to recover the shortfall. A misrepresentation is generally regarded as actionable only if it is relied upon by the innocent party. That requirement is relaxed in the case of fraud. In *Hayward v Zurich Insurance Company Plc*,[110] H was injured at work in June 1998 and submitted a claim of £419,316.59 against his employers. Liability insurers took over the negotiations and reached a settlement in the sum of £134,973.11, embodied in a court order in October 2003. Two years later, the employer received information from H's neighbours indicating that H was not as seriously injured as he had claimed. The insurers, who had been suspicious of H at the time of the settlement, sought to have it overturned for fraud. The Supreme Court, allowing the action, held that the insurers' suspicions did not preclude their right to set aside the settlement for fraud, and the test was not whether H's statements or conduct had induced them to enter into the settlement but, rather, whether the fraud was one of the material causes of them doing so.

At common law, a settlement agreement can be overturned for mistake in exceptional circumstances only. In *Great Peace Shipping Ltd v Tsavliris Salvage (International) Ltd, The Great Peace*,[111] the Court of Appeal confirmed that there was no supplementary equitable jurisdiction that rendered a contract voidable for any mistake that was less than fundamental. In so deciding, the Court of Appeal doubted the correctness of its own earlier decision in *Magee v Pennine Insurance Co Ltd*,[112] where a settlement was avoided in equity following the insurers' discovery that the policy itself could have been avoided for non-disclosure. However, if the mistake is fundamental, then it is irrelevant whether the mistake is of fact (eg the nature of the circumstances giving rise to the loss)[113] or of law affecting the validity or otherwise of the claim, including a retrospective change in the law by reason of a decision of the courts.[114] To avoid these uncertainties, it is now standard practice for settlement contracts to be stated to be final and binding, and not subject to factual or legal issues 'known or unknown'. A clause of similar width was tested in *ECH Holdings Ltd v Vero Insurance New Zealand Ltd*,[115] where the insured's building was damaged by earthquakes in 2010 and 2011, but the policy was renewed for the years 2013–17. In 2018 the damage claim was settled on the basis that the building had been totally lost, the settlement providing that it was in

> full and final settlement and discharge of the Claim and any claims, rights, demands and set-offs … arising directly or indirectly out of, or in connection with the … Policy whether such claims arise under statute, common law, or equity …

The insured's claim for recovery of the premiums paid in the years following the loss, on the basis that the consideration for them had totally failed, was dismissed by the New Zealand

[110] [2016] UKSC 48. See E Bant, 'Unravelling Fraud in the Wake of Hayward v Zurich Insurance' [2019] *Lloyd's Maritime and Commercial Law Quarterly* 91.

[111] [2002] 4 All ER 689.

[112] [1969] 2 QB 507.

[113] As in *Norwich Union Fire Insurance Society Ltd v Price* [1934] AC 455.

[114] *Bank of Credit and Commerce International v Ali* [2001] 1 All ER 961; *Southern Response Earthquake Services Ltd v Dodds* [2020] NZCA 395; *Sneesby v Southern Response Earthquake Services Ltd* [2022] NZHC 262.

[115] [2021] NZHC 3104.

High Court on the ground that the settlement extended to the premiums as well as to the sums paid.

In many cases, particularly involving small claims or consumer policies, payment is simply made by the insurers without any settlement agreement. The question then arises as to whether the sums are recoverable if the insurers can show that they were paid under mistake of fact or law. The House of Lords has determined[116] that there is no distinction between law and fact, as was once thought to be the case, subject to the usual defences available in restitutionary claims. Such defences are limited, and it does not suffice for the payee to show that the payment was made in accordance with the law as it was understood at the time and that the law has changed only subsequently. Nor is it a defence to show that the payee acted in the honest belief that he or she was entitled to the payment. The most important defence is change of position, where the payee's position has changed so fundamentally in reliance on the payment that restitution would be inequitable.[117] However, the payee must prove that his position has changed by reason only of the payment, so that the payee would not have incurred expenditure on goods or services had the payment not been made.[118]

[116] *Kleinwort Benson Ltd v Lincoln City Council* [1998] 4 All ER 513.

[117] *Lipkin Gorman v Karpnale Ltd* [1991] 2 AC 548.

[118] *Avon County Council v Howlett* [1983] 1 All ER 1073; *Scottish Equitable Plc v Derby* [2001] 3 All ER 818; *Moore v National Mutual Life Association of Australasia Ltd* [2011] NSWSC 416.

12

Indemnity and Reinstatement

1. The Principle of Indemnity

1.1. The Meaning of Loss

1.1.1. Damage

Non-marine insurance recognises two forms of loss where the subject matter has been damaged: total loss, consisting of the complete destruction of the insured subject matter; and partial loss, where the insured subject matter is damaged and is capable of repair. Marine insurance accepts a third possibility, namely, constructive total loss, consisting of partial loss whose repair is more costly than the subject matter would be worth when repaired.[1] The important difference between total loss and partial loss is the measure of indemnity: where there is a total loss, the insured is entitled to recover the full value of the insured subject matter (at least, up to the maximum sum insured under the policy); but where there is a partial loss, the insured's measure of indemnity is the reduction in the value of the subject matter by reason of the insured peril, generally reflected in repair costs. There will, of course, be cases where the cost of repairing partially damaged property is out of all proportion to its repaired value, but there is still only a partial loss in such a case.[2] Interestingly, this throws doubt upon the practice of motor insurers in 'writing off' a vehicle that has been seriously damaged and not worth repairing, as it is apparent that there is only a constructive total loss and the insured can – unless the policy otherwise provides – insist upon full repair costs up to the maximum sum insured. This point was recognised by Rix LJ in *Masefield AG v Amlin Corporate Member Ltd*,[3] although he did not elaborate. It may nevertheless be the case that damage short of total destruction amounts to total loss, as where spare parts are unavailable or reinstatement is impracticable.[4]

[1] Although marine policies today define constructive total loss by reference to the insured value (and sometimes 80% of the insured value): see ch 18 below.

[2] *Marriott v Vero Insurance New Zealand Ltd* [2014] NZCA 447; *Mobis Parts Australia Pty Ltd v XL Insurance Company SE* [2017] NSWSC 1321.

[3] [2011] EWCA Civ 24.

[4] Recognised in *Marriott* [2014] NZCA 447, paras [107]–[108].

Property policies are concerned with physical loss and not loss of use: the latter form of cover, most importantly in the form of business interruption, may be added as an extension to a property policy. Business interruption insurance is rarely a stand-alone form of cover and insurance is contingent upon there having been damage to property leading to interruption to the business, although property policies do contain non-damage business interruption extensions and these have been extensively litigated in the light of the COVID-19 pandemic.[5] Loss of use is not damage: that was held to be the case in *Kraal v The Earthquake Commission*,[6] where an order to the insured to evacuate his undamaged house for fear of a landslide was held not to give rise to an insurance claim. The primary cover of a property policy is, therefore, damage to the insured subject matter. Many policies refer to physical loss or damage, and although there is an argument that 'loss' of property is a wider concept than 'damage' to property, most policies refer to 'physical loss or damage', making it clear that there must be a physical impact on the insured subject matter. Marine cases involving paper losses, as where goods ordered are not supplied, illustrate that there is no coverage in the absence of some sort of financial loss extension.[7]

The search is thus for some physical change to the insured subject matter which has in some way led to a reduction in its value. The cases show that the change can be invisible and even sub-molecular, but there must be a physical impact. In *Ranicar v Frigmobile Pty Ltd*,[8] scallops stored for a short period at a temperature higher than recommended, thereby making them unsaleable even though perfectly safe and edible, were held to be damaged. In *Technology Holdings Ltd v IAG New Zealand Ltd*,[9] a number of electronic payment terminals were stored in a premises which flooded. The terminals did not come into contact with water, but the subsequent humidity rendered the warranties on them void so that their value was accordingly reduced, and they were held to have been damaged. The leading English authority is *Quorum A/S v Schramm*,[10] where a Degas pastel, *La Danse Greque*, stored in a strongroom was exposed to smoke from a fire breaking out on the premises. There was no visible damage, but the scientific evidence was that there would have been sub-molecular damage to the paint, albeit undiscoverable without investigation that would have damaged the painting. The reduction in market value was held to be recoverable. The importance of these cases is that they demonstrate that a virus such as COVID-19, which sits on surfaces until wiped away or naturally losing potency, cannot be said to have caused damage to property:[11] this is discussed in chapter 19 below.

1.1.2. Loss of Possession

In non-marine insurance there is a total loss of property if the insured is irretrievably deprived of possession, whereas if there is any realistic possibility of recovery then there is no loss at all. By contrast, marine insurance recognises that property will be a constructive

[5] See ch 19 below.
[6] [2014] NZHC 919.
[7] Compare *Engelhart CIP (US) LLC v Lloyd's Syndicate 1221* [2018] EWHC 900 (Comm) with *ABN Amro Bank NV v Royal & Sun Alliance plc* [2021] EWCA Civ 1789, discussed in ch 17 below. In *Quadra Commodities SA v XL Insurance Company SE* [2022] EWHC 431 (Comm) it was asserted that a cargo of grain insured against loss or damage had never existed so that there was no coverage under the policy, a defence rejected on the facts by the court.
[8] [1983] Tas LR 113.
[9] (2009) 15 ANZ Ins Cas 61-786.
[10] [2002] Lloyd's Rep IR 292.
[11] *Swiss Re International SE v LCA Marrickville Pty Ltd* [2022] FCAFC 17.

total loss if it is unlikely to be recovered within a reasonable time.[12] The difference between the two sets of rules is illustrated by *Moore v Evans*,[13] where a quantity of pearls insured under an all risks policy and sent to a potential customer in Germany were placed on deposit in a German bank following the outbreak of war. The House of Lords ruled that there was no loss of the pearls, but only a deprivation of the immediate right to possession, and that it was necessary to wait and see whether they would be returned to the insured. Loss of possession must therefore be permanent if there is to be an insurance claim. The same approach may be seen in *Scott v Copenhagen Reinsurance Co (UK) Ltd*,[14] a claim brought for a British Airways aircraft that landed at Kuwait's airport during the Iraqi invasion on 1 August 1990.[15] The aircraft was left on the ground and – unlike 15 Kuwaiti aircraft also at the airport –not seized or flown elsewhere. The BA aircraft was later destroyed in a bombing attack on the airport by US forces. The question was whether the BA aircraft had been lost at the same time as the Kuwaiti aircraft[16] in that its recovery at that point seemed to be unlikely. The Court of Appeal held, contrasting the position with that in marine insurance, that there was no immediate loss and that it was necessary to wait and see what transpired. The loss did not take place until the aircraft was destroyed.

If the insured is tricked into parting possession with goods to a fraudster whose payment is later dishonoured, the loss is to be regarded as one of the goods themselves and not of the proceeds of sale.[17]

1.2. Measurement of Loss

1.2.1. The Meaning of Indemnity: Valued and Unvalued Policies

Where the subject matter of the policy is property, whether real or personal, the insured is precluded from recovering more than the value of the actual loss sustained. This is because 'indemnity' means that the insured is to be put back to the position he would have been in had the loss not occurred, less any excess which the insured has agreed to bear and capped at the maximum sum insured.[18] The position should be contrasted with contingency insurance, for example life and accident policies, where the loss is by its nature incapable of measurement in financial terms and so the sum recovered is fixed by the terms of the policy. The governing principle was stated by Brett LJ in *Castellain v Preston*,[19] a case in which the Court of Appeal considered the nature of a fire insurance policy:

> Every contract of marine or fire insurance is a contract of indemnity, and indemnity only, the meaning of which is that the assured in case of a loss is to receive a full indemnity, but is never to

[12] See ch 17.

[13] *Moore v Evans* [1918] AC 185.

[14] [2003] Lloyd's Rep IR 696.

[15] Quite what it was doing landing during a hostile takeover of the airport remains a mystery. The various theories include a secret SAS surveillance mission, an attempt to rescue the Kuwaiti Royal Family or a plain 'cock up'. To date, one television documentary and two books by Stephen Davis have favoured the first of these possibilities.

[16] For aggregation purposes.

[17] *Dobson v General Accident Fire and Life Assurance Corp* 1989] 3 All ER 927, by implication affirming *Webster v General Accident Fire and Life Assurance Corp* [1953] 1 QB 520 and departing from *Eisinger v General Accident Fire and Life Assurance Corp Ltd* [1955] 2 All ER 897.

[18] See further A Lewis, 'A Fundamental Principle of Insurance Law' [1979] *Lloyd's Maritime and Commercial Law Quarterly* 275; J Birds, 'The Measure of Indemnity in Property Insurance' (1980) 43 *MLR* 456.

[19] (1883) 11 QBD 380.

> receive more. Every rule of insurance law is adopted in order to carry out this fundamental rule, and if ever any proposition is brought forward, the effect of which is opposed to this fundamental rule, it will be found to be wrong.

The overriding requirement of indemnity can be seen to underlie the rules which operate in the event of an insured loss.

There is one important exception to the notion of indemnity, in the form of the use of 'valued' policies. A valued policy is defined by section 27 of the Marine Insurance Act 1906 as one which specifies the agreed value of the subject matter and which renders the valuation conclusive in the absence of fraud. In the event of a total loss, the agreed value is payable, and in the event of a partial loss the sum recoverable is the appropriate proportion of the agreed value. This is calculated by determining the ratio which the actual value of the damaged property bears to the insured sum. In *Elcock v Thomson*,[20] a mansion was insured against loss or damage by fire. The agreed value – conclusive for the purposes of any claim – was £106,850. A fire occurred which partially destroyed the property. The actual value of the property before the fire was £18,000 and after the fire it stood at £12,600, which represented a depreciation of 30 per cent. The property was not reinstated, and the insured claimed under the policy. The issue for the court to decide was how much the insurers should pay. It was held that the agreement as to value applied not just in the event of total loss, but also partial loss. The insurers were therefore liable to pay 30 per cent of £106,850, which was £32,055. Morris J, construing the policy, stated:

> The respective words 'loss' and 'damage', as used in the policy, seem to be synonymous. It would not seem to be the case that the word 'loss' is only referable to complete destruction … The result is that in my judgment, the percentage of actual depreciation resulting from the fire should be applied to the agreed values as set out in the policy so as to arrive at the amount recoverable.[21]

By contrast, in the case of an unvalued policy, which by section 28 of the 1906 Act is one that does not specify the amount recoverable in the event of a loss, the insured will recover actual loss subject to the maximum sum insured. The financial limit of indemnity thus has a different role in valued and unvalued policies: in a valued policy, it is the sum recoverable (or the basis of recovery in the event of a partial loss); in an unvalued policy, it is the maximum sum recoverable once the insured has proved the actual amount of the loss. Valued policies are not regarded as wagers, so that as long as the insured has a valid insurable interest, the policy is lawful.[22]

Whether a policy is valued or unvalued is a matter of construction. Normally the difference is clear, in that valued policies are typically used for subject matter which is unique or otherwise not easily susceptible to accurate valuation, in which case it is more straightforward for the parties to agree the value in advance so as to remove disputes in the event of loss. One form of notoriously ambiguous wording is a reference to the 'sum insured', but it is now clear that the phrase refers to an unvalued policy.[23]

[20] [1949] 2 KB 755. See also *Global Private Investments RSC Ltd v Global Aerospace Underwriting Managers Ltd* [2021] ADGMCFI 0008.

[21] ibid 761.

[22] See the discussion of insurable interest in ch 6 above.

[23] *Kyzuna Investments Ltd v Ocean Marine Mutual Insurance (Europe), The Solveig* [2000] Lloyd's Rep IR 513; *Quorum AS v Schramm* [2002] Lloyd's Rep IR 292; *Thor Navigation Inc v Ingosstrak Insurance, The Thor II* [2005] Lloyd's Rep IR 54.

1.2.2. Unvalued Policies on Buildings

The starting point for the analysis is the seminal judgment of Leggatt LJ in *Sartex Quilts and Textiles Ltd v Endurance Corporate Capital Ltd*.[24] The insured obtained insurance on its manufacturing premises, the insuring clause providing that the insurers would provide indemnity 'against loss or destruction or damage to the property' on the basis of 'reinstatement of the property'. A disastrous fire occurred on 25 May 2011. The insurers denied liability and the insured commenced proceedings. At the date of the trial the premises had not been repaired, although there was a factual finding by the trial judge that the insured had at the date of the fire intended to use the premises in the manufacturing business. The question for the Court of Appeal was whether the insured was entitled to the value of the premises at the date of the fire or at the date of the trial.

Leggatt LJ applied the settled principle that the obligation of the insurers is to hold the insured harmless, so that a claim arises as soon as the insured peril occurs.[25] The amount of the insured's loss is accordingly to be ascertained at the date of the insured peril, so that the value of the premises to the insured is based on the difference between the value immediately before the occurrence of the peril and immediately after the occurrence of the peril. The insured is entitled to a sum representing that loss, and in the absence of a policy term requiring the insured to use the insurance monies to repair or reinstate the building, the assured is free to apply the sum paid in any way that the insured thinks fit – including not reinstating at all. It follows that what happens after the occurrence of the insured peril is irrelevant to the measure of loss, and Leggatt LJ chose not to follow the comment of Chrisopher Clarke LJ in *Great Lakes Insurance (UK) SE v Western Trading Ltd*[26] that it was doubtful whether an insured who had no intention of using the insurance monies to reinstate the premises was entitled to indemnity based on the cost of reinstatement. Leggatt LJ's view was that if the insured had intended immediately before the occurrence of the insured peril to use the premises as part of the business, then the loss was the cost of reinstatement and it was irrelevant whether or not the insured actually used the money to reinstate. That principle resolved the *Sartex* case: the insured's intention immediately before the fire was to use the premises for manufacturing, and the insured was entitled to be indemnified for reinstatement costs. The fact that the insured had not reinstated the premises by the time of the trial was irrelevant: post-peril intentions and actions are not relevant to the calculation.

The default position, therefore, is that the insured is entitled to recover diminution in value by reason of the peril, and that is generally reflected in reinstatement costs. It is, of course, possible that the insured did not at the date of the peril intend to use the premises in the future. By way of example if the insured intended to sell the building, then the loss is not the repair costs but rather the reduction in the market value. This figure may amount to less than the cost of reinstatement. For example, in *Leppard v Excess Insurance Co Ltd*,[27] the claimant purchased a cottage for the express purpose of reselling it, the market value being £3000. He insured the cottage against fire for £10,000. The proposal form stated that the sum insured represented the 'full value' of the property: 'full value' was defined

[24] [2020] EWCA Civ 308. R Merkin, 'The Measure of Indemnity under Property Insurances' (2020) 136 *LQR* 360.

[25] See ch 11 above.

[26] [21016] EWCA Civ 1003.

[27] [1979] 2 All ER 668.

as 'the amount which it would cost to replace the property in its existing form should it be totally destroyed'. Upon renewal of the policy, the sum insured was increased to £14,000. Before any sale took place, the property was totally destroyed by fire. The claimant claimed the rebuilding cost, some £8000. The insurer contested the claim, arguing that the claimant was entitled only to £3000, the market value of the property at the time of the fire. The Court of Appeal held that under the terms of the policy the insurers agreed to indemnify the insured in respect of loss or damage caused by fire. It being an indemnity contract, the claimant could not recover the cost of reinstatement but only the market value of the cottage at the date of the fire (£3000). In their reasoning, both Megaw and Geoffrey Lane LJJ emphasised that the principle of indemnity operated to restrict the amount recoverable to the actual loss suffered by the insured and no more.[28] There may be other cases where the insured is not entitled to reinstatement costs. These will include where, before the occurrence of the peril, the insured intended to demolish the building so that it was of no value at all.[29]

The right of the insured to recover reinstatement costs is subject to the important requirement for the insured to mitigate the loss, which means that the insured must not insist upon reinstatement in a form that no reasonable person would demand. The principle is derived from a breach of contract case, *Ruxley Electronics and Construction Ltd v Forsyth*,[30] where the claimant sued contractors who had installed a swimming pool for the cost of removing and replacing the pool because it was not of the correct depth. The House of Lords ruled that the pool was perfectly functional and that no reasonable person would have made the demand made by the claimant: accordingly, there was a failure to mitigate, and the claimant was entitled only to nominal damages. Leggatt LJ applied *Ruxley* to insurance cases. If the insured had used the building purely for functional purposes, then reinstatement costs would generally exclude reinstatement of particular ornate elements of the building that were of little or no value to the insured, because no reasonable insured would demand reinstatement of those features.[31] By contrast, if the value of the building to the insured was its ornate features, then it would not be for the insured to insist upon like-for-like reinstatement. In *Reynolds v Phoenix Assurance Co Ltd*,[32] business premises which had been purchased for £18,000 were insured for £628,000, covering the buildings (£550,000), machinery (£28,000) and stock (£50,000). A fire occurred which destroyed some seven-tenths of the buildings. Exercising their right under the terms of the policy, the insurers elected not to reinstate.[33] The claimants sued, claiming an indemnity which amounted to the cost of reinstatement of the buildings. The insurers argued that the claimants' loss should be determined by the value of the buildings as used for the purposes intended by the claimants, and that this should be measured either by market value or modern replacement value. Further, the insurers claimed that reinstatement, even if genuinely intended by the claimants, was not appropriate in that no commercial man would think of spending £1.25 million in rebuilding obsolete premises if he could buy modern premises for £30,000. It was held that the claimants' intention to rebuild the damaged premises if awarded an adequate sum to do so was genuine and was not based upon some eccentricity. The sum claimed was a true indemnification.

[28] ibid 674 and 676, respectively.

[29] *Bakerland Pty Ltd v Coleridge* [2002] NSWCA 30 (the Coogee Palace Aquarium in Sydney, now a hotel).

[30] [1996] AC 344.

[31] *Exchange Theatre Ltd v Iron Trades Mutual Insurance Co* [1983] 1 Lloyd's Rep 674.

[32] [1978] 2 Lloyd's Rep 440.

[33] The policy in question contained a pay, reinstate or replace clause.

Where the insured possesses only a limited interest in the insured property, recovery in the event of a loss is limited to the actual value of the interest in question. Examples include creditors who insure the value of their security interests in an asset, and tenants (lessees) who insure the value of their property. Where several creditors have security interests in the same property, the total sum recoverable in the event of a loss may exceed the actual value of the property.[34]

A lessee who has covenanted to repair or insure the property against fire damage will receive the cost of reinstatement. Recovery is not limited to the market value of the lease. The point has also been taken that even in the absence of such a covenant, a tenant will recover more than the value of his interest where the loss results in the tenant losing his home.[35]

1.2.3. Unvalued Policies on Goods

Where goods have been totally lost, the courts will take the market value of the items as a means of determining the sum recoverable by the insured. In assessing market value, account will be taken of the time and place of the insured loss.[36] The test is what would it cost the insured to replace the lost goods,[37] and their aesthetic or sentimental value is to be disregarded. The principle was cogently stated by Cockburn CJ in *Chapman v Pole*[38] when summing up for the jury: 'You must not run away with the notion that a policy of insurance entitles a man to recover according to the amount represented as insured … he can only recover the real and actual value of the goods.'[39]

If the lost item is second-hand, the insured will recover no more than its reasonable second-hand value as at the time of the loss:

> Many an assured who has had an armchair burned to pieces has put forward the proposition: 'Well I want an armchair to sit upon. This one is destroyed and I can only get one to sit upon by buying a new one.' In some circumstances, if the law were otherwise, that might be very reasonable, but very often it is not recognised and he realises to his chagrin that all he can recover is not his armchair to sit upon, but the reasonable value of the second-hand armchair that has been destroyed.[40]

The measure of second-hand value is subject to an important ambiguity that it sometimes, but not always, resolved by the policy wording. Does the value of the subject matter refer to the amount for which it could have been sold by the insured prior to the loss or does it relate to the cost to the insured of buying a replacement in the same condition as before the loss? In tort law, the replacement cost to the insured is the correct measure, so the facts that the claimant had obtained the subject matter cheaply, below market price, and that any sale in the open market by the insured may have been to a dealer, who would have offered a lower price to include mark-up, are to be left out of account.[41] In New Zealand the view has been

[34] *Westminster Fire Office v Glasgow Provident Society* (1888) 13 App Cas 699.
[35] *Castellain v Preston* (1883) 11 QBD 380.
[36] *Chapman v Pole* (1870) 22 LT 306.
[37] *Rice v Baxendale* (1861) 7 H & N 96, 100 (Bramwell B).
[38] (1870) 22 LT 306.
[39] ibid 307.
[40] *Ewer v National Employers' Mutual General Insurance Association Ltd* (1937) 157 LT 16, 21 (Mackinnon J).
[41] *Dominion Mosaics Co v Trafalgar Trucking Co* [1990] 2 All ER 246.

taken that the insured is entitled to the amount that a reasonable person would have paid for the subject matter.[42]

In the case of partial loss of goods, the default measure is the diminution in market value. In the case of goods that can be repaired, the cost of restoring the goods to their pre-loss condition is generally regarded as a useful surrogate test. However, there may be cases where the goods are not repairable and they have no market value as such. Thus, in the case of a rare antique, the court will generally take the price which the item could have been sold for immediately prior to the loss. In the case of a work of art, for example a film, that may mean that the amount recoverable could be lower than the costs involved in producing the film.[43] The difficulties of assessing the value of a damaged work of art can be seen in *Quorum AS v Schramm*,[44] which – it will be recalled from the above discussion – concerned sub-molecular smoke damage to the Degas pastel, *La Danse Grecque*. After the fire the parties negotiated an endorsement to the policy governing partial loss:

> In the event of partial loss or damage … the amount of the loss shall be the cost and expense of restoration plus any resulting depreciation in value. Underwriters' liability shall be limited to that proportion of such loss or damage which the sum insured bears to the market value of the item immediately prior to the loss and in no event shall underwriters be liable for more than the insured value of the item.

The court had to assess both the value of the painting before the fire and its value after the ensuing damage. With respect to the first issue, Thomas J stated that, as with the approach taken in relation to sale of goods and valuation for tax purposes, the task of the court is to ascertain the price that could be achieved between a willing seller and a willing buyer in the relevant market. If there is an open market price, that should be ascertained. Expert evidence should be taken into account, including evidence of prices obtained at auctions. The judge held, on the basis of the authorities and the views of expert valuers, that the court should have regard to the market where the painting was likely to obtain a higher price. On the facts, this was the dealers' market. Turning to the second issue, Thomas J was faced with conflicting expert evidence as to the level of depreciation of the damaged painting, which ranged from 20 per cent to 80 per cent. He noted that the range of those interested in the painting in its damaged state would be far fewer. He also accepted that in valuing it after the fire, he needed to look at the risks of further deterioration. On the facts, it was held that the painting's value before the fire was US$3.6 million, while its damaged value was US$2.2 million.

It is all but inevitable that, following the repair of damaged goods, their value would have been reduced: damaged and repaired is plainly worth less than undamaged. The difference between the two, known as 'accelerated depreciation', is recoverable in tort,[45] but the position in insurance depends upon the wording of the policy. The matter was tested in the Abu Dhabi Commercial Court before retired English High Court Judge Sir Andrew Smith, in *Global Private Investments RSC Ltd v Global Aerospace Underwriting Managers Ltd*.[46] An aircraft was insured under an all risks aviation policy against 'physical loss of or damage'. In the event of partial loss, the insurers were to pay the 'cost of repairs', defined as covering transportation, personnel and test flight costs. The issue between the parties

[42] *State Insurance Office v Bettany* [1992] 2 NZLR 275.
[43] *Richard Aubrey Film Productions Ltd v Graham* [1960] 2 Lloyd's Rep 101.
[44] [2002] Lloyd's Rep IR 292.
[45] *Payton v Brooks* [1974] 1 Lloyd's Rep 241.
[46] [2021] ADGMCFI 0008.

was whether the definition of cost of repairs was exhaustive or whether other forms of loss – including accelerated depreciation – were recoverable under the policy. Sir Andrew Smith held that the definition was exhaustive and that there was no coverage for any other form of loss. The court rejected the further argument that the word 'repairs' required the insurers to ensure that the insured had not suffered any loss, but that there had been accelerated depreciation loss: while the word itself could be construed as meaning to make good any loss, the present context made it clear that the policy was concerned only with physical repair costs.

2. Limits on Recovery

2.1. Betterment

The concept of betterment, which is known to both tort and insurance law, arises where the claimant/insured uses the funds derived from his claim to repair or reinstate the damaged subject matter and thereby obtains something better than the previously undamaged subject matter. As noted above, this is unlikely to arise with domestic goods, including cars, and it is in any event the case that 'new for old' policies, whereby the replacement value rather than the market value of the insured property is covered, are now common. Betterment is a far greater possibility for repairs effected to buildings and commercial goods. Betterment has its origins in eighteenth-century marine cases which recognised that insurance recoveries to repair a wooden vessel other than one on a maiden voyage should be reduced by one-third to reflect the likely increase in value: this 'customary deduction' is codified by section 69 of the Marine Insurance Act 1906, although by the time the Act was passed it had fallen into disuse with the demise of wooden vessels. There are numerous statements in the authorities that betterment should be taken into account. In *Reynolds v Phoenix Assurance Co Ltd*,[47] betterment was held to be minimal because the claimants intended to use second-hand building materials and other substances of inferior quality as far as possible, but Forbes J explained the underlying basis of the doctrine of betterment in the following terms:

> [T]he principle of betterment is too well established in the law of insurance to be departed from at this stage even though it may sometimes work hardship on the assured. It is simply that an allowance must be made because the assured is getting something new for something old.[48]

The judge subjected the principle of indemnity as it applies to real property to detailed consideration. Citing the Irish case of *Murphy v Wexford County Council*,[49] which concerned statutory compensation to persons whose property had suffered malicious damage, Forbes J noted that the difficulty in assessing *quantum* lies in reaching a figure which does not amount to enrichment or impoverishment. He stressed that the determination of the proper measure of indemnity is a question of fact and degree to be decided on the circumstances of the case; and in its deliberations, the court should take account of the factors indicated by

[47] [1978] 2 Lloyd's Rep 440.
[48] ibid, 453. See also *Dominion Mosaics & Tile Co Ltd v Trafalgar Trucking Co Ltd* [1990] 2 All ER 246 (CA), 255.
[49] (1921) 2 IR 230.

Sir James Campbell C in *Murphy*: 'Would [the insured] for any reason that might appeal to an ordinary man in his position rebuild [the premises] if he got replacement [costs] or is his claim for such [costs] a mere pretence?'[50]

The judgment of Leggatt LJ in *Sartex Quilts and Textiles Ltd v Endurance Corporate Capital Ltd*[51] has now established a principled basis for betterment.[52] Three possibilities were identified. First, the insured chose to make improvements to the subject matter, eg by installing double glazing in place of the original single glazing: the additional cost required to make such improvements was to be deducted from the insured loss by reason of betterment.[53] Secondly, the repair or reinstatement incidentally and unavoidably resulted in improvements, as where a damaged machine was replaced with a new one because an equivalent machine could not be found: there was no betterment and no deduction in that situation. Thirdly, the repairs or reinstatement conferred upon the upon the insured a real pecuniary advantage, as where a damaged machine was replaced with another that was more efficient[54] and thus produced real savings, or where an item with an expected remaining life of eight years is replaced with another with an expected life of 30 years:[55] the pecuniary benefits could be deducted by way of betterment.

2.2. Under-insurance and the Principle of Average

Where the sum insured under the policy is lower than the actual value of the subject matter and there is a total loss, the insured must bear the shortfall: in the case of a valued policy, the insured recovers the agreed value; and in the case of an unvalued policy, the insured recovers the actual loss but capped at the maximum sum insured. The principle of average arises where there is a partial loss, and is enshrined in section 81 of the Marine Insurance Act 1906, which deems the insured to be his own insurer for any difference between the insured value of the subject matter and its actual value. That means that responsibility for any partial loss is borne by the insurers and the insured in proportion to their respective contributions. If, for example, a cargo which is actually worth £50,000 is insured for £25,000, and as a result of a partial loss £10,000 is required to repair it, the insured will only recover £5000. Without average, the insured would recover the full £10,000. Marine policies are subject to average unless they otherwise provide. In other forms of insurance there is no implied average term, although average clauses are sometimes found in policies on commercial buildings. Describing a policy as 'subject to average' is something of a hidden trap for an ordinary policyholder, and average clauses are not found in domestic policies. It may be noted that in Australia average clauses in consumer policies are banned,[56] and in New Zealand an average clause may not be used in a policy on a dwelling and in all cases other than in marine insurance is enforceable only if specifically drawn to the insured's attention.[57]

[50] ibid 240.

[51] [2020] EWCA Civ 308.

[52] Applying his own judgment in *Thai Airways International Public Co Ltd v KI Holdings Co Ltd* [2015] EWHC 1250 (Comm).

[53] *Tonkin v UK Insurance Ltd* [2007] Lloyd's Rep IR 283.

[54] These were the facts of *British Westinghouse Electric & Manufacturing Co Ltd v Underground Electric Railways Co of London Ltd* [1912] AC 673.

[55] *Voaden v Champion, The Baltic Surveyor* [2002] EWCA Civ 89.

[56] Insurance Contracts Act 1984, s 44.

[57] Insurance Law Reform Act 1985, ss 15 and 16.

2.3. The Excess Clause

An excess clause, otherwise known as a deductible or self-insured retention, is used almost universally in all forms of insurance. The clause provides that the insured will bear the first part of any loss. Such a clause is generally expressed by way of a sum of money or, in some commercial policies, by way of a percentage of any loss.[58] The insured is his own insurer for the amount of the excess. The excess is not regarded as part of the insured loss and, as will be seen in chapter 13, that has important implications for subrogation recoveries. It is sometimes said that an excess gives the insured a personal stake, so that there is some incentive for the insured to take care to avoid loss. This is a doubtful justification: even assuming that policyholders are aware of the amount of any excess, it is difficult to imagine that their behaviour is greatly impacted by its existence. The real function of the excess is recognition that the vast majority of losses are small, so that imposing an excess can greatly reduce the amount of the premium and, indeed, the costs of the insurance industry as a whole. The amount of the excess reflects the underwriting risk. For example, a motor policy may have an ordinary excess for first party damage[59] of £100, rising to, say, £400 if the vehicle is being driven by an inexperienced driver. Some insurers offer policies without an excess, but the premium for them is disproportionately higher, and other insurers allow the insured to choose the level of excess with appropriate adjustment of the premium. In the commercial world some excesses may run into millions of pounds, and the market offers 'deductible buy-back' insurance whereby the excess is insured under a separate policy.

An excess clause is not regarded as an exclusion, so the burden of proving that a loss is greater than the excess is borne by the insured and not the insurers. The point was crucial in *Ted Baker Plc v Axa Insurance UK Plc (No 2)*,[60] where the insured bore an excess of £5000 for 'each and every loss'. An employee of the insured systematically stole stock over a period of four years, and when his house was searched goods to the value of £367,000 was discovered. However, the claim failed. There was no evidence of the frequency and amount of the thefts, and the insured could thus not show that any one theft had exceeded £5000.

2.4. The Franchise Clause

Franchise clauses have the effect of relieving the insurer from liability completely unless the loss exceeds a stated figure, in which case the insurer will be liable for the whole loss. However, separated losses falling below the stated sum cannot be aggregated in order to defeat a franchise clause.[61] This type of clause has its origins in the Lloyd's SG wording, whereby claims for damage to specified commodities were uninsured unless the loss reached a given percentage or the vessel was stranded. That wording is no longer used.

[58] It has been held in New Zealand that the agreed percentage is to be deducted from the sum recoverable under the policy and not from the totality of the loss where part of it is uninsured: *QBE Insurance (International) Ltd v Wild South Holdings Ltd and Maxims Fashions Ltd, Marriott v Vero Insurance, Crystal Imports Ltd v Certain Underwriters at Lloyd's of London* [2014] NZCA 447.

[59] Excesses are not permitted for liability to third parties: see ch 14 below.

[60] [2014] EWHC 3548 (Comm). There was no appeal on this point when the matter went to the Court of Appeal, [2017] Lloyd's Rep IR 682.

[61] *Stewart v Merchant's Marine Insurance Co* (1885) 16 QBD 619.

2.5. Aggregation

2.5.1. *The Importance of Aggregation*

Of all the issues that arise in insurance and reinsurance law, aggregation comes close to the top in terms of frequency and importance. Its significance is easily explained. We have seen in this chapter that all policies have excesses and policy limits, but it becomes crucial to know how many excesses and how many policy limits are applicable to any one claim. By way of example, a factory is insured against liability for damage caused to neighbouring houses. The policy has a limit of £1,000,000 for any one event, and the insured has to bear an excess of £100,000 for any one event. There is an explosion at the factory, causing severe damage to 10 neighbouring houses. Each house is damaged to the extent of £500,000, so the total loss is £5,000,000. The amount that the insured recovers depends upon the meaning of 'event'. If event means the explosion, then there is one event and the insured recovers the policy limit of £1,000,000 minus one excess of £100,000, ie £900,000. By contrast, if the damage to each individual house is a separate event, then the policy applies separately to each of them: the insured recovers £500,000 minus the excess of £100,000 excess on 10 separate occasions, a figure of £4,000,000. The difference between the two calculations becomes even more apparent if it is assumed that the damage to each house is only £100,000. If there is one event, the insured recovers an aggregate of £1,000,000 for the explosion giving rise to the damage to each of the houses, minus one excess of £100,000, again £900,000. However, if each house is an event, then although the insured has 10 claims, none of those claims is greater than the £100,000 excess applicable to each of them, so that nothing would be recovered under the policy. What is apparent from these examples is that the effect of aggregation will vary depending upon whether the issue is the number of claims with separate limits of indemnity that may be made or the number of excesses that must be borne. As a broad generality, the assured will want to recover as many policy limits as possible while bearing as few excesses as possible, whereas the insurers will want to limit the policy coverage to one event while arguing for as many excesses as possible. It is for that reason that aggregation clauses cannot be construed *contra proferentem*, because until the nature of the losses and the figures are known it cannot be said whether it is beneficial or disadvantageous for the insured to argue for one event or a number of events.

Aggregation can be expressed in a number of different ways. Typical phrases found in policies require aggregation for policy limits or excess purposes of all losses arising from any one 'originating cause', 'cause', source', 'event', 'occurrence', 'accident', 'claim' or 'happening'. Each of these phrases has been given detailed consideration by the courts, and in general terms it may be said that causes and sources are very broad and are the underlying reason why losses have been suffered, whereas events and occurrences focus on the loss itself. As was said in *Countrywide Assurance v Marshall*,[62] the cause is the 'why' whereas the event or occurrence is the 'what'. The decided cases are far from straightforward or reconcilable on the application of this distinction.

2.5.2. *Event and Occurrence*

These two words are interchangeable. An event is, in the words of Lord Mustill in *Axa Reinsurance (UK) Plc v Field*,[63] 'something which happens at a particular time, at a

[62] [2002] EWHC 2082 (Comm).
[63] [1996] 3 All ER 517.

particular place and in a particular way', as opposed to the underlying cause or general state of affairs that has led to what has happened. So, if a series of losses is to be aggregated, those losses are required to satisfy the 'unities' of time, place and motive, and there must also be a connection to the aggregating event. The connection is looser than the ordinary doctrine of proximate cause,[64] but the weaker the link between the losses, the more difficult it is to establish that the losses are the result of a single event. There are numerous illustrations of events and occurrences in the decided cases. The most straightforward of them concern individual losses arising out of a state of affairs, eg each train derailment on a rail network and each speed restriction arising out of a general failure to maintain the network,[65] individual acts of theft,[66] the seizure of Kuwait airport, so that each of the 15 Kuwaiti planes on the ground at the time were lost by reason of a single event,[67] and each individual looting of supermarkets in Jakarta as part of an organised political campaign.[68]

One question that has arisen in a number of jurisdictions in both courts and arbitrations in insurance and reinsurance disputes is the classification of the attacks on the World Trade Center on 11 September 2001. The building itself consisted of two parallel towers, connected only at their base. Each tower was attacked by terrorists flying a hijacked aircraft into it. The attacks took place within 15 minutes of each other, although they were designed to have coincided and failed to do so because one of the aircraft was delayed in taking off. Applying the unities to this situation has been a matter of controversy. One view is that the attacks took place at the same place, at the same time and with a common motive. The alternative view, accepted by Field J in *Aioi Nissay Dowa Insurance Co Ltd v Heraldglen Ltd*,[69] is that there were two events. It was necessary to focus not on New York, but rather on the individual circumstances affecting each of the aircraft: the security arrangements for each were deficient, the aircraft took off from different airports in the USA and the hijackings occurred at different times. It suffices to say that there is no consensus on this matter.

2.5.3. Originating Cause

The terms 'original/originating cause', 'cause' and 'source' are interchangeable[70] and refer to a state of affairs. The classic statement is that of Lord Mustill in *Axa v Field*:[71]

> A cause to my mind is something altogether less constricted. It can be a continuing state of affairs; it can be the absence of something happening. Equally, the word 'originating' was in my view consciously chosen to open up the widest possible search for a unifying factor in the history of the losses which it is sought to aggregate. To my mind the one expression [originating cause] has a much wider connotation than the other [event].

A cause is on this basis the reason that individual losses have occurred, and although there has to be sufficient connection between the losses and the cause so that they are not too remote from it, the test is not one of proximate cause.[72] Matters that have been described

[64] See ch 10 above.

[65] *Midland Mainline Ltd v Commercial Union Assurance Co Ltd* [2004] Lloyd's Rep IR 22.

[66] *Dornoch Ltd v Mauritius Union Assurance Co Ltd and Mauritius Commercial Bank Ltd (No 2)* [2007] Lloyd's Rep IR 350; *Ted Baker Plc v Axa Insurance UK Plc (No 2)* [2017] Lloyd's Rep IR 682.

[67] *Kuwait Airways Corp v Kuwait Insurance Co SAK* [1996] 1 Lloyd's Rep 664; *Scott v Copenhagen Reinsurance Co (UK) Ltd* [2003] Lloyd's Rep IR 696.

[68] *Mann v Lexington Insurance* [2001] Lloyd's Rep IR 179.

[69] [2013] EWHC 154 (Comm).

[70] *Spire Healthcare Ltd v Royal & Sun Alliance Insurance Ltd* [2022] EWCA Civ 17.

[71] [1996] 3 All ER 517.

[72] *Spire Healthcare Ltd v Royal & Sun Alliance Insurance Ltd* [2022] EWCA Civ 17.

as causes include: failure by the insured financial services company to give proper training to its agents, leading the agents to mis-sell products to customers;[73] a 'blind spot' in the form of a propensity by an underwriter to act negligently in writing reinsurance risks to be accepted by his syndicate;[74] failure by a fund manager to make appropriate investments, leading to losses by investors;[75] prolonged rain, leading to serious flooding;[76] and the outbreak of a pandemic.[77] The leading authority is *Spire Healthcare Ltd v Royal & Sun Alliance Insurance Ltd.*[78] Here, a consultant breast surgeon employed by the insured was found to have performed a number of operations by using a technique generally regarded as inappropriate and also without the informed consent of the patients. The surgeon also fraudulent carried out a series of procedures that were not clinically necessary, presumably in order to earn fees from patients. Numerous claims were made, and these were settled. The insured's policy was subject to a £10 million limit for all losses attributable to one source or cause. The trial judge held that there were two separate causes – negligence in carrying out necessary operations and fraud in carrying out unnecessary operations – so that the insured could recover for up to £10 million for a group of claims. The Court of Appeal disagreed and held that there was just one cause, namely, the dishonesty of the surgeon, his failure to seek informed consent and his lack of care for his patients. The Court of Appeal held that these matters could be 'identified either singly or collectively as a unifying factor in the history of the claims' so that they were one originating cause.

The distinction between event and cause is easy to state, but is very difficult to apply at the margins. *Simmonds v Gammell*[79] was a rather different claim arising out of the World Trade Center. The Port of New York (PONY) was insured against liability for the period including the terrorist attack, and the insurers were reinsured under a contract imposing a $1.5 million excess for all loss arising from one event. PONY settled many claims brought by police and firefighters injured in the rescue operation who alleged that their injuries had been sustained through PONY's failure to provide adequate equipment and training. An arbitration tribunal held that the terrorist attacks constituted one event so that the reinsured was required to bear only one excess. An appeal against the award was dismissed by the court, ruling that the tribunal had applied the correct legal principle so that the result was not capable of challenge. The court notably failed to comment on the correctness of the award, and it is strongly arguable that the terrorist attack was too remote from the injuries suffered to constitute the relevant aggregating event and that PONY's failings were a cause rather than an event, so that aggregation would not have been available to the reinsured and multiple excesses would have applied.

2.5.4. Series Clauses

Aggregation is very commonly achieved by the use of a 'series' clause.[80] Typical wording would allow aggregation of all losses arising from a series of related events, or from a series

[73] *Countrywide Assured Group Plc v Marshall* [2002] EWHC 2082 (Comm).
[74] *Caudle v Sharp* [1995] LRLR 433; *Cox v Bankside Members Agency Ltd* [1995] 2 Lloyd's Rep 43.
[75] *Ace European Group v Standard Life Assurance Ltd* [2012] EWCA Civ 1713.
[76] *Tokio Marine Europe Insurance Ltd v Novae Corporate Underwriting Ltd* [2013] EWHC 3362 (Comm).
[77] *Financial Conduct Authority v Arch Insurance* [2021] UKSC 1.
[78] [2022] EWCA Civ 17.
[79] [2016] EWHC 2515 (Comm).
[80] K Wu, 'Interpretation of "Series"-Based Aggregation Clauses: When Can the Insurance Claims Be Aggregated?' [2021] *Journal of Business Law* 384.

of related acts or omissions. It will be appreciated that on this type of wording there are two separate elements: the need for a series and the need for the events or acts/omissions to be related to each other. A logical interpretation of such wording would be that the word 'series' implies no more than a sequence, and that the requirement for the matters to be 'related' sets out the circumstances in which a sequence of events can be treated as one event. In *Lord Bishop of Leeds v Dixon Coles and Gill*,[81] the first instance judge noted that the word 'series' taken alone was ambiguous and could mean a sequence of events or a related sequence of events,[82] but it was not necessary for the court to decide the point given that there was a further requirement for the events to be related.

The question thus becomes, when is a series of events related so as to permit aggregation? The point was discussed inconclusively by the House of Lords in *Lloyds TSB General Insurance Holdings v Lloyds Bank General Insurance Co Ltd*,[83] where the insured financial services company faced multiple claims for pensions mis-selling by its agents. The professional indemnity policy provided for a per claim excess of £1 million and for the aggregation of excesses where 'a series of third party claims shall result from any single act or omission (or a related series of acts or omissions)'. It was held that each act of negligence bore its own deductible, with the result that little or nothing was covered by the policy, and the words in brackets could not undermine that basic wording. Lord Hobhouse expressed the view that the bracketed words might operate to aggregate separate losses arising from one act of mis-selling (eg a presentation to a number of customers), but that was questioned by Lord Hoffmann, who did not proffer his own opinion. Subsequently, wordings were altered and the brackets were dropped. In *AIG Europe Ltd v Woodman*,[84] solicitors obtained professional indemnity insurance under which liability was capped at £3 million for any 'series of related matters or transactions'. The case involved two proposed developments, one in Turkey and one in Morocco, attracting a total of 214 investors whose funds were used to buy the land and pay for the construction. The solicitors were bound to the investors not to release any funds without security. They did release the sums without security, but the developments did not take place and the investments were lost. The solicitors asserted that the individual investments were not related and so the insurers were liable for up to £3 million in respect of each individual claim by an investor. Lord Toulson, delivering the leading judgment, held that the relevant transactions were the two developments, and that investors for each of the developments were investing in a common development and were effectively co-beneficiaries under a common trust, so a £3 million limit of indemnity applied separately to each of the developments. The two developments themselves were not related, in that although they had a common source and operated in the same way, they had no actual connection with each other. 'Related' referred to a connection between the two investments, not to a similarity between them.

Woodman was applied in *Baines v Dixon Coles & Gill*,[85] where one partner in a firm of solicitors engaged over a period of years in embezzling funds from two client accounts. The policy imposed a per claim limit of £2 million, a claim being defined as including 'one series of related acts or omissions'. The Court of Appeal held that there were two separate series. As was the case in *Woodman*, the only connection between the two groups of embezzlements

[81] [2020] EWHC 2809 (Ch).
[82] The latter view was adopted in *Moore v IAG New Zealand Ltd* [2020] NZCA 319, discussed in ch 19 below.
[83] [2003] Lloyd's Rep IR 623.
[84] [20177 UKSC 18.
[85] [2021] EWCA Civ 1211. See also *Bank of Queensland Ltd v AIG Australia Ltd* [2019] NSWCA 190.

was that they had been carried out and covered up in the same way. That, however, did not make them 'related', as there was no connection between the two client accounts.

Mention may also be made of 'hours' clauses commonly found in property policies insuring against natural catastrophes. The effect of an 'hours' clause is to treat all losses arising from a single occurrence within a given period (ranging from 48 hours to 168 hours) as constituting a single loss for policy limits and excess aggregation purposes.

---

3. Late Payment[86]

3.1. The Common Law Background

It is perhaps self-evident that where an insurer unreasonably delays in settling a claim the consequences for an insured can be disastrous. *Sprung v Royal Insurance (UK) Ltd*[87] is a paradigm case. The insured, Sprung (S), owned a factory which processed animal waste. He effected two insurance policies: the first covered him against theft and the second provided cover in relation to the plant and machinery against 'sudden and unforeseen damage that necessitates immediate repair of the plant before it can resume normal working'. Condition 6 of the second policy permitted him to carry out minor repairs 'without prejudice to the liability of the insurers' provided they were given notice together with a schedule of repairs. However, it was stipulated that major repairs required the prior sanction of the insurers. When vandals broke into the premises and destroyed the machinery, S submitted a claim. It was rejected by the insurers on the basis that the evidence did not point to theft and, with respect to the second policy, that cover was not provided against wilful damage. S lacked the financial resources to repair the machinery pending resolution of his dispute with the insurers and was not able to raise the necessary credit facility. The business's goodwill evaporated and he ceased trading six months later. The insurers continued to deny liability for almost four years before finally indemnifying him for the lost machinery. S, having lost his livelihood, brought an action seeking consequential damages in the sum of £75,000. Appearing in person and aided by the judges, he based his claim on two grounds: first, late payment; and, second, that the insurer's failure to accept liability constituted a breach of contract.

Sprung's claim failed. To understand the Court of Appeal's reasoning, it is necessary to appreciate the considerable weight of established legal principle that bound the court and which, therefore, operated to defeat the claim. The point has already been made that an insurance claim amounts to a claim for unliquidated damages for breach of contract, in that the insurers have failed in their obligation to hold the insured harmless.[88] While damages may be awarded for late payment of debt, no such remedy lies for late payment of damages.

[86] F Arnold-Dwyer, 'Insurance Law Reform by Degrees: Late Payment and Insurable Interest' (2017) 80 *MLR* 489.

[87] [1999] 1 Lloyd's Rep IR 111. See J Lowry and P Rawlings 'Insurers, Claims and the Boundaries of Good Faith' [2005] *MLR* 82.

[88] *Jabbour v Custodian of Absentee Property for the State of Israel* [1954] 1 WLR 139; *Hardcastle v Netherwood* (1821) 5 B & Ald 93; *Castelli v Boddington* (1852) 1 E & B 66; *Luckie v Bushby* (1853) 13 CB 864; *Lloyd v Fleming* (1872) 7 QBD 299; *Pellas & Co v Neptune Marine Insurance Company* (1879) 5 CPD 34; *Swan and Cleland's Graving Dock and Slipway Co v Maritime Insurance Co and Croshaw* [1907] 1 KB 116, 123–24; *Baker v Adam* (1910) 15 Com Cas 227; *William Pickersgill & Sons Ltd v London and Provincial Marine and General Insurance Co Ltd* [1912] 3 KB 614, 622; *Callaghan v Dominion Insurance Co* [1997] 2 Lloyd's Rep 541.

This point assumed major significance in *Sprung*. The classic statement of this rule was delivered by Lord Brandon in *The Lips*:[89] 'There is no such thing as a cause of action in damages for late payment of damages. The only remedy which the law affords for delay in paying damages is the discretionary award of interest pursuant to statute.' In *The Fanti*,[90] a case on indemnity insurance, Lord Goff stated that:

> [A]t common law, a contract of indemnity gives rise to an action for unliquidated damages, arising from the failure of the indemnifier to prevent the indemnified person from suffering damage, for example, by having to pay a third party. I also accept that, at common law, the cause of action does not (unless the contract provides otherwise) arise until the indemnified person can show actual loss … This is, as I understand it, because a promise of indemnity is simply a promise to hold the indemnified person harmless against a specified loss or expense. On this basis, no debt can arise before the loss is suffered or the expense incurred; however, once the loss is suffered or the expense incurred, the indemnifier is in breach of contract for having failed to hold the indemnified person harmless against the relevant loss or expense.[91]

Given that indemnity in insurance is characterised as damages, a claim for loss caused by late payment falls foul of the rule outlined by Lord Brandon in *The Lips*. However, the use of the term 'damages' in the context of insurance payments is curious. 'Damages' in this context is used in a sense different from its common (compensatory) meaning. As Pearson J has pointed out,

> its use is puzzling and seems to be used in a rather unusual sense, because the right to indemnity arises, not by reason of any wrongful act or omission on the part of the insurer (who did not promise that the loss would not happen or that he would prevent it) but only under his promise to indemnify the insured in the event of a loss.[92]

The common law categorisation of an insurance claim as a claim for unliquidated damages for breach of contract gives rise to the unfortunate consequence that if an insurer wrongfully refuses to settle a claim, it will not be liable for damages for the losses suffered by the insured because of the principle laid down in *The Lips*. The reasoning of Hirst J in *Ventouris v Mountain, The Italia Express (No 2)*[93] is instructive. The claimant insured a vessel against war risks under an agreed value policy. While it was undergoing repairs, the vessel was totally lost when it was sunk by explosives attached to its hull. The insurers initially denied liability, arguing that the loss was caused by the wilful misconduct of the claimant in procuring the sinking. On the thirty-seventh day of the trial, following rulings by the Court of Appeal on the admissibility of certain evidence relied on by the underwriters in their defence, they withdrew their allegations and submitted to judgment on liability. Judgment was entered in favour of the claimant in the sum of $4 million, the insured value of his vessel. The claimant went on to claim damages for other losses consequent upon the insurers' delay in meeting the claim: loss of income which would have been earned by a replacement vessel; loss suffered by virtue of increase in the capital value of a replacement vessel; and damages for hardship, inconvenience and mental distress. The issue which fell for determination was whether such heads of damages were recoverable as a matter of law.

[89] *President of India v Lips Maritime Corp* [1988] AC 395, 424.
[90] *Firma C-Trade SA v Newcastle P & I Association, The Fanti* [1991] AC 1.
[91] ibid 35.
[92] *Jabbour v Custodian of Absentee Property for the State of Israel* [1954] 1 WLR 139.
[93] [1992] 2 Lloyd's Rep 281.

It was common ground between both parties that a contract of insurance is an agreement by the underwriter to hold the insured harmless against loss or damage from the peril insured against and that the remedy for breach of that obligation is a claim in damages. However, the parties diverged in their analysis of the nature of the obligation to 'hold the insured harmless'. The claimant argued that the underwriters failed to hold him harmless against the loss of his vessel in that if the $4 million was not paid immediately following the demand for payment then at that point the underwriter was in breach of contract and their secondary obligation to pay damages at large (which were not limited to $4 million) was triggered. The claimant thus contended that in property insurance, as opposed to liability insurance, the underwriters were not in breach until a demand for immediate payment of the indemnity has been made. On the other hand, the underwriters argued that their primary obligation was to prevent the occurrence of the loss and that this obligation was broken the moment the vessel sunk. On this analysis, it followed that no demand for payment was necessary and that there was no subsequent separate breach of contract by the underwriter's failure to meet the claim. Thus, there was no distinction between liability and property insurance in this respect. Further, relying on section 67 of the Marine Insurance Act 1906, the underwriters argued that an agreed value clause in the policy is equivalent to a liquidated damages provision which limits the measure of indemnity to the agreed value of the vessel.[94] Hirst J, on the basis of the statutory language, rejected the claimant's contention. He held that the underwriters were in breach of contract the moment the vessel sank, and therefore from the time when the peril occurred they came under a secondary obligation to pay damages to the insured which were limited by the amount agreed in the policy. As a matter of law, the underwriter's liability was fixed at $4 million by the policy and the claimant could not recover additional special or general damages for this as this would be tantamount to allowing damages for the late payment of damages. Further, Hirst J took the view that although *The Fanti* was a liability insurance decision, it was nevertheless of general application and extended to property insurance.

While, strictly speaking, *The Italia Express (No 2)* is an authority dealing purely with the construction of section 67 of the Marine Insurance Act 1906, it has not been viewed in this light in subsequent non-marine cases. The reasoning of Hirst J and the approach taken by Lord Goff in *The Fanti* both proved to be determinative in *Sprung*. At first sight, it appears that the insured's plight in *Sprung* was caused by the insurer's failure to pay within a reasonable time. However, this was not the view taken by the Court of Appeal. Noting that they had not heard a detailed argument on the point, the court nevertheless dismissed Sprung's claim as amounting to no more than a claim for late payment of damages.[95] Evans LJ was prepared to hold that there was an implied term obliging the insurers to respond promptly to the insured's claim and that the defendants' delay did in fact amount to breach of that implied obligation. However, as a matter of law, this did not result in any liability for consequential loss except in relation to interest for late payment. The insurer's initial denial of liability placed Sprung in a position where he was entitled – and, indeed, bound – to proceed as if he was uninsured. He could have reinstated or repaired the damaged property, and if he had done so the insurer

> would not then be in a position to allege by way of defence that there had been a breach of condition (6) [of the policy]; in other words, they would have disqualified themselves from saying

[94] See ch 17 below.
[95] [1999] 1 Lloyd's Rep IR 111, 116 (Evans LJ).

> that, the repairs having been carried out without their consent, the claimant was not entitled to recover the promised indemnity under the policy.[96]

Evans LJ was thus driven to conclude that the insured became author of his own misfortune for which the insurer was in no way liable:

> What has to be said, however hard it may seem to say it, is that in such circumstances the cause of any loss which the plaintiff suffered must be regarded as the consequence of his own decision not to proceed with repair or reinstatement, whether that decision was voluntary or not. In other words, if, unfortunately, through his own financial circumstances he is unable to do so without assistance from the defendants, he cannot allege that the defendants were in breach of contract by failing to accept liability at that stage.[97]

It was with 'undisguised reluctance' that Evans LJ held that Mr Sprung's claim should fail. Similarly, Beldam LJ felt constrained by the authorities in holding that an insured has no cause of action for damages for non-payment of damages. He thought that no distinction could be drawn between a breach of the term in the contract (Condition 6) that required the insurers to inspect or give consent to the repairs promptly and a requirement that they should meet their obligations under the policy with due expedition. Thus, Beldam LJ also thought that if the insured had carried out his repairs after learning of the insurers' refusal to meet the claim or after unreasonable delay on the insurers part, the court would not entertain any argument on the insurer's part that they were not liable because of breach by the insured of the policy conditions.

The English view of the common law has been followed in Australia. It has been held in New South Wales that the insured's action is for unliquidated damages arising at the date of the insured peril,[98] and it follows that there can be no claim for damages for failing to pay damages.[99] By contrast, the New Zealand courts have recognised an implied contractual term that payment will be made within a reasonable period,[100] and in Canada the position is that punitive damages may be awarded for reprehensible failure to pay in a timely fashion.[101]

3.2. The Reform Process

The English and Scottish Law Commissions examined the law in this area in Issues Paper 6, published in March 2010. They argued strongly for reform, on four grounds. (1) The law lacked principle. The idea that the insurer's primary obligation is to prevent a loss occurring is a fiction which ignores commercial reality. (2) The law appeared unfair and biased against the interests of policyholders. (3) The law appeared to reward inefficiency and dishonesty amongst insurers. (4) The law led to injustice. The Law Commissions proposed to overturn the decision in *Sprung* and, in reliance on Scottish law, argued that the insurer's primary obligation should be to pay valid claims after due opportunity for a reasonable

[96] ibid 118.
[97] ibid.
[98] Globe Church Inc v Allianz Australia Insurance Ltd [2019] NSWCA 27.
[99] Worth v HDI Global Speciality SE [2021] NSWCA 185.
[100] *Young v Tower Insurance Ltd* [2016] NZHC 2969, where the court (without attribution) quoted verbatim from the Insurance Act 2015, s 13A, discussed below, as representing the common law.
[101] *Whiten v Pilot Insurance Co* [2002] 1 SCR 595, where allegations of arson following a fire in a family home were maintained without any evidence: the insured loss was only \$160,000, but punitive damages of \$1,000,000 were additionally awarded. See also *Stewart v Lloyd's Underwriters* 2019 BCSC 1582, where \$100,000 was awarded following an 'overwhelmingly inadequate' investigation of a claim under a travel policy and conduct designed to restrict liability for medical bills.

investigation and that damages should be awardable on ordinary contractual principles of remoteness as laid down in *Hadley v Baxendale*.[102] They also proposed that an insurer should be liable for any foreseeable losses, subject to any variation by the express terms of a contract. Consultation demonstrated concern that the introduction of this test would increase speculative claims, as the remit of consequential losses might be wide. Further, insurers argued that there ought to be a limit on the level of damages an insured should receive because the level of loss may be larger than the claim itself. The Law Commissions were undaunted, and in the December 2011 consultation paper *Reform of Insurance Law*[103] proposed a regime under which: insurers would be under a contractual obligation to pay claims within a reasonable time; the period for consideration would not start to run until insurers had received all material information from the insured and had been afforded an opportunity to consider the claim; it would not be possible to contract out of this liability to consumers, but exclusions in business policies would be permitted as long as the insurers had acted in good faith; and damages for distress should be awarded to consumers.

The Law Commissions' July 2014 report *Business Disclosure; Warranties; Insurers' Remedies for Fraudulent Claims; and Late Payment*[104] confirmed the earlier proposals and included a draft Bill. However, the Insurance Bill published by the government immediately afterwards excluded the late payment provisions. The view was that they were too controversial to be included in a Law Commission Bill subject to an expedited parliamentary procedure, and that the correct means of reform was in a government Bill so that there could be full discussion. The fear of the insurance industry was that late payment rights might open the door to the sort of bad faith claims coupled with punitive damages common in a number of US states. It was also suggested by commentators that awarding damages for late payment is akin to awarding free business interruption cover under property policies.[105] Attempts in Parliament to amend the Insurance Bill to include late payment provisions were rejected. It was initially thought that the government might not follow through with its promise to bring the late payment provisions forward in another Bill, but the government was as good as its word and the proposals were added to the Enterprise Bill 2015. The Law Commissions' draft survived the parliamentary process unscathed, other than the addition of a short limitation period for the bringing of claims for damages for late payment. The Enterprise Act 2016 duly added two new sections to the Insurance Act 2015: section 13A, the basic right to damages for late payment; and section 16A, regulating contracting out. In addition, section 5A has been added to the Limitation Act 1980, setting out the limitation period for late payment claims.

3.3. Statutory Provision for Late Payment

3.3.1. The Right to Damages for Late Payment

Section 13A of the Insurance Act 2015 provides as follows:

> (1) It is an implied term of every contract of insurance that if the insured makes a claim under the contract, the insurer must pay any sums due in respect of the claim within a reasonable time.

[102] [1854] EWHC Exch J70.
[103] Law Com CP No 201/Scot Law Com CP 152.
[104] Law Com CP No 353/Scot Law Com CP 238 (Cm 8898).
[105] As to which, see ch 19 below.

(2) A reasonable time includes a reasonable time to investigate and assess the claim.
(3) What is reasonable will depend on all the relevant circumstances, but the following are examples of things which may need to be taken into account –
    (a) the type of insurance,
    (b) the size and complexity of the claim,
    (c) compliance with any relevant statutory or regulatory rules or guidance,
    (d) factors outside the insurer's control.
(4) If the insurer shows that there were reasonable grounds for disputing the claim (whether as to the amount of any sum payable, or as to whether anything at all is payable) –
    (a) the insurer does not breach the term implied by subsection (1) merely by failing to pay the claim (or the affected part of it) while the dispute is continuing, but
    (b) the conduct of the insurer in handling the claim may be a relevant factor in deciding whether that term was breached and, if so, when.
(5) Remedies (for example, damages) available for breach of the term implied by subsection (1) are in addition to and distinct from –
    (a) any right to enforce payment of the sums due, and
    (b) any right to interest on those sums (whether under the contract, under another enactment, at the court's discretion or otherwise).

A number of points may be made about this provision.

First, the duty of the insurer to make payment within a reasonable time takes effect as an implied term (subsection (1)), so that any breach of the term sounds in damages to be assessed by the ordinary rules of remoteness in contract. There is nothing in subsection (5) that caps damages at the sum insured by the policy, nor does the section restrict the total amount recoverable for the claim and by way of damages at the sum insured under the policy. Accordingly, Mr Sprung might well now recover for the loss of his business under the section, and possibly even for loss of opportunity to expand his business.[106] The application of the ordinary rules of remoteness also means that in appropriate circumstances in consumer cases an award can be made for distress and inconvenience,[107] but it has been held in Australia that a claim by an insured for personal injuries after he was refused payment for storm damage to his roof and who fell off a ladder while attempting to effect repairs himself was too remote.[108] It will be noted that the implied term is about payment only: it says nothing about an insurer's failure to reinstate or repair the subject matter in a reasonable time where that is the appropriate means of indemnification under the policy.[109] Punitive damages, while recognised in Canada, are almost certainly not available in England.[110]

Secondly, interest is awardable in addition to damages. Interest is awardable by a court under section 35A of the Senior Courts Act 1981 on sums not paid by the date of judgment,[111] and interest is payable on the judgment debt itself at a statutory rate of

[106] See the West Australian case *Maxwell v Highway Hauliers Pty Ltd* [2013] WASCA 115, affirmed without appeal on this point [2014] HCA 33.

[107] See *Stuart v Guardian Royal Exchange Assurance of New Zealand Ltd (No 2)* (1988) 5 ANZ Ins Cas 60-844 (New Zealand High Court).

[108] *Sharma v Insurance Australia Ltd* [2017] NSWSC 55. This was obiter. At the time of the incident the insurers had not had a full opportunity to investigate the damage, and medical evidence showed that the insured's injury was an old one.

[109] In New Zealand an implied term to rebuild within a reasonable time, based upon the implied term to pay within a reasonable time, has been recognised: *Bruce v IAG New Zealand Ltd* [2018] NZHC 3444.

[110] *Morris-Garner v One Step (Support) Ltd* [2018] UKSC 20.

[111] The court may vary the rate of interest, or grant interest rests, for the relevant period, based upon the respective conduct of the parties. For the assessment of interest, see *Hellenic Industrial Development Bank v Atkin, The Julia* [2003] Lloyd's Rep IR 365.

8 per cent.[112] It may well be that in many cases there is no additional loss so that the measure of damages is interest on money wrongly withheld.

Thirdly, by subsection (2) the insurers have a reasonable time to investigate and assess the claim. The burden of proving unreasonable conduct is borne by the insured. Subsection (3) provides a non-exhaustive list of factors to be taken into account, and at this stage of the inquiry the fact that the insurers believed that they had a defence to the claim is to be left out of account: that becomes material only if unreasonable delay is found, and provides a defence under subsection (4), discussed below. The type of insurance and the size and complexity of the claim are obvious points. Regulatory requirements may include money-laundering checks, required before substantial sums of money are paid over. Factors outside the insurers' control may include disputes between co-insurers, logistical problems with undertaking surveys of damage to property[113] and the failure of the insured to comply with valid requests for information. It is not clear whether control means 'physical' or 'legal' control. An insurer who is refused an indemnity by reinsurers until further investigations have been made by them is presumably still able to pay even though that may threaten its reinsurance recovery, and the remedy would be against the reinsurers for their own late payment.

Finally, by subsection (4)(a), if the insured has shown a breach of the implied term, then the insurers have a defence if they can show that there were reasonable grounds for disputing the claim. It is irrelevant that they were wrong in their assessment: the defence is having reasonable grounds.[114] An insurer is almost certain to have received legal advice, and it is far from clear from the subsection that acceptance of that advice is automatically reasonable grounds or whether the grounds must be objectively justifiable so that if the advice is wrong the insurers are in breach. Subsection (4)(b) states the insurer's conduct in handling the claim may amount to a breach. This may already have been taken into account under subsection (3)(b), so it is relevant only where the delay was directed solely to a dispute as to the insurers' liability.

3.3.2. Limitation Period

New section 5A of the Limitation Act 1980 puts late damages claims into a special category. The usual six-year period, running from the date of the insured peril under section 5 of the Limitation Act, is disapplied, and instead

> [a]n action in respect of breach of the term implied into a contract of insurance by section 13A of the Insurance Act 2015 (late payment of claims) may not be brought after the expiration of one year from the date on which the insurer has paid all the sums referred to in subsection (1) of that section.

Although this section was inserted during the parliamentary discussion of the Enterprise Bill in order to mitigate the effects of the section 13A cause of action, it is unlikely to have any practical effect. The assumption is that, following a dispute, payment is made late and the insured then has a further year to consider its position and to sue for damages for late payment. However, if the late payment sum is of a size worth pursuing, it is very likely that

[112] Judgments Act 1838, s 17.

[113] As in *Quadra Commodities SA v XL Insurance Company SE* [2022] EWHC 431 (Comm), where the cargo was located in Ukraine and evidence of what had occurred was unavailable and otherwise conflicting.

[114] *Quadra Commodities SA v XL Insurance Company SE* [2022] EWHC 431 (Comm).

proceedings for the insured sum itself would have been commenced, and they would have included a claim for damages for late payment. So it will be relatively uncommon for an insured who has received payment to initiate entirely fresh proceedings.

3.3.3. Contracting Out

Section 16A of the Insurance Act 205 provides as follows:

> (1) A term of a consumer insurance contract, or of any other contract, which would put the consumer in a worse position as respects any of the matters provided for in section 13A than the consumer would be in by virtue of the provisions of that section (so far as relating to consumer insurance contracts) is to that extent of no effect.
> (2) A term of a non-consumer insurance contract, or of any other contract, which would put the insured in a worse position as respects deliberate or reckless breaches of the term implied by section 13A than the insured would be in by virtue of that section is to that extent of no effect.
> (3) For the purposes of subsection (2) a breach is deliberate or reckless if the insurer –
> (a) knew that it was in breach, or
> (b) did not care whether or not it was in breach.

Following the familiar structure for contracting out of the 2015 Act, a distinction is drawn between consumers and businesses. Subsection (1) prohibits contracting out for consumers. As for businesses, subsection (2) permits contracting out, but precludes reliance on an exclusion where the insurer has deliberately or recklessly broken its obligation to make a timely payment. Subsection (3) defines a deliberate or reckless breach as one where the insurer knew or did not care about breach.

4. Reinstatement

4.1. Contractual Reinstatement

The default position at common law is that where buildings or goods have been damaged the insured is entitled to payment for the loss of value, and the insured 'is quite entitled simply to put the money into pocket without in any way reinstating the building'.[115] However, policies have long provided for reinstatement or repair of damaged property, in part to make it easier to handle the various different insured interests that may exist in the subject matter and in part to provide a disincentive for an insured to commit deliberate damage in an attempt to obtain cash for the asset: as was said by Forbes J in *Reynolds v Phoenix Assurance Co Ltd*,[116] the mischief which reinstatement is designed to address is 'the temptation to an ill minded owner to set fire to the building in order to pocket the insurance money'. Policies may confer upon the insured the option to elect for reinstatement rather than payment; but it is far more common for that option to be conferred upon the insurers.

[115] *Reynolds v Phoenix Assurance Co Ltd* [1978] 2 Lloyd's Rep 440, 462 (Forbes J). See also *Rayner v Preston* (1881) 18 Ch D 1, 6 (Cotton LJ), 9–10 (Brett LJ); *Re Law Guarantee Trust & Accident Society Ltd* [1914] 2 Ch 617, 639 (Kennedy LJ). The point was confirmed in *Sartex Quilts and Textiles Ltd v Endurance Corporate Capital Ltd* [2020] EWCA Civ 308.
[116] 1978] 2 Lloyd's Rep 440, 462.

Where there is an option for the insurers to reinstate, and they choose not to exercise it but to pay instead, the measure of indemnity is that based on the value of the property to the insured and not the reinstatement cost. That was held in *Leppard v Excess Insurance Co*,[117] the facts of which were given earlier, where the insured sought to overcome the principle that the loss was confined to market value by reason of the insured's pre-fire intention to sell the property by arguing that the insurer's option to reinstate meant that there was agreement that the sum to be paid was the reinstatement cost. The Court of Appeal rejected that argument: once the insurers had opted to pay rather than reinstate, the only question was the calculation of the measure of indemnity based upon the value of the property to the insured, which on the facts was the market price.

If the policy provides that the insurer has the option to either pay insurance monies to the insured or require him to reinstate or repair, the insurer must make an election.[118] The election must be made within the period fixed by the policy or, if none is stipulated, within a reasonable time of the claim.[119] The insurer must communicate its election to the insured in unequivocal terms; and once an election is made, it is irrevocable.[120] Merely making an offer to settle by way of payment may be viewed as a mere negotiating step and will not necessarily pre-empt the insurer from subsequently making an election should the offer be rejected by the insured.[121] In practice, the election is communicated by the insurer informing the insured of its intention to reinstate or, conversely, of its intention to pay insurance money.[122]

Once an election has been made to reinstate, the insurers have a further choice: they may either undertake the work themselves; or they may instruct the insured to carry out the work using builders and other professionals approved by (and often introduced by) the insurers.

If the insurers opt to undertake the reinstatement work themselves, the contract is to be viewed as if it originally required the insurer to carry out the act so elected.[123] Thus, the policy becomes a repair or rebuild contract, and as such the insurer will be responsible for the quality of the reinstatement carried out by the contractor. If the work is defective, the insured may sue the insurer for damages to remedy the defect.[124] The insured has no contract with the contractor and so has no direct claim against the contractor;[125] equally, the contractor cannot sue the insured for the cost of repairs if the insurers default in making payment to the contractor.[126] The standard of repair required depends upon the policy: as noted in chapter 19, there is a distinction between 'as new' (based on equivalence with the

[117] [1979] 2 All ER 668.

[118] *Kammins Ballrooms Co Ltd v Zenith Investments (Torquay) Ltd* [1971] AC 850, 883 (Lord Diplock).

[119] *C&S Kelly Properties Ltd v Earthquake Commission* [2015] NZHC 1690, which holds that the court will exercise the option for the insurers rather than simply award damages for breach of contract.

[120] *Scarf v Jardine* (1882) 7 App Cas 345, 360 (Lord Blackburn).

[121] *Sutherland v Sun Fire Office* (1852) 14 D (Ct Sess) 775.

[122] *Scottish Amicable Heritable Securities Association Ltd v Northern Assurance Co* (1883) 11 R (Ct Sess) 287; *Skyward Aviation 2008 Ltd v Tower Insurance Ltd* [2014] NZCA 76; *Domenico Trustee Ltd v Tower Insurance Ltd* [2015] NZHC 981.

[123] *Brown v Royal Insurance Co* (1859) 1 El & El 853, 859 (Lord Campbell CJ); *Robson v New Zealand Insurance Co Ltd* [1931] NZLR 35.

[124] *Alchorne v Favill* (1825) LJ Ch 47.

[125] But see *Charnock v Liverpool Corporation* 1968] 1 WLR 1498 and *Brown & Davis Ltd v Galbraith* [1972] 2 Lloyd's Rep 1, in each of which separate additional arrangements were found to have been made between the insured and the contractor.

[126] *Godfrey Davis Ltd v Culling and Hecht* [1962] 2 Lloyd's Rep 349; *Cooter & Green Ltd v Tyrrell* [1962] 2 Lloyd's Rep 377. Contrast *Brown & Davis Ltd v Galbraith* 1972] 2 Lloyd's Rep 1 and *AJ Building and Plastering Ltd v Turner* [2013] EWHC 484 (QB), where the insured was found to have undertaken to pay uninsured costs to the contractor.

original condition of the property) and 'when new' (based on the actual original condition). Normal contractual damages principles apply to reinstatement contracts and it has recently been confirmed that an insured may be able to claim 'modest' damages for distress and inconvenience where the reinstatement has not been completed within a reasonable time.[127] The insurer will be liable for any further damage caused to the property in question after it has entered into possession in order to reinstate.[128] The insurer's liability to reinstate will not be discharged because the work is more expensive than anticipated.[129] Should reinstatement become impossible before an election is made, the insurer will be liable to indemnify the insured by paying the insurance monies.[130] Where, however, impossibility occurs after the election to reinstate has been made, the doctrine of frustration may operate to discharge the obligation to repair or rebuild.[131] In this situation, the policy would convert to a contract to pay insurance monies,[132] but only if the frustrating event is itself an insured peril. In *Wright, Stephenson, and Co Ltd v Holmes*,[133] a vehicle under repair by the insurers was destroyed by an earthquake, which was not an insured peril, and it was held that there was no recovery at all. The insurers may plead the Law Reform (Frustrated Contracts) Act 1943,[134] so that if the insured has 'obtained a valuable benefit' before the contract was frustrated, he may be required to pay such sum as 'the court considers just, having regard to all the circumstances of the case'.[135] It is difficult to see how any deduction could be made, as there is no obvious benefit to the insured in having property only partly repaired and incapable of further repair.

Alternatively, the insurers may choose not to reinstate themselves but to require the insured to do so. Policies typically provide that the insurers will indemnify the insured for costs incurred and the work must be carried out with reasonable despatch. This has been construed as meaning that the insurers will indemnify the insured for liability incurred to pay contractors and not for actual payment, as that would mean that insureds unable to fund payment would be left without indemnity.[136] A contractor who defaults is liable to the insured in the usual way for breach of the repair contract, but the position of the insurer depends upon the wording of the policy. It was held in *University of Newcastle v GIO General Ltd*[137] that the insurer was liable to make good the defects in the contractor's work. The basis for that decision is uncertain, as it was simply assumed that the policy imposed a duty on the insurers to provide a reinstated building. The point was clarified by the

[127] *AXA Insurance UK v Cunningham Lindsey UK plc* [2007] EWHC 3023.

[128] *Ahmedbhoy Habbibhoy v Bombay Fire and Marine Insurance Co* (1912) 107 LT 668.

[129] *Brown v Royal Insurance Co* (1859) 1 El & El 853; *Carlyle v Elite Insurance Co* (1984) 56 BCLR 331; *Government Insurance Office of New South Wales v Atkinson-Leighton Joint Venture* [1981] HCA 9; *Lumley General Insurance Ltd v Vintix Pty Ltd* (1991) 24 NSWLR 652.

[130] *Anderson v Commercial Union Assurance Co* (1885) 55 LJQB 146.

[131] *Brown v Royal Insurance Co* (1859) 1 El & El 853, which was decided before the courts developed the doctrine of discharge by virtue of impossibility or frustration.

[132] *Anderson v Commercial Union Assurance Co* (1885) 55 LJQB 146.

[133] [1932] NZLR 815.

[134] s 1(1) of which provides: 'Where a contract governed by English law has become impossible of performance or been otherwise frustrated, and the parties thereto have for that reason been discharged from the further performance of the contract, the following provisions of this section shall, subject to the provisions of section two of this Act, have effect in relation thereto.'

[135] s 1(3) of the 1943 Act. Although by s 2(5)(b), the Act does not apply to contracts of insurance, it will be recalled that after the election has been made by the insurers, the policy becomes a contract to reinstate.

[136] *Medical Assurance Society New Zealand Ltd v East* [2015] NZCA 250; *Manchikalapati v Zurich Insurance Plc* [2019] EWCA Civ 2163; *Sartex Quilts and Textiles Ltd v Endurance Corporate Capital Ltd* [2020] EWCA Civ 308.

[137] (1995) 8 ANZ Ins Cas 61-281.

New Zealand High Court in *Sleight v Beckia Holdings Ltd*,[138] where the insurers exercised their policy option to provide an indemnity for 'the cost of repairing or rebuilding the home to a condition as similar as possible to when it was new, using current materials and methods'. Contractors nominated by the insurers but appointed by the insured carried out earthquake damage repairs negligently, and the insured sought remediation costs from the insurers, the contractors having become insolvent. Gendall J held that the insurers were not vicariously liable for the defective work, but that their obligation under the policy was to restore the building to a 'when new' condition, and they had failed to do so. Their liability under the policy thus remained in place.

4.2. Fires Prevention (Metropolis) Act 1774, Section 83

A statutory form of reinstatement is provided by the Fires Prevention (Metropolis) Act 1774 whereby any 'person interested' can require the insurer to reinstate irrespective of whether such a person is a party to the contract of insurance. The Act is expressly designed to address the temptation to an ill-minded owner to set fire to his insured building in order to pocket the insurance money. Section 83 of the 1774 Act therefore authorises and requires fire insurers, upon suspicion of fraud or arson on the part of the insured, to use the insurance monies, so far as they will go, to reinstate the building instead of paying it to the insured. To avoid the danger that there may be other persons interested in the building whose 'lives and fortunes … may be lost or endangered', section 83 also requires the insurers to reinstate if requested to do so by such a person or persons.

The Act is restricted to fire insurance and applies to 'offices for insuring houses or other buildings'. Fire insurance on personal chattels is therefore excluded from its ambit. Thus, it has been held that section 83 does not apply to a tenant's trade fixtures,[139] or to the contents of buildings.[140] Despite the Act's short title, the courts have extended its application to England and Wales on the basis that the mischief addressed by the statute was not confined to London. In *ex p Gorely*,[141] where the insured property was in Dover, Lord Westbury LC reasoned that:

> [W]hen we approach the 83rd section we find, in the first place, that the enactment therein contained is heralded by a particular preamble of its own, which recites a general and universal evil as being the occasion of its being passed. We should be prepared, therefore, to infer, from the statement in that preamble of a general evil which the Legislature was desirous to redress, viz, that the enactment would, in fact, be co-extensive with the evil stated to have been intended to be redressed; and in point of fact, that general inference is confirmed by the language of the enactment itself, which is in itself general, and does not contain the words, 'within the limits aforesaid'; words which were evidently omitted, and omitted designedly. In my judgment, therefore, this particular section is intended to be of general and universal application.[142]

However, in *Westminster Fire Office v Glasgow Provident Investment Society*,[143] Earl Selborne and Lord Watson held that the Act does not apply to Scotland because it was originally

[138] [2020] NZHC 2851.
[139] *Ex p Gorely* (1864) 4 De G J & S 477.
[140] *Sinnot v Bowden* [1912] 2 Ch 414.
[141] (1864) 4 De G J & S 477.
[142] ibid 480–81.
[143] (1888) 13 App Cas 699, 714 and 716, respectively.

introduced to amend earlier legislation which did not extend to Scotland. It should also be noted that the scope of section 83, which is expressed to apply to the 'governors or directors of the several [fire] insurance offices', is restricted to insurance companies only and does not therefore apply to members of Lloyd's. The point has been made that 'the corporation of Lloyd's do not insure anybody against anything. It is the underwriters who undertake the burden of insurances.'[144]

As has been noted, a 'person interested' may request reinstatement under section 83. Obviously this term encompasses a person who, while not being a party to the insurance contract, nevertheless has an insurable interest in the property, irrespective of whether such interest is full or limited. However, it excludes the insured, so the latter cannot require reinstatement.[145] The effect of section 83 is to give a 'person interested', although not a party to the contract, a statutory right to direct the insurers to expend the insurance monies in a particular way. Generally, any person with a legal or equitable interest in the building will be a 'person interested'. Such a person will include a mortgagee,[146] a tenant,[147] a lessor,[148] a purchaser of real property prior to completion[149] and a lessee.[150] In *Lonsdale & Thompson Ltd v Black Arrow Group plc*,[151] it was held that a tenant could request the landlord's insurers to reinstate following a fire even though the landlord had contracted to sell the property before the loss and therefore no longer possessed any insurable interest in it. The court construed the policy as enuring for the tenant's benefit despite the sale of the freehold.

The request to reinstate must be distinct and it should include some reference to the statutory right. In *Simpson v Scottish Union Insurance Co*,[152] a landlord let two houses to a tenant who insured them as required to do so by his lease. When the houses were destroyed by fire, the landlord visited the insurers' offices, claimed the benefit of the policy and requested to have the insurance monies applied towards the rebuilding costs. Although the secretary of the insurers' agreed to his request, the insurers nevertheless settled with the tenant. The landlord, having rebuilt the houses, sued the insurers. The court held that as his request did not make reference to the Act, it amounted to nothing more than the landlord claiming to be the person interested under the insurance policy. There had been no distinct request before the settlement with the tenant.

Where an insurer fails to comply with a due and proper request to reinstate, the person interested cannot reinstate himself and claim the cost from the insurer. The redress available is probably a mandatory injunction compelling the insurer's compliance.[153] However, it has been held that the appropriate remedy is an injunction to prevent the insurer paying the insured since enforcing the mandate may prove impossible.[154]

The Law Commissions initially propose to reform section 83 because its main use has proved to be different from that which was envisaged when the statute was enacted.[155]

[144] *Portavon Cinema Co Ltd v Price and Century Insurance Co Ltd* [1939] 4 All ER 601, 608 (Branson J).
[145] See *Reynolds v Phoenix Assurance Co Ltd* [1978] 2 Lloyd's Rep 440, 462 (Forbes J).
[146] *Sinnot v Bowden* [1912] 2 Ch 414. See the Law of Property Act 1925, s 108(3).
[147] *Wimbledon Golf Club v Imperial Insurance Co* (1902) 18 TLR 815.
[148] *Matthey v Curling* [1922] 2 AC 180, 198 (Atkin LJ).
[149] *Rayner v Preston* (1881) 18 Ch D 1, 15 (James LJ).
[150] *Portavon Cinema Co Ltd v Price and Century Insurance Co Ltd* [1939] 4 All ER 601.
[151] [1993] 2 Lloyd's Rep 428.
[152] (1863) 1 H & M 618.
[153] ibid 629 (Sir W Page-Wood V-C).
[154] *Wimbledon Golf Club v Imperial Insurance Co* (1902) 18 TLR 815.
[155] 'Reforming Insurance Contract Law Introductory Paper: Section 83 of the Fires Prevention (Metropolis) Act 1774: Should It Be Reformed?' (March 2009) paras 1.5–11.16.

As noted above, the original purpose was designed to deter arson and insurance fraud; however, it creates rights for non-policyholders.[156] The Commissions sought responses as to whether the statute should be repealed, replaced or left as is. The main driver behind the proposal to repeal section 83 was to 'remove any controversies about its territorial extent, and its use or abuse'.[157] The Law Commissions were only willing to remedy these issues if convinced that there was 'a serious problem'.[158] After receiving responses to their paper, the Law Commissions concluded that, although the area could benefit from reform and clarity, 'the case is not strong enough'.[159] The Act has thus remained untouched by the subsequent reforms.

[156] ibid para 1.13–1.14.
[157] ibid para 1.31.
[158] ibid para 1.35.
[159] 'Section 83 – Summary of Responses' (February 2010) para 1.28.

13

Subrogation and Contribution

1. Subrogation

1.1. The Nature of Subrogation[1]

1.1.1. Origins and Purposes

Subrogation is a general principle of law whereby if A provides an indemnity to B for a loss suffered by B, A is entitled to exercise B's rights against C if C was responsible for B's loss. Insurance is perhaps the most important practical application of the subrogation principle, and as early as 1782 Lord Mansfield was able to say that 'every day the insurer is put in the place of the assured'.[2] It has long been recognised that an insurer cannot refuse to pay merely on the ground that the insured has a claim against a third party: the insured 'does not receive [money from the insurers] because of the accident, but because he has made a contract providing for the contingency'.[3] Equally, the third party cannot deny liability on the ground that the insurer has or will indemnify the insured.[4] The underlying purpose of

[1] SR Derham, *Subrogation in Insurance Law* (Sydney, The Law Book Company, 1985); JG Fleming, 'The Collateral Source Rule and Loss Allocation in Tort Law' (1966) 54 *California Law Review* 1478; J Birds, 'Contractual Subrogation in Insurance' [1979] *Journal of Business Law* 124; R Hasson, 'Subrogation in Insurance Law: A Critical Evaluation' (1985) 5 *OJLS* 416; RC Horn, *Subrogation in Insurance Theory and Practice* (Homewood, IL, Richard D Irwin, 1964); G Jones, *Goff and Jones: The Law of Restitution* (London, Sweet & Maxwell, 2009) ch 3; C Mitchell, 'Defences to an Insurer's Subrogated Action' [1996] *Lloyd's Maritime and Commercial Law Quarterly* 343; C Mitchell, *The Law of Subrogation* (Oxford, Oxford University Press, 1994); HN Sheldon, *The Law of Subrogation* (Frederick, MD, Beard, 2000); RM Walmsley, *Subrogation and Contribution in Insurance Practice* (London, Witherby, 2001); C Mitchell and S Watterson, *Subrogation: Law and Practice* (Oxford, Oxford University Press, 2007). For the early history of the doctrine, see ML Marasinghe, 'An Historical Introduction to the Doctrine of Subrogation' [1975] 10 *Valparaiso University Law Review* 45, 275. For a comparative view, see 'International Comparative Review of Subrogation Law' [2009] 18 *LLID Supp* 4.

[2] *Mason v Sainsbury* (1782) 3 Doug 61, 64.

[3] *Bradburn v The Great Western Railway Co* (1874) LR 10 Exch 1, 3 (Pigott B). See also *Mason v Sainsbury* (1782) 3 Doug 61; *Yates v Whyte* (1838) *Cullen v Butler* (1816) 5 M & S 461; *Yates v Sainsbury* (1838) 1 Arn 85; 4 Bing (NC) 272; *Dickenson v Jardine* (1868) LR 3 CP 639; *Collingridge v Royal Exchange Assurance* (1877) 3 QBD 173, 176–77; *Caledonia North Sea Ltd v British Telecommunications plc* [2002] Lloyd's Rep IR 261.

[4] *Parry v Cleaver* [1970] AC 1.

subrogation is to prevent the insured from recovering more than an indemnity by obtaining funds both from his insurers and also from the third party causing the loss:

> The very foundation, in my opinion, of every rule which has been applied to insurance law is this, namely, that the contract of insurance contained in a marine or fire policy is a contract of indemnity, and of indemnity only, and that this contract means that the assured, in case of a loss against which the policy has been made, shall be fully indemnified, but shall never be more than fully indemnified. That is the fundamental principle of insurance, and if ever a proposition is brought forward which is at variance with it, that is to say, which either will prevent the assured from obtaining a full indemnity, or which will give to the assured more than a full indemnity, that proposition must certainly be wrong.[5]

A subrogation action is brought in the name of the insured, so that notionally the insurers are not party to the proceedings against the third party. This means that the insurers have exactly the same rights as the insured against the third party. As will be seen below, the insurers cannot bring a subrogated claim until they have indemnified the insured, and the insurers cannot make a profit from a subrogation action, so they must pay over to the insured any sums received from the third party that exceed the amount of the indemnity provided under the policy.

The indemnity principle underlying subrogation manifests itself in three ways. First, if the insured has received the policy monies from the insurers, the insured's rights against the third party responsible for the loss are to the extent of the insurers' payment transferred to them. A simple example is *Castellain v Preston*,[6] where a house was damaged by fire after a contract of sale had been signed but before the date of completion so that the purchaser remained liable to make payment. The vendor was paid by his insurers for the loss. The purchase was then completed and the price paid to the vendor. The insurers were allowed to recover their payment out of the sale proceeds of the house. Secondly, if the insured has received damages from the third party, the insurers are discharged from liability to the extent that the insured has been compensated; the principle here is that insurers are the indemnifiers of last resort, so that their liability is secondary to that of the third party.[7] Thirdly, if the insured has been paid by both the insurers and the third party, the insurers have a right to recover their payment by way of money had and received.[8] Mitchell has cogently argued that only the first constitutes subrogation.[9] In the second situation the payment by the insurer is made under a mistake of fact, namely, the belief that the insured has not been indemnified. Here, the means of recovering the excess is an action for money had and received. In the third situation the insurer has an equitable lien over the money in the hands of the insured.[10] While accepting the logic of this view, it is perhaps too late to retrieve the limited and more exact definition of subrogation in the face of more than 120 years of judicial bad habits, so these three aspects will be dealt with together in this chapter. In recent years, subrogation has been recognised by academics in particular as a

[5] *Castellain v Preston* (1883) 11 QBD 380, 386 (Brett LJ).

[6] ibid.

[7] *Hamilton v Mendes* (1761) 2 Burr 1198, 1210 (Lord Mansfield CJ); *Burnand v Rodocanachi* (1882) 7 App Cas 333, 339 (Lord Blackburn).

[8] *Randal v Cockran* (1748) 1 Ves Sen 98; *Blaauwpot v Da Costa* (1758) 1 Ed 130; *Commercial Union Assurance Co v Lister* (1874) LR Ch App 483; *Castellain v Preston* (1883) 11 QBD 380, 389 per Brett LJ; *Assicurazoni Generali De Trieste v Empress Assurance Corporation Ltd* [1907] 2 KB 814.

[9] Mitchell, *The Law of Subrogation* (n 1) 68–74; Mitchell and Watterson (n 1). See the comments of the court in an Australian case, *British Traders Insurance Co Ltd v Monson* (1964) 111 CLR 86, 94.

[10] *Lord Napier and Ettrick v Hunter* [1993] 1 Lloyd's Rep 10.

restitutionary remedy and there has been attempts to integrate subrogation into the restitution family. As a result, the simplicity of the basic notion has been somewhat overlooked. This chapter is concerned purely with subrogation as it operates in insurance.

It would nevertheless be misleading to say that subrogation is purely a negative doctrine which prevents the insured recovering more than an indemnity. The codification of subrogation in section 79 of the Marine Insurance Act 1906 refers to the insurers, on payment, being 'subrogated to all the rights and remedies of the assured', and it has been held in Singapore, in *Sompo Insurance Singapore Pte Ltd v Royal & Sun Alliance Insurance plc*,[11] that insurers who had indemnified the insured for loss suffered by a breach of contract by a contractor were entitled to claim under a performance bond issued to the insured to cover the contractor's defaults. Further, as will be seen below, an insured who has compromised the insurers' subrogation rights by settling with the third party wrongdoer may face a claim by the insurers for loss of those rights. So, although it is right to say that the indemnity principle is at the heart of subrogation, the doctrine operates to confer positive rights upon the insurers.

In recent years there has been a great deal of discussion as to whether subrogation is an equitable principle or whether it is an incident of the contract of insurance. Lord Diplock has suggested that subrogation is an implied term,[12] but it is apparent from the earliest authorities on subrogation that it was regarded as rooted in equity,[13] and the matter was given detailed consideration by the House of Lords in *Napier and Ettrick (Lord) v Hunter*.[14] This case is analysed below; it suffices to say here that the conclusion was that subrogation is an equitable doctrine which springs from the contract between the parties and therefore is subject to contractual variation. Many policies contain subrogation clauses which modify equitable principles, eg by permitting the insurers to require the insured to seek interim relief against the third party to prevent the third party from removing assets from the jurisdiction.

1.1.2. Is Subrogation Discretionary?

Equitable remedies are discretionary and can be refused by the courts in closely defined circumstances. The question has inevitably arisen as to whether subrogation, as an equitable remedy, can be refused where the court thinks that it might operate unfairly. In *Lister v Romford Ice and Cold Storage Co Ltd*,[15] a father and son were both employed by the defendant company. The son negligently injured his father while reversing a lorry, thereby rendering the defendant vicariously liable for a claim by the father. The insurers provided an indemnity to the defendant, and then exercised subrogation rights against the son seeking to recover their money. The House of Lords held that there was nothing in the employment contract between the defendant and the son whereby the defendant relieved the son from responsibility simply because insurance was in place, and on that basis a subrogation action lay. The decision was rapidly reversed by an agreement between the government and the insurance industry under which employers' liability insurers undertook not to pursue

[11] [2021] SGHC 152.

[12] *Hobbs v Marlowe* [1978] AC 16.

[13] *Randal v Cockran* (1748) 1 Ves Sen 98; *Blaaupot v Da Costa* (1758) 1 Ed 130; *White v Dobinson* (1844) 14 Sim 273.

[14] [1993] 1 Lloyd's Rep 10.

[15] [1957] AC 555.

employees of their insureds. However, that agreement applied only to the employer's own employees, which became apparent in *Morris v Ford Motor Co.*[16] Morris was an employee of a firm that undertook cleaning work for Ford. Under the contract between the parties, Ford was to be indemnified in respect of liability for injury caused by the negligence of the employees of either company. Morris was injured by the negligent act of Roberts, one of Ford's employees. Morris sued Ford as Roberts's employer, Ford sought an indemnity from the cleaning firm and this, in turn, led to the argument that since the cleaning firm was obliged to provide an indemnity, there was a right to sue Roberts. The case for the cleaning firm seemed fairly strong in view of the decision in *Lister*. Lord Denning MR in *Morris* did not really bother to conceal his distaste for *Lister*, which he called 'an unfortunate decision', and he duly proceeded to ignore it. Since the two cases were not precisely similar, in that *Lister* involved two people employed by the same firm and *Morris* two people employed by different firms, he was technically able to distinguish them. In any event, Lord Denning formulated a very broad principle:

> [W]here the risk of a servant's negligence is covered by insurance, his employer should not seek to make that servant liable for it. At any rate, the courts should not compel him to allow his name to be used to do it.[17]

His justification was simple:

> Everyone knows that such risks as these are covered by insurance. So they should be, when a man is doing his employer's work, with his employer's plant and equipment, and happens to make a mistake. To make the servant personally liable would not only lead to a strike. It would be positively unjust.[18]

He suggested that since subrogation rights were equitable, the court had discretion, and in circumstances such as these Ford would not be compelled to lend its name to an action against one of its employees. Ford expected the cleaning firm to insure, and it had; the insurance company had received premiums and everyone would have expected the insurers, not the employee, to bear the loss. In addition, it was 'not just and equitable' to endanger industrial relations by forcing Ford to sue its own employee.[19] There is much to be said for the flexibility of Lord Denning's approach.[20] James LJ avoided these difficulties by concluding that the rights of subrogation were excluded by an implied term in the insurance contract.

It is of interest to note the position in Australia. Under section 65 of the Insurance Contracts Act 1984 (Cth), a subrogation action is not permitted where the insured could not reasonably have been expected to sue the defendant by reason of a family or other personal relationship, although subrogation is permitted where the defendant was guilty of serious or wilful misconduct. In employment cases, section 66 prohibits a subrogation action against the insured's employee, again other than in cases of serious or wilful misconduct.

It has also been held that the right of an insurer to exercise subrogation rights is not subject to an overriding equitable discretion exercised by the courts. An insurer who

[16] [1973] QB 792.

[17] At 801.

[18] ibid. Lord Denning referred to the informal agreement drawn up by the insurance industry in the wake of *Lister*.

[19] Lord Denning argued in the alternative that if the right of subrogation originated in an implied term, he would not imply such a term into this contract.

[20] *Woolwich Building Society v Brown* [1996] CLC 625, 629 (Waller J); *The Surf City* [1995] 2 Lloyd's Rep 242. See *Patent Scaffolding Co v William Simpson Construction Co* 64 Cal Rptr 187 (Calif 1967).

wrongfully refuses to accept liability at the outset is not to be deprived of subrogation rights once payment has been made.[21]

1.1.3. Subrogation, Contribution, Abandonment and Assignment

It is important to distinguish subrogation from other legal principles that reinforce the indemnity principle and may operate to give insurers rights against third parties.

Contribution, which is discussed in detail later in this chapter, arises where two or more insurers are liable to the insured for the same loss. The insured can claim from any one of the insurers up to the limit of indemnity, but the paying insurer has a right of proportional contribution from other insurers who could have been called upon to pay. Contribution exists only between insurers. In all other cases the paying insurer has a right of subrogation. That may be seen from *Caledonia North Sea Ltd v British Telecommunications Plc*,[22] where the insured, the operator of the North Sea oilrig Piper Alpha, faced liability for the deaths of 167 workers and crew and for personal injuries to numerous others as a result of the explosion of the rig on 6 July 1988. The insured had liability insurance covering the claims, and also had a contractual indemnity from contractors whose employees were killed or injured. The House of Lords held that contractual indemnifiers were not in the same position as insurers, and that as between an insurer and a contractual indemnifier the former had subrogation rights even though the liability of both was based on contract. Contribution is thus confined to claims between insurers.

Abandonment arises where an insurer has paid for a total loss of property. The insurer is entitled to require the insured to abandon whatever is left of the property to the insurer. The definition of total loss, as shown in chapter 12 above, is destruction or permanent seizure of the subject matter, so in most cases there is very little for the insurer to claim. Where abandonment is of crucial importance is in marine insurance,[23] where the principle of constructive total loss allows the insured to claim for the full sum insured for an economic rather than physical total loss: if the subject matter is repairable but not worth repairing, there is a marine constructive total loss. The role of abandonment is discussed in chapter 17 below, but it is important to distinguish between subrogation and abandonment.[24] Subrogation is concerned with the transfer of a cause of action relating to the insured's loss, whereas abandonment is concerned with the transfer of the property itself. The two may well operate together, as where a third party negligently collides with the insured's vessel or inflicts severe damage on the insured's cargo, in which case the insurers, having paid for a total loss, have subrogation rights against the third party and also the right to treat what remains of the property as abandoned to them.

Assignment consists of a contractual transfer of legal rights from the insured to the insurers. An assignment of a claim as a chose in action can take effect at law if the requirements of section 136 of the Law of Property Act 1925 are satisfied, namely that the assignment is absolute, in writing signed by the assignor and notice has been given to the debtor. An

[21] *England v Guardian Insurance Ltd* [2000] Lloyd's Rep IR 404.

[22] [2002] Lloyd's Rep IR 261. See also *Cape Distribution Ltd v Cape Intermediate Holdings Plc* [2016] Lloyd's Rep IR 499.

[23] Motor insurers may also stipulate that if a vehicle is damaged beyond economic repair they will write it off and pay under the policy but remove the vehicle for scrap.

[24] The two concepts are, somewhat confusingly, intertwined in the statutory definition in s 79 of the Marine Insurance Act 1906.

assignment not satisfying these requirements may be recognised in equity if it is made for good consideration and notice has been given to the debtor. Legal assignment differs from subrogation in a number of important respects: the insurers obtain legal title to the claim and thus sue in their own name rather than that of the insured; a subrogated insurer is entitled to retain from the sum obtained from the third party only an amount equivalent to its indemnity payment to the insured, whereas an insurer who has taken an assignment owns the claim and can retain its full amount; and a subrogated claim can be brought only where the insurers have indemnified the insured, whereas an assigned claim can be brought at any time. Some policies contain a term whereby the insurers can require the insured to assign third party claims to them. The disadvantage for insurers in suing under an assignment is that their involvement in the case is both before the court and also public.

1.2. The Requirements for Subrogation

1.2.1. The Policy Must Be an Indemnity Policy

If the primary purpose of subrogation is to hold the insured to an indemnity, it follows that if the policy is not one of indemnity then subrogation rights do not arise under it. The most important form of insurance excluded from subrogation rights is life and accident.[25] Plainly it is impossible to put an actual value on life or limb, and the law accordingly allows the insured to accumulate whatever recoveries he can, from insured and non-insured sources. However, if the loss is measurable, then the policy is one of indemnity and subrogation can operate. A policy against medical expenses[26] or loss of income following injury[27] would fall into this category. Not surprisingly, no right of subrogation exists if the insurance contract is void. A marine policy in which no proof of an insurable interest is required (a 'ppi' contract) is void under the Marine Insurance Act 1906, section 4(1) and (2) and will not, therefore, give rise to the right of subrogation because any payment made by the insurer is not pursuant to an obligation to indemnify the insured.[28]

1.2.2. The Provision of an Indemnity

There is some ambiguity in the requirement that the insured must receive an indemnity. This could mean an indemnity under the policy, ie that the insurers have paid up to the limits imposed by the policy, or it could mean an absolute indemnity, ie that the insured has not suffered any uninsured loss. The point was clarified by the House of Lords in *Lord Napier and Ettrick v Hunter*. The insurers must have discharged their liability under the policy to the insured in order to obtain subrogation rights, but the insured retains the right to control the conduct of the proceedings against the third party if any part of the loss is uninsured.

The first point is illustrated by *Page v Scottish Insurance Corporation*.[29] Mr Forster's car was involved in an accident as a result of the negligent driving of Mr Page, a mechanic. Both

[25] *Solicitors' and General Life Assurance Society v Lamb* (1864) 1 De GJ & Sm 251; *Theobald v Railway Passengers Assurance Co* (1854) 10 Ex 45.

[26] *Bupa Australia Pty Ltd v Shaw* [2013] VSC 507.

[27] *Insurance Commission of Western Australia v Kightly* [2005] WASCA 154.

[28] *John Edwards and Co v Motor Union Insurance Co Ltd* [1922] 2 KB 249.

[29] (1929) 140 LT 571.

Forster's car and a car owned by a Mr Stobart were damaged. Forster's insurers agreed to let Page undertake the repairs to Forster's car, but failed to pay him. Page sued and the insurers responded by suing Page, as the wrongdoer, for a sum equivalent to the cost of the repairs. The Court of Appeal held that the insurers had no right to be subrogated to Forster's rights of action because they had not settled in full all the claims under the policy relating to the accident, including those brought by Stobart against Forster and Page jointly. Similarly, in *Scottish Union & National Insurance Company v Davis*,[30] when a Bentley car owned by Mr Davis was damaged by a coping stone falling from a building, the insurers agreed that the car should be repaired by a particular firm. The firm failed to carry out the repairs, but submitted a bill, which the insurers paid. Davis then received a sum of money in settlement of a claim against the owner of the building and his insurers sought to recover that money. The Court of Appeal held that the right of subrogation only arose when the insurers settled the claim, and in this case, although they had paid out money, they had not settled because the car had not been repaired as the policy required. Pending full indemnification under the policy, the insurers have no rights.

As to the second point, the right of subrogation arises when the insurers have paid out for the loss to the extent required by the policy, even if the actual loss exceeds that figure. However, if there is uninsured loss, then the control of the proceedings against the third party vests in the insured. *Lord Napier and Ettrick v Hunter* has established an important exception here, in that the amount of any deductible is to be disregarded in determining whether the insured has suffered any uninsured loss: the deductible is a sum that the insured is required to bear, and is therefore to be disregarded. Thus, the right of the insured to control the proceedings where there is uninsured loss applies where the uninsured loss is outside the scope of the policy or above policy limits, but not where it merely consists of the deductible. The principles are illustrated by the New South Wales decision, *Johnson v Endeavour Energy*.[31] A major fire broke out in Blue Mountains, North of Sydney, as a result of the defendant's alleged negligence. Representative proceedings were brought by affected householders, some 565 of whom were insured against property damage by the insurers, IAG. Payments were made by IAG up to policy limits, but the householders were underinsured and still faced substantial losses. The proceedings against the defendant were thus maintained. IAG, without seeking the consent of their policyholders, withdrew them from the proceedings, and unsurprisingly they objected. The court ruled that IAG had no power to act in that way. As long as there were uninsured losses, the policyholders retained the right to decide when and how to pursue the proceedings against the defendant and to recover uninsured sums for their own benefit.

The fact that the insurers have no say over the proceedings against the third party until they have provided indemnity has led to the use of express clauses in policies whereby the insured is under an express duty to take steps in advance of indemnification to preserve the insurers' rights. The clause may include issuing proceedings against the third party in the limitation period[32] and seeking interim measures to preserve the potential defendant's assets by freezing order or arrest of the vessel. The insured will be entitled to an indemnity for costs from the insurers, and in practice the actions are taken by the insurers themselves with the consent of the insured.

[30] [1970] 1 Lloyd's Rep 1.

[31] [2015] NSWSC 1117.

[32] This is particularly important in cargo claims, where the contractual limitation is almost always 12 months from the completion of the cargo's discharge.

1.2.3. The Insurance Payment Must Relate to a Loss under the Policy

The equitable maxim 'equity does not assist a volunteer' suggests that if insurers pay a claim ex gratia, then they cannot rely upon equity to confer a subrogation action. The courts have rejected that proposition, and have recognised that the insurers will also acquire the right of subrogation where they have made a payment for a loss even if it is not covered by the policy, as long as that payment was 'honestly and reasonably' made. In *King v Victoria Insurance Co Ltd*,[33] the insured bank made a claim for a lost cargo of wool over which it had security. The insurers, having indemnified the bank under a settlement agreement, sought to exercise subrogation rights against the operators of the lighters from which the wool had been lost. The defence was that the claim was not covered by the policy so that the payment by the insurers was ex gratia and did not support a subrogation action. The Privy Council rejected the defence, holding that it was

> a very startling proposition to say that when insurers and insured have settled a claim of loss between themselves, a third party who caused the loss may insist on ripping up the settlement, and on putting in a plea for the insurers which they did not think it right to put in for themselves.

It may be that 'honestly and reasonably' making the payment does not suffice, and that it is necessary also that the payment was designed to reduce the insured's loss. That point was made in *AAI Ltd v Technology Swiss Pty Ltd*,[34] where insurers settled with the insured for a single sum that covered both insured and uninsured losses but did not distinguish between the two. It was held that subrogation did not arise simply because a settlement had been reached in good faith, and that it was necessary for the insurers to demonstrate that the payment had been made to reduce losses insured under the policy. In the absence of any form of allocation between insured and uninsured losses, a subrogation action could not proceed. *HSBC Rail (UK) Ltd v Network Rail Infrastructure Ltd*[35] illustrates the same point. HSBC leased rolling stock to GNER, a train operator, on terms that GNER was to assume all risk of loss. The contract required GNER to take out all risks property insurance in the names of both itself and HSBC; the proceeds were payable to HSBC and would be applied in discharging GNER's obligation to HSBC. The rolling stock was damaged due to the admitted negligence of the defendant. The insurers indemnified HSBC, and the insurers then sought to exercise subrogation rights against the defendant. The Court of Appeal held that they could not. HSBC, as a bailor, could sue only for damage to the reversionary interest, and there had been no loss. Although HSBC argued that they have suffered no loss only because they had been compensated by the insurance, the court held that it was GNER that was indemnified under the policy, not HSBC.[36] It was 'unrealistic to regard an insurance policy which insures the respective rights and liabilities of both HSBC and GNER as indemnifying HSBC rather than GNER'.[37] Longmore LJ summarised: 'The reality of this case is that HSBC, as lessor, has in the event suffered no damage to its reversionary interest because GNER has fully indemnified it, not because it has been indemnified by insurance.'[38]

[33] [1896] AC 250.
[34] [2021] FCAFC 168.
[35] [2005] EWCA Civ 1437.
[36] ibid [34].
[37] ibid.
[38] ibid [38].

1.2.4. The Sum Received from the Third Party Must Relate to the Insured Loss

Not all sums received by the insured must be taken into account as reducing the insured loss. The money must be paid for that reason and not, for example, to provide personal compensation to the insured. The leading cases on this point relate to compensation received from governments following a loss for which they were responsible.[39] In two of the earliest cases on subrogation, *Randal v Cockran* and *Blaaupot v Da Costa*, the British government distributed sums to shipowners for losses suffered by them at the hands of Spanish vessels. The insurers, who had already paid the losses, were held to be entitled to claim those sums. Those cases were distinguished in the difficult case of *Burnand v Rodocanachi*.[40] By an arbitration award in 1872, the British government was found to be liable to pay to the US government the sum of US$15.5 million by way of compensation to US shipowners and merchants who had suffered losses in the American Civil War from the activities of three vessels, *Alabama*, *Shenandoah* and *Florida*, which had been built in Britain and permitted to fall into the hands of the Confederacy. The sums were paid by the US government to those suffering uninsured losses. One such victim, the defendant in the present proceedings, had two valued policies for £15,000 on a cargo of tobacco. The cargo was seized and the insurers paid the sum insured. Subsequently the insured received just under £2803 from the compensation fund, on the basis that the cargo had been underinsured and loss in excess of the agreed value had been suffered. The insurers claimed that sum, arguing that the valuation of £15,000 was conclusive and so there was no uninsured loss. The House of Lords agreed with the insurers that, had the sum from the compensation fund been paid in respect of insured loss, then the insurers could have recovered it, but their Lordships ruled that sums paid from the fund did not reduce insured losses and were to be left out of account. Obiter, it was suggested that the reason was that such sums were a gift.

Burnand has rightly been regarded as an exceptional case,[41] and it has been distinguished in later cases. The correct principle is that sums paid to the insured in a commercial context by a third party are almost – but not quite – inevitably designed to reduce the insured's loss and are not to be payment on an ex gratia basis for injured feelings or personal compensation.[42] That point was made in *Colonia Versicherung AG v Amoco Oil Co*,[43] where payment by the carriers to the insured for loss of a cargo of oil was held to be by way of indemnification and therefore to be deducted from the sum insured so that the insured had suffered no loss, which was unfortunate for the carriers because they had taken, in return for the payment, an assignment of the insured's worthless insurance claim. An interesting contrast is *Merrett v Capitol Indemnity Corp*,[44] where brokers voluntarily paid for the insured's loss pending proceedings by the insured against the insurers: that was held to be a purely voluntary payment to maintain a business relationship, so that the insured could recover from the insurers and the brokers had no right of recoupment given that they had paid as volunteers.

[39] For a modern illustration of the issue in the context of COVID-19, see ch 19 below.

[40] (1882) 7 App Cas 333. The full story is told in R Merkin, 'Alabama: The Devil Fools with the Best Laid Plans' (2019) 30 *Industrial Law Journal* 65.

[41] But for the agreement to go to arbitration, there could easily have been a war between Britain and the USA, and it would have been unthinkable for the London insurance market to take back any of the sums paid to the USA, so *Burnand* is a highly political decision.

[42] *Stearns v Village Main Reef Gold Mining Co Ltd* (1905) 21 TLR 236, where compensation was paid by the South African government for the seizure of gold during the Boer War.

[43] [1995] 1 Lloyd's Rep 570, affirmed [1997] 1 Lloyd's Rep 261.

[44] [1991] 1 Lloyd's Rep 169.

1.2.5. The Action Must Be Brought in the Name of the Insured

A subrogation action must be brought in the name of the insured. That procedural requirement has a number of implications for insurers.

First, given that the claimant is the insured, it is obvious that the wrongdoer cannot be the insured himself. That was decided in *Simpson v Thomson, Birrell*,[45] where the insurers were precluded from exercising rights of subrogation where two ships owned by the same insured collided. In *Midland Insurance Co v Smith*,[46] Mrs Smith burnt down the insured property, and the insurers responded to a claim on the policy with an action against Mr Smith, the policyholder, arguing that – as the law stood then – he was responsible for the actions of his wife. The court held that, while it might have been possible to argue that the claim by the insured was not within the terms of the policy (although the court felt it unlikely that this would have succeeded because Mr Smith was not implicated in the arson), it was not possible to assert, as the insurers were implicitly doing, that it was within the terms of the policy to pay out to Mr Smith and, at the same time, seek an indemnity from him. If the husband is responsible for the actions of his wife, then he cannot sue her, since that would be the same as suing himself.

Secondly, any defence that the third party has against the insured is binding on the insurers: this is of particular importance where the arrangements between the insured and the third party have expressly or impliedly excluded any right of action, or where after the loss the insured has settled with the third party: each of these situations is discussed below.

Thirdly, if the insured is a company that has been dissolved, it has no legal existence and proceedings cannot be commenced in its name. In those circumstances the insurers must apply to the court to restore the company to the register under section 1030 of the Companies Act 2006. That section can generally be used only within six years of the date of dissolution, but a change in the law in 2018 has removed the time limit when the purpose is to resurrect the company for the purposes of bringing a subrogation action in its name.[47] A related issue arises where the insured company is in liquidation and the liquidator has exercised the power in section 178 of the Insolvency Act 1986 to apply to the court to disclaim the contract. This occurred in *Re Ballast plc*.[48] The company, a civil engineering firm, appointed M to undertake work on a project that the company was constructing. Out of that work there arose an alleged claim against M for breach of contractual duty of care, but the company was in liquidation. The liquidator, faced with a counterclaim and believing that the company's claim against M lacked merit, made a section 178 application to disclaim the contract. The insurers' assertion that they had proprietary rights over the claim was rejected: a subrogation action was simply a claim to the proceeds of the action, and there was no basis for refusing the liquidator's application.

Fourthly, the insurers are bound by any restrictions on the cause of action, including a jurisdiction or arbitration clause, a choice of law clause or a limitation period.

[45] (1877) 3 App Cas 279. If the two ships are owned by different companies the result will be different, even if those companies are owned by the same person: ibid 294 (Lord Blackburn). See also *Co-operative Retail Services Ltd v Taylor Young Partnership* [2002] UKHL 17 (HL). For a critique of *Simpson*, see PS James, 'The Fallacies of *Simpson v Thomson*' (1971) 22 *MLR* 149.

[46] (1881) 6 QBD 561.

[47] Third Parties (Rights against Insurers) Act 2010 (Consequential Amendment of Companies Act 2006) Regulations 2018, SI 2018/1162.

[48] [2006] EWHC 3189 (Ch). For a critique, see L Chan Ho (2007) 23(4) *Insolvency Law & Practice* 103.

Fifthly, the measure of damages is represented by the loss to the insured looked at independently of the insurance.

In *Sousa v London Borough of Waltham Forest*,[49] the claimant was required by his policy to use a specified firm of solicitors with whom the insurers had a collective conditional fee agreement, including a success fee. The claim was settled on the basis that the defendant paid the claimant's costs, but the defendant refused to pay the success fee on the ground that it had not been reasonable for the claimant to have entered into a conditional fee agreement (CFA) because he had the benefit of a full indemnity against costs provided by the insurers under the terms of the policy. The Court of Appeal held that the success fee was recoverable by the insurers exercising rights of subrogation. Ward LJ held that the question of whether the success fee is recoverable:

> depends on the application of the rules to the facts of the case. The court always has to ask whether the costs have been unreasonably incurred or are unreasonable in amount. In considering that, the court must take all the circumstances of the case into account and in particular must have regard to the Practice Direction which requires the court in deciding whether a percentage increase is reasonable to take into account the other methods of financing the costs that were available to the receiving parties.[50]

Thus, he said 'If one is looking at the realities, one has to look at the position of the insurers and consider the reasonableness of the insurer entering into this CFA'.[51] The fact that the claim was being controlled by the insurers under their subrogation rights and that the insured would be indemnified was irrelevant.[52] Thus, the decision confirms that the insurer, when exercising their rights of subrogation, has the same rights as an insured: the insured would have been able to enter into a CFA and therefore the insurer can compel the insured to do so.[53]

Finally, the loss must be looked at from the point of view of the insured and not from the point of view of the insurers. In *Bee v Jenson (No 2)*,[54] the insured's vehicle was damaged in a motor accident caused by the defendant. The insured's policy allowed the hire of a replacement vehicle at the expense of the insurers. They sought to recover the hire charges from the defendant by way of subrogation. The defendant argued that the insurers should have deducted an introduction fee from the car hire because this represented an unjustified profit at the defendant's expense, and that the insurers could have obtained a replacement vehicle more cheaply by utilising corporate rates available to it. Morison J confirmed 'that contractual subrogation (as in insurance cases) and subrogation as a remedy to prevent unjust enrichment are two distinct institutions and must not be confused':[55]

> '[S]ubrogation' is concerned solely with the mutual rights and liabilities of the parties to the contract of insurance. It confers no rights and imposes no liabilities upon third parties who are strangers to that contract. It vests in the insurer who has paid a loss no direct rights or remedies against anyone other than the assured. He cannot sue such parties in his own name; he is bound by any release given by the assured to a third party. The insurer's rights against the assured cannot be affected by any subsequent contract, or dealings between the assured and a third party.

[49] [2011] EWCA Civ 194.
[50] ibid [23].
[51] ibid [28].
[52] ibid [24] and [25].
[53] ibid.
[54] [2008] Lloyd's Rep IR 221.
[55] ibid [8]. See Mitchell and Watterson (n 1).

Morison J held that the insured was entitled to hire a replacement car, and as long as it was at a reasonable rate and for a reasonable period, the sums could be recovered. That decision was not affected by whether the insurers had made 'a large profit or a profit on their insurance arrangements'.[56] The amount recoverable by the insurers was based on the insured's loss, and the fact that collateral benefits had been received by the insurers was irrelevant, particularly as contractual subrogation was not governed by principles of unjust enrichment. Morison J also rejected the argument that insurers could have obtained a lower rate as had the claimant, as it would be tantamount to saying that in 'reality the insurers' claim and that the insurers are to be treated as parties to the action. That is not the law; on the contrary, the law is blind to insurance arrangements and recoveries in claims such as this.'[57] Therefore, the claimant could not be confined in his claim to the cost of hiring a car on corporate as opposed to spot rates.

1.3. The Allocation of Subrogation Recoveries

If damages relating to an insured loss have been recovered from a third party, the question arises as to how they are to be allocated as between the insured and the insurers. There is no particular difficulty if the full sum insured is recovered from the third party, but a problem arises where the damages obtained from the defendant are less than the sum insured. There are two guiding principles relating to allocation: the insured must be full indemnified; and the insurers must not make a profit. There is a further question of the status of funds received from the third party.

1.3.1. The Insured Must Be Fully Indemnified

The insured is entitled to a full indemnity, so that the sums recovered from the third party must be allocated to any uninsured loss suffered by the insured. Uninsured loss may be a form of loss simply not covered by the policy, in which case the insured has first claim over the proceeds in respect of it. For instance, if a motor policy does not cover the cost of hiring a replacement vehicle following an accident, then the part of any compensation received that relates to this expenditure should not be brought into the calculation for the purposes of apportionment of that compensation between the insured and the insurer. Uninsured loss may also be in the form of underinsurance of the subject matter, ie where the insured has been paid up to policy limits but the payment does not represent the full amount of the insured's loss in respect of the subject matter. The general principle that the insured is entitled to an indemnity means that the damages are to be allocated to the uninsured loss, and only the balance can go to the insurers. To that there are important modifications.

First of all, if the policy is valued, the valuation is conclusive of the amount of the insured's loss, so it is not open to the insured to argue that a greater sum has been lost than that agreed under the policy in respect of the insured subject matter. For example, where the agreed value of a ship was £6000, even though its real value was £9000, and the insurers paid for a total loss, they were entitled to the whole of a payment of £5000 received as compensation from the wrongdoer.[58]

[56] ibid [14].

[57] ibid [17].

[58] *North of England Iron Steamship Insurance Association v Armstrong* (1870) LR 5 QB 244. See also *Thames & Mersey Marine Insurance v British and Chilean Steamship Co* [1915] 2 KB 214 (affirmed at [1916] 1 KB 330); for

Secondly, the excess/deductible is to be left out of account, as that is not regarded as any part of the insured's loss. That issue came before the House of Lords in *Lord Napier and Ettrick v Hunter*,[59] where the loss was £160,000 but the sum insured on a liability policy was only £125,000, of which the insured was liable for the first £25,000 of the loss (the excess). The insurer, therefore, paid £100,000 in full settlement of the claim under the terms of the policy. Compensation of £130,000 was later received from the wrongdoer. The House of Lords held that the insured was his own insurer for the first £25,000 and that he had agreed to bear any loss over the insured sum of £125,000. Out of the compensation, the insured was, therefore, entitled to £35,000. This was the uninsured loss of £60,000 (the first £25,000 and the amount of the loss that was not covered, which was £35,000) less £25,000, which was the amount of the excess. The insurer received the rest of the compensation, that is £95,000 (£130,000 less £35,000). The House of Lords held that the excess clause (the first £25,000 of the loss) entitled the insurers to priority over the insured's claim to be compensated for the amount of that excess.

Only Lords Templeman and Jauncey went on to look at the other aspect of the problem, the amount by which the loss exceeded the value in the contract (that is, the amount over £125,000 which was not covered by the policy: £35,000).[60] Lord Templeman said that there were three insurances: the first was for £25,000 (the excess), the second was for the next £100,000 (the part for which the insurer was liable under the policy) and the third was for the remaining £35,000 (the amount by which the actual loss exceeded that covered by the policy). The compensation is applied from the top down: that is, first, to the insurer of the last slice (£35,000), then the insurer of the second slice (£100,000) and finally, if any is left, to the insurer of the third slice (£25,000). This meant that the insured, who covered the top slice, received £35,000 and the insurers took the rest (£95,000). Since that came to £130,000, there was nothing left to pay the loss suffered by the insured on the excess (£25,000).[61] Lord Jauncey agreed with Lord Templeman on the outcome of the calculations, but disagreed on the method used. For him, the loss that was not covered by the compensation from the wrongdoer was £30,000, which he arrived at by deducting £130,000 (the compensation paid) from £160,000 (the loss). Then he deducted the excess of £25,000 from this amount and arrived at a figure of £5000, which was due to the insured from the insurers. In other words, of the £130,000 paid by the wrongdoer, the insurers receive £95,000 and the insured £35,000.

> When an insured loss is diminished by a recovery from a third party, whether before or after any indemnification has been made, the ultimate loss is simply the initial loss minus the recovery and it is that sum to which the provisions of the policy of assurance apply including any provision as to an excess.[62]

The costs of proceeding against the third party follows the allocation of the sums received.[63]

a case of a valued policy where there was only a partial loss, *Goole & Hull Steam Towing Co Ltd v Ocean Marine Insurance Co Ltd* [1928] 1 KB 589.

[59] See [1993] 1 Lloyd's Rep 10. See also MC Hemsworth, 'Subrogation: The Problem of Competing Claims to Recovery Monies' [1998] *Journal of Business Law* 111.

[60] The insurers had conceded that the insured was entitled to this sum, so it was not necessary to decide the point.

[61] In support of Lord Templeman's approach, see *Kuwait Airways Corpn v Kuwait Insurance Co SAK* [2000] 1 Lloyd's Rep 252.

[62] [1993] 1 Lloyd's Rep 10, 748 (Lord Jauncey).

[63] *England v Guardian Insurance Ltd* [2000] Lloyd's Rep IR 404.

1.3.2. The Insurers May Not Make a Profit

If the compensation received from the wrongdoer exceeds the payment made by the insurers, the surplus belongs to the insured because the action taken against the wrongdoer is in law that of the insured and because, although it is often said that the insured must not be allowed to make a profit, it is more accurate to say that the objective of subrogation is to prevent double recovery by the insured. In *Yorkshire Insurance Co Ltd v Nisbet Shipping Co Ltd*,[64] after the insurers had paid for a total loss of £72,000, a successful action was brought against the wrongdoer by the insured with the consent of the insurers. The damages were assessed in Canadian dollars and, because of a shift in the value of that currency, this produced a sum in sterling of £126,000. It was held that the insurers were entitled only to the amount paid to the insured and the insured could retain the surplus. Of course, the parties may avoid this consequence by providing for the distribution of such an excess in their agreement.[65] Where the insurers exercise their right of subrogation and receive damages from a third party which exceed the payment made to the insured on the claim, then the insurers hold that surplus on trust for the insured.[66]

1.3.3. Holding the Proceeds

As already noted, if the insurers have paid on a claim and compensation is later paid to the insured, the insurers can recoup their payment by a common law action for money had and received. It is clear that the insurers also have an equitable interest in the compensation itself. In *Lord Napier and Ettrick v Hunter*,[67] compensation from the wrongdoer had been paid to the insured's agent. The problem was not that the insured denied the insurers' right to recoupment from that fund, but that if the only remedy available to the insurer was a common law action for money had and received, then, since the insured was a Lloyd's syndicate made up of 246 individuals, an action would have to be brought against each individual and this would create certain difficulties: some of these people lived abroad in jurisdictions where there might be little sympathy for the insurers, and recovery would also be prejudiced if any were bankrupt because the insurer would not have priority over the other creditors. The House of Lords held that the insurer has an equitable lien over the compensation paid by the wrongdoer to the insured's agent up to the amount paid by the insurer to the insured in settlement of the claim under the policy. There is also a right under the contract that the insured will pay to the insurer the amount to which the insurer is entitled out of the monies received in reduction of the loss.[68] According to Lord Templeman, equity will 'ensure that the insured person exercises his right of action against the wrongdoer in good faith and that the insurer is recouped out of the damages recovered from the wrongdoer'. The lien also gives the insurers priority over other creditors in the event of an insured becoming insolvent or bankrupt.[69] The lien does avoid the need to bring actions against insureds in their

[64] [1962] 2 QB 330.

[65] *Lucas v Export Credit Guarantee Department* [1974] 1 WLR 909.

[66] *Lonrho Exports Ltd v Export Credits Guarantee Department* [1996] 2 Lloyd's Rep 649.

[67] [1993] 1 Lloyd's Rep 10.

[68] An injunction was granted preventing the insured's agent from paying to the insured (and the insured from receiving) any part of the fund. The House of Lords decided that the money was not held on trust because this would place too onerous a duty on the insured as trustee and because it was more than was required to protect the insurers' interests.

[69] *Re Miller, Gibb & Co* [2000] Lloyd's Rep IR 404.

country; the insurer need only pursue the money wherever it is. Moreover, the insurer's right to enforce the lien will not be undermined by an allegation of inequitable conduct because the lien is a proprietary right in the monies, which cannot be defeated by the insurer's conduct.[70] This equitable interest in the money will be lost if the compensation has been paid to the insureds, or if it has been acquired by a bona fide purchaser for value without notice. Lord Templeman also expressed the opinion that the insurers might have an equitable interest in any cause of action available to the insured if, were that action to be successful, it would result in a fund in which the insurers would have an equitable lien:

> [P]romises implied in a contract of insurance with regard to rights of action vested in the insured person for the recovery of an insured loss from a third party responsible for the loss confer on the insurer an equitable interest in those rights of action to the extent necessary to recoup the insurer who has indemnified the insured person against the insured loss.

The reasoning behind this rests on the principle that where there is a payment of compensation by a third party that relates to the payment of a claim under the policy, the insurers have an equitable interest in that compensation so long as it forms a separate identifiable fund. That led Lord Templeman to the rather radical proposition that the insurers will have an equitable interest in the cause of action that might lead to such payment of compensation. If this is right, then where the insurers have indemnified the insured, they might have an action against a wrongdoer who, having notice of the interests of the insurers (merely knowing that the claim has been paid might be sufficient notice), settles with the insured on terms that are unfavourable to the interests of the insurers.

1.4. Subrogation Immunity and Third Parties[71]

1.4.1. Joint Insurance

It was seen in chapter seven above that two or more persons can be insured under a single policy, but that a fundamental distinction is drawn between joint insurance and composite insurance. Joint insurance arises where the interests of the parties in the insured subject matter are indivisible, as in the case of (and probably only) matrimonial or partnership property. The principle here, as set out in *Simpson v Thomson, Birrell*,[72] is that the insurers cannot bring a subrogation action against their own insured. So, if A and B jointly own and insure property, and it is negligently damaged by B, then the insurers must pay the sum insured and have no subrogation claim against B. If B deliberately destroyed the property, then there would be no claim under the insurance in any event, as the rights of A and B stand or fall together.

1.4.2. Composite Insurance

The position is quite different in the case of composite insurance, where two or more persons are insured under the same policy. As noted in chapter seven above, it is not fully

[70] *England v Guardian Insurance Ltd* [2000] Lloyd's Rep IR 404.

[71] O Gurses, 'Subrogation Against a Contractual Beneficiary: A New Limitation to Insurers' Subrogation?' [2017] *Journal of Business Law* 557; W Feng, 'The Doctrine of Subrogation in Joint Insurance – The Ocean Victory' (2017) 23 *Journal of International Maritime Law* 191.

[72] (1877) 3 App Cas 279.

clear whether composite insurance consists of a single contract with multiple insureds or a series of individual policies within the same document, but on either analysis each composite insured has a separate interest in the insured subject matter and claims are unaffected by the rights, acts and omissions of the other composite insureds. The issue that has arisen here is whether the insurers, having paid for a loss suffered by co-insured A caused by co-insured B, can pursue co-insured B by way of subrogation. A good illustration of the issue comes from the construction industry, where head contractor A has hired a number of subcontractors (but we will focus on just one, subcontractor B) to perform specific tasks, and the head contractor has insured himself and all subcontractors under a property policy against damage to the works and existing buildings. If a subrogated claim is brought against B, does he have immunity? Three theories for immunity have been put forward.

The first is the theory of circuity propounded by Lloyd J. If the insurers indemnify A and claim against B, then B has the right himself to sue for the damage, B having a pervasive insurable interest in the entire works by virtue of the loss that he will suffer if the work cannot continue by reason of damage.[73] Therefore any subrogation claim is pointless.

The second is the implication into the policy of a term whereby insurers agree to sue a co-insured by way of subrogation. That was the suggestion of Colman J.[74]

Thirdly, under what is now the settled view, subrogation immunity comes not from the insurance, but rather from the arrangements between the co-insureds. It is obvious that if A does not have a claim against B, then the insurers, having indemnified A, can themselves have no claim against B, as subrogation does not confer better rights on the insurers than had been possessed by the insured. That approach was pointed at by the decision of the House of Lords in *Co-operative Retail Services Ltd v Taylor Young Partnership*,[75] where a subrogation claim was rejected because any right of action was precluded by the contract between A and B, and endorsed by Rix LJ in *Tyco Fire & Integrated Solutions (UK) Ltd v Rolls Royce Motor Cars Ltd*.[76] It is now the case that subrogation immunity rests upon whether, by the terms of the contract, A has exonerated B from liability, and that question is answered by examining the insurance and liability provisions in the contract. If A has agreed to insure on behalf of B, then that promise carries the almost inevitable implication that A is also agreeing that A is surrendering any cause of action against B in favour of reliance on the insurance.[77] Thus, if A recovers from the insurers, he cannot recover from B, and if for some reason A has not taken out the agreed policy, then B's immunity is not changed because – leaving aside the fact that A is in breach of contract – the arrangement is that A will rely on sums that ought to have been recovered from insurers rather than suing B.[78] What is required for the subrogation immunity of a co-insured is thus some form of undertaking by A that he will insure in his own and B's name, and it is clear from the arrangement that A is to look to the insurers and not to B. Not all insurance provisions in the contract between A and B will have that effect. It may be, for example, that the obligation to insure is purely for A's benefit and B is co-insured simply to reflect the fact that

[73] *The Yasin* [1979] 2 Lloyd's Rep 45, as modified in *Petrofina (UK) Ltd v Magnaload Ltd* [1984] QB 127.

[74] *National Oilwell (UK) Ltd v Davy Offshore Ltd* [1993] 2 Lloyd's Rep 582; *Stone Vickers Ltd v Appledore Ferguson Shipbuilders Ltd* [1991] 2 Lloyd's Rep 288, reversed without challenging the reasoning [1992] 2 Lloyd's Rep 578.

[75] [2002] UKHL 17 (HL); J Birds, 'Denying Subrogation in Co-Insurance and Similar Situations' [2001] *Lloyd's Maritime and Commercial Law Quarterly* 193.

[76] [2008] EWCA Civ 286, [2008] 1 CLC 625.

[77] *Rathbone Brothers plc v Novae Corporate Underwriting Ltd* [2014] EWCA Civ 1464.

[78] *Scottish & Newcastle Plc v GD Construction (St Albans) Ltd* [2003] EWCA Civ 16.

A is to use any insurance monies to reinstate the works so that B can continue to perform the contract,[79] or that the insurance obligation is clearly negatived by an obligation on B to indemnify A for any loss caused by B.[80] Further, the obligation of A to look only to the insurers and not to B will not operate if B has deliberately caused the loss or B's conduct causes a loss falling outside the terms of the insurance.[81]

The position was confirmed by the Supreme Court in *Gard Marine & Energy Ltd v China National Chartering Ltd*,[82] although the outcome was a 3:2 split on the precise facts. A vessel was chartered by A to B on terms that B would obtain insurance to cover the interests of both A and B. The vessel was sub-chartered to C and then to D. All of the charters contained a 'safe port warranty' under which the charterer was responsible for any lack of safety at any port visited by the vessel. The vessel suffered loss in port and the insurers, having indemnified both A and B, sought to pursue C and D by way of assignment and subrogation for breach of the safe port warranty. The Supreme Court unanimously dismissed the claim on the basis that there had not been a breach of the safe port warranty, but views were expressed as to the immunity of C and D had there been such a breach. Lords Mance, Hodge and Toulson thought that C and D would be immune, in that the insuring provisions of the head charter were designed to provide a code whereby A would look only to the insurers in the event of a loss. Lords Clarke and Sumption, by contrast, thought that the safe port warranty overrode the insuring clause. The reasoning thus prevented any liability from arising in the first place, so that no question of subrogation could arise.

In short, the issue in every case is the interpretation of the contract to determine how the risk of loss was to be allocated between A and B.[83] This is consistent with the general view of contract law as being all about the allocation of risk.

1.4.3. Third Party Immunity

The courts have considered in a number of cases the position of a third party who does not have co-insurance arrangements and who is not named or identified in the policy as a co-insured. The absence of co-insurance does not necessarily mean that subrogation proceedings are possible, as once again the issue is whether the contractual arrangements between the insured party and the third party are such that the insured party is to look to the insurers and not to the third party in the event that the third party causes a loss. Once again, at the root of the cases is the question of risk allocation. In *Mark Rowlands Ltd v Berni Inns*,[84] a tenancy agreement stipulated that the lessor insure against fire and use any insurance monies to rebuild. The tenant was required to contribute to the premium and was relieved of any duty to repair where damage was caused by fire. The Court of Appeal held that the insurers, who paid out on the policy following a fire, could not recover against the tenant. Although the tenant was not mentioned in the policy, it was clear from the lease that it was effected on behalf of both the landlord and the tenant, that he also contributed to the premium and that the lease excluded the tenant's liability for fire.

[79] That was the position in *Tyco* itself.

[80] *Haberdashers' Aske's Federation Trust Ltd v Lakehouse Contracts Ltd* [2018] EWHC 558 (TCC).

[81] *Tate Gallery (Trustees) v Duffy Construction Ltd* [2007] EWHC 361 (TCC).

[82] [2017] UKSC 35. See also *Cape Distribution Ltd v Cape Intermediate Holdings Plc (No 2)* [2016] Lloyd's Rep IR 499.

[83] *Rugby Football Union v Clark Smith Partnership* [2022] EWHC 956 (TCC).

[84] 1986] QB 211. See J Birds, 'Landlords, Tenants and Subrogation' (1986) 6 *OJLS* 304. See also *Barras v Hamilton* 1994 SC 544; *Frasca-Judd v Golovina* [2016] EWHC 497 (QB).

The insurers were not a party to this arrangement, nor was it disclosed. Nevertheless, the Court of Appeal held that the intention of the parties was that in the event of a fire the lessor's loss should be recouped from the insurance policy and there would be no other claim against the tenant by the lessor, or, therefore, by the lessor's insurer. The commercial sense of this will be appreciated. If the tenant faced subrogation proceedings, he would need to take out his own insurance and would thereby be paying twice. A similar decision is *Herculito Maritime Ltd v Gunvor International BV*,[85] in which the owners chartered their vessel to charterers on terms that the owners would insure against war risks on the basis that the premiums would be paid by the charterers. The vessel was seized by Somali pirates and released only after payment of a ransom of US$7.7 million by the insurers. General average was declared, so that all of the persons interested in the voyage were required to contribute to the ransom payment made for the common good to the amount of their respective interests in the saved property.[86] A claim of US$4.8 million was on that basis made against the charterers and the owners of the cargo. They claimed immunity on the ground that the terms of carriage evidenced in the bills of lading incorporated the provisions of the charter and in particular the obligation on the vessel's owners to insure. It was held that the charterers were immune because they had paid the premiums and were – while not parties to the insurance – intended beneficiaries of it. However, that did not apply to the cargo owners: they were not the intended beneficiaries of the insurance and had not paid any of the premiums. The obligation to pay premiums is not a necessary precondition of immunity. It may be that a promise to insure by the insured party is enough to amount to an agreement by that party to look only to the insurers if the loss falls within the terms of the insuring obligation. But for the promise, the other party would have to take out his own insurance and therefore might not be willing to pay as much to the insured party under the terms of the contract between them. So in every case it is a question of ascertaining objectively the intentions of the parties as regards risk allocation.

A promise to insure will not give subrogation immunity for loss falling outside the insuring obligation. In *Lambert v Keymood Ltd*,[87] the tenant's bonfire caused damage to the leased premises, the tenant having previously been warned that bonfires were too close to the premises. The court's view was that the landlord's promise to insure extended to accidental losses only, and not – as here – loss inflicted recklessly. In *Prezzo Ltd v High Point Estates Ltd*,[88] the landlord's insuring obligation was held to apply only to the part of the building comprised in the lease, so that there was held to be nothing to prevent a subrogation action by insurers where the tenant damaged other parts of the building. In *Bank of New York Mellon (International) Ltd v Cine-UK Ltd*,[89] the landlord's obligation to insure against loss of rent in the event of physical damage to the leased premises was held not to relieve the tenant from the obligation to pay rent when the premises were forced to be closed in the COVID-19 lockdown, as there was no physical damage involved even though the premises could not be used for their intended purpose.

[85] [2021] EWCA Civ 1828.
[86] For general average, see ch 17 below.
[87] [1999] Lloyd's Rep IR 80.
[88] [2018] EWHC 1851 (TCC).
[89] [2021] EWHC 1013 (QB).

1.4.4. Effect of Contractual Arrangements Removing or Restricting Subrogation Rights

As has been seen in the preceding paragraphs, contractual arrangements between the insured and the third party may operate to exempt the third party from any liability. The absence of subrogation rights is potentially a material fact for insurers requiring disclosure under the insured's duty of fair presentation, assuming that the insurers can prove both objective materiality and also inducement in that they would have acted differently as regards policy terms or premium had the arrangements been disclosed. In practice, potential subrogation recoveries are not usually an element in the calculation of premium as they are surrounded by too many uncertainties, and if there are such recoveries they are treated as a windfall by insurers. On that basis, a plea of non-disclosure has a relatively limited prospect of success, and in *Tate & Sons v Hyslop*[90] the Court of Appeal held that an insurer has constructive knowledge of the manner in which the insured's class of business operates so that it is only where contractual immunities are exceptional that there is even a possibility of a successful plea of non-disclosure. In that case it was held that the cargo owner's agreement that goods would be unloaded 'without recourse to lightermen' was sufficiently unusual to have merited disclosure, but the exceptional nature of the case was emphasised.

The position is somewhat different if, after the policy has been entered into, the insured agrees to exempt or limit the liability of the defendant, eg because the insured knows that any future claim is covered by insurance. The insurers have no subrogation rights at this stage, and it has been held in Australia[91] that there is no implied term barring the insured from making such arrangements as long as the intention to do so did not exist before the insurance was entered into. Insurers agree to carry any increase of risk, and such an agreement seems to fall into that category.

A further possibility is that, after a loss has occurred and before the insurers have provided an indemnity – so that the insured retains the right to control the claim – the insured settles with the third party in a manner that necessarily removes or restricts subrogation rights. Here, the courts have formulated a broad principle requiring the insured not to act to the prejudice of the rights of the insurers.[92] The insured must not reach any agreement which undermines the rights of the insurers. If the insured abandons a claim against the wrongdoer, that may amount to a breach of the insurance contract, which will entitle the insurers who have not paid to refuse to do so and the insurers who have paid to recover from the insured damages for the prejudice suffered.[93] Likewise, if the insured reaches a settlement with the wrongdoer which prejudices the insurers' rights, the insured incurs personal liability to the extent of that prejudice.[94] There is no breach of contract if the insured acted in good faith, although what amounts to a bona fide settlement is not clear.[95] It may simply be that if there is no collusion between the insured and the wrongdoer and, in the circumstances, the settlement is reasonable, the insurers may find it difficult to show they have been prejudiced. In *Horwood v Land of Leather Ltd*,[96] the claimants commenced

[90] (1885) 15 QBD 368.

[91] *State Government Insurance Office (Qld) v Brisbane Stevedoring Pty Ltd* (1969) 123 CLR 228.

[92] *Commercial Union Assurance Co Ltd v Lister* (1874) LR Ch App 483.

[93] *West of England Fire Insurance Company v Issacs* [1897] 1 QB 227; *Horse, Carriage and General Insurance Company (Ltd) v Petch* (1917) 33 TLR 131.

[94] *Boag v Standard Marine Insurance Co Ltd* [1937] 2 KB 113, 128 (Scott LJ); *Phoenix Assurance Co v Spooner* [1905] 2 KB 753.

[95] *Commercial Union Assurance Co v Lister* (1874) LR Ch App 483.

[96] 2010] EWHC 546 (Comm).

proceedings against the assured for personal injuries. The assured became insolvent and the claim proceeded against the assured's product liability insurers under the Third Parties (Rights against Insurers) Act 1930. Clause 3 of the policy, which was a condition precedent, was a claims control clause under which the assured was not to

> except at his own cost, take any steps to compromise or settle any claim or admit liability without specific instructions in writing from the Insurer nor give any information or assistance to any person claiming against him, but the Insurer shall for so long as they shall so desire have the absolute conduct and control of all proceedings (including arbitrations) in respect of any claims for which the Insurer may be liable under this policy, and may use the name of the Insured to enforce for the benefit of the Insurer any order made for costs or otherwise or to make or defend any claim for indemnity or damages against any third party or for any other purpose connected with this policy.

At the end of 2007, and following complaints about allergies, the assured decided to stop selling products provided by Linkwise, and it was agreed that Linkwise would provide compensation of US$900,000, although the court found that there was no agreement as to how and when the money should be paid. The release provided that '[the assured] also confirm they will make no further claim on Linkwise in respect of alleged allergic reactions to their products though no proof exists that the cause was Linkwise products'. The insurers contended that the release contravened the claims control clause. The court ruled that the claims control clause applied not just to claims made against the assured, but also to claims made by the assured, and accordingly it had been broken. In regard to the formation and breach of an implied term relating to an insurers' subrogation rights, Teare J stated that:

> The implied term arises because the insurer has a right to be subrogated to the rights of the insured when he indemnifies him pursuant to the policy of insurance. If the insured acts without regard to that contingent right he may harm the value of that right to the insurer. The most obvious harm occurs where the insured settles a claim he may have against a third party for an indemnity and so deprives the insurer of its benefit in whole or in part. But in principle harm may be caused to the insurer's rights of subrogation where the claim against the third party is not lost or reduced in value by settlement. For example, the documents necessary to establish such claim may be destroyed. I therefore consider that the implied duty must be one which obliges the insured to act in good faith and reasonably with regard to the interests of the insurer.[97]

Thus, had the point arisen, the court would have found that there was an implied term in the policy that the assured would act in good faith and reasonably with regard to the interests of the insurers so as to preserve the insurers' subrogation rights and, by entering into a settlement contract, that implied term had been broken.

1.4.5. Subrogation Waiver by the Insurers

Insurers may expressly agree to waive their subrogation rights. This possibility arises in particular where there is a close relationship between the insured and potential defendants. For example, a cargo policy may waive subrogation rights against the carrier of the cargo where the cargo owner and the carrier form part of the same group of companies. At common law, in the absence of co-insurance, a subrogation waiver clause was ineffective, in that the doctrine of privity of contract prevented reliance upon it by the defendant,[98]

[97] ibid [67].
[98] *National Oilwell (UK) Ltd v Davy Offshore Ltd* [1993] 2 Lloyd's Rep 582.

subject only to the insured seeking to enforce the waiver by seeking an injunction against the insurers. There was a suggestion by Clarke J in *The Surf City*[99] that it would be inequitable to allow insurers to exercise subrogation rights against a third party where they had previously agreed with the insurers that they would not do so, but, as has already been suggested, the authority for this approach is not strong.

The position has been transformed by the Contracts (Rights of Third Parties) Act 1999. The third party may rely upon the subrogation waiver clause as long as he is the beneficiary of that promise, he is identified by name or class in the policy and it was intended that the third parties could rely upon the promise. The last of these requirements was significant in *Haberdashers' Aske's Federation Trust Ltd v Lakehouse Contracts Ltd*,[100] where the policy taken out by a contractor waived subrogation rights against all subcontractors. The defendant subcontractor fell within the relevant description, but it was nevertheless held that there had not been any intention on the part of the contractor to include that particular subcontractor in the waiver, given the contractual arrangements between them under which the subcontractor was to arrange its own insurance. It was irrelevant, therefore, that the subcontractor on the face of things fell within the class of persons to whom subrogation immunity had been extended.

Subrogation may also be waived by an insurer after the loss has occurred. This occurred in *Kitchen Design and Advice Ltd v Lea Valley Water Co*,[101] where the claimant's property insurers entered into a settlement agreement with the defendant's liability insurers. After the settlement had been entered into, the claimant made additional claims against its property insurers, but the settlement precluded any further recovery from the defendant's liability insurers. An attempt was made to sidestep the settlement by the device of a subrogation action, brought on the basis that neither the claimant nor the defendant was a party to any settlement, the agreement being between their insurers only. The court was able to find with some ease that the two insurers had been acting under authority conferred by the respective policies and so the settlement bound the claimant and defendant as well as their insurers.

---

2. Double Insurance and Contribution

2.1. Double Insurance

2.1.1. Significance and Meaning

There is no prohibition against double insurance, so a person may effect multiple policies on the same property against identical risks. This practice was a necessary protection in the era when insurance was taken out with individual underwriters at Lloyd's, given the risk of insolvency, and the practice was recognised by section 32 of the Marine Insurance Act 1906. In such a case, the insured is free to claim payment from whichever insurer he chooses, subject to the overriding principle that not more than an indemnity can be recovered. As is stated in section 32(2)(a) of the Act, 'The assured, unless the policy otherwise provides,

[99] 1995] 2 Lloyd's Rep 242.
[100] [2018] EWHC 558 (TCC).
[101] [1989] 2 Lloyd's Rep 221.

may claim payment from the insurers in such order as he may think fit, provided that he is not entitled to receive any sum in excess of the indemnity allowed by this Act'.[102] In these days of strict solvency controls on insurers, pure double insurance is largely unnecessary. However, double insurance may arise accidentally or incidentally. Goods in the boot of a car may be covered by both household and motor insurance. Travel insurance may be available to an insured from the insured's employer and also from the insured's bank. Further, the insured may wrongly believe that a policy has been cancelled or does not cover a particular risk, and so insures under a different policy. There is no intention to doubly insure in any of these cases, but that may be the effect of the arrangements.

The definition of double insurance is important for two reasons. First, as is recognised by section 32(2)(a) of the 1906 Act, there may be contractual restrictions prohibiting double insurance or regulating how the respective insurers are to make payment where double insurance exists. Secondly, where there is double insurance, the paying insurer has a right of contribution against any other insurer liable for the same claim. Each of these matters is considered below. There are numerous decisions on the definition of double insurance. The effect of them is that double insurance exists where the two policies cover the same subject matter, the same insured and the same interest. Whether two policies cover the same subject matter is a question of construction, as in *Boag v Economic Insurance Co Ltd*,[103] where a cargo of cigarettes insured under an all risks transit policy were held not to fall within a fire policy on premises where the cigarettes had been stored temporarily so that there was no double insurance. Premises insured separately by the landlord and the tenant,[104] or goods insured separately by the bailor and the bailee,[105] cannot be said to have been doubly insured. There is no unity of interest as between a primary layer policy and an excess layer policy, in that although they cover the same subject matter, they provide indemnity for different parts of the loss. The two policies must also be in effect at the same time. A ship called the *Aladdin* was insured on its voyage to Calcutta and for 30 days after arrival. When it arrived, the owners effected another insurance with the same insurers to cover the ship at Calcutta and during a proposed voyage to Bombay. The ship sank in Calcutta, and the question was whether the reinsurers of the second policy (under which the claim was made) were entitled to a contribution from the insurers. The court construed the intention of the parties as being that the first policy terminated on the making of the second policy.[106] As will be seen in chapter 19, there may be double insurance as between policies taken out in consecutive years where the loss can be regarded as having taken place in each of those years. However, liability policies written on a claims made basis commonly exclude claims arising out of circumstances notified in previous years, so the effect is that there is simply no cover for a claim made in the policy year arising out of circumstances notified to a previous insurer.[107]

[102] The remainder of the section deals with the complexities raised where one of the policies is valued (the valuation being conclusive) and the other is unvalued. A claim under the valued policy is limited to the sum insured under that policy even if the loss is greater, so anything obtained under the unvalued policy must be deducted from the agreed value. For that reason, it is necessary to claim under the valued policy first, so that the balance of any loss can be recovered under the unvalued policy. See *Bruce v Jones* (1863) 1 H & C 769.

[103] [1954] 2 Lloyd's Rep 581.

[104] *Portavon Cinema v Price* [1939] 4 All ER 601.

[105] *North British and Mercantile Insurance Co v London, Liverpool and Globe Insurance Co* (1877) 5 Ch D 569.

[106] *Union Marine Insurance Co Ltd v Martin* (1866) 35 LJCP 181.

[107] *National Employers Mutual General Insurance Association Ltd v Haydon* [1980] 2 Lloyd's Rep 149.

If the requirements for double insurance are satisfied, there is no need for the policies themselves to be of the same type or, indeed, substantially on the same risks: double insurance arises where two policies of whatever type happen to cover the same loss.

2.1.2. Contractual Variations on Double Insurance

Although double insurance is permitted by the general law, and in most cases is not deliberate, from an insurer's point of view double insurance – like overvaluation – may be an indication of an intention on the part of the insured to perpetrate a fraud. For this reason, policies have long contained provisions restricting the insured's statutory rights under section 32 of the 1906 Act to obtain two policies on the same risk and, if there is double insurance, to claim against the insurers in such order as the insured thinks fit.

In order to prevent double insurance, a policy term may as a condition precedent to liability require the insured to notify the insurers of any further policy taken out on the insured subject matter, as in *Australian Agricultural Co v Saunders*,[108] where a fire policy on a cargo of wool was held to respond to the loss of the wool in a warehouse fire despite the fact that the insured had taken out a later marine policy, as the latter was construed as applying only to goods in transit. A similar decision is *Equitable Fire & Accident Office v Ching Wo Hong*,[109] where the condition was held to be inapplicable because the insured had not paid the premium under the second policy so that it never became effective. In *Home Insurance Co of New York v Gavel*,[110] the policy provided that it would not come into existence if there was any earlier insurance. There may also be express questions to the insured as to the existence of other insurance when the policy is effected, a false answer being misrepresentation that could lead to avoidance.

There are three main devices used by insurers to regulate the order of recovery under two policies covering the same risk. An 'escape' clause provides that if there is any other insurance in force in respect of a claim, there is no cover. An 'excess' clause provides that if there is any other insurance in place, the policy takes effect as an excess cover only so that the other insurance pays first and the excess insurers pick up only any loss beyond the financial limits of that other insurance. A 'rateable proportion' clause provides that the policy covers only a proportion of the loss, with the remainder of the loss being borne by the other party. Each of these devices works perfectly well taken alone, but complications appear when the affected policies all contain one or more of these devices. The courts have adopted the starting point that it is necessary to avoid the absurdity of the insured finding that he or she has no cover at all in spite of having paid two premiums. This was established in two motor cases. In *Gale v Motor Union Insurance Co*,[111] the policies both contained escape and rateable proportion clauses. It was held that the escape clauses were modified by the rateable proportion clauses, so that each insurer was liable to pay one half of the loss. This case left open the question of how two policies each containing escape clauses but not rateable proportion clauses would respond, the answer given by Rowlatt J in *Weddell v Road Traffic and General Insurance Co Ltd*[112] (where just one of the policies contained a rateable

[108] (1875) LR 10 CP 668.
[109] [1907] AC 96.
[110] (1928) 30 Ll L Rep 139.
[111] [1928] 1 KB 359.
[112] [1932] 2 KB 563. See also *Structural Polymer Systems Ltd and Structural Polymer Technologies Ltd v Brown* [2000] Lloyd's Rep IR 64.

proportion clause) that 'the reasonable construction is to exclude from the category of co-existing cover any cover which is expressed to be itself cancelled by such co-existence, and to hold in such cases that both companies are liable'. The same approach has been adopted where one policy contains an escape clause and the other an excess clause,[113] and where each of the policies seeks to convert itself into an excess cover if other insurance exists.[114]

Rateable proportion clauses operate in a straightforward manner, and operate to apply the contribution principle at the claims stage: rather than one insurer paying the loss and seeking contribution, each insurer only pays its own share at the outset. There is an obvious unfairness, given that the insured has to make two claims rather than one. The problems that arise where one policy contains an escape or excess clause and the other a rateable proportion clause were addressed by Gavin Kealey QC in *National Farmers Union Mutual Insurance Society Ltd v HSBC Insurance (UK) Ltd*.[115] The sellers of a property were insured by NFU. There was an extension in the policy in favour of buyers, stating that:

> *We* will not pay any claim if any loss, damage or liability covered under this insurance is also covered wholly or in part under any other insurance except in respect of any excess beyond the amount which would have been covered under such other insurance had this insurance not been effected.

The buyers were insured by HSBC, the policy stating that 'If when you claim there is other insurance covering the same accident, illness, damage or liability, we will only pay our share'. A fire broke out on the insured property between exchange of contracts for the sale of the property and completion. The sale was completed despite the fire. The buyers claimed under their HSBC policy and were indemnified. HSBC sought contribution from NFU, but the claim was refused. The court's view of the arrangement was that the NFU policy did not apply to the buyers if the buyers had their own cover. The 'rateable proportion' clause was overridden by the 'excess' clause. The buyers' policy did not exclude liability to the buyers in the event that there was some other insurance in place, and the only relevant provision was a rateable proportion clause, which restricted liability in the case of double insurance. However, there was no double insurance by reason of the excess clause. The judge reiterated that

> the right to a contribution between insurers depends in general on the existence of co-ordinate liabilities to make good one loss, it can be varied or excluded by contract: either by contract between the co-obligors or by contract between insured and insurer.[116]

Construing the terms of the two policies, he found that the seller's policy was to continue up and until completion of the sale of the property; this was because it covered losses which the seller would suffer if the completion of sale did not take effect.[117] The clause did extend to any loss which may be suffered by buyers of the property, up and until completion of the sale had taken effect, but this extension was qualified in that there was only cover if the buyers themselves had not taken out any insurance.[118] The judge found that there 'would be no good reason in a contract of insurance between HSBC and the sellers for HSBC to

[113] *Allianz Insurance Australia Ltd v Certain Underwriters at Lloyd's of London* [2019] NSWCA 271.
[114] *Foster v QBE European Underwriting Services (Australia) Pty Ltd* [2018] NSWSC 440.
[115] [2010] EWHC 773 (Comm).
[116] ibid [16].
[117] ibid [19].
[118] ibid [20].

extend insurance protection to those same buyers',[119] and there would be no commercial reason to confer a benefit on buyers who were not its original insured and had paid no premium. Accordingly, there would be 'no commercial reason to confer on the insurers of those buyers a benefit that would accrue in the event of double insurance'.[120]

2.2. Contribution

2.2.1. *The Nature of Contribution*

Where there is double insurance and one insurer has paid the claim, that insurer has a right of contribution against any other insurer also liable to indemnify the insured. Contribution is not based on contract, and is an equitable right akin to subrogation based on the maxim 'equality is equity', extending to all cases of co-indemnification and not just insurance. The law was codified by the Marine Insurance Act 1906, section 80:

> (1) where the assured is overinsured by double insurance, each insurer is bound, as between himself and the other insurers, to contribute rateably to the loss in proportion to the amount for which he is liable under the contract; and
> (2) if an insurer pays more than his proportion of the loss, he is entitled to maintain an action for contribution against the other insurers, and is entitled to the like remedies as a surety who has paid more than his proportion of the debt.

Some confusion has arisen over the question whether insurance contribution remains governed by equitable principles or whether the law has been superseded by the Civil Liability (Contribution) Act 1978.[121] Section 1(1) of the 1978 Act sets out the principle that 'any person liable in respect of any damage suffered by another person may recover a contribution from any other person liable in respect of the same damage (whether jointly with him or otherwise)'. Section 6(1) provides that contribution applies whatever the basis of legal liability for the damage, whether 'tort, breach of contract, breach of trust or otherwise'. By section 7(3), the Act supersedes any right, other than an express contractual right, to recover contribution. It is apparent that insurance contribution on the face of things falls within this Act, because the liability of an insurer to the insured is one based on breach of contract. However, if the 1978 Act does supersede the 1906 Act, it means that contribution as of right under the 1906 Act is replaced with the court's discretion to award contribution on a 'just and equitable basis' under section 2(1) of the 1978 Act. The matter was discussed by the Supreme Court in *Zurich Insurance PLC UK Branch v International Energy Group Ltd*,[122] where Lord Mance favoured the 1906 Act whereas Lord Sumption felt that the 1978 Act now prevailed. In *RSA Insurance Plc v Assicurazioni Generali*,[123] HHJ Rawlings reviewed the authorities and concluded that Lord Sumption was correct. The consequence of that ruling was that the two-year limitation period for contribution claims under the 1978 Act, rather than absence of a limitation period for claims in equity, was applicable and defeated the claim. An appeal was settled, so the current view is that section 80 of the 1906 Act no longer has currency and that the grant and quantum of contribution is in the discretion of

[119] ibid [21].
[120] ibid [20].
[121] Re-enacting on this matter the Law Reform (Married Women and Joint Tortfeasors) Act 1935.
[122] [2015] UKSC 33.
[123] [2018] EWHC 1237 (QB).

the court. The point awaits clear determination, but in what follows it will be assumed that the 1978 Act would be applied in the same way as the 1906 Act.

2.2.2. *The Timing of a Contribution Claim*

As with subrogation, there can be a contribution claim only by an insurer who has actually made payment and who faced liability to the insured. An ex gratia payment does not in principle suffice, because of the equitable maxim 'equity does not assist a volunteer'. However, the courts have proved flexible on the point, recognising that every incentive should be given to an insurer to indemnify the insured, and they have allowed an insurer who has made a voluntary payment to seek indemnification by an insurer actually liable for the loss. The point first arose in *Legal and General Assurance Society Ltd v Drake Insurance Co Ltd.*[124] A motorist was insured by two policies, by LG and Drake, each of which contained the usual rateable proportion clause. A claim was made against LG alone, and LG paid the full amount of the loss. Its contribution claim against Drake was rejected. LG was liable only for 50 per cent of the loss, so the additional 50 per cent had been paid voluntarily. However, that case was distinguished – and in effect not followed – by the Court of Appeal in *Drake Insurance Co Ltd v Provident Insurance Co Ltd.*[125] Here, both Drake and Provident were the insurers in respect of a personal injury claim by a third party against the insured. The policies contained rateable proportion clauses. Provident relied upon an arbitration clause in their policy[126] and obtained an arbitration award establishing their right to avoid the policy. Drake paid the claim and sought to recover half of its payment from Provident by way of contribution. The Court of Appeal allowed the action. The arbitration award was not binding on Drake as a third party, and the Court of Appeal was satisfied that the award was not correct as a matter of law. That meant that Drake had established that Provident was liable to the insured. That left the argument that Drake had paid as a volunteer, in that it was only liable for 50 per cent of the loss. The Court of Appeal held that in the circumstances Drake had not acted as a volunteer, in that it had sought at every stage to involve Provident in the settlement but Provident refused and instead relied upon the arbitration award. Thus, if the paying insurer pays beyond its own liability, but does so only because the other insurer has refused to participate, it cannot be said that the payment is voluntary.

Given that the claim by the paying insurer (A) may only be made against another insurer (B) who was also liable for the loss, the question arises as to whether B's liability for the loss is to be assessed at the date of the occurrence of the insured peril or the date on which A makes payment to the insured. The point is significant because if at the time of the loss both A and B are liable to the insured but a claim is made only against A, then by the time that A has made payment and seeks contribution from B it may be that B has obtained a defence against the insured based on breach of a condition precedent relating to the making of a timely claim or providing documents. These were more or less the facts of *Legal and General Insurance Society Ltd v Drake Insurance Co Ltd.* The Court of Appeal held that the correct analysis is that as soon as the insured loss occurs, A has a contingent contribution claim against B, and when A makes payment, the claim crystallises. That means that in the intervening period between the occurrence of the peril and the payment by A, B cannot

[124] [1992] QB 887.
[125] [2004] Lloyd's Rep IR 277.
[126] This is no longer permissible in consumer cases: see ch 11 above.

acquire a defence to A's equitable contribution claim: the position as between B and the insured is irrelevant, as the claim by A is not under B's policy but in equity. However, the point is not free from doubt. In *Eagle Star Insurance Co v Provincial Insurance Plc*,[127] the Privy Council disapproved the reasoning of the Court of Appeal and held that the correct analysis was that there could not be a contribution claim unless B was liable to the insured at the date of A's payment. In *O'Kane v Jones*,[128] the insured obtained a hull and machinery policy with A, but the premiums were not paid. The insured's managers, wrongly believing that A's policy had been cancelled, obtained a further hull and machinery policy with B. In fact, A's policy was never cancelled, with the result that at the date of the loss both policies were in force. It was then agreed that B's policy would be cancelled and the premiums refunded. A paid the claim and sought contribution. The court, following *Legal and General*, upheld the claim for contribution: as soon as the loss occurred, A had a contingent contribution claim against B, and it could not be defeated by any post-loss defences acquired by B.[129] There is no clear authority on whether *O'Kane v Jones* was correctly decided, but the very facts of the case demonstrate that a test based on the date of payment can create serious problems for a paying insurer.

2.2.3. Calculating Contribution

There are two broad approaches to the calculation of contribution. The independent liability test focuses on the liability of each of the insurers for the claim. Thus, if policy A has a limit of £100,000 and policy B has a limit of £200,000, each of the insurers is liable for a claim of up to £100,000 and so any loss up to that sum would be divided 50:50. Any loss in excess of £100,000 is to be apportioned by reference to the respective liabilities of A and B. Thus, if the loss is £150,000, based on independent liability, A is liable for £100,000 and B is liable for £150,000, so the loss would be divided in those ratios. The maximum liability test, unlike the independent liability test, focuses on policy limits rather than the actual claim. So, on the facts given above, any loss would be divided in proportion to the maximum sum insured by each insurer, namely 1:2. There is no clear authority on which of these tests is to be applied in any one case, although in *Commercial Union Assurance Co Ltd v Hayden*[130] the Court of Appeal applied the independent liability test to a liability policy on the basis that the maximum sum insured was a notional figure only. The same argument is less persuasive in a property policy, where the sum insured is a key determinant of the premium, and also in a case where the two policies are entirely different in nature.

[127] [1993] 3 All ER 1, on appeal from the Bahamas.

[128] [2005] Lloyd's Rep IR 174.

[129] B relied upon other defences (lack of insurable interest by the manager, and non-disclosure of the default in paying the premium under A's policy) that would have rendered the policy void *ab initio* so that there was never any liability. These defences were rejected by the court.

[130] [1977] 1 Lloyd's Rep 1.

14

Motor Insurance

1. Requirements of Compulsory Insurance

1.1. Compulsory Liability Cover

1.1.1. The Obligation to Insure

The Road Traffic Acts 1930 and 1934 made cover for third party liability compulsory for all those who used a motor vehicle on a road.[1] The legislation was amended on a number of occasions and was codified in Part VI of Road Traffic Act 1988.[2] Although the basic structure of the law remains in place, the UK regime has been amended in significant respects on a number of occasions in order to implement a series of five EU directives on compulsory motor insurance between 1973 and 2000, culminating in a sixth consolidated directive in 2009.[3] Those directives were designed to further the principle of free movement of persons, and they lay down minimum insurance requirements as well as establishing a regime whereby compensation can be recovered in the victim's home state irrespective of where in the EU the accident occurred. The departure of the UK from the EU with effect from 1 January 2021 has led to modification of the law, particularly in respect of the rights of visitors to and from the UK injured in motor accidents, but in other respects established principles of EU law in the decided cases remain binding on the UK courts until amending legislation has been passed. The position at time of writing is, therefore, far from straightforward, the law being that set out in the amended 1988 Act along with supplementary statutory instruments and also in the decisions of the Court of Justice of the European Union before 1 January 2021. The UK courts may 'have regard' to later CJEU decisions, but they are not binding.[4]

[1] See generally R Merkin and M Hemsworth, *The Law of Motor Insurance*, 2nd edn (London, Sweet & Maxwell, 2015).

[2] Road Traffic Act 1988, Part VI, ss 143–62.

[3] European Parliament and Council Directive 2009/103/EU. For the background to the EU legislation, see J Marson, K Ferris and A Nicholson, 'Irreconcilable Differences? The Road Traffic Act and the European Motor Vehicle Insurance Directives' [2017] *Journal of Business Law* 51.

[4] All of this is the effect of s 6 of the European Union (Withdrawal) Act 2018.

The primary aim of the legislation is to ensure that compensation is provided for those who are killed or injured, or who suffer damage to property by the acts or omissions of road users, by requiring that all motorists have a minimum level of liability insurance. In addition, the motor insurance industry has created a scheme to compensate those who have suffered loss that is within the cover required under the 1988 Act, but where the wrongdoer is uninsured or cannot be traced. The scheme is administered by the Motor Insurers' Bureau (MIB) under agreements with the government first entered into in 1946 for uninsured drivers and in 1969 for untraced drivers. The MIB incorporates the Motor Insurers' Information Centre, where information about vehicles and insurance is held to facilitate compensation for victims of motor accidents.[5] The legislation is not concerned with first party cover, only liability cover: the driver of a vehicle who suffers injury or property damage through his or her own fault is not protected by the 1988 Act.[6] The minimum form of cover on the market is 'third party, fire and theft', although first party cover in the form of 'fully comprehensive insurance' is the market norm.

It is a criminal offence under the Road Traffic Act 1988 for anyone to use, or cause or permit another to use, a motor vehicle on a road or other public place unless, in relation to the use of that vehicle by that person, there is in force an insurance policy in respect of certain third party risks (section 143(1), (2)). It was at one point permissible to sidestep the insurance obligation by providing security in the form of a deposit, but that possibility was repealed with effect from November 2021 by the Motor Vehicles (Compulsory Insurance) (Miscellaneous Amendments) Regulations 2019.[7] There is a defence to prosecution under section 143(3) for a person if he can demonstrate that the vehicle did not belong to him and was not in his possession under any contract of hiring or loan, that he was using the vehicle in the course of his employment and that he neither knew nor had reason to believe that he was not insured while using the vehicle. These are cumulative conditions. The employment defence aside, liability is strict even if the user had been assured by a third party that there was insurance in place.[8] The insurance obligation is, by section 144, removed from a variety of public bodies, including local authorities, health service bodies and the police. There is a policy for the purpose of the Act, even though it is voidable on account of, for instance, non-disclosure.[9]

The Road Safety Act 2006, section 22 introduced the additional offence of being the registered keeper of a vehicle which does not meet statutory insurance requirements. The offence is not based on the use of the vehicle, merely its keeping. Schedule 5 of the same Act makes provision for the immobilisation, removal and disposal of vehicles where it appears the new offence is being committed. These provisions make amendments to the Road Traffic Act 1988 by adding five new sections (144A, 144B, 144C, 144D and 159A) and one new schedule (schedule 2A). They introduce the offence of being the registered keeper of

[5] Motor Vehicles (Compulsory Insurance) (Information Centre and Compensation Body) Regulations 2003 (2003/37), regs 3–9. The Regulations were initially implemented to facilitate cross-border claims, so that persons domiciled in the EU and injured in the UK could obtain the necessary insurance information to facilitate a direct claim against the insurers (see below). Reciprocal arrangements operated throughout the EU, so that UK victims of foreign accidents could acquire the necessary insurance information. Brexit put an end to that, and led to the modification of the Regulations to confine them to vehicles normally based in the UK.

[6] *Cooper v Motor Insurers' Bureau* [1985] QB 575.

[7] SI 2019/1047.

[8] *R (on the Application of Chaplin) v Wood Green Crown Court* [2012] EWHC 3773 (Admin).

[9] *Adams v Dunne* [1978] RTR 281. Where a contract is avoided, under the criminal law this does not mean it was void *ab initio*: *Goodbarne v Buck* [1940] 1 KB 771.

a vehicle which does not have insurance cover but provide that liability for the offence may be discharged on payment of a fixed penalty fee of £100. The Motor Vehicles (Insurance Requirements) Regulations 2011,[10] which came into force on 4 February 2011, prescribe the particulars and declarations to be furnished for the purposes of exceptions to the offence, create a new exception to the offence, provide for a reduced fixed penalty upon prompt payment and require MIB data to be provided for enforcement purposes.

1.1.2. The Policy of Insurance

The policy must, by section 145(2) of the 1988 Act, be issued by an insurer authorised to carry on motor insurance business under the Financial Services and Markets Act 2000. By section 143(3) of the 1988 Act, the policy must insure against four classes of risk.

First, by section 145(3)(a), it must cover

> such person, persons or classes of person as may be specified in the policy in respect of any liability which may be incurred by him or them in respect of the death of or bodily injury to any person or damage to property caused by, or arising out of, the use of the vehicle on a road or other public place in Great Britain.

Liability for personal injury must be unlimited, and for property damage arising out of any one accident must be at least £1.2 million (section 145(4)(b)). A policy may identify a named driver and also other drivers fitting a given description, eg driving with the insured's consent.[11] Section 148(7) supplements this provision by imposing liability on the insurer to indemnify any person covered by the policy, thereby creating a mandatory statutory exception to the doctrine of privity. There is a wealth of authority in support of the contention that where, as is usually the case, the policy refers to a particular vehicle, the insurers will not be liable if the insured has parted with ownership of that vehicle, even if the policy is stated to cover any car that is 'being used instead of the insured car'. Motor cover runs with the ownership of the vehicle specified in the policy, so that if the vehicle has been sold there is no 'insured car' and the policy terminates.[12] However, these authorities should be regarded as unreliable in light of the most recent decision on the matter in *Dobson v Dobson*.[13] It was held that a policy with similar wording to that in previous cases did not have the effect of bringing the insurance contract to an end in the event that the car to which the policy relates was sold. The insured retained an interest in the policy because he or she might drive other vehicles or go on to purchase another vehicle.

There are various limits to the requirements of a policy issued under section 145(3)(a). The policy is not required to extend to: liability for damage to the vehicle itself when it has been used by a third party (section 145(3)(c)); liability for damage to goods being carried for hire or reward, or under the user's custody or control (section 145(3)(d), (e)); and contractual liability other than that covered by the other provisions of section 145(3) (section 145(3)(f)).

[10] SI 2011/20.

[11] In *Singh v Rathour* [1988] 1 WLR 422, where it was held that consent for the use of a vehicle for the user's own purpose did not offer consent for the user to drive a group of people to a wedding. It was decided in *Kelly v Cornhill Insurance Co Ltd* [1964] 1 All ER 321 that the death of the owner did not revoke permission until the user (his son) had received notice of the death and a reasonable period had elapsed.

[12] *Rogerson v Scottish Automobile & General Insurance Co Ltd* (1932) 41 Ll L Rep 1; *Tattersall v Drysdale* [1935] 2 KB 174; C Parsons, 'Termination of Motor Policies: Some Issues of Law and Practice' (1993) 3 *Insurance Law & Practice* 43.

[13] [2001] Lloyd's Rep IR 278.

The most important restriction relates to employment. As will be seen in chapter 14, it is compulsory for an employer to insure against liability to an employee for injury suffered in the course of employment. To reflect that point, section 145(4)(a) removes from the compulsory motor insurance requirement an obligation to insure against liability incurred by the employer in the course of employment. However, the duty to insure is reinstated by section 145(4A) in the case of a person carried in or upon a vehicle or entering, getting onto or alighting from a vehicle unless there is insurance in place under the 1969 Act. The subsection was added to comply with EU law, and applies essentially to a passenger (whether or not an employee), because the 1969 Act does not apply to any employee carried in or upon a vehicle, or entering, getting onto or alighting from a vehicle. The demarcation line between the two regimes is not always clear. In *Miller v Hales*,[14] it was held that a police constable who had clung onto a vehicle to stop it being stolen and who was injured in the process was not being 'carried', and in *Axa Insurance UK Plc v Norwich Union Insurance Ltd*[15] an employee standing in a hoist on the back of his employer's vehicle was similarly not being 'carried', so that the 1969 Act rather than the 1988 Act was engaged in both cases. Neither Act applies to an employee driving a vehicle who is injured in the absence of negligence.[16]

Secondly, in the case of a vehicle normally based in the EU, it must cover the use of the vehicle in Great Britain (section 145(3)(aa)). The cover required must match that of the EU Member State where the vehicle is normally based if it is more extensive than that set out in section 145(3)(a). A vehicle is normally based where it is registered.

Thirdly, in the case of a vehicle normally based in Great Britain, it must cover liability in any EU Member State (section 145(3)(b)). If the law of the Member State in question imposes greater insurance requirements than those in section 145(3)(a), the policy must satisfy those requirements.

Fourthly, it must cover any liability under statute for emergency treatment. Until 1999, insurers were required to pay relatively small sums to hospitals and for roadside emergency treatment (sections 157–60). The law was transformed by the Road Traffic (NHS Charges) Act 1999, replaced with effect from 2007 by the Health and Social Care (Community Health and Standards) Act 2003. The 2003 Act, which replicates the position on social security payments,[17] has confined the provisions of the 1988 Act to private hospitals. As far as state medical services are concerned, insurers are now liable to meet the cost of hospital treatment.

1.1.3. The Certificate of Insurance

A compulsory motor policy is of no effect until a certificate of insurance is delivered by the insurers to the insured (section 147(1)). The certificate must be delivered electronically[18] or otherwise by the insurer within four days of the issue of the policy and must be in the form specified in the Motor Vehicles (Third Party Risks) Regulations 1972.[19] As a result of amendments made by the Deregulation Act 2015, insurers who have issued a policy face

[14] [2007] Lloyd's Rep IR 54.
[15] [2008] Lloyd's Rep IR 122.
[16] *R v Secretary of State for Transport Ex p National Insurance Guarantee Corp Plc* 1996, unreported.
[17] See ch 15 below.
[18] Electronic delivery is permitted by s 147(1A)–(1E), added by the Motor Vehicles (Electronic Communication of Certificates of Insurance) Order 2010.
[19] SI 1972/1217, as amended.

liability to indemnify the insured for any third party claim even though a certificate has not been delivered at the date of the accident.[20] A further change made by the 2015 Act is that insurers cease to be liable on the cancellation of the policy, whereas previously they had to secure return of the certificate in order for their liability to be terminated. A certificate is not a policy of insurance, so in the event of conflict the policy has to prevail,[21] and the wording of the certificate cannot be used to extend cover not specified in the policy.[22]

The certificate has a number of formal purposes: a police officer may demand production of the certificate if there are reasonable grounds for him to believe that the vehicle was being driven without insurance (section 165);[23] in the event of an accident, the insured is required to produce the certificate to a police officer, and although the victim has no right to demand the certificate, the victim will have a claim for damages if the driver refuses to provide insurance information or gives false information (sections 154 and 170); a certificate is required to obtain a vehicle excise licence under the Vehicles Excise Registration Act 1994 (although this happens automatically if an online application is made); and a certificate is prima facie evidence that there is insurance in place so that the offence of driving without insurance has not been committed. Forging a certificate is a criminal offence (section 174).

1.2. 'Use'

The obligation to insure attaches to any 'user' of the vehicle. That is obviously the driver, but passengers in the car may also be regarded as users in appropriate circumstances. The determinative issue here is control. The English courts took the view that a passenger who negligently opened a car door and injured a pedestrian was not in control of the vehicle,[24] although the CJEU has come to the opposite conclusion[25] and the latter ruling would under the Brexit legislation appear to prevail. A passenger may otherwise enter into a joint enterprise with the driver to use the vehicle[26] where it is being driven under the passenger's direction or control, eg where the driver was incapacitated,[27] or where the driver and passenger were engaged in some form of joint enterprise.[28] Moreover, 'use' does not simply refer to the act of driving: there may be use where the engine does not work,[29] or the vehicle has been abandoned.[30]

The words 'caused by, or arising out of the use of' a vehicle (section 145(3)(a)) expand the scope of insurance that a driver must obtain, in that it must extend not just to losses

[20] In *Motor & General Insurance Co Ltd v Cox* [1990] 1 WLR 1443, the Privy Council had reached this position as long as the certificate had been delivered by the date of judgment so that it took effect retroactively.

[21] *Biddle v Johnston* [1965] 2 Lloyd's Rep 121.

[22] *R&S Pilling v UK Insurance Ltd* [2019] UKSC 16.

[23] In *Pryor v Chief Constable of Greater Manchester Police* [2011] EWCA Civ 749, the police were found to be liable in damages for seizing a vehicle after the insured had produced the certificate, although in *Gray v The Commissioner of Police of the Metropolis* [2016] EWCA Civ 1360 damages were refused when the insured failed to produce the certificate and simply informed the police that it was available online.

[24] *Brown v Roberts* [1965] 1 QB 1.

[25] Case C-648/71 *BTA Baltica Insurance Company v Baltijas Apdrošināšanas Nams AS* ECLI:EU:C:2018:917.

[26] *Hatton v Hall* [1999] Lloyd's Rep IR 313; *Leathley v Tatton* [1980] RTR 21; *O'Mahoney v Jolliffe* [1999] Lloyd's Rep IR 321.

[27] *Stinton v Stinton* [1995] RTR 157.

[28] *Leathley v Tatton* [1980] RTR 358 (joint theft).

[29] *Elliott v Grey* [1960] 1 QB 367, although not if it is immobile and beyond repair, in which case it may be neither a motor vehicle nor in 'use': *Pumbien v Vines* [1996] RTR 37.

[30] *Williams v Jones* [1975] RTR 433.

proximately caused by driving, but also to losses that 'arise out' of the use of a car. There will be borderline cases. On one side of the line, a person who runs out of petrol and causes an accident while leaving the vehicle to secure a lift to a garage is to be regarded as having incurred liability out of the use of a vehicle.[31] By contrast: a person who dashes across a road in order to obtain a lift in a minibus and is hit by an oncoming vehicle has not suffered injuries arising out of the use of the minibus;[32] a person carrying out welding work on a vehicle in a workshop and who accidentally causes a fire damaging neighbouring properties has not caused damage arising out of the use of the vehicle;[33] and a person using his taxi to drug and assault women[34] or to defraud a customer[35] has not inflicted injury arising out of its use.

1.3. 'Cause or Permit'

It is an offence to 'cause or permit any other person' to use a vehicle if that person is not insured (section 143(1)(b)). While 'cause' imports the notion of a positive command or authority to use the vehicle, the word 'permit' has been interpreted quite widely to include not just express words of permission, but circumstances in which permission can be inferred, such as where the vehicle is placed by its owner in the control of someone else in circumstances which 'carry with it a reasonable implication of a discretion or liberty to use it in the manner in which it was used'.[36] In *McLeod v Buchanan*,[37] a man was given a car for business and private use by his employer. The car proved unsatisfactory and the employer authorised the purchase of a van. This vehicle was insured only for business, although the driver also used it for private purposes. The court held that since the van was bought for the same purposes as the car and the employee had not been told to use it only for business, the employer had permitted its use by another without insurance. It is not just the owner who can commit this offence. Anyone who has control over the vehicle and causes or permits an uninsured person to use it commits an offence,[38] such as a commercial traveller who lends a company car to an uninsured friend. On the other hand, someone who is not the owner and does not have control over its use will not come within the offence.[39]

An honest but mistaken belief that the driver is insured is no defence,[40] even if that mistake was induced by the driver's misrepresentation. This means that an offence will be committed if no condition is imposed or if a condition is imposed that, as the owner knows, will be ignored. In *Lloyd-Wolper v Moore*,[41] it was alleged that the owner had been misled by the driver's representations that he was 17 years old and had a full driving licence, whereas he was 16 and had no licence. Unsurprisingly, the Court of Appeal seemed somewhat

[31] *Dunthorne v Bentley* [1999] Lloyd's Rep IR 560.
[32] *Slater v Buckinghamshire County Council* [2004] Lloyd's Rep IR 432.
[33] *R & S Pilling v UK Insurance Ltd* [2019] UKSC 16.
[34] *AXN v Worboys* [2012] EWHC 1730 (QB).
[35] *Carroll v Taylor* [2020] EWHC 153 (QB).
[36] *McLeod (or Houston) v Buchanan* [1940] 2 All ER 179, 187 (Lord Wright).
[37] ibid.
[38] *Lloyd v Singleton* [1953] 1 QB 357.
[39] *Watkins v O'Shaughnessy* [1939] 1 All ER 384.
[40] *Baugh v Crago* [1976] 1 Lloyd's Rep 563.
[41] ibid.

sceptical about the owner's claim not to have known the truth of these matters since the driver was his son; nevertheless, the judges held that permission to drive had been given even if the claim were true since consenting on the basis of a mistaken belief did not amount to the imposition of a condition. In *DPP v Fisher*,[42] the owner lent the car to someone who, as the owner knew, was uninsured, on the condition that this person would only allow an insured person to drive. The car was lent to someone who was not known to the owner and who did not have insurance. It was held that the permission of the owner to the second person was unconditional and, therefore, amounted to the offence. This principle means that a driver who takes their car into a garage for repair and who permits it to be driven will have given unconditional permission for an uninsured mechanic to use it.[43] Yet, there are cases in which a rather softer approach has been taken.[44] Mackenna J was of the opinion that 'Permission connotes knowledge or that which is in criminal law the equivalent of knowledge, a deliberate blindness to obvious facts which it would be inconvenient to know'.[45] It was held in *Newbury v Davis* that if the person giving permission makes it a condition of using the vehicle that the driver obtains insurance, then there will be no offence, because 'A permission subject to a condition which was not fulfilled was no permission'.[46] It was said in *DPP v Fisher*[47] that *Newbury* should be confined to its particular facts and this view is to be preferred, although in a subsequent Scottish decision, *Macdonald v Howdle*,[48] it was held that an owner would not have given permission to the driver had she not been told by her friend that his policy covered him and, therefore, her permission was conditional on the driver being insured.

1.4. 'Motor Vehicle'

The Act only applies to a 'motor vehicle', which is defined in section 185(1) as 'a mechanically propelled vehicle intended or adapted for use on the roads'.[49] A motor car comes within this definition even if it is not capable of being driven because the engine has been removed, so long as its immobility is only temporary.[50] On the other hand, a car will not be regarded as a motor vehicle if it is in such disrepair or has been dismantled to such an extent that there is little prospect of it ever being made mobile and it is, in reality, simply a pile of spare parts.[51] A motorcycle that can be pedalled is not a motor vehicle if essential parts of the engine have been removed.[52]

[42] [1992] RTR 93.

[43] *Lyons v May* [1948] 2 All ER 1062.

[44] *Sands v O'Connell* [1981] RTR 42.

[45] *Sheldon Deliveries Ltd v Willis* [1972] RTR 217, 220 (MacKenna J).

[46] *Newbury v Davis* (1974) 118 Sol Jo 222.

[47] 1992] RTR 93.

[48] 1995 SLT 779.

[49] The s 189(1) exemptions are for grass cutters, vehicles controlled by pedestrians and electrically assisted pedal cycles.

[50] *Lawrence v Howlett* [1952] 2 All ER 74, 75 (Devlin J); *Newberry v Simmonds* [1961] 2 QB 345.

[51] *Smart v Allan* [1963] 1 QB 291.

[52] *Lawrence v Howlett* [1952] 2 All ER 74. In *Floyd v Bush* [1953] 1 WLR 242, a similar bicycle was classified as a motor vehicle because the engine was intact and capable of propulsion, even though the engine was not being used. It will be the same where there is merely a temporary defect: *R v Tahsin* [1970] RTR 88.

The vehicle must also be 'intended or adapted for use on the roads'. It is not sufficient that it is capable of being used on the road if it was not intended or adapted for that use. However, if it is so intended or adapted, it does not matter that it is not normally used on the road. The test is 'what would be the view of the reasonable man as to the general user of this particular vehicle, not the particular user to which this particular appellant put it'.[53] This test may be satisfied by evidence that the device in question is widely used as a motor vehicle within the meaning of the Act, even if it does not conform to statutory vehicle safety standards and the manufacturer warns owners not to use it on the road.[54] On that basis, a dumper truck used on a building site but stolen and driven on a road was held to be a motor vehicle.[55] A family car that is always used on a motor racing circuit will be a motor vehicle under the Act if on an occasion it is used on a road; on the other hand, a go-kart is certainly capable of being used on the road, but it is not intended for such use and will not come within the definition, unless adapted for the road.[56] The courts have also held that a vehicle which is intended for only occasional use on the road will not be within the Act, unless there is evidence that the intention is that such will be its general use: a dumper truck designed for carrying building materials which occasionally travelled short distances on the highway was not intended for general use on the road and was not, therefore, a motor vehicle.[57]

1.5. 'Road or Other Public Place'

Under the original version of the 1988 Act, cover was required only for the use of a vehicle on a 'road', defined as 'any highway and other road to which the public has access, and includes bridges over which a road passes' (section 192(1)). It therefore includes private roads where they are used by the public in general, as opposed to a particular section.[58] The courtyard of a hotel, which was private property but was used by the public without hindrance by the hotel's owners as a means of access to the hotel and to cut a corner, was a 'road'.[59] A road serving an industrial estate and leading off a public road is a 'road', for access to the industrial estate was open to members of the public at large.[60] A private road used only by the customers of a particular shop was not a road within the Act,[61] nor was a private road leading to a farm that was used, with permission, by anglers and picnickers and to gain access to a caravan site owned by the farmer. In both cases, this was because only a restricted class of the public had access and the number of people in that class was irrelevant.[62] The definition of 'road' was found to have serious shortcomings in *Clarke v General Accident Fire and Life Assurance Corpn plc* and *Cutter v Eagle Star Insurance Co Ltd*,[63]

[53] *Chief Constable of Avon and Somerset v Fleming* [1987] 1 All ER 318, 322 (Glidewell LJ). See also *Burns v Currell* [1963] 2 QB 433, 440 (Lord Parker CJ).

[54] *Chief Constable of North Yorkshire Police v Saddington* [2001] RTR 15.

[55] *Lewington v Motor Insurers Bureau* [2017] EWHC 2848 (QB).

[56] *Burns v Currell* [1963] 2 QB 433. In *Chief Constable of Avon and Somerset v Fleming* [1987] 1 All ER 318, a motorcycle which had been originally constructed in such a way as brought it within the Act was later adapted for scrambling and taken outside the Act by those modifications.

[57] *Chalgray Ltd v Apsley* (1965) 109 *Sol Jo* 394.

[58] *Randall v Motor Insurers' Bureau* [1968] 1 WLR 1900.

[59] *Bugge v Taylor* [1941] 1 KB 198.

[60] *Evans v Clarke* [2007] Lloyd's Rep IR 16.

[61] *Thomas v Dando* [1951] 2 KB 620.

[62] *R v Beaumont* [1964] Crim LR 665.

[63] [1998] 4 All ER 417.

cases involving car parks laid out as roads and with public access. The House of Lords ruled that a road: has to be clearly defined, as opposed to being an open space such as a field; it must be a means by which vehicles can travel to a destination; and it must have a surface (prepared or produced by constant use) suited to this purpose.[64]

The restrictions imposed by those cases were removed by the Motor Vehicles (Compulsory Insurance) Regulations 2000, which add to 'road' in section 143 the words 'or other public place'. There is no definition of this term in the 1988 Act, but it is used in numerous places in the legislation for the purposes of the offences of causing death or serious injury by dangerous driving or driving without due care and attention, general dangerous driving and driving while intoxicated. The numerous authorities were reviewed in *Brown v Fisk*,[65] where an accident occurred in the entrance yard for premises used by the 400 or so members of a bonfire society. The yard was surrounded by a fence and access was through gates that were normally left unlocked. It was held that the yard was not a public place even though members of the public used it for access from time to time to attend events and to buy tickets, and that occasional public use did not amount to 'truly an actual public purpose'.

English law does not, therefore, contemplate that liability for injuries inflicted on private land are required to be covered by insurance. Further, the cases are consistent in saying that if the injury actually occurs on private land, then the fact that the vehicle involved has left a road in order to access that private land does not mean that the injury arises out of the use of the vehicle on the road.[66] By contrast, before Brexit, the CJEU had established that liability for injuries suffered on private land fell within the compulsory insurance requirement in the directives. That was the effect of *Vnuk v Zavarovalnica Triglav*,[67] which arose where the victim was knocked off a ladder by a tractor and trailer on the insured's farm. The CJEU ruled that the directives required cover for any 'accident caused by a vehicle in the course of its use, if that use is consistent with the normal function of that vehicle'. The *Vnuk* ruling had, in accordance with the direct effect principles of EU law, no impact on private claims, and as a result of Brexit *Vnuk* no longer has any application in the UK. The matter was put beyond doubt by the Motor Vehicles (Compulsory Insurance) Act 2022, which added a new s 156A to the 1988 Act. Under that section, the obligation to insure applies only to the use of a motor vehicle on a road or other public place.

---

2. Third Party Claims

2.1. The Liability of the Insured: Breach of Statutory Duty

The insured under a motor policy who causes death, personal injury or property damage deliberately or negligently is liable in tort to the victim. Where the owner has permitted use of their vehicle by a person who is not covered by the insured's policy and does not have his

[64] ibid.

[65] [2021] EWHC 2769 (QB).

[66] *Inman v Kelly* [2001] PIQR P18; *Clarke v Motor Insurers Bureau* [2012] EWHC 2118 (QB); *Lewis v Tindale* [2018] EWHC 2376 (QB), affirmed on other grounds *Motor Insurers Bureau v Lewis* [2019] EWCA Civ 909; *UK Insurance v Holden* [2019] UKSC 16.

[67] Case C-162/13, [2015] Lloyd's Rep IR 142.

own insurance, it was held in *Monk v Warbey*[68] that the victim can sue the insured for breach of statutory duty in causing or permitting the uninsured use of the vehicle. That case was decided in the early years of the legislation and before the formation of the MIB, so that there was no other remedy for the victim of an uninsured driver. The MIB has rendered the *Monk v Warbey* statutory tort more or less redundant for third party claims, particularly given the decision of the Court of Appeal in *Bretton v Hancock*[69] that only losses falling within the insurance requirements of the 1988 Act are within the scope of the tort. Nevertheless, the fact that there is a remedy against the MIB does not preclude an action by the third party under *Monk v Warbey*.[70] The principle nevertheless retains vitality in the sense that if the MIB pays a claim in these circumstances, then it has a subrogated claim against the insured and the insured's own insurers are not liable to indemnify the insured for that subrogated liability.[71]

2.2. Action against Insurer to Enforce a Judgment

2.2.1. Elements of the Enforcement Action

The 1988 Act, re-enacting the earlier legislation, confers upon a victim who has obtained judgment against the insured the right to enforce the judgment against the insured's insurers. The conditions for the direct action are that the policy has been issued, the liability falls within the compulsory insurance requirements of the 1988 Act and the policy covers the use of the vehicle in question (section 151(1), (2)). There are restrictions on the defences that an insurer may use in such a case. Terms in the policy concerning cover will be ignored if they are invalid against a third party by virtue of section 148 (see below) and exclusions of liability that are permitted will be narrowly construed.[72] It is irrelevant that the insurers were entitled to avoid or cancel, or have avoided or cancelled, the policy (section 151(6)). The insurers cannot seek to defend the action by showing that the driver was not authorised to drive the vehicle, or indeed was not licensed to drive the vehicle (section 151(3)), so the effect is that the insurers face liability to meet a judgment against any person using the vehicle even if that person is a thief (section 151(2)(b)). The only exception to liability for unauthorised drivers arises where the victim was a passenger in a vehicle that he knew or had reason to believe[73] had been stolen or unlawfully taken[74] (section 151(4)). Section 151 can even be used where the vehicle involved in the accident has been identified but the driver has not been identified: that was so held by the Supreme Court in *Cameron v Liverpool Victoria Insurance Co Ltd*.[75]

[68] *Monk v Warbey* [1935] 1 KB 75.
[69] [2005] Lloyd's Rep IR 454.
[70] *Corfield v Groves* [1950] 1 All ER 488; *Norman v Aziz* [2001] Lloyd's Rep IR 52.
[71] *Sahin v Havard* [2016] EWCA Civ 1202; *Cameron v Hussain* [2017] EWCA Civ 366.
[72] *Keeley v Pashen* [2004] EWCA Civ 1491.
[73] Which requires actual or 'blind eye' knowledge, and not merely negligence: *McMinn v McMinn* [2006] EWHC 827 (QB); *Stych v Dibble* [2012] EWHC 1606 (QB).
[74] The latter phrase including the situation where a vessel was borrowed with permission but put to an unauthorised use: *McMinn v McMinn* (ibid); *Stych v Dibble* (ibid).
[75] [2019] UKSC 6. S Gee, 'Suing Persons Unknown, the EC Motor Insurance Directive and Cameron v Liverpool Victoria' [2019] *Journal of Business Law* 416.

In the event of having paid in respect of the liability of an uninsured person, the insurer can recover that amount from anyone who is insured by the policy and who has caused or permitted the use of the vehicle which gave rise to the liability (section 151(8)). However, the compatibility of this provision with EU law was called into question in circumstances where the insured was also the victim of the uninsured driver's negligence. In *Churchill v Wilkinson*,[76] the claimant's parents bought him a car and insured him as a named driver through Churchill Insurance. The claimant incurred serious injuries in an accident while the car was being driven by his friend F, who the claimant knew was not insured. Following the accident, the claimant sought to recover under the policy, but Churchill refused to make payment, relying on section 151(8) of the Road Traffic Act 1988. It was not at issue whether Churchill would be liable to satisfy any judgment that the claimant might obtain against F under section 151 of the 1988 Act, but rather whether section 151(8) gave the insurers the right to recover such sums from the claimant. At first instance,[77] Blair J held that section 151(8) was contrary to EU law, which provides that where a provision or clause restricts cover by reference to the authorisation of the driver, it is to be void against all persons except those who knowingly enter a stolen vehicle. He concluded that the correct approach would be to allow the claimant to enforce judgment, free of section 151(8), and it was the proper function of contributory negligence to determine how much of that judgment should be awarded to the claimant. In a joined appeal, Waller LJ held that 'the effect of section 151(8) as a matter of English law must be to exclude from the benefit of insurance a passenger who is the insured but has given permission to an uninsured driver to drive'.[78] The point was referred to the CJEU, which ruled[79] that EU law required compensation to be paid to a passenger, and that, at worst, the passenger might face a deduction from the damages awarded against the driver to the extent that the passenger contributed to his own loss. The case was remitted to the Court of Appeal,[80] which held that section 151(8) did not bar a claim and that the amount recoverable would be proportionate and based on the precise circumstances of the case. This ruling, being pre-Brexit, remains good law.

2.2.2. Defences to an Enforcement Action

Section 152 of the 1988 Act sets out four cases in which there is no liability under section 151.

First, unless, before or within seven days after the commencement of the proceedings in which the judgment was given the insurer had notice of the bringing of the proceedings (section 152(1)(a)). There is much authority on the meaning of 'notice', and the cases show[81] that notice must be clear and unconditional, and given in circumstances that the insurer was not taken by surprise. An insurer who was aware of the likelihood of proceedings before they have been issued may be taken to have waived notice, but in the absence of notice an insurer who has after the proceedings have commenced taken steps to defend the insured will not be taken to have waived notice unless its conduct amounts to a representation relied upon by the claimant so as to give rise to an equitable estoppel.[82]

[76] *Churchill Insurance Co Ltd v Wilkinson; Evans v Equity Claims Ltd* [2010] EWCA Civ 556.
[77] [2009] EWHC 1297 (QB).
[78] [2019] UKSC 6.
[79] Case C-442/10 *Churchill Insurance Co v Wilkinson; Evans v Equity Claims Ltd* ECLI:EU:C:2011:799.
[80] [2012] EWCA Civ 1166.
[81] They were summarised in *Wylie v Wake* [2001] RTR 20.
[82] ibid.

Secondly, in respect of any judgment so long as execution on the judgment is stayed pending an appeal (section 151(2)(b)).

Thirdly, if, before the happening of the event which was the cause of the death or bodily injury or damage to property giving rise to the liability, the policy was cancelled by mutual consent or by virtue of any provision contained in it (section 152(2)(c)). As a result of the Deregulation Act 2015, there is no longer a need for the insurers to have secured the surrender of the certificate by the date of the event, and it suffices that the policy was cancelled.

Finally, if, before the happening of the event which was the cause of the death or bodily injury or damage to property giving rise to the liability, the insurer has either: (a) obtained a declaration that the insurer was entitled to avoid the policy under either of the relevant insurance enactments on the ground that it was obtained by the non-disclosure of a material fact, or by a representation of fact which was false in some material particular; or (b) avoided the policy on that ground that he was entitled so to do. For these purposes, 'material' means of such a nature as to influence the judgement of a prudent insurer in determining whether he will take the risk and, if so, at what premium and on what conditions (section 152(2), (3)). The original version of this section permitted the insurer to seek a declaration within three months of the commencement of the proceedings against the assured. That defence was held to be incompatible with EU law,[83] and it was modified by Article 6 of the Motor Vehicles (Compulsory Insurance) (Miscellaneous Amendments) Regulations 2019[84] so as to confine the defence to action taken by the insurer before the insured event occurred.[85] It will be recalled from chapter four that there is no longer a duty of disclosure on consumers, and that for both consumer and non-consumer policies there is no automatic remedy of avoidance for breach of duty and a lesser remedy may be awarded. The statutory defence to an enforcement action is thus limited to cases where the breach of duty was such as to justify avoidance.[86]

2.3. Direct Action against Insurers

In anticipation of pending changes to EU law, the European Communities (Rights against Insurers) Regulations 2002[87] conferred upon the victim of a motor accident a direct claim against the insurers without first having obtained judgment against the insured. The measure was initially designed to facilitate cross-border claims, by allowing a third party injured in any EU Member State to bring a direct action against the insurers of the driver in the courts of the third party's own domicile. The Regulations remain in force following Brexit.

Under the Regulations, the third party may proceed directly against the insurer without having first obtained judgment against the driver (regulation 3(2)). The third party must be

[83] *RoadPeace v Secretary of State for Transport* [2017] EWHC 27225 (Comm).

[84] SI 2019/1047.

[85] Accidents occurring before this change in the law did not go uncompensated. Because the EU was not directly effective between private parties, the insurers were entitled to rely upon s 152(2) even though the UK was in breach of EU law in allowing avoidance (*Colley v Shuker* [2019] EWHC 781 (QB)) but the MIB faced default liability under the Uninsured Drivers Agreement because there was no insurance in place (*Colley v Motor Insurers' Bureau* [2022] EWCA Civ 360).

[86] The cases on the operation of this provision – *Tesco Underwriting Ltd v Achunche* [2016] EWHC 3869 (QB), *Southern Rock Insurance Co Ltd v Hafeez* [2017] CSOH 127 and *Ageas Insurance Ltd v Stoodley* [2019] Lloyd's Rep IR 1 – were discussed in ch 4.

[87] SI 2002/3061.

'an entitled party', which means a resident of one of the EEA states (regulation 2(1)), and must have a right of action in tort against an insured person (regulation 3(1)). That action must have arisen from an accident on a road or public place in the UK that was caused by the use of any vehicle that is insured according to the requirements of section 145 and is normally based in the UK (regulation 2). The Regulations do have some disadvantages when compared with an action brought under section 151. Since the effect of the Regulations is to put the third party into the same position as the insured with regard to the insurer, defences available to the insurer, which could not be used under section 151, may be available. For instance, where the third party is injured by the deliberate act of the insured, it is clear that the insured – and therefore the third party – has no right of action under the Regulations against the insurer, but, as discussed below, the third party will have such a right of action under section 151.

The 2002 Regulations are important also for a pending new form of liability. The Automated and Electric Vehicles Act 2018 anticipates the widespread use of remote, or self-driving, vehicles. The technology for such vehicles is still at the developmental stage and it may be some time before the UK's roads have been adapted for their use. Nevertheless, legislation has been put in place to deal with the challenges posed by remote vehicles. The main issue is that there is no driver required, so that the traditional negligence action will not be relevant, and any accidents are most likely to be the result of equipment, software or satellite failure. The 1988 Act is amended (although the amendments are not yet in force) to require insurance to be issued, and the insurer bears strict liability for any death, personal injury or property damage arising out of an accident caused by a remote vehicle. A direct claim can thus be made against the insurers under the 2002 Regulations. Policies may exclude liability where the owner of the vehicle has made unauthorised modifications to the software or has failed to install software updates. There are also deductions for contributory negligence and a right of recoupment or contribution from third parties fully or partly responsible for the accident.

2.4. Claims by Passengers

Before 1971, English law drew a distinction between passengers carried for hire or reward and other passengers, with only the former being protected by compulsory insurance in their favour. That distinction, which proved elusive where a private vehicle was used to transport work colleagues,[88] was removed by the Motor Vehicle (Passenger Insurance) Act 1971, with the result that all passengers fell within the compulsory insurance requirement. That position is maintained by section 145 of the 1988 Act. The EU similarly requires passengers to be protected. The English courts have held also that while a liability policy does not protect the driver of a vehicle, the insured owner of the vehicle benefits from compulsory insurance where the vehicle is being driven by another person with the consent of the insured.[89]

There may nevertheless be limits on the circumstances in which a passenger can make a claim against the driver and thus against the insurers in the form of defences to tort, namely voluntary assumption of risk, contributory negligence and public policy. The first of these

[88] *Albert v Motor Insurers Bureau* [1971] 2 Lloyd's Rep 229, where the House of Lords by a majority found that such arrangements were for hire or reward.

[89] *Churchill Insurance Co Ltd v Wilkinson; Evans v Equity Claims Ltd* [2010] EWCA Civ 556. If the driver was uninsured, the owner of the vehicle faces a recourse claim by the insurers under s 151(8).

possibilities has been removed by section 149 of the 1988 Act, under which any agreement between the driver and passenger relieving or limiting the former's liability is a nullity, and the fact that a person has willingly accepted the risk of negligent driving does not negative the driver's liability. It was held in *Pitts v Hunt*[90] that the pillion passenger on a motorcycle being driven at speed and in a reckless fashion by an intoxicated driver was not debarred from proceeding against the driver's estate – and thus his insurers – by the principle of voluntary assumption of risk. The 1988 Act does not, however, prevent the driver from relying upon the defence of contributory negligence, so that a court may under the Law Reform (Contributory Negligence) Act 1945 reduce damages to the extent that the passenger has caused his own loss. Deductions may thus be made for failure to wear a seatbelt or crash helmet. Public policy is discussed in the following paragraph.

2.5. Public Policy

The most complex of defences to a claim in tort is that of public policy. This will typically apply where the driver and victim were engaged in a joint criminal enterprise, and the principle here is that there is no recovery if there is a causal link between the criminality and the injuries suffered. There are numerous illustrations of the operation of these principles as regards claims by passengers: a bank robber cannot sue the driver of the getaway vehicle for injuries inflicted in a high-speed chase culminating in a crash;[91] a pillion passenger who has encouraged the driver of a motorcycle to ride in a reckless fashion is engaged in a joint enterprise and has no claim against the driver,[92] although the passenger will have an action against the driver of a van who has negligently collided with the motorcycle;[93] a passenger in the back of a speeding van with its back door open so that he could hold onto a stolen ladder had no claim against the driver when he fell from the van;[94] and a passenger carrying a quantity of cannabis for resale is not precluded from claiming against the negligent driver for personal injury as there is no causal link between the criminality and the injury.[95]

Public policy may be relevant other than in passenger claims where there is a joint enterprise between the driver and the victim. One example might be that of a bank robber who is accidentally run over by the getaway driver before entering the car. However, it will generally be difficult for the driver to establish a causal link between negligent driving and the injuries suffered by a person outside the vehicle. In *Flint v Tittensor*,[96] the parties were engaged in an altercation, following which the defendant deliberately drove his car at the claimant and caused injury. While the defendant had been at fault, it was held that his conduct was not such as to deprive him of the right to damages. In *Wallett v Vickers*,[97] two drivers, who did not know each other, were both driving on a dual carriageway. An impromptu race

[90] [1990] 3 All ER 344.
[91] *Ashton v Turner* 1981] QB 137.
[92] *Pitts v Hunt* [1990] 3 All ER 344.
[93] *McCracken v Smith* [2015] EWCA Civ 380.
[94] *Joyce v O'Brien* [2013] EWCA Civ 546.
[95] *Delaney v Pickett* [2011] EWCA Civ 1532.
[96] [2015] EWHC 466 (QB). See also *Clarke v Clarke* [2012] EWHC 2118 (QB).
[97] [2018] EWHC 3088 (QB).

developed between them and reached the point where the road narrowed into a single lane. One of the drivers was killed, and his representatives brought a claim against the other alleging negligent driving. The court ruled that the joint enterprise defence was not available: the two drivers might have had a common goal, but it could not be said that they had engaged in a joint enterprise.

2.6. Deliberate Running Down[98]

Section 145 requires insurance to be in place for 'any liability' which may be incurred arising out of the use of a motor vehicle on a road or other public place. Although the vast majority of claims arise from negligence, there will be cases where injuries are inflicted through the use of a vehicle as a weapon, and the 1988 Act does not draw any distinction based on intention for the purposes of the obligation to insure. However, the obligation to insure does not mean that the policy will by its terms provide coverage. Most policies are restricted to accidents, and in *Charlton v Fisher*[99] it was held that an insured who had deliberately rammed another vehicle had no claim under the policy because the conduct was not accidental. Nevertheless, it has been held in a series of cases involving deliberately inflicted injury or damage[100] that the victim has a direct claim against the insurers under section 151 of the 1988 Act, on the basis that the insured's conduct imposes only a personal bar on recovery and does not affect third party claims: as noted earlier, there is no direct claim against the insurers under the 2002 Regulations, because by their terms the victim has no better rights than the insured. There is a further possibility that the driver has no insurance at all, in which case the liability must be picked up by the MIB (see below).

3. Hire of Replacement Vehicles

Where a vehicle is damaged in a motor accident, the victim has the right in tort to claim both for repair costs and for the cost of replacing the vehicle in the period of repairs. The latter right is nevertheless subject to the overriding obligation of the victim to mitigate loss, which means that hiring costs that are unnecessary or excessive cannot be recovered. The principle was stated by Aikens LJ in *Pattni v First Leicester Buses Ltd*:[101]

> The loss of use of a car as a result of the car being damaged by the negligence of another driver is a loss for which, in appropriate circumstances, the innocent claimant can recover damages, even where the car is 'non-profit earning'. It is the duty of the innocent claimant to mitigate his loss. If the loss of use of a car can be mitigated or avoided by the hire of a replacement car, the cost of that replacement car will be the measure of damages recoverable for the loss of use of the car.

[98] M Hemsworth, 'Insurance Obligations, the Road Traffic Act 1988 and Deliberately Caused Damage' [2013] *Journal of Business Law* 354.

[99] [2001] 1 Lloyd's Rep IR 287.

[100] *Hardy v Motor Insurers Bureau* [1964] 2 QB 745; *Gardner v Moore* [1984] AC 548; *Bristol Alliance Ltd Partnership v Williams* [2013] QB 806; *AXN v Worboys* [2012] EWHC 1730 (QB).

[101] [2011] EWCA Civ 1384.

In every case there are two main issues: is it necessary for the victim to hire a replacement vehicle; and, if so, is the rate of hire excessive?

The victim will satisfy the first requirement by demonstrating that the vehicle was used for work or domestic purposes. However, damages based on the hiring of a replacement vehicle will not be appropriate where the victim has other vehicles at his disposal, in which case damages will be based upon interest and capital deployed, along with any depreciation, in the repair period.[102] In the case of a taxi or similar vehicle used in trade, the correct measure of damages will be the lower of loss of profit or hire charges, although both may be recoverable if the victim can show that the vehicle was used also for social purposes, if the loss of the use of the vehicle threatened future profits in that clients might choose to look elsewhere or if the victim was impecunious and could not afford to continue working.[103]

The basic principle regarding the recovery of the cost of hiring a replacement car, as established in *Dimond v Lovell*,[104] is that a claimant can only recover the reasonable costs of hiring a replacement vehicle, which would normally be the spot rate – subsequently referred to in the cases as the basic hiring rate (BHR), the lowest reasonable local rate – for hiring an equivalent car. The period of hire must be reasonable: a victim who delays for a lengthy period before replacing a vehicle damaged beyond repair will be held to damages for a reasonable period.[105] The type of replacement vehicle hired by the victim must also be reasonable: as was said by Aikens LJ in *Pattni*, the victim will not have acted reasonably in hiring a car bigger or better than the damaged vehicle, and damages are to be assessed by reference to the hire cost of an equivalent vehicle. There may be situations in which the victim is impecunious and cannot afford to pay hire fees. To cover that situation, a market has developed for credit hire, an arrangement under which the victim is provided with a car but with charges deferred until the victim – or at least the credit hire company – under assigned rights has recovered damages from the insured. Alternatively, if damages are not recovered, the charges are paid under an insurance policy issued for that purpose. So, in all events, the victim pays nothing. It is obvious that a credit hire arrangement is more expensive than ordinary hire, and provides not just a hire car, but also ancillary benefits in the form of freedom from charges and a damages recovery service. The courts have held that the right to use credit hire is confined to victims who are impecunious and who could not afford to hire a replacement vehicle without credit hire. The House of Lords so decided in *Lagden v O'Connor*.[106] The authorities on the appropriate BHR for credit hire were discussed in *McBride v UK Insurance Ltd*,[107] and Flaux LJ drew from them the proposition that the victim had to establish the BHR by producing evidence of actual local hiring rates and then showing that he had opted for the lowest reasonable rate quoted by a mainstream supplier for the hire of the vehicle in question. That test was thought to eliminate the argument that the victim had unreasonably obtained benefits from credit hire in addition to the hiring of the vehicle itself.

The joined cases of *Copley v Lawn* and *Maden v Haller*[108] dealt with the issue of whether a claimant is obliged to accept an offer of a replacement vehicle from the defendant's insurers

[102] In *Beechwood Birmingham Ltd v Hoyer Group UK Ltd* [2010] EWCA Civ 647.
[103] *Hussain v EUI Ltd* [2019] EWHC 2647 (QB).
[104] [2002] 1 AC 384.
[105] *Zurich Insurance Plc v Umerji* [2014] EWCA Civ 357, where the victim's delay of a year produced hire charges of £95,130 on a vehicle worth around £8000.
[106] [2004] Lloyd's Rep IR 329. See also *Putta v Royal Sun Alliance Insurance Plc* [2020] EWHC 117 (QB).
[107] [2017] EWCA Civ 144.
[108] [2009] EWCA Civ 580.

or if the claimant is entitled to make their own arrangements. In the first case, Mrs Copley's car was damaged by the negligence of Mr Lawn. She required a replacement vehicle and so entered into an agreement with Helphire under which she agreed to hire a replacement vehicle at a rate of £39.00 per day while her car was being repaired. Later that same day, Mrs Copley received a telephone call from Mr Lawn's insurers, offering her a free replacement car. That offer was not accepted; Mrs Copley maintained the agreement with Helphire and then, after 71 days, when her car was repaired, sent the Bill to Mr Lawn's insurers. In the second case, Captain Maden's car was damaged as a result of Mr Haller's negligence. He was contacted within 24 hours by Mr Haden's insurers and offered a free replacement car. He chose to ignore this offer and instead hired a replacement car from Helphire at a rate of £156.80 per day for a period of three days. He then sought to recover this sum from Mr Haller's insurers. In both instances the insurers refused to pay, stating that both Mrs Copley and Captain Maden had failed in their duty to mitigate their loss when they unreasonably rejected the insurers offers of a free replacement vehicle. Both cases were heard by HHJ Langan, who dismissed them, upholding the reasoning that refusal of an offer of a 'free' car amounted to a failure by the claimants to take reasonable steps to mitigate their loss. The Court of Appeal, however, found in favour of the claimants and stated that only if the insurers had made an offer for a replacement car and made it clear that the cost was less than the claimant was intending to pay could the refusal to accept that offer be a failure to mitigate. In these two cases, the insurers gave no such information regarding cost, so it was not unreasonable for the claimant to reject them.[109] Although it was not therefore necessary for the Court of Appeal to comment on the consequences of a failure to mitigate, Longmore LJ stated that if it was found that the claimant failed to mitigate, this would not deprive them of all damages because it was clear that they had suffered a loss – the claimant would be able to recover the actual reasonable cost of hire.[110] It was subsequently held by the Court of Appeal in *Sayce v TNT (UK) Ltd*[111] that a victim who, at the scene of the accident, was given details of a free replacement service operated by the driver's employers, was under no obligation to accept the offer by way of mitigation. The victim was entitled to consider whether to accept the offer or to opt for credit hire and had not failed to mitigate by refusing the offer.

4. The Effect of Exclusions in the Policy

4.1. Third Party Claims

Section 148(1) states:

> Any parts of the policy which purport to restrict the cover of the persons insured by reference to any matters mentioned in [section 148(2)] shall, as respects such liabilities as are required to be covered by a policy under section 145 of this Act, be of no effect.

In short, the insurers are constrained as to the restrictions they can place in the policy with regard to cover for liability to third parties, including passengers. If a vehicle is used

[109] ibid [22]–[24] (Longmore LJ).
[110] ibid [25]–[31].
[111] [2011] EWCA Civ 1583, [2012] 1 WLR 1261.

in a way that means it is not covered by the policy and that restriction does not fall within section 148(1), the insurers will not be liable, and even if the exclusion is within section 148(1) so that the insurers are liable to a third party, they may be able to recoup the payment from the insured if the terms of the policy allow this (section 148(6)). It is to be stressed that section 148 applies only to third party claims. The contractual provisions barred by section 148 are fully enforceable where the claim is made by the insured himself for his own injuries or for damage to his vehicle.

The restrictions referred to in section 148(1) are (section 148(2)): (a) the age or physical or mental condition of drivers; (b) the condition of the vehicle; (c) the number of passengers the vehicle carries; (d) the weight or physical characteristics of goods the vehicle carries; (e) the times at which or the areas within which the vehicle is used; (f) the horsepower or cylinder capacity or value of the vehicle; and (g) the carrying of any particular apparatus or (h) of any means of identification other than as required under the Vehicle Excise and Registration Act 1994. In addition, under section 148(5) the insurers cannot avoid their liability to third parties and passengers by making it subject to 'some specified thing being done or omitted to be done after the happening of the event giving rise to a claim'. So, the requirement in a policy that the insured must notify the insurers of an accident within a particular period of time will not defeat a claim by a third party. To modern eyes, the logic of section 148(2) is unclear. Why have these matters been selected as ones for which the insurers should remain responsible if there is a third party claim, while others have been missed off the list? For example, why are the insurers liable if the car is in an unroadworthy condition or is carrying more than the stipulated number of passengers, but not if the accident occurred while the insured, who was covered for social and pleasure use, was driving to a business meeting? The reason is to be found in the history of the provision: the list dates back to the Road Traffic Act 1934, as a response to judicial criticism that it was straightforward for insurers to evade the compulsory insurance requirement in the 1930 Act by inserting policy exclusions[112] and the list was devised to deal with the most common exclusions at that time. It has never been updated.

However, it is far from certain that insurers can rely upon policy exclusions not contained in this list. As a matter of pure English law, it is clear that policy exclusions outside section 148 can be relied upon against third parties. However, doubts were raised by a series of EU decisions, beginning with *Bernaldez*,[113] where the CJEU stated that the effect of the directives was to 'preclude an insurer from being able to rely on statutory provisions or contractual clauses to refuse to compensate third party victims of an accident caused by the insured vehicle'. The English cases have been at odds on the question whether *Bernaldez* had the effect of prohibiting all contractual restrictions. The authorities were considered at length in *RoadPeace v Secretary of State for Transport*[114] by Ouseley J, who concluded that the language in *Bernaldez* was not as wide ranging as it at first sight appeared and that section 148 did not in its limited form infringe EU law. Thus, when Brexit occurred, there was no binding decision that section 148 was deficient, and that still remains the position. Accordingly, contractual defences outside section 148 may be relied upon by insurers in third party claims, and of course section 148 has no application to first party claims.

[112] *Zurich General Accident and Liability Insurance Co Ltd v Morrison* [1942] 2 KB 53.
[113] [1996] All ER (EC) 741.
[114] [2017] EWHC 27225 (Comm).

4.2. Contractual Limits on Coverage

Policies contain a plethora of restrictions on coverage.

There will normally be restrictions on the persons entitled to drive the car. Coverage may be limited to drivers identified by name, class or persons authorised by the named driver. The age and qualifications of the driver may also be the subject of contract terms, with young drivers either being uninsured or insured but with a far higher excess than a driver with more experience.

The condition of the vehicle will also be the subject of policy terms. In construing a clause which stipulated that the vehicle must not be driven while in 'an unsafe or unroadworthy condition', Goddard J drew an analogy with the warranty of seaworthiness implied into marine policies by the Marine Insurance Act 1906 and said that the condition will be satisfied if the vehicle was roadworthy at the commencement of the particular journey.[115] That analogy seems difficult to sustain – and, indeed, the Privy Council has refused to follow it[116] – if only because the discovery of a defect during a journey poses quite different problems for a car driver from those faced by a ship's crew, if only because, while the driver will usually be able to pull over, that option is not likely to be available to the ship's crew. There seems, therefore, less reason not to impose a continuing duty that the car be roadworthy while it is being driven and, in practice, the terms of modern policies specify such an obligation. The requirement that the car be roadworthy may be breached by the use of the car as well as by its condition: permitting nine passengers to travel in a car suitable for only four renders it unroadworthy.[117] It is enough that the car is unroadworthy for the term to be breached; it is irrelevant that the insured honestly believes, and has taken reasonable precautions to ensure, that the vehicle is roadworthy. If, however, the policy only requires that the insured 'shall take all due and reasonable precautions to safeguard the property insured and to keep it in a good state of repair', the insured need only take reasonable care to ensure that the car is roadworthy. Similarly, where the policy requires the vehicle to be kept in an 'efficient condition' and a defect in the brakes can only be discovered by dismantling them, the insured will be covered,[118] unless the insurers are able to show that there was no reasonable system for periodical inspection of the vehicle.[119] Following this reasoning, there was a breach where the defect related to the condition of the tyres, since these could be readily inspected.[120] If the insured is in breach of such a term, the insurer may, nevertheless, be liable to an injured third party (see below), but may be able to claim for damages from the insured for that breach (section 148(4)).[121] Policies also commonly contain prohibitions on modification of the vehicle.

It is normal to restrict cover for private motor vehicles to 'social, domestic and pleasure purposes', although its precise meaning is not easy to convey. The words should be

[115] *Barrett v London General Insurance Co* [1935] 1 KB 238.

[116] *Trickett v Queensland Insurance* [1936] AC 159.

[117] *Clarke v National Insurance and Guarantee Corp Ltd* [1964] 1 QB 199.

[118] *Conn v Westminster Motor Insurance Association Ltd* [1966] 1 Lloyd's Rep 407; *Lefevere v White* [1990] 1 Lloyd's Rep 569.

[119] *Brown v Zurich Accident and Liability Insurance Co Ltd* [1954] 2 Lloyd's Rep 243. The insurer must show the insured (and not just an employee) was negligent: *Amey Properties Ltd v Cornhill Insurance plc* [1996] LRLR 259.

[120] *Conn v Westminster Motor Insurance Association Ltd* [1966] 1 Lloyd's Rep 407; *Lefevere v White* [1990] 1 Lloyd's Rep 569.

[121] There may be a remedy for breach of contract: *National Farmers' Union Mutual Insurance Society v Dawson* [1941] 2 KB 424.

interpreted according to 'their natural, ordinary, normal and reasonable meaning',[122] and according to the context of the policy in which they are contained. Travelling to a meeting, at which a business deal was to be negotiated, was not covered, even though it was chosen as a comfortable (that is, a pleasurable) means of travel.[123] Indeed, travelling to work does not come within the phrase 'social, domestic and pleasure', although policies are now routinely extended to cover such travel as well. A motorist was not covered when he helped out a friend's taxi business by picking up a customer, even though he did not charge for the journey.[124] On the other side is the decision in *Keeley v Pashen*.[125] Pashen's policy covered only 'social, domestic and pleasure including travel to and from permanent place of business' and expressly excluded 'use for hire or reward'. He used the car in a taxi business and deliberately drove at Keeley, a customer whom he had just dropped off. Keeley was killed and the insurers were held liable because at the time of the accident Pashen was not driving for hire or reward: Keeley had been dropped off and Pashen's purpose was to go home, even if in doing so he drove at Keeley in order to frighten him. In another case, the use of a local authority vehicle to transport visitors from France who had come to promote a town twinning was held to be within such cover on the grounds that the use in connection with the visit was social and voluntary and had nothing directly to do with the official duties of the local authority, in the sense of those which they were obliged to undertake by statute or by convention.[126] Where the insurance covers use of the vehicle for a particular business, there will be no cover if it is used for another type of business. Moreover, if the vehicle is used for two or more purposes simultaneously and one of those purposes is specifically excluded by the policy, the insurers will not be liable. For instance, there was no liability where a policy allowed the use for pleasure but not in connection with the motor trade and it was driven, with permission, by a mechanic who, while taking his family for a ride, also used the journey to check the car for faults.[127] In such cases the courts look at the essential character of the journey.[128]

Where, as is normal in a policy designed for private motorists, the insured driver is restricted by the policy to the use of the vehicle for specified purposes of a non-commercial nature, such as for social, domestic and pleasure purposes, or it excludes the use of the vehicle for hire or reward, for business or commercial use, or for specified purposes of a business or commercial character, then, with regard to the claims which are required to be covered under section 145, the use of the vehicle on a journey during which one or more passengers are carried at separate fares[129] will be treated as falling within either the specified use or outside the exclusions (section 150(1)). This will only be the case if: the vehicle is not adapted to carry more than eight passengers and is not a motor cycle; the fare or aggregate of fares does not exceed the running costs (including depreciation and general wear); and the fare arrangements were made before the journey began (section 150(2)). These provisions not only conform with the overall objective of the legislation, which is to ensure that third parties, including passengers, are covered by insurance, but also fit in with the desire

[122] *Wood v General Accident Fire and Life Assurance Corpn* (1948) 82 Ll L Rep 77, 81 (Morris J).
[123] ibid.
[124] *Orr v Trafalgar Insurance Co Ltd* (1948) 82 Ll L Rep 1.
[125] [2004] EWCA Civ 1491.
[126] *DHR Moody (Chemists) Ltd v Iron Trades Mutual Insurance Co Ltd* [1971] 1 Lloyd's Rep 386.
[127] *Browning v Phoenix Assurance Co Ltd* [1960] 2 Lloyd's Rep 360.
[128] *Seddon v Binions* [1978] 1 Lloyd's Rep 381.
[129] As defined in Public Passenger Vehicles Act 1981, s 1(4) (Road Traffic Act 1988, s 150(4)).

of the government to encourage car-sharing schemes and thereby, it is fondly hoped, reduce road congestion.[130]

5. Uninsured and Untraced Drivers

5.1. The Motor Insurers' Bureau

In spite of the provisions of the legislation, there will be occasions on which a third party has no real remedy, such as where the driver is uninsured and has insufficient means to meet a claim, or where the driver simply cannot be traced, as in a 'hit-and-run'. In 1937 a Departmental Committee chaired by Sir Felix Cassel recommended the creation of arrangements with respect to uninsured drivers, although not the victims of hit-and-run accidents. This led to an agreement in 1946 between the government and those insurers who undertook compulsory motor insurance. The agreement was replaced in 1988, 1999 and again in 2015. In 1969 an agreement on compensating the victims of untraced drivers was also signed following judicial condemnation of the lacuna.[131] This was replaced by further agreements in 1972, 1996, 2003 and, following a CJEU ruling that the 2003 agreement was incompatible with EU law,[132] in 2017. The MIB administers the schemes. Although the agreements are made between the MIB and the government, and, technically, cannot be enforced by a victim, for obvious reasons the MIB has not argued this point to defeat claims and the courts have never raised it as an issue.[133]

5.2. The Uninsured Drivers Agreement 2015

The Uninsured Drivers Agreement 2015 applies where a claimant has obtained a judgment in respect of a liability required to be covered under the 1988 Act but the judgment has not been satisfied, and it is immaterial that there is insurance in force: what triggers the MIB's liability is non-payment (clause 3). An interim payment may be ordered against the MIB pending judgment if it is clear that there will ultimately be an award in the claimant's favour (Civil Procedure Rules, rule 25.7). Once the claimant has received compensation from any other source (other than the Criminal Injuries Compensation Scheme), the MIB's liability is discharged to that extent (clause 6). The claimant is entitled to recover both the amount of the judgment and any legal costs (clause 1.1), and the MIB is also liable to make payments for medical expenses under the Health and Social Care (Community Health and Standards) Act 2003. The MIB is not liable for injuries caused by vehicles exempted from the compulsory insurance requirement under section 144 of the 1988 Act unless there happens to be

[130] Since 1975 insurers have agreed not to regard contributions to petrol costs as falling within a term of the policy which excludes liability if the vehicle is used for hire or reward. The Transport Act 1980 added to the Road Traffic Act 1972 the provision which is now s 150.

[131] *Adams v Andrews* [1964] 2 QB 347.

[132] *Evans v Secretary of State for the Environment* [2004] Lloyd's Rep IR 391. The procedure was held to be permissible, but there were deficiencies as regards the payment of costs and interest by the MIB.

[133] *Albert v Motor Insurers' Bureau* [1972] AC 301, 312 (Lord Donovan).

insurance in place (clauses 4 and 5). The 2015 Agreement was amended in 2017 to provide cover where the vehicle is used for terrorist purposes.

The MIB's liability for damage to the claimant's vehicle is capped at £1.2 million, the figure in the 1988 Act (clause 11), and is removed where the vehicle was uninsured and the claimant knew or ought to have known that that was the case (clause 7). The MIB's liability for passenger claims is limited by clause 8, which applies where a claimant who, at the time of the use giving rise to liability, was voluntarily allowing himself to be a passenger in the vehicle and, either before the start of the claimant's journey in the vehicle or after its start if the claimant could reasonably be expected to have alighted from it, knew or had reason to believe[134] either that the vehicle had been stolen or unlawfully taken or that the vehicle was uninsured[135] contrary to the requirements of the 1988 Act. The phrase under earlier versions of the Agreement was 'knew or ought to have known', which had, in order to comply with EU law, been construed in *White v White* as meaning actually knew or had blind eye knowledge. It has yet to be determined whether the revised wording has achieved any change, but following Brexit the UK courts are free to reach their own decision on this point. The exclusion applies only where the claimant was being driven with consent, and it was held in *Pickett v Motor Insurers' Bureau*[136] that a claimant who revokes consent in the course of the journey and before the accident is entitled to recover from the MIB. In *Pickett*, the Court of Appeal by a majority held that the passenger had not revoked her consent by shouting 'for God's sake stop the car' when the driver of an uninsured vehicle began to drive recklessly by speeding and carrying out handbrake turns, and that something akin to false imprisonment on the part of the driver was required: it is difficult not to have sympathy for Pill LJ's dissenting judgment that the majority test paid insufficient attention to the actual position before the accident.

The Uninsured Drivers Agreement lays down a series of procedural requirements. An application has to be made in the correct form (clause 12) and the MIB has to be joined to the proceedings against the defendant unless the claimant has a reasonable belief that the defendant is insured (clause 13). The MIB may under clause 14 require the claimant to commence proceedings against the driver and any person who caused or permitted the uninsured use of the vehicle, subject to indemnification for costs, and the MIB may require a claimant who has obtained an unsatisfied judgment to assign the judgment to the MIB so that it can be enforced (where possible) for the MIB's benefit. Any decision by the MIB on whether or not to provide compensation must be in writing and reasoned (clause 16), with disputes to be resolved on paper by a sole arbitrator (clause 17).

Actual payment is made in accordance with Article 75 of the MIB's memorandum and articles of association. The general principle is that if there is an insurer in place but the insurer has a defence to the claim, that insurer will be nominated by the MIB to pay the claim as 'Article 75 insurer'. Any dispute as to whether an insurer is an Article 75 insurer are resolved by the Technical Committee with an appeal to an arbitrator.[137]

[134] [2001] Lloyd's Rep IR 493.

[135] If the vehicle is insured but the driver is not covered by the insurance to the knowledge of the passenger, the exclusion will not apply: the exclusion refers to knowledge of the existence of a policy, not to the persons covered by the policy. See *Colley v Motor Insurers' Bureau* [2022] EWCA Civ 360.

[136] [2004] Lloyd's Rep IR 513.

[137] *Haven Insurance Company Ltd v EUI Ltd* [2018] EWCA Civ 2494.

5.3. The Untraced Drivers Agreement 2017

The MIB's liability arises where death, personal injury or property damage, liability for which was required to be insured under the 1988 Act, has occurred (clause 3) but the driver has not been identified. As with the Uninsured Drivers Agreement, the MIB is not liable for accidents involving vehicles exempt from the insurance requirement under section 14 (clauses 4 and 5), and the sums payable are reduced by anything received by the claimant from any source other than the Criminal Injuries Compensation Scheme (clause 6). Clause 8 of the 2017 Agreement replicates clause 8 of the Uninsured Drivers Agreement, removing cover for a passenger in a vehicle stolen or unlawfully taken.

The conceptual difficulty with claims under the 2015 Agreement is that the precise circumstances of the accident may not be known. There are formal requirements to the making of a claim, including informing the police as well as the MIB (clause 10). The MIB under clause 12 carries out an investigation and then reaches a reasoned written decision as to whether or not payment will be made. If the claimant disputes the decision, there is a right of appeal to an arbitrator, and if the dispute is to quantum, the arbitrator cannot award an amount lower than that offered by the MIB (clauses 15–22). The amount payable by the MIB is that which would have been awarded by a court, subject to any deduction for contributory negligence (clause 11). Interim payments may be made, and the final award must include interest and costs. In the case of personal injury, the MIB must pay health charges under the Health and Social Care (Community Health and Standards) Act 2003. In the case of property damage (clause 7), the maximum sum recoverable is £1.2 million, subject to an excess of £400. There is also an important anti-fraud device, addressing the problem that a claimant may falsely assert that property damage to a vehicle was the result of a collision with an unidentified vehicle. For that reason, property damage is recoverable only if the claimant has also sustained 'significant personal injury' requiring at least two nights in hospital or three sessions of outpatient treatment.

6. Cross-border Accidents: The Green Card Scheme

The Green Card Scheme, which the UK joined in 1968, is an international arrangement promulgated by the United Nations under which a person insured in any one Contracting State is to be treated as insured for driving in any other Contracting State as long as that person has secured a Green Card complying with statutory regulations.[138] During the UK's membership of the EU, Green Cards were not required for a UK motorist driving in other EU Member States, and although Brexit ended that freedom, the UK and the EU reached a post-Brexit agreement under which, with effect from August 2021, EU countries have waived the need for the production of Green Cards. The Scheme is administered under the Multilateral Guarantee Agreement between National Insurers' Bureaux 1996. If a person suffers injury in a Green Card state by a vehicle registered in another Green Card state, the local bureau (in the UK, the MIB) will provide compensation to the victim, although there is a right of recourse from the national bureau of the Green Card state in which the vehicle was

[138] Motor Vehicles (International Motor Insurance Card) Regulations 1971, SI 1971/792, as amended by Motor Vehicles (International Motor Insurance Card) (Amendment) Regulations 2021, SI 2021/720.

registered. The participating nations are: Albania, Andorra, Austria, Azerbaijan, Belarus, Belgium, Bosnia-Herzegovina, Bulgaria, Croatia, Cyprus, the Czech Republic, Denmark, Estonia, France, Finland, Germany, Greece, Hungary, Iceland, Iran, Ireland, Israel, Italy, Latvia, Lithuania, Luxembourg, Malta, Moldova, Montenegro, Morocco, the Netherlands, North Macedonia Norway, Poland, Portugal, Romania, Russia, Serbia, Slovak Republic, Slovenia, Spain, Sweden, Switzerland, Tunisia, Turkey, Ukraine and the UK.

There remains an important post-Brexit gap in coverage, which is that if a person domiciled in the UK is injured in a road accident elsewhere in the EU by an uninsured or untraced driver, it is no longer possible for the victim to recover from the local insurers' bureau, and the MIB is responsible for providing compensation only for liabilities required to be covered by the 1988 Act, ie in the UK. Such victims will go uncompensated unless they have their own first party insurance, although since Brexit there have been bilateral and reciprocal agreements between the UK and individual EU countries under which the local compensation body will provide compensation. Thus far no agreement has been reached with France in this regard.

15

Liability Insurance

1. Principles Applicable to Liability Policies

1.1. Importance of Liability Insurance

Insurance effected against the risk of incurring liability to a third party is now almost universal. The fear to individuals or businesses that they may be confronted with a claim by a third party which could not be met out of their own resources has led to the rapid expansion of liability insurance over the last 70 years or so. Although a liability policy is designed to protect the insured against liabilities and is to be construed in that fashion, the reality of liability insurance is that it provides a source of compensation for the victims of the insured. The overwhelming majority of personal injury claims arise on the road and in the workplace: since 1930 – and now with the Road Traffic Act 1988 – it has been compulsory for road users to insure against liability, coupled with various mechanisms whereby the victim can bring direct proceedings against the driver's insurers;[1] and since the Employers Liability (Compulsory Insurance) Act 1969 it has been mandatory for employers to insure against liability to their employees. Other fields of activity are also subject to compulsory insurance, whether by legislation,[2] by international convention[3] or under contract. As any person tendering for the provision of construction or other works, or professional services, will testify, pretty much the first question they will be asked is the scope of their liability cover, and any subsequent contract will make express provision for insurance.[4] Public liability policies are not compulsory, but any organisation that allows members of the public onto its premises will have insurance arrangements in place to protect against claims under the Occupiers Liability Acts 1957 (visitors) and 1984 (trespassers). In all cases, under the Third Parties (Rights against Insurers) Act 2010, replacing the Third Parties (Rights against Insurers) Act 1930, the victim can bring a direct action against the liability insurers of

[1] See ch 14 above.

[2] Key professional services – including dentists, solicitors, osteopaths, psychiatrists, estate agents, insurance brokers – may be carried on only with compulsory liability insurance. Other matters covered by compulsory insurance include nuclear energy, package holidays, dangerous animals and riding schools.

[3] Mainly aviation and shipping, the latter including oil pollution and wreck removal.

[4] See ch 14 above.

a deceased or insolvent defendant. Although student textbooks cling to the fiction that tort cases are between a claimant and a defendant, the reality is that the vast majority of property and financial loss cases[5] are between a subrogated first party insurer and the defendant's liability insurers, the parties themselves being largely irrelevant.[6] Apart from the cases of motor insurance and death or insolvency of the insured, a liability policy does not confer rights on any third party claimant under the Contracts (Rights of Third Parties) Act 1999 unless the third party is identified by name, class or description. Although the third party is the ultimate beneficiary, the claim has to be brought against the insured, and it is only where a judgment is not satisfied by reason of insolvency that the third party has a claim against the insurers.

1.2. Types of Liability Policy

1.2.1. Occurrence Policies

Property liability policies and personal injury liability policies are written on an occurrence basis, so that the policy responds to a loss occurring during the policy year. The relevant occurrence may be an act that gives rise to the damage, or it may be the damage itself. In most cases this is a distinction without a difference, because most acts give rise to immediate damage. However, there may be situations where the negligent act does not cause damage for some years afterwards. By way of example, a negligently constructed wall may collapse some years after it has been built, damaging neighbouring property; and an employee exposed to a potentially harmful substance may not become ill for some time. In such cases it is necessary to ascertain whether it is the policy in force when the negligent act was committed or the policy in force (if there is one) in the later year when the damage or injury occurred that is applicable. This question was crucial in the mesothelioma litigation discussed in chapter 19 below.

The insured will be under an obligation, generally in the form of a condition precedent to liability, to notify the insurers of any event which may or is likely to give rise to a claim. 'May' is a wider test than 'likely' in that the former refers to a possibility whereas the latter means more likely than not. The courts have recognised that not every incident giving rise to injury or damage is caught by either of these formulations. In *Jacobs v Coster*,[7] the claimant slipped on a patch of oil at the insured's garage. The claimant immediately said that it was his own fault. The insured thought no more of it until a claim was subsequently made. It was held by the Court of Appeal that a claim in those circumstances was not likely and the insured was not in breach of the clause. By way of contrast, in *Arch Insurance (UK) Ltd v McCullough*,[8] an accident occurred at the insured's motor cycle track, injuring a young girl. The insured believed that no claim would be made and did not notify the event until proceedings were issued. It was held that it was obvious from the outset that a claim was likely, and accordingly that the insured was in breach of the notification clause.

[5] There is no subrogation for personal injury cases: see ch 13 above.
[6] R Merkin and J Steele, *Insurance and the Law of Obligations* (Oxford, Oxford University Press, 2013).
[7] [2000] Lloyd's Rep IR 506. See also *Zurich Insurance Plc v Maccaferri Ltd* [2016] EWCA Civ 1302.
[8] [2021] EWHC 2798 (Comm).

1.2.2. Claims Made Policies

Professional indemnity policies – including policies taken out by company directors – are, by contrast, written on a claims made basis. This type of policy has two triggers. The primary trigger is a third party claim made against the insured in the year of cover, and if a claim is made the insured is required by condition precedent to notify that claim to the insurers as soon as practicable.[9] There is a secondary, and in practice far more important, trigger, under which an insured is entitled to notify to the insurers circumstances known to the insured which 'may' (or 'are likely' – the wording varies) at some future point give rise to a claim. If the circumstances are duly notified in the policy year, then any subsequent claim made against the insured is deemed to have been made in the year in which the circumstances were notified. In other words, the notification of circumstances takes effect as notification of a claim by a third party even though the claim itself is not made until a later year. The importance of the 'notification of circumstances' extension is that if an insured becomes aware of circumstances that may give rise to a future claim, then when the policy is renewed those circumstances will be material facts that have to be disclosed to the insurers and the insurers may decline any renewal or they may renew with an exclusion for any claim arising out of those circumstances. The ability to secure cover by notifying the circumstances themselves is a crucial protection for insureds. In England the 'notification of circumstances' extension is universal.

Claims made policies are thought to be easier and cheaper to administer for professional liabilities than losses occurring policies, in that the insurers are given early notice of potential liability and can take immediate steps to investigate and, if appropriate, to settle. Claims made policies are to some extent retroactive, in that they apply to negligent acts that may have occurred in an earlier year and the acts may not give rise to a claim or notifiable circumstances until the later year in which the policy is in force. Insurers typically limit the retroactive effect of such policies by imposing a 'retroactive date', and this may give rise to causation issues. By way of example, in *ARC Capital Partners v Brit Syndicates Ltd*[10] a professional indemnity policy was renewed in October 2013, and provided that: 'This … Insurance shall not indemnify the Assured against any claim and or claims arising from or in any way involving any act, error or omission committed or alleged to have been committed prior to 5th June 2009.' The claim against the insured arose out of a contract made in 2008 and negligently implemented in 2010: it was held that the relevant act or omission was in 2010 and so was within the cover, the 2008 contract being no more than the background to the claim and not giving rise to the claim. Some policies have a very short retroactive date, sometimes the commencement of the policy itself, so that events occurring before the policy incepts are to be disregarded. It should be borne in mind that the limitation period under section 2 of the Limitation Act 1980 for professional liability claims is normally six years, so unless proceedings against the insured are issued within six years from the date of the damage, then there is no tort liability in any event.

The primary trigger for coverage is the making of a claim against the insured in the policy year. A claim is a demand for compensation from the insured,[11] normally in the form of a

[9] Some claims made policies require notification within the year of cover: these are known as 'claims made and notified' covers.

[10] [2016] EWHC 141 (Comm). See also *Murray Goulburn Co-operative Co Ltd v AIG Australia Ltd* [2021] FCA 288.

[11] *TSB Bank Plc v Robert Irving and Burns* [1999] Lloyd's Rep IR 528.

letter before action,[12] but on occasion by the service of a claim form without prior warning. The issue of a claim form without service probably constitutes the making of a claim,[13] but if there is no service then the insured cannot know of it and therefore will not be in breach of the notification clause up to the point of service. A claim should be distinguished from a preliminary communication in which the insured is informed of a possible problem by a client but no actual demand is made: that is not a 'claim', but is plainly a circumstance that may give rise to a claim and is therefore notifiable. It was held in *Rothschild Assurance Ltd v Collyear*[14] that a direction to the insured by the financial services regulator, the Financial Services Authority (now the Financial Conduct Authority), to undertake an investigation to determine whether there has been any mis-selling of its products and to pay compensation where appropriate constitutes a notifiable claim even though clients were not at that stage involved.

As noted above, the most important trigger for coverage is the right of the insured to notify circumstances that may or are likely to give rise to a claim. The root decision on the interpretation of this type of extension clause is *HLB Kidsons v Lloyd's Underwriters*.[15] The action arose out of professional negligence claims made against Kidsons in relation to the activities of its tax-planning subsidiary. General Condition 4 of the policy provided that 'The Assured shall give to the Underwriters notice in writing as soon as practicable of any circumstance of which they shall become aware … which may give rise to a loss or claim against them'. The insured's subsidiary sold products which minimised tax liabilities. The insured was alerted to potential risks by an employee, and sent a series of communications to the insurers. (1) On 27 September 2001 a letter was sent, stating that while the products had all been validated, the Inland Revenue might be critical of some procedures followed in them and the board of the subsidiary was invited to investigate. The letter added that 'There is no sign of a claim arising at the present time but the Board feels that it is appropriate in the circumstances to advise what is happening and to take your instructions'. (2) On 17–18 October 2001 the same letter was sent, but this time accompanied by details of five cases. (3) On 18–19 April 2002 a letter was sent to some of the insurers confirming possible procedural problems with the scheme. (4) In July 2002 the Lloyd's market was sent the same material as the April communication. The issue for the Court of Appeal was whether these letters and other documents relied upon by Kidsons constituted valid and effective notice of circumstances to the underwriters.

The *Kidsons* judgment contains a detailed discussion of timing and knowledge issues. In determining whether a notification has been made as soon as practicable after the insured has become aware of circumstances which may give rise to a claim, four separate elements must be considered: the insured must be aware of the circumstances; the insured must appreciate that the circumstances may give rise to a claim, although the Court of Appeal was divided on whether the test was wholly subjective or whether there had to be an objective basis for believing that a claim might be made, the latter view now being the accepted approach;[16] the relevant knowledge could be imputed to the insured from those responsible for managing the business; and the notification must be given as soon as practicable.

[12] *Thorman v New Hampshire Insurance Co Ltd* [1988] 1 Lloyd's Rep 7.
[13] Rule 7.2 of the Civil Procedure Rules states that proceedings are 'started' on issue.
[14] [1999] Lloyd's Rep IR 6.
[15] [2008] EWCA Civ 1206.
[16] *Aspen Insurance UK Ltd v Pectel Ltd* [2009] Lloyd's Rep IR 440.

As to the facts, it was not contended that the first letter was a notification of circumstances, and Rix LJ doubted whether the concerns of an employee that a scheme might be defective were sufficient to amount to 'circumstances'. As to the second letter, Rix LJ highlighted that General Condition 4 said nothing about how a notification was to be made, other than that it had to be in writing and given as soon as practicable after awareness of circumstances which may give rise to a claim. Rix LJ regarded this as a 'fairly loose and undemanding test'.[17] On that basis, the second letter constituted a valid notification of circumstances. The correct question was what the presentation reasonably conveyed to its recipient. In the circumstances, the second letter 'was on all objective criteria intended to be a notification of circumstances'. The third letter updated the second letter. As to the fourth letter, Rix LJ held that this was out of time and that the Lloyd's market recipients were not bound by it: the information had been available to the insured and the entire market should have been notified.

Later cases have discussed the detail required for a valid notification, and in particular whether what has become known as a 'hornet's nest' notification is permissible. The English courts have accepted this possibility. In *McManus v European Risk Insurance Co*,[18] the insured firm of solicitors took over the business of another firm. Soon afterwards, a small number of claims relating to conveyancing transactions forming part of the acquired business were made against the insured, and these were duly notified as claims. The insured undertook a random review of some 110 files, and discovered a series of failures of the same type, leading the insured to conclude that all of the acquired files might be affected by the same failures. The insured duly notified the insurers that there were at least 5000 problematic files, and the notification included a spreadsheet of the matters possibly affected. The insurers rejected the notification on the ground that it had not identified

> the specific incident, occurrence, fact, matter, act or omission which would give rise to a Claim on each individual file. Simply stating that [the predecessor] worked on the files in the List and Spreadsheet does not constitute a valid notification, and as such, the notifications are firmly rejected in their entirety and without question.

The trial judge held that the rejection was unjustified and that there was no need for actual matters and potential claimants to be identified. There was an appeal on a procedural issue only, and the thrust of the decision was not challenged in the Court of Appeal.

The possibility of broad notifications raises a final issue concerning the required connection between the notified circumstances and the claim subsequently made. That turns on the proper interpretation of the notification in order to determine its scope. In *Kajima UK Engineering Ltd v Underwriter Insurance Co Ltd*,[19] Kajima was a main contractor employed to design and build a block of flats in Leeds which involved the relatively novel application of the installation on five stories of a stacked pre-constructed pod and flat-pack construction. The Underwriter Insurance Company Limited provided professional indemnity insurance on a claims made basis to Kajima for the period 20 May 2000 to 19 May 2002. The policy permitted notification of circumstances 'which might reasonably be expected to produce a claim' notified during a period of insurance. On 22 February 2001 Kajima provided written notification to the insurers that the accommodation pods were 'settling and moving

[17] ibid [86].

[18] [2013] EWCA Civ 1545.

[19] [2008] EWHC 83 (Comm). See also *Cultural Foundation v Beazley Furlonge Ltd* [2018] EWHC 1083 (Comm), where an initial notification was held not to encompass problems which were unknown at the time.

excessively causing adjoining roofing and balconies and walkways to distort under differential settlement'. There was reference to other possible damage and risk, and to the fact that 'an investigation was presently underway to identify/confirm cause & potential effects/risk'. Such investigation as there was over the months that followed immediately determined that the problem was an anticipated one and that it had stabilised. There was no dispute as to the effectiveness of this notification. Over the years that followed, a number of further problems arose in relation to the project, some of which were in the physical area of the matters notified but others of which were not, and some of which were not of the same type as or, arguably, directly associated with what had been specifically notified by Kajima to the insurers in February 2001. The issue therefore surrounded whether, and if so to what extent, the defects and damage which emerged were the subject matter of what was notified in February 2001. Kajima sought to rely on the notification to cover all the problems faced on the ground that the investigation referred to in the notification led, in time, to further investigations resulting in further defects being revealed and they therefore related to notified circumstances; Kajima effectively said that there was a 'continuum' from 2001 onwards and the losses, costs and liabilities incurred by them all in effect therefore arose from the notified circumstances.[20] On the contrary, the insurers argued that the notification concerned relatively narrow circumstances; the 'investigation' mentioned was clearly intended to be an investigation into the notified circumstances as opposed to some general investigation into the possible existence of other defects.[21] Akenhead J, finding for the insurers, concluded that the notification was only effective in relation to the specific circumstances that were notified or those losses which were caused or related to the circumstances notified; it was insufficient that there was a historical 'continuum' of investigation which coincidentally revealed further defects which have not or may not have anything to do with the notified circumstances. Furthermore, Akenhead J held that Kajima ought to have made further notifications to the insurers as they became aware of further circumstances which may give rise to a claim – in the event, the insurers would not have been liable for these defects because many of the problems for which Kajima claimed arose after the expiry of the policy.[22]

Kajima was distinguished by the Court of Appeal in *Euro Pools Plc v Royal & Sun Alliance Insurance Plc*,[23] a case instructive for those wishing to know the mechanics of swimming pool manufacture. The insured, a manufacturer of swimming pools, used a system of booms that were raised or lowered in order to divide pools into sections. The system used up to February 2007 pumped into and removed air from steel tanks in the booms, but by that time leakage problems had developed and the insured switched to an airbag system to raise and lower the booms. When the policy was renewed in June 2007, the insurers were informed that the use of the original air drive system might give rise to future claims by clients whose pools had been fitted with that system but that the cost of repairs was unlikely to exceed the deductible in the policy. The airbags proved to be unsatisfactory, and in March 2008 the insured gave a further notification of circumstances and changed to a hydraulic system. The Court of Appeal held that the February 2007 notification encompassed all future problems with the booms and the claim fell under the original policy. There had been a problem with

[20] ibid [101].
[21] ibid [102].
[22] ibid [111].
[23] [2019] EWCA Civ 808.

the booms, and it was immaterial that the insured did not know, and could therefore not notify, the cause, extent or solution to the problem. There was accordingly a valid 'hornet's nest' notification encompassing all matters relating to the booms.

One particularly valuable feature of claims made policies is that they make provision for an individual who has retired from professional work but who later faces claims from events arising during the period of work. This is known as run-off cover.

1.3. Scope of Liability Policies

1.3.1. Forms of Liability

A liability policy is aimed primarily at liability in the tort of negligence. Typical wording will refer to liability at law for damages or compensation. Liability for loss deliberately caused is excluded by the common law principle of fortuity and also by express wording,[24] although the Court of Appeal in *Lancashire County Council v Municipal Mutual Insurance Ltd*[25] held that a local authority facing vicarious liability for the deliberate wrongdoing of its employees – police officers – could recover from its insurers the punitive damages awarded as part of its total liability in damages. The position is doubtless different if punitive damages are incurred personally by the insured, as an insurance indemnity would deprive the award of any effect. Restitutionary claims are also outside the scope of cover because a restitutionary claim is in essence one for the return of money that the insured should not have possessed in the first place.[26] It was seen in chapter 10 above that the law does not countenance indemnity for sums incurred by an insured to prevent a future loss from occurring, eg preventing further pollution by repairing leaks.[27]

Contractual liability is generally excluded, although only where, but for the contract, the law would not impose liability. The usual reference is to liability assumed by the insured except to the extent that the liability would otherwise have been imposed by law. There is accordingly coverage in cases where a professional fails to live up to the required standard of care, because the liability is both contractual and tortious. By contrast, there is no coverage where a seller supplies defective products,[28] because there is no tort involved unless the goods are dangerous and cause damage to the purchaser or a third party. It should be noted that liability policies do not as a general rule cover claims arising from a contract. In *Tesco v Constable*,[29] the question to the court was whether Tesco, the claimant insured, could recover from the defendant excess public liability insurers a large sum which it became liable to pay under the terms of a deed of covenant for economic loss to a third party affected by its activities. The case concerned a project embarked upon by Tesco to build a supermarket over a railway – a tunnel was to be built over the railway and then the supermarket would be built on the infill site above. During construction, part of the tunnel collapsed and the railway line had to be closed for 51 days. The actual railway track was owned by Network

[24] See ch 10 above.
[25] [1996] 3 All ER 545.
[26] *Stone & Rolls Ltd (in liquidation) v Moore Stephens (A Firm)* [2009] 1 AC 1391.
[27] *Yorkshire Water v Sun Alliance* [1997] 2 Lloyd's Rep 21; *Marketform Managing Agency Ltd v Amashaw Pty Ltd* [2018] NSWCA 70.
[28] Claims against manufacturers are protected by product liability insurance: see below.
[29] [2008] EWCA Civ 362.

Rail, but Chiltern Railway Co Ltd operated the railway under a Track Access Agreement. Chiltern had entered into a deed of covenant with Tesco which required Tesco to pay on demand such sums to compensate them for any costs losses or expenses resulting from the work. As part of the deal with Network Rail, Tesco was required to take out public liability insurance to the sum of £155 million. Chiltern subsequently made a claim against Tesco under the deed of covenant for loss of passenger revenues; Tesco agreed liability and the matter was settled. Tesco then looked to their insurers to indemnify them for their loss.

At first instance,[30] Field J held that Tesco's liability to Chiltern was in respect of contractual economic loss and therefore not within the scope of the insurance policy, which only contemplated loss for which there was liability in tort. On appeal, Tesco contended that the judge had attached too much importance to the fact that it was a public liability policy, and argued that the wording of the policy was wide enough to include contractual claims. Tuckey LJ held that public liability policies provide cover against liability to the public at large and, by contrast, private liability arises from contracts entered into between individuals. He stated that public liability in this sense arises in tort and cannot arise only in contract. Furthermore, he highlighted that as a general rule a claim in tort cannot be founded upon pure economic loss and, accordingly, the judge at first instance was correct in emphasising the nature of the policy.[31] Tuckey LJ recognised that it was possible for the wording in such a policy to extend to cover third party claims in contract, even for pure economic loss, but, based on the facts of the case, this was not made out.

Liability imposed by statute is recoverable where it takes the form of damages or compensation. It was held in *Bartoline Ltd v Royal & Sun Alliance Insurance Plc*[32] that an obligation on the insured under the Water Resources Act 1991 to pay the costs of cleaning up pollution did not constitute 'liability at law by way of damages'. By contrast, in *Bedfordshire Police Authority v Constable*,[33] the insured police authority was able to recover from its insurers sums payable under the Riot (Damages) Act 1886[34] for property damage caused by rioting within its local area: although liability was strict, the payments to local householders were compensatory in nature and thus constituted a liability for damages. In personal injury cases, the Health and Social Care (Community Health and Standards) Act 2003 imposes liability upon insurers to reimburse the Department of Work and Pensions for any social security benefits paid to the victim of a tort.[35]

1.3.2. Classification of the Claim against the Insured

A liability policy responds not to the manner in which the claim against the insured is framed but rather to the actual substance of the claim.[36] There is little point in a third party alleging fraud against an insured, because insurers do not face liability for harm deliberately inflicted. Accordingly, the third party is more likely to allege negligence and to obtain judgment on that basis. That happened in *McDonnell Information Systems v Swinbank*,[37] where

[30] [2007] EWHC 2088.
[31] ibid [14].
[32] [2007] Lloyd's Rep IR 423.
[33] [2009] Lloyd's Rep IR 607.
[34] See ch 16 below.
[35] For the history of the legislation, see *Aviva Insurance Ltd v Secretary of State for Work and Pensions* [2022] EWCA Civ 15.
[36] *West Wake Price & Co v Ching* [1957] 1 WLR 45.
[37] [1999] Lloyd's Rep IR 516. The court refused to follow *Redbridge LBC v Municipal Mutual Insurance Ltd*, in which it had been held that a judgment against the insured was conclusive on the nature of the liability faced by the insured.

it was held that it was open to the insurers to argue that there had in fact been fraud and that they had a defence. The point operates in the converse fashion: if there is judgment against the insured on a ground not covered by the policy, it remains open to the insured to argue that there was parallel liability falling under the policy. In *Omega Proteins Ltd v Aspen Insurance UK Ltd*,[38] Christopher Clarke J ruled that an underlying judgment finding an insured liable to a third party for breach of contract for supplying contaminated goods did not conclusively determine the basis of liability for the purposes of a claim under the insurance policy which contained a contractual liability exclusion. Accordingly, it was open to the insured either to argue that the underlying judgment was incorrect or to contend that there was parallel liability in tort for supplying a dangerous product.[39]

1.3.3. Insured Activities

A liability policy will identify the insured activities in respect of which an indemnity is payable. A householder's policy will cover liability incurred by the insured as occupier.[40] A commercial liability policy will refer to liability arising from the insured's stated business. The nature of the restriction can be seen from a series of cases on policies taken out by solicitors[41] where coverage was restricted to liability arising out of or in connection with the provision of services in private practice as a solicitor. The question which arises is whether the activity giving rise to liability arose out of the services of a solicitor. A solicitor who incurred liability under a guarantee given for a debtor client was held not to be acting in connection with the usual services provided by a solicitor.[42] The point is often reinforced by an express exclusion for trading debts or liability for the supply or use of any goods or services. In *Impact Funding Solutions Ltd v Barrington Support Services Ltd*,[43] the Supreme Court held by a 4:1 majority that the exclusion applied to solicitors' liability under an agreement with a litigation funder under which the solicitors agreed to indemnify the funder for costs incurred in failed claims for industrial deafness. The liability was not one incurred to clients, which was the purpose of the policy, but rather arose out of a separate agreement designed to support the business of the firm.

1.4. Claims

1.4.1. The Trigger for Coverage

Assuming that the claim made by the insured falls within the terms of the policy, it is a precondition of indemnification that the insured's liability to the third party has been established and quantified. Liability policies respond only to liability and not to ex gratia payments made by the insured for the purpose of maintaining a commercial relationship

[38] [2010] EWHC 2280.
[39] See ibid [49].
[40] This may give rise to difficult questions as to when property is occupied by the insured. See *Oei v Foster* [1982] 2 Lloyd's Rep 170.
[41] It was held in *Zurich Professional Ltd v Brown* [2010] EWHC 3300 (Ch) that a solicitor who had been struck off had not provided a solicitor's services because he had not held himself out as a solicitor.
[42] *Halliwells LLP v NES Solicitors* [2011] EWHC 947 (QB). See also *Sutherland Professional v Bakewells* [2011] EWHC 2658 (QB).
[43] [2016] UKSC 57, [2017] AC 73, reversing [2015] EWCA Civ 31, [2015] 4 All ER 319.

with the third party. A recent example is *Cruise and Maritime Services International Ltd v Navigators Underwriting Agency Ltd, The Marco Polo*,[44] where a travel agent provided ex gratia compensation to passengers on a cruise disrupted by an outbreak of norovirus. Establishing and quantifying liability to the third party can happen in one of three ways: there is a judgment against the insured in favour of the third party; there is an arbitration award against the insured in favour of the third party; or a settlement has been reached between the insured and the third party. Although none of these are conclusive of liability and quantum, they are an essential starting point in that the burden then shifts to the insurers to challenge the basis of the judgment, award or settlement.

Turning first to judgments and arbitration awards, the principle that a judgment or award is conclusive of the rights of the parties – giving rise to an issue estoppel that prevents the points decided from being reargued in later proceedings – applies only as between the parties. The insured's liability insurers, even though they may have paid for the defence of the proceedings, are not parties and therefore are not bound by the outcome. There are decisions to the effect that English judgments are binding and that foreign judgments are binding unless they are manifestly perverse,[45] but more recently Christopher Clarke LJ has stated,[46] obiter, that:

> In the event of dispute the existence of liability has to be established to the satisfaction of the insurer, or, failing that, by the judge or arbitrator who has jurisdiction to decide such a dispute. It is not, therefore, necessarily sufficient for the insured to show that he has been held liable to a claimant by some court or tribunal or that he has agreed to settle with him. In practice the fact that this has occurred may cause or persuade the insurer to pay, but, if it does not, the insured must prove that he was actually liable. Under English law the ultimate arbiter of whether someone is liable, if insured and insurer cannot agree, is the tribunal which has to resolve their disputes (or any relevant appeal body). It may hold that there was in fact no actual liability and that an insured who thought, or another tribunal which decided, that there was, liability was in error either on the facts or the law or both.

As for settlements, the principle here is that the question is not whether the settlement was reasonable but whether the insured can show on the balance of probabilities that the settlement sum was no greater than the amount for which the insured would have faced liability had the matter been tested in the courts or in arbitration.[47] If there are numerous claims against the insured, as where all of the passengers on disrupted cruises seek recovery, the principle applies to the aggregate settlement sum,[48] so that the investigation of each individual claim is not necessary and the insurers cannot complain that the settlement does not allocate a sum to each claim.[49]

In general, payment of the claim by the insured is not a prerequisite for indemnification. The one important exception to that principle found in operation is in the rules of

[44] [2017] 1 Lloyd's Rep 575. The insurers were not liable for the entirely separate reason that the agent was not an insured person under the policy.

[45] *Commercial Union Insurance v NRG Victory Reinsurance* [1998] Lloyd's Rep IR 439.

[46] *AstraZeneca Insurance Co Ltd v XL Insurance (Bermuda) Ltd* [2013] EWHC 349 (Comm), para [17].

[47] *Commercial Union Insurance v NRG Victory Reinsurance* [1998] Lloyd's Rep IR 439; *Structural Polymer Systems Ltd v Brown* [2000] Lloyd's Rep IR 64.

[48] *P&O Steam Navigation Co v Youell* [1997] 2 Lloyd's Rep 136.

[49] *Enterprise Oil Ltd v Strand Insurance Co Ltd* [2007] Lloyd's Rep IR 186, Aikens J rejecting the decision in *Lumbermans Mutual Casualty Co v Bovis Lend Lease Ltd* 2005] 1 Lloyd's Rep 494 where Colman J thought that allocation was necessary so that a settlement which did not allocate losses as between claims did not qualify as a settlement at all.

protection and indemnity (P&I) clubs offering liability insurance to member shipowners, whose cover operates on a 'pay to be paid' basis. The effect of this provision is that an insolvent insured unable to make payment to the third party will confer a windfall benefit on the insurers, and outside of the maritime context such clauses have been described in Australia as 'inimical' to the concept of insurance.[50] We have already seen in chapter 12 above that pay to be paid provisions in property policies for the funding of repairs are construed as entitling the insured to an indemnity on incurring liability to a repairer to make payment rather than requiring that the payment is actually made. The real significance of pay to be paid clauses is where the insured becomes insolvent, because in those circumstances the claim is transferred to the third party and plainly the third party cannot fulfil the payment obligation: for that reason, the Third Parties (Rights against Insurers) Act 2010 prevents the use of pay to be paid clauses by P&I clubs where the third party claim is for death or personal injury: this point is discussed below.

1.4.2. The Duties of the Insured in the Claims and Settlement Process

The insured's duties once the insurers have been informed of a possible claim falling within the policy will depend upon the terms of the policy. The insured will normally be under a duty to co-operate with the insurers, including the provision of information. If the clause fails to specify a time limit for the insured to provide information, it is an implied term that the information will be provided within a reasonable time. The issue that has been litigated is that of what constitutes a reasonable time. These issues were discussed in chapter 11 above, where it was noted that if the contractual requirements are expressed to be conditions precedent, then any breach of them will defeat the insured's claim.

There will generally be a restriction in the policy on the insured admitting liability, and for that reason most settlements provide that liability is not admitted. In *Terry v Trafalgar Insurance Co Ltd*,[51] the claimant, who was involved in a motor collision with a third party, apologised to him at the scene of the accident and later that day wrote admitting liability. The claimant's policy with the defendant insurers contained the following clause: 'No liability shall be admitted or legal expenses incurred nor any offer promise or payment made to Third Parties without the Company's written consent.' This was described in the policy as a condition precedent to the liability of the insurers. Initially, the claimant sought to settle with the third party, but upon being informed that the damage to the vehicle was more severe than was first appreciated, he sought to claim on his insurance. The insurers denied liability. The claimant argued, first, that the policy condition was contrary to public policy insofar as it tended to cause the insured to lie about what happened, or at least conceal the truth, and secondly, that the condition was subject to the implication that no liability should be admitted if it was to the prejudice of the insurers. Judge Graham Rogers held that the claimant's first line of argument was based on a false premise. He said:

> [T]his is a fanciful argument; the condition does not require the insured to lie, but to refrain from admissions of liability. There is a world of difference between giving a factual account of what happened, without giving any expression of opinion as to blame, and an admission of liability. This is and has been for many years a standard condition of motor insurance policies, and in my view it is clearly a necessary and proper one for the protection of insurance companies.[52]

[50] *Lambert Leasing Inc v QBE Insurance Ltd (No 2)* [2015] NSWSC 1196.
[51] [1970] 1 Lloyd's Rep 524.
[52] ibid 526.

With respect to the claimant's second contention, the judge held that, whether or not the condition should be read as being subject to any proviso as to prejudice, the insurers were, in any case, certainly prejudiced by the claimant's admission of blame: 'by his letter, written within hours of the accident, the defendants were shut out from any negotiations, and deprived of a possible chance of a favourable settlement'.[53]

1.4.3. The Duties of the Insurers in the Settlement Process

In practice, policy terms will remove the liability of the insurers in the event of a settlement that they have not participated in or approved, and there is reinsurance authority for the proposition that the insurers are, by virtue of implied term or principles of utmost good faith, required to act rationally and may not refuse their approval for reasons unconnected with the merits of the settlement, eg to put pressure on the insured in respect of other claims.[54]

Distillers-Bio-Chemicals (Australia) Property Ltd v Ajax Insurance Co Ltd[55] arose out of the thalidomide scandal of the 1970s, in which drugs prescribed to pregnant women containing thalidomide caused severe physical damage to their unborn foetuses. It was alleged that Distillers were negligent in their failure to detect the side effects of the drug before releasing it for prescription. Distillers, who had public liability insurance with Ajax, wished to settle with the third parties who had commenced an action against the company in negligence. Ajax, however, refused to consent to this and also declined to conduct the company's defence. It was held by the High Court of Australia that Ajax could refuse its consent without incurring liability. Stephen J observed that in relation to the question of whether to settle with a third party, the interests of the insured and the insurer are often tangentially opposed. While the insured will wish to settle the claim at any figure provided it is within the policy limits, the insurer may wish to use the deterrent of protracted litigation in order to negotiate a relatively low settlement figure. Where the third party's case is strong and a damage award above the sum insured is likely, the urgency of settlement will become a matter of paramount concern to the insured. Against this, the insurer's financial interest will be best served by seeking to avoid liability to indemnify altogether. In this situation it will not wish to exercise the right to defend the claim and by withholding its consent to a settlement the insurer may well procure a breach of condition should the insured go ahead and settle without first obtaining the insurer's consent. Given the vulnerable position of the insured, the judge stressed that the insurer's power to prevent a settlement cannot be used arbitrarily but must be

> exercised in good faith having regard to the interests of the insured as well as to its interests and in the exercise of its power to withhold consent the insurer must not have regard to considerations extraneous to the policy of indemnity.[56]

Thus, if the third party's case is strong and it is likely to succeed in any ensuing litigation, the insurer should not unreasonably withhold its consent to a settlement within the policy

[53] ibid 527.
[54] *Gan Insurance v Tai Ping (Nos 2 and 3)* [2001] Lloyd's Rep IR 667. See ch 18 below.
[55] (1974) 130 CLR 1.
[56] ibid 26–27.

limits. Where consent is refused but the insured nevertheless negotiates a reasonable settlement figure with the third party, the insurer will be liable to indemnify him. But if the third party's case is weak and the insured seeks to settle in order, for example, to avoid damaging publicity, the insurer's refusal to grant its consent may, in the circumstances, be justified.

1.4.4. The Insurers' Duties in Defending the Insured

The obligations of the insurers in defending claims made against the insured will depend upon the policy terms. If there is a discretion but not a duty to defend, the insurers are required by implied term or principles of utmost good faith to reach their decision on rational grounds and not for reasons unconnected with the merits of the matter. The principle has been accepted by the English courts[57] and the duty of the insurers to take account of the interests of the insured has been described by Longmore LJ in *K/S Merc-Scandia XXXXII v Certain Lloyd's Underwriters, The Mercandian Continent*,[58] as one of the few genuine examples of a post-contractual duty of utmost good faith.

Where an insurer decides to exercise its right to take over and conduct the defence or settlement of a claim on behalf of the insured, it does not necessarily follow that it will be estopped from subsequently avoiding liability because, for example, it discovers that the insured is in breach of a policy term or has failed to disclose a material fact. In order for estoppel to operate in this context, two conditions must be satisfied: first, that the insurer's conduct in taking over the defence of the claim amounted to an unequivocal representation that it was liable on the policy; and secondly, it must be shown that the insured acted upon the insurer's representation. There are dicta to the effect that simply defending the insured does not necessarily estop the insurer from subsequently denying liability, the reason being that the insurer's conduct is not in itself unequivocal. In *Soole v Royal Insurance Co Ltd*,[59] Shaw J stated that:

> [T]he assumption of control of the proceedings is equivocal. It does not necessarily imply a representation by the insurers that they regard the claim which is the subject matter of those proceedings as one which *must* give rise to a liability to indemnify the insured. It indicates no more that it appears that it may give rise to such liability. Hence the insurers would not be estopped from asserting that the particular claim was, in the event, never within the ambit of the policy.[60]

If, on the other hand, the insurer has knowledge of the insured's breach prior to defending him, the insured may be able to assume that the insurer has waived the breach.[61]

The conduct of the insurers in conducting the insured's defence is capable of causing additional loss to the insured. The most important manifestation will be where the insurers refuse an offer of settlement from the third party claimant – and it is very common for the

[57] *Eagle Star Insurance Co Ltd v Cresswell* [2004] EWCA Civ 602, a reinsurance case. See ch 17 below.

[58] [2001] Lloyd's Rep IR 802.

[59] [1971] 2 Lloyd's Rep 332. The decision was approved in *Kosmar Villa Holidays Plc v Trustees of Syndicate 1243* [2008] Lloyd's Rep IR 489.

[60] ibid 339–40. Waiver has to be judged by the insurer's conduct towards the insured and not the third party claimant: see *Spriggs v Wessington Court School* [2005] EWHC 1432.

[61] See *Fraser v Furman (Productions) Ltd* [1967] 1 WLR 898, 909, in which Diplock LJ observed that 'one of the terms of the [liability] policy is that the insurers take over the conduct of the action, and, if they did so and failed to repudiate with knowledge of the facts, they would be estopped from doing so thereafter'. See also *Evans v Employers' Mutual Insurance Association Ltd* [1936] 1 KB 505.

third party to make an offer at policy limits, with each side bearing its own costs – and insist upon defending the proceedings. If the case is lost, there is a possibility that the judgment against the insured may exceed the limits of the policy, therefore exposing the insured to uninsured liability. There are comments in English cases to the effect that insurers must take into account the interests of the insured in deciding whether or not to settle,[62] and there are decisions from Canada[63] and Hong Kong[64] holding that the insurers face liability in damages to the insured, over and above policy limits, if their unreasonable conduct exposes the insured to uninsured losses of this type. This situation is avoided in professional indemnity policies by the use of the 'QC clause', under which the insurers will pay a claim against the insured unless they have at their own expense obtained an opinion from a QC to the effect that the claim is likely to fail.

1.4.5. Costs

A crucial part of the cover provided by a liability policy is that for the insured's defence costs. Such costs are invariably included in the policy, sometimes as a part of the overall limit of indemnity and sometimes in addition to the overall limit of indemnity. It is usual for insurers to be required to pay defence costs if proceedings are commenced against the insured, although some policies confer a discretion on the insurers as to whether or not defence costs are to be paid, normally tempered by the requirement that the insurers' permission for the insured to incur defence costs will not be unreasonably withheld.[65] The common law in any event requires the insurers, by way of implied term or the duty of utmost good faith, to reach a decision on the provision of defence costs on rational grounds connected to the claim and not for any extraneous purpose.[66] The policy may remove a duty or discretion to pay defence costs if the claim made by the insured plainly falls outside the coverage of the policy, but it has been held[67] that if the claim arguably falls within the scope of cover, then the policy obligations in respect of defence costs remain applicable up to the point in the proceedings where it becomes apparent that there is no coverage. It may be that there are both insured and uninsured claims made against the insured, and in that situation the leading authority – the decision of the Privy Council in *New Zealand Forest Products Ltd v New Zealand Insurance Co Ltd*[68] – has taken the view that the correct approach is not to apportion the costs but rather to ask whether the uninsured claims would have increased the costs expenditure in defending the insured claims, so that only the excess is irrecoverable. This case concerned US proceedings against directors insured under a directors' and officers' liability policy and also against a number of uninsured defendants, and it was held that the full amount of the costs of the insured directors was recoverable even if there was indirect benefit conferred upon the uninsured defendants. The same approach has been

[62] *Groom v Crocker* [1939] 1 KB 194; *Beacon Insurance v Langdale* (1939) 65 Ll L Rep 57.

[63] *Plaza Fibreglass Manufacturing Ltd v Cardinal Insurance Co* 68 DLR (4th) 586 (1990); *Fredrickson v Insurance Corp of British Colombia* 69 DLR (4th) 399 (1990).

[64] *Insurance Ltd v Metropolitan Electrical Appliance Manufacturing Co Ltd* [2009] HKCFI 1132.

[65] *Hulton & Co v Mountain* (1929) 8 Ll L Rep 249, where the withholding of consent based on the incorrect assertion that the claim fell within the insured's deductible was found to be unreasonable.

[66] *Gan Insurance Co Ltd v Tai Ping Insurance Co Ltd (Nos 2 and 3)* [2001] Lloyd's Rep IR 667.

[67] *John Wyeth & Bros Ltd v Cigna Insurance Co of Europe SA NV* [2001] Lloyd's Rep IR 420. There is much authority on this point in Canada: see, most recently, *Henderson v Northbridge General Insurance Corporation* 2021 BCSC 1841.

[68] [1996] 2 NZLR 20, applied in *Thornton Springer v NEM Insurance Co Ltd* [2000] Lloyd's Rep IR 590.

adopted in respect of insured and uninsured claims (the latter falling outside the year of cover) against a single insured defendant.[69]

So much for the insured's legal costs. What of the legal costs incurred by a successful claimant against the insured that are awarded against the insured as defendant in the proceedings? Such costs fall within the standard wording of any liability policy, and an issue arises in respect of them only where the combined sums of liability plus claimant costs exceed the limit of indemnity under the policy. In such a case it is possible for the claimant to bring proceedings directly against the insurer for the amount of costs under section 51 of the Senior Courts Act 1981. This section confers an absolute discretion on the court to award costs, and in exceptional circumstances costs may be awarded against a person who was not a party to the proceedings but who in some way supported the proceedings and caused them to be protracted. It has been held by the courts in a series of cases that a liability insurer is caught by this exceptional category, and that costs may be awarded under section 51 if five conditions are satisfied:[70] (1) the insurers had taken the decision to defend the claim; (2) the defence of the claim had been funded by the insurers; (3) the insurers had conducted the litigation; (4) the insurers had fought the claim exclusively to defend their own interests; and (5) the defence had failed in its entirety. The conditions will be met where the insured is insolvent or has no interest in defending the proceedings (eg because the insured business has ceased trading), so that the conduct of the defence is purely to limit the insured sum payable under the policy. The issue was given detailed consideration by the Supreme Court in *Travelers Insurance Co Ltd v XYZ*.[71] The claimants in this case were women who had undergone breast transplant surgery. The implants were defective and many ruptured. A group litigation order was made, and 623 of the claimants joined the action against the manufacturer, Transform. In the course of the proceedings, in May 2014, it became apparent that only 197 of the claims were covered by the policy: the remaining 426 claims were excluded either because the injuries had occurred outside the policy period or because the claimants' implants had not ruptured so that no injuries had been sustained (a group referred to as the 'worried well'). The insurers nevertheless defended all of the claims, and when judgment was given for the claimants in June 2015 the insurers paid the damages and costs of the 197 covered claims but did not pay either damages or costs for the 426 uninsured claims. The 426 successful but uncompensated claimants brought the present proceedings against the insurers under section 51 of the 1981 Act, seeking to recover their costs. It was apparent that these claimants had not discontinued their action in May 2014 because, although they appreciated that they would not receive compensation, they at least expected to recover their legal costs.

The 426 claimants were unsuccessful. The Supreme Court held that a distinction was to be drawn between insured and uninsured claims. In the case of an insured claim, the question was whether the insurers were the real defendants, based upon the five conditions set out in the earlier cases. However, in the case of an uninsured claim, the insurers could be liable for costs under section 51 only if they had in some way 'intermeddled'. Where there were both insured and uninsured claims, and they were connected, an insurer who defended the insured claims and thus had some say or influence in the conduct of the defence of the uninsured claims could not be said to have intermeddled. This was the majority view,

[69] *John Wyeth & Brothers Ltd v Cigna Insurance Co of Europe SA NV* [2001] Lloyd's Rep IR 420.
[70] *TGA Chapman Ltd v Christopher* [1998] 2 All ER 873.
[71] [2019] UKSC 48.

expressed in the judgment of Lord Briggs. Lord Sumption would have been even more restrictive, and suggested that even in a case involving the defence only of insured claims, an insurer should face liability under section 51 only if it was an intermeddler.

2. Specific Forms of Liability Insurance

2.1. Employers' Liability Insurance

2.1.1. The Duty to Insure

The liability of employers for industrial injuries or disease caused to employees continues to be one of the most litigated areas of the tort of negligence.[72] Operating in tandem with the common law, there are a range of statutory duties imposed on employers in respect of employee safety under, in particular, the Factories Act 1961, the Health and Safety at Work Act 1974 and the Employers Liability (Defective Equipment) Act 1969. The state scheme for industrial injuries provides for compensation without the need to prove fault. However, actions in negligence remain the preferred route for claimants because of the higher level of common law damages. As with actions against impecunious defendants, little is gained from litigation if a damage award cannot be actually recovered. In order to ensure that an employee who is awarded damages for negligence against an employer receives the compensation due to him, the Employers' Liability (Compulsory Insurance) Act 1969 requires employers to insure against liability for injuries sustained by employees in the course of their employment.[73] The Act is supplemented by the Employers' Liability (Compulsory Insurance) Regulations 1998,[74] which fleshes out the detail of the requirements of the Act itself. Section 1(1) of the Act provides that, subject to certain exceptions contained in sections 2 and 3,

> every employer carrying on any business in Great Britain shall insure, and maintain insurance, under one or more approved policies with an authorised insurer or insurers against liability for bodily injury or disease sustained by his employees, and arising out of and in the course of their employment in Great Britain in that business, but except insofar as regulations otherwise provide not including injury or disease suffered or contracted outside Great Britain.[75]

The term 'business' includes any trade or profession carried on by an incorporated or unincorporated person. Under section 1(3) the employer must be carrying business in Great Britain and have a place of business in Great Britain. The Act has been extended to employees working outside Great Britain on offshore installations,[76] but otherwise an employee not ordinarily resident in Great Britain is outside the insuring obligation by reason of section 2(2). The insurance need extend only to liability for bodily injury or disease, and not to damage to employees' own equipment or possessions.

[72] D Bennett, *Munkman on Employer's Liability*, 17th edn (London, LexisNexis, 2019).

[73] The Act entered into force on 1 January 1972.

[74] SI 1998/2573.

[75] An employers' liability policy, together with any tort claims, is transferred on the sale of the business: the Transfer of Undertakings (Protection of Employment) Regulations 1981; see *Martin v Lancashire CC* [2000] Lloyd's Rep IR 665.

[76] Offshore Installations and Pipeline Works (Management and Administration) Regulations 1995, SI 1995/738.

The term 'employee' for the purposes of the statutory duty borne by employers to insure against their liability for personal injury to employees is defined by section 2(1) of the 1969 Act. This provides that an employee is 'an individual who has entered into or works under a contract of service or apprenticeship with an employer whether by way of manual labour, clerical work or otherwise, whether such contract is express or implied, oral or in writing'. The duty to insure does not therefore extend to independent contractors who work under a contract for services. The distinction between a contract of service and a contract for services can be particularly narrow and it has long vexed the courts.[77]

Section 2(2) of the Act relieves the employer from insuring employees who are close relatives, such as the employer's spouse, parent, grandparent, step-parent, child, grandchild, stepchild or sibling, including half-brother or half-sister. There is no insurance obligation on a sole trader who has adopted a corporate form but has no other employees.[78] Sections 3(1) and 3(2) of the 1969 Act, taken with regulation 9 of the 1998 Regulations, exempt certain employers from the statutory duty to insure. In general, these are government departments, foreign governments, local authorities, health service bodies, nationalised bodies, and judicial and educational bodies.

Under the 1998 Regulations, risks which must be covered under a motor insurance policy by virtue of the Road Traffic Act 1988 need not be included in an employers' liability policy. The key to determining the scope of the employer's duty to insure against liability to employees lies in the meaning of the phrase contained in section 1(1) above, namely, 'arising out of and in the course of their employment'. This form of wording also appears in the Road Traffic Act 1988, section 145 and in the old workmen's compensation legislation. In *Moore v Manchester Liners Ltd*,[79] Lord Loreburn defined 'the course of employment' as meaning that the event, normally an accident, giving rise to the employee's claim must 'arise when the employee is doing what a man so employed might reasonably do during a time during which he was employed and at a place where he may reasonably be during that time to do that thing'.[80]

As a general rule, an employee's journey to and from his place of work is not ordinarily in the course of employment unless the journey in question is so closely connected with the employee's work that the general principle ceases to apply.[81] In *Smith v Stages*,[82] an employee, M, a peripatetic lagger, had been instructed to work away from his usual workplace at the Drakelow power station in Staffordshire to undertake urgent work at Pembroke power station in Wales. As soon as the work was completed, M was driven back to his home in Staffordshire on a Bank Holiday Monday by a colleague so that he could resume work at his usual place of employment the next day. During the journey the car left the road and crashed into a brick wall. Both men were seriously injured. M was paid by his employers for the day he needed to travel back on the same basis as any normal working day. The House

[77] The most recent decision on the point is that of the Supreme Court in *Pimlico Plumbers Ltd v Smith* [2018] UKSC 29, where the relevant authorities are discussed.

[78] Employers' Liability (Compulsory Insurance) (Amendment) Regulations 2004, SI 2004/2882.

[79] [1910] AC 498.

[80] ibid 500–01.

[81] In *Smith v Stages* [1989] AC 928, 955, Lord Lowry stated that: 'The paramount rule is that an employee travelling on the highway will be acting in the course of his employment if, and only if, he is at the material time going about his employer's business. One must not confuse the duty to turn up for one's work with the concept of already being "on duty" while travelling to it.'

[82] ibid. See also *Elleanor and Cavendish Woodhouse Ltd v Comerford* [1973] 1 Lloyd's Rep 313; *Paterson v Costain & Press (Overseas) Ltd* [1979] 2 Lloyd's Rep 204.

of Lords held that at the time of the accident M was acting in the course of his employment. Lord Goff, having reiterated the fundamental principle that an employee remained in the course of his employment when he is doing what he is employed to do or anything reasonably incidental to his or her employment,[83] stressed that in determining the course of employment there are a number of factors to be taken into account, none of which are decisive.[84] In this respect, Lord Goff went on to state that:

> [T]he fact that a man is being paid by his employer in respect of the relevant period of time is often important, but cannot of itself be decisive ... I approach the matter as follows. I do not regard this case as an ordinary case of travelling to work ... In my opinion, in all the circumstances of the case, [M] was required by the employers to make this journey ... and it would be proper to describe him as having been employed to do so ... the Monday, a normal working day, was made available for the journey, with full pay for that day to perform a task which he was required by the employers to perform ... the journey was therefore made in the course of his employment.[85]

On the other hand, in *Vandyke v Fender*,[86] V and F, who were both employed by the same company as skilled moulders and who worked some distance from home, were provided with a car by their employer so that F could drive himself and V to their place of work. The employer also contributed towards the cost of petrol. During a journey to work they were involved in an accident caused by F's negligence in which V was seriously injured. V brought an action in negligence for damages against F and the employer. The employer joined as third party its insurers under an employers' liability policy. One of the issues before the court was whether the employers' liability policy covered this risk or whether the claim should be directed to the relevant motor insurer. It was held that the employers' liability insurer was not liable as the accident did not occur during the course of R and F's employment. Driving to work is not the same as driving at work and, in any case, V was under no obligation to travel in the car. Lord Denning MR, having reviewed the authorities,[87] observed that:

> They show, to my mind quite conclusively, that when a man is going to or coming from work, along a public road, as a passenger in a vehicle provided by his employer, he is not then in the course of his employment – unless he is *obliged* by the terms of his employment to travel in that vehicle. It is not enough that he should have the right to travel in the vehicle, or be permitted to travel in it. He must have an *obligation* to travel in it. Else he is not in the course of his employment.[88]

Whether or not an employee was acting in the course of employment is a question of law which, as indicated by Lord Goff in *Smith*, is determined by a range of indecisive tests which have been devised by the judges on a case-by-case basis. The application of these legal tests to a particular case is, of course, a matter of fact. Given the sheer diversity of employment relationships, these questions of fact often cause considerable difficulty, with the consequence that attempting to predict a particular outcome is generally a fatuous exercise.

2.1.2. Approved Policies

The reference in section 1(1) of the 1969 Act to 'approved policies' is defined in section 1(3). The policy must be issued by an insurer authorised in the UK to carry on this class of

[83] See *R v National Insurance Commissioner, ex p Michael* [1977] 1 WLR 109.
[84] Citing the judgment of Sir John Donaldson MR in *Nancollas v Insurance Officer* [1985] 1 All ER 833, 836.
[85] [1989] AC 928, 938–39.
[86] [1970] 2 QB 292.
[87] The two leading cases being *St Helen's Colliery Co Ltd v Hewitson* [1924] AC 59 and *Weaver v Tredegar Iron & Coal Co Ltd* [1940] AC 955.
[88] [1970] 2 QB 292, 305.

business. The policy must also be one 'not subject to any conditions or exceptions prohibited for these purposes by regulations'. The 1988 Regulations lay down four prohibited conditions 'in whatever terms'. In general, any term which is a condition precedent to liability is prohibited for the purposes of the Act. More particularly, Regulation 2(1) provides that:

> [T]here is prohibited in any contract of insurance any condition which provides (in whatever terms) that no liability (either generally or in respect of a particular claim) shall arise under the policy, or that any such liability so arising shall cease, if:
>
> (a) some specified thing is done or omitted to be done after the happening of the event giving rise to a claim under the policy;[89]
> (b) the policy holder does not take reasonable care to protect his employees against the risk of bodily injury or disease in the course of their employment;[90]
> (c) the policy holder fails to comply with the requirements of any enactment for the protection of employees against the risk of bodily injury or disease in the course of their employment; or
> (d) the policy holder does not keep specified records or fails to provide the insurer with or make available to him information from such records.[91]

It will be appreciated that the list of prohibited terms compares unfavourably with those in section 148 of the Road Traffic Act 1988.[92] By way of further unfavourable comparison with the 1988 Act, there is nothing in the statute which prevents an insurer avoiding the policy for breach of the duty of fair presentation. This point was highlighted in *Komives v Hick Lane Bedding Ltd.*[93] The employer's terms of employment were in effect those of modern slavery. The claimant employees suffered serious injuries at their place of work by reason of almost total disregard of health and safety requirements. They obtained judgment against the employer, but the employer's insurers avoided the policy for the employer's non-disclosure and misrepresentation as to working conditions, leaving the employees with unsatisfied judgments. It was held that the insurers had been entitled to avoid the policy, and were not prevented from doing so by anything in the 1969 Act. The only contentious point was the effect of ICOBS 8 in the Financial Conduct Authority's rulebook,[94] under which an insurer must act reasonably in reaching avoidance decisions. May J held that ICOBS did not confer rights on claimants against the insured, but only on the insured itself, and in the

[89] See also the Road Traffic Act 1988, s 148(5), considered further in ch 14 above. The failure to give notice of a claim within a specified time limit or the failure to comply with a co-operation clause by, for example, admitting liability (see ch 11 above) will be caught by this provision.

[90] Obviously, as in liability insurance generally, a primary reason for effecting the policy is to cover the risk of liability arising from the tort of negligence. In *Woolfall and Rimmer Ltd v Moyle* [1941] 3 All ER 304, the Court of Appeal held that a condition which stated that 'the insured shall take reasonable precautions to prevent accidents' is not broken by a negligent act by a competent foreman selected by the employers to supervise their employees. Lord Greene MR stated (309): 'If the delegation was reasonable, and, if, in selecting that particular foreman to perform the task, the [insured] took reasonable precautions, their obligation under this condition was, in my opinion, an end.' The prohibition in para (b) therefore confirms the common law position. See the discussion of reasonable care clauses in ch 10 above. However, a condition which provides that the insured's recklessness will relieve the insurers from liability may be enforceable. See further RA Hasson, 'The Employers' Liability (Compulsory Insurance) Act – A Broken Reed' [1974] *Industrial Law Journal* 79.

[91] Premiums are generally fixed by reference to an employer's wages bill and the breach of an express term requiring the maintenance of records in this respect will not, according to para (d), invalidate an employer's claim under a policy.

[92] See ch 14 above.

[93] [2020] EWHC 3288 (QB), affirmed [2021] EWHC 3139 (QB).

[94] The *FCA Handbook*. See ch 2 above.

circumstances the insurers had acted perfectly reasonably in avoiding the policy for flagrant breaches of presentation duties by the insured.

Section 1(2) of the 1969 Act states that regulations may provide for the 'amount for which an employer is required by this Act to insure and maintain'. Regulation 3(1) of the 1998 Regulations stipulates a minimum sum insured of £5 million 'in respect of claims relating to any one or more of [the insured's] employees arising out of any one occurrence'.[95] The ambiguity in the term 'occurrence', which could apply to an incident giving rise to a series of injuries or to each injury separately, was noted in chapter 12, but the issue is not a live one as the practice of the market is to issue policies with no limit of liability. Regulation 2(2) prohibits the imposition of requirement for the employer to pay the first part of any claim by way of policy deductible. However, there is nothing to prevent an insurer from requiring the employer to repay any part of the insurance proceeds, which are in practice paid directly to the claimant employee and not to the employer.[96] By this means a deductible can be indirectly imposed, but the risk of the employer's insolvency is borne by the insurers and not the claimant employee, and an employer is entirely free to take out separate insurance against having to repay to the employer's liability insurers a sum equivalent to a deductible.[97]

There is nothing in the legislation to stipulate the form of policy, but it is apparent that only a policy which responds to the employer's act or default giving rise to liability can provide the proper protection. That is particularly important for diseases resulting from exposure to harmful substances. A policy that provides an indemnity in the year in which the employee is injured will be deficient where the negligent act occurred some years earlier and by the time the injury occurred the victim had ceased to be an employee. As was said by Lord Mance in *Durham v BAI (Run-Off) Ltd*:[98]

> An obligation to have a policy in force only at or by the time when injury is actually experienced would leave employees or ex-employees at the mercy of compliance with the statute by their employers or ex-employers at uncertain future dates. It would also leave such employees or ex-employees at the mercy of employers who, for whatever reason, ceased to carry on business either in Great Britain or (for example due to insolvency) at all.

One of the issues that may arise with such policies is that the negligent act may have taken place many years before the injury occurred, and although there would have been insurance in place at the time of exposure, the employer may have ceased trading by the date of the claim and the identity of the insurers cannot be ascertained. This matter is partially addressed by regulation 4 of the 1998 Regulations, which requires an employer to retain a record of insurance for 40 years, and also by the Employers' Liability Tracing Office, which has since 2011 operated an electronic database of relevant policies.[99]

2.1.3. Enforcement

The 1969 Act opted for a curious means of enforcement. At a time when much of British industry was unionised, it was thought sufficient to provide for union enforcement. The

[95] Reg 3.

[96] *Amlin UK Ltd v Geo-Rope Ltd* [2016] CSOH 165.

[97] See *T&N v Sun Alliance* [2004] Lloyd's Rep IR 102.

[98] [2012] UKSC 14. This case is discussed in detail in ch 19 below, where it is noted that the policy was construed as applying to exposures and not to subsequent injury.

[99] For further information, see the Employers' Liability Tracing Office website, www.elto.org.uk/home.

scheme adopted, and retained by the 1988 Regulations, is to require every employer to display at its place of business a certificate of insurance in statutory form and of the requisite size issued by the insurers.[100] The absence of a certificate would prompt inquiry by the relevant trade union or by employees. Although the power of unions has declined, the self-enforcement mechanism is unaltered, though inspectors appointed by the Secretary of State are permitted to demand sight of certificates. The display requirement was modified by the Employers' Liability (Compulsory Insurance) (Amendment) Regulations 2008,[101] which permit electronic record keeping as an alternative to display. Readers will have seen such certificates on working premises, including restaurants and bars, although very few would have given little thought as to why they are there.

Section 5 of the 1969 Act provides that an employer who fails to effect liability insurance in accordance with the Act shall be liable on summary conviction to a fine of up to £1000 per day. In *Richardson v Pitt-Stanley Ltd*,[102] the Court of Appeal, by a majority,[103] held that the statute did not confer upon the claimant, an injured employee, the right to bring a civil action against the directors and secretary of the company for their failure to effect liability insurance. The claimant had sought to claim damages from the company which, having gone into liquidation, lacked sufficient assets to satisfy the judgment he had obtained against it. The decision is curious when viewed against the mischief which the statute was clearly intended to address and, as such, it has been strongly criticised.[104] Unlike the position in motor insurance, there is no fallback body providing compensation where an employer is uninsured, and a suggestion for the creation of an Employers' Liability Insurance Bureau equivalent to the Motor Insurers Bureau was rejected by the Department of Work and Pensions in 2012.

2.2. Product Liability Insurance

Product liability insurance offers cover, normally on a claims made basis, against liability for death, personal injury or property damage resulting from a defective product supplied, manufactured or repaired by the insured. The relevant liabilities are imposed upon a manufacturer by the common law, and upon a supplier by the Consumer Protection Act 1987, whereby a supplier who has imported or put his name onto a product faces liability as if he were the manufacturer. There is no liability in tort for a product that does not cause any harm but simply fails to perform its function, although there will be contractual liability under the Sale of Goods Act 1979 or the Consumer Protection Act 2015. Claims based on the failure of the product to fulfil its stated function are excluded from product liability policies,[105] thereby removing any possibility of claims for pure economic loss only. A good

[100] Regs 4 and 5.

[101] Employers' Liability (Compulsory Insurance) (Amendment) Regulations 2008, SI 2008/1765.

[102] [1995] QB 123.

[103] Russell and Stuart-Smith LJJ, Sir John Megaw dissenting.

[104] See, eg J O'Sullivan, 'Industrial Injuries and Compulsory Insurance – Adding Insult to Injury' [1995] *CLJ* 241, 243, who argues that if Parliament leaves the issue of civil liability silent, the courts must address a policy question, which in this case was: 'Who should bear the risk that a company, which has carried on business in breach of safety regulations (so that an employee is disabled) and without compulsory insurance, goes bust unable to meet the employee's damages? Should it be the culpable controllers of that company, skulking behind the corporate veil, or the injured employee? English law saddles the employee …'

[105] *Horbury Building Systems Ltd v Hampden Insurance* [2007] Lloyd's Rep IR 247.

illustration of the point is *Pilkington United Kingdom Ltd v CGU Insurance Plc*,[106] where the insured supplied and installed some 3000 glass panels in the roof of Waterloo Station. Thirteen of the panels showed signs of cracking, and they were removed and replaced before falling and causing injury. It was held that there was no insurance cover, in that the only problem was a defect in the product itself, which reduced its value but which did not cause any external harm. Policies also exclude the costs of putting right any defect in the product itself, although there may be coverage for product recall costs.

A product liability policy covers only products and not services, and there is commonly an exclusion for defective workmanship. There is no standard definition of 'product', but typical wording would refer to any goods manufactured, constructed, repaired or supplied by the insured after they have left the insured's care, custody or control. In *Aspen Insurance UK Ltd v Adana Construction Ltd*,[107] the Court of Appeal addressed the question whether a building could be a product. The insured in this case built onsite a concrete base designed to support a crane. The base was attached to four piles by metal dowels. The base collapsed, damaging the crane, and it was demonstrated that the dowels had been incorrectly fitted to the piles. The base was held not to be a product because it did not possess the qualities of being supplied and thereafter moveable. The only products supplied were the dowels, but they were not defective and had simply failed to perform their function.[108]

2.3. Directors and Officers Liability Insurance

This form of insurance, long in use in the USA, did not become available in the UK until 1989, when the prohibition on a company indemnifying its directors for liability for breach of duty was removed from the companies legislation. The validity of directors' and officers' liability (D&O) insurance now rests upon sections 232 and 233 of the Companies Act 2006, under which a company may purchase and maintain insurance for its directors against any liability for negligence, default, breach of duty or breach of trust. The various duties and liabilities faced by directors to their companies are set out in the 2006 Act, and as a matter of both express term and public policy there is no cover for acts designed to cause harm or for restitutionary claims in respect of money that the director had no right to receive. A policy will also provide cover for the costs of legal proceedings and regulatory investigations, including proceedings in which fraud or dishonesty has been alleged. although it is generally provided that there is coverage for defence costs up to the point at which fraud or dishonesty is proved or admitted. The importance of this form of insurance is such that few individuals will take up directorships in major companies unless insurance is in place.[109]

[106] [2004] Lloyd's Rep IR 891. See also *James Longley & Co v Forest Giles Ltd* [2002] Lloyd's Rep IR 421; *AXA Insurance UK Plc v Thermonex Ltd* [2012] EWHC B10 (Mercantile); *Metricon Homes Pty Ltd v Great Lakes Insurance SE* [2017] VSC 749. The principle that a product liability policy does not cover the condition of the subject matter supplied is often reflected in an express exclusion relating to repair costs, as in *AXA Insurance UK Plc v Thermonex Ltd* [2013] Lloyd's Rep IR 323.

[107] [2015] EWCA Civ 176.

[108] There is conflicting authority on the question of whether a building can be a product. An affirmative answer has been given in New Zealand, in *Body Corporate 83501 v Christchurch City Council* [2013] NZHC 2472, and in Australia, in *Metricon Homes Pty Ltd v Great Lakes Insurance SE* [2017] VSC 749, but the most recent decision from Australia: *Liberty Mutual Insurance Company Australian Branch v Icon Co (NSW) Pty Ltd* [2021] FCAFC 126 favours the *Aspen* approach.

[109] A Paolini and D Nambisian, *Directors' and Officers' Liability Insurance* (London, Routledge, 2008); J Tarr, 'Directors' and Officers' Insurance: Recent Critical Issues in Australia and New Zealand' [2016] *Journal of Business Law* 1.

A D&O policy may consist of three forms of cover. Side A cover indemnifies the directors for claims against them when the company itself has not provided an indemnity. Liability must be sustained in the capacity of director and not as professional adviser, as the latter form of liability falls within a professional indemnity policy. The distinction is not always easy to draw, but in general terms it may be said that statements made by the director to raise funds for or otherwise promote the company are within D&O,[110] whereas the services provided by the directors to the company's clients are for professional indemnity insurance. Side B cover indemnifies the company for any sums that they pay to the director to indemnify the director for claims. Side C cover indemnifies the company for its own liability. The insured under a D&O policy is the company itself, and the directors are beneficiaries who may enforce the policy either because the company is their agent or under the terms of the Contracts (Rights of Third Parties) Act 1999. The insurance is composite, so that the position of each director is distinct from that of the others: the fraud of one may prevent that director from recovering, but does not taint possible claims by other directors.[111]

---

3. Third Parties (Rights against Insurers) Act 2010

3.1. Background to the 2010 Act

At common law, where a person who had liability insurance became bankrupt, or if a company went into liquidation, a third party with an outstanding claim was left in a vulnerable position because he would have to prove in the bankruptcy or liquidation proceedings that he was an ordinary creditor of the insured. The position was that once an insured became insolvent, any insurance monies paid by way of indemnity went into the general pool for the benefit of all the insured's general creditors.[112] The common law position was manifestly unjust, so the Third Parties (Rights against Insurers) Act 1930 was passed to confer on third parties the right to claim directly against insurers of third party risks where the insured is insolvent. The 1930 Act was intended to supplement the introduction of compulsory motor insurance under the Road Traffic Act 1930, allowing the victim of a motor accident to proceed against the driver's insurers where the driver was insolvent. However, the Road Traffic Act 1934 introduced a specific means of protecting the victims of motor accidents in the form of a right to enforce against the insurers a judgment obtained against the driver. That remains in place, under what is now section 151 of the Road Traffic Act 1988,[113] but it meant that it became unnecessary to use the 1930 Third Parties Act in motor cases and instead it became relevant to the rapidly developing market in liability insurance for professional negligence and accidents at work.

[110] *Murray Goulburn Co-operative Co Ltd v AIG Australia Ltd* [2021] FCA 288.

[111] See ch 7 above.

[112] See *Re Harrington Motor Co Ltd* [1928] Ch 105, 124, in which Atkin LJ, commenting on the anomaly produced by the common law position, said: 'it would appear as though a person who is insured against risks and who has general creditors whom he is unable to satisfy, has only to go out in the street and to find the most expensive motor car or the most wealthy man he can to run down, and he will at once be provided with assets, which will enable him to pay his general creditors quite a substantial dividend'. See also *Hood's Trustees v Southern Union General Insurance Co of Australasia Ltd* [1928] 1 Ch 793.

[113] See ch 14 above.

The 1930 Act placed the third party claimant in the shoes of the insured by means of a statutory assignment or subrogation, so that once the insured had become insolvent, the claim could be continued or, if judgment had been obtained against the insured, enforced against the insured's liability insurers. The 1930 Act was a well-meaning and in many cases highly effective measure, but its limits were exposed by a series of judicial rulings. These were highlighted by reports of the English and Scottish Law Commissions published in 2001, containing wide-ranging proposals and a draft Bill.[114] No action was taken for a further nine years, when the reports were adopted as the Third Parties (Rights against Insurers) Act 2010. Ironically, by this time the courts had taken it upon themselves to remedy some of the defects in the 1930 Act. In the event, the 2010 Act was not brought into immediate effect, as there was a minor error in the measure that required amending legislation. The Insurance Act 2015 conferred power upon the Secretary of State to modify the 2010 Act, and the necessary step was taken by the Third Parties (Rights against Insurers) Regulations 2016.[115] The 2010 Act came into force with respect to injury or damage suffered on or after 1 August 2016.[116]

3.2. Conditions for the Application of the 2010 Act

3.2.1. Scope of the 2010 Act

The 2010 Act applies to liability policies, including the liability coverage conferred on shipowners by membership of a P&I club. By section 16, the Act applies also to policies that cover liability assumed under contract by the insured. That section codifies the decision in *Re OT Computers*.[117] The insured was a supplier of computing equipment and offered extended warranties to its customers. A finance company which provided credit for the purchase of computers was jointly and severally liable under the warranties by virtue of section 75 of the Consumer Credit Act 1974. The insured became insolvent and the finance company continued to honour the warranty claims; in so doing, it thus became subrogated to the customers' claims against the insured. Relying on the 1930 Act, the finance company sought to recover its payments from the suppliers' liability insurers. Longmore LJ, overruling earlier first instance decisions, allowed the claim and vigorously rejected the argument that contractual liabilities were not covered by the 1930 Act. By section 15, the 2010 Act does not apply to reinsurance, which was also the position under the 1930 Act.

It was unclear if and how the 1930 Act applied to a claim with some cross-border element. One view was that if the policy was governed by English law, then a claim could be brought even though the liability was incurred abroad. Another possibility was that what mattered was the place where the tort was committed. The issue has been resolved by section 18 of the 2010 Act, which adopts the principle that the 2010 Act is in effect an insolvency measure in that it affects the way in which the sums available for distribution to the insured's creditors are to be dealt with. On that basis, the 2010 Act applies if the insolvency procedure in question is being conducted in the UK.

[114] Law Com No 272/Scot Law Com No 184 (Cm 5217, 2001).

[115] SI 2016/570.

[116] Third Parties (Rights against Insurers) Act 2010 (Commencement) Order 2016, SI 2016/550, as construed in *Redman v Zurich Insurance Plc* [2017] EWHC 1919 (QB).

[117] [2004] Lloyd's Rep IR 669.

The 2010 Act is mandatory. By section 17, any policy term which directly or indirectly avoids or terminates a policy, or alters the rights of the insured, in the event that the insured becomes insolvent or an individual dies insolvent is deprived of effect. Insolvency freezes the insured's rights under the policy and they cannot be removed thereafter. The 2010 Act, like its predecessor, says nothing about agreements between the insured and the insurers prior to insolvency. It may be, for example, that the insured is faced with one or more substantial claims and enters into a settlement contract with the insurers fixing their liability at the agreed sum. If the insured then becomes insolvent, the settlement remains effective and it will bar recovery in excess of the settlement sum by the third party. It has been suggested that a settlement made in bad faith and designed to defeat the rights of the third party would amount to a conspiracy or otherwise would not be binding,[118] but the possibility of such behaviour by an insurer must be considered remote in the extreme.

3.2.2. Transfer of Rights

The rights of the insured against liability insurers to the extent of the liability of the insurers for the claim[119] are transferred to the third party claimant against the insured when the insured becomes a 'relevant person' (section 1). This term is defined at length in sections 4, 5, 6, 6A and 7 of the 2010 Act and catches all of the statutory possibilities for insolvency proceedings. The most important are bankruptcy, administration, liquidation and the various voluntary arrangements available under the Companies Act 2006 and the Insolvency Act 1986. Three situations may arise: (a) the insured may become a relevant person before the proceedings against the insured have commenced, in which case the proceedings are to be brought against the insurers in the place of the insured; (b) the insured may become a relevant person in the course of the proceedings, in which case the proceedings can continue, but against the insurers; and (c) the insured may become a relevant person after there has been a judgment against the insured, in which case the third party can enforce the judgment against the insurers. In case (c), the 2010 Act gives the third party a claim under the policy, although it is, of course, open to the insurers to defend the claim on the basis that the liability did not fall within the terms of the policy. By contrast, in cases (a) and (b), the insurer becomes the defendant in the proceedings brought by the third party, and the insurers have the right to defend the claim on two grounds: that the insured did not face liability; or, if the defendant did face liability, that the liability did not fall within the coverage of the policy. In cases (a) and (b), section 2 of the 2010 Act permits the third party to seek a declaration either that the insured faced liability or that the policy responds to liability if it is established. By this means, an expensive trial on both issues can be sidestepped. Thus, if there is a dispute as to whether there is policy coverage involving a point of construction that can be dealt with fairly easily and cheaply, it can be determined by declaration that it is only necessary to proceed to a factual trial on the further question of whether the insured faced liability once the preliminary coverage point has been resolved in the third party's favour. If the proceedings are against the insurers, the insured does not necessarily drop out of the picture, because there may be a shortfall where the claim against the insured exceeds the limit of indemnity in the policy or where there is a policy deductible. Section 14 of the 2010

[118] *Rowe v Kenway* (1921) 8 Ll L Rep 225; *AB v Transform Medical Group (CS) Ltd* [2020] CSOH 3.

[119] Under s 8, if the liability of the insured is less than the available indemnity, eg because defence costs are also insured, then only the liability claim is transferred.

Act allows the third party to maintain the claim against the insured for any shortfall, but insofar as the claim is covered by insurance, it can be brought only against the insurers.[120]

Under the 1930 Act the liability of the insured had to be established and quantified by the third party, and if the insured then became insolvent the judgment could be enforced against the insurers. An action against the insurers was premature in the absence of a judgment, award or settlement establishing the insured's liability.[121] A crucial change effected by the 2010 Act is that it is no longer necessary for the third party to establish and quantify the insured's liability as a precondition for proceeding against the insurers, and the sole trigger for the direct claim is the insured becoming a 'relevant person'. The significance of this change may be illustrated by decision of the House of Lords in *Bradley v Eagle Star Insurance Co Ltd*.[122] The claimant, who had been employed by the insured company which operated a cotton mill, developed a respiratory disease caused by the inhalation of cotton dust. The company was wound up in 1975 and dissolved by removal from the register of companies in 1976. In 1984 the claimant instituted an action against her former employer's insurers. The House of Lords rejected the claim. The effect of the dissolution of the company was to deprive it of any legal existence, and it was not possible for the claimant to sue a non-existent company. It therefore became impossible for her to establish and quantify the company's liability, with the result that the 1930 Act could not apply. Lord Templeman in his dissenting judgment questioned whether Parliament could have intended that 'the protection afforded against a company in liquidation should cease as soon as the company in liquidation reaches its predestined and inevitable determination in the dissolution of the company'.[123] Following the decision in *Bradley*, Parliament intervened to allow a struck-off company to be restored to the register at any time after its dissolution for the purposes of a personal injury claim, and within two years for all other claims. The reform was retroactive, so that Mrs Bradley's claim was preserved.

The effect of the 2010 Act is to remove the need for a dissolved company to be restored to the register. As soon as the company has gone into liquidation, the company becomes a 'relevant person' and the rights of the company under the policy are automatically transferred to the third party.

3.2.3. Insurers' Defences under the Policy

Under the 2010 Act, the third party is in no better position against the insurers than the insured would have been. This maintains the policy of the 1930 Act, where the third party was not permitted to pull out the plums and leave the duff behind.[124] The limits of liability are effective against the third party, and if there are competing claims to the insurance monies exceeding the amount available, then the 2010 Act follows the common law 'first past the post' approach[125] that insurance monies are to be allocated in the order in which claims against the insured are established and quantified.[126] The policy defences open to

[120] This confirms the interpretation put on the 1930 Act by the Court of Appeal in *Centre Reinsurance International Co v Freakley* [2005] EWCA Civ 115.
[121] *Post Office v Norwich Union* [1967] 1 All ER 577.
[122] [1989] AC 957.
[123] ibid 970.
[124] The colourful language used in *Post Office v Norwich Union* [1967] 1 All ER 577.
[125] *Teal Assurance Company Ltd v WR Berkley Insurance (Europe) Ltd* [2013] UKSC 57. See ch 18 below.
[126] *Cox v Bankside Members Agency Ltd* [1995] 2 Lloyd's Rep 437. Phillips J rejected arguments for a pro rata approach (regarded as impracticable because the sums owing to all claimants may not be determined for many years) and also that on the facts the claimants had agreed between themselves on a pro rata distribution.

the insurers against the insured are available also against the third party, eg avoidance for breach of the duty of fair presentation, as are obligations relating to claims such as arbitration clauses and choice of law provisions. There are, however, some important modifications to this general principle.

First, the 2010 Act corrects a problem that arose under the 1930 Act, namely, that an insolvent insured had no particular incentive either to notify a potential claim to the insurers or, once the claim had been made by the third party, to give any assistance to the insurers in respect of it. Where, as is usual, compliance was a condition precedent to the insurers' liability, the insured's defaults would grant the insurers a defence to a claim by the insured. Section 9 deals with the problem by preventing the insurers from relying upon the obligation of the insured to notify a claim or circumstances that may give rise to a claim, and thereafter the duty to satisfy the insured's obligations is transferred to the third party where the insured has died or is a dissolved company.

Secondly, the 2010 Act mitigates the effect of 'pay to be paid' clauses. As noted above, such clauses are rarely found in liability policies other than the cover provided by P&I clubs, where such clauses are universal. The operation of pay to be paid clauses gave rise to difficulty under the1930 Act as a result of the decision of the House of Lords in *The Fanti.*[127] The Lords ruled that the third party was bound by any obligation imposed on the insured, and also it could not be said that the imposition of a pay to be paid clause contravened the prohibition on contracting out of the 1930 Act – now section 17 of the 2010 Act discussed above – because the rights of the insured were the same both before and after insolvency, namely to pay in order to recover. The suggestion that the ruling undermined the very purpose of the legislation, in that the only time that the 1930 Act would be needed – when the shipowner was insolvent – was the very time when it would not be available, was waved away by Lord Goff, who reasserted that the purpose of the 1930 Act was simply to give the third party the same rights as possessed by the insured. The matter has been addressed by the 2010 Act. Under section 9(5), pay to be paid clauses can no longer be relied upon. However, there is an exception for marine policies in section 9(6), which permits pay to be paid clauses in all cases other than claims for death or personal injury. The effect of these provisions is relatively minor, given that pay to be paid clauses are in practice used only by P&I clubs, and the result is that cargo, collision and other claims can be the subject of pay to be paid clauses whereas personal injury claims must be satisfied without any prepayment requirement.

Thirdly, if there are unpaid premiums, section 10 permits the insurers to set off the sum owing against the monies due under the policy. The right of set-off is confined to premiums payable under that policy. There may be other sums owing to the insurers by the insured, eg under other policies, and they are not subject to any right of set-off.

Fourthly, the insurers may have a defence against the insured based on public policy, such as where the insured committed a criminal act giving rise to liability. It was suggested by Mance J in *Total Graphics Ltd v AGF Insurance Ltd*[128] that public policy was no more than a personal bar on a claim by the insured and that it did not preclude an action against the insurers by the innocent third party victim. Those comments were considered by May J in *Komives v Hick Lane Bedding Ltd*,[129] an avoidance case. It was held that there was noth-

[127] *Firma C-Trade SA v Newcastle Protection and Indemnity Association* [1991] 2 AC 1.
[128] [1997] 1 Lloyd's Rep 599.
[129] [2021] EWHC 3139 (QB).

ing in the legislation that afforded the third party any better rights than those possessed by the insured. Mance J's comments were obiter and the same may be said of those of May J, as the issue in that case was non-disclosure of criminality rather than post-contractual criminal conduct.

3.2.4. Obtaining Insurance Information

The 1930 Act made no provision for a third party to be able to ascertain whether a defendant who was, or who was likely to become, insolvent had any valid insurance coverage. Plainly there is no point in pursuing an uninsured insolvent defendant. Before the passing of the 2010 Act, the Court of Appeal in *Re OT Computers*[130] suggested that the third party could obtain the relevant information, but the precise means was not clarified. Section 11 of and schedule 1 to the 2010 Act partially fill this gap, and the rules are mandatory and not capable of being varied by policy terms. Where the insured has become insolvent, and the third party reasonably believes that the insured has incurred liability, the third party may give notice to the insured requiring the production of the basic terms of the policy and details of any disputes between the insured and the insurers. That will permit the third party to make a judgement as to whether, if the claim proceeds, the insurers will ultimately face liability to meet it. However, there is no provision for securing information from the insured short of insolvency: in such a case, the third party must take its chances in the same way as any other litigant: English procedural rules do not provide for 'cards on the table'.[131] Information may alternatively be sought from another person, eg a broker, who is in possession of the relevant details. In all cases, a request that is not satisfied can be enforced by an application to the court. In the case of a dissolved company, its ex-directors and ex-employees may be required to provide the necessary insurance information.

[130] [2004] Lloyd's Rep IR 669.

[131] *West London Pipeline and Storage Ltd v Total UK Ltd* [2008] Lloyd's Rep IR 688; *Peel Port Shareholder Finance Company Ltd v Dornoch Ltd* [2017] EWHC 876 (TCC).

16

Specific Insurances

1. Property Insurance

1.1. The Nature of Property Insurance

Property policies insure against damage to buildings or goods; they do not cover damage to the land itself and they do not extend to consequential financial loss unless extended to business interruption[1] (the issues arising from business interruption insurance, highlighted by the COVID-19 pandemic, are discussed in chapter 19 below). They normally respond to damage suffered by the property in the policy year, whether or not it has been or could have been discovered at that time. Some policies may instead respond to a peril occurring in the policy year and subsequently giving rise to damage. The latter form of cover may give rise to problems in exceptional cases where perils occur in consecutive years and the damage does not become apparent until later: in order to recover, the insured must be able to point to which of the perils was the proximate cause. The insured in *Kelly v Norwich Union Fire and Life Insurance Ltd*[2] held an events occurring policy and came unstuck when a pipe burst under his house on two separate occasions, one before the policy incepted and one during its currency. The insured was unable to prove that the cracking to his walls was the result of the second burst pipe and thus was unable to recover. The result would, of course, have been different if the policy responded to damage and not to the event causing the damage.

Policies may be against specified risks, or they may be written on an 'all risks' basis. The latter type of insurance, used for marine cargoes and other goods in transit, commercial stock and even household property, does not cover every eventuality. All risks policies always contain a series of exclusions, and the effect of an 'all risks' policy is to permit the insured to recover simply by proving that a fortuitous loss has occurred: the burden of proof then switches to the insurers to show that, on the balance of probabilities, one of the exclusions was the proximate cause.[3] The epithet is potentially misleading – a point made in *Tektrol Ltd v International Insurance Co of Hanover Ltd*[4] by Carnwath LJ, who bemoaned

[1] *Re Wright and Pole* (1834) 1 Ad & E 621.
[2] [1989] 2 All ER 888.
[3] *British & Foreign Marine Insurance Co v Gaunt* [1921] 2 AC 41.
[4] [2006] Lloyd's Rep IR 38.

an all risks policy on the basis that 'one has to search long and hard, through a bewildering and apparently comprehensive list of exclusions, to discover the extent to which any risks are in fact covered'.

Property policies are generally written against accidental, sudden or unforeseen events when looked at from the insured's point of view. An event is not accidental if it is inevitable, as in *Leeds Beckett University v Travelers Insurance Company Ltd*,[5] where student accommodation constructed from a disused brewery collapsed because the foundations did not have adequate drainage. The meaning of 'sudden' was considered by the Nova Scotia Court of Appeal in *Zurich Insurance Company Ltd v Halifax Regional Municipality*,[6] which involved hydrocarbon contamination at a transit bus depot in Dartmouth, Nova Scotia. This was traced to a discharge of diesel fuel from an underground pipe at the depot. The Municipality incurred significant costs in cleaning up the contaminated soil and sought indemnity from their insurers. The policy provided coverage for the cost of decontaminating the Municipality's property 'resulting from the sudden and accidental actual, not suspected discharge, release, escape, dispersal, seepage or migration of such contaminants occurring at the premises'. It was conceded that the escape was accidental, the only issue was whether it was 'sudden'. The Court held that the word referred to something 'abrupt, unexpected and unintentional', so that every escape was sudden but there was nothing to limit coverage to short-term effects. The Court gave the example of a dam unexpectedly failing, causing flooding that lasted for several weeks: in ordinary language, it would be said that the flood was sudden and accidental. This reasoning effectively relegates the word 'sudden' to meaning no more than an unexpected event. The authorities are not consistent. In other jurisdictions it has been held that the outcome will depend upon whether by the terms of the policy the event giving rise to the loss has to be sudden, as in *Halifax* itself and also where a sudden mechanical breakdown gave rise to losses,[7] or whether the loss itself has to be sudden, in which case the gradual solidification of a liquid causing damage to a tank is sudden even though the cause is gradual.[8]

The need for the happening of some sort of event leading to property damage means that damage resulting from inherent vice – the very nature of the subject matter – is not insurable.[9] Ordinary wear and tear, which has been defined in *JSM Management Pty Ltd v QBE Insurance (Australia) Ltd*[10] as meaning 'ordinary and natural deterioration or abrasion which an object experiences by its expected contacts between its component parts and outside objects during the period of its natural life expectancy', is also not insurable, although it was decided in this case that damage caused to an area of hardstanding by the use of a heavy container forklift for a period of eight months was not wear and tear as the damage was neither inevitable nor ordinary.

1.2. Fire and Explosion

In determining whether a loss was caused by fire, the court will eschew technical discussions as to the nature of fire: ignition is an essential element; damage by mere overheating or

[5] [2017] EWHC 558 (TCC).
[6] 2021 NSCA 43.
[7] *Sun Alliance & London Insurance Group v North-West Iron Co Ltd* [1974] 2 NSWLR 625.
[8] *Pacific Chemicals Pte Ltd v MSIG Insurance (Singapore) Pte Ltd* [2012] SGHC 198.
[9] For inherent vice, see ch 17 below.
[10] [2011] VSC 339.

scorching will not make the insurers liable.[11] In the absence of an agreement to the contrary, the cause of the fire is normally irrelevant, eg where the fire is the result of an explosion[12] or lightning. A fire caused by the negligence of the insured will not preclude a claim since covering this eventuality is 'one of the objects of insurance against fire':[13] when an insured lit a fire in her grate, forgetting that she had hidden jewels there, the insurers were held liable.[14] Similarly, an act of arson will not prevent an insured from claiming, unless committed – or colluded in – by the insured,[15] in which case public policy will preclude a claim.[16] For example, in *Porter v Zurich Insurance Co*,[17] the court dismissed a claim under a policy of insurance for losses caused by a fire which the claimant had himself started, finding recovery to be contrary to public policy, the general law of insurance and the specific terms of the policy.

Once a fire has ignited, then consequential damage to the insured property will be covered, such as explosion, damage by smoke or by the roof collapsing on to insured goods as a result of being weakened by the fire,[18] as will 'any loss resulting from an apparently necessary and *bona fide* effort to put out a fire',[19] such as damage caused by spraying water to extinguish the fire or by action to prevent fire spreading to the property.[20] However, the property must be affected by fire or by 'an actual existing state of peril of fire, and not merely a fear of fire'.[21]

Explosion in the absence of fire is generally an insured peril. The word 'explosion' has been given its technical rather than colloquial meaning by the courts, so that what is required is a physical or chemical reaction:[22] on that basis, it was held in *Commonwealth Smelting Ltd v Guardian Royal Exchange Assurance*[23] that the fracturing of an engine casing by a part of the engine breaking off and being forced outwards by compressed air was not an explosion. The fact that a bystander would have described the events as an 'explosion' – and it would indeed be difficult to think of any other possibility – did not sway the Court of Appeal. It was held in *Aegis Electrical and Gas International Services Co Ltd v Continental Casualty Co*,[24] following *Commonwealth Smelting*, that what was required was 'violence and manifest violence[25] … [and] a shattering destruction [caused by] a very rapid chemical or nuclear reaction, or the bursting out of gas or vapour under pressure'. That test was not

[11] *Austin v Drewe* (1816) 4 Camp 360; *Fleming v Hislop* (1886) 11 App Cas 686; *Tempus Shipping Co v Louis Dreyfus & Co* [1930] 1 KB 699.

[12] *Everett v London Assurance* (1865) 19 CBNS 126.

[13] *Shaw v Robberds, Hawkes and Stone* (1837) 6 Ad & E 75, 84 (Lord Denman CJ).

[14] *Harris v Poland* [1941] 1 KB 462.

[15] The burden of proving the insured's involvement being on the insurers: *McLennan v Insurance Australia Ltd* [2014] NSWCA 300.

[16] *Midland Insurance Co v Smith a* (1881) 6 QBD 561, 568 (Watkin Williams J).

[17] [2009] EWHC 376 (Comm).

[18] *In re An Arbitration between Hooley Hill Rubber and Chemical Co Ltd, and Royal Insurance Co Ltd* [1920] 1 KB 257, 271 (Scrutton LJ).

[19] *Stanley v Western Insurance Co* (1868) LR 3 Ex 71.

[20] *Canada Rice Mills Ltd v Union Marine and General Insurance Co Ltd* [1941] AC 55; *Symington & Co v Union Insurance Society of Canton Ltd* (1928) 34 Com Cas 23.

[21] *The Knight of St Michael* [1898] 30, 35 (Gorell Barnes J).

[22] eg a volcanic eruption: *Martini Investments v McGinn* [2001] Lloyd's Rep IR 374.

[23] [1984] 2 Lloyd's Rep 608.

[24] [2008] Lloyd's Rep IR 17.

[25] It has been held in New Zealand in *Golden Bay Cement Co Ltd v South British Insurance Co Ltd* [1980] 1 NZLR 348 that there can be an explosion even where nobody was aware of it, as where the roof of a silo was lifted off and dropped back down again by reason of air pressure, the only sound being a hissing which was inaudible against the other noise on the premises.

satisfied by the bulging and cracking of a reactor unit following an attempt to repressurise it after a power cut.[26]

Policies may impose upon the insured obligations to take steps to minimise the risk of fire. Commercial premises are generally subject to such conditions, particularly where the business activity involves heat processes. There may, for example, be an obligation not to store oily rags overnight[27] or to store combustible material away from machinery.[28] The use of oxyacetylene cutting equipment and blowlamps without proper safety precautions may be prohibited.[29] Restaurants and hotels are subject to requirements for regular maintenance of kitchen equipment to ensure that ducts, extractors and the like are kept free from grease.[30] It will be recalled from chapter eight above that sections 10 and 11 of the Insurance Act 2015 prevent an insurer from relying upon a breach of a policy term if the circumstances of the loss were unrelated to the term, so that if an insured fails to maintain a sprinkler system the insurers cannot plead that as a defence to a claim for theft from a break-in.

1.3. Burglary and Theft

Where terms of art such as 'theft', 'burglary' or 'robbery' are used, they are given the definition ascribed to them by the criminal law unless the policy expressly provides another meaning. Theft is defined by section 1 of the Theft Act 1968 as occurring if one person 'dishonestly[31] appropriates property belonging to another with the intention of permanently depriving[32] the other of it'.[33] That definition is wider than it might appear at first sight, and, as was seen in chapter nine above, it was held in *Dobson v General Accident Fire and Life Assurance Corporation plc*[34] that there is theft where the owner of property voluntarily transfers possession to a fraudulent buyer whose payment is not honoured. The term 'theft' may be redefined by the policy, eg by requiring that the theft is 'committed by persons present on the premises of the assured': it was held in *Deutsche Genossenschaftsbank v Burnhope*[35] that all of the elements of theft had to be satisfied on the premises, so there was

[26] See also *Pacific Chemicals Pte Ltd v MSIG Insurance (Singapore) Pte Ltd* [2012] SGHC 198 (buckling of a tank following a change in temperature was not an explosion).

[27] *Transthene Packaging Co v Royal Insurance* [1996] LRLR 32.

[28] *Wheeldon Brothers Waste Ltd v Millennium Insurance Company Ltd* [2018] EWHC 834 (TCC), where it was held that storage required some degree of permanence and that combustible material did not simply mean paper and cardboard that might catch fire.

[29] *LEC (Liverpool) Ltd v Glover* [2001] Lloyd's Rep IR 315; *Bonner Williams v Peter Lindsay Leisure Ltd* [2001] 1 All ER (Comm) 1140.

[30] *Paine v Catlins* [2005] Lloyd's Rep IR 665; *The Seashell of Lisson Grove Ltd v Aviva Insurance Ltd* [2011] EWHC 1761 (Comm).

[31] If goods are seized by strikers demanding payment of wages there is no theft because there is no dishonesty: *Clothing Management Technology Ltd v Beazley Solutions Ltd* [2012] EWHC 727 (QB). See also *Nishina Trading Co Ltd v Chiyoda Fire and Marine Insurance Co Ltd* [1969] 2 All ER 776.

[32] It is for this reason that joyriding does not constitute theft, but there is a separate offence in s 12 of the Theft Act 1968 of taking a conveyance without permission.

[33] In *Masefield AG v Amlin Corporate Member Ltd, The Bunga Melati Dua* [2011] EWCA Civ 24, the Court of Appeal recognised the extended meaning of 'theft' under the Theft Act 1968, s 6(1), which provides 'A person appropriating property belonging to another without meaning the other permanently to lose the thing itself is nevertheless to be regarded as having the intention of permanently depriving the other of it if his intention is to treat the thing as his own to dispose of regardless of the other's rights'.

[34] [1990] 1 QB 274, approved in *R v Gomez* 1993] 1 All ER 1.

[35] [1993] 2 Lloyd's Rep 518.

no cover when securities were honestly collected from the premises by an agent and then later given to the agent's principal, who dishonestly appropriated them.

Burglary is defined by section 9 of the Theft Act 1968 as entering a building as a trespasser with intent to steal, cause grievous bodily harm or do unlawful damage to property. Robbery is, by section 8 of the Theft Act 1968, committed by a person if 'he steals, and immediately before or at the time of doing so, and in order to do so, he uses force on any person or puts or seeks to put any person in fear of being then and there subjected to force'. In *Canelhas Comercio Importacao e Exportacao Ltd v Wooldridge*,[36] a jeweller's policy excluded robbery at a time when the premises were open for business or when any employee was present. The insured's family was kidnapped and, under orders, he went to the premises during working hours and removed emeralds to be used as a ransom payment. This loss was held not to be a robbery within this exclusion, because there was no threat of violence to anyone on the premises when the emeralds were removed. Commonly, a burglary policy requires violent and forcible entry onto the premises. The word 'violent' requires some aggression to be demonstrated, whereas the word 'forcible' simply means any form of physical effort, including turning a key in a lock, so clandestinely stealing keys to a building from the insured's car and using them to enter the building is 'forcible' but not 'violent'.[37] The policy may also provide cover for forcible and violent entry when the premises are unoccupied, or the use of or threat of violence when they are occupied: it was held in *Anders & Kern Ltd v CGU Insurance Plc*[38] that there had to be an actual threat of violence, so that the insured could not recover when a nightwatchman left premises unoccupied fearing that he might be in danger.

Employee theft falls within the meaning of 'theft,'[39] but typically is excluded from theft cover and instead is available under a fidelity insurance extension to the cover. An extension of this type will include embezzlement of money and securities, but it does not extend to an employer indemnifying a customer against fraud committed against it by one of the employer's employees, as that is liability rather than first party loss.[40] The trigger for fidelity coverage is dishonesty on the part of the employee, and some policies provide that the employee's 'manifest intent' must be to steal from or defraud the employer, which has been held to mean 'a clear, obvious or apparent' intent.[41]

Theft and burglary policies contain a number of safeguards. Goods in transit policies provide that the subject matter must not be 'left unattended'. The root case on this wording is *Starfire Diamond Rings v Angel*,[42] where the driver of a vehicle parked it on the roadside, walked 37 yards and then devoted his full attention to a tree with his back to the vehicle. The Court of Appeal held that he had left the vehicle unattended, the test being whether there was someone present and able to intervene in the event of attempted theft. It has been held

[36] [2004] Lloyd's Rep IR 915.

[37] *Nash v Prudential Assurance Co Ltd* [1989] 1 Lloyd's Rep 379. See also *Re Calf and Sun Insurance Office* [1926] 2 KB 366, where goods stolen by a person who entered the premises, hid in the basement until they were closed and then broke into the ground and first floors were held to be lost by violent and forcible means. That decision throws doubt on *Re George and Goldsmiths and General Burglary Insurance Association Ltd* [1899] 1 QB 595, where the facts were not dissimilar but there was held not to have been violent and forcible entry.

[38] [2008] Lloyd's Rep IR 460.

[39] *Ted Baker Plc v Axa Insurance UK Ltd* [2012] EWHC 1406 (Comm).

[40] *New Hampshire Insurance Co v Philips Electronics North America Corporation* 1999] Lloyd's Rep IR 58.

[41] ibid.

[42] [1962] 2 Lloyd's Rep 217. See also *Sanger v Beazley* [1999] Lloyd's Rep IR 424 and *QBE Insurance Ltd v Patterson Fine Jewellery Pty Ltd* (2004) 13 ANZ Ins Cas 61–610, in each of which the driver visited an indoor facility for the same purpose.

in later cases that even if the driver can see the vehicle, it is left unattended if he is unable to reach it quickly,[43] but it is not left unattended if the driver is in close proximity and his or her back is turned for only a few seconds.[44] There is a requirement for the premises not to be left unoccupied,[45] left unattended[46] or without an inhabitant for more than a given number of days. Burglar alarms are generally to be fitted to commercial premises, and obligations in respect of alarms have been construed generously. In *Victor Melik & Co Ltd v Norwich Union Fire Insurance Society Ltd*,[47] a condition specifying that a burglar alarm be kept in working order was not broken when the alarm had, unknown to the insured, stopped working, and in *AC Ward & Sons Ltd v Catlin (Five) (No 2)*[48] a condition that 'all defects … must be promptly remedied' was confined by the court to defects in the burglar alarm of which the insured was aware.

It is common for property policies on cargo, jewellery and other valuables to incorporate a clause excluding 'mysterious disappearance and stocktaking losses', ie excluding coverage for loss of property if the cause of the loss cannot be identified. Such clauses are found even where the policy is written on an all risks basis, but it is not clear what significance they can have in a policy where the insured merely has to show loss in order to recover. The courts have struggled with the point. In *Widefree Ltd v Brit Insurance Ltd*,[49] the insured's jewellery shop was visited by two women who examined some items but did not buy anything. It was later discovered that a valuable ring had gone missing. The insurers' argument that the disappearance was mysterious was undermined by CCTV footage showing theft by the women, and the clause did not in any event apply because the loss was not discovered during stocktaking, but the court was of the view that if the insurers could show that there was no explanation for the loss then the exclusion would apply. In *AXL Resources Ltd v Antares Underwriting Services Ltd*,[50] the claimant metal trading company was insured against all risks of loss, under a Lloyd's marine open cargo policy, which incorporated a clause excluding 'mysterious disappearance and stocktaking losses'. A cargo of cobalt belonging to the assured disappeared from a warehouse in Antwerp in unexplained circumstances sometime between 21 October 2008 and 27 January 2009, and the insurers denied liability when a claim was brought. The insured subsequently sought summary judgment. The insured's case was that because the policy covered all risks, the insured had to prove no more than the fact of the accidental loss, and it was not its burden to disprove mysterious disappearance. In the event, by the time of the trial, the Belgian police had gathered evidence of an organised theft and accordingly it was held that the insured was entitled to summary judgment. Although this meant that there was no need to explore the relationship between the all risks policy and the exclusion clause, Gloster J did comment that while it is for the insured to prove that there has been a fortuitous loss, thereafter, the burden of proof switches to the insurer to prove that the loss fell within the 'mysterious disappearance' exclusion.

[43] *Ingleton Ltd v General Accident Fire and Life Assurance Corp* [1967] 2 Lloyd's Rep 179.

[44] *Langford v Legal and General Assurance Society* [1986] 2 Lloyd's Rep 103; *Sanger v Beazley* [1999] Lloyd's Rep IR 424.

[45] Premises are occupied if the unoccupancy is purely temporary: *Winicofsky v Army and Navy General Assurance Association* (1919) 88 LJKB 1111; *Simmonds v Cockell* [1920] 1 KB 843.

[46] Held in *Milton Furniture Ltd v Brit Insurance Ltd* [2015] EWCA Civ 671 to have the same meaning as in goods in transit cases, a test not satisfied on the facts of the case by two employees sleeping on the premises.

[47] 1980] 1 Lloyd's Rep 523.

[48] [2009] EWHC 3122 (Comm).

[49] [2011] Lloyd's Rep IR 63.

[50] [2010] EWHC 3244 (Comm).

1.4. Natural Perils

Wording commonly found in property policies refers to 'storm, tempest and flood'. Dictionary definitions of 'storm' refer to prolonged wind and rain, although in one Scottish case it has been held that a snowstorm not accompanied by high winds, leading to the collapse of a roof from the weight of the snow, constituted storm damage.[51] A 'tempest' is a more violent storm.[52] A 'flood' in the context of this phrase takes its meaning from 'storm' and 'tempest', and thus requires water accumulating in a 'violent, sudden and abnormal' fashion,[53] but in the absence of those surrounding words the existence of a flood is measured by the volume of water and not the manner in which it reached its unintended destination.[54] The key decision on the matter is now *Tate Gallery (Trustees) v Duffy Construction Ltd*,[55] in which work was being carried out in the basement of the Tate Gallery in London. Work stopped for a few days for the Easter break, and when the workers returned they found that a pipe had become detached from a water main, leading to an ingress of water to the depth of 1.4 metres. Jackson J could not contemplate that an accumulation of water of that depth did not constitute a flood simply because it had not been the result of some violent event, and it was instead ruled that it was necessary to consider

> (a) whether the source of the water was natural; (b) whether the source of the water was external or internal; (c) the quantity of water; (d) the manner of its arrival; (e) the area and character of the property upon which the water was deposited; (f) whether the arrival of that water was an abnormal event.

Applying those criteria, there was clearly a flood. There is also coverage for 'bursting or overflowing of water tanks, apparatus or pipes', although what is required here is some form of internal pressure causing the release of water and not an external event such as an object being dropped onto a pipe and fracturing it.[56]

---

2. War and Related Risks

2.1. War

War and related risks are commonly excluded from property policies, and in the marine market the standard Institute Hull and Cargo Clauses exclude all war risks, which are instead insurable under specific Institute War Risks Clauses. The meaning of the various terms used to describe war and related risks have been the subject of numerous decisions.

A war between nations exists even if there has not been a declaration of war as long as the court determines that, in fact, a state of war exists.[57] The word 'war' includes civil war,

[51] *Glasgow Training Group (Motor Trade) Ltd v Lombard Continental Plc* 21 November 1988, unreported.
[52] *Oddy v Phoenix Assurance Co Ltd* [1966] 1 Lloyd's Rep 134; *Young v Sun Alliance Insurance* [1976] 2 Lloyd's Rep 189, 192.
[53] *Young v Sun Alliance Insurance* [1976] 2 Lloyd's Rep 189. See ch 9 above.
[54] *Rohan Investments Ltd v Cunningham* [1999] Lloyd's Rep IR 190.
[55] [2007] Lloyd's Rep IR 758, followed in *Tyco Fire & Integrated Solutions (UK) Ltd v Rolls-Royce Motor Cars Ltd* [2007] EWHC 3159 (TCC) (there was no appeal on this point).
[56] *Computer & Systems Engineering Plc v John Lelliott (Ilford) Ltd* (1990) 54 BLR 1.
[57] *Kawasaki Kisen Kabushiki Kaisha of Kobe v Bantham SS Co Ltd* [1939] 2 KB 544.

although it is usual to refer to both in the policy. It has been said by Mustill J in *Spinney's (1948) Ltd v Royal Insurance Co Ltd*[58] that in determining whether there is a state of civil war, the court must consider: whether there were opposing sides; what the objectives of those sides were and how they set about pursuing them; and what was the scale both of the conflict and of its effect on public order and on the life of the inhabitants. Applying these criteria to Lebanon in 1975, he said that although the fighting was serious, it was not the case that one side was seeking to wrest political power from the other or to seize power by violence: for instance, the president had been criticised and his resignation suggested, but there had been no attempt at that time to remove him by violent means, and the prime minister enjoyed fairly broad support. Although the government was largely powerless to prevent the fighting, no faction sought to remove it. In addition, he took the view that there were no 'sides' in existence because there was a lack of common leadership or unanimity of purpose. The fighting was sporadic and incoherent. He therefore concluded that matters had not advanced from 'massive civil strife and virtual anarchy to the stage of civil war' at that time.[59] Conflict short of civil war, such as guerrilla war, will also constitute 'war' for insurance purposes, as long as the guerrillas are purporting to act on behalf of a group that asserts sovereignty as a government.[60] An uprising, such as the Irish Rebellion of 1916, may be defined as a 'war' for this purpose.[61]

War risks clauses refer also to civil commotion, rebellion, insurrection and military or usurped power. For a civil commotion:

> The element of turbulence or tumult is essential; an organised conspiracy to commit criminal acts, where there is no tumult or disturbance until after the acts, does not amount to civil commotion. It is not, however, necessary to show the existence of any outside organisation at whose instigation the acts were done.[62]

There need be no evidence of a revolt against the government, but 'the disturbances must have sufficient cohesion to prevent them from being the work of a mindless mob'.[63] Clearly, such would also amount to a riot, but civil commotion has been described as one of the various stages between riot and civil war.[64] So, for instance, fighting between different factions in Lebanon in the 1970s was held to be a civil commotion.[65] Where the exception in the policy relates to 'civil commotion assuming the proportions of or amounting to a popular rising', then, while it is impossible to be precise about the meaning of these additional words, the commotion 'must involve a really substantial proportion of the populace, although obviously not all the population need participate, and … there should be tumult and violence on a large scale'.[66]

In that same case, Mustill J also considered the exceptions for rebellion and insurrection. He referred to the *Oxford English Dictionary*, where rebellion is defined as 'organised

[58] [1980] 1 Lloyd's Rep 406.
[59] ibid 431–32.
[60] *Pan American World Airways Inc v Aetna Casualty & Surety Co* [1975] 1 Lloyd's Rep 77.
[61] *Curtis & Sons v Matthews* [1919] 1 KB 425.
[62] *Levy v Assicurazioni Generali* [1940] AC 791, 800 (Luxmoore LJ).
[63] *Spinney's (1948) Ltd v Royal Insurance Co Ltd* [1980] 1 Lloyd's Rep 406, 438 (Mustill J).
[64] *Republic of Bolivia v Indemnity Mutual Marine Assurance Co Ltd* [1909] 1 KB 785, 801 (Farewell LJ).
[65] *Spinney's (1948) Ltd v Royal Insurance Co Ltd* [1980] 1 Lloyd's Rep 406. See also *Cooper v General Accident Fire and Life Assurance Corpn* (1922) 128 LT 481; *Motor Union Insurance Co Ltd v Boggan* (1923) 130 LT 588. Contrast the situation in Palestine in 1936, when the civil authorities were still in control and the violence, although severe, was to some extent contained by the authorities: *Levy v Assicurazioni Generali* [1940] AC 791.
[66] *Spinney's (1948) Ltd v Royal Insurance Co Ltd* [1980] 1 Lloyd's Rep 406, 438 (Mustill J).

resistance to the ruler or government of one's country; insurrection, revolt'. To this Mustill J added 'the purpose of the resistance must be to supplant the existing rulers or at least to deprive them of authority over part of their territory'.[67] An insurrection is 'an incipient or limited rebellion' and implies 'a lesser degree of organisation' than a rebellion. But the two shade into each other, and in both cases there must be 'action against the government with a view to supplanting it'.[68] Although they would normally involve personal violence, it has been held that economic sabotage, such as the blowing up of an oil pipeline in Mozambique, can come within both terms.[69] This action amounted to an insurrection: there was widespread internal discontent with the Frelimo government in Mozambique; the group which committed the act, Renamo, had the aim of overthrowing that government; Renamo had substantial support from large numbers of Mozambican dissidents and from the Rhodesian and South African governments; and yet it could not be said that Renamo was merely a puppet organisation of those governments, which might have taken away the crucial element of internal strife.[70]

'Military power' is the action of invading forces from outside the country, including an air raid,[71] or the damage caused by the domestic army attempting to repel such an invasion or defeat rebels.[72] 'Usurped power' 'consists of the arrogation to itself by the mob of a law-making and law-enforcing power which properly belongs to the sovereign'.[73] In other words, there are elements of treason, organisation and leadership, and in the spectrum of violent disturbances, it is therefore closer to rebellion or civil war than to riot. Even if the action is not designed to overthrow the government, it will amount to a usurpation of power if it involves taking on some of the functions of government.

There are important causation points arising in relation to war clauses. The loss in question has to be proximately caused by the event in question and must not be too remote from it. The mere fact that a war or invasion is threatened cannot, for example, be regarded as the proximate cause of looting, just as the existence of a wartime blackout causing the insured to trip and suffer injury will not justify war being regarded as the proximate cause of the injury.[74]

2.2. Riot

English law has legislated against rioters since 1549. At common law, a riot constituted disorderly conduct by three or more persons, and attracted the death penalty. The Riot Act 1714 provided a measure of compensation to those whose property was damaged by rioters, to be paid by the local authority (hundred) on the principle that it was the authority's duty to protect inhabitants against rioters. Liability was strict, so there was no need for a claimant to prove any fault on the part of the authority. Insurers who insured property against riot had subrogation rights against the local authority.[75] The 1714 Act referred to

[67] ibid 436.
[68] ibid 436–37.
[69] *National Oil Company of Zimbabwe (Private) Ltd v Sturge* [1991] 2 Lloyd's Rep 281.
[70] ibid. Since this meant the insurers were not liable on the policy, Saville J did not consider fully whether this was an act of rebellion or civil war.
[71] *Rogers v Whittaker* [1917] 1 KB 942.
[72] *Curtis & Sons v Matthews* [1919] 1 KB 425.
[73] *Spinney's (1948) Ltd v Royal Insurance Co Ltd* [1980] 1 Lloyd's Rep 406, 435 (Mustill J).
[74] *Coxe v Employers' Liability Assurance Corporation Ltd* [1916] 2 KB 629, discussed in ch 9 above.
[75] *Mason v Sainsbury* (1782) 3 Doug 61, the Gordon Riots.

persons 'unlawfully, riotously and tumultuously' assembled and who failed to disperse after the public reading of a statutory proclamation, giving rise to a phrase that has passed into modern usage: 'reading the riot act'. The 1714 definition was amended by the Seditious Meetings Act 1817 to read 'riotously or tumultuously assembled', although the 1714 wording was restored by the Remedies against the Hundred Act 1827 until further altered by the Riot (Damages) Act 1886 to read 'persons riotously and tumultuously assembled together'.

The insurance cases on 'riot' applied the legal definition, leading to the bizarre decision in *London and Lancashire Fire Insurance Co v Bolands*,[76] in which recovery for losses sustained in an armed robbery of a bakery was held to fall within a policy exclusion for 'riot' in that it had been conducted by armed men who had caused the insured to fear for his life. The law was modified by section 1 of the Public Order Act 1986, under which a riot occurs when 12 or more people, who are present together, threaten unlawful violence for a common purpose in such a manner as would cause a person of reasonable firmness to fear for his personal safety.

Compensation under the 1886 Act was to be paid by the local authority responsible for policing in the affected area. A series of cases decided under the 1886 Act concluded: that the words 'riotously' and 'tumultuously' were not cumulative, so it sufficed if either was satisfied, and that a 'tumult' meant a gathering of considerable size and agitation;[77] that compensation was limited to property damage and did not extend to financial loss flowing from an inability to carry on business consequent on that damage;[78] that a body exercising contracted-out public functions, including the operation of a detention centre, could recover for damage inflicted by rioters at the premises;[79] and that a public liability policy held by a police authority covering its legal liability to pay damages extended to compensation under the 1886 Act.[80] As a result of the last of these decisions, some liability insurers chose to exclude expressly liability for compensation awarded under the 1886 Act.

The law was transformed with the repeal of the 1886 Act by the Riot Compensation Act 2016, as supplemented by the Riot Compensation Regulations 2017.[81] This Act addresses for the first time the relationship between available compensation and insurance. A claim for compensation may be made against the local policing authority, again on the basis of strict liability, where there has been riot as defined by the Public Order Act 1986, and the word 'tumult' has been removed from the legislation. The affected subject matter may be a building, a motor vehicle or property on land being used for business purposes or within a building. If the property is uninsured or underinsured, then the claim may be made by the person whose property was damaged. If, by contrast, the property is insured and payment has been made under the policy, that insurance payment is to be deducted from the compensation payable to the victim under the Act and instead the claim may be brought directly by the insurers. The sum available is capped at £1 million per claim, and the amount is to be assessed on a fair and reasonable basis. Loss suffered by the rioters themselves is excluded. The Act and Regulations lay down detailed procedures for the making and handling of claims, and for appeals against decisions on the award of compensation.

[76] [1924] AC 836.
[77] *Mitsui Sumitomo Insurance Co (Europe) Ltd v Mayor's Office for Policing and Crime* [2014] EWCA Civ 682.
[78] *Mayor's Office for Policing and Crime v Mitsui Sumitomo Insurance Co (Europe) Ltd* [2016] UKSC 18.
[79] *Yarl's Wood Immigration Centre Ltd v Bedfordshire Police Authority* [2009] EWCA Civ 1110.
[80] *Bedfordshire Police Authority v Constable* [2009] EWCA Civ 64.
[81] SI 2017/371.

3. Accident Insurance

An accident policy is one which covers death or personal injury as the result of an accident. Such policies provide for a fixed sum to be paid and since such a policy is not an indemnity, then, as has been seen, the insurers have no right of subrogation and the insured can recover not only under the policy, but also from the tortfeasor.[82] It is, however, not uncommon for accident policies to include a term requiring the insured to declare the existence of other policies covering the same loss. The Life Assurance Act 1774 has been held to apply to such policies.[83]

Much of the litigation on accident policies concerns the issue of whether the loss was caused by an 'accident': this involves construing the word within the terms of the contract and deciding whether the cause – as determined by common law principles unless there are express terms on causation – was accidental.[84] The issue of causation arose in *Blackburn Rovers Football and Athletic Club v Avon Insurance*,[85] where the insurance policy in question provided that there would be cover in the event that the insured player sustained accidental bodily injury which, independently of any other cause, occasioned the player permanent total disablement. The claim made by Blackburn Rovers related to one of their players, MD, who suffered an injury during training on 21 October 1997. He underwent a scan and physiotherapy, and consulted a number of specialists, but despite attempts to return to fitness and to the game, MD retired from professional football on 5 July 1999. It was claimed that the retirement was a result of an injury causing him total disablement within the meaning of the policy. The insurers declined to pay out on the policy, submitting that MD was suffering from constitutional degenerative disc disease, meaning that any back pain or disc lesion he suffered during training was caused wholly or in part and directly or indirectly by his degenerative disc disease, thereby disqualifying him from the policy. After taking the expert evidence into account, Dobbs J held that while it was proven that MD did suffer an accidental bodily injury on 21 October 1997, and it was on that date that he suffered permanent total disablement, the accidental bodily injury was not sustained solely and independently of any other cause.[86] In fact, Dobbs J held that the medical evidence was 'overwhelming one way' in favour of the argument that the cause was the degenerative disc disease. In any event, she concluded that 'it need not be *the* cause, so long as it is *a* cause, in order to fail to come within the insuring clause'.[87]

It has been said that 'accident' implies 'some violence, casualty, or vis major' and that it is manifested in some external injury,[88] and indeed it is common for policies to use words such as 'outward, violent and visible means' or 'violent, accidental, external and visible means'. These phrases should be taken as a whole and not broken down into their component parts.[89] It seems that, although physical injury is required, it may be sufficient that such

[82] See ch 12 above.
[83] *Shilling v Accidental Death* (1857) 2 H & N 42.
[84] See ch 9 above.
[85] [2006] EWHC 840 (QB).
[86] ibid [96]–[108].
[87] ibid [108].
[88] *Sinclair v The Maritime Passengers' Assurance Co* (1861) 3 El & El 478, 485 (Cockburn CJ).
[89] *De Souza v Home and Overseas Insurance Co Ltd* [1995] LRLR 453, 462 (Mustill LJ).

injury is purely internal in the sense of not being visible. Drinking poison can, therefore, amount to an accident, even though its effects do not manifest themselves externally on the body.[90] Nervous shock, on the other hand, is not an injury which comes within the terms of an accident policy, unless the shock suffered has some physical consequences: where a policy covered accidental injury which prevented the insured from working and the nervous shock he suffered did so incapacitate him, then he was able to claim.[91]

As has been seen in chapter 10, insurers have been keen to reduce their liability for accidental injury or death by extending the search for the cause of the injury or by attempting to exclude liability where the insured has failed to take particular precautions.[92] In *Marcel Beller Ltd v Hayden*,[93] a personal accident policy covered death caused by an accident but excluded death 'directly or indirectly resulting from deliberate exposure to exceptional danger or insured's own criminal act'. The motorist, who was killed, had driven with a blood-alcohol level more than three times the permitted maximum and had crashed while taking a corner at a speed in excess of the permitted limit. Judge Edgar Fay said that the crash was an accident. It would only have not been an accident if 'the running of the danger was a conscious act of volition',[94] and voluntarily exposing oneself to risk was not the same as deliberate exposure to risk: speeding was dangerous, but there was nothing to show that the driver had consciously taken on that risk; rather, the fact that he was drunk would suggest that he would have been less aware of it.[95] However, although the judge concluded that this was an accident, the claim was defeated by the exclusion. Therefore, a criminal act of inadvertence or negligence would not have defeated the claim, but here he had driven while drunk and had driven dangerously, and these actions were, either 'directly or indirectly', causes of the accident.

In *Morley and Morley v United Friendly Insurance plc*,[96] where the policy excluded injury which resulted from 'wilful exposure to needless peril', the deceased was held not to have wilfully exposed himself to needless peril by jumping on the bumper of a car driven by his fiancée. It is not enough to show that 'intentional acts done by the insured resulted in his being exposed' to needless peril. Moreover, the exposure to peril must go beyond negligent exposure to needless peril: there must be shown to have been 'a conscious act of volition, which can include recklessness, directed at the running of the risk',[97] or else it must be shown that

> at the time of his actions the insured was mindful of a real risk of the kind of injury for which benefit was provided by the policy and that he either intended to run that risk or exposed himself to it not caring whether he sustained such injury or not.[98]

[90] *Cole v Accident Insurance Co Ltd* (1889) 5 TLR 736 (the claim failed on the wording in the policy which excluded liability for death by poison).

[91] *Pugh v The London, Brighton and South Coast Railway Co* [1896] 2 QB 248, particularly 253 (AJ Smith LJ).

[92] See also *Cornish v Accident Insurance Co Ltd* (1889) 23 QBD 453.

[93] [1978] QB 694.

[94] ibid 704.

[95] An earlier case on drunken driving was more cautious: it seemed to have made a difference that the driver had not become deliberately drunk, nor put himself deliberately into a position where he would drive while drunk, so that even though in the end he did drive, the judge regarded this as an act of folly rather than premeditation: *James v British General Insurance Co Ltd* [1927] 2 KB 311, 325 (Roche J).

[96] [1993] 1 WLR 996.

[97] ibid 1000 (Neill LJ).

[98] ibid 1004 (Beldam LJ).

It is necessary to consider all the circumstances, but most particularly, the likelihood of the insured injury happening if the risk is taken, and the opportunity for reflection before the risk is taken. The test is to ask whether the insured 'appreciated that he was exposing himself to the risk at least of fracture of one of the major bones of the body or that he embarked on that conduct not caring whether he sustained such injury or not'.[99] If the answer to either of these questions is yes, then the insurers are not liable. Here, Beldam LJ thought the answer to both was no. It was not reasonable to infer from the momentary act of stupidity in jumping onto the bumper of the car that the deceased appreciated that he was exposing himself to the peril of any injury; after all, he knew the driver was sober and that, as his fiancée, she loved him. Such an exclusion will, however, probably mean the insurers will not be liable if the insured takes part in some form of extreme sport, such as motor racing, hang-gliding or boxing, because there is an appreciable risk of injury and the insured will, presumably, have had time to reflect on that risk, though the insurers may be liable where the insured takes part in a contact sport like football.[100]

Mustill LJ, in *De Souza v Home and Overseas Insurance Co Ltd*,[101] found the authorities on accident were not only confusing and contradictory, but they also led to conclusions which defied common sense. He defined accident as involving 'the idea of something fortuitous and unexpected, as opposed to something proceeding from natural causes; and injury caused by accident is to be regarded as the antithesis to bodily infirmity by disease in the ordinary course of events'.[102] However, he was, perhaps, more struck by a less technical test: referring to the heat stroke which led to the death of the insured in that case, he said:

> If one … asked an ordinary literate lay member of the public whether this sad event entailed that Mr De Souza had been the victim of an accidental bodily injury, I believe that he or she would say: – 'Of course not'.[103]

He concluded that there were two categories of accident.[104] The first is where 'the injury is the natural result of a fortuitous and unexpected cause'. Here, 'the element of accident manifests itself in the cause of the injury',[105] as, for instance, where the insured is hit by a train.[106] The second is where 'the injury is the fortuitous and unexpected result of a natural cause'.[107] Here, 'the element of accident manifests itself, not in the cause, but in the result', as where someone is doing something ordinary and normal which unexpectedly leads to an injury, such as the insured who, while putting on a sock, scratched his leg with a thumbnail and died as a result of the wound becoming infected.[108]

An injury is not caused by an accident, Mustill LJ said, 'when it is the natural result of a natural cause'.[109] Someone who dies as a result of an undetected heart condition is not killed by an accident, but by natural causes. It is the same if the heart attack, which kills that person, is brought on by running for a train. There was no accident when the insured,

[99] ibid.
[100] ibid 1000 (Neill LJ).
[101] [1995] LRLR 453.
[102] ibid 458.
[103] ibid 454.
[104] ibid 458–59.
[105] ibid 458.
[106] *Lawrence v Accident Insurance Co Ltd* (1881) 45 LT 29.
[107] *De Souza v Home and Overseas Insurance Co Ltd* [1995] LRLR 453, 458.
[108] *Mardorf v Accident Insurance Co Ltd* [1903] 1 KB 584.
[109] *De Souza v Home and Overseas Insurance Co Ltd* [1995] LRLR 453, 459.

during the course of his employment, ejected a customer from licensed premises and died because this exertion strained his heart, which, unbeknown to him, was weak.[110] Here, there is no element of intervening chance: the person deliberately ran for the train and the publican intended to eject the customer. There is nothing, according to the common understanding of the word, that could be described as accidental in either example. Similarly, when Mr De Souza chose to overexpose himself to the sun on holiday and as a result died of sunstroke, it was no accident.[111] It does not become an accident merely because the consequences of the deliberate action were not foreseen, and therefore not actually intended, so long as those consequences follow naturally from the deliberate action:

> A man must be taken to intend the ordinary consequences of his acts, and the fact that he did not foresee the particular consequence or expect the particular injury does not make the injury accidental if, in the circumstances, it was the natural and direct consequence of what he did, without the intervention of any fortuitous cause.[112]

So, in the case on the publican, it was said 'It is true that Scarr did not foresee the effect, but this, in my opinion, cannot make it accidental if it was the natural and direct consequence' of a deliberate act of the deceased.[113] In *Weyerhaesur v Evans*,[114] when Mr Weyerhaesur died as the result of an infection, which originated in a pimple, his estate was unable to prove that the pimple had been treated by a friend and that this was the cause of the infection; therefore, the insurers were not liable on an accident policy. Another illustration of this principle is provided by *Dhak v Insurance Co of North America (UK) Ltd*.[115] A nurse, who was covered by a personal accident insurance policy, suffered an accidental injury to her back at work. To ease the pain, she began to drink heavily and six months later died in her sleep as a result of choking on her own vomit. Neill LJ concluded that as a nurse she must have known the risks associated with heavy drinking and her deliberate assumption of those risks was the proximate cause of her death, not the accident. He said that where the insured undertook a deliberate action that led to injury, it must be asked, did she intend to inflict the injury on herself or take a calculated risk of suffering injury, or was the injury the natural and direct consequence of a deliberate act? If the answer is yes to any of these questions, there will be no recovery, unless some fortuitous cause intervened between the deliberate act and the injury.

If some chance event does intervene, which is not the deliberate act of the insured (even though it may be the deliberate act of a third party or the negligent act of the insured) and which diverts events from their natural course, then the result may be an accident. It depends on the circumstances in which the injury is received. If the weak-hearted walker does not intend to run, but enters a field without knowing that it contains a bull and, as a result, is forced to run, then the running is not the intentional act of the insured. In *Hamlyn v Crown Accidental Insurance Co*,[116] a shopkeeper stooped to pick up a marble and because

[110] *In re Arbitration between Kate Scarr and the General Accident Assurance Corpn Ltd* [1905] 1 KB 387.

[111] *De Souza v Home and Overseas Insurance Co Ltd* [1995] LRLR 453.

[112] ibid 459 (Mustill LJ).

[113] *In re Arbitration between Kate Scarr and the General Accident Assurance Corpn Ltd* [1905] 1 KB 387, 393 (Bray J).

[114] (1932) 43 Ll L Rep 62.

[115] [1996] 1 WLR 936.

[116] [1893] 1 QB 750. See the interpretation placed on this case by Bray J in *In re Arbitration between Kate Scarr and the General Accident Assurance Corpn Ltd* [1905] 1 KB 387, 394 and by Mustill LJ in *De Souza v Home and Overseas Insurance Co Ltd* [1995] LRLR 453, 461.

it rolled away from him, he bent forward and, in doing so, wrenched his knee. This was held to be an accident because the court took the view that he had not intended the extra exertion involved: the man did not intend to do the act which wrenched his knee.

There are, however, some severe difficulties with this line of reasoning and, perhaps, the problem lies with the distinction between accidental results and accidental means that has been disinterred by the judges in *De Souza* and *Dhak*. It had long been supposed that the Court of Appeal in *Hamlyn* had rejected the idea of a distinction between accidental result and accidental means, and famously the American judge Cardozo J castigated those who would make such a distinction for plunging 'this branch of the law into a Serbonian bog'.[117] Neill LJ in *Dhak* was not deterred. Drawing on the judgment of Lord Justice Mustill in *De Souza*, he maintained that the judges in *Hamlyn*, in which there was a similarly worded policy, had acknowledged this distinction. The policy in *Dhak* covered 'bodily injury resulting in death … caused directly or indirectly by the accident', and the words 'caused by accidental means' were construed as requiring the court to look at the cause of the injury and determine whether it was accidental, so there would be no cover if the insured's deliberate act led to the injury. The problem is that if *Dhak* is correct, then, however one reads the judgments in *Hamlyn*, its conclusion must surely be wrong in finding the insurers liable since the man deliberately bent forward to pick up the marble and that action led to the injury, which was its natural consequence. Other jurisdictions have rejected the distinction. For instance, in the Scottish case of *MacLeod v New Hampshire Insurance Co Ltd*,[118] the injury to the insured's back occurred when he threw a tire into his truck. The policy covered injury caused by 'accidental, violent, visible and external means' and the court held the insurers liable. Even though the injury was a natural and foreseeable consequence of an intentional act, this result was not intended and therefore, according to the ordinary meaning of the word, this was an accident. The word 'accidental' merely emphasised the distinction between an accidental injury and one resulting from an existing infirmity.

4. Litigation Insurance

4.1. Legal Expenses Insurance

Cover for costs incurred in litigation is standard in liability policies where the insured is the defendant.[119] In addition, both claimant and defendant costs may also be covered by way of extension under householders' or commercial policies. Such cover is not automatic and will rest upon the insurers being satisfied that the insured has reasonable prospects of success. UK measures implementing EU legislation, which have remained in place despite Brexit, are designed to protect the holder of legal expenses cover from any conflict of interest where the claimant's legal expenses insurer is also the liability insurer of the potential defendant.

[117] *Landress v Phoenix Mutual Life Insurance* (1934) 54 S Ct 461, 463. It should be pointed out that he dissented in that case.

[118] 1998 SLT 1191. See *Sargent v GRE (UK) Ltd* [2000] Lloyd's Rep IR 77 for some encouraging signs that the Court of Appeal may be moving away from the rather complex method of construing policies that has, it might be suggested, led to the difficulties of *De Souza* and *Dhak*.

[119] See ch 15 above.

The Insurance Companies (Legal Expenses Insurance) Regulations 1990[120] provide that legal expenses cover must either be in a separate policy or in a separate section of the policy. To avoid conflicts, the insurer must adopt one of three possible types of arrangement: (a) no member of staff who is concerned with management of claims under legal expenses policies, or with legal advice in respect of such policies, may carry on the same activity in relation to any other class of business; (b) legal expenses claims must be dealt with by a separate company; or (c) as soon as a claim arises, the insured may appoint a lawyer of his choice. Whichever approach is adopted, once proceedings have been issued, the insured may choose his or her own lawyer, and the insurers cannot insist that the insured appoints a lawyer from the insurer's own panel of approved lawyers or that the insurer's permission be obtained for the appointment of a non-panel lawyer. However, the insurers cannot be required to make payment of legal fees above the rates charged by panel solicitors unless the insured can prove that the panel rates were unreasonably low and in practice operated as a barrier to the insured's right to appoint a lawyer of their own choice.[121]

4.2. After the Event Insurance

The abolition of legal aid in 1999 meant that another form of funding legal claims had to be found. The solution adopted was that in section 29 of the Access to Justice Act 1999. This recognised a comparatively new form of insurance – after the event (ATE) – whereby a claimant could take out an insurance policy against the risk of losing the claim and thus facing liability for the defendant's costs. The scheme of an ATE policy was to give the claimant credit for the amount of the premium until the judgment in the proceedings brought by the claimant had been handed down. If the claimant was unsuccessful, the premium would not have to be paid. By contrast, if the claimant succeeded, the effect of section 29 was that the claimant could recover the amount of the ATE premium from the defendant by way of costs. Litigation was thus risk-free. The system was administered through solicitors appointed to the panels of ATE insurers. If the solicitors could confirm that the claim had at least a 50 per cent chance of success, the claimant would be put forward for support under the ATE policy, the premium resting upon the prospects of success and the complexity of the case. Solicitors themselves would participate in the funding process by, in accordance with section 58 of the Courts and Legal Services Act 1990. adopting conditional fee arrangements whereby fees could be uplifted in the event of a successful claim and the uplift could also be claimed from the losing defendant by way of costs.

The system produced a spiralling of litigation and also a series of disputes in which unsuccessful defendants challenged the amount of premium that they were being asked to pay by way of costs. It is no longer necessary to dwell on these matters. In December 2009 Lord Justice Jackson published a report entitled *Review of Civil Litigation Costs*. His broad conclusion was that the costs of litigation were excessive and disproportionate, and that in particular it should no longer be possible to recover ATE premium costs and success fee uplifts. The proposals were implemented in the Legal Aid, Sentencing and Punishment of Offenders Act 2012. The 2012 Act added section 58C to the 1990 Act, removing the power

[120] SI 1990/1159.

[121] *Brown-Quinn v Equity Syndicate Management Ltd* [2012] EWCA Civ 1633. See also *Pine v Das Legal Expenses Insurance Co Ltd* [2011] EWHC 658 (QB).

of the court to award ATE premiums by way of costs other than in cases specified by regulations made under the section. The relevant regulations – the Recovery of Costs Insurance Premiums in Clinical Negligence Proceedings (No 2) Regulations 2013[122] – permit recovery of reasonable premium only if: (a) the claim is for more than £1000; (b) the insurance covers the risk of liability to pay for an expert medical report; and (c) the premium does not exceed that part of the premium which relates to the risk of incurring liability to pay for an expert. Section 58C of the 1990 Act also allows ATE premiums to be recovered in mesothelioma cases.

[122] SI 2013/739. See: *Peterborough & Stamford Hospitals NHS Trust v McMenemy* [2017] EWCA Civ 1941; *West v Stockport NHS Foundation Trust* [2019] EWCA Civ 1220.

17

Marine Insurance

1. Interpreting the Marine Insurance Act 1906

The Marine Insurance Act 1906[1] was a codification by parliamentary draftsman Sir Mackenzie Chalmers of some 3000 cases decided in the preceding 250 years.[2] The Act did not purport to codify anything other than marine law, although a small number of the provisions of the 1906 Act have been regarded by the courts as being of general application. This chapter focuses on those matters confined to marine insurance. Issues such as presentation of the risk, warranties, insurable interest, subrogation and double insurance, which are much the same in both marine and non-marine insurance, are discussed at the relevant points in this book.

The intention of the 1906 Act was to codify the common law and the approach taken to the interpretation of that type of legislation was established by Lord Herschell in a case on the Bills of Exchange Act 1882:

> I think the proper course is in the first instance to examine the language of the statute and to ask what is its rational meaning, uninfluenced by any considerations derived from the previous state of the law, and not to start with inquiring how the law previously stood, and then, assuming that it was probably intended to leave it unaltered, to see if the words of the enactment will bear an interpretation in conformity with this view.[3]

Viscount Finlay adopted this approach when it came to interpreting the 1906 Act, adding:

> When the law has been codified by such an Act as this, the question is as to the meaning of the code as shown by its language. It is, of course, legitimate to refer to previous cases to help in the explanation of anything left in doubt by the code, but, if the code is clear, reference to previous authorities is irrelevant.[4]

[1] J Gilman, C Blanchard, M Templeman, P Hopkins, N Hart and D Walsh, *Arnould's Law of Marine Insurance*, 20th edn (London, Sweet & Maxwell, 2021); Ö Gürses, *Marine Insurance Law*, 2nd edn (London, Routledge, 2016).

[2] R Merkin, *Marine Insurance: A Legal History* (Cheltenham, Edward Elgar, 2021).

[3] *The Governor and Company of the Bank of England v Vagliano Brothers* [1891] AC 107, 144–45.

[4] *P Samuel & Co Ltd v Dumas* [1924] AC 431, 451.

The Act was not intended to change the law, merely to set out what the state of the law was in 1906. However, the codification has not been an unqualified success. The hope that it would not be necessary to go behind the codification to examine the earlier case law has not been fulfilled. There are many gaps in the legislation, either because issues were simply not addressed or because the wording is ambiguous, and very many cases decide since 1906 have found it necessary to analyse the pre-Act authorities. The Act has, in a small number of cases and probably unintentionally, changed the law: the definition of constructive total loss is a clear example of where the statute has diverged from the common law.[5] The Act reflects only the decided cases and not insurance market clauses which have in many instances altered the common law rule: one example is the common law's refusal to recognise mechanical breakdown as an insured peril,[6] a position partially reversed by the insurance market immediately afterwards. In that regard, it should be stressed that the rules laid down in the 1906 Act represent the common law default position and are thus subject to contrary agreement. It is also important to note that the Act does not seek to codify common law principles applicable to all contracts. Under section 91(2), 'The rules of the common law including the law merchant, save insofar as they are inconsistent with the express provisions of this Act, shall continue to apply to contracts of marine insurance'.[7] The point, therefore, is that a reader wishing to understand the law of marine insurance must be careful to treat the 1906 Act as the starting point but by no means the destination.

The Act refers to 'assured' rather than 'insured', and that will be followed in the present chapter.

2. The Form of a Marine Insurance Policy

A marine insurance contract does not have to be in a particular form, but it will not be admitted in evidence unless it is 'embodied in a marine policy', although the policy can be issued at the time of the contract or afterwards (section 22), even after a loss has occurred.

The policy must specify the name of the assured,[8] or the assured's agent (section 23(1)); the subject matter must be designated with reasonable certainty, although there is no need for the assured's interest to be identified (section 26); and it must be signed by or on behalf of the insurer or, in the case of a corporation, it may be sealed (section 24). The English and Scottish Law Commissions in October 2010 published Issues Paper 9, on the need to retain the formal requirement in section 22 of the Marine Insurance Act 1906 for a policy document. The Commissions argued that section 22 is out of date because it originated from the imposition of stamp duty in 1795 and was designed to prevent the parties from agreeing insurance contracts without paying tax. As stamp duty was abolished in 1970, its original justification has disappeared, and it has the potential to cause problems for assureds and for recent contract certainty initiatives. The recommendation that section 22 should be repealed was not, however, adopted in the Insurance Act 2015.

[5] *Polurrian Steamship Co Ltd v Young* [1915] 1 KB 92.

[6] *Hamilton, Fraser & Co v Thames and Mersey Marine Insurance Company Ltd* (1887) 12 App Cas 484.

[7] For an example of such a common law rule, see *British and Foreign Marine Insurance Co Ltd v Samuel Sanday & Co* [1916] 1 AC 650.

[8] It need not specify the nature and extent of the assured's interest in the subject matter (s 26(2)); *Mackenzie v Whitworth* (1875) 1 Ex D 36), although of course the assured must have an insurable interest.

The 1906 Act includes, in schedule 1, the form of policy commonly in use at the time known as the 'SG form'. The inadequacies of this archaic wording, which dates back to at least the seventeenth century before being formally adopted at Lloyd's in 1779, has been constantly criticised by judges and authors, perhaps most famously in these words: 'If such a contract were to be drawn up for the first time to-day, it would be put down as the work of a lunatic endowed with a private sense of humour.'[9] Various amendments were made to the SG Policy in the following century, but in 1884 the Institute of London Underwriters (ILU), formed by Lloyd's and marine insurance companies, produced a series of Institute Clauses, which were used to supplement the SG Policy. It was not until 1983 that the market abandoned the SG Policy, replacing it with a short-form document, the MAR Policy Form, to which the relevant Institute Clauses are appended. The ILU merged with the London International Insurance and Reinsurance Market Association in 1998 to form the International Underwriting Association. The marine wordings nevertheless remain known as the Institute Clauses. These clauses differ according to the type and subject matter of the policy: so, for example, there are Institute Voyage Clauses (Hulls) (IVCH) and Institute Time Clauses (Hulls) (ITCH) for ships, as well as Institute Cargo Clauses (ICC), and each comes in several versions. The Institute Time Clauses were updated by the International Hulls Clauses (IHC) 2003, and, although most policies are still written on the ITCH 1983 (ITCH(83)) terms, there are some that are written on IHC 2003 terms, so these provisions will also be discussed below. Similarly, the Institute Cargo Clauses were updated in 2009 as a result of the work of a Joint Cargo Committee, made up of members of the International Underwriting Association and the Lloyds Market Association. Unlike IHC 2003, these clauses are now in common use.

Schedule 1 to the 1906 Act contains definitions of terms used in the Lloyd's SG Policy, and section 30 provides that the definitions are to be used in the construction of the policy. Many of the defined terms have fallen into disuse since the abandonment of that policy form, but others remain in use the current MAR Policy Form. It has generally been assumed that the schedule 1 definitions hold good in the interpretation of the MAR Form.

3. The Nature of Marine Insurance

> A contract of marine insurance is a contract whereby the insurer undertakes to indemnify the assured, in manner and to the extent thereby agreed, against marine losses, that is to say, the losses incident to marine adventure.[10]

A 'marine adventure' is one in which: any ship, goods or other moveables[11] (the 'insured property') is exposed to maritime perils; 'the earning or acquisition of any freight, passage money, commission, profit or other pecuniary benefits, or the security for any advances, loan, or disbursements is endangered by the exposure of insurable property to maritime perils';

[9] D Owen, *Ocean Trade and Shipping* (1914), 158.

[10] Marine Insurance Act 1906, s 1.

[11] Moveables 'means any tangible property, other than the ship, and includes money, valuable securities, and other documents' (s 90).

and 'any liability to a third party may be incurred by the owner of, or other person interested in or responsible for, insurable property, by reason of maritime perils' (section 3(2)). According to section 30(2), schedule 1, rule 15, a ship includes

> the hull, materials and outfit, stores and provisions for the officers and crew, and, in the case of vessels engaged in a special trade, the ordinary fittings requisite for the trade, and, also, in the case of a steamship, the machinery, boilers, and coals and engine stores, if owned by the assured.

'Goods' means 'goods in the nature of merchandise, and does not include personal effects or provisions and stores for use on board' (section 30(2), schedule 1, rule 17). So, it does not include the food to be consumed during the voyage or the jewellery worn by the passengers, but it will include food or jewels being transported as cargo.

Marine policies on hull and goods are concerned with physical loss or destruction in the course of a voyage. The Institute Hull Clauses list the perils insured against by the policy. These fall into two groups. The first group consists of external perils, which are covered in all circumstances. These consist of: perils of the seas; fire; explosion; violent theft by persons from outside the vessel; jettison;[12] contact with land conveyance, dock or harbour equipment or installation; earthquake, volcanic eruption or lightning; accidents in loading, discharging or shifting cargo, fuel, stores or parts; and contact with satellites, aircraft, helicopters or similar objects, or objects falling therefrom. The second group consists of perils over which the assured may have some control, and these are subject to due diligence being exercised by the assured: if the insurers can prove the assured's negligence, there is no cover.[13] That list consists of:

> bursting of boilers or breakage of shafts; any latent defect in the machinery or hull; negligence of Master, Officers, Crew or Pilots;[14] negligence of repairers or charterers provided such repairers or charterers are not an Assured under this insurance; barratry of Master, Officers or Crew.[15]

The Institute Clauses also cover pollution hazards and three-quarters collision liability. Other forms of liability incurred by shipowners, including damage to cargo and injury to

[12] Where goods are thrown overboard to preserve others.

[13] *Venetico Maritime SA v International General Insurance Co Ltd* [2013] EWHC 3644 (Comm).

[14] Crew negligence has from the earliest times left unaffected the assured's right to claim under a policy. Crew negligence is not regarded as a peril in its own right, so if there is an insured peril, then the fact that it was caused by crew negligence is immaterial and what matters is the insured peril itself. See, eg *Busk v Busk v Royal Exchange Assurance Co* (1818) 2 B & Ad 73, where a fire started by the crew got out of control, but the loss was held to have been proximately caused by the insured peril of fire. The point was codified by s 55(2)(a) of the 1906 Act, stating that the assured can recover for an insured peril 'even though the loss would not have happened but for the misconduct or negligence of the master or crew'. Given that principle, quite what is intended to be covered by the Hull Clauses is unclear, and presumably it can only be referring to crew negligence leading to a peril that was otherwise uninsured.

[15] Barratry, master and crew fraud, is typically covered by marine policies (see eg ITCH(83), cl 6.2.5 or IHC 2003, cl 2.2.5). It 'includes every wrongful act wilfully committed by the master or the crew to the prejudice of the owner [of the ship], or, as the case may be, the charterer' (s 30(2), sch 1, r 11). A loss caused by the misconduct of the crew is an insured peril at common law, although not if the misconduct was with the connivance of the assured (Marine Insurance Act 1906, s 55(2)(a); also ITCH(83), cl 6.2.3 or IHC 2003, cl 2.2.3). The act need not be criminal and need not be intended to injure the owner of the ship, but it must prejudice the owner. The question arises as to whether it is for the owner to prove lack of consent or for the insurers to prove consent. Bingham J felt that, in the absence of authority, he would have held that the owner had to prove lack of consent, but in view of a decision by the Court of Appeal in *Elfie A Issaias v Marine Insurance Co Ltd* (1923) 15 Ll L Rep 186, where it was declared to be 'the very cornerstone of British justice' that a wrongful act must be proved by the person alleging it, Bingham J felt obliged to hold that it was for the insurers to establish 'to the high standard required for proof of fraud in a civil case that the owners consented': *N Michalos & Sons Maritime SA v Prudential Assurance Co Ltd* [1984] 2 Lloyd's Rep 264, 272. See SJ Hazelwood, 'Barratry – The Scuttler's Easy Route to the "Golden Prize"' [1982] *Lloyd's Maritime and Commercial Law Quarterly* 383.

passengers and crew, are generally not covered by ordinary marine policies but are insured separately with protection and indemnity (P&I) clubs, which operate on a mutual basis rather than for profit.

The Institute Cargo Clauses are in three forms: A, B and C. The A clauses provide for all risks cover, so that any peril other than one specifically excepted is insured against. The B and C clauses contain different lists of insured perils, and are obviously cheaper. The vast majority of cargo cover is nevertheless all risks. Financial loss, eg where there has been a fraud on a purchase of cargo and damaged goods, or an insufficient number of goods has been shipped, is not covered. The former situation arose in *Engelhart CIP (US) LLC v Lloyd's Syndicate 1221*,[16] where worthless slag was shipped in the place of the agreed cargo, and the latter situation arose in *Coven Spa v Hong Kong Chinese Insurance Co.*[17]

Financial loss must, therefore, be specifically insured. The most important example is insurance against loss of freight, defined as 'the profit derivable by a shipowner from the employment of his ship to carry his own goods or moveables, as well as freight payable by a third party' (section 90).[18] Freight will normally be lost where the voyage is not successfully completed or the cargo is lost en route, so a marine casualty is likely to result in a loss of freight. It is possible for a hull or cargo policy to cover financial loss consequent upon physical damage, but clear words are needed. Such a case was *ABN Amro Bank NV v Royal & Sun Alliance plc*,[19] where a marine policy issued to a bank which had taken security over cargo in return for loans expressly included coverage for loss of resale value.

By 'maritime perils' is meant perils 'consequent on, or incidental to, the navigation of the sea' (section 3(2)). The result of these definitions is that the insurances effected by the owner of a ship, the owner of goods that are being sent by sea and the shareholder in a company that is laying an electric cable on the seabed[20] are all marine insurances. A contract of marine insurance can be extended to cover journeys on inland waters or on land 'which may be incidental to any sea[21] voyage', or to cover the construction of a ship (section 2(1), (2)).

4. Time and Voyage Policies

The 1906 Act distinguishes between time and voyage policies. A time policy is one written for 'a definite period of time' (section 25(1)) and is widely used for the insurance of vessels and freight.[22] It is common to include a clause which, on notification to the insurers, extends the cover until the ship reaches its destination: ITCH(83) provide that 'should the vessel at the expiration of this insurance be at sea or in distress', then as long as previous notice

[16] [2018] EWHC 900 (Comm).

[17] [1999] Lloyd's Rep IR 565. See also *Fuerst Day Lawson Ltd v Orion Insurance Co Ltd* [1980] 1 Lloyd's Rep 656. Contrast *Quadra Commodities SA v XL Insurance Company SE* [2022] EWHC 431 (Comm), where the suggestion that there was no cargo in existence and so it could not have been lost was rejected on the facts.

[18] Sums payable by passengers ('passage money') are excluded from the definition of freight and have to be insured in their own right.

[19] [2021] EWCA Civ 1789.

[20] *Wilson v Jones* (1867) LR 2 Exch 139.

[21] 'Sea' includes any tidal estuary: *Mercantile Mutual Insurance (Australia) Ltd v Gibbs* [2003] HCA 39.

[22] See ch 1 for discussion of the starting and finishing dates for time policies.

has been given to the underwriters, the ship will be held covered at a pro rata premium. Similarly, IHC 2003 provide that if the ship is at sea and 'in distress or missing' or in port and 'in distress', then as long as the insurers are notified as soon as possible, the ship will be held covered until it arrives at the next port in good safety at a pro rata premium. Under clause 4.1 of ITCH(83) and clause 13 of IHC 2003, cover is terminated automatically after change of the classification society of the vessel, or an alteration of the class within that society. The standing of the particular society by which the vessel is classified and the class within which that vessel is placed are both important indicators of the seaworthiness of the vessel. Cover is also automatically terminated where there are certain changes in ownership or use of the ship, such as change of owner, flag or management (clause 4.2).

A voyage policy covers a 'voyage from one place to another' (section 25(1)). Such policies may be used for vessels and freight, but cargo insurance is by its very nature for the duration of the voyage on which the cargo is to be carried and not for a fixed period. The wording used in the nineteenth century – as reproduced in section 42 of the 1906 Act – referred to coverage commencing 'at and from' a particular place, subject to an implied condition that the voyage was commenced within a reasonable time. The risk terminates when the vessel arrives at the destination and is moored in good safety for the period specified in the policy. Clause 8 of the Institute Cargo Clauses make detailed provision for the commencement and termination of a cargo policy. The risk attaches when 'the subject-matter insured is first moved in the warehouse or at the place of storage for the purpose of the immediate loading into or onto the carrying vehicle … for the commencement of transit' and terminates on the earlier of the completion of unloading from the carrying vehicle in or at the final warehouse or 60 days after completion of discharge of the subject matter at the final port of discharge where it has not been conveyed to the final warehouse. A cargo policy thus covers not just the voyage, but also loading and storage risks. Cargo that has been temporarily landed and unloaded at an intermediate port remains insured, as in *Bayview Motors Ltd v Mitsui Marine and Fire Insurance Co*,[23] where two cargoes of cars in transit to the Turks and Caicos Islands were unloaded at a stop in the Dominican Republic, where they were stolen by local customs officials.

There are important legal differences between a voyage and a time policy. As will be seen below in the discussion of section 39, the requirement for the vessel to be seaworthy takes effect as an implied warranty for voyage policies but merely as a causal exclusion for time policies. The 1906 Act lays down a series of rules for the conduct of the voyage under a voyage policy. Under section 43, the risk does not attach if the voyage sails from a place other the specified place: thus, where a voyage policy on a ship covers a voyage from Liverpool to Calais, the risk will not attach if the voyage begins from Bristol (section 43); however, if the voyage begins at Liverpool and at that time the intention is that it will end at Calais, the risk attaches. There is an implied condition that the voyage will commence within a reasonable period of time, unless the circumstance that caused the delay was known to the insurer before the contract was concluded or the insurer waived the condition (section 42).[24] Unless there is a lawful excuse, the voyage must be prosecuted with 'reasonable dispatch' and the insurer is discharged from the point at which any delay becomes unreasonable (section 48).[25]

[23] [2003] 1 Lloyd's Rep 131.

[24] There is nothing in s 42 permitting the assured to excuse the delay by showing that it was involuntary or there was a lawful excuse (contrast with ss 45 and 48).

[25] *Samuel v The Royal Exchange Assurance Co* (1828) 8 B & C 119.

If, after the commencement of the risk, the destination is voluntarily changed, this will amount to a change of voyage (section 45(1)).[26] The insurers are discharged from liability from 'when the determination to change [the destination] is manifested', even if the loss happens before the ship has actually changed voyage,[27] although the insurers remain liable for losses incurred beforehand (section 45(2)). The policy may include an express term that permits a change of voyage provided notice is given immediately after receipt of advices and any amended terms and additional premium are agreed.[28] A change of voyage must be distinguished from a change of destination. The latter occurs where, although a particular destination is specified in the policy, the vessel sails for a different destination. In those circumstances, the risk never attaches (section 44). The distinction between a change of voyage and a change of destination rests on the point in time when the decision was made: there will be a change of destination where there is no intention at the start of the voyage to go to the specified destination so the risk never attaches and a change of voyage where at some point after the risk attached it is decided to go to a different destination.[29] It was pointed out in *Nima SARL v Deves Insurance Plc*[30] that there was inconsistency between the section 44 principle that the risk does not attach when the vessel sails for a different destination and the provisions of the Institute Cargo Clauses, under which the risk attaches as soon as the goods are moved for loading. The Court of Appeal there held that the Act took priority and that the risk did not attach. The point was addressed by clause 10 of the 2009 version of the Clauses, under which the coverage provided by the Cargo Clauses remains in place where the vessel sails for a different destination without the knowledge of the assured or its employees.

A deviation from the route without lawful excuse will discharge the insurers from liability, even if the ship later returns to the original route (section 46(1)). The policy may specify the route to be taken, but if it does not, it is implied that the customary course between the places specified will be taken (section 46(2)(b)). This is presumed to be the direct geographical route, although that presumption can be rebutted where a less direct route is not unreasonable having regard to those interested in the voyage. Put another way, the route must be 'usual and reasonable in a commercial sense'. What this means may change, for example, as fuel prices in different ports vary.[31] A deviation is not a change of voyage because the destination remains the same; it is a change in the route to that destination. Unlike the situation where there is a change of voyage, there must be an actual deviation – a mere intention to deviate will not discharge the insurers (section 46(3)). Once again, the insurers will be liable for losses incurred before the deviation (section 46(1)).[32] Some policies include a clause giving the ship liberty to 'touch and stay' at any port; this 'does not authorise the ship to depart from the course of her voyage from the port of departure to the port of destination' (section 30(2), schedule 1, rule 6). In other words, only those ports that are both properly on the route and visited for purposes connected to the adventure contemplated by the policy can be entered. If this were not the case, 'there can be no limit, either

[26] A change of voyage will not be voluntary where, for instance, the ship is ordered into a port by the government: *Rickards v Forestal Land, Timber and Railways Co Ltd* [1941] 3 All ER 62.

[27] *Tasker v Cunninghame* (1819) 1 Bligh 87.

[28] The 'held covered' clause found in the Institute Hull Clauses.

[29] *Wooldridge v Boydell* (1778) 1 Doug KB 16. A held covered clause will, of course, not excuse a change of destination because in such a circumstance the risk will not have attached.

[30] [2002] Lloyd's Rep IR 752.

[31] *Reardon Smith Line Ltd v Black Sea and Baltic General Insurance Co Ltd* [1939] AC 562, 576 (Lord Wright).

[32] *Kewley v Ryan* (1794) 2 H Bl 343; *Hare v Travis* (1827) 7 B & C 14.

of time or place, to the risk described in this policy'.[33] The Marine Insurance Act 1906, section 49(1) lists deviations and delays which will be excused: where authorised by the policy; where caused by circumstances beyond the control of the master and the master's employer; where reasonably necessary to comply with a warranty or for the safety of the ship or subject matter insured; for the purpose of saving human life or aiding a ship in distress if life may be in danger; where reasonably necessary for obtaining medical aid for anyone on board; or where caused by the barratrous conduct of the master or crew, if barratry is one of the insured perils. Once the excuse ceases to operate, the ship must resume course (section 49(2)), which, in the case of the ship driven off its original course, will mean taking the most direct route to its destination.[34] The Institute Clauses expressly continue coverage in case of deviation, provided that notice is given to the insurer immediately after the assured is notified and any amended terms and additional premium are agreed. The insurer will be liable if the assured has complied with the notice requirement, even though this occurs after the loss.[35]

---

5. Warranties

5.1. Express and Implied Warranties

As discussed in chapter eight, much of the common law relating to warranties was repealed and replaced by the Insurance Act 2015. Warranties may still be used but, subject to the various limitations to sections 10 and 11 of the 2015 Act discussed in that chapter, breach of a warranty merely suspends the risk, and during the period of suspension the assured may recover for loss not causally related to the breach. The use of express warranties in marine policies has all but been abandoned, and the remaining issues relate to the warranties implied into marine policies by sections 36–42 of the 1906 Act. There is no need to dwell upon the interpretation of a warranty of neutrality (section 36), the absence of any warranty of nationality (section 37) and the warranty of good safety (section 38): the first two belong to the Napoleonic era, and the third relates to words no longer employed in marine policies. It is necessary to discuss only two of the statutory provisions: seaworthiness (sections 38 and 39); and legality (section 40).

5.2. Seaworthiness

5.2.1. Seaworthiness in Voyage Policies

The 1906 Act implies a warranty in a voyage policy that, at the commencement of the voyage, the ship is seaworthy and reasonably fit to carry the goods to the destination specified (sections 39(1) and 40(2)), although there is no implied warranty that the goods be

[33] *Tenant v Brown* (1826) 5 B & C 208, 219 (Abbott CJ).

[34] *Phyn v The Royal Exchange Assurance Co* (1798) 7 TR 505, where there was a deviation when the master of a ship, which had been blown off course, mistakenly took a less direct route to its destination.

[35] *Greenock Steamship Co v Maritime Insurance Co* [1903] 1 KB 367.

seaworthy (section 40(1)).[36] The commencement of the voyage is, normally, when the ship leaves the port and goes out to sea without any intention of returning, even if bad weather forces a return to port.[37] It is up to the insurers to prove that the ship was unseaworthy at this point,[38] although where a ship sinks in calm weather shortly after commencing its voyage, then it is a reasonable assumption that it was unseaworthy at the time of sailing.[39] If the policy attaches while the ship is in port, there is an implied warranty that it 'shall be reasonably fit to encounter the ordinary perils of the port' (section 39(2)) and seaworthy when it commences its sea voyage. Similarly, if the ship is undertaking a voyage in stages, such as part by river and part by sea (section 39(3)),[40] it must be seaworthy at the start of each stage. In *Garnat Trading & Shipping (Singapore) Pte Ltd v Baominh Insurance Corporation*,[41] Clarke J summarised the law relating to the doctrine of stages:

> By reason of the 'doctrine of stages' it is sufficient if the ship is seaworthy for some definite, well recognised and separate stage of the voyage, even though some work, or change, to the vessel, her equipment, supplies or crew is required before she is fit for a second or later stage of the voyage. Different parts of a sea voyage can be separated into distinct stages. Indeed, in many cases the circumstances of the voyage are such that it will be necessary to introduce an intermediate stage before the commencement of the open sea voyage.

If seaworthy at the time of sailing, 'then it mattered not how soon after she became otherwise':[42] the warranty is not breached since 'the assured makes no warranty to the underwriters that the vessel shall continue seaworthy'.[43]

What amounts to seaworthiness has been the subject of much debate. According to the Act, a ship is seaworthy 'when she is reasonably fit in all respects to encounter the ordinary perils of the seas of the adventure insured' (section 39(4)). In general terms, the ship must be 'in a fit state as to repairs, equipment, and crew, and in all other respects, to encounter the ordinary perils of the voyage insured, at the time of sailing upon it'.[44] This means that the hull must be sound and able to carry cargo without endangering either the ship or the cargo,[45] the engine must function properly, and there must be an adequate level of competent crew and equipment to meet the ordinary perils of the insured voyage.[46] The ship will be unseaworthy if, although apparently seaworthy on commencing the voyage, there is some latent defect which means that it is not fit for the voyage: so, for example, insufficient fuel for the voyage will render an otherwise sound ship unseaworthy.[47] On the other hand, a ship is not rendered unseaworthy by a trivial defect that can ordinarily be remedied by a competent crew, even though the defect is not, in fact, remedied. This is because a ship's seaworthiness

[36] *Koebel v Saunders* (1864) 17 CB (NS) 71. See generally CB Anderson, 'The Evolution of the Implied Warranty of Seaworthiness in Comparative Perspective' (1986) 17 *Journal of Money Laundering Control* 1.

[37] *Price v Livingstone* (1882) 3 QBD 679 (a case on charterparties).

[38] *Pickup v The Thames and Mersey Marine Insurance Co Ltd* (1878) 3 QBD 594; *C Hoffman & Co v British General Insurance Co* (1922) 10 Ll L Rep 434, 436 (Bailhache J).

[39] *Pickup v The Thames and Mersey Marine Insurance Co Ltd* (1878) 3 QBD 594, 600 (Brett LJ).

[40] *Claude Bouillon et Cie v Lupton* (1863) 15 CB (NS) 113.

[41] [2010] EWHC 2578 (Comm), 160 (affirmed on different grounds [2011] EWCA Civ 773).

[42] *Parker v Potts* (1815) 3 Dow 23, 30 (Lord Eldon LC).

[43] *Dixon v Sadler* (1839) 5 M & W 405, 414 (Parke B).

[44] The elements of seaworthiness are clearly set out by Cresswell J in *Papera Traders Co Ltd v Hyundai Merchant Marine Co Ltd, The Eurasian Dream* [2002] 1 Lloyd's Rep 719.

[45] *Stanton v Richardson* (1875) 45 LJCP 78.

[46] *Tait v Levi* (1811) 14 East 481; *Phillips v Headlam* (1831) 2 B & Ad 380, 383 (Parke J).

[47] *Greenock Steamship Co v Maritime Insurance Co Ltd* [1903] 1 KB 367; *Thin v Richards & Co* [1892] 2 QB 141 (a case on the warranty as to seaworthiness in a charterparty).

is assessed as it was at the time of departure and not in the light of later events.[48] Cargo will make the ship unseaworthy only if it affects the condition of the ship itself, such as it may if poorly stowed, but not if the only impact is on other cargo. A boat constructed for river use will usually not be seaworthy without modifications. It may be seaworthy, however, if it is merely being sent across the sea to a place where it will act as a river boat and, as far as was possible with a boat of that construction, temporary modifications were made to fit it for the voyage even though they 'might not make her as fit for the voyage as would have been usual and proper if the adventure had been that of sending out an ordinary seagoing vessel'.[49] This should cause no difficulties, since the insurer will be aware of the risk involved in such a venture.

It does not matter who or what caused the ship to be unseaworthy, or even that the assured had no way of knowing its condition.[50] In a case on the implied warranty of seaworthiness in a bill of lading, it was said that 'the shipowner contracts, not merely that he will do his best to make the ship reasonably fit, but that she shall really be reasonably fit for the voyage'.[51] In *C Hoffman & Co v British General Insurance Co*,[52] even though neither the owner, who acted honestly and reasonably, nor a professional surveyor could detect the problem, the ship's unseaworthy condition meant the insurers were relieved of liability. However, for the purpose of cargo policies, the 2009 Institute Clauses provide that 'The Insurers waive any breach of the implied warranties of seaworthiness of the ship and fitness of the ship to carry the subject-matter insured to destination'.

At common law, the insurers are discharged from liability even though the ship is subsequently rendered seaworthy: where a ship commenced a voyage from Cuba to Liverpool without the proper number of seamen, the fact that additional sailors were picked up shortly afterwards did not remedy the breach of the implied warranty.[53] Lord Redesdale, speaking in 1816, was clear about the reasons for the strict application of this implied warranty:

> Unless the assured were bound to take care that the vessel was in every respect seaworthy, the consequence would be most mischievous: for the effect of insurance would be to render those chiefly interested much more careless about the condition of the ship, and the lives of those engaged in navigating her.[54]

The effect of sections 10 and 11 of the Insurance Act 2015 is a matter of some debate. As was seen in chapter eight, section 10 provides that a breach of warranty does not bring the risk to an automatic end but, rather, suspends the risk until the breach has been remedied, so that a loss occurring after that date is unaffected by the earlier breach. However, the question is whether a warranty that applies once and for all can conceptually ever be remedied: the obligation of the assured was to commence the voyage with a seaworthy vessel, and if that obligation has been broken, then it is difficult to see how subsequently rendering the vessel seaworthy can retrospectively remove the breach. All that may be said is that the Law Commissions' illustrations of the operation of section 10 assumed that it would apply to the

[48] *Hedley v Pinkney and Sons Steamship Co Ltd* [1892] 1 QB 58 (a case on the criminal offence of sending an unseaworthy ship to sea). Compare *Steel v The State Line Steamship Co* (1877) 3 App Cas 72 with *GE Dobell & Co v The Steamship Rossmond Co Ltd* [1895] 2 QB 408.

[49] *Burges v Wickham* 3 B & S 669, 696. See also *Harocopos v Mountain* (1934) 49 Ll L Rep 267.

[50] *Douglas v Scougall* (1816) 4 Doug 269, 276 (Lord Eldon LC).

[51] *The Glenfruin* (1885) 10 PD 103, 108 (Butt J).

[52] (1922) 10 Ll L Rep 434.

[53] *Forshaw v Chabert* (1821) 3 Brod & B 158. See also *Quebec Marine Insurance Company v Commercial Bank of Canada* (1870) LR 3 PC 234, where defects in the vessel had been repaired by the time of the loss.

[54] *Wilkie v Geddes* (1815) 3 Dow 57, 60. See also *Douglas v Scougall* (1816) 4 Doug 269, 276 (Lord Eldon LC).

seaworthiness warranty, and that it would be somewhat curious if the statutory reversal of the common law 'no cure' rule did not apply in the very context in which that rule was developed. Assuming that section 10 does apply to allow a claim where there was no breach of warranty at the time of the loss, a further question becomes whether section 11 of the 2015 Act rescues an assured who was in breach of warranty at the time of loss but the warranty had no causal connection to the manner in which the loss occurred. The problem here is that it is uncertain whether section 11 can apply to the seaworthiness warranty. A term falls within section 11 only if the term relates to loss at a particular time, at a particular place or in a particular manner, none of which seem apposite to a general seaworthiness obligation. Further, section 11 does not apply to a term that defines the risk as a whole, and there is a good argument that an upfront seaworthiness warranty is exactly of that type.

5.2.2. Seaworthiness in Time Policies

There is no implied warranty as to seaworthiness in a time policy. The view of the courts was that a time policy might incept in the course of a voyage, and it was therefore inappropriate to impose a term requiring seaworthiness in circumstances where the assured would be most unlikely to know the condition of the vessel at the time the policy took effect, and even if the assured did know that the vessel was unseaworthy, the insurers were adequately protected by the duty of disclosure.[55] Nevertheless, the courts decided that insurers would not be liable under a time policy if the assured was aware that the ship was unseaworthy at the start of the voyage and this caused the loss.[56] That rule was codified in section 39(5) of the Marine Insurance Act 1906:

> In a time policy there is no implied warranty that the ship shall be seaworthy at any stage of the adventure, but where, with the privity of the assured, the ship is sent to sea in an unseaworthy state, the insurer is not liable for any loss attributable to unseaworthiness.

The owner must have had actual knowledge, or had reason to believe the ship was unseaworthy and deliberately failed to undertake an examination of the ship. Simple negligence in not taking precautions against the possibility that the ship is unseaworthy is not sufficient.[57] There must be a 'conscious realisation of the implication of the facts making the ship unseaworthy'.[58] If the ship owner honestly believes as a prudent owner that a crew of 10 is sufficient, then the fact that a court might regard the ship unseaworthy because it required 12 sailors does not mean the assured is in breach of the implied warranty. Where there are two defects which make the ship unseaworthy and the owner is only aware of one of these, the insurers are liable if the loss is caused by the condition of which the assured is not aware.[59]

There may be cases involving time policies where the vessel was sent to sea in an unseaworthy condition but without the assured's knowledge. In such a case, section 39(5) has

[55] *Gibson v Small* (1853) 4 HL Cas 353; *Thompson v Hopper* (1858) EB & E 1038; *Fawcus v Sarsfield* (1856) 6 E & B 192; *Dudgeon v Pembroke* (1877) 2 App Cas 284.

[56] *Dudgeon v Pembroke* (1877) 2 App Cas 284.

[57] *Compania Naviera Vascongada v British & Foreign Marine Insurance Co Ltd* (1936) 54 Ll L Rep 35, 58 (Branson J). See also *Compania Maritima San Basilio SA v Oceanus Mutual Underwriting Association (Bermuda) Ltd* [1977] 1 QB 49; *Manifest Shipping & Co Ltd v Uni-Polaris Insurance Co Ltd, The Star Sea* [1995] 1 Lloyd's Rep 651.

[58] *Compania Maritima San Basilio SA v Oceanus Mutual Underwriting Association (Bermuda) Ltd* (1936) 54 Ll L Rep 35, 76–77 (Roskill LJ).

[59] *Thomas v Tyne & Wear SS Freight Insurance Association* [1917] 1 KB 938. For an example concerning ITCH, see *Martin Maritime Ltd v Provident Capital Indemnity Fund Ltd, The Lydia Flag* [1998] 2 Lloyd's Rep 652.

no application, and the assured will be able to recover if it can be shown that the loss was caused by a peril of the seas: unseaworthiness is the remote cause only and is to be left out of account. That was decided by Mustill J in *JJ Lloyd Instruments Ltd v Northern Star Insurance Co Ltd, The Miss Jay Jay*,[60] where a vessel with numerous defects giving rise to unseaworthiness was lost at sea in difficult but perfectly ordinary sea conditions. It was held that the proximate cause of loss was fortuitous perils of the seas, and that where there is a chain of causation running from unseaworthiness to adverse weather, loss of watertight integrity and damage, there is recovery. On appeal, the Court of Appeal preferred to treat the facts as involving concurrent proximate causes, with the insured peril of the seas prevailing over the uninsured unseaworthiness,[61] but the correctness of Mustill J's reasoning was subsequently confirmed by the Supreme Court in *Syarikat Takaful Malaysia Berhad v Global Process Systems Inc, The Cendor MOPU*.[62]

5.3. Warranty of Legality

Section 41 of the 1906 Act states that there is an implied warranty in all marine policies, first, that the adventure insured is lawful and, secondly, that 'so far as the assured can control the matter, the adventure shall be carried out in a lawful manner' (section 41; also section 3(1)). This is one of the most curious sections in the 1906 Act, in that there was no common law authority elevating illegality to the status of warranty, and the courts have refused to extend the warranty to non-marine policies.[63] The common law position was simply that a contract illegal as formed could not be enforced by either party; and a contract legal as formed but performed illegally could not be enforced by the guilty party. The first principle is illustrated by *Cunard v Hyde*.[64] The insured ship was allowed to sail without a certificate relating to the safe stowage of the cargo having first been obtained. The insurers were not liable when the cargo was lost, even though the illegal act did not cause the loss. The reasoning behind this was explained by Tindal CJ: 'A policy on an illegal voyage cannot be enforced; for it would be singular, if, the original contract being invalid and therefore incapable to be enforced, a collateral contract founded upon it could be enforced.'[65]

The second principle is illustrated by *Pipon v Cope*,[66] where the owner ignored the smuggling activities of the crew in spite of the ship having been seized on three previous voyages, and he was not allowed to recover on a policy because his failure to take action amounted to consent. The common law principles applicable to insurance in the context of trading with the enemy were considered by Lord Davey in *Janson v Driefontein Consolidated Mines Ltd*.[67] First, 'the King's subjects cannot trade with an alien enemy, ie, a person owing allegiance to a Government at war with the King, without the King's licence. Every contract made in violation of this principle is void.' Secondly, 'no action can be maintained against an insurer of an enemy's goods or ships against capture by the

[60] [1987] 1 Lloyd's Rep 32.
[61] See ch 10 above.
[62] [2011] UKSC 5.
[63] *Euro-Diam Ltd v Bathurst* [1990] 1 QB 1.
[64] (1859) 2 El & El 11. See also *Parkin v Dick* (1809) 11 East 502.
[65] *Redmond v Smith* (1844) 7 Man & G 457, 474.
[66] *Pipon v Cope* (1808) 1 Camp 434, as explained in *Trinder, Anderson & Co v Thames and Mersey Marine Insurance Co* [1898] 2 QB 114, 129 (Collins LJ).
[67] [1902] AC 484, 499.

British Government'. This is so even where the insurance is taken out before the war and also where the person claiming on the policy is a neutral or British subject, if the insurance is effected for an alien enemy. Thirdly, if a loss occurs before the war, the claim is suspended until the restoration of peace.

Although section 41 is expressed in absolute terms, the preceding common law was more flexible and required the illegality to be more than incidental. In *Redmond v Smith*,[68] a statute prohibiting the use of seamen who were not under articles was breached, but since this legislation aimed only to provide them with a better method of enforcing their contracts, it was held that the illegality did not affect the contract of insurance. In recent times, notably in *Patel v Mirza*,[69] the courts have affirmed the flexible approach to illegality generally, and will refuse a remedy by balancing three considerations: the underlying purpose of the illegality; public policy implications of allowing or denying recovery; and whether denial of recovery would be a proportional response to the illegality. There does not seem any obvious reason why marine insurance should impose a more rigid standard, and recent cases have suggested that the section 41 warranty is to be construed in line with general principles. The courts have construed the section as requiring illegality to affect the adventure as a whole, so that an incidental element of illegality does not amount to breach of warranty. In *Royal Boskalis v Mountain*,[70] the Court of Appeal held that the making of an unlawful payment to secure the vessel's release was too far removed from the adventure to preclude recovery. In the most recent authority, *Suez Fortune Investments Ltd v Talbot Underwriting Ltd, The Brilliante Virtuoso*,[71] it was held that a conspiracy between the owner of a vessel and the charterers to defraud the Chinese revenue authorities did not render the adventure an unlawful one and had no impact upon the ability of the assured mortgagee bank to recover under the hull policy. Further, even where the warranty does apply, *Suez Fortune* confirms that it is concerned with breaches of English law only, reflecting the common law principle that the English courts are not concerned with foreign illegality.

6. Perils of the Seas

The Lloyd's SG Policy provided cover for a list of perils, the most important of which was 'perils … of the seas'. The list, which was otherwise concerned with captures and seizures, concluded with the words 'all other perils, losses, and misfortunes'. The numerous pre-Act cases on losses at sea sought to define 'perils of the seas', and the cases were concerned also with the question whether a loss that did not strictly constitute a peril of the seas fell within the concluding general words. Those words were held not to be unlimited and were to be construed as covering similar causes.[72] The sweeping-up phrase is no longer used, and it is now necessary to determine whether a loss results from a cause recognised by the courts as a peril of the seas. The term, which is used also in charterparties, is defined by schedule 1,

[68] (1844) 7 Man & G 457.

[69] [2016] UKSC 42.

[70] [1997] 2 All ER 929. See also *Sea Glory Maritime Co v Al Sagr National Insurance Co, The Nancy* [2013] EWHC 2116 (Comm).

[71] [2019] EWHC 2599 (Comm).

[72] *Thomas Wilson, Sons & Co v The Owners of the Cargo per The 'Xantho'* (1887) 12 App Cas 503.

rule 7 as follows: 'The term "perils of the seas" refers only to fortuitous accidents or casualties of the seas. It does not include the ordinary action of the wind and the waves.'

According to Lord Herschell:

> I think it clear that the term 'perils of the sea' does not cover every accident or casualty which may happen to the subject-matter of the insurance on the sea. It must be a peril of the sea. Again, it is well settled that it is not every loss or damage of which the sea is the immediate cause that is covered by these words. They do not protect, for example, against that natural and inevitable action of the winds and waves, which results in what may be described as wear and tear. There must be some casualty, something which could not be foreseen as one of the necessary incidents of the adventure. The purpose of the policy is to secure an indemnity against accidents which may happen, not against events which must happen. It was contended that those losses only were losses by perils of the sea, which were occasioned by extraordinary violence of the winds or waves. I think this is too narrow a construction of the words, and it is certainly not supported by the authorities, or by common understanding. It is beyond question, that if a vessel strikes upon a sunken rock in fair weather and sinks, this is a loss by perils of the sea. And a loss by foundering, owing to a vessel coming into collision with another vessel, even when the collision results from the negligence of that other vessel, falls within the same category.[73]

The statutory definition was analysed by the Supreme Court in *The Cendor MOPU*.[74] Here, a cargo policy was an oil rig to be transported by barge. The assured, with the insurers' knowledge, decided that the oil rig would not be dismantled but instead would be laid on its back, with its three legs protruding into the air. The rig was unable to withstand ordinary sea conditions, and vibration caused one of the legs to fall off. That destabilised the entire rig, leading to the other legs coming off and the rig becoming a total loss. The Supreme Court held that the loss was caused by perils of the seas.

Turning first to fortuity, it was held that a loss satisfied that requirement as long it was accidental, unintended and not inevitable. The trial judge, Blair J, found as a matter of fact that the rig could have survived the voyage, and even though loss was likely, it was not inevitable. There was no appeal from that factual finding. The Supreme Court made it clear that the fact that a loss could have been anticipated did not prevent the loss from being fortuitous. The deliberate scuttling of a vessel is not a fortuitous loss,[75] and was held by the House of Lords in *Samuel & Co v Dumas*[76] that where the vessel was scuttled by her owner, the mortgagee bank which was co-insured under the hull policy and entirely innocent of the fraud was nevertheless unable to recover simply because there was no insured peril.[77] The burden of proving that a fortuitous act has occurred is borne by the assured, so that if a vessel simply disappears and there is no evidence whatsoever as to the cause of the loss, the assured will be unable to recover. That was the sad outcome in *Rhesa Shipping Co v Edmunds, The Popi M*,[78] where a fishing vessel was lost in calm seas off Scotland. The assured suggested that the only possible cause of the loss could have been a collision of

[73] ibid 509; *The Lapwing* [1940] 112, 120–21 (Hodson J).

[74] [2011] UKSC 5.

[75] See Marine Insurance Act 1906, s 55(2)(a), stating that the insurer is not liable for loss attributable to the wilful misconduct of the assured. This is a principle of law rather than construction and cannot be excluded by agreement of the parties.

[76] [1924] AC 431.

[77] Contrast the position for all other perils, where fortuity is not a precondition and so a deliberate act bars recovery only by the person committing that act: *Burnett v International Insurance Company of Hanover Ltd* [2021] UKSC 12, discussed in ch 10 above.

[78] [1985] 2 All ER 712.

some kind, but, in the absence of any evidence to that effect, the House of Lords concluded that the assured had not proved that there had been any fortuity and it did not suffice for the assured to show that collision was the least unlikely of all of the possibilities. The same point arose in the curious circumstances found in *Kastor Navigation Co Ltd v Axa Global Risks (UK) Ltd, The Kastor Too*,[79] where a vessel was seriously damaged by fire (an insured peril) and sank the following day for unexplained reasons entirely unconnected with the fire. It was held that there could not be a claim for the sinking because perils of the sea could not be established, although – as explained below – the Court of Appeal permitted a claim for the fire.

Secondly, in the phrase 'ordinary action of the wind and the waves', the adjective 'ordinary' qualified the noun 'action' and not 'the winds and waves'. That meant that the focus was not on whether the wind and waves were ordinary, but on whether the effect of the wind on the waves was extraordinary. As was stated by Lord Mance, the phrase 'ordinary action of the wind and waves' draws attention to the question whether the winds and waves have had some extraordinary effect, rather than whether they were extraordinary in themselves. In *The Cendor MOPU* itself, there had been nothing exceptional about the wind and the waves, but their effect on the oil rig was extraordinary and gave rise to a claim. This principle was applied in *Venetico Marine SA v International General Insurance Co Ltd*,[80] where a mechanical failure led to the vessel drifting and then running aground. Here, the fortuity was the failure of the vessel's equipment, which caused it to drift and run aground. The grounding was fortuitous, and it was irrelevant that the weather conditions at the time were not unexpected or unusual.

Thirdly, the loss must be of the sea, ie, as the result of being at sea. Some early cases drew a distinction between perils *of* the seas and perils *on* the seas, and on that basis it was held in *De Vaux v Salvador*[81] that a collision was not a peril of the seas. However, that distinction was rejected by the House of Lords in *The Xantho*, a charterparty case involving a collision, where it was said that there was no distinction between a loss caused by a sunken rock, an iceberg or another vessel. The loss must also be one that is capable of happening only at sea. Thus, where rats damaged bags holding cargo, that was held not to be a peril of the sea.[82] Again, in *Thames & Mersey Marine Insurance Co Ltd v Hamilton, Fraser & Co, The Inchmaree*,[83] an engine used for pumping water into the main boilers of a ship was damaged because a valve, which should have been left open, was closed, either by accident or by the negligence of the engineer. The insurers were held not to be liable since the loss was of a type which could have happened on land as easily as at sea. The actual decision was reversed by the adoption immediately afterwards of the Inchmaree Clause, which has been extended over the years and now forms the 'due diligence' set of perils contained in the Hull Clauses as set out earlier in this chapter. There is cover for damage caused by 'bursting of boilers or breakage of shafts' and 'any latent defect[84] in the machinery or hull'. It will be noted that the insurance is against damage caused by those events and not for the repair of the boiler, shaft or latent defect. Thus, if a shaft breaks as a result of a latent defect, the insurers will

[79] [2004] EWCA Civ 277.

[80] [2014] 1 Lloyd's Rep 349.

[81] (1836) 4 A & E 420.

[82] *Hamilton, Fraser & Co v Pandorf & Co* (1887) 12 App Cas 518 (contract of affreightment), codified in Marine Insurance Act 1906, s 55(2)(c).

[83] (1887) 12 App Cas 484, codified in Marine Insurance Act 1906, s 55(2)(c).

[84] That is any defect that is hidden and not reasonably discoverable: *Prudent Tankers Ltd SA v Dominion Insurance Co, The Caribbean Sea* [1980] 1 Lloyd's Rep 338.

not be liable for its loss, but they will be liable where a piece of it holes the hull.[85] However, the cost of repairs is recoverable where such repairs are necessary to make good the damage caused by the event in question,[86] and the IHC 2003 now extend the insurance to repairs where an additional premium is paid.

The proximate cause test as applied to perils of the seas focuses on the underlying reason why the vessel has been damaged and not the damage itself. This can be most clearly seen in cases of water entering the vessel. The courts here have focused not on an ingress of water, but rather on the event that has caused the ingress of water. As long as that event is fortuitous, there is a peril of the seas. Illustrations include rats gnawing through a pipe allowing water into the vessel,[87] crew negligently leaving open a valve or pipe[88] and vandals smashing windows and forcing open the vessel's hatches.[89]

If the loss is due to action taken to prevent a loss by a peril of the seas, then the insurers will be liable, as, for instance, where ventilators were closed to prevent the incursion of the sea during rough weather and this caused the cargo of rice to overheat.[90] Negligence will not preclude liability for a loss by perils of the seas since it 'provides the fortuitous circumstances which entitles the [assured] to recover under the terms of the policy'.[91]

7. Exclusions from Marine Policies

7.1. Delay

By section 55(2)(b) of the 1906 Act, 'unless the policy otherwise provides, the insurer on ship or goods is not liable for any loss proximately caused by delay, although the delay be caused by a peril insured against'. This implements the principle that a marine policy on a vessel or cargo is against physical damage and not against consequential financial loss. The principle does not extend to freight, but the 'time charter' clause in use in the London market since the 1890s operates to exclude recovery for freight consequent upon delay following a casualty.[92]

7.2. Inherent Vice

Section 55(2)(c) of the 1906 Act provides that 'unless the policy otherwise provides, the insurer is not liable for ordinary wear and tear, ordinary leakage and breakage, inherent vice

[85] *Oceanic Steamship Co v Faber* (1906) 11 Com Cas 179, 187 (Walton J) (on appeal (1907) 13 Com Cas 28); *Scindia Steamships (London) Ltd v The London Assurance* [1937] 1 KB 639.

[86] See *Promet Engineering (Singapore) Pte Ltd v Sturge, The Nukila* [1997] 2 Lloyd's Rep 146 (recovery for the cost of repairing cracks in the base of the legs of an oil rig, as the cracks caused additional damage to the legs themselves).

[87] *Hamilton, Fraser & Co v Pandorf & Co* (1887) 12 App Cas 518.

[88] *Seashore Marine SA v Phoenix Assurance Plc* [2001] EWHC 536 (Comm); *Versloot Dredging BV v HDI Gerling Indusrie Versicherung AG, The DC Merwestone* [2013] EWHC 1666 (Comm); *CCR Fishing Ltd v Tomenson, The La Pointe* 69 DLR (4th) 112 (1990). Crew negligence is not of itself a 'peril': what matters is whether the negligence has given rise to an insured peril.

[89] *McKeever v Northernreef Insurance Co SA* [2019] 2 Lloyd's Rep 161.

[90] *Canada Rice Mills Ltd v Union Marine and General Insurance Co Ltd* [1941] AC 55.

[91] *The Lapwing* [1940] P 112, 121 (Hodson J).

[92] *Naviera de Canarias SA v National Hispanica Aseguradora SA* [1978] AC 853.

or nature of the subject-matter insured'. The 'inherent vice' exclusion has been the subject of conflicting case law and commentary over many years. The Supreme Court decision in *Syarikat Takaful Malaysia Berhad v Global Process Systems Inc, The Cendor MOPU*[93] has confirmed two important points. First, the term 'inherent vice' was correctly defined by Diplock LJ in *Soya v White*[94] as meaning 'the risk of deterioration of the goods shipped as a result of their natural behaviour in the ordinary course of the contemplated voyage without the intervention of any fortuitous external accident or casualty'. Secondly, section 55(2)(c) does not lay down a causation test but rather defines the circumstances in which there is not a peril of the seas, so that the two are mutually exclusive and a loss is either a peril of the seas or it is a loss by inherent vice.

The importance of these rulings can be seen by considering *Mayban General Assurance BHB and others v Alstom Power Plants Ltd*,[95] decided shortly before *The Cendor MOPU*. In *Mayban*, the inherent vice limitation was successfully applied when a transformer was damaged on a journey from England to Malaysia as a result of the vessel's pitching and rolling in the bad weather. Moore-Bick J found in favour of the insurers on the basis that there was no evidence of exceptionally bad weather and thus no peril of the seas, and instead the proximate cause of the damage to the transformer was its inability to withstand the usual incidents of the marine voyage. However, the Supreme Court in *Global Process Systems* considered that the test applied in *Mayban* was too wide in scope and needed reconsideration. As we have seen, in this case an oil rig was being carried by a barge with its legs elevated above the deck. Fatigue cracking, caused by the repeated bending of the legs under the motion of the barge as it was towed, caused the starboard leg and the other two legs to break off and be lost. The policy in question covered all risks of loss or damage to the subject matter insured, subject to the exclusion that 'in no case shall this insurance cover loss or damage or expense caused by inherent vice or nature of the subject-matter'. The question to the court, in light of the fact that the action of the waves was no greater than would be reasonably expected at that time, was whether the proximate cause of the loss was due to the perils of the sea or rather to inherent vice and therefore excluded from the policy.

At first instance,[96] Blair J applied *Mayban*. He began by highlighting that this case was concerned with causation. He argued that under section 55 of the Marine Insurance Act 1906, the question should be framed in terms of the 'proximate cause' of the loss of the legs of the oil rig, based on the common sense of the ordinary businessman or seafarer.[97] He concluded that, based on the evidence presented, the proximate cause of the loss was the fact that the legs were not capable of withstanding the normal incidents of the insured voyage, including the weather reasonably to be expected. The proximate cause of the loss was therefore not the perils of the sea but inherent vice, and thus excluded from the policy.[98] This decision was overturned in the Court of Appeal,[99] where Waller LJ argued that the correct question to ask in such a case was 'was the cause an inability to withstand the ordinary incidents of the voyage?' and the answer to this was not to be found by reference to what might reasonably be foreseeable as the ordinary incidents of the voyage, but rather by

[93] [2011] UKSC 5.
[94] [1983] 1 Lloyd's Rep 122, 125.
[95] [2005] Lloyd's Rep IR 18.
[96] *Global Process Sytems Inc, Global Process Systems (Asia Pacific) Sdn Bhd v Syarikat Takaful* [2009] EWHC 637 (Comm).
[97] ibid [84].
[98] ibid [111].
[99] *Global Process Systems Inc & Anr v Syarikat Takaful Malaysia Berhad* [2009] EWCA Civ 1398.

reference to wind or wave, which, it would be the common understanding, would be bound to occur as the ordinary incidents on any normal voyage of the kind being undertaken.[100] He concluded that metal fatigue was not the sole cause of the loss of the legs, but rather:

> A leg breaking wave, not bound to occur in the way it did on any normal voyage round the Cape of Good Hope, caused the starboard leg to break off. That led to the others being at greater risk and then breaking off. It was not certain that that would happen and although with the benefit of hindsight we know that it was highly probable, that high probability was unknown to the insured and that was a risk against which the appellants insured.[101]

Thus, Waller LJ adopted a narrower test than the one used in *Mayban* and as a result it was deemed a risk against which the rig owners had insured.

The Supreme Court, dismissing the insurers' appeal, was unanimous in deciding that the inherent vice defence should be limited to situations where the loss has been proximately caused by something internal to the insured subject matter, and not as a consequence of some external fortuity. Four judges, Lords Saville, Mance, Collins and Clarke, gave concurring judgments, each perhaps slightly differing in emphasis, with all of whom Lord Dyson agreed. The Court stressed that, by virtue of section 55(1) of the Marine Insurance Act 1906, the key enquiry in a case such as this is to establish the proximate cause of the loss and the answer to this should be based on fact and common-sense principles.[102] Lord Mance began by stating that if the decision in *Mayban* were followed as a rule of law, namely that if the insured subject matter was unable to withstand all bad weather conditions which it would foreseeably meet during the insured venture then the assured would not be able to recover in respect of any resulting loss or damage, this would place a stringent limit on the scope of marine insurance cover.[103] He argued that this would 'lead to disputes about the fitness of cargo to travel, and leave Cost, Insurance and Freight (CIF) buyers in doubt about whether to look to their insurers or sellers or both, quite possibly in different fora'. As to the excepted perils included in section 55(2) of the Act, Lord Mance stated that in this case, it would only be if the loss or damage could be said to be due either to uneventful wear and tear (or 'debility') in the prevailing weather conditions or to inherent characteristics of the hull or cargo not involving any fortuitous external accident or casualty that insurers would have a defence. In attempting to define what 'ordinary wear and tear' and 'inherent vice' meant, Lord Mance suggested that:

> [O]rdinary wear and tear and ordinary leakage and breakage would thus cover loss or damage resulting from the normal vicissitudes of use in the case of a vessel, or of handling and carriage in the case of cargo, while inherent vice would cover inherent characteristics of or defects in a hull or cargo leading to it causing loss or damage to itself – in each case without any fortuitous external accident or casualty.[104]

Based on the facts of the case, Lord Mance concluded that the rig suffered the loss of the three legs not just because of the cracking that developed, but ultimately only after the first, and then each other, leg was caught, in just the 'right' way, by a leg-breaking wave. The loss of the three legs overboard was a fortuitous external accident or casualty, insured under the all risks insurance, rather than the result of inherent vice. He stated that to hold that the insurance did not cover such a loss would be to 'deprive it of much of its

[100] ibid [62].
[101] ibid [64].
[102] ibid [46] (Lord Saville).
[103] ibid [52].
[104] ibid [81].

utility'.[105] Lord Collins concluded that the breaking of the legs occurred under the influence of a leg-breaking wave, and even though this loss occurred in 'the ordinary course of the contemplated voyage', the way in which it occurred was fortuitous; the proximate cause of the loss was the result of a fortuity, and not the susceptibility of the legs to crack as a result of metal fatigue.[106] Similarly, Lord Saville concluded that:

> [T]he proximate cause of the loss, applying common sense principles, was not inherent vice nor indeed ordinary wear or tear or the ordinary action of the wind and waves, but an external fortuitous accident or casualty of the seas. This took the form of the rolling and pitching of the barge in the sea conditions encountered catching the first leg at just the right moment to produce stresses sufficient to cause the leg to break off, thereby leading to increased stresses on the remaining legs and their subsequent breakage.[107]

Thus the 'leg-breaking wave' was the proximate cause that provided the necessary element of external fortuity to enable the insured to recover under the policy; in order for a loss to be regarded as having been caused by inherent vice, the sole reason for that loss must have been the nature of the insured subject matter, such that it would suffer loss irrespective of external fortuitous events.

7.3. War and Strikes Risks[108]

The Institute Clauses cover only marine risks. War and strikes risks are excluded, but such risks are insurable under matching Institute War and Strikes Risks Clauses or by War Mutual Clubs formed by shipowners. The war perils treated in this way are:

> [W]ar, civil war, revolution, rebellion, insurrection, or civil strife arising therefrom, or any hostile act by or against a belligerent power; capture, seizure, arrest, restraint or detainment and the consequences thereof or any attempt thereat; derelict mines, torpedoes, bombs or other derelict weapons of war.

The strike provisions relate to 'strikers, locked-out workmen, or persons taking part in labour disturbances, riots or civil commotions'. The Institute Hull Clauses exclude also 'loss, damage, liability or expense arising from any terrorist; any person acting from a political motive; and the use of any weapon or the detonation of an explosive by any person acting maliciously or from a political motive'.

Since 2005 piracy has been treated as a war risk other than for Institute Cargo Clauses A. The term is defined by schedule 1, rule 8 as including 'passengers who mutiny and rioters who attack the ship from the shore'. The essence of piracy is robbery. The distinguishing features of piracy are that: it is confined to the high seas so that inland waterways are excluded;[109] violence must be involved in the robbery, so that clandestine theft followed by an altercation in the course of escape[110] or boarding a vessel by subterfuge[111] are not piracy; and robbery must be purely for private gain and not to further the interests of a state.[112]

[105] ibid [87].
[106] ibid [97].
[107] ibid [46]
[108] For war risks generally, see ch 16 above.
[109] *Republic of Bolivia v Indemnity Mutual Marine Assurance Co Ltd* [1909] 1 KB 785.
[110] *The Andreas Lemos* [1983] 1 All ER 591.
[111] *Suez Fortune Investments Ltd v Talbot Underwriting Ltd, The Brilliante Virtuoso* [2019] EWHC 2599 (Comm).
[112] *Republic of Bolivia v Indemnity Mutual Marine Assurance Co Ltd* [1909] 1 KB 785. State sponsored taking at sea is privateering rather than piracy.

The term 'seizure' refers to any taking at sea where there has been the use of the force of law or the force of arms.[113] Not all takings are seizures. Where there is insurance for seizure, there are generally exclusions for confiscation: for infringement of customs or trading regulations;[114] in the course of ordinary judicial process;[115] for action taken for the purpose of enforcing or securing payment of a claim; and for failure to provide security for a claim.[116]

8. Measure of Indemnity[117]

8.1. Forms of Loss

8.1.1. Total, Loss and Partial Loss

Non-marine insurance recognises two forms of loss: total loss, where the subject matter is destroyed in its entirety; and partial loss, where the subject matter is damaged but capable of repair.[118] Marine insurance, by contrast, in section 56 of the 1906 Act, recognises an intermediate form of loss – constructive total loss – which is in essence a loss that falls short of complete destruction but renders the subject matter uneconomic to repair or retrieve. In the case of a constructive total loss, the assured has the option to treat the loss as total and to recover an indemnity based upon total loss, or to treat the loss as partial and to recover an indemnity based upon partial loss. That option is exercised by abandoning the insured subject matter to the insurers and serving a 'notice of abandonment' on them. The difference between marine and non-marine insurance in this regard dates back to the end of the eighteenth century and the fact that many vessels and their cargoes were seized by the enemy and taken to a prize court for condemnation and sale. Claims were made by owners in advance of prize proceedings, and it became settled that the assured was entitled to claim for a total loss immediately on seizure, in return for granting the insurers all rights over the subject matter should it be recaptured or otherwise returned. By that means the assured would be paid immediately and the insurers, in return, obtained rights that might prove to be valuable. By contrast, in the case of non-marine insurance, a bright line could be drawn between a total loss and a partial loss.

Partial loss – rather confusingly referred to by section 64 as a 'particular average loss' – is simply any loss that is not a total loss. An actual total loss is defined by section 57 as arising 'where the subject-matter insured is destroyed, or so damaged as to cease to be a thing of the kind insured, or where the assured is irretrievably deprived thereof'. There is a total loss where there is no possibility of repair or recovery.[119] That may also arise where damage is suffered in a remote part of the world and there are no available repair facilities. An assured is not irretrievably deprived of property if it is legally and physically possible to recover it,

[113] *Cory v Burr* (1883) 8 App Cas 393.
[114] *Atlasnavios-Navegacao LDA v Navigators Insurance Company Ltd (No 2)* [2018] UKSC 26.
[115] *Melinda Holdings SA v Hellenic Mutual War Risks Association (Bermuda) Ltd* [2011] EWHC 181 (Comm).
[116] *Svenska Handelsbanken AB v Dandridge, The Aliza Glacial* [2002] 2 Lloyd's Rep 421.
[117] R Khurram, 'Total Loss and Abandonment in the Law of Marine Insurance' (1994) 25 *Journal of Money Laundering Control* 95.
[118] See ch 12 above.
[119] *Venetico Maritime SA v International General Insurance Co Ltd* [2014] 1 Lloyd's Rep 349; *Quadra Commodities SA v XL Insurance Company SE* [2022] EWHC 431 (Comm).

even if such recovery can only be achieved by disproportionate effort or expense.[120] There will be an actual total loss of goods if they have lost their character. The test is,

> whether, as a matter of business, the nature of the thing has altered … [I]f the nature of the thing is altered, and it becomes for business purposes something else, so that it is not dealt with by business people as the thing which it originally was, the question for determination is whether the thing insured, the original article of commerce, has become a total loss. If it is so changed in its nature by the perils of the sea as to become an unmerchantable thing, which no buyer would buy and no honest seller would sell, then there is a total loss.[121]

After a sunken ship had been raised, it was found that its cargo of dates was impregnated with sewage, so that, although still resembling dates in appearance and of value for distillation into spirit, they were no longer merchantable as dates. It was held that the cargo was an actual total loss.[122] But if part of the cargo survives in its original form, then there is no actual total loss. When a cargo of rice became immersed in water but, following kiln drying, was later sold as rice, although for a much lower price than if undamaged, it was held to be a partial and not a total loss.[123] Freight is only payable if the cargo is delivered, but if the cargo is delivered, whether in part or damaged, then freight is payable. If the cargo is not delivered and that failure is caused by an insured peril, then there will be a claim for the total loss of freight. A ship that has gone missing may be presumed to be a total loss after lapse of a reasonable time (section 58).

The issue of whether the seizure and ransom of a vessel and its cargo by pirates amounts to actual total loss was considered by the Court of Appeal in *Masefield AG v Amlin Corporate Member Ltd, The Bunga Melati Dua*.[124] The vessel in question was carrying the assureds' cargo of biodiesel on a voyage between Malaysia and Rotterdam when captured on 19 August 2008 in the Gulf of Aden by Somali pirates and taken with the crew into Somali coastal waters. Negotiations for the payment of a ransom for the release of the vessel, the crew and cargo were almost immediately commenced by the vessel's owners, MISC, a Malaysian state-owned shipping company. The assured was still out of possession of the cargo on 18 September 2008 when it served a notice of abandonment on its insurers. The notice was rejected, but proceedings were by agreement deemed to have been commenced on that day. The vessel, the crew and cargo were released some 11 days later on payment of a ransom of US$2 million by MISC. The voyage to Rotterdam was completed on 26 October 2008. The cargo had not deteriorated during the delay, but it had missed its market in the meantime. The market for biofuel is seasonal, and effectively closes after the end of September. The assureds' two parcels therefore had to be stored until the following year, when it was sold at a price substantially less than its insured value. The assureds, despite having their economically impaired consignment restored to them, claimed an indemnity from their cargo insurers for its actual total loss by piracy,[125] less the salvage sale price. The assureds relied on two submissions: first, that capture by pirates created an immediate actual total loss, whatever the prospects of recovery might be, an argument supported by *Dean v Hornby*,[126] where a piratical seizure was held to give rise to an immediate total loss;

[120] *Masefield AG v Amlin Corporate Member Ltd, The Bunga Melati Dua* [2011] EWCA Civ 24, [24] (Rix LJ).
[121] *Asfar & Co v Blundell* [1896] 1 QB 123, 127 (Lord Esher MR).
[122] ibid.
[123] *Francis v Boulton* (1895) 1 Com Cas 217.
[124] [2011] EWCA Civ 24.
[125] Constructive total loss was pursued as an alternative at first instance but this was, perhaps in error, not argued on appeal.
[126] (1854) 3 E & B 180.

and second, that in any event the law would not or could not take account of the payment of a ransom as a relevant, legitimate reason for calculating the possibilities of recovery. As to whether the owners had been irretrievably deprived of their property, as required in order to successfully claim actual total loss, Rix LJ held that:

> [P]iratical seizure in the circumstances of this case, where there was not only a chance, but a strong likelihood, that payment of a ransom of a comparatively small sum, relative to the value of the vessel and her cargo, would secure recovery of both, was not an actual total loss. It was not an irretrievable deprivation of property. It was a typical 'wait and see' situation.[127]

Furthermore, he held that there was no rule of law that capture or seizure by pirates amounts to an actual total loss. In fact, he stated that the subject matter is not amenable to a rule of law at all; it is all ultimately a question of fact.[128] Rix LJ did state that there could be circumstances where a piratical seizure could be deemed as an actual total loss, eg in the absence of a policy of ransom, where the pirates escape with their prize for their own use and there is no prospect whatever of finding or recovering vessel or cargo.[129]

As to the issue of public policy, the assureds argued that the payment of ransom, which amounted to submission to extortion, was so undesirable from the point of view of the public interest and universal principles of morality that it could be no part of an insured's duty to preserve his property from loss by succumbing to a ransom demand. That being the case, they argued that the property concerned must be considered to have been irretrievably lost, physically and/or legally, where the only means of recovering it was to do something which an insured could not reasonably be expected or required to do. In response to this, Rix LJ began by highlighting Parke B's dictum in *Egerton v Brownlow*,[130] which concerned the circumstances in which public policy could be invoked by a court, where he stated that: '[T]he doctrine should only be invoked in clear cases in which the harm to the public is substantially incontestable, and does not depend upon the idiosyncratic inferences of a few judicial minds'.[131] Furthermore, in concluding that the payment of a ransom cannot be against public policy, Rix LJ stated that there is no legislation against the payment of ransoms, which is therefore not illegal,[132] and that, as observed in *Royal Boskalis Westminster NV v Mountain*,[133] a form of loss akin to a ransom (abandoning a good claim under duress) was a proper sue and labour expense under the Marine Insurance Act, section 78(4).[134]

8.1.2. Constructive Total Loss

Section 60 of the 1906 Act sets out six situations in which there is a constructive total loss of the insured subject matter. The section is not drafted in straightforward fashion, and it is possible to summarise the various classes of constructive total loss as follows.

[127] [2011] EWCA Civ 24, [56].
[128] ibid.
[129] ibid. That was the position in *Dean v Hornby*, where the vessel had remained in the hands of pirates and the assured had never been in a position to try to recover the vessel.
[130] (1853) 4 HLC 1.
[131] [2011] EWCA Civ 24, [123].
[132] ibid [63].
[133] [1999] QB 674.
[134] [2011] EWCA Civ 24, [64] and [75].

First, where the subject matter insured is reasonably abandoned because its actual total loss from an insured peril appears to be unavoidable (section 60(1)). The phrase 'reasonably abandoned' refers not to any legal concept, but rather to the physical act of walking (or sailing) away from the goods because their loss appears unavoidable. At first instance in *Masefield v Amlin*[135] it was held that goods in the possession of pirates had not been reasonably abandoned, because payment of a ransom would almost certainly have secured their release.

Second, where the expenditure necessary to preserve it from actual total loss would exceed its value after the expenditure had been incurred (section 60(1)). The common law, as codified by sections 27(4) and 60(2), tested this by measuring the cost of repairs against the repaired value, but the market has modified this rule by measuring the cost of repairs against the insured value.[136] The reasonable cost of repairs is measured by the sum that would have been incurred by a prudent shipowner who did not have insurance,[137] and includes salvage costs incurred by the assured in the aftermath of the casualty.[138]

Third, where the assured is deprived of possession of ship or goods by an insured peril and it is unlikely that the ship or goods will be recovered (section 60(2)(i)(a)). The common law rule was that there was a constructive total loss if recovery was uncertain, but the 1906 Act changed the test to unlikely.[139] The word 'unlikely' is to be read as meaning 'within a reasonable time': it was held on that basis in *Clothing Management Technology Ltd v Beazley Solutions Ltd*[140] that the detention of women's fashion goods could be regarded as a constructive total loss if they were unlikely to be returned within a relatively short period, given the very limited shelf-life of such items. It is somewhat surprising that this provision was not relied upon in *Masefield v Amlin*.

Fourth, where the assured is deprived of possession of ship or goods by an insured peril and the cost of recovery would exceed the value when recovered (section 60(2)(i)(b)).

Fifth, where a ship is so damaged by an insured peril that the cost of repair would exceed the value of the repaired ship (section 60(2)(ii)). As is the case with preservation costs, market clauses compare repair costs with the insured value.[141]

Sixth, where the cost of repair and of forwarding goods to their destination would exceed their value on arrival (section 60(2)(iii)).

In addition to the list in the 1906 Act, there is a common law rule that where goods are insured from the port of loading to the port of destination, the voyage is frustrated by the detention of those goods for an indefinite period (not merely a temporary delay) and this occurs as the result of an insured peril, the owner can elect to recover from the insurers for a constructive total loss: so, in one case, the owner of goods was able to claim following an indefinite interruption of the voyage by war.[142]

[135] [2010] EWHC 280 (Comm).

[136] *Venetico Maritime SA v International General Insurance Co Ltd* [2013] EWHC 3644 (Comm); *Involnert Management Inc v Aprilgrange Ltd* [2015] EWHC 2225 (Comm). The IHC 2003 go further and specify that there is a constructive total loss if the repair costs exceed 80% of the insured value.

[137] *Suez Fortune Investments Ltd v Talbot Underwriting Ltd, The Brillante Virtuoso* [2019] EWHC 2599 (Comm).

[138] *Sveriges Angfartygs Assurans Forening v Connect Shipping Inc* [2019] UKSC 29. See W Feng, 'What Types of Expenses Should Be Taken into Account when Calculating Constructive Total Loss?' [2019] *Journal of Business Law* 504.

[139] *Polurrian Steamship Co v Young* [1915] 1 KB 922.

[140] [2012] 1 Lloyd's Rep 571.

[141] 80% of the insured value under the IHC 2003.

[142] *British and Foreign Marine Insurance Co Ltd v Samuel Sanday & Co* 1916] 1 AC 650. This rule applies only to goods and is excluded in the Institute War Clauses (Cargo), cl 3.7 and the Institute Strikes Clauses (Cargo), cl 3.8.

As might be imagined, there is plenty of scope for disputes over the boundary between an actual total loss and a constructive total loss. According to Lord Abinger CB:

> If, in the progress of the voyage [the subject matter] becomes totally destroyed or annihilated, or if it be placed by reason of the perils against which [the insurer] insures, in such a position, that it is wholly out of the power of the assured or of the underwriter to procure its arrival, he is bound by the very letter of his contract to pay the sum insured.[143]

If a ship retains its character as a ship and could be repaired, it is not an actual total loss, but it may be a constructive total loss where the cost of those repairs would exceed its repaired value. On the other hand, when 'reduced to a mere congeries of planks, the vessel was a mere wreck, the name which you may think fit to apply to it cannot alter the nature of the thing'.[144] A pile of planks is not a ship. In one case in which it was said that a ship was not an actual total loss, Potter LJ remarked:

> Albeit it was grounded and incapable of proceeding without salvage and a degree of repair, its essential components were not so damaged or dissipated that its role and function as a dead ship susceptible of being towed away for scrap had been totally destroyed.[145]

The ship in that case was in one piece and the possibility or even probability that it might have had to be broken into two in order to salvage it was irrelevant in deciding whether or not it was an actual total loss.[146] There will be an actual total loss if the ship has been missing for a reasonable time, although the assured must, of course, show on the balance of probabilities both that this loss can be presumed to have occurred within the period of the insurance and that it was caused by an insured peril. When, during the First World War, a ship disappeared rapidly in an area where there were stray British and German floating mines and German submarine patrols, the court held that the loss was by enemy action, which was not an insured peril.[147]

The date on which the existence or otherwise of a constructive total loss is to be ascertained is at common law the dates on which legal proceedings are commenced against the insurers.[148] However, as a matter of practice, it is normally agreed that the assessment is to be made at the date the notice of abandonment is served by the assured. Where there is an agreement to that effect, events occurring after the service of the notice of abandonment are to be disregarded. That point was recognised by the House of Lords in *Sailing Ship Blairmore Co Ltd v Macredie*,[149] where at the time the notice of abandonment was served the insured vessel was submerged. Thereafter the insurers, at their expense, raised the vessel and asserted that the vessel was a partial loss only. Their Lordships ruled that the nature of the loss crystallised when the notice of abandonment was served, and it was not open to the insurers to alter the nature of that loss thereafter.

[143] *Roux v Salvador* (1836) 3 Bing NC 266, 286.
[144] *Cambridge v Anderton* (1824) 2 B & C 691, 692–93 (Abbott CJ).
[145] *Fraser Shipping Ltd v Colton* [1997] 1 Lloyd's Rep 586, 591.
[146] See also *Barker v Janson* (1868) LR 3 CP 303.
[147] *Macbeth & Co v King* (1917) 86 LJKB 1004.
[148] *Hamilton v Mendes* (1761) 2 Burr 1199, a case involving recapture of the insured vessel by the date of the legal proceedings, extended in *Ruys v Royal Exchange Assurance Corporation* [1897] 2 QB 135 to the restoration of the vessel after proceedings had commenced but before judgment.
[149] [1898] AC 593.

8.1.3. Notice of Abandonment

Where there is an actual total loss, the assured does not have to give notice of abandonment to the insurers (section 57(2)), although under certain versions of the Institute Clauses notice must be given to the insurers promptly after the assured becomes aware of the loss so that a surveyor may be appointed[150] and notice more than 180 days after the loss will discharge the insurers.[151] In the event of a constructive total loss, the assured has the choice to treat the loss as a partial loss or to abandon the subject matter to the insurers and treat it as if it were an actual total loss (section 61). Until that choice has been made there is no abandonment: in other words, unless the assured gives notice of abandonment to the insurers, the loss can only be treated as a partial loss (section 62(1)). Notice need not take any particular form (section 62(2)), but it must be given 'with reasonable diligence after the receipt of reliable information of the loss' (section 62(3)).

The purpose of the notice of abandonment is, primarily, to give the insurers the opportunity to take action to preserve the subject matter or to determine if there is a subrogation claim against a third party. If, in the circumstances, there is no possibility of the insurers taking action, notice is unnecessary (section 62(7)). That was the position in *The Kastor Too*,[152] where the assured was excused this obligation as there was a fire onboard the vessel and the vessel sank the following day, there being no opportunity to give notice in the circumstances. Similarly, the owners of the *Litsion Pride* were similarly excused when the ship sank in a war zone in the Persian Gulf after being hit by a missile because there was no possibility of salvage in that place.[153] The rejection of the claim by the insurers before a notice of abandonment has been served does not remove the need for service: if the assured wishes to preserve its right to assert that there has been a constructive total loss, service remains essential.[154] The requirement of notice can be waived by the insurers (section 62(8)), although the Institute Clauses stipulate that actions to protect or recover the subject matter will not amount to a waiver.

It is worth making clear the difference between abandonment and notice of abandonment. Abandonment is

> a legal concept rather than an act, physical or mental. The legal concept is the cession of the ship to the insurer (see … sections 63 and 79 of the Act). That cession occurs in both forms of total loss, actual as well as constructive … The cession, however, only occurs upon payment, and only if the underwriter is willing to accept the cession.[155]

A constructive total loss does not depend on the assured issuing a notice of abandonment: in any particular factual situation there is a single legal answer to the question 'has there been a constructive total loss?' Giving notice signifies the assured's election to treat it as a constructive total loss, but such notice can only be given if there has been a constructive total

[150] eg IHC 2003, cl 44.1: 'notice must be given to the Leading Underwriter(s) as soon as possible after the date on which the Assured, Owners or Managers become aware of such loss, damage, liability or expense so that a surveyor may be appointed'. However, ITCH(83) cl 10.1 simply provides that 'notice shall be given to the Underwriters prior to survey and also, if the vessel is abroad, to the nearest Lloyd's Agent so that a surveyor may be appointed'.

[151] eg IHC 2003, cl 43.2.

[152] [2004] EWCA Civ 277.

[153] *Black King Shipping Corporation and Wayang (Panama) SA v Mark Ranald Massie* [1985] 1 Lloyd's Rep 437, 478 (Hirst J).

[154] *Involnert Management v Aprilgrange* [2015] EWHC 2225 (Comm), [2015] 2 Lloyd's Rep 289.

[155] *Kastor Navigation Co Ltd v Axa Global Risks (UK) Ltd* [2004] EWCA Civ 277.

loss. The absence of notice is, in effect, an election by the assured to treat what amounts to a constructive total loss as merely a partial loss. Notice is an offer to cede, which, on payment of the claim, the insurer can take up or reject and which, before that time, can be withdrawn by the assured. Where notice of abandonment is not required, there still must be an election by the assured through conduct or omission to act. Unless the assured makes an election to treat the loss as a constructive total loss it will be treated as only a partial loss, and while the former election is revocable up to the time of acceptance by the insurer, the latter is not.[156]

Once there has been acceptance of the notice of abandonment by the insurers, which can be expressly inferred from their conduct, although silence on its own is not acceptance (section 62(5)), then by section 62(6) the acceptance is conclusive and irrevocable, and amounts to an admission of liability unless it is vitiated by mistake.[157] In practice, insurers reject the notice of abandonment, although that does not necessarily amount to a rejection of the claim: liability may be admitted while the insurers reserve their right to dispute whether there is a constructive total loss or merely a partial loss. Rejection does not prejudice the right of the assured to seek to recover for constructive total loss (section 62(4)), although the assured remains free to withdraw the notice of abandonment.

8.1.4. Rights over the Abandoned Subject Matter

The fate of the insured subject matter following abandonment by the assured rests upon the action of the insurers. The starting point of the analysis is that the property can be claimed by the insurers only on making payment for a total loss. Once payment has been made, the insurers are, under section 79, subrogated to the rights of the assured and may – but are not obliged to – take over the interest of the assured in the remains of the subject matter insured. If the subject matter is a ship, they are entitled to any freight which is being earned and is earned after the loss, as well as reasonable remuneration for carrying the shipowner's goods after the loss (section 63(2)).[158] The rule entitling the insurers to acquire the assured's rights in the subject matter following payment for a total loss is, like subrogation, connected to the principle of indemnity. Nevertheless, subrogation and abandonment give rise to distinct sets of rights.[159] As Lord Blackburn pointed out:

> My Lords, I have no doubt at all that where the owners of an insured ship have claimed or been paid as for a total loss, the property in what remains of the ship, and all rights incident to the property are transferred to the underwriters as from the time of the disaster in respect of which the total loss is claimed for and paid. The right to receive payment of freight accruing due but not earned at the time of the disaster is one of those rights so incident to the property in the ship, and it therefore passes to the underwriters because the ship has become their property, just as it would have passed to a mortgagee of the ship who before the freight was completely earned had taken possession of the ship … This is at times very hard upon the insured owner of the ship; he can, however, avoid it by claiming only for a partial loss, keeping the property in himself, and so keeping the right to earn the accruing freight. In such a case he recovers an indemnity for the amount of the loss actually sustained, in calculating which all the benefits incident to the property retained by the shipowner must be considered. But the right of the assured to recover damages from a third

[156] *Stringer v English and Scottish Marine Insurance Co Ltd* (1869) LR 4 QB 676.
[157] *Norwich Union Fire Insurance Society Ltd v WH Price Ltd* [1934] AC 455.
[158] See *Yorkshire Insurance Co Ltd v Nisbet Shipping Co Ltd* [1962] 2 QB 330, 339 (Diplock J). The right to freight earned after abandonment is typically expressly waived in contracts of marine insurance: see, eg the Institute Time Clauses Hulls, cl 20; *Coker v Bolton* [1912] 3 KB 315.
[159] Marine Insurance Act 1906, s 79(1).

> person is not one of those rights which are incident to the property in the ship; it does pass to the underwriters in case of payment for a total loss, but on a different principle. And on this same principle it does pass to the underwriters who have satisfied a claim for a partial loss, though no property in the ship passes.[160]

If the insurers opt to assert ownership of the subject matter following payment for a total loss, they will take any rights that come with that subject matter: they will be entitled 'to every benefit to which the assured is entitled in respect of the thing to which the contract of insurance relates, but to nothing more'.[161] In *Attorney General v Glen Line Ltd*,[162] the insurers paid for a total loss following the seizure of a ship by the German government during the First World War. After the war, the ship was recovered and sold for more than had been paid to the assured. It was held that the insurers were entitled to retain the whole of the proceeds of the sale. Abandonment does not pass to the insurers the right to recover damages from a third party. Such a right is not an incident of the ownership of the property acquired by the insurers through abandonment because the property had already been damaged by the tortfeasor before the insurers acquired it.[163] So, unless the assured assigns the right to sue a third party, the insurers must take any action against the wrongdoer in the name of the assured under their right of subrogation.[164]

Asserting ownership of the subject matter following payment can present the insurers with problems: for instance, the owner of a sunken ship which is blocking sea lanes may be required to pay for its removal.[165] It may, therefore, be that the insurers will not wish to exercise the right to acquire ownership of the subject matter. If the assured has abandoned the subject matter to the insurers but they have refused to accept it, there is some authority for the proposition that the property becomes *res nullius*, that is, it is owned by no one and reverts to the Crown.[166] The alternative view is that ownership remains with the assured. There is no modern decision on the point.

The above principles leave unresolved the question of ownership of, or rights over, the subject matter in the period between the service of the notice of abandonment and payment for a total loss by the insurers. If the insurers reject the notice of abandonment, they have no rights over the subject matter at that point, so the assured is free to sell the subject matter; by so doing, the notice of abandonment is effectively withdrawn and it is then for the purchaser to make a claim against the insurers, which may include serving a fresh notice of abandonment. By contrast, if the insurers accept the notice of abandonment, then there is some uncertainty as to whether they have by doing so agreed that they will accept the insured subject matter as soon as payment for a total loss has been made: that is thought to be the effect of section 63(1), although there is no authority on the point. It is to avoid that possibility that notices of abandonment are rejected, so that when payment is actually made the insurers retain their section 79 discretion to claim or reject the subject matter. What is clear,

[160] *Simpson v Thomson, Birrell* (1877) 3 App Cas 279, 292 (Lord Blackburn). The 'different principle' is, of course, subrogation. See also *Page v Scottish Insurance Corporation* 140 LT 571, 575 (Scrutton LJ).

[161] *Sea Insurance Co v Hadden & Wainwright* (1884) 13 QB 706, 718 (Lindley LJ).

[162] (1930]) 37 Ll L Rep 55.

[163] Anon, 'Abandonment and Subrogation in Marine Insurance' (1917) 30 *Harvard Law Review* 383, 384.

[164] *Simpson v Thomson, Birrell* (1877) 3 App Cas 279.

[165] *Arrow Shipping Co Ltd v Tyne Improvement Commissioners, The Crystal* [1894] AC 508. In that case, the House of Lords decided that the crucial time was not when the ship became an obstruction (at which time it was owned by the assured) but when the authority, under statutory powers, incurred expenses in the removal (at which time it was owned by the insurer).

[166] *Allgemeine Versicherungs-Gesellschaft Helvetia v Administrator of German Property* [1931] 1 KB 672.

however, is that by accepting a notice of abandonment, the insurers immediately obtain an equitable lien over the subject matter, so that it cannot be sold by the assured, and once the insurers have paid for a total loss they retain their lien pending a decision on whether or not to take over the subject matter, so that any purported sale will override their equitable rights only in the unlikely event that the purchaser is a bona fide purchaser without notice of the lien.

The most likely scenario is that in which the insurers refuse to accept the notice of abandonment but then pay for a total loss. The position of the subject matter pending a decision by the insurers to assert their section 79 right to claim ownership was considered at length by Tomlinson J in the unique circumstances of *Dornoch Ltd v Westminster International BV*.[167] In March 2007 a huge hopper dredger was damaged off the coast of China and, on 27 March 2007, a notice of abandonment was tendered. The insurers declined this and the vessel was towed to a dockyard in Thailand. By 16 April 2008 all the primary and excess layer insurers made payments for constructive total loss in their respective portions, and in July 2008 the insurers also paid the salvage removal claim. When a dispute arose as to the value of the vessel in December 2008, a majority of the insurers (77.5 per cent of the primary layer insurers and 85 per cent of the excess layer insurers) exercised their right to take over the interest of the assured in the vessel. In January 2009 the owners, who were keen to avoid the vessel falling into the hands of a competitor, decided to frustrate the insurers' intentions by selling the vessel to a related Nigerian company, without notice to the insurers, for a nominal consideration (€1000). After the sale of the vessel the remaining insurers purported to elect to take over the vessel. The main issues to be determined related to the question of whether English law recognised that the claimant insurers had any equitable proprietary interest in the vessel. The claimants submitted that, on payment for total loss, or alternatively upon payment of the salvage claim some three months later, they had acquired an equitable lien over the vessel. Alternatively, they submitted that the express election by the majority of underwriters to take over the vessel gave those underwriters an equitable lien or a beneficial interest under a trust.

The court first dealt with the issue of whether the insurers had obtained an equitable lien by virtue of their payment for total loss. Tomlinson J stated that, in general, insurers have it within their power to create in their favour proprietary rights in the vessel either by acceptance of notice of abandonment or, if it is different, by irrevocable election to take over, on the promised payment for a constructive total loss, the interest of the assured in the wreck.[168] He then highlighted that the mere fact that underwriters decline notice of abandonment cannot without more in the ordinary way deprive underwriters of their right to take over the assured's interest in the subject matter insured, which right becomes available on payment for a constructive total loss as a result of section 79(1).[169] As to the important question of whether an equitable lien arises where insurers, having declined to accept notice of abandonment, subsequently pay for a constructive total loss but without either expressly claiming or disclaiming the interest of the assured in the wreck, Tomlinson J held that there is no general rule that insurers should gain a security interest by virtue of their paying a constructive total loss. In fact, he ruled that in these circumstances it would be 'arguably unconscionable that equity should impose a security interest over the vessel in favour of

[167] [2009] EWHC 889.
[168] ibid [43].
[169] ibid [44].

insurers' since to impose a lien would 'reserve to the insurers all the benefits which might flow from taking over the interest of the assured in the wreck whilst imposing none of the corresponding burdens of ownership'.[170] He stated that equity will secure the position of an insurer who exercises an election to take over the vessel but it would not intervene to secure an insurer's position while they took the time to decide whether to accept those benefits/burdens.[171] Based on this, Tomlinson J concluded that the insurers had not obtained an equitable lien by virtue of their payment of the constructive total loss.[172] Furthermore, he highlighted that this position was not altered by the later payment of the salvage removal claim.[173]

Having made this decision, Tomlinson J then turned his attention to the effect of the decision by the majority of the insurers to take over the vessel. The owners submitted that the reference in section 79(1) of the Act to payment for a total loss of the whole of the subject matter insured has the result that an election to take over the assured's interest in the subject matter insured can only be made by an insurer who pays the entirety of the loss.[174] However, Tomlinson J rejected this argument, stating that it was 'misconceived' because it ignored the fact that each insurer has a separate contract with the insured and each would gain the separate right of election once he had paid his proportion of the indemnity.[175] Accordingly, he held that each of the insurers who had subsequently elected to take over the interest of the owners had acquired a beneficial interest in the vessel under a trust; they therefore became co-owners of the vessel together with the assured in their respective proportions and they were entitled to have the appropriate number of shares transferred to them and registered in their name.[176] With regard to the issue surrounding the sale of the vessel, Tomlinson J highlighted that, on the assumption that the Nigerian company was a bona fide purchaser for value, in the event that those underwriters, who had elected in December 2008, became legal as opposed to beneficial co-owners of the vessel as tenants in common at law, they would as a matter of English law remain legal co-owners after the purported sale. Furthermore, he concluded that those underwriters who had not elected before the purported sale enjoyed no equitable interest and so their later election after the sale is on any view ineffective if by the sale the first defendant divested itself of legal title.[177]

8.2. Sums Recoverable

By section 27(1) of the Marine Insurance Act 1906, a marine policy may be either valued or unvalued. A valued policy is, by section 27(2) of the 1906 Act, one 'which specifies the agreed value of the subject-matter insured'. The valuation agreed by the parties is, in the absence of fraud, conclusive (section 27(3)) and forms the basis for the measure of indemnity. An unvalued policy, as defined by section 28, is one 'which does not specify the value of the subject-matter insured, but, subject to the limit of the sum insured, leaves the insur-

[170] ibid [50].
[171] ibid [55].
[172] ibid.
[173] ibid [57].
[174] ibid [59].
[175] ibid [60].
[176] ibid [61]–[63].
[177] ibid [64].

able value to be subsequently ascertained'. The default rule for the measure of indemnity under an unvalued policy, as set out in section 16, is the value of the vessel, cargo or freight at the date the policy was taken out. That is at odds with the rule applicable to all other forms of insurance, where the sum recoverable under an unvalued policy is measured by the diminution in value immediately before and immediately after the occurrence of the insured peril.[178] The market has, however, reversed the marine rule so that the measure of indemnity is common to marine and non-marine policies.[179]

The calculation of the sums payable under a policy depends upon whether the policy is valued or unvalued. In the case of a total loss under a valued policy, the sum recoverable is the agreed valuation (section 68(1)), and if the policy is unvalued, then the measure of indemnity is the diminution in the value of the subject matter measured at the date of the loss (section 68(2)).

The sum recoverable for the partial loss of a vessel is: if the vessel has been repaired, the reasonable cost of repairs (section 69(1)); if the vessel has been partially repaired, the reasonable cost of repairs plus depreciation arising from unrepaired damage (section 69(2)); and if the vessel has not been repaired and has not been sold, reasonable depreciation in market value (and not insured value)[180] arising from the unrepaired damage (section 69(3)). The Act does not deal with the situation in which an unrepaired vessel has been sold, but it has been held that the measure of indemnity is the difference between the undamaged value immediately before the loss and the sum received from the third party.[181] At common law there was a customary deduction of one-third for a wooden ship not on a maiden voyage, representing depreciation. Although section 69 refers to customary deductions, it was never clear whether the common law rule applied to iron ships, and there is no provision for deduction in the Institute Hull Clauses.

The sum recoverable for partial loss of freight is such proportion of the sum as is fixed by the policy in the case of a valued policy, or in the case of an unvalued policy the proportion of freight lost by the assured as against the whole freight at the risk of the assured under the policy (section 70). The same principles apply to partial loss of goods (section 71).

In all cases, the amount recoverable is subject to section 81, which sets out the principle of 'average'.[182] This applies where the subject matter is underinsured. Under this provision, the assured is deemed to be his or her own insurer for the uninsured proportion, so that the amount of the full loss recoverable is reduced by the proportion of underinsurance.

8.3. General Average

It is in the interests of all the parties – the owners of the ship, of the cargo and of the freight, and the crew – that the captain and crew are free to act as necessary to protect the whole of the common adventure. Where expenditure is incurred or a sacrifice of something is made to save the adventure, then it is not unreasonable to expect that all those who benefit by this action should bear a proportion of the loss: for instance, if cargo is thrown overboard to prevent the ship from sinking, the others – such as the ship's owner and the owners of

[178] See ch 12 above.
[179] *Clothing Management Technology Ltd v Beazley Solutions Ltd* [2012] 1 Lloyd's Rep 571.
[180] *Suez Fortune Investments Ltd v Talbot Underwriting Ltd, The Brilliante Virtuoso* [2019] EWHC 2599 (Comm).
[181] *Pitman v Universal Marine Insurance Co* (1882) 9 QB 192.
[182] See ch 12 above.

the freight and the remaining cargo – benefit and should, therefore, contribute to the loss suffered by the cargo owner. This, in essence, is the purpose of the law of general average. It is a subject of broad significance in maritime law, which cannot be covered in great detail here; nevertheless, its impact on marine insurance requires that its main features be discussed.[183]

A general average loss 'is a loss caused by or directly consequential on a general average act' (section 66(1)), and there is a general average act 'where any extraordinary sacrifice or expenditure is voluntarily and reasonably made or incurred in time of peril for the purpose of preserving the property imperilled in the common adventure' (section 66(2)). According to the York–Antwerp Rules 1994,[184] rule A:

> There is a general average act, when, and only when, any extraordinary sacrifice or expenditure is intentionally and reasonably made or incurred for the common safety for the purpose of preserving from peril the property involved in a common maritime adventure.[185]

The captain of the ship must have voluntarily, intentionally and reasonably incurred extraordinary expenditure (a general average expenditure),[186] or made an extraordinary sacrifice of equipment or goods (general average sacrifice), to save more than one subject from a common peril which threatened both the interest claiming the contribution and the interest from whom the contribution is claimed.

In explaining why, in one case, the action taken had been extraordinary, Blackburn J said

> this expenditure was not incurred on behalf of the master as agent of the shipowner, performing his contract to carry on the cargo to its destination and earn freight, but was an extraordinary expenditure for the purpose of saving the property at risk.[187]

Elsewhere, it has been observed that 'there must be expenditure abnormal in kind or degree, and it must have been incurred on an abnormal occasion for the preservation of the property'.[188] An expenditure or a sacrifice that might properly and ordinarily have been incurred by the captain in undertaking the contract of carriage of goods is not general average. Moreover, there must be an intentional sacrifice: if goods are lost overboard by the action of the waves, there is no obligation to contribute. The peril must actually exist and not merely be believed to exist, even if that belief is reasonable: where a master soaked the hold in the mistaken belief that there was a fire and thereby damaged the cargo, there was no general average loss.[189] On the other hand, the master does not have to wait until damage has actually occurred, although 'the peril must be imminent, which means that it must be substantial and threatening and something more than the ordinary peril of the seas'.[190] There is no right of contribution where the loss was caused by the fault of the interest claiming the contribution, so the owner of a ship that is unseaworthy at the start of the voyage

[183] R Cornah, *Lowndes and Rudolph on General Average*, 15th edn (London, Sweet & Maxwell, 2018); J Macdonald, 'General Average Ancient and Modern' [1995] *Lloyd's Maritime and Commercial Law Quarterly* 480.

[184] Now York–Antwerp Rules 2004.

[185] The York–Antwerp Rules 2004 form a code on various aspects of general average. The rules are not compulsory, but are commonly expressly incorporated into marine policies.

[186] An example of general average expenditure would be the cost of towage and the harbour dues paid when, in order to save it from an immediate peril, a ship is towed into port.

[187] *Hingston v Wendt* (1876) 1 QBD 367, 370.

[188] *Société Nouvell D'Armementv Spillers & Bakers Ltd* [1917] 1 KB 865, 871 (Sankey J).

[189] *Joseph Watson and Son Ltd v Firemen's Fund Insurance Co of San Francisco* [1922] 2 KB 355.

[190] *Société Nouvell D'Armement v Spillers & Bakers Ltd* [1917] 1 KB 865, 871 (Sankey J).

cannot claim a general average contribution.[191] Similarly, if a latent defect in the cargo is the cause of the loss – as, for instance, where coal spontaneously combusts and is damaged as a result of the operation to extinguish the fire – the cargo owner cannot claim a general average contribution, although a contribution may be awarded to the owners of freight lost when the damaged coal is unloaded before the destination is reached.[192]

The interest on whom a general average loss falls is entitled 'to a rateable contribution from the other parties interested', known as the general average contribution (section 66(3)). Subject to any express term of the policy, an assured who has incurred a general average expenditure can recover from insurers 'in respect of the proportion of the loss which falls upon him'; this is contrasted with the situation in general average sacrifice, where the insured may recover 'in respect of the whole loss without having enforced his right of contribution from the other parties liable to contribute' (section 66(4)). An assured who has paid, or is liable to pay, a general average contribution can recover from the insurer (section 66(5)), which in other words means the insurer is liable for the assured's share of the contribution. In addition, where the assured has incurred general average expenses and the contributions of all the interested parties (including the assured's own share) fall below the expenditure, the insurer is liable for the shortfall because it is 'the proportion of the loss which falls' on the assured.[193] Although this reasoning came from a case where the shortfall was caused by a diminution in the value of the cargo, there seems no reason for not applying it more widely, so that, whatever the reason for the shortfall, the assured can ultimately claim from the insurer. The only difference from the position in general average sacrifice is that the other parties must be approached before a claim can be made against the insurer for the loss that does not form part of the assured's share. Where the ship, freight and cargo, or any two of these, are owned by the same assured, the insurers' liability for general average loss or contributions is determined as if they were owned by different people (section 66(7)).

Under section 73 of the Act, 'where the assured has paid, or is liable for, any general average contribution, the measure of indemnity is the full amount of such contribution, if the subject-matter liable to contribution is insured for its full contributory value'. Insurers are only liable for losses covered by the policy, so they will not be liable for any general average loss or contribution 'where the loss was not incurred for the purpose of avoiding, or in connection with the avoidance of, a peril insured against' (section 66(6)). However, the Institute Clauses include a term covering general average incurred 'to avoid or in connection with the avoidance of loss from any cause', with certain exceptions.[194] This means that the insurers will be liable if part of the cargo is thrown overboard to enable a ship to escape from a peril, which, while not specifically excluded, is not expressly covered.

The Marine Insurance Act 1906 makes the law of general average subject to the contrary express agreement of the parties, and the Institute Clauses all include provisions incorporating the York–Antwerp Rules.[195] The adjustment of general average is determined by the policy, failing which it will be in accordance with the law of the port of destination. If the

[191] *Schloss v Heriot* (1863) 14 CB (NS) 58.
[192] *Pirie & Co v Middle Dock Co* (1881) 44 LT 424.
[193] *Green Star Shipping Co Ltd v London Assurance Co, The Andree* [1933] 1 KB 378.
[194] ICC (B), (C), cl 2 (these remain unchanged under the 2009 clauses).
[195] eg IVCH(95), cl 8.3.

adventure ends at another port, then it will be in accordance with the law of that port and, where that port is not in the UK, the adjustment is a foreign adjustment, which will bind the assured and insurers.[196]

9. Suing and Labouring

9.1. The Duty to Sue and Labour

The Lloyd's SG Policy, codifying earlier wordings, included a term authorising the assured

> to sue, labour, and travel for, in and about the defence, safeguards, and recovery of the said goods and merchandises, and ship, &c., or any part thereof, without prejudice to this insurance; to the charges whereof we, the assurers, will contribute.[197]

It was clearly in the interest of the insurers that the assured be encouraged to avert or reduce the loss from insured perils, and allowing the assured to recover expenditure for doing so was the chosen means. Suing and labouring at common law was, therefore, seen in terms of compensating the assured for efforts in mitigating loss, and there were no cases supporting the proposition that the assured owed some sort of duty to sue and labour. However, when the law was codified in 1906 Act, section 78(4) provided that 'it is the duty of the assured and his agents in all cases to take such measures as may be reasonable for the purpose of averting or minimising a loss'. Despite the lack of common law authority, the statutory provision has been picked up by the market: there is a similar obligation in the Institute Clauses: under ITCH(83), clause 13.1 and IHC 2003, clause 9.1, it is the duty of the assured or their servants/employees and agents 'to take such measures as may be reasonable for the purpose of averting or minimising a loss which would be recoverable under this insurance'. The pre-Act cases turned on causation rather than duty, and recognised that in exceptional circumstances the assured's own act or omission might constitute the proximate cause of a loss rather than an insured peril. That view is supported by section 55(2)(a), which permits recovery even though there has been negligence by the master or crew. In *Astrovianis Compañia Naviera SA v Linard, The Gold Sky*,[198] section 78(4) was thought to be a drafting error, and the reconciliation of sections 55(2)(a) and 78(4) there suggested was that the latter applied only to the assured personally and to agents other than master and crew, thereby reducing section 78(4) to virtual meaninglessness. That approach was subsequently rejected,[199] and the courts have now reverted to the original common law by rejecting the word 'duty' and regarding the matter as one of causation.[200] It will be in exceptional circum-

[196] ITCH(83), cl 11.2 and IHC 2003, cl 8.2 expressly provides for this.

[197] Generally, AL Parks, 'Marine Insurance: The Sue and Labor Clause' (1977) 9 *Journal of Money Laundering Control* 415; BP O'Sullivan, 'The Scope of the Sue and Labor Clause' (1990) 21 *Journal of Money Laundering Control* 545; P MacDonald Eggers, 'Sue and Labour and Beyond: The Assured's Duty of Mitigation' [1998] *Lloyd's Maritime and Commercial Law Quarterly* 228.

[198] [1972] 2 Lloyd's Rep 187.

[199] The authorities were reviewed in *Melinda Holdings SA v Hellenic Mutual War Risks Association (Bermuda) Ltd* [2011] EWHC 181 (Comm).

[200] *National Oilwell (UK) Ltd v Davy Offshore Ltd* [1993] 2 Lloyd's Rep 582; *State of Netherlands v Youell* [1998] 1 Lloyd's Rep 236; *Orica Australia Pty Ltd v Limit (No 2) Ltd* [2011] VSC 65.

stances only where the chain of causation is broken by the imminence or occurrence of an insured peril and the assured's response to it. Phillips LJ has observed that there appeared to have been no examples of the subsection providing insurers with a defence to a claim since the enactment of the legislation in 1906.[201] Since that comment was made, the only case in which the assured's claim has been affected by post-casualty conduct is *Linelevel Ltd v Powszechny Zaklad Ubezpieczen SA, The Nore Challenger*,[202] where a small deduction was made from the sum due under the policy for the assured's continued use of an unrepaired damaged vessel in a manner that exacerbated the necessary repairs.

9.2. Payment for Suing and Labouring Expenditure

Where the assured does undertake expenditure, the insurers are required to make payment for sums reasonably incurred. Section 78(1) states:

> Where the policy contains a suing and labouring clause, the engagement thereby entered into is deemed to be supplementary to the contract of insurance, and the assured may recover from the insurer any expenses properly incurred pursuant to the clause, notwithstanding that the insurer may have paid for a total loss …

Although the section (curiously, unlike section 78(4)) is based on the existence of a suing and labouring clause, such clauses are all but universal, and even in the absence of a clause the obligation to indemnify would be implied.[203] Section 78(1) makes it clear that the sums payable by way of suing and labouring expenses are additional to the sums insured, so that even if the assured's attempts are unsuccessful and there is a loss, the insurers must pay both the loss and the expenses. There are a number of important limits on the right of recovery.

First, section 78(3) states that 'expenses incurred for the purpose of averting or diminishing any loss not covered by the policy are not recoverable under the suing and labouring clause'. That is an obvious point, in that if the peril is not covered by the policy, then the expenditure cannot be for the insurers' benefit.

Secondly, the expenditure must have been 'properly incurred'. That has two elements. The expenditure must have been in respect of a peril that had actually occurred or, at the very least, was 'in the teeth of the peril', and not simply in anticipation that a peril might occur at some point in the future.[204] Further, the expenditure must have been reasonable in the circumstances: Lord Keith in *Stephen v Scottish Boatowners Mutual Insurance Association, The Talisman*[205] set out the test as being whether 'any ordinary competent skipper would have acted differently'. Thus, the cost of feeding a cargo of cattle to prevent them from dying can be recovered.[206] In *Masefield AG v Amlin Corporate Member Ltd*,[207] it was confirmed that, in the case of the seizure and ransom of a vessel and its cargo by pirates, the

[201] *State of Netherlands v Youell* [1998] 1 Lloyd's Rep 236, 238. See similarly Rix LJ in *Masefield AG v Amlin Corporate Member Ltd* [2011] EWCA Civ 24, [76]; *Melinda Holdings SA v Hellenic Mutual War Risks Assoc (Bermuda) Ltd* [2011] EWHC 181 (Comm).

[202] [2005] 2 Lloyd's Rep 534.

[203] *Netherlands Insurance Co (Est 1845) Ltd v Karl Ljungberg & Co AB* [1986] 2 Lloyd's Rep 19. Modern restitutionary principles would seem to put this beyond doubt.

[204] *BN Amro Bank NV v Royal & Sun Alliance plc* [2021] EWHC 442 (Comm).

[205] [1989] 1 Lloyd's Rep 535, 540.

[206] *The Pomeranian* [1895] P 34.

[207] [2011] EWCA Civ 24.

payment of a ransom in order to procure the release of the vessel amounted to a sue and labour expense. Legal expenses incurred in seeking to protect or recover insured property also fall within the clause.[208]

Thirdly, general average losses and contributions and salvage charges, as defined by this Act, are not recoverable under the suing and labouring clause. It was seen above that general average contributions arise by operation of maritime law and fall within the indemnity granted by the policy itself rather than the suing and labouring clause. Charges incurred by the assured in appointing salvors to rescue subject matter are payable under general maritime law independently of contract, as assessed in amount by admiralty law principles, and fall within the policy indemnity itself: that was the position at common law as codified by section 65(1). However, charges incurred by the assured under contract – referred to by section 65(2) as 'particular charges' – are not recoverable under the contract itself. Instead, they fall within the suing and labouring clause, which means that the insurers have the right to challenge the reasonableness of any contractual arrangements made by the assured. In practice, salvage is almost always conducted under contract, on the terms of the Lloyd's Open Form. Disputes as to quantum are resolved by arbitration.

---

10. Successive Losses

The assured may be unfortunate enough to suffer more than one loss. The question then arises as to how a policy responds to a series of unfortunate events. The position is laid out in part by section 77 of the 1906 Act and in part by the common law. The various possibilities are as follows.[209]

First, where in the same policy period there are a series of partial losses, the policy itself will determine whether the assured is entitled to recover for each of them even though their total exceeds the sum insured (section 77(1)). Most policies do place an aggregate cap by reference to the sum insured, and successive losses are subject to the indemnity principle so that a further claim for a ship or cargo in a damaged and unrepaired state cannot be made for the same damage. The total sum recoverable for a series of unrepaired partial losses is determined at the date the policy comes to an end.[210]

Secondly, where in the same policy period there is a partial loss which has not been repaired, followed by a total loss, the partial loss merges into the total loss and the assured is restricted to claiming for the latter. That is set out in section 77(2) and is based on *Livie v Janson*,[211] where a vessel ran aground (insured peril) and before repairs were possible the vessel was confiscated for breaking an embargo (an uninsured peril): the latter alone was relevant, so there was no recovery. If, by contrast, the partial loss has been repaired, the assured can recover for the total loss at least if the policy does not impose an aggregate cap on the amount recoverable.

[208] *Quadra Commodities SA v XL Insurance Company SE* [2022] EWHC 431 (Comm).
[209] See ch 19 below for the position in non-marine insurance.
[210] *Kusel v Atkin, The Catariba* [1997] 2 Lloyd's Rep 749.
[211] (1810) 12 East 648.

Thirdly, where there is a partial loss during the policy and it is unrepaired by the date the policy terminates, the assured may recover for that loss. It is irrelevant that the vessel became a total loss by another peril after that date.[212]

Fourthly, and perhaps the most difficult, where a constructive total loss is followed by an actual total loss, the assured may rely upon either of them, although not both. That unusual possibility arose in *The Kastor Too*,[213] a case in which a disastrous fire (an insured constructive total loss) was followed immediately by an unrelated sinking (an uninsured event as there was no evidence of fortuity). It has already been noted that the assured was not able to serve a notice of abandonment in this case, but the circumstances made that impossible.

[212] *British & Foreign Marine Insurance Co v Wilson Shipping Co Ltd* [1921] 1 AC 188.
[213] [2004] EWCA Civ 277.

18

Reinsurance[1]

1. Introduction

Reinsurance is insurance taken out by insurers to protect themselves against exposure to a massive claims liability and to allow them to participate in risks which would otherwise be beyond their resources. By spreading risks between insurers worldwide, it becomes possible to issue cover for major and often international risks which would otherwise be uninsurable and to support national insurance markets which are too small in capacity to cover domestic risks.[2] Reinsurance also enables insurers to protect their own solvency, and, indeed, the rules made by the Financial Conduct Authority and the Prudential Regulatory Authority under the Financial Services and Markets Act 2000 requires insurers to have adequate reinsurance in place as a guarantee of their solvency margin. Reinsurance is written by Lloyd's syndicates, ordinary insurance companies and specialist reinsurers. In practice, many reinsurance contracts written on the London market cover 100 per cent of the underlying risk in respect of policies written by overseas insurers who themselves lack the sophistication or resources to underwrite the business, a practice known as 'fronting'. The local reinsurer bears none of the risk and passes the premium to the reinsurers, retaining only a small part, typically 5 per cent, by way of commission for facilitating the arrangement. The use of fronting has become of increased importance following Brexit, which removed the possibility of UK insurers selling insurance directly into EU countries. The solution adopted by Lloyd's was to establish a subsidiary in Belgium to write all EU risks and to reinsure them back into Lloyd's underwriters in London on a 100 per cent fronting basis.

Reinsurance was in its origins viewed with some suspicion as facilitating gambling by underwriters and was banned by the Marine Insurance Act 1745.[3] The prohibition was not lifted until a series of partial measures between 1864 and 1867.[4] Reinsurance contracts

[1] See generally *Butler and Merkin on Insurance Law* (London, Sweet & Maxwell, 1985 to date, updated, looseleaf); T O'Neill and J Wolonecki, *The Law of Reinsurance*, 5th edn (London, Sweet & Maxwell, 2021); C Edelman et al, *The Law of Reinsurance*, 2nd edn (Oxford, Oxford University Press, 2020); Ö Gürses, *Reinsuring Clauses* (London, Informa, 2010).

[2] The importance of reinsurance is explained in *Bonner v Cox Dedicated Corporate Member Ltd* [2005] EWCA Civ 1512 and *Sovereign Assurance Co Ltd v Commissioner of Inland Revenue* [2013] NZCA 652.

[3] R Merkin, *Marine Insurance: A Legal History* (Cheltenham, Edward Elgar, 2021), paras 6-603–6-604.

[4] ibid para 14-007.

were written in that period, but it was not possible to lay down legal principles applicable to such contracts. Having struggled through the definition of an insurance contract, the reader will not find it too surprising to learn that it is rather difficult to arrive at an all-embracing definition of a reinsurance policy. There is no statutory definition of reinsurance, although there are statutory references to the activity, and there is no exhaustive judicial definition because of the sheer variety of different types of reinsurance. According to Lord Lowry, 'Reinsurance is prima facie a contract of indemnity ... under which the reinsurer indemnifies the original insurer against the whole or against a specified amount or proportion ... of the risk which the latter has himself insured'.[5] More simply, Viscount Cave LC said that 'by a contract of reinsurance the reinsuring party insures the original insuring party against the original loss'.[6]

Reinsurance is to be distinguished from co-insurance, insurance arranged in layers and double insurance, in each of which cases the insured has a separate contract of insurance with each underwriter. Reinsurance is also not an assignment of the direct policy by the reinsured to the reinsurers,[7] neither is it a partnership between the reinsured and the reinsurers.[8] There is no privity of contract between the insured and the reinsurers so that the insured's only action is against his own insurers,[9] although some reinsurance agreements contain cut-through clauses under which the insured is given a direct action against the reinsurers, albeit generally only in the event of the reinsured's insolvency,[10] and in principle it is perfectly possible for reinsurers to agree to accept direct liability to the insured.[11] A cut-through clause is potentially enforceable by the insured under the Contracts (Third Parties) Act 1999,[12] although there is some doubt as to whether a cut-through clause is valid under the English insolvency rule of equal treatment of unsecured creditors.[13] The Third Parties (Rights against Insurers) Act 2010, section 15 specifically excludes reinsurance contracts, so that an insured has no direct claim against reinsurers in the event of the reinsured's insolvency.

There has long been a debate as to whether reinsurance is a further policy on the direct subject matter or something akin to a liability policy under which the reinsured obtains indemnity when it faces liability to the direct insured. For regulatory purposes, under

[5] *Forsikringsaktieselskapet Vesta v Butcher* [1989] AC 852, 908. See also *Travelers Casualty & Surety Co of Europe Ltd v Commissioners of Customs and Excise* [2006] Lloyd's Rep IR 63, where it was held by a VAT tribunal that reinsurance is the reinsurance of the business of an insurer even though that business is not strictly insurance (eg the issue of fidelity bonds).

[6] *Forsikringsaktieselskabet National (of Copenhagen) v Attorney-General* [1925] AC 639, 642 (Viscount Cave LC). See also *ERC Frankona Reinsurance v American National Insurance Co* [2005] EWHC 1381 (Comm).

[7] *Re Lancashire Plate Glass Fire and Burglary Insurance Co Ltd* [1912] 1 Ch 35.

[8] *Re Norwich Equitable Fire* (1887) 57 LT 241.

[9] Marine Insurance Act 1906, s 9(2); *In re Law Guarantee Trust and Accident Society Ltd. Liverpool Mortgage Insurance Company's Case* [1914] 2 Ch 617, 647–48 (Scrutton J); *Phoenix General Insurance Co of Greece SA v Halvanon Insurance Co Ltd* [1985] 2 Lloyd's Rep 599, 614 (Hobhouse J): 'The relationship of a reassured and a reinsurer is not that of agent and principal; it is one as between principals. The reinsurer is in no sense a party to the contract of original insurance and has no rights under it.' See also *Equitas Ltd v Wave City Shipping Co Ltd* [2005] EWHC 923 (Comm) (reinsurers not liable to insured for the tort of inducing breach of contract simply by the reinsurers having agreed to pay profit commission to the reinsured).

[10] But not always: the clause in *Randgold Resources Ltd v Santam Ltd* [2018] EWHC 2493 (Comm) was expressed in general terms.

[11] See *Grecoair Inc v Tilling* [2005] Lloyd's Rep IR 151, where there was no evidence of any such intention even though the reinsurers took over all responsibility for handling the insured's claim.

[12] *Randgold Resources Ltd v Santam Ltd* [2018] EWHC 2493 (Comm), where the court permitted an insured to seek a declaration as to the reinsurer's liability to the reinsured.

[13] The rule in *British Eagle International Air Lines Ltd v Compagnie Nationale Air France* [1978] 1WLR 758.

the 2000 Act reinsurance is deemed to be of the class of direct insurance to which the contract relates;[14] as such, it falls within the Insurance Act 2015.[15] However, these statutes aside, it is clear that reinsurance shares many of the characteristics of a liability policy, not least that the reinsurers' liability is triggered by the reinsured establishing and quantifying its loss in exactly the same way as an insured under a liability policy.[16] The authorities are inconsistent.[17] The matter was given consideration by the House of Lords in *Wasa International Insurance Co v Lexington Insurance Co*,[18] where the argument for the reinsured was that the reinsurers were required to provide an indemnity whenever the reinsured faced liability under the direct policy. The House of Lords ruled that a reinsurance contract is generally to be construed as further insurance on the underlying subject matter so that the reinsurers had the right to assert that the direct loss did not fall within the coverage of the reinsurance, although their Lordships all recognised that it is perfectly possible to frame a reinsurance agreement as a liability cover. In *Feasey v Sun Life of Canada*,[19] for instance, a reinsurance agreement covering personal accident claims was originally drafted in liability terms, but the wording was subsequently altered so that the agreement was expressed as one which responded to accidents rather than the reinsured's liability to make payment for accidents. The reinsurance was held to be a life policy and thus subject to the rules on insurable interest in the Life Assurance Act 1774.[20]

For the most part, the same principles apply to reinsurance policies as to insurance policies in general, and therefore in this chapter only the features which are peculiar to reinsurance will be examined.

---

2. Types of Reinsurance Contracts

Reinsurance agreements[21] may be proportional or non-proportional. Under a proportional agreement, the reinsured retains a proportion of the risk and cedes the balance to

[14] *Re NRG Victory Insurance* [1995] 1 All ER 533; *Re Friend's Provident Life* [1999] Lloyd's Rep IR 547.

[15] The definition of insurance does not include reinsurance, but reinsurance is referred to in s 4(5)(b) for the purposes of defining knowledge of facts that have to be disclosed, and this reference was thought by the government to suffice to show that reinsurance was intended to be covered.

[16] See ch 14 above.

[17] Thus, in *British Dominion General Insurance Co Ltd v Duder* [1915] 2 KB 394, 400, Buckley LJ described reinsurance of direct fire policies as 'in effect a policy of insurance against loss by or incidental to fire'. See also *Forsikringsaktieselskabet National (of Copenhagen) v Attorney-General* [1925] AC 639, 642 (Viscount Cave LC); *British Dominion General Insurance Co v Duder* [1915] 2 KB 394, 400 (Buckley LJ); *Re NRG Victory Reinsurance* [1995] 1 All ER 533; *Toomey v Eagle Star Insurance Co Ltd* [1994] 1 Lloyd's Rep 516, 522–24 (Hobhouse LJ); *CGU International Insurance plc v Astrazeneca Insurance Co Ltd* [2005] EWHC 2755 (Comm). According to the Marine Insurance Act 1906, s 9(1): 'The insurer under a contract of marine insurance has an insurable interest in his risk and may re-insure in respect of it.' But in *Charter Reinsurance Co Ltd v Fagan* [1996] 2 Lloyd's Rep 113, 117, Lord Mustill did not rule out the possibility that there might be cases in which the reinsurance is not an insurance of the subject matter of the primary contract. As Lord Mustill pointed out, the main issue in contention here is the regulation of insurance business, although there are other issues, such as the requirement of a policy in marine insurance under Marine Insurance Act 1906, s 22, and the applicability of the Life Assurance Act 1774.

[18] [2009] UKHL 40. See also the judgment of Lord Sumption in *Zurich Insurance Plc UK Branch v International Energy Group Ltd* [2015] UKSC 33.

[19] [2003] Lloyd's Rep IR 637.

[20] The root decision of *Dalby v India & London Life* (1854) 3 CB 364 may indeed be regarded as an early example of the same point.

[21] Other than those which are pure fronting arrangements.

the reinsurers. The premium paid to the reinsured is (minus brokerage and ceding commission) payable to the reinsurers to reflect the parties' proportions. Under a non-proportional agreement, the reinsured retains a given sum (referred to as the 'deductible', and much the same as an excess clause in a direct policy) and the reinsurers accept liability for an amount in excess of that sum up to a given maximum sum. The premium under a non-proportional agreement is not necessarily based on the direct premium. The reinsured may on occasion be required by a reinsurance of either type to retain the deductible for its own account, thereby giving the reinsurers some guarantee that the business accepted by the reinsured is of the appropriate quality, although in most cases there is no such provision and the reinsured is free to reinsure the amount of its deductible elsewhere.[22] A deductible is normally to be construed as applying to the amount of the reinsured's liability for a claim and not to the totality of the claim itself.[23]

The simplest form of reinsurance is facultative, which is the reinsurance of a single risk. By way of example, A insures a ship with B and B enters into facultative reinsurance with C to cover the liability undertaken in the first agreement. This type of reinsurance is nearly always proportional. Until the introduction of the Market Reform Contract in 2009, facultative reinsurance was written in the London market by a short form 'slip policy', making it clear that no further reinsurance policy wording would be issued which had appended to it the terms of the underlying insurance. The key term provision in a facultative policy is the 'full reinsurance' clause, of which the following is typical: 'being a reinsurance of and warranted same terms and conditions as original, and to follow the settlements'. These days it is commonly abbreviated to 'as original'.

Treaty reinsurance is appropriate where the reinsured wishes to obtain cover for a portfolio of risks. The reinsurance may extend to the reinsured's entire business ('whole account' reinsurance) or it may be confined to a part of that business (eg the marine account). A treaty is a framework arrangement under which the parties agree that all risks of the type described are to fall within the scope of the treaty. Treaties may be obligatory or non-obligatory. Under the former, any risks accepted by the reinsured are automatically ceded to the reinsurance without either party having any discretion in the matter: there may be an obligation on the reinsured to inform the reinsurers on a regular basis[24] of risks accepted, but failure to notify the reinsurers will not prevent the risk from attaching even if notification is not made until after the loss has occurred.[25] If the contract is non-obligatory, the reinsured has the right to decide whether to proffer a risk for acceptance, and the reinsurers have the right to refuse any particular risk. The treaty here is an agreed machinery for the presentation of proposals by the reinsured. A hybrid is a facultative-obligatory contract under which the reinsured has the right to decide which risks to cede but the reinsurers have no right to reject what is presented to them. This arrangement is unfavourable to reinsurers

[22] *Great Atlantic Insurance v Home Insurance* [1981] 2 Lloyd's Rep 219; *Phoenix General Insurance of Greece v Halvanon Insurance* [1985] 2 Lloyd's Rep 599; *Societe Anonyme d'Intermediaries Luxembourgeois v Farex Gie* [1995] LRLR 116; *GE Reinsurance Corporation v New Hampshire Insurance Co* [2004] Lloyd's Rep IR 404.

[23] See *Allianz Marine Aviation (France) v GE Frankona Reinsurance Ltd London* [2005] EWHC 101 (Comm), in which the reinsured's subscription to the direct policy was 45.238%. The total loss was US$17,857,901.85, the reinsured's share being US$8,078,557. It was held that the US$5,000,000 deductible was to be applied to the latter figure and not to the former.

[24] Often monthly and by the use of 'bordereaux'.

[25] *Glencore International AG v Ryan, The Beursgracht* [2002] 1 Lloyd's Rep 574.

as they are more or less at the mercy of the reinsured, who may decide to offload poor business on the reinsurers,[26] and a 'fac-oblig' contract imposes an obligation on the reinsured to inform the reinsurers of risks which have been ceded, as in the absence of a declaration the reinsured cannot be seen to have exercised the option to cede.[27]

Treaties come in various proportional and non-proportional forms. Quota share and surplus treaties are both proportional, the reinsured retaining an agreed proportion of each risk and the reinsurers taking the remainder. The most important form of non-proportional treaty is excess of loss, under which the reinsurers accept liability for sums in excess of the reinsured's 'ultimate net loss', a figure defined as the total aggregate of liabilities, excluding fixed costs, arising out of an event or occurrence. Stop loss reinsurance is a guarantee of solvency and comes into play when the reinsured's loss reach an agreed figure. Lloyd's operates reinsurance to close which enables syndicates of members to place limits on their liabilities. A syndicate's accounts for each year remain open for three years for the receipt of premiums and the payment of claims; the account is then closed and future liabilities are reinsured by another Lloyd's syndicate.[28]

Where the amounts at stake are large, a combination of the various forms of reinsurance may be used. In particular, there may be a number of different excess layers of reinsurance.[29] Reinsurers may themselves take out cover, known as retrocession, and there may often be a large number of contracts at different levels. The London market in the 1980s and 1990s operated the London Market Excess of Loss (LMX) Spiral, which consisted of a chain of excess of loss treaties, sometimes involving many thousands of contracts.[30]

There has been some discussion as to whether all reinsurance treaties are insurance contracts. If the reinsurers are obliged to accept risks ceded to them, then there seems no difficulty in seeing this as a contract of insurance.[31] But where there is no such obligation, then this is not reinsurance; rather, it is, as Gatehouse J expressed it, 'simply a procedural mechanism which, if operated as both parties no doubt hoped and expected, would secure considerable commercial benefit to both sides'.[32]

Reinsurance treaties are generally long-term contracts which last for more than the one year traditional for direct policies. Three-year agreements are common. Provision is made in such agreements for annual review of the contract, so that if the reinsured's losses are unusually high, the reinsurers may have the right either to cancel the agreement on its anniversary date or at the very least give notice of a premium increase.[33]

[26] *Aneco Reinsurance Underwriting Ltd v Johnson & Higgins* [1998] 1 Lloyd's Rep 565.

[27] See *Glencore International AG v Alpina Insurance Co* [2004] 1 Lloyd's Rep 111, where it was held that a declaration could not be made after the insured (this was a direct declaration policy) had become aware that a loss had occurred.

[28] *Toomey v Eagle Star Insurance Co Ltd* [1994] 1 Lloyd's Rep 516, 520 (Hobhouse LJ); *Baker v Black Sea and Baltic General Insurance Co Ltd* [1996] LRLR 353, 358 and 360–61 (Staughton and Millett LJJ).

[29] For a description of the operation of the market and the use of a 'spiral' of reinsurance contracts involving business which was loss-making but for reinsurance protection, see the important judgment of Thomas J in *Sphere Drake Insurance Ltd v Euro International Underwriting Ltd* [2004] Lloyd's Rep IR 525, where brokers were held to have engaged in a fraud by arranging a succession of unnecessary reinsurance contracts from which they derived commission.

[30] For a description of the LMX spiral, see *IRB Brasil Resseguros SA v CX Reinsurance Company Ltd* [2010] EWHC 974 (Comm).

[31] *Forsikringsaktieselskabet National (of Copenhagen) v Attorney-General* [1925] AC 639.

[32] *Société Anonyme d'Intermediaries Luxembourgeois v Farex Gie* [1995] LRLR 116, 135.

[33] *Charman v New Cap Reinsurance Corporation Ltd* [2004] Lloyd's Rep IR 373.

3. Formation of the Contract

Reinsurance is subject to all the rules applied to other insurance contracts, including the particular requirements of a marine or life policy, where appropriate. As noted above, the reinsureds' insurable interest is either the risk under the primary policy or the risk of having to indemnify the reinsured. If the insured under the primary policy has no insurable interest, the reinsureds will also have no insurable interest and neither policy will be enforceable.[34]

Reinsurance is frequently formed in advance of insurance. If the risk is a particularly large or unusual one and it is likely that existing reinsurance arrangements do not confer adequate protection, the broker will appreciate that the task of finding willing insurers will be greatly eased when it is possible to offer additional reinsurance coverage to a subscribing insurer. Alternatively, the broker may approach an insurer and receive a conditional acceptance, depending upon the broker securing adequate reinsurance. This raises as yet unresolved questions as to the agency of the broker appointed by the insured to place the direct policy – as it is clear that the broker cannot be acting for the insured unless he has been expressly authorised to place reinsurance[35] – and the status of the reinsurance agreement prior to direct policy being allocated to it. The courts have for the most part sidestepped these problems and have resorted to the traditional contractual analysis that an agreement to reinsure amounts to a standing offer which can be accepted by any insurer by accepting the direct risk and thus becoming entitled to the benefit of the reinsurance.[36]

Reinsurance agreements are normally the result of protracted negotiations, with formal agreement being reached by the scratching of, in London, the Market Reform Contract. As with other London market placements, the Market Reform Contract constitutes a series of bilateral contracts between the reinsured and each reinsurer. It is possible for a contract to come into existence prior to the scratching of the Market Reform Contract, where the parties have reached agreement on all material points, although this is relatively unusual.[37] Terms cannot be imposed unilaterally after agreement has been reached.[38]

The duty of fair presentation applies to reinsurance in the same way as at the direct level.[39] The reinsurers thus have to prove that a statement has been made[40] or a fact has been

[34] For instance, a 'ppi' policy (ie a proof of policy interest policy under which the insurers agree to pay whether or not the insured has an insurable interest) cannot be the subject of an enforceable reinsurance policy: *Re Overseas Marine Insurance Co Ltd* (1930) 36 Ll L Rep 183.

[35] *SAIL v Farex Gie* [1995] LRLR 116.

[36] *GAFLAC v Tanter, The Zephyr* [1985] 2 Lloyd's Rep 529; *Youell v Bland Welch (No 2)* [1990] 2 Lloyd's Rep 431; *Kingscroft v Nissan (No 2)* [1999] Lloyd's Rep IR 603; *Tryg Baltica International (UK) Ltd v Boston Compania De Seguros SA* [2005] Lloyd's Rep IR 40; *Bonner v Cox Dedicated Corporate Member Ltd* [2005] EWCA Civ 1512.

[37] *ERC Frankona Reinsurance v American National Insurance Co* [2005] EWHC 1381 (Comm); *Allianz Insurance Company Egypt v Aigaion Insurance Company SA* [2008] EWCA Civ 1455. For an exception, see *Sun Life Assurance Co of Canada v CX Reinsurance Co Ltd* [2004] Lloyd's Rep IR 86.

[38] *Allianz Insurance Co Egypt v Aigaion Insurance Co SA (No 2)* [2008] EWHC 1127 (Comm).

[39] *Highlands Insurance Co v Continental Insurance Co* [1987] 1 Lloyd's Rep 109.

[40] The statement has to be sufficiently specific to amount to a representation, so that the statement that the reinsured maintained the highest standards in writing risks is too vague to be actionable: *Limit No 2 Ltd v Axa Versicherung AG* [2008] EWCA Civ 1231. A statement of intention or opinion is only a misrepresentation if the intention or opinion is not held: *Rendall v Combined Insurance Company of America* [2005] EWHC 678 (Comm); and such a statement, if made when the contract is taken out, is unlikely to be regarded as having been repeated on renewal: *Limit No 2 Ltd v Axa Versicherung AG* [2008] EWCA Civ 1231.

withheld, the fact was objectively material and the presentation by the reinsured induced the reinsurers to accept the risk on the specified terms and for the specified premium. There are, however, two important modifications to ordinary principles to be borne in mind. The first is that the facts which may be material for reinsurance purposes are quite different from those which are material under a direct policy. Material facts will include:

- the reinsured's underwriting policy;[41]
- the liabilities faced by the reinsured under the direct cover,[42] including the amount of the cover[43] and facts which render the direct risk a particularly acute one,[44] such as the nature of the insured subject matter[45] and any moral hazard affecting the direct insured;[46]
- the reinsured's claims experience;[47]
- the manner in which the reinsured sets aside reserves for actual and potential claims, as the figure for reserves may mislead the reinsurers into thinking that there are few outstanding claims if the reinsured adopts an unusual reserving policy which omits many potential claims;[48] and
- the amount of the premium charged by the reinsured.[49]

The second important modification is that the duration of the duty depends upon the nature of the reinsurance agreement. As far as a treaty is concerned, it was held by Aikens J in *HIH Casualty and General Insurance v Chase Manhattan*[50] that the duty of fair presentation does not attach to a treaty which is a contract *for* insurance rather than a contract *of* insurance, and that the reinsurers' remedies are those generally available at common law, including avoiding for misrepresentation. However, the nature of the treaty in that case was not in issue, and it may be that the duty of disclosure depends upon whether the treaty is obligatory or non-obligatory. If the treaty is obligatory, so that the reinsurers cannot refuse proffered declarations, it is arguable that the reinsured's duty of disclosure exists when the treaty is set up, although it is clear that there is no separate duty of disclosure in respect of each individual declaration. If the treaty is non-obligatory, so that the reinsurers can refuse individual risks, then *HIH* is plainly right and the duty of disclosure applies only to declarations and not to the treaty itself.[51]

[41] *Limit No 2 Ltd v Axa Versicherung AG* [2008] EWCA Civ 1231; *Crane v Hannover Ruckversicherungs-Aktiengesellschaft* [2008] EWHC 3165 (Comm).

[42] *Abrahams v Mediterranean Insurance and Reinsurance Co* [1991] 1 Lloyd's Rep 216; *Aneco Reinsurance Underwriting Ltd v Johnson & Higgins* [2002] Lloyd's Rep IR 91; *ERC Frankona Reinsurance v American National Insurance Co* [2005] EWHC 1381 (Comm).

[43] *Toomey v Banco Vitalico de Espana de Seguros y Reaseguros* [2004] EWCA Civ 622.

[44] *Property Insurance v National Protector Insurance* (1913) 108 LT 104.

[45] *WISE Underwriting Agency Ltd v Grupo Nacional Provincial SA* [2004] Lloyd's Rep IR 764.

[46] *Brotherton v Aseguradora Colseguros SA (No 3)* [2004] Lloyd's Rep IR 774.

[47] *Aiken v Stewart Wrightson* [1995] 3 All ER 449; *Groupama Insurance Co Ltd v Overseas Partners Re Ltd* [2003] EWHC 34 (Comm); *Axa Versicherung AG v Arab Insurance Group* [2017] EWCA Civ 96.

[48] *Assicurazioni Generali SpA v Arab Insurance Group* [2002] Lloyd's Rep IR 131.

[49] *Allianz Via Assurance v Marchant* 1996, unreported; *Mander v Commercial Union Assurance Co plc* [1998] Lloyd's Rep IR 93; *Markel International Insurance Company Ltd and another v La Republica Compania Argentina de Seguros Generales SA* [2005] Lloyd's Rep IR 90.

[50] [2001] Lloyd's Rep IR 191.

[51] *SA d'Intermediaries Luxembourgeios v Farex Gie* [1995] LRLR 116.

4. Express and Implied Terms

4.1. Express Terms and Incorporation of Terms

As noted above, the practice of the London market in relation to the creation of facultative contracts is to use a minimal amount of wording, often no more that the full reinsurance clause. The first part of the full reinsurance clause states 'warranted terms and conditions as original' or its equivalent. The balance of authority holds that this wording is effective to incorporate the terms of the direct policy into the reinsurance, although there are some comments to the contrary. Lord Griffiths in *Forsikringsaktieselskapet Vesta v Butcher* expressed 'regret that so little thought was apparently given to the difference between a primary insurance contract and a reinsurance contract at the time the reinsurance was placed with Lloyd's',[52] and his Lordship, dissenting on this point, concluded that the full reinsurance clause amounted to no more than a warranty by the reinsured that the terms of the direct policy disclosed to the reinsurers were accurately stated. In *Toomey v Banco Vitalico de Espana de Seguros y Reaseguros*,[53] Thomas LJ, speaking for the Court of Appeal, refused to reach a concluded decision on the point, and instead held that there had been an express warranty to the effect that the terms of the direct policy were as represented to the reinsurers.

Assuming that the full reinsurance clause does have an incorporating effect, incorporation will plainly extend to the basic cover granted by the direct policy. However, claims conditions and other policy provisions will be incorporated only if consistent with the nature of reinsurance. The precise conditions for incorporation were laid down by David Steel J in *HIH Casualty and General Insurance v New Hampshire Insurance*[54] as follows: (i) the term must be germane to the reinsurance; (ii) the term must make sense, subject to permissible 'manipulation' of the words used, in the reinsurance agreement; (iii) the term must be consistent with the express terms of the reinsurance;[55] and (iv) the term must be apposite for inclusion in the reinsurance. Notice provisions have thus been held to be capable of incorporation only if they make sense in a reinsurance context.[56] In *Home Insurance Co of New York v Victoria-Montreal Fire Insurance Co*,[57] the reinsurance agreement consisted of a slip containing special terms of reinsurance with attached to it a primary fire policy of the type issued by the original insurers, which had been amended to a minimal extent – so, for instance, the syllable 're' had been inserted before 'insure'. As might be expected, almost none of the terms of the primary fire policy were appropriate for a reinsurance policy, in particular a term which prohibited an action on the policy once 12 months had elapsed since the fire. The Privy Council approached this document on the basis that the primary fire policy was attached merely for information, as showing the origin of the liability which

[52] [1989] 1 All ER 402, 406 (also 420 (Lord Lowry)).

[53] [2004] EWCA Civ 622.

[54] [2001] Lloyd's Rep IR 191.

[55] See *Heath Lambert Ltd v Sociedad de Corretaje de Seguros* [2004] Lloyd's Rep IR 905, where incorporation of a premium payment clause was rejected for that reason.

[56] *Home Insurance of New York v Victoria-Montreal Fire* [1907] AC 59; *Municipal Mutual Insurance Ltd v Sea Insurance Co Ltd* [1996] LRLR 265; *CNA International Reinsurance v Companhia de Seguros Tranquili-dade* [1999] Lloyd's Rep IR 289; *Prifti v Musini Sociedad Anonima de Seguros y Reaseguros* [2004] Lloyd's Rep IR 528; *Hanwha Non-Life Insurance Co Ltd v Alba Pte Ltd* [2011] SGHC 271.

[57] [1907] AC 59.

was the subject of the reinsurance policy. Since the reinsurers only became liable once claims had been settled and they had no control over when claims would be settled, the Privy Council concluded that the term could not apply to the reinsurance policy.

The leading authority on the point is now the decision of the Court of Appeal in *HIH v New Hampshire*,[58] In *HIH*, the clause in issue was a waiver of defences clause in the underlying contract. The reinsurance was 'as original', and it was held by both David Steel J and the Court of Appeal that the clause had been incorporated into the reinsurance by the general words of incorporation (the Court of Appeal disagreed with David Steel J that there had been incorporation by express reference in the reinsurance to a 'cancellation clause' as the clause was held by the Court of Appeal not to relate to cancellation). David Steel J held that the wording of the incorporated clause could be 'manipulated' so as to give it sense in the reinsurance context: accordingly, as manipulated, the clause operated as a waiver of reinsurers' rights of avoidance in the event of a breach of the duty of fair presentation by the reinsured. The Court of Appeal rejected this analysis and held that it was not possible to manipulate the wording of the incorporated clause as it contained references which could not be translated to the reinsurance context. The Court of Appeal's view was that the clause was incorporated only in unmanipulated form, which meant that it did not amount to a waiver of reinsurers' rights of avoidance for independent breaches of duty by the reinsured. Instead, it operated only to: (i) allow the reinsured to recover from reinsurers in circumstances where the reinsured's own right of avoidance against the insured had been lost by reason of the clause (ie it was a form of follow the settlements clause); and (ii) allow the reinsured to recover where there had been a common presentation of the risk to the reinsured and reinsurers, so that both parties had agreed to waive their rights and the result was back-to-back cover. Rix LJ pointed out that giving the clause the wider meaning accepted by David Steel J would prevent the reinsurance from being back-to-back with the insurance, as the reinsurance would contain a waiver of rights independent of the insurance itself.

Terms which are ancillary to the direct policy will not be incorporated unless express reference is made to them in the reinsurance agreement. The most important terms which fall into this category involve dispute resolution, namely exclusive jurisdiction clauses,[59] arbitration clauses[60] and choice of law clauses.[61] A leading underwriter clause in the direct policy is also to be regarded as ancillary to reinsurance and thus will not be incorporated by general words: reinsurers will not, therefore, be bound by variations to the direct risk agreed to by the leading direct underwriter for the other reinsureds.[62]

It should be added that the strict rules on incorporation in respect of dispute resolution provisions apply only where there is purported incorporation from one contract into another. If there is incorporation from a document other than a contract involving a different party, eg standard market clauses, then the rule is applied less strictly and incorporation may be recognised even though there is no direct reference in the reinsurance agreement to the clause in question.[63]

[58] [2001] Lloyd's Rep IR 702.

[59] *AIG Europe (UK) Ltd v The Ethniki* [2000] Lloyd's Rep IR 343; *Cigna Life Insurance Co of Europe SA-NV v Intercaser SA de Seguros y Reaseguros* [2001] Lloyd's Rep IR 821; *AIG Europe SA v QBE International Insurance Ltd* [2002] Lloyd's Rep IR 22; *Prifti v Musini Sociedad Anonima de Seguros y Reaseguros* [2004] Lloyd's Rep IR 528; *Catlin Syndicate Ltd v Weyerhaueser* [2018] EWHC 3609 (Comm).

[60] *Pine Top Insurance v Unione Italiana* [1987] 1 Lloyd's Rep 476; *Excess Insurance v Mander* [1995] LRLR 358; *Tryg-Hansa v Equitas* [1998] 2 Lloyd's Rep 439.

[61] *Gan Insurance Co Ltd v Tai Ping Insurance Co Ltd* [1999] Lloyd's Rep IR 472.

[62] *American International Marine Agency of New York v Dandridge* [2005] EWHC 829 (Comm).

[63] *Axa Re v Ace Global Markets Ltd* [2006] EWHC 216 (Comm).

4.2. Implied Terms

The limited requirement for disclosure under obligatory and facultative/obligatory treaties is justified by the implication of terms to protect the reinsurers from the reinsured's acceptance of bad risks and settling losses unreasonably: the terms were set out in *Phoenix General Insurance of Greece v Halvanon Insurance*,[64] a case involving a proportional treaty. The terms are:

(a) keeping proper records and accounts of risks accepted, premiums received and claims made or notified;
(b) investigating all claims and confirming that there is liability before liability is accepted;
(c) investigating risks offered prior to acceptance of them;
(d) keeping full and accurate accounts showing sums owing and owed;
(e) ensuring that all amounts owing are collected promptly, and that all amounts payable are paid promptly; and
(f) making all documents reasonably available to the reinsurers.

The argument that there is a general obligation on the reinsured to keep the retention for its own account was rejected in *Halvanon* itself. *Baker v Black Sea*[65] held that the implied terms are not conditions precedent to the reinsurers' liability, so that if the reinsured breaks any of the terms, the reinsurers remain liable. In *Bonner v Cox Dedicated Corporate Member Ltd*,[66] substantial doubt was cast upon the width of the implied terms recognised in *Halvanon*, at least in respect of excess of loss contracts. In that case, the reinsured had engaged in 'writing against' the reinsurance, ie accepting risks which were likely to give rise to net losses without reinsurance but which were perfectly profitable with reinsurance. The Court of Appeal rejected the notion that the reinsured under an excess of loss contract owes any duty of care or continuing duty of good faith to the reinsurers, so that it was not a breach of contract for the reinsured to 'write against' the insurance by accepting risks which, but for reinsurance coverage, could not have been profitable. In so deciding, the Court of Appeal distinguished proportional from non-proportional reinsurance, so that *Phoenix v Halvanon* was merely distinguished and not overruled, although Waller LJ, giving the leading judgment in the Court of Appeal, doubted that even a reinsured under a proportional contract might owe the various implied duties to the reinsurers recognised by Hobhouse J in *Halvanon*.

4.3. Interpretation of Reinsurance Contracts: The Presumption of Back-to-Back Cover

Irrespective of incorporation, there is a general presumption that the cover granted by a proportional reinsurance agreement is 'back-to-back' with the underlying insurance, as the parties can be regarded as 'co-adventurers' even though as a matter of law they are simply contracting parties. Back-to-back cover is particularly important for fronting arrangements, as the reinsured is not itself the risk-taker, receives only a notional premium and is facilitating the reinsurer's access to the market in cases where the reinsurer cannot for legal or other

[64] [1985] 2 Lloyd's Rep 599.
[65] [1995] LRLR 287.
[66] [2005] EWCA Civ 1512.

reasons itself act as insurer.[67] The presumption of back-to-back cover, which is a principle of construction rather than a rule of law, was emphasised in *Forsakrings Vesta v Butcher*, in order to overcome problems arising where the reinsurance and the insurance are governed by different applicable laws. In that case, the direct policy, which was governed by the law of Norway, contained a warranty that the insured fish farm would be under 24-hour watch. The reinsurance, which was governed by English law, incorporated the terms of the direct policy, so that the same warranty was contained in the reinsurance. A loss occurred at a time when the insured was in breach of warranty, which under Norwegian law did not provide a defence to the insurers because it was not causative of the loss, but the reinsurers nevertheless denied liability to the insurers and relied upon the then stricter English rule – now abolished by sections 10 and 11 of the Insurance Act 2015[68] – that a breach of warranty has an automatic discharging effect. The House of Lords was unwilling to accept the defence, and resorted to the presumption of back-to-back cover to conclude that it was appropriate to construe the reinsurance agreement in the same manner as the insurance agreement, ie in accordance with principles of Norwegian law, even though the reinsurance was governed by English law. The outcome is welcome, but the reasoning is curious.[69] The back-to-back analysis has been followed on numerous occasions.[70]

The presumption of back-to-back cover was arguably taken to extreme lengths in *Groupama Navigation et Transports v Catatumbo CA Seguros*.[71] In this case an English law reinsurance policy incorporated the terms of an underlying Venezuelan law marine policy. The insurance contained a classification warranty, and the reinsurance itself included a classification warranty, albeit similarly worded. The insured failed to comply with the class warranty, but as their breach was not causative of the loss the insurers were not discharged from liability. The reinsurers nevertheless pleaded their own warranty and argued that the presumption of back-to-back cover had been ousted by the use of an express English law provision. The Court of Appeal disagreed and applied the *Vesta* case to the facts. Mance LJ, delivering the leading judgment, took the view that the reinsurance warranty had been inserted on a provisional basis only to guard against the possibility that there was no classification warranty in the direct policy, and that once it became clear that there was such a warranty then the reinsurance warranty ceased to operate, and the principle of back-to-back cover applied. This case comes close to allowing a rule of construction to override the express terms of the reinsurance.

The back-to-back cover presumption as applied to warranties is no longer relevant in the light of the changes to the English law of warranties brought about by the Insurance Act 2015. That aside, the principle has important limitations. There is no such

[67] *British-American Insurance (Kenya) Ltd v Matelec Sal* [2013] EWHC 3278 (Comm) demonstrates the mechanism of arranging the reinsurance first and then finding a willing local insurer to act as front. The case demonstrates also that as a matter of law the insurance and the reinsurance are entirely distinct contracts and that any attempt to include them in a single document will inevitably lead to a confusion of concepts.

[68] See ch 8.

[69] It should be noted that the finding that the full reinsurance clause had incorporated the direct policy's terms into the reinsurance was the root cause of the problem. Had the House of Lords rejected the incorporation theory, as per Lord Griffiths, the same result could have been reached without doing violence to the rule that the applicable law governs the construction of the contract.

[70] *Commercial Union Assurance v Sun Alliance* [1992] 1 Lloyd's Rep 475; *Ace Insurance SA-NV v Zurich Insurance Co* [2001] Lloyd's Rep IR 504; *Goshawk Syndicate Management Ltd and others v XL Speciality Insurance Co* [2004] Lloyd's Rep IR 683; *Gard Marine & Energy Ltd v Tunnicliffe* [2011] EWHC 1658 (Comm); *Amlin Corporate Member Ltd v Oriental Assurance Corp* [2012] EWCA Civ 1341; *Tokio Marine Europe Insurance Ltd v Novae Corporate Underwriting Ltd* [2013] EWHC 3362 (Comm).

[71] [2001] Lloyd's Rep IR 141.

presumption in non-proportional reinsurance contracts, as in those cases the parties are not co-adventurers and the reinsurance premium is assessed independently of the premium paid to the reinsured.[72] That fundamental point aside, the notion of back-to-back cover cannot operate to strike out or override those express terms of the reinsurance agreement which are inconsistent with the underlying terms.[73] In *Aegis Electrical and Gas International Services Co Ltd v Continental Casualty Co*[74] it was held that reinsurers were not liable to indemnify the reinsured for fire damage to machinery in an an oil refinery where the reinsurance contained its own definitions of the peril insured and those definitions confined cover to sudden mechanical breakdown and to boilers. Again, if the terms of the underlying insurance are altered but there are no corresponding change to the reinsurance, interpretation on a back-to-back basis is no longer possible.[75]

A further, although perhaps exceptional, restriction was imposed upon the principle of back-to-back cover by the House of Lords in *Wasa International Insurance v Lexington Insurance*.[76] In this case the reinsured, Lexington, issued property damage cover for the period 1977–80 to a major US corporation, Alcoa, in respect of all of its sites. The insurance did not contain any choice of law or jurisdiction provisions, and instead provided in a service of suit clause that Lexington would submit to the jurisdiction of any court of competent jurisdiction in the USA. Claims were brought by Alcoa in Washington in respect of loss which had occurred not just in the insured period, but also for a period totalling some 50 years, running both before and after the insured period. The Washington court held that, under Washington conflict of laws rules, the claims were governed by the law of Pennsylvania. Under Pennsylvania law, as it had developed in the 1980s, an insurer was liable for the entirety of any damage as long as some of it occurred during the policy period, and Lexington duly settled the claims against it on that basis. Lexington had placed facultative proportional reinsurance governed by English law with the defendant reinsurers on 'as original' terms, and it was common ground that the terms of the insurance had been incorporated into the reinsurance. The period of cover for the reinsurance was 36 months and exactly matched that of the underlying policy. The House of Lords held that this was an exceptional case in which the reinsurers were entitled to rely upon the English law interpretation of the 36-month coverage clause in the reinsurance contract even though such reliance meant that the two contracts were not treated as back-to-back. *Vesta* and *Catatumbo* were distinguished as decisions in which it was known from the outset which law was going to govern the direct policies, and so the reinsurers could be taken to have assumed liability to indemnify the reinsureds for claims made against them under the known applicable law. However, in *Wasa*, it was not known at the outset which law would be applied to the claims under the direct policies, and it could not have been predicted that the dispute would be resolved under the law of Pennsylvania. In the absence of an identified applicable law, the House of Lords thought that the reinsurers could not be taken to have agreed to provide coverage which rested on the principles of an unknown law, and for that

[72] *Axa Reinsurance v Field* [1996] 3 All ER 517.

[73] *Youell v Bland Welch (No 1)* [1992] 2 Lloyd's Rep 127; *Municipal Mutual Insurance Ltd v Sea Insurance Co Ltd* [1996] LRLR 265; *GE Reinsurance Corporation v New Hampshire Insurance Co* [2004] Lloyd's Rep IR 404; *Allianz Australia Insurance Ltd v General Cologne Re Australia Ltd* [2004] NSWCA 433; *MetLife Insurance Ltd v RGA Reinsurance Company of Australia Ltd* [2017] NSWCA 56.

[74] [2007] EWHC 1762 (Comm).

[75] *Munich Re Capital Ltd v Ascot Corporate Name Ltd* [2019] EWHC 2768 (Comm).

[76] [2009] UKHL 40.

reason the reinsurers could rely upon the English law interpretation of significant clauses, including the duration clause. It appears that the majority view was that the outcome would have been different had it been clear from the outset that Pennsylvania law was going to be the applicable law,[77] in that the reinsurers took the risk that there might be changes in the known applicable law between the date of the contract and the date of the claim. However, what they could not be taken to have agreed to is the risk that some completely unpredictable applicable law might apply to the claims. This decision has both its supporters and its detractors,[78] although there is now a great deal of uncertainty as to the borderline between *Vesta* and *Wasa*, and reinsurance markets have sought methods of overcoming the outcome and making sure that reinsurers provide an indemnity in cases where they have taken a proportion of the premium and have reinsured on identical terms.

---

5. Losses and Claims

5.1. Loss

The reinsured is entitled to indemnity under a reinsurance contract if it can can prove that there is liability under the insurance and also that the claim falls within the terms of the reinsurance. The first of these requirements is satisfied where the reinsured is able to show that its liability to the insured has been established and quantified by judgment, arbitration award or binding settlement.[79] The second turns on the terms of the reinsurance.

In the absence of express wording, reinsurers are not liable for extra-contractual damages awarded against a reinsured, eg by way of punitive damages for late payment available under the law of many US states,[80] or for the costs incurred by the reinsured in defending claims brought by the insured.[81] The six-year limitation period under section 5 of the Limitation Act 1980 for a claim against the reinsurers will also run from the date on which liability has been established and quantified.[82] The fact that the reinsured has not made payment under

[77] Lord Mance took a narrower view of coverage and felt that even an express choice of Pennsylvania law would not have resolved the issue. This view is, however, hard to reconcile with *Vesta v Butcher*.

[78] See A Mecz and A Bailey, '*WASA v Lexington*: Buyer Beware' [2010] *Journal of Business Law* 1; A Schaff, '*WASA v Lexington*: The Limits to "Back to Back" Presumption' [2010] *Journal of Business Law* 9; Ö Gürses, 'The Construction of Terms of Facultative Reinsurance Contracts: Is *WASA v Lexington* the Exception or the Rule?' (2010) 73 *MLR* 119; R Merkin, 'Commercial Certainty in the Reinsurance Market' (2010) 126 *LQR* 24.

[79] *Baker v Black Sea & Baltic General Insurance Co Ltd* [1995] LRLR 261; *Halvanon Insurance Co Ltd v Companhia de Seguros do Estado de Sao Paulo* [1995] LRLR 303; *North Atlantic Insurance Co Ltd v Bishopsgate Insurance Ltd* [1998] 1 Lloyd's Rep 459; *Sphere Drake Insurance plc v Basler Versicherungs-Gesellschaft* [1998] Lloyd's Rep IR 35. This is the same test applicable to liability policies. It is possible to vary this by express wording, and to specify that the reinsurers' duty to provide an indemnity arises on the happening of a given event, which may arise where the reinsurance is on the direct subject matter rather than on liability: see *Feasey v Sun Life of Canada* [2003] Lloyd's Rep IR 637.

[80] But note – as discussed in ch 12 – that under s 13A of the Insurance Act 2015, damages for late payment are contractual and not extra-contractual, so that it becomes possible for a reinsured to argue that damages awarded under English law in favour of the insured are recoverable under the reinsurance. Note also that by virtue of s 13A a reinsurer who pays sums under the reinsurance unreasonably late may be liable in damages to the reinsured independently of any responsibility for damages awarded against the reinsured.

[81] *Baker v Black Sea and Baltic General Insurance Co Ltd* [1998] Lloyd's Rep IR 327.

[82] *North Atlantic Insurance Co Ltd v Bishopsgate Insurance Ltd* [1998] 1 Lloyd's Rep 459; *Sphere Drake Insurance plc v Basler Versicherungs-Gesellschaft* [1998] Lloyd's Rep IR 35.

the direct policy is not a relevant consideration. A problem has arisen in relation to excess of loss treaties, as many ultimate net loss clauses contain wording to the effect that the reinsured 'shall actually have paid'. Decisions of the English courts,[83] culminating in that of the House of Lords in *Charter Reinsurance v Fagan*,[84] have reached the conclusion that this type of wording does not oust the principle that payment is not a condition precedent to recovery from the reinsurers. In *Charter Re* itself, the reinsured had become insolvent and was unable to make payment to its policyholders, which meant that, given the wording, a literal interpretation would have fortuitously relieved the reinsurers from any possible liability. The outcome has more to do with commercial considerations than with the meaning of the words used,[85] and it may be that clearer wording could achieve the result that the liability of reinsurers is postponed until the date of payment by the reinsured.[86]

In the event that there has been a judgment or arbitration award in favour of the insured against the reinsured, the judgment or award will generally be accepted at face value and be determinative on the issue of whether the reinsured has established and quantified its liability to the insured. However, as a matter of law, it appears that a judgment or award is not legally binding on the reinsurers. Given that the reinsurers will not have been parties to the judicial or arbitral proceedings, there is no issue estoppel against the reinsurers and it is not abuse of process for the reinsurers to challenge the outcome in any claim brought by the reinsured. In *Commercial Union Assurance Co v NRG Victory Reinsurance Ltd*,[87] the Court of Appeal suggested obiter that reinsurers could challenge a judgment from a foreign court only if it was 'manifestly perverse'. However, Lord Mance in *Wasa International Insurance Co v Lexington Insurance Co*[88] expressed the opinion that any judgment or award could be challenged by the reinsurers, and that view was endorsed by Christopher Clarke LJ in *AstraZeneca Insurance Co Ltd v XL Insurance (Bermuda) Ltd*,[89] speaking in the analogous context of liability insurance, as discussed in chapter 15.

5.2. The Effect of a Settlement by the Reinsured

Settlements raise different issues, as they mean that there is no authoritative – even if only persuasive – decision or award holding that the reinsured faces liability to the insured. The principle adopted by the Court of Appeal in *Commercial Union Assurance Co v NRG Victory Reinsurance Ltd*[90] is that a settlement is not binding on the reinsurers, and that the reinsured can be called upon to prove that as a matter of law it faced liability to the insured under

[83] *Home Insurance Co v Mentor Insurance* [1989] 3 All ER 74; *Re A Company No 0013734 of 1991* [1992] 2 Lloyd's Rep 413.

[84] [1996] 3 All ER 46.

[85] This is plain from a reading of the speech of Lord Mustill. For Lord Hoffmann's brave if unconvincing attempt in the speech of Lord Hoffmann to demonstrate that the words of the ultimate net loss clause are concerned with establishing the amount payable rather than the date of payment, see ch 9 above.

[86] This has been recognised at the direct level, in the form of 'pay to be paid' clauses in liability policies which have been construed as having this very effect: *The Fanti and the Padre Island* [1990] 2 All ER 705. Under New York law, actual payment is required of the reinsured: *Cleaver and Bodden v Delta American Reinsurance Co* [2002] Lloyd's Rep IR 167.

[87] [1998] Lloyd's Rep IR 421.

[88] [2009] UKHL 40.

[89] [2013] EWCA 1660.

[90] [1998] Lloyd's Rep IR 421, reversing [1998] 1 Lloyd's Rep 80. See also *New Zealand Local Government Insurance Corp Ltd v R+V Versicherung AG* [2013] NZHC 690.

the direct policy. The reinsured was the insurer of the *Exxon Valdez*, which ran aground in 1989. The insured incurred substantial losses, including clean-up costs, and sought to recover clean-up costs from the reinsured. Proceedings were commenced against the reinsured in Texas, and in the course of those proceedings the reinsured settled on the basis that it was liable for the clean-up costs. The reinsurers denied liability under the reinsurance, on the basis that as a matter of law the direct policy excluded clean-up costs. Clarke J at first instance accepted that the reinsured had to prove its loss, and that required proof of actual liability to the insured; it was not enough that the reinsured had reached a settlement which was bona fide and businesslike. Clarke J further ruled that, in determining legal liability, the matter should be approached not from the point of view of an English court (even though the direct insurance was governed by English law), but rather from the point of view of the court which would have determined the matter had the action against the reinsured proceeded to judgment. At the time of the settlement, the matter was pending in an action in Texas, and Clarke J was satisfied by the evidence of a US lawyer that the court in Texas would in all probability have ruled in favour of the reinsured had the matter gone to a non-expert judge and to a jury, and accordingly he held that the reinsured was entitled to summary judgment. On appeal, the Court of Appeal set aside the summary judgment. The Court of Appeal agreed with Clarke J on the need of the reinsured to prove its loss, but held that the learned judge had been wrong to rely upon the prediction in the evidence of the US lawyer as to the outcome of the Texas proceedings, as that prediction had been based on a variety of non-legal as well as legal considerations. It was necessary for the reinsured to go further and to demonstrate that there was legal liability as a matter of law. The result, therefore, is that the insured cannot settle proceedings brought against it in a foreign court, and seek to recover from its reinsurers, unless the settlement is based upon the absence of any arguable defence in those proceedings: it is not enough that the settlement is advantageous to the reinsured, in that it limits costs and removes the possibility of a large award of punitive damages by a foreign court, or that the foreign court may well find against the reinsured for reasons other than the strict application of the law applicable to the insurance agreement.[91]

It was decided, in *Lumberman's Mutual Casualty Co v Bovis Lend Lease Ltd*,[92] a direct liability case, that a global settlement which encompasses various claims and cross-claims can be taken into account only if it contains a clear allocation of sums to each of the various items within its scope. In the absence of such allocation, the settlement has no legal effect on the reinsurers and there can be no claim under the reinsurance even if the reinsured is able to prove its liability as a matter of law. The decision was widely regarded as unsupportable, given that global settlements very rarely seek to allocate sums in this way[93] and because a settlement which purports to apportion liabilities will almost inevitably result in the reinsured breaking its obligation not to admit liability. Subsequently, in *Enterprise Oil Ltd v Strand Insurance Co Ltd*,[94] Aikens J refused to follow the decision and held that the policyholder can present a settlement to underwriters whether or not it seeks to apportion individual losses, and that it suffices that the policyholder can establish and quantify the loss for which indemnity is sought.

[91] In the subsequent trial, *King v Brandywine Reinsurance Co (UK) Ltd* [2005] Lloyd's Rep IR 509, it was held that the reinsured had not proved that it faced liability for clean-up costs, so that the reinsurers were not liable to provide an indemnity.

[92] [2005] Lloyd's Rep IR 74.

[93] Reaching a settlement on that basis is a far less likely prospect as a matter of practice.

[94] [2006] EWHC 58 (Comm).

5.3. Follow the Settlements

To overcome the problems raised by the principles recognised in *Commercial Union v NRG Victory*, most facultative reinsurance agreements today contain 'follow the settlements' clauses, normally as the second part of the 'full reinsurance clause' referred to earlier. These clauses originally appeared in facultative agreements in the 1930s, in order to prevent the reinsurers from reopening the reinsured's settlements. In the leading authority, *Insurance Co of Africa v Scor (UK) Reinsurance*,[95] the Court of Appeal accepted the general rule that reinsurers are liable to the reinsured if, in the words of Goff LJ: (i) 'in settling the claim the insurers have acted honestly and have taken all proper and business like steps in making the settlement'; and (ii) 'the claim so recognised by [the reinsured] falls within the risks covered by the policy of reinsurance as a matter of law'.[96] The Court of Appeal went on to hold that the effect of a follow the settlements clause is to modify the first of these requirements, and that instead of having to prove its loss as a matter of law it is enough that the reinsured has settled with the insured in a bona fide and businesslike fashion.[97]

There is little authority on the meaning of 'bona fide and businesslike', although it is established that the burden of proof is on the reinsurers to show that the settlement was not bona fide and businesslike.[98] What is clear is that the settlement must be a genuine compromise, and that any payment by the reinsured which is purely ex gratia for its own business purposes is not within the scope of a follow the settlements clause. The reinsured must also show that it has made appropriate investigations into the circumstances of the loss and has taken advice from local lawyers as to the meaning of the direct policy.[99] The fact that other reinsureds have settled is some evidence that the reinsured has acted in a bona fide and businesslike fashion by following their lead.[100]

There is a potential difficulty in ascertaining the relationship between the two principles in *Scor* that the settlement must be bona fide and businesslike and that the loss must fall within the scope of the reinsurance. In the case of facultative proportional reinsurance, the insurance and reinsurance will be on the same terms, either by incorporation of the terms or by reason of the 'back-to-back' cover presumption. That, of course, is not always the case, and there will be situations in which the two contracts are not back-to-back either because they are differently worded or because the reinsurers have otherwise not agreed to run exactly the same risk faced by the reinsured.[101] The problem arises where the reinsured reaches a settlement on the basis of its view that it probably faces liability under the direct policy but the reinsurers deny liability on the basis that they are not liable under the identical words in the reinsurance agreement. If the reinsurers are allowed to act in this way, the follow the settlements clause is undermined as the settlement can be indirectly reopened, but if they are not allowed to act in this way then the second condition of liability as set out in *Scor* is removed. The matter was addressed by the Court of Appeal in *Assicurazioni Generali Spa v CGU International Insurance plc*.[102] The Court of Appeal rejected the reinsurers'

[95] [1985] 1 Lloyd's Rep 312.

[96] The two limbs in *Scor* were approved by the House of Lords in *Hill v Mercantile & General* [1996] LRLR 160.

[97] An alternative formulation used in many reinsurances, although mainly from outside England, is that the reinsurers are to 'follow the fortunes' of the reinsured. There is no English authority on this wording, and there is a difference of view among practitioners as to whether these words replicate 'follow the settlements' or whether they impose additional burdens on reinsurers.

[98] *Insurance Co of the State of Pennsylvania v Grand Union Insurance* [1990] 1 Lloyd's Rep 208.

[99] See generally *Gan Insurance v Tai Ping Insurance (No 3)* [2002] Lloyd's Rep IR 612.

[100] *English and American Insurance Co Ltd v Axa Re SA* [2006] EWHC 3323 (Comm).

[101] See the discussion of *Wasa International Insurance v Lexington Insurance* [2009] UKHL 40 above.

[102] [2004] Lloyd's Rep IR 457.

suggestion that they were always entitled to rely upon the incorporated wording of the reinsurance, and it also rejected the reinsured's most extreme argument that there was an automatic right to recovery if the settlement was bona fide and businesslike. Instead, the Court of Appeal adopted a middle approach,[103] namely that the reinsured was entitled to recover if: (i) the settlement was bona fide and businesslike; and (ii) the basis on which the claim was accepted by the reinsured was one which fell, or at least arguably fell, within the scope of the direct policy and the reinsurance.

The effect of this reasoning is that the reinsurers cannot challenge the facts as found by the reinsured, and they cannot challenge the reinsured's conclusions as to the coverage of the direct policy: all that they can do is to put the reinsured to proof of the basis upon which the claim had been admitted, to ensure that the facts and the wording have not been disregarded. If the reinsured simply pays a claim without considering whether or not it falls within the terms of the direct policy, the reinsured cannot be said to have 'recognised' the claim on the basis that it was covered by the direct policy; in that situation, the reinsured cannot rely upon the follow the settlements clause and must prove its loss as a matter of law.[104] It was argued in *Tokio Marine Europe Insurance Ltd v Novae Corporate Underwriting Ltd*[105] that the Court of Appeal had erred in *Generali* and that the true principle was that reinsurers were bound to follow a settlement only if: (i) the insurance claim as recognised arguably fell within the terms of the insurance policy; and (ii) the reinsurance claim on the balance of probabilities fell within the terms of the reinsurance agreement. Hamblen J clearly thought that as a matter of principle the reinsurers were right on this point. While *Generali* worked well enough where the insurance and reinsurance were on identical terms, the formulation in *Generali* effectively precluded the reinsurers from relying upon their own wording if it was not materially identical to that in the insurance. However, Hamblen J recognised that he was bound by the decision in *Generali* and that the test laid down there was to be applied. In *Tokio* itself the wording of the insurance and the reinsurance on the relevant point – the operation of a deductible – were identical, and accordingly the reinsurers were bound by the reinsured's settlement.

These principles may, of course, be varied by the express terms of the reinsurance, and the obligations of the reinsurers may be restricted. The standard 'loss settlements' clause, which states that the reinsured can recover for a settlement provided that the reinsured was liable to the insured as a matter of law, does little more than replicate the common law and requires the reinsured to prove its loss.[106] Further, where the follow the settlements clause states that the reinsurers will only recognise settlements which are not excluding 'without prejudice and ex gratia', the phrase is be construed as providing two alternative defences so that a claim which is settled on a 'without prejudice' basis but not 'ex gratia' disapplies the follow the settlements clause and the reinsured is required to prove its loss as a matter of law.[107] In principle, a follow the settlements clause may grant extended coverage to the reinsured, although there is no case in which alternative wording has been held to have that effect: the courts have decided that the obligation on reinsurers to follow settlements 'whether liable or not'[108] or 'without question'[109] does not vary the general rule laid down in *Generali*.

[103] Predicated by Evans J in *Hiscox v Outhwaite (No 3)* [1991] 2 Lloyd's Rep 524.
[104] *Aegis Electrical and Gas International Services Co Ltd v Continental Casualty Co* [2007] EWHC 1762 (Comm).
[105] [2013] EWHC 3362 (Comm).
[106] *Hill v Mercantile and General* [1996] LRLR 341.
[107] *Faraday Capital Ltd v Copenhagen Reinsurance Co Ltd* [2007] Lloyd's Rep IR 23.
[108] *Charman v Guardian Royal Exchange Assurance plc* [1992] 2 Lloyd's Rep 607.
[109] The formulation in *Assicurazioni* itself.

5.4. Proof of Loss under Treaties

Proof of loss under a facultative policy is relatively straightforward. Where there is no follow the settlements clause, the reinsured has to prove its loss as a matter of law, and if there is a follow the settlements clause, then the onus switches to the reinsurers to show that the settlement was not reached in a bona fide and businesslike fashion. The position under a treaty is somewhat more complicated, because the claim may relate to a large number of losses and not simply a single loss. The problem is most acute in the context of excess of loss treaties, because the reinsured is able to recover only by showing that the aggregate of individual losses has reached the figure necessary to trigger reinsurance coverage. If it is necessary for the reinsured to prove each individual loss, recovery under the treaty could be delayed indefinitely. Further, many of the losses presented by the reinsured to the reinsurers will themselves be aggregated losses, such as where the insured is insured under a liability policy and the insured and insurers have settled a class action for a global sum based upon a rough-and-ready calculation of the total liability faced by the insured. It would plainly be impossible for the reinsured to prove the quantum of liability for each of the underlying claims in order to show that the global settlement did not exceed the amount that would have been payable if each individual claim had been litigated.

The courts have taken a pragmatic approach to this question. In *Equitas Ltd v R&Q Reinsurance Company (UK) Ltd*,[110] the reinsured sought to recover under an excess of loss treaty which formed a part of the LMX Spiral, so that it was one of very many such treaties. The treaty contained a 'loss settlement' clause which required the reinsured to prove its loss as a matter of law. Two claims were made against the London market, one in respect of the loss of aircraft in Kuwait and the other in respect of pollution liability incurred by the owners of the grounded *Exxon Valdez*. Court decisions subsequently established that the claims were smaller than had originally been believed, and at that point the reinsurers stopped all payments.[111] It was not disputed that the reinsurers bore some liability, at least 80 per cent of the claims, but they refused to make any payment at all in the absence of proof of the actual sums owing. However, such proof could not be provided because it was impossible for the LMX Spiral to be recreated and individual liabilities assessed. Gross J, recognising that it would be absurd if the reinsurers faced no liability at all, held that the reinsured was entitled to prove its loss on the balance of probabilities, and on the facts had done so by commissioning actuarial models which, so far as possible, replicated the effect of the LMX Spiral.

Equitas v R&Q was followed by Burton J in *IRB Brasil Resseguros SA v CX Reinsurance Company Ltd*.[112] This was a more typical case in which the reinsured had settled a series of class actions brought against its insureds, in respect of claims relating to asbestos, contaminated blood products, defective breast implants and contamination caused by genetically modified plants. Each settlement was for a global figure, and it was almost inevitable that individual claimants would not have received the precise amounts due to them: some would have been overcompensated and some would have been undercompensated. Once again, the reinsurance contained a loss-settlements clause rather than a full follow the settlements clause. The court held that it was not necessary for the reinsured to prove that the insured

[110] [2009] EWHC 2787 (Comm).

[111] Respectively *Scott v Copenhagen Reinsurance Co (UK) Ltd* [2003] Lloyd's Rep IR 696 and *King v Brandywine Reinsurance Co (UK) Ltd* [2005] Lloyd's Rep IR 509.

[112] [2010] EWHC 974 (Comm).

would have been liable to each and every claimant, and that instead it was required only to prove its loss on the balance of probabilities. The reinsured had shown that the settlements were reasonable and had thereby satisfied that burden. The effect of these decisions is that the reinsured's burden under a treaty is effectively regarded as more or less the same as if there was a follow the settlements clause.

5.5. Allocation of Losses

The reinsured may be faced with the situation in which it has suffered losses over a period of years and it becomes necessary to allocate those losses to individual years of reinsurance cover. In most cases this is a straightforward process, because the year in which the reinsured loss has occurred will be obvious. However, there will be situations in which it cannot be said with any certainty in which year losses were suffered by the reinsured. In that type of case the reinsured will undoubtedly seek to maximise its reinsurance recovery by allocating the losses in the manner which suits it best: if there is a small number of large losses, it may be in the reinsured's interest to allocate them to different years so that the limits of indemnity for any one year are not exceeded. By contrast, if the reinsured has faced a large number of small losses, each of which bears a deductible, the reinsured will wish to treat them as a single loss in one policy year so that only one deductible has to be borne.

In the USA, this problem is treated as one of following the settlements, in that if the reinsurers are required to follow settlements, then they must accept an allocation which is made in a bona fide and businesslike fashion. The English cases, by contrast, show that the reinsured does not have an absolute right to allocate as it thinks fit, and that if the date of losses cannot be proved, then there is a presumption that losses have occurred in a regular and linear fashion. In *Municipal Mutual Insurance v Sea Insurance*,[113] the insured port authority suffered a series of thefts of property in its custody, for which it faced liability to the owners. The thefts occurred over a period of 18 months, which straddled three years of reinsurance coverage – the last three months of the first policy, the full duration of the second policy and the first three months of the third policy. The Court of Appeal held that it had to be assumed that the pattern of the losses was regular, and accordingly the losses were to be apportioned one-sixth, two-thirds and one-sixth to the three policies. The reinsured was not permitted to treat all of the losses as falling into a single policy year so that it had to bear only one deductible. As will be seen from chapter 19 and the discussion of the Court of Appeal in *Equitas Insurance Ltd v Municipal Mutual Insurance Ltd*[114] concerning the allocation of mesothelioma claims to reinsurers in circumstances where losses could be regarded in each of several consecutive years of cover, allocation is to be presumed to be regular across policy years.

The point that the reinsured does not have an entirely free hand in using allocation to maximise reinsurance recoveries was confirmed by *Teal Assurance Company Ltd v WR Berkley Insurance (Europe) Ltd*,[115] where the allocation related to layers of cover in a single year rather than allocation across years. Here, the reinsured, a captive insurer, issued a

[113] [1998] Lloyd's Rep IR 421, applied in *IRB Brasil Resseguros SA v CX Reinsurance Company Ltd* [2010] Lloyd's Rep IR 974 (Comm).
[114] [2019] EWCA Civ 718.
[115] [2013] UKSC 57.

number of liability policies in layers, constituting the 'professional indemnity (PI) tower', which covered all claims. The top layer cover – the general policy – excluded US losses. The reinsurance matched the primary cover: there was reinsurance for the PI tower which covered all losses, and there was an excess policy which excluded US losses. The insured companies received a number of claims both from the USA and from other sources in respect of defects in construction projects, and an issue arose as to how the losses were to be allocated as between the PI tower and the general policy. The Supreme Court held that the allocation had to take place on a strictly chronological basis and in accordance with the rule that the obligation on a liability insurer to provide indemnity arises when the insured has established and quantified its liability. It followed that the allocation of losses had to take place in the order in which judgments were given against the insured, and it was not open to Teal to treat the US losses as having occurred first so that they could be allocated to the PI tower rather than to the general policy. The Supreme Court warned that it was not permissible for a reinsured to manipulate the order of losses in order to maximise recovery. The ruling was applied in subsequent proceedings, *WR Berkley Insurance (Europe) v Teal Assurance Co Ltd (No 2)*.[116] These concerned a settlement of certain non-US claims by the insured under which a payment of US$13,460,531 was made into an escrow account, and the claimant against the insureds was able to withdraw funds from the account to fund the effecting of repairs to the buildings. The Court of Appeal held that the establishment of the account had not established and quantified the relevant liabilities, and that this occurred only on the later dates when funds were actually withdrawn from the account. That ruling worked in favour of the insured, as it operated to postpone its non-US liabilities so that US liabilities came first and fell within the PI tower.

5.6. 'Claims Co-operation' or 'Claims Control' Clauses

A claims co-operation clause requires the reinsured to give initial notification of a loss to the reinsurers[117] and thereafter to provide information to them. The clause will generally give the reinsurers the ultimate right to consent to any settlement in order to be bound by it at the reinsurance level.[118] A claims control clause takes negotiations with the insured out of the reinsured's hands and confers upon reinsurers the right to negotiate with the insured. These types of clauses have come into widespread use relatively recently, in order to remove the possibility that reinsurers might face liability to indemnify the reinsured in circumstances where there are valid doubts as to the veracity of a judgment, award or settlement which establishes and quantifies the reinsured's liability. Claims control clauses are particularly important where the insurance is simply a fronting operation for London market reinsurers, as it is obvious that the reinsured has no real interest in the outcome of

[116] [2017] EWCA Civ 25.

[117] What has to be notified depends upon the terms of the contract. In *Royal and Sun Alliance Insurance plc v Dornoch Ltd* [2004] Lloyd's Rep IR 82, it was held that the reinsured's obligation to notify losses of which it had knowledge referred to losses suffered by claimants against the insured, so that until there was a settlement of the claims between the claimants and the insured it could not be said that any loss had been established. Contrast *AIG Europe (Ireland) Ltd v Faraday Capital Ltd* [2007] EWCA Civ 1208, where it was apparent from the outset that the claimants against the insured had suffered losses (in the form of a dramatic drop in the share value of the insured company) and those losses were known to the reinsured at an early stage, so notification following settlement was, therefore, out of time.

[118] *Beazley Underwriting Ltd v Al Ahleia Insurance Co* [2013] EWHC 677 (Comm).

any claim by the insured, given that the reinsurers are providing an indemnity of 100 per cent. It was held in *Federal Mogul Asbestos Personal Injury Trust v Federal-Mogul Ltd*[119] that the phrase in a reinsurance agreement conferring upon the reinsurers 'full, exclusive and absolute authority, discretion and control, which shall be exercised in a businesslike manner in the spirit of good faith and fair dealing', did not operate as a blanket authority to settle claims, but rather required the reinsurers to act fairly both in the procedure adopted for handling the claim and in the ultimate settlement reached.

It is apparent that the obligation of reinsurers to follow settlements can scarcely be reconciled with their right to approve or even control settlements. The relationship between follow the settlements clauses and claims clauses was authoritatively determined by the Court of Appeal in the *Scor* case, Goff LJ laying down the principle that the claims clause has priority and 'emasculates' any obligation to follow settlements. However, it was further held in *Scor* that if the claims clause is not a condition precedent, then its breach will not affect the right of the reinsured to recover, provided that he can prove his loss as a matter of law, by being sued to judgment or establishing liability in proceedings against the reinsurers. By contrast, if compliance with the claims clause is a condition precedent to the liability of the reinsurers, then non-compliance with the clause is fatal, even if there is a judgment against the reinsured in favour of the insured. The reinsurers are under a duty of utmost good faith at common law[120] in exercising their rights under a claims clause, and must not arbitrarily refuse to approve a settlement[121] or refuse to take over the negotiations with the insured where there can be no liability unless the negotiations are conducted by the reinsurers.[122] The test for breach is not one of reasonableness, as this would require the court to second-guess the commercial judgment of the reinsurers: the test is whether the reinsurers have, in reaching their decision, taken into account considerations extraneous to the merits of the claim.

Reinsurers may waive the right to rely upon a claims co-operation or claims control clause. If the clause is not a condition precedent, then waiver is not likely to be an issue, because breach is unlikely to have any adverse effect upon the reinsured's right to claim. By contrast, if it is a condition precedent, then the principle in *Kosmar Villa Holidays plc v Trustees of Syndicate 1243*[123] means that nothing short of estoppel will suffice for the reinsured. In *Lexington Insurance Co v Multinacional de Seguros SA*,[124] the reinsurers informed the reinsured that they intended to refuse to make payment by reason of a breach of the claims provisions. The reinsured thereafter proceeded to settle with the insured and presented a claim to the reinsurers. At that point, the reinsurers abandoned their initial defence and relied instead upon the fact that the reinsured had not, after the initial denial of liability by the reinsurers, failed to seek their consent to the settlement in breach of the claims clause. It was held that the initial denial of liability did not exempt the reinsured from its obligation to comply with the claims condition, so that failure to seek consent was fatal to the claim. The reinsurers were not estopped from relying upon the clause by reason of their initial denial of liability.

[119] [2014] EWHC 2002 (Comm).

[120] That proposition is now reinforced by the amendments to s 17 of the Marine Insurance Act 1906 by s 14 of the Insurance Act 2015. See ch 9 above.

[121] *Gan Insurance Co Ltd v Tai Ping Insurance Co Ltd (Nos 2 and 3)* [2002] Lloyd's Rep IR 667.

[122] *Eagle Star Insurance Co Ltd v Cresswell* [2004] EWCA Civ 602.

[123] [2007] EWCA Civ 147.

[124] [2008] EWHC 1170 (Comm).

19

Case Studies

1. Introduction

This book has set out the general principles of insurance law. As has been seen, insurance is about risk assessment, and many of the authorities are concerned with the inevitable question of what risks have been agreed to be transferred to the insurers under the policy. That may be difficult enough to ascertain when the risks are foreseeable, but matters become greatly contemplated where the losses are of a type or on a scale that could not reasonably have been contemplated. This chapter focuses, in the form of case studies, upon three recent sets of circumstances that have given rise to insurance claims in a manner affecting almost all of the legal principles already discussed. Readers may find that the principles are more conveniently explained if they are set in context rather than scattered in various places throughout the book. As will be seen, the law has been required to embrace important modifications in order to face challenges exposed by such risks.

2. Mesothelioma and Liability Insurance[1]

2.1. Liability in Tort for Mesothelioma

The dreadful disease mesothelioma is a form of lung cancer that is commonly caused by the lodgement of asbestos fibres in the lungs following exposure to the substance. About 3 per cent of exposures lead to disease, and about 3 per cent of diseased lungs go on to develop the condition itself. The typical progression of the disease is: exposure; damage to the lungs many years later, sometimes some 30–40 years after exposure; the manifestation of illness and diagnosis around 2–3 years after damage; and fatality within a further 14 months. Almost all of the legal issues that the courts and Parliament have faced in determining

[1] R Merkin, 'Insurance and Reinsurance in the *Fairchild* Enclave' (2016) 36 *Legal Studies* 302; KV Krishnaprasad, 'Unjust Enrichment in the "Fairchild Enclave": *International Energy Group Ltd v Zurich Insurance Plc*' (2017) 80 *MLR* 1150.

tortious liability for exposure, and insurance coverage for those responsible for exposure, flow from the problem that it remains beyond the ability of medical science to pinpoint from a series of exposures the individual exposure or exposures that have caused mesothelioma. The law can do no better than work on the balance of probabilities that damage is more likely to have been caused where the period of exposure has been either or both lengthy and intense.

The matter was first considered by the House of Lords in *Fairchild v Glenhaven Funeral Services Ltd*,[2] where the victim had been exposed to asbestos by different employers, and it was impossible to determine which of the employers, let alone which of the exposures, had caused the disease. The House of Lords, faced with the prospect of having to deprive the victim of any common law compensation by applying strict causation principles, took the bold step of holding that in cases where there had plainly been negligence and breach of duty but medical science could not provide proof of cause, each of the employers faced liability. Such tampering with the rules of causation created academic outrage[3] and the House of Lords by a majority took a step back in *Barker v Corus UK Ltd*,[4] holding that *Fairchild* did not inflict 100 per cent liability on each employer guilty of exposing the employee to asbestos, but rather imposed only a proportionate liability based upon its own contribution to the risk: that was generally accepted to be based on the length of each employer's period of exposure. It followed from *Barker* that if, for example, employer A had exposed the employee for five years, employer B had exposed the employee for four years and the employee had had a one-year period of self-employment during which there was exposure to asbestos, A would face 50 per cent liability and B would face 40 per cent liability, and proceedings would have to be brought against each of them. There would be no tort recovery for 10 per cent of any potential damages. It was subsequently decided by a majority of the Supreme Court in *Durham v BAI (Run off) Ltd, Employers' Liability Trigger Litigation*[5] that *Fairchild* had not created a new tort of contributing to the risk of loss but, rather, had adopted a 'weak causation' test where negligence had been established. There may well be an earlier thickening of the walls of the lungs (pleural plaques), but that may not develop into actual injury. In *Johnston v NEI International Combustion*,[6] it was held that a person diagnosed with pleural plaques but with no actual injury had no claim against the person responsible for exposure for fear or distress. Such claimants have become known as the 'worried well'.

Barker had by this time been reversed by legislation, to restore the position that had been thought to have been established by *Fairchild*. By section 3 of the Compensation Act 2006, the victim of exposure to asbestos can recover the full amount of damages from any one person responsible for any of the exposures if the victim can demonstrate that: mesothelioma had been contracted by exposure to asbestos; the person sued faced liability in tort for the exposure; and medical science could not determine which exposure had led to the injury. The effect of the 2006 Act was to allow the victim to bring a single action for damages, encompassing all periods of exposure, including those where the victim was responsible for their own exposure. The basis for such liability is that each exposure is a tort, and there

[2] [2003] 1 AC 32.

[3] Typical of which is J Morgan, 'Lost Causes in the House of Lords: *Fairchild v Glenhaven Funeral Services*' (2003) 66 *MLR* 277.

[4] [2006] 2 AC 572.

[5] [2012] UKSC 14. Lord Phillips, dissenting, held that *Fairchild* created a new tort so that proof of causation remained necessary.

[6] [2007] UKHL 39.

is no need for the victim to demonstrate a causal link between any one exposure and the onset of injury. However, liability under the Act is joint and several, so that the nominated defendant has a right to seek contribution under the Civil Liability (Contribution) Act 1978 from others responsible for exposing the victim to asbestos. Although the point has yet to be tested, it is generally assumed that contribution claims are based upon proportional duration of exposure. There is no contribution claim against the victim representing any self-exposure period, but the defendant may plead contributory negligence.

As an alternative to tort claims, the Mesothelioma Act 2015 provides a state compensation scheme for victims first diagnosed with the disease on or after 25 July 2012. The state benefits are not available to a victim who has also pursued a tort claim.

2.2. Insurance Issues Arising from Mesothelioma

The vast majority of instances of exposure occurred at the workplace, although some would be on premises to which the public have access, such as state or local authority offices. The Employers' Liability (Compulsory Insurance) Act 1969, which came into force on 1 January 1972, made – with some minor exceptions – insurance against liability for injury at work compulsory.[7] It should be obvious that in the absence of insurance coverage, many claims against employers would be worthless: the tortious exposures would have taken place decades before the infliction of injury could have been known, and in the meantime smaller employers at least would have ceased trading or been removed from the register of companies. It thus became necessary to establish the coverage provided by employers' liability policies and (for non-employment claims) public liability policies. It was noted in chapter 15 that policies covering liability for personal injury and other forms of physical damage may be written on one of two bases: liability for negligent acts committed within the period of insurance; and liability for injury suffered within the period of insurance. In most cases the difference between the two is not important, because negligence and injury will occur simultaneously, as where there is a motor accident or injury caused in the workplace by faulty mechanical equipment. However, the difference is important for exposure injuries because the negligent exposure giving rise to the disease, and the injury suffered by the disease itself, may occur at different times. Mesothelioma is perhaps the most extreme example, where the gap is generally one of decades. In the case of employers' liability insurance, typical wording refers to 'injury sustained' or 'disease contracted' by an employee in the year when the policy was in force. If those words are construed as meaning the onset of injury in the form of lung damage, and assuming a gap of, say, 30 years between exposure and that injury, there is a very strong probability that the victim will not have remained in the employment of that employer when the injury finally occurred: the employer may have gone out of business, or the victim may have changed employers (very few employees stay with one employer for that length of time) or retired. That would mean that the victim would not be an 'employee' at the date of injury, so it could not be said that the injury had been sustained or the disease contracted by an 'employee'. By contrast, if 'injury sustained' or 'disease contracted' means exposure, then the victim would have been exposed when employed and thus the insurance cover would be triggered.

[7] See ch 15 above.

The point was tested in *Bolton Metropolitan Borough Council v Municipal Mutual Insurance & Commercial Union Assurance*,[8] although this was a claim against a council rather than an employer. The Council's insurance covered liability for 'accidental bodily injury'. The Court of Appeal ruled that 'bodily injury' did not occur on exposure but required physical injury to the victim, which took place many years later, when the victim's lungs became damaged. The result was that the insurer on risk in the year of injury, rather than the insurer on risk in the year of exposure, faced liability to indemnify the Council. Because this was not an employment case, the victim was not at risk of receiving no compensation all and the issue was, rather, which of the successive insurers faced liability. Applying this ruling to the employment situation would remove the most important source of compensation from most victims. However, when the matter was tested in the employment context in the *Trigger* case, the Supreme Court by a majority concluded that the insuring clauses referred to exposure, thereby opening the door to insurance claims by employers found to be liable to employees for exposure injuries. The Supreme Court made little attempt to disguise that the ruling was designed to ensure that the tweaks – and, some would argue, distortions – to the law of causation in *Fairchild* were not in vain. Much was made in argument in the case that applying date of injury would create a 'black hole' for victims, a point plainly not lost on the majority in the Supreme Court. The decision nevertheless created a dichotomy between public liability insurances (to be construed as applying to the date of injury) and employers' liability insurances (to be construed as applying to the date of exposure), and the Supreme Court chose not to explore the correctness or otherwise of *Bolton*.

Trigger, while settling the coverage issue, gave rise to a further question of allocation between successive insurers. A victim bringing an action against an employer who has exposed the victim to asbestos over a period of, say, five years, does not need to show the year in which the killing exposure took place. Indeed, *Fairchild* is predicated on the victim's inability to do so. It follows that the employer is unable to point to the actual year for which insurance coverage is sought. That will not matter if there has been a single insurer on risk for the entire period, because the insurer is plainly liable in each of those years, and it should be added that such policies rarely have a financial cap on liability (despite the 1969 Act permitting a cap of £5 million), so there is no need for the employer to worry about policy limits having been reached in any one year.

Where identification of the year of the killing exposure is important is where the employer has changed insurers during the five-year period. The point came before the Supreme Court in *Zurich Insurance PLC UK Branch v International Energy Group Ltd*,[9] a panel of seven having been convened by reason of the significance of issues raised. The case concerned a single employer[10] in Guernsey, IEG, which had exposed one of its employees to asbestos throughout the period of his employment from 13 November 1961 to 31 December 1988. He was diagnosed with mesothelioma and in 2008 issued proceedings against IEG. These were settled for the sum of £250,000 plus £15,300 costs, and IEG had to bear its own costs of £13,150. IEG had no insurance until December 1978; IEG, being a Guernsey company,

[8] [2006] EWCA Civ 50.

[9] [2015] UKSC 33.

[10] The added complexity of other employers equally guilty of exposure did not arise. Had there been other insurers, then, given that the Compensation Act 2006 did not extend to Guernsey, each of the employers would have been liable based on their respective proportions of the duration of the total period of exposure, as held in *Barker v Corus*. But that would have left unaffected the actual question in *IEG*, namely, allocation between any one employer's successive insurers.

was not bound by the 1969 Act and thus had no obligation to insure. IEG nevertheless obtained an employers' liability policy issued by XL Insurance from December 1978 to December 1980. Cover was renewed for the period December 1982 to December 1988 with Midland Insurance, a company later acquired by Zurich. Thus, of the 27 years during which the employee had been exposed to asbestos: for 19 years there was no insurance; for two years the insurer was XL; and for six years the insurer was Midland/Zurich. A claim was made against Zurich for the full amount of the claim plus costs. IEG's case was that the full amount of the loss fell into any of the 27 years of exposure, that it was open to IEG to 'spike' the claim into any year of its choice and that IEG had opted to seek indemnity from Zurich without the need to specify which of the six years of coverage had been triggered. Zurich's case was that the loss should be spread on a 'time on risk' basis, so that Zurich should be liable for no more than 6/27ths of the full amount of the claim. In short, the question was whether the *Fairchild* principle should be extended to insurance.

The majority of the Supreme Court, represented by Lord Mance, upheld IEG's claim against Zurich. The logic of *Fairchild* was that it was impossible to determine the year of exposure into which any claim should fall, and that there was a claim against the employer in any one of the years. If IEG was liable on that basis, then equally its insurers were subject to the same principle. The minority of the Supreme Court, represented by Lord Sumption, vehemently rejected that analysis. The minority view was that *Fairchild* was designed to ensure that the victim had a cause of action, and that *Trigger* was designed to ensure that there was insurance coverage. There was no need at the insurance level to create unfairness by imposing the full amount of the claim on any one insurer, and the correct analysis was that Zurich was liable for 6/27 of the loss, XL was liable for 2/27 of the loss and IEG had to bear the remaining 19/27 of the loss itself, as it was 'self-insured' for that period.

The majority recognised that imposing 27/27ths liability on Zurich even though it had been on risk for only 6/27ths of the period of exposure was disproportionate and unfair, but thought that the ruling was in principle necessary to protect the victim of an employer against the risk that one or more of the insurers on risk in the period of exposure might have ceased business or become insolvent. The Supreme Court thereby allowed the insured to 'manipulate' the losses as between insurers so as to secure maximum cover.[11] Lord Mance suggested two important mitigating considerations. First, if there was any other insurer on risk in the relevant period, the paying insurer should have a right of contribution based on time on risk against that insurer. On the facts, Zurich had a 2/27ths right of contribution from XL. In so concluding, Lord Mance was sanctioning an extension of the ordinary rules of contribution, discussed in chapter 13. Contribution had up to this point been held to operate where two or more insurers were on risk in the same policy period, with the paying insurer entitled to recover a proportionate share – based on the respective amounts of liability under the policy – from the other insurers on risk. This reasoning reflected an extension of existing principles in two respects: (a) the insurers were not concurrent, but consecutive, in time; and (b) the time on risk principle was essentially a novelty – applying traditional principles of contribution to concurrent insurances, issues of time on risk were simply not relevant (as each insurer would have been liable for a one-year period and the loss fell on a day when both policies were in force). Thus, to achieve an equitable result, it was necessary to manipulate established contribution principles to fit the new scenario created by *Fairchild*.

[11] A possibly rejected by the Supreme Court itself in *Teal Assurance Company Ltd v WR Berkley Insurance (Europe) Ltd* [2013] UKSC 57, discussed in ch 18 above.

Secondly, Lord Mance was of the view that IEG's decision to self-insure for 19/27ths of the period of exposure should not allow it to escape liability even though IEG was not an insurer and thus not subject to contribution rules. The majority thus sanctioned the adoption of a 'recoupment' principle', whereby Zurich was given a restitutionary remedy against IEG for recovery of 19/27ths of its payment. This was in essence replicating contribution, but from the assured rather than from another insurer. The novelty of this analysis should be emphasised: the only other context in which the policyholder has been required by the law to bear a proportion of its own loss is that of valued policies where there is underinsurance.

2.3. Reinsurance Issues Arising from Mesothelioma

The tort and insurance cases have acquired the epithet '*Fairchild* Enclave', as they represent something of a departure from earlier principles but in a manner necessary to secure compensation for the victims of exposure to asbestos. It was all but inevitable that the liability faced by insurers would give rise to further questions at the reinsurance level. The following, much simplified example – simplified by stripping out the possibilities of consecutive exposure by different employers (a matter governed by *Fairchild* and the Compensation Act 2006) and changes in insurance coverage by those employers during the period of exposure (the issue in *IEG v Zurich*) – may illustrate the issue. An employer has exposed an employee to asbestos for a period of five years. The employer was insured by the same insurer for that entire period. The insurer was itself reinsured for the first four years by reinsurer A and for the final year by reinsurer B. Claims are made by the employee against the employer, and under *Fairchild* the employer faces full liability for each exposure, so that the claim could be brought in any one of the five years. However, there is no need for the victim to choose a year; it suffices for him to rely upon exposure by that employer without having to show which exposure caused the injury. The employer, following *IEG* in extending *Fairchild* to the insurance level, can recover from the insurer without having to determine the year in which its liability arose, because each exposure has given rise to liability. The consequence for the insurer is that it faces liability in each of the five years of coverage. How, then, is the insurer to present its claim to the reinsurers? In short, is the insurer entitled to 'spike' its claim into any of the five years of coverage?

The issue was referred to arbitration before Flaux J, sitting as a judge-arbitrator. The insurer, MMI, issued employers' liability policies for the period 1 January 1950 to 31 December 1981, and reinsured its liabilities with various syndicates at Lloyd's. Those liabilities were transferred to Equitas under the Lloyd's Reconstruction and Renewal Scheme in 1996. The reinsurances were in the form of annual excess of loss treaties[12] arranged in financial layers. Over the years, the amount of cover and the identities of the subscribing syndicates changed, so that the reinsurance varied in one or more respects over the entire period of reinsurance. The question was whether MMI was entitled to 'spike' its reinsurance claims into the most favourable years of coverage under the treaties. By an arbitration award, which is confidential and which has never been published, Flaux J ruled that there were no restrictions on MMI in the treaties, and that the natural extension of *Fairchild* meant that MMI could place its losses wherever it felt fit. Permission to appeal against

[12] See ch 18 above.

the arbitration award on the ground that it was open to serious doubt[13] was granted by the Court of Appeal in *Equitas Insurance Ltd v Municipal Mutual Insurance Ltd*.[14] In the substantive hearing of the appeal,[15] the Court of Appeal overturned the award and held that spiking was not permissible. The Court of Appeal noted that *Fairchild*, *Trigger* and *IEG* had all been decisions intended to secure compensation to the victims of mesothelioma, but that reinsurance was one step removed from that problem and there was no obvious need to extend the '*Fairchild* Enclave' to reinsurance. In terms of legal analysis, the Court of Appeal held that there should be implied into the reinsurance agreements a term whereby claims would be made on a time on risk basis, so that an equal share of the loss was borne by each year's reinsurers. That term was that the right of MMI

> to present its reinsurance claims must be exercised in a manner which is not arbitrary, irrational or capricious, and that in that context rationality requires that they be presented by reference to each year's contribution to the risk, which will normally be measured by reference to time on risk …

The Court of Appeal regarded the implied term as essential to give effect to the intentions of the parties. It was argued for the reinsurers in the alternative that MMI was constrained by the principle of utmost good faith[16] to take into account the interests of all of the parties to the treaties and to allocate its losses proportionately amongst the reinsurers. Leggatt LJ, who alone considered the argument in detail, was tempted by it and suggested that the court might

> imply a term as to the manner in which a contractual power may be exercised so as to ensure that the power is not abused and is exercised in good faith. The doctrine of good faith in this context requires a contractual power to be exercised in a way which is consistent with the justified expectations of the parties arising from their agreement, construed in its relevant context.

However, Leggatt LJ did not go so far as to rely upon utmost good faith as an independent ground for his ruling in favour of the reinsurers. There was ultimately no appeal to the Supreme Court and the dispute was settled.

---

3. COVID-19 and Business Interruption Insurance

3.1. The Nature of Business Interruption Insurance

COVID-19 began to appear in the UK mid-February 2020. On 4 March the government published guidance on social distancing and on 5 March 2020 COVID-19 was made a 'notifiable disease', so that any doctor coming across a case was required to notify the matter to the Health Authorities. On 12 March those with symptoms were instructed to self-isolate for seven days. On 21 March the Health Protection (Coronavirus, Business Closure) (England) Regulations 2020 imposed restrictions on business premises selling food and drink. On 23 March the Prime Minister issued an instruction to the British people to stay at

[13] The test for the grant of permission to appeal against an arbitration award of general public importance, under section 69 of the Arbitration Act 1996.

[14] [2018] EWCA Civ 991.

[15] [2019] EWCA Civ 718.

[16] See ch 4 above.

home, on 24 March holiday accommodation providers were told to close their premises for commercial use, on 25 March 2020 the Coronavirus Act 2020 was passed, regulating matters such as food supplies, and on 26 March the Health Protection (Coronavirus, Restrictions) (England) Regulations 2020 revoked the 21 March Regulations and required the closure of all businesses and facilities offering goods and services to the public. The Regulations also issued a general prohibition against people leaving their residences without reasonable excuse, including obtaining basic necessities or medical advice and taking exercise. Since those early days there have been a variety of changes to the rules, in the form of relaxations, reimpositions and announcements of freedom.

Although COVID-19 gave rise to numerous claims under travel and health policies, the most complex issues have arisen under business interruption (BI) policies taken out by operators in the leisure industry, including pubs, restaurants, cafes, hotels and golf clubs. To provide clarity to some 380,000 affected policyholders, the Financial Conduct Authority sponsored a test case relating to 21 representative policies, which reached the Supreme Court as *FCA v Arch Insurance*.[17] The purpose of the test case was to determine the meaning of common wordings in BI policies so that the rulings could be applied to individual claims; the case did not of itself resolve any claims, and many of those may well turn on issues not discussed in the *Arch* case. It is not outrageous to suggest that the entire process was an exercise in trying to fit unanticipated events into contract wording that was never designed for that purpose. There was indeed pandemic insurance on offer (after SARS in 2012), but very few policyholders opted for it.

BI is rarely stand-alone cover, and typically forms part of a policy against physical damage. The trigger event for BI is material damage to the property insured under the policy, and once such damage can be shown for which there is a valid claim, then there is an entitlement to recover BI losses caused by the damage to the property. Obvious examples are flood and fire, leading to shutdown. A policy covering a group of companies each of which is identified as an insured will apply separately to each of them, so the limit of indemnity under the policy is to be construed as available to each of them and is not an aggregate figure.[18] By means of extension, some BI policies do not require the material damage that has given rise to the BI loss to be of property insured under the policy itself: some refer to property owned or used by the insured, while others cover BI losses where the property damaged is that of suppliers to the insured business who by reason of damage are unable to maintain those supplies.

BI insurance almost universally contains a series of extensions, often referred to as 'non-damage' triggers, which permit recovery of BI losses in the absence of physical damage. As is shown by the *Arch* case, these fall into three broad categories: (a) disease or public health issues on, or in the vicinity of, the premises (sometimes specified as 25 miles), affecting the business conducted on the premises; (b) closure or restriction or loss of access ordered by public authorities by reason of disease; and (c) closure or restriction or loss of access ordered by public authorities for any reason. The non-damage triggers are sometimes expressed as having 'sub-limits', meaning that the sum recoverable is capped at – typically – 10 per cent of the amount that would been recoverable if there had been material damage.

The sum recoverable under a BI policy is the loss of revenue caused by the material damage (or other trigger). The parties agree an 'indemnity period', which can be anything from a week to a number of years – it is up to the policyholder to decide how long it is worth

[17] [2021] UKSC 1.

[18] *Corbin & King Ltd v AXA Insurance UK Plc* [2022] EWHC 409 (Comm).

insuring against BI loss. As was seen in chapter three, a broker charged with calculating the relevant period when placing cover may face negligence liability if the period proves to be too short. The amount recoverable is the revenue that would have been earned in the indemnity period had the damage or other trigger not occurred. The loss is usually measured by comparing previous years' revenue results with the sum actually obtained in the indemnity period. However, to eliminate other matters that might have affected performance in previous years or in the indemnity period, the 'Trends Clause' requires those matters to be discounted. Thus, if a hotel suffers a fire and suffers a loss of revenue in the indemnity period, it is necessary to examine whether there were any independent matters that had artificially lowered or raised the revenue in previous years (eg the employment of a Michelin star chef) or whether there were any independent matters that would have lowered or raised revenue in the indemnity period 'but for' the occurrence of the trigger (eg notice given by the chef that would have expired after the fire). Although the loss cannot be fully ascertained until the end of the indemnity period, it has been held in Ireland that the statutory limitation period for issuing proceedings against the insurers runs for the six year statutory period from the date of the occurrence of the insured peril giving rise to the running of the indemnity period.[19]

3.2. BI Triggers

The most important trigger is material damage. The question then becomes whether COVID-19 can cause damage to property. The key feature of COVID-19, like any other virus, is that it cannot survive for long or replicate outside the living cell of a host. If property is contaminated by COVID-19, it may be capable for a short period of causing infection to any person who is in contact with the property, but the physical characteristics of the property itself are left unaffected, such alteration being the definition of damage.[20] The Australian Federal Court in the Australian test case *LCA Marrickville Pty Ltd v Swiss Re International SE*[21] accordingly concluded that there was no material damage caused by a virus with a relatively short period of viability which did not attack the structure of the property and did not require remediation. If there is to be recovery, it has to be under one or other of the non-damage triggers. In *TKC London Ltd v Allianz Insurance plc*,[22] a café was forced to close its premises and consequently to dispose of stocks of food either by selling at a loss or by throwing the food away. It was argued that the loss of the food was physical damage resulting from COVID-19. The argument was rejected on two grounds: COVID-19 had not itself caused any damage; and the damage that had been suffered was not the result of COVID-19 but rather of deterioration – inherent vice – so that nothing fortuitous was involved.

As far as public health triggers are concerned, typical wording refers to 'interruption or interference with the business following any occurrence [manifestation] of a notifiable [infectious] disease on or within a radius of 25 miles [vicinity] of the premises'. Such a clause would generally encompass other local events, including burst water mains, gas explosion,

[19] *Bann Carraig Ltd v Great Lakes Reinsurance (UK) PLC* [2021] NIQB 63.
[20] See ch 12 above.
[21] [2022] FCAFC 17.
[22] [2020] EWHC 2710 (Comm).

bank robbery or road closure. The most important construction issues in *Arch* arising out of this type of wording were the following:

(1) *'Interruption'* did not require a complete closure but only a partial closure of a severable sector or premises: a restaurant forced to close its doors to sitting customers but able to operate takeaway has suffered 'interruption'.
(2) *'Occurrence'* and *'manifestation'* were different concepts. 'Occurrence' did not require diagnosis; 'manifestation' by contrast required either symptoms or diagnosis, and not simply an undiagnosed case.
(3) *'Notifiable/infectious disease'*: the UK has a system of 'notifiable' diseases, if one is discovered by doctor then authorities must be informed. There is a list of notifiable diseases set out in legislation and it can be amended from time to time. Plainly COVID-19 was not notifiable before early 2021. Some policies covered any notifiable disease, and that included a disease that became notifiable after the policy had been made. Other policies laid down a fixed list of notifiable or infectious diseases, but what of new notifiable or infectious diseases emerging after the policy had been made that are not on the policy list? In *Rockliffe Hall Ltd v Travelers Insurance Co Ltd*[23] the policy was written in July 2019, before Covid-19 had been heard of let alone become notifiable. The policy gave a fixed list of 'infectious diseases' including Plague, Acute Encephalitis and Meningitis. It was held that the list was exhaustive; and none of the listed items included COVID-19. 'Plague' was not ambiguous and referred only to bubonic plague, and there was no evidence that COVID-19 could lead to Acute Encephalitis and Meningitis.

The second form of non-damage trigger was the hybrid trigger, typically worded in terms such as

> loss resulting from an interruption to your business activities caused by your inability to use the insured premises due to restrictions imposed by a public authority following occurrence or manifestation of an infectious or contagious disease on or within 25 miles of the premises.

The Supreme Court in *Arch* construed the key words as follows:

> (1) *'Restrictions'* did not need to be legally binding but could include instructions issued by authorities albeit not backed by force of law. Restrictions also included instructions or duties imposed upon the public and not necessarily on the business itself.
> (2) *'Inability to use'* was satisfied if the policyholder was unable to use the premises for a discrete part of its business activities or if it was unable to use a discrete part of its premises for its business activities. Thus, if a golf course was allowed to continue to operate but with the clubhouse closed, there would be an inability to use a divisible part of the premises.
> (3) *'Closure'* meant closure of any part of the premises. It did not mean a forced or voluntary cesser of business, as where a factory that was not required to shut down decided to cease or limit production or where a shop not required to shut down decided to limit opening hours or the number of people permitted at any one time.[24]

The third type of non-damage trigger was concerned with loss or prevention of access. That could be for any reason. A typical wording refers to closure, prevention of access to or

[23] [2021] EWHC 412 (Comm), followed in Ireland in *Brushfield Ltd v Arachas Corporate Brokers Ltd* [2021] IEHC 263.

[24] *LCA Marrickville Pty Ltd v Swiss Re International SE* [2022] FCAFC 17.

inability to use the premises due to the actions or advice of a government or local authority due to an emergency on or within one mile of the premises which is likely to endanger life or property. Such clauses typically do not refer to disease. An immediate question arising here is whether a loss of access clause can apply to closure by reason of disease where there was a separate disease trigger in the same policy. This question has prompted different views. In *Various Policyholders v China Taiping Insurance*,[25] an arbitration award by Lord Mance that was made public, it was held that the two clauses, although overlapping, could operate independently of each other so that it was open to the policyholder to seek to recover under either of them. By contrast, the Federal Court of Australia in *LCA Marrickville Pty Ltd v Swiss Re International SE*[26] ruled that the two clauses were mutually exclusive so that disease closures fell within the disease trigger only, and all other administrative closures were to be considered under the loss of access trigger. *China Taiping* was distinguished on the basis that the two clauses in that case were both specifically drawn and so each should be construed in accordance with its terms, whereas in *Marrickville* the loss of access clause was drafted in very general terms and the disease coverage clause was narrow and contained a number of restrictions on cover. It was thus appropriate to give priority to specific wording over general wording, failing which the limitations on disease cover in the specific wording would be sidestepped by reliance on the loss of access clause.

The wording of the prevention of access clause in *Corbin & King Ltd v AXA Insurance UK Plc*[27] provided cover for loss

> resulting from interruption or interference with the business where access to your premises is restricted or hindered … arising from the actions taken by … any statutory body in response to a danger or disturbance at your premises or within a 1 mile radius of your premises.

The clause went on to exclude 'notifiable diseases' as listed in the schedule to the policy. The policy was taken out before COVID-19 had raised its head, so the list of excluded infectious diseases did not refer to COVID-19. Cockerill J held that there was cover under the clause for a national event with local impact. The phrase 'danger or disturbance' encompassed two separate concepts – 'disturbance', which suggested that the relevant event was purely local, and 'danger', which was of general application – and there was no reason to construe 'danger' in a limited fashion simply because it appeared in the same phrase as 'disturbance'.[28] That construction was consistent with the specific exclusion for listed diseases, in that the exclusion would have been superfluous had diseases not fallen within the main part of the clause.

Some Australian policies restrict prevention of access triggers to specified causes. Those policies have given rise to an interesting issue of construction related to that in *Corbin & King*. In that case the question was whether two words contained in the same phrase but with different meanings were to be construed in a consistent fashion, whereas in the Australian cases the question was whether the addition of 'other' affected the position. It seems that it does. In *Star Entertainment Group Ltd v Chubb Insurance Australia Ltd*[29] and

[25] 10 September 2021.
[26] [2022] FCAFC 17.
[27] [2022] EWHC 409 (Comm).
[28] In so doing, Cockerill J refused to follow *Brushfield Ltd v AXA Insurance Designated Activity Company* [2021] IEHC 263, which had concluded that 'danger' was, by reason of the context, to be taken as referring only to purely local events.
[29] [2022] FCAFC 16.

LCA Marrickville Pty Ltd v Swiss Re International SE,[30] the wordings covered 'loss resulting from or caused by any lawfully constituted authority in connection with or for the purpose of retarding any conflagration or other catastrophe'. In *Star Entertainment*, Allsop CJ at first instance[31] was firmly of the view that COVID-19 was in ordinary language a 'catastrophe', but it was necessary to examine the word in the context in which it appeared.[32] He held that the phrase 'or other catastrophe' was confined by the word 'conflagration' to physical damage and did not extend to closure by reason of the COVID-19 outbreak. That analysis was adopted by Jagot J at first instance in *Marrickville*.[33] The question was given detailed consideration in the *Marrickville* appeal. The full court agreed with the first instance judges that the phrase 'or other catastrophe' had to be construed in its context, and took its meaning from 'conflagration'[34] and also from the reference to 'retarding', a word that could not easily be applied to restrictions on the movement of people. In the context of the policy, therefore, the phrase meant 'the sudden onset of a physical event of substantial magnitude which results in widespread destruction or loss of life and necessitates physical action to retard it'. However, the full court disagreed with the judges' view that COVID-19 would independently of context have been a catastrophe, and that dictionary definitions required a catastrophe 'to be sudden or, at the very least, for it to have a commencement which is relatively certain in time and tend to eschew the inclusion of a state of affairs which emerges relatively slowly or progressively over time'.

3.3. Causation

Assuming that the requirements of the non-damage triggers had been satisfied, the major difficulty for claimants under the disease and hybrid remains proved to be the locality requirement imposed by many of the triggers.

In the first place, the insured peril under many of the wordings was closure by reason of something happening on or in the locality of the premises, whether in the form of a local outbreak of disease or some other event giving rise to official action. However, the reality was that what actually caused the lockdown and the loss of business was not any individual local outbreak, but the pandemic. On the face of things, it was not possible to establish a causal link between the local outbreak and the closure.

Secondly, in the official action clause cases, the trigger for cover was lockdown. However, there had been loss independently of lockdown. People would not have gone out even if there had not been a forced closure of premises, so in the indemnity period losses were the result of both lockdown and also private decisions (which were not insured). Also, there were losses before lockdown which had reduced revenue, and under the trends clause the fact that revenue was falling before the lockdown meant that the loss in the indemnity period merely continued the previous downward trend and could not be the result of the lockdown. It could not therefore be said that the lockdown was the cause of the loss.

[30] [2022] FCAFC 17.
[31] [2021] FCA 1206.
[32] See ch 8 above.
[33] [2021] FCA 907.
[34] The court noted that it was more difficult to apply a contextual analysis where general words such as 'or other' followed just one enumerated peril, but felt that the overall context of physical damage was strongly supportive.

The leading case on these issues before *Arch* was that of Hamblen J in *Orient-Express Hotels Ltd v Assicurazioni Generali SpA*.[35] In August 2005 New Orleans was battered by Hurricanes Katrina and Rita, leaving large areas of the city devastated by wind damage and flooding. On 27 August 2005 a curfew was imposed, and the following day an evacuation was ordered on safety grounds. Occupants were not permitted to return until the beginning of October 2005. The insured operated a luxury hotel in New Orleans, which was insured against material damage and BI under fairly standard wording. The BI insuring clause provided cover against loss due 'to interruption or interference with the Business directly arising from [Material] Damage'. The trends clause provided that the insured could recover only that revenue which it would have obtained 'but for' the occurrence of the insured peril. The hotel sustained significant physical damage, and was not able to reopen until 1 November 2005. Revenue had been lost as a result of the hurricanes, but there were two immediate causes of loss: the damage caused by the hurricane (an insured peril); and the closure of the city, which necessarily prevented any potential customers from reaching the hotel. The insured's claim was rejected on causation grounds, and the matter went to arbitration. The tribunal ruled that the wording of the policy, and in particular the 'but for' test in the trends clause, made it necessary to ask what would have happened if there had not been any material damage to the hotel. If there would have been loss independently of the material damage, then the 'but for' test precluded recovery for such loss. The tribunal thus postulated an undamaged hotel in a damaged city, and concluded that the loss would have occurred independently of the material damage. That ruling was upheld by Hamblen J in an appeal against the award.

The reasoning in *Orient-Express* created a serious barrier to recovery in the *Arch* case. If there had not been a local outbreak, the national impact of the pandemic would still have led to a closure of the premises, so it could not be said that the locality requirement in the triggers had been satisfied. Again, even if there had not been local outbreaks and official closure of the premises, business would still have been hit by the unwillingness of people to venture into hospitality venues, so again it could not be said that there would have been no loss but for the local outbreaks or official closures. The Supreme Court in *Arch*, including Lord Leggatt (one of the arbitrators in *Orient-Express*) and Lord Hamblen, held that *Orient-Express* had been wrongly decided: the two gracefully accepted that they had been in error. The correct analysis was that every single case of COVID-19, wherever occurring, was a cause of the lockdown. So, in any one locality, a business would suffer loss by reason of (a) the local outbreak (insured) and (b) the national outbreak (uninsured). There were accordingly two concurrent causes, and the law was that in the case of one insured and one uninsured concurrent cause, the insured concurrent cause took priority. Given that there was an insured cause in (a), the uninsured causes in (b) could be disregarded. The insurers' argument that this gave disproportionate weight to the local cause in (a) was rejected by the Supreme Court. As for the trends clause, the Supreme Court ruled that the insured peril was disease, and everything to do with the disease had to be ignored in ascertaining the loss. So, loss before the lockdown attributable to the disease had to be disregarded and loss in the indemnity period attributable to the disease (albeit not the result of lockdown) was also to be disregarded. The *Arch* reasoning was primarily concerned with disease clauses, but in *Corbin & King Ltd v AXA Insurance UK Plc*[36] the analysis was extended to loss of access

[35] [2010] EWHC 1186 (Comm).
[36] [2022] EWHC 409 (Comm).

clauses requiring an outbreak of disease within a given radius of the premises giving rise to closure: if a national pandemic led to the introduction of closure measures, then as long as there was an incidence of the disease in the locality of the insured premises, it could be regarded as a concurrent proximate cause.

This reasoning is consistent with the rules on concurrent independent causes arising from a common source, discussed in chapter 10 above. If the concurrency is between an insured peril and an excluded peril, then there is no coverage. However, if the concurrency is between an insured peril and an uninsured peril, then there is coverage. In *Arch* and *Corbyn & King*, there were no excluded perils operating, only uninsured perils: it would, of course, have been different if the policies had excluded pandemics, but that was not the case. It is also clear from *Arch* that it is not relevant to weight the potency of the insured and uninsured perils.

3.4. Subrogation Issues

On the outbreak of COVID-19, the UK government, like many others, introduced various schemes to provide financial assistance to businesses which faced losing some or all of their income as a result of lockdown measures. The main UK measure was a 'furlough', by which the state took over responsibility for wage costs. The question raised by this payment is whether it is deductible from sums payable by business interruption insurers. In principle, this should be the case. As was seen in chapter 13 above, insurers are indemnifiers of last resort, so that any sum received by the insured which is designed to diminish an insured loss is to be deducted from the amount payable by the insurers. Furlough payments appear to fall within this category, in that business interruption losses incurred by an insured include wages payable to employees who are by reason of the occurrence of the insured peril unable to carry out work for the insured employer. At first instance in *Marrickville*,[37] Jagot J held that the test was whether the sums received by the insured were designed to reduce the insured loss or whether they were paid for some other purpose. The court thus ruled that JobKeeper payments, the equivalent of UK furlough payments, although in some respects more extensive because they extended to most self-employed persons, were to be deducted from the sum recoverable from the insurers, as were waivers of rent and franchise payments otherwise due from insureds. However, Jagot J held that grants from state authorities were not to be deducted, as they constituted 'grace' payments. The full court on appeal in *Marrickville*[38] held the position to be rather more nuanced. The full court focused on the terms of the policy wording before it, whereby 'sums saved in consequence of the interruption or interference' could be deducted from the indemnity. This provision was exhaustive of the insurers' rights, so there was no room for the application of ordinary subrogation principles. The words 'interruption or interference' referred to interruption or interference from an insured peril, which was a local outbreak of disease, and therefore sums could be regarded as saved only if they were concerned with the disease itself. On the facts, the payments were not to mitigate the effects of disease but, rather, to relieve the insureds from financial hardship whether or not there had been a local outbreak of disease. It followed that JobKeeper and other payments from the authorities did not fall to be deducted. There

[37] [2021] FCA 907.
[38] [2022] FCAFC 17.

was no appeal against Jagot J's decision that rent and franchise payment waivers were to be deducted from the indemnity, presumably on pure indemnity grounds.

---

4. Earthquakes and Property Insurance[39]

4.1. The Canterbury Earthquakes

On 4 September 2010 the Canterbury region of the South Island of New Zealand was rocked by a major earthquake measuring 7.1 on the Richter scale. This was centred on the city of Christchurch, to which much damage was done. On 22 February 2011 there was a second earthquake, technically an aftershock, which greatly exacerbated the harm to what was already a badly hit area. It was less intense, measuring only 6.3 on the Richter scale, but it was on a fault line close to the city. It caused the collapse of a building in which 185 people lost their lives, wrecked the cathedral and more or less flattened the central business district, including public buildings. A third earthquake hit on 10 June 2011. The damage done by the earthquakes may be explained by the facts that Christchurch is built on compressed sandy soil, and the vibrations from the shallow earthquakes broke up the soil and led to the escape of pressurised water that turned the ground into mud, a process known as liquefaction.

It proved necessary to evacuate much of the city, and the Canterbury Earthquake Recovery Authority was established to assist those affected, including buying up houses that were located in unsafe areas. New Zealand also has a statutory scheme for the protection of domestic premises from natural catastrophes, under the Earthquake Commission Act 1993. The broad effect of the Act at the time was to provide compensation for land damage (which is not covered by property insurance) plus $100,000 for damage to buildings and $20,000 for damage to contents. These sums are available only to a person who holds property insurance, and the private insurance tops up the sums available from the Earthquake Commission (EQC). The scheme is funded by levies on property insurance premiums. One of the major issues that has arisen from the tens of thousands of claims against insurers has been the relationship between private insurers and the EQC in investigating and assessing losses, often leading to serious delays in settling claims where the two could not agree. This matter was addressed following the Kaikoura earthquake on 14 November 2016, 112 miles north of Christchurch: the EQC and the leading insurers agreed various protocols whereby their efforts would not be duplicated. The 1993 Act was amended by the Earthquake Commission Amendment Act 2019, raising the property damage coverage to $150,000 and repealing that for contents. The delays in settling claims led to the establishment by legislation of the Canterbury Earthquakes Commission Tribunal in June 2019, a body charged with the task of resolving Canterbury earthquake insurance disputes in a fair, speedy, flexible and cost-effective way. At time of writing, legislation is before the New Zealand Parliament, the Natural Hazards Insurance Bill 2022, under which: the EQC is to be renamed the Natural Hazards Commission; claims are to be lodged with insurers rather than the EQC, to avoid the duplication that proved to be so damaging to the handling of claims; and the cap for cover will be raised to NZ$300,000.

[39] R Merkin, 'The Christchurch Earthquakes: Insurance and Reinsurance Issues' (2012) 18 *Canterbury Law Review* 119.

4.2. Insurance Coverage for Property Damage[40]

(1) The first issue concerns whether the building is capable of repair. Property policies recognise only total loss and partial loss. If damage is not repairable, the loss is total and the measure of indemnity is based on the full value of the property; if the damage is repairable, then the loss is generally based on reasonable repair costs. Whether property has been destroyed or damaged is not a straightforward question and, as was said in *Marriott v Vero Insurance New Zealand Ltd*,[41] factors may include:

> any special character or features of the building, the insurer's promise to pay the costs of reinstating (subject to policy limits) that particular building, and the insured's preferences so far as they are not eccentric or unreasonable … The physical feasibility of repairs is a relevant consideration, but not the only one. The only answer that can be given in the abstract to the question whether the insured property has been destroyed is that the question is one of fact, to be answered in all the circumstances.

Some New Zealand policies contain a definition of total loss, including 'beyond economic repair', 'by reason of damage, cannot be repaired'[42] and, more recently, if the total cost of repairs exceeds 80 per cent of the insured value of the property.[43]

(2) Property policies generally respond only to physical damage; sometimes the policy refers to 'damage' and sometimes to 'physical damage', but the two are interchangeable. The economic consequences of loss of use do not suffice in the absence of clear wording to that effect. In *Kraal v Earthquake Commission*,[44] the New Zealand Court of Appeal held that this did not fall within the phrase 'physical loss or damage to the house'. The word 'loss', while capable of referring to loss of use, was prefixed with the limiting term 'physical' and thus had been rendered redundant.

(3) Assuming that there is a claim for repairable damage, the question arises as to whether the building is to be repaired by the insurers, whether repairs are to be funded by the insurers or whether the assured is entitled to a cash payment. Normally, by the terms of the policy, the choice between reinstatement or payment is one for the insurers.[45]

(4) Where the indemnity is to be provided in the form of cash rather than repairs, the measure of indemnity is typically one to be decided by the insured – and not the insurers – from a range of options set out in the policy. These may include full repair costs where the insured chooses to repair, or the diminution in the value of the property if the insured chooses not to repair. If there is no measure in the policy itself, then the common law test requires the insured to prove the amount of the loss. The settled rule, as reaffirmed in *Prattley Enterprises Ltd v Vero Insurance New Zealand Ltd*,[46] is that:

> [T]he measure of loss for which the insured is indemnified may depend on the insured's intentions for the property and the reasons for owning it. That is a factual enquiry and must be made in light of the circumstances applying in each claim event.

[40] For the general principles, see ch 12 above.

[41] [2015] NZCA 246.

[42] *Vero Insurance New Zealand Ltd v Morrison* [2015] NZCA 246.

[43] *Islington Park Ltd v Ace Insurance Ltd* [2014] NZCA 446.

[44] [2015] NZCA 13. See also *O'Loughlin v Tower Insurance Ltd* [2013] NZHC 670; *Rout v Southern Response Earthquake Services Ltd* [2013] NZHC 3262.

[45] *O'Loughlin v Tower Insurance Ltd* [2013] NZHC 670; *Prattley Enterprises Ltd v Vero Insurance New Zealand Ltd* [2015] NZSC 1444; *Skyward Aviation 2008 Ltd v Tower Insurance Ltd* [2015] NZSC 185.

[46] [2015] NZHC 1444, [83]. These comments were approved on appeal: [2016] NZCA 67.

(5) The New Zealand earthquake sequence gave rise to problems not previously encountered in a non-marine context, namely, the effect of successive losses in the same policy year. The rules as set out in section 77 of the Marine Insurance Act 1906 and cases decided on it are as follows: (a) the insurer is liable for successive repaired partial losses in the same policy year, even if their aggregate exceeds the sum insured under the policy; (b) if there has been an unrepaired partial loss followed by a further loss, there can be recovery for each of the losses if the damage caused by each is different;[47] (c) if there has been an unrepaired partial loss followed by a further partial loss, and it is not possible to repair the second loss without also making good the first loss, then, applying the principle of indemnity, the first loss will be regarded as having been subsumed by the second loss, although there may be difficult questions of proof in that situation;[48] (d) if there is an unrepaired partial loss followed by a total loss, the former is subsumed into the latter, otherwise – as in (c) – the assured would be recovering for a notional loss; (e) if there is a repaired partial loss followed by a total loss, then the assured is fully entitled to recover for the total loss despite having been indemnified for the partial loss; and (f) if there is an unrepaired partial loss at the end of the policy year, the insured is entitled to recover for that loss irrespective of what happens thereafter, so that if there is a total loss a few days later the insured can recover the initial damage under the first policy and the value of damaged property under the renewed policy.

The principle in (d) is generally referred to as the doctrine of merger. In *Ridgecrest NZ Ltd v IAG New Zealand Ltd*,[49] the New Zealand Supreme Court was faced with a policy under which the limit of indemnity was NZ$1,984,000 for diminution of value on each 'happening'. The house was damaged in the first earthquake on 4 September 2010, suffered further damage in a minor earthquake on 26 December 2010 and was totally destroyed by the big earthquake on 22 February 2011. Only minor repairs had been effected between earthquakes. The insured claimed both the full sum insured for the total loss and also lesser sums for each of the partial losses, even though those losses could never be repaired independently and no expenditure on them had been incurred. The Supreme Court somewhat surprisingly allowed the claim, and held that the doctrine of merger had no application to non-marine cases. The Supreme Court ruled that policy properly construed regarded the damage caused by each earthquake as a crystallised loss for diminution of value for which there could be recovery independently of later events. That decision was much criticised by insurers, and was effectively distinguished out of existence by a New Zealand Court of Appeal decision in three joined cases, *QBE Insurance (International) Ltd v Wild South Holdings Ltd*, *Marriott v Vero Insurance* and *Crystal Imports Ltd v Certain Underwriters at Lloyd's of London*, just days later.[50] The Court of Appeal accepted that *Ridgecrest* had removed the possibility of merger, but went on to hold that *Ridgecrest* had left unaffected the principle of indemnity under which it was not possible for an insured to recover for earlier unrepaired damage as well as for the subsequent total loss. *Ridgecrest* was thus confined to the wording of that particular policy, which unsurprisingly is no longer in use. Later cases have refused to apply *Ridgecrest* outside the particular wording used in that policy, and, by applying the indemnity principle, have effectively recognised the merger principle under another name.

[47] *Vero Insurance New Zealand Ltd v Morrison* [2015] NZCA 246.
[48] See the evidential issues arising in *Sadat v Tower Insurance Ltd* [2017] NZHC 1550.
[49] [2014] NZSC 117.
[50] See also *Morrison and Cross v Vero Insurance New Zealand* [2014] NZHC 2344, affirmed [2015] NZCA 246.

Point (f) is illustrated by *Mathieson v Tower Insurance Ltd*.[51] The insured property was damaged in the September 2010 and February 2011 earthquakes, and was not repaired. The policy then renewed and there was further damage. It was held that the renewal was a fresh contract under which the insured could recover for diminution in the value of the property for post-renewal damage. The insured retained the right to claim under the earlier policy for unrepaired damage.

(6) To overcome the issues flowing from consecutive losses in the policy period, many policies contain reinstatement clauses under which, following damage insured under the policy, cover for the original sum insured is reinstated. That means that successive losses are insured. It is generally the case that the policy requires payment of an additional premium for reinstatement. In *Annex Developments Ltd v IAG New Zealand Ltd*,[52] the policy provided that: 'After we have paid a claim under this policy, we will reinstate your sum insured. We may ask you to pay an additional premium for this. If we do, you must pay the additional premium.' It was held that this wording required actual payment of the earlier claim, so that, because the insurers had failed to pay the claim, the reinstatement could not take effect. In the absence of a stated means of calculating the reinstatement premium, it may be that this type of clause is no more than an agreement to agree and thus unenforceable as a matter of general contract law.

(7) The earthquake cases have also raised important issues of aggregation. In *Moore v IAG New Zealand Ltd*,[53] a house was insured for the period 13 November 2010 to 13 November 2011. The policy stated that 'The most we pay for any loss (or series of losses caused by one event) is [NZ$2,500,000]'. The word 'event' was defined as meaning 'a single event or series of events which have the same cause'. Damage was caused to the house by the earthquakes in February and June 2011. The scientific evidence was that the two earthquakes were aftershocks from the September 2010 earthquake. The insured asserted that the damage had two separate causes, namely, each of the earthquakes, and that there were two limits of indemnity rather than a single limit. The insurers contended that the earthquakes constituted a 'series of events' and that their common cause was the September 2010 earthquake. The insurers' argument was accepted by the trial judge but rejected by the Court of Appeal. In its view, the 2011 earthquakes were independent of the September 2010 earthquake and each constituted an event in its own right. The phrase 'series of events' required some form of connection between the events in the series, and it did not suffice that they were sequential. Further, each earthquake was a 'cause' in its own right, as it could not be said that the September 2010 earthquake was the proximate cause of the later earthquakes. As has been seen in chapter 12, the narrow reading of 'series' is open to dispute, in that in the absence of the usual further express requirement for the series of events to be 'related', it is far from obvious that some form of relationship requirement between the events should have been implied. Further, as also noted in chapter 12, the word 'cause' has generally been regarded as the underlying reason for individual losses rather than the proximate cause of those losses, and a more orthodox application of the English authorities would have led to the conclusion that the relevant cause was the fact that New Zealand is situated on a major tectonic fault and not each earthquake itself.

[51] [2020] NZHC 136.

[52] [2017] NZHC 706. *cf Mathieson v Tower Insurance Ltd* [2020] NZHC 136, where the policy provided for reinstatement 'after we meet any claim'.

[53] [2020] NZCA 319.

(8) Finally, the earthquake cases have given the New Zealand courts the opportunity to consider whether there is any remedy for late payment. The law in New Zealand replicates that in England, namely that a claim under an insurance policy is one for unliquidated damages, so that in principle there cannot be an award of damages for failure to pay damages. As was seen in chapter 12, the UK response to that problem, set out in section 13A of the Insurance Act 2015, is to imply a term whereby there is an implied term for timely payment so that failure to make payment within a reasonable time constitutes a separate breach of contract giving rise to damages in addition to the sums due under the policy. In *Young v Tower Insurance Ltd*,[54] the insured's claim for damages for late payment was rejected on the factual basis that the insurers had not been guilty of culpable delay, but the High Court accepted that the duty of utmost good faith took effect as an implied term under which insurers were required to make payment within a reasonable time. The criteria laid down for assessing whether payment had been timely were taken directly from section 13A of the 2015 Act, although the measure was not referred to by the Court. In subsequent cases the Court of Appeal has rejected the notion of a generalised duty of utmost good faith but has accepted that it is possible to imply specific terms whereby obligations are imposed upon insurers in the claims process.[55]

4.3. Reinstatement

Most policies confer upon the insurers the option to reinstate the damaged property, to fund reinstatement or to pay an indemnity in accordance with the policy measure. If the insurers have opted to pay rather than to reinstate or fund reinstatement, then, as discussed above, any policy discretions relating to the measure of indemnity are generally a matter for the insured. That was held to be the correct interpretation of the wording in *Skyward Aviation 2008 v Tower Insurance Ltd*,[56] a case in which it was also held that the insurers, in their correspondence with the insured, had not unequivocally opted to pay but were merely engaged in negotiations.[57] Insurers who fail to exercise their right of election within a reasonable time will forfeit that right and the insured is entitled to apply to the court for directions.[58] In principle, that may well include an order for the insurers to exercise the option most favourable to the insured.

The standard of repair required of the insurers who opt to reinstate or to fund reinstatement will depend upon the wording of the policy. There are two broad standards: 'as new' and 'when new'. The former, 'as new', refers to equivalence to the original condition of the property, and the relevant clause requires 'building materials and construction methods in common use at the time of repair or rebuilding'. In *Turvey Trustee Ltd v Southern Response Earthquake Services Ltd*,[59] it was held that the clause required equivalence to the 'as new' condition of the property rather than precise reproduction, and that equivalence required a building the same 'by size, functionality, relative quality and reasonably addressing the

[54] [2016] NZHC 2956, an analysis applied also in *Bruce v IAG New Zealand Ltd* [2018] NZHC 3444 and *Kilduff v Tower Insurance Ltd* [2018] NZHC 704.
[55] *Southern Response Earthquake Services Ltd v Dodds* [2020] NZCA 395; *Taylor v Asteron Life Ltd* [2020] NZCA 354.
[56] [2015] NZSC 185.
[57] See also *Domenico Trustee Ltd v Tower Insurance Ltd* [2015] NZHC 981.
[58] *C&S Kelly Properties Ltd v Earthquake Commission* [2015] NZHC 1690.
[59] [2012] NZHC 3344.

re-creation of character and appearance'. The phrase 'in common use' does not justify the insurers adopting an untested mode of repair, as occurred in *Young v Tower Insurance Ltd*,[60] where insurers who proposed to adopt a new means of settling the house, by winching, were held not to have complied with their obligations and the assured was accordingly entitled to the default means of calculating indemnity, namely full rebuilding costs. The latter phrase, 'when new', imposes a stricter obligation on the insurers and requires restoration to the original condition and not just equivalence, although there is no bar on using modern materials where there is no discernible difference.

A decision by the insurers to reinstate can take two forms: the insurers undertake to indemnify the insured for the costs of reinstatement up to policy limits; or the insurers undertake to effect the reinstatement themselves. It was held in *Medical Assurance Society New Zealand Ltd v East*[61] that the obligation to indemnify the insured for reinstatement costs will not be construed as a 'pay to be paid' obligation. The policy here undertook to provide compensation against unforeseen physical loss or damage on a replacement value basis, meaning that the insurers would 'cover the cost of rebuilding or restoring the dwelling to a condition substantially the same as new, so far as modern materials allow'. The New Zealand Court of Appeal ruled that the words 'cover the cost' referred to the actual cost of repairs and not the estimated cost of repairs, so that there had to be some sort of obligation on the insured in respect of reinstatement. However, that did not mean that the insured was under an obligation to fund the repairs himself and then to seek repayment from the insurers. It was recognised that such an obligation would preclude recovery in many cases, and that the preferable construction was that the insurers' obligation would be triggered as soon as the insured assumed contractual liability to the builders for the rebuilding to be carried out.

A clear distinction should be drawn between an insurer who opts to effect repairs and an insurer who opts to pay repair costs but only once they have been incurred by the insured. In the former situation the insurers undertake to effect the reinstatement themselves. Any repairing contract is between the insurers and the builders, so that if the builders carry out the work in a defective or negligent fashion, the insurers themselves are in breach of the obligation to rebuild and have the responsibility for putting matters right. It also follows that there is no contractual relationship between the insured and the builders. By contrast, if the insurers choose to fund the cost of repairs, they will typically recommend a builder with whom the insured is to contract. In that situation the insured's primary remedy if the repairs are defective is against the builder. In *Sleight v Beckia Holdings Ltd*,[62] the New Zealand High Court considered the question whether the insured had any fallback remedy against the insurers for defective repairs in circumstances where no remedy could be obtained from the builders themselves. In this case the insurers were required to pay 'the cost of repairing or rebuilding the home to a condition as similar as possible to when it was new, using current materials and methods'. Following earthquake damage, the insured entered into a repair contract with builders who had, in turn, been nominated by a project manager appointed by the insurers. The work was carried out in a defective manner, but the builders became insolvent and were unable to effect repairs. The insured's claim against the insurers for the cost of putting right the defective work was upheld. While it was the case that the insurers were not vicariously liable for the defects of their contractors, they were

[60] [2016] NZHC 2956.
[61] [2014] NZHC 3399, affirmed [2015] NZCA 250. See also *Kilduff v Tower Insurance Ltd* [2018] NZHC 704.
[62] [2020] NZHC 2851.

liable under the insuring clause itself, as they had undertaken to fund the cost of putting the building into a 'when new' condition. Until that had happened, the insurers' obligation remained in place. Thus, the liability of the insurers in this type of case is purely contractual and arises under the policy itself.

4.4. Sale of Damaged Buildings

As a result of the delays faced by insureds in receiving payment from insurers to enable them to repair damaged buildings, many insureds chose to sell their buildings and to assign their claims to the purchaser of the building. Typically the purchaser would pay the insured close to the value of the building when repaired. Although this type of arrangement is perfectly sensible and allows the insured to receive payment at an earlier stage, it faces legal obstacles. The initial problem is that any assignment of the claim does not change the identity of the insured,[63] so that the measure of indemnity is based upon the insured's loss. However, if the insured has received the full value of the insured subject matter from the purchaser, then the insured has not suffered any loss. It is to be remembered that insurers are indemnifiers of last resort,[64] so that if the insured receives a sum from another source designed to reduce the loss, that sum is to be deducted from any insurance recovery. That point became apparent in *Toomey v IAG New Zealand Ltd*,[65] where the insured repaired his earthquake-damaged house from an insurance payment and then sold the house to a purchaser along with the benefit of the insurance policy. Further damage was later discovered and a claim was made by the purchaser in respect of that damage. The claim was struck out. The insured had received the full value of the house from the purchaser and therefore had suffered no loss. While the purchaser had suffered loss in that it had paid more for the house than it was worth, the claim did not belong to the purchaser.

The problem raised by this principle is not insurmountable. One device that has been used is for the purchaser to pay the full value of the property, but to allocate all but $1 of the purchase price to the land, which is not within the scope of the insurance, so that the insured does not obtain more than $1 by way of payment for the damaged building. The efficacy of this has yet to be tested. Even if this does work, a further problem became apparent in *Xu v IAG New Zealand Ltd*.[66] Here, a house was insured under a home insurance policy which stated that, in the event of loss or damage, the insured would receive an indemnity based on 'the cost of restoring [your home] to a condition as nearly as possible equal to its condition when new'. However, if the insured opted not to carry our restoration work, the amount payable would be the lesser of the amount of damage or the estimated restoration costs. The house was damaged in the earthquakes in 2010 and 2011. In February 2015 the insured sold the house to the claimants for $217,000 and assigned their rights under the policy. The claimants sought to recover the rebuilding costs of $353,888 from the insurers. The New Zealand Supreme Court by a 3:2 majority ruled that it was not open to the claimants to exercise the option to restore the property and to claim the costs of doing so. The right to restore was one that was personal to the insured and could not be exercised by the claimants. So, as a result of *Xu*, even it is possible to recover a basic indemnity for the damage, it is not possible to recover the enhanced indemnity available for a restored building.

[63] See ch 7 above.
[64] See ch 13 above.
[65] [2019] NZHC 2882.
[66] [2019] NZSC 68, applying *Bryant v Primary Industries Ltd* [1990] NZHC 142.

Index

Introductory Note: References such as '178–79' indicate (not necessarily continuous) discussion of a topic across a range of pages. Wherever possible in the case of topics with many references, these have either been divided into sub-topics or only the most significant discussions of the topic are listed. Because the entire work is about 'insurance', the use of this term (and certain others which occur constantly throughout the book) as an entry point has been restricted. Information will be found under the corresponding detailed topics.